RICHARD ENGLISH

IRISH FREEDOM

The History of Nationalism in Ireland

MACMILLAN

First published 2006 by Macmillan
an imprint of Pan Macmillan Ltd
Pan Macmillan, 20 New Wharf Road, London N1 9RR
Basingstoke and Oxford
Associated companies throughout the world
www.panmacmillan.com

ISBN-13: 978-1-4050-4189-8 HB
ISBN-10: 1-4050-4189-7 HB
ISBN-13: 978-0-230-01660-6 TPB
ISBN-10: 0-230-01660-X TPB

1 3 5 7 9 8 6 4 2

A CIP catalogue record for this book is available from
the British Library.

Typeset by SetSystems Ltd, Saffron Walden, Essex
Printed and bound in Great Britain by
Mackays of Chatham plc, Chatham, Kent

FOR

C.M.C., J.H.E. and A.F.E.

Contents

PART THREE
THE LONG TWENTIETH CENTURY

PART FOUR
CONCLUSION

Acknowledgements

As ever, research and writing have left me with debts of gratitude to many people. I first developed an interest in Irish nationalism when I was a student at Oxford: the subtle guidance of my then tutor David Eastwood had a profound and lasting effect, as have our many conversations about history and politics over subsequent years. My PhD supervisor at Keele University, Charles Townshend, likewise taught me much about the writing of history, and he has remained a source of very sharp insight into the past. All students of Irish nationalism owe a great deal to George Boyce, whose pioneering work on the subject has illuminated all our reading; I myself have also learned much from my many discussions with him over the years, concerning Irish nationalism. Roy Foster's scholarship, friendship and wise advice have all had a decisive influence upon my thinking, and have been truly invaluable.

In Belfast, I have benefited greatly from conversations with many friends and colleagues. Historians such as Graham Walker, Alvin Jackson, Peter Hart, Paul Bew, Margaret O'Callaghan, Keith Jeffery, Henry Patterson, David Fitzpatrick, Sean Connolly, Liam Kennedy, David Hayton, Joost Augusteijn, Ben Levitas, Brian Walker, Fearghal McGarry, Jane Leonard, Patrick Maume, Marie Coleman and Peter Gray – though resident in the city for varying periods and with various kinds of institutional affiliation – have none the less collectively represented an informal Belfast School of Irish History; their combined influence on our understanding of Irish nationalism has been very impressive, and my personal debt to them has been considerable. Belfast-based scholars with other areas of specialism have also shaped my thinking in important ways: it's a pleasure to thank Harvey Whitehouse, Mark Burnett, Hastings Donnan, David Livingstone, Colm Campbell, Christopher Marsh, Vincent Geoghegan and Shane O'Neill for the ways in which their arguments have informed my thinking. I'm also grateful for the help and advice which have been given by many other people, including Marianne Elliott, Joseph

ix

Morrison Skelly, Cormac O'Malley, David Adamson, Tim Smyth, Cormac Kinsella and Cameron Watson. Maxine Cresswell, Roy Foster, Ian McBride and Charles Townshend generously took the time to read draft chapters of the book; each offered extremely valuable advice, and I'm deeply grateful to them all.

The staffs of many research institutions have offered great assistance during the years of my work on this book, and I would particularly like to thank those who have helped me at the following: the Public Record Office of Northern Ireland (Belfast); the Linen Hall Library (Belfast) – especially Yvonne Murphy in the Northern Ireland Political Collection; the Library of Queen's University, Belfast; the Belfast Central Newspaper Library; the British Library (London); the Archives Department of University College, Dublin; the National Library of Ireland (Dublin); the National Archives (Dublin); the National Archives at Kew; the House of Lords Record Office (London). I would also like to thank all those people who have kindly allowed me to interview them during my years of research into Irish nationalism.

The Leverhulme Trust generously awarded me a Research Fellowship, thereby providing time for the completion of the book; Queen's University, Belfast, was consistently supportive of the project and provided an excellent setting for research and writing. George Morley and her team at Macmillan have offered invaluable advice, support and encouragement, while Bruce Hunter's wise counsel has, as ever, been of great benefit throughout.

Richard English
Belfast

List of Abbreviations

ACA	Army Comrades' Association
ADUCD	Archives Department, University College, Dublin
AFIL	All-For-Ireland League
AOH	Ancient Order of Hibernians
AP	*An Phoblacht*
APL	Anti-Partition League
AP/RN	*An Phoblacht/Republican News*
BT	*Belfast Telegraph*
CBS	Christian Brothers' School
CE	Christian Era
DJ	*Derry Journal*
DUP	Democratic Unionist Party
FJ	*Freeman's Journal*
GE	*Galway Express*
GHQ	General Headquarters
GPO	General Post Office
HLRO	House of Lords Record Office (London)
ICA	Irish Citizen Army
IICD	Independent International Commission on Decommissioning
IN	*Irish News*
INLA	Irish National Liberation Army
IP	*Irish Press*
IPP	Irish Parliamentary Party
IRA	Irish Republican Army
IRSP	Irish Republican Socialist Party
ISRP	Irish Socialist Republican Party
IT	*Irish Times*
LHLPC	Linen Hall Library Political Collection (Belfast)

LLL	Ladies' Land League
MEP	Member of the European Parliament
MP	Member of Parliament
NAD	National Archives, Dublin
NAL	National Archives, London
NGA	National Graves Association
NICRA	Northern Ireland Civil Rights Association
NLI	National Library of Ireland (Dublin)
POW	Prisoner of War
PRONI	Public Record Office of Northern Ireland (Belfast)
RIC	Royal Irish Constabulary
RN	*Republican News*
RSF	Republican Sinn Féin
RUC	Royal Ulster Constabulary
SDLP	Social Democratic and Labour Party
TCD	Trinity College, Dublin
TD	Teachta Dála (Dáil Deputy, Member of the Dáil)
UCD	University College, Dublin
UIL	United Irish League
UUP	Ulster Unionist Party
UVF	Ulster Volunteer Force

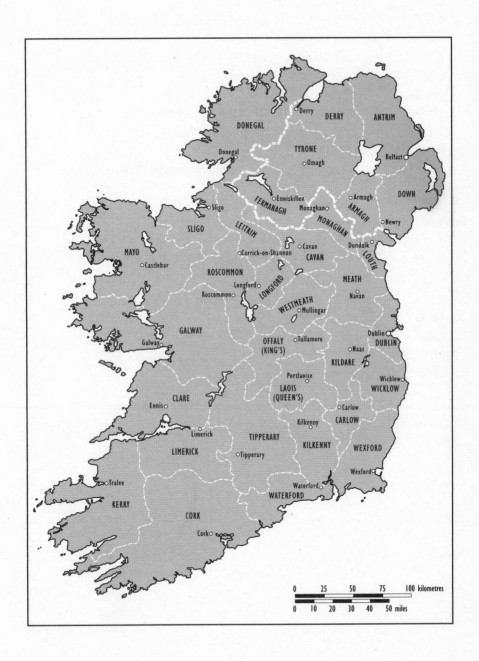

INTRODUCTION

1

Just outside the County Donegal town of Buncrana, in the northern part of Ireland, lies a stone memorial to the eighteenth-century United Irishman Theobald Wolfe Tone. This small monument to the celebrated Irish republican faces westward across the quiet water of Lough Swilly, towards the beautiful Fanad peninsula, and it maintains a silent devotion:

> In memory of Theobald Wolfe Tone who was arrested near this spot in November 1798 and of the heroic efforts that he and his comrades in the United Irishmen made 'To abolish the memory of past dissension' and to establish in the land they loved a civil order governed by the principles of Liberty, Equality and Fraternity.

Tone had sailed from France in September 1798 on board the seventy-four-gun French flagship, the *Hoche*, and had headed for Ireland with rebellious, anti-English intention in that year of failed risings. On 12 October, a severe storm having broken as Tone and his comrades reached the Irish north coast, the *Hoche* was engaged in a dawn battle by British forces. Tone himself was fully engaged in this fight, and he was captured when his fatally damaged ship was surrounded and taken. On 31 October, after more than two weeks of continuing storm, the *Hoche* was then towed into Lough Swilly ('one of the most beautiful bays in Ireland',[1] as the later Irish nationalist Alice Milligan put it), and Tone was brought on shore with other prisoners at Buncrana on 3 November.

A short drive from Buncrana to the other side of the Inishowen peninsula takes you to Tremone Bay, a small Donegal beach arrived at via narrowly winding roads. At one end of this bay lies another memorial to another rebel, a small, grey-stoned monument dedicated to a nineteenth-century Irish nationalist who escaped after the 1848 Rising: 'Erected to commemorate the escape of Thomas D'Arcy McGee (1825–1868) from Tremone Bay to America in September 1848. He was a key figure in the Young Ireland movement'. Also on Inishowen, further north towards Malin Head, lies the glorious Five Finger Strand. As you stand on this vanilla-sanded Donegal beach, a beautiful crescent of land surrounds you: away in front and to the right are the five knuckles of rock which give the strand its name, then nearer towards you and still on your right are high cliffs, with sheep precariously grazing on their sloping grass. Behind you are the triangular dunes which back on to the beach itself, while off to the left, beyond occasional and isolated houses, lie hauntingly shadowed mountains – County Donegal possessing what IRA man and writer Ernie O'Malley once described as 'a mountainous core extending in every direction'.[2] Directly in front of you is the 'cold-lipped Atlantic'[3] (as another literary Irish republican, Donegal IRA novelist Peadar O'Donnell, once phrased it): a permanent sea symphony, enthralling in any weather. And ahead of you in that sea silently lies Glashedy Island where, allegedly, poteen – powerful, illicit whiskey – used to be made in the nineteenth century. As you look around you on this beach, there are 360 degrees of beauty. And in the dunes here at Five Finger Strand the Provisional IRA buried arms dumps during the 1980s in their long struggle against the British state in Ireland.

2

These Donegal stories could be echoed across much of Ireland. And, for all the great differences between them, the people mentioned here – Theobald Wolfe Tone, Alice Milligan, Thomas D'Arcy McGee, Ernie O'Malley, Peadar O'Donnell and the Provisional IRA – were all variously engaged in an Irish expression of the most important and powerful force in human history. For nationalism has substantially determined and shaped the modern world.[4] It has caused and fuelled wars; stabilized and destabilized states; defined political and cultural life across the globe. Nationalism has triumphantly outlived communism, and it has transcended social class and religious attachment alike: not all nationalists espouse particular (or even any) religious beliefs, and nationalists come from diverse social backgrounds; yet the vast majority of religious people and of people from diverse social classes possess nationalist views, attachments, loyalties and ideas. People have defined themselves (and scholars have sought to define them) in terms of various historical forces and categories – class, religion, gender, civilization – but nationalism has proved more persistently and pervasively powerful than any of these. It remains an inescapably central feature of human life,[5] and nobody can comprehend the modern world without understanding and explaining this most definitive of all forces in our history.

It has certainly been the most crucial force in the history of Ireland. For centuries, nationalist campaigns and anti-nationalist politics have between them provided the context for Irish historical development. Even if one were to begin only with the familiar story from the late eighteenth century onwards, the record is clear enough: the United Irishmen, the O'Connellite campaigns for Catholic Emancipation and Repeal of the Union, the Young Irelanders of the 1840s, the late-nineteenth-century Fenian movement, the Home Rule politics of Parnell and Redmond, the early-twentieth-century world of Sinn Féin and other republicans, the politics of independent Ireland after 1922, the post-1968 Northern Ireland Troubles – in each of these cases, nationalist politics have centrally defined Irish life. So, too, the politics of those who have strenuously opposed Irish nationalism (whether Irish unionists, or anti-nationalist British politicians operating in Ireland), have themselves been framed by nationalist assumptions. Unionist and British views frequently involve their own species of nationalism, and they have often been moulded in response to challenges set by nationalist Ireland. Indeed, the terrain on which anti-Irish-nationalist battles have been fought has been land worked often enough by nationalist hands: the politics of opposing Repeal, of opposing Home Rule, or of combating the IRA, were all politics partly

determined by the agenda of Irish nationalists themselves. The shape
of modern Ireland, for good or ill or both, has been sculpted largely
by nationalism.

So this book explores a subject of paramount international and also
local, national importance. In doing so it has three main aims.

The **first**, and most straightforward, is to tell the compelling story
of Irish nationalist history through the extraordinarily vivid and
wide-ranging sources which have been left to us by Irish nationalists themselves. Through archives, pamphlets, memoirs, newspapers,
novels, diaries, plays, poems, paintings, music, maps, censuses, parliamentary debates, films, interviews, ballads, correspondence, speeches,
opinion polls, election materials and other sources, I hope that the
dramatic tale of nationalist Ireland will here be brought to vigorous
and entertaining life.

The book's **second** aim is to provide readers with an authoritative
but accessible, up-to-date, single-volume account of what scholars now
think and know (or think that they know) about Irish nationalism.
There are libraries full of specialist studies which focus on different
periods, individuals, movements, themes and problems relating to Irish
nationalism. But most people simply don't have the time to spend
their lives reading through this vast monograph literature, and so
there's a danger that scholarly understanding will just lie buried in
micro-studies which few people read. I hope that *Irish Freedom* will,
among other things, provide a comparatively short and enjoyable route
– in one volume – towards finding out what scholars now think about
this great subject. Perhaps strangely, no such book currently exists.
There are several superb general treatments of nationalism in Ireland,
but none would claim to disseminate the current state of the art of
scholarship on Irish nationalism.[6] There are also very fine general
histories of Ireland,[7] but these books necessarily have to consider far
more than nationalism; as a result, they don't have the space to tell the
full story of scholarly thinking about nationalism in Ireland. So, in the
course of telling the story of Irish nationalism, this current book will
also reflect and summarize much of the existing literature on this
subject.

As I say, my desire to write a book which serves this purpose is
one which arises partly from an anxiety that the over-specialization
of historical research has led to an unhelpful compartmentalization of

history-writing. There are now so many micro-studies (local, biographical, period-specific) and so many sub-fields of specialization (military history, women's history, social history, family history, and so on), that it is sometimes difficult for readers to grasp the ways in which all these different histories meaningfully link together, in life lived across rather than within such categories. There's a danger that such a situation might lead people to feel cut off from current understandings of the past, and more particularly of *their own* past, and this would be unfortunate. So, in part, this book has been written as a kind of public history, intended to make available to a wider audience what at present lies buried in obscure articles, archives or academic seminar discussions.

And it should be noted that our scholarly understanding of the past emerges, not merely from the work of those in university history or politics departments, but also from the profound insights of people from a wide range of other disciplinary backgrounds. *Irish Freedom* is primarily a work of political history; but I hope that it also represents a new kind of historical writing in that it draws throughout on important work by people from a very broad range of disciplines (including psychology, political science, sociology, law, anthropology, theology, philosophy, political theory, literature, economics, geography, biology, archaeology and music).

My **third** aim in writing this book is the most ambitious and difficult of the three, and it concerns my desire not just to tell the Irish nationalist story, but also to explain it: to address the deeper question 'Why?' as well as the more traditional question 'What?' In order to do this, it will be necessary not just to offer a chronicle of Irish nationalists' actions, arguments and experiences over the years, but also to weave into this tale some precise consideration of what *nationalism* itself actually is as a political phenomenon (its precise nature, causes, dynamics and consequences), and in particular why it is that it has been so persistently dominant in people's lives.

Most studies of Irish nationalist history – monographs on particular movements or periods or individuals – have tended to avoid such precise conceptual reflection and definition regarding the nature of nationalism itself.[8] The basic assumptions of nationalism (whether Irish, British or Ulster unionist) have become so deeply internalized, it seems, that even those who have studied the details of the phenomenon have tended simply to take it somewhat for granted: nationalism itself has effectively been treated as an inevitable or given context within which we have all operated. So the question of what nationalism actually *is* – of why and when it arose, and of why it has proved so lastingly, pervasively powerful – has tended all too often to be ignored. Nationalism is assumed simply to be a given reality and framework, and one which therefore requires no sustained interrogation. This is true of most specialist micro-studies, but it is also true of more general treatments of Irish nationalism (several of which have been excellent).[9] That people have expressed their desire for landownership, or social revolution, or parliamentary authority, through nationalism rather than through other ideological media or within other political frameworks, has too often been simply taken for granted; and most scholars have shied away from the difficult task of precise and informed conceptual definition of the phenomenon in question.[10] The dominant force in modern Ireland has been treated as though its existence were inevitable and natural, and as though it required no conceptual delineation or explanation.

But while Irish historians have favoured empirical over philosophical precision (producing, it should be said, much outstanding and very detailed historical work in the process), the approach of scholars studying nationalism as a global phenomenon has often suffered from an opposing bias. An impressive and vast literature exists on the subject of nationalism as such, but the authors of most of these studies have ignored Ireland; less forgivably, they have not tended to test the validity of their theories through empirically detailed consideration of the case of any one nation over a sustained period of time in the kind of detail which historians would demand. So countless general definitions of nationalism have been offered, refined and refuted; and innumerable explanations have been proffered for its emergence, sustenance and influence. But these arguments have rarely been tested in ways that an historian would consider necessary: against the lengthy, unique, detailed and messy experience of a particular national community, in a particular place, studied under the microscope over time.[11]

So philosophers and sociologists of nationalism have been better at saying why something called nationalism arose as a global phenomenon than at explaining why – in particular places at specific times – some nationalists within a movement took one path and others another in, for example, schism or civil war; why some nationalists were socialist and others anti-socialist within the same nationalist movement, place and period; why some classmates – sharing similar social and geographical, educational and even family influences – joined a particular nationalist movement, while others sitting near them in class vehemently opposed it; why particular periods of nationalist politics were marked by varying regional intensities and timings; how and why nationalist ideas reached particular people and places and made such sense among them; and so on. And these questions of detailed human intricacy do not concern trivial surface symptoms, for they have been and they remain decisive in terms of people's lives and – all too frequently – their deaths.

What I'm suggesting is that there has been a significant problem with our understanding of Irish nationalism, arising from the fact that these two different traditions of studying the phenomenon have failed to listen to each other with sufficient care. What might be called the 'sociologists' of nationalism have spoken in one language (general and theoretical), while historians have spoken in another (local and empirical); what we now need is to approach the subject bilingually. As an historian who has spent his professional life working in a university politics department, I've attempted to achieve at least some degree of simultaneous fluency in these rival languages, and so this book aims both to narrate vividly and to explain deeply at the same time. If theorists have offered philosophical precision, while lacking sufficient appreciation of the unique and the contingent; and if historians have been strong on the particular but less adept at conceptual or comparative reflection,[12] then a marriage of the two approaches offers the possibility of a more full understanding of this vital subject than would be attainable by either school operating on its own.

To alter the metaphor, we might think of the process as involving two maps. One has been large-scale, outlining the broad contours of global nationalism as a whole, but insufficiently detailed to explain or to guide us regarding the particularities of any localized region. The other has been a small-scale map of a local area, illuminating that region's specific features in closely focused fashion but leaving us in the dark about how and where it fits into the broader world picture. Until now, the two sets of cartographers producing these maps have operated far too independently of each other, with the result that the two maps fail to fit each other accurately or closely enough. What is needed is that these two maps should be produced and refined as part of the same process, and that they should be able to fit on to one another precisely: what we know of the local detail should exactly match what we know of broad, global realities and explanations, and vice versa.

So this book offers a theory of 'nationalism' as well as the story of 'Irish nationalism', and it attempts to relate the two phenomena to each other in a way that will enrich our understanding of both. The theory (first set out very briefly in the final section of this Introduction) explains what nationalism is, what drives it, and why it has been so powerful and dominant in the modern world. Chapters One to Six of the book will then tell the Irish nationalist story, and the Conclusion ('Explaining Irish Nationalism') will both elaborate and justify the theory of nationalism more fully, and relate this in some detail to the Irish historical experience: the aim will be to show how a thorough understanding of nationalism itself is the only way of making deeper sense of the nationalist story in Ireland over the centuries.

So I hope that this book offers an original integration of narrative detail with analytical reflection on nationalism as such: it's a dramatic story of what people have thought and done, but it is also an interpretive one concerning the ultimate reasons for their having thought and acted in these ways. My aim has been to write history which relates theoretical understanding to the messy practicality of lived experience, in a way which allows each to explain how and why the other operates as it does. It's a challenging task. But unless the conceptual and the empirical are deployed in this kind of explanatory relationship with each other, then it seems to me unlikely that we will properly understand nationalism anywhere.

A few other points might briefly be mentioned at this stage. In trying to re-create Irish nationalists' thought and action through their own words, I've aimed to show the extraordinary variety, richness and particularity of people's lives. This has involved not merely the famous elite (prominent though they have to be in such a story), but also the rank and file of nationalist movements and populations; and it necess- arily involves women as well as the men who often monopolize text and footnotes in such studies. Such an account records the experiences of those who have been victims, as well as those who have been practitioners of nationalist politics and violence; and it considers many localities as well as the famous metropolitan sites of action. In all of this I hope that some often-ignored voices will be made rather more audible. Readers tend to be familiar with names such as Theobald Wolfe Tone, Robert Emmet, Daniel O'Connell, Thomas Davis, John Mitchel, Charles Stewart Parnell, Patrick Pearse, Michael Collins, Eamon de Valera, John Hume, Bobby Sands and Gerry Adams; and *Irish Freedom* will indeed examine the vital role of these and other main players in the Irish nationalist drama. But we also possess many other vivid sources, recording the experiences of less eminent figures in the story, and enabling us to understand the plot much more fully. Far fewer readers will be familiar with the names of Leonard Magill or Patrick O'Neill, Joseph Skeffington or Eithne Coyle, Jeremiah Mac-Veagh or Joseph Connellan, Lily FitzSimons or Alex Comerford, Denis Haughey or Sean Coleman. But it's vital to hear the voices of such people if we are properly to understand the story of nationalist Ireland, and so I've tried to give them their place.

I would like to think that this rounded picture will demonstrate the rich and multi-layered nature of Irish nationalism. This is emphatically a story of Irish *nationalisms* (fluid and layered) rather than of any homogeneous nationalism (static and monochrome). The terms and aspirations and even the vocabulary of nationalists have altered dramatically over time, and the competing varieties of nationalism evident in Ireland at any one point are equally telling. This is a tale of Irish nationalist conflict with England and Britain; but it's also a story of conflict between Irish people – nationalist-versus-nationalist as often as nationalist-versus-unionist.

A word about the reader, and the author. I hope that the book contains material of interest and importance for the scholar and the connoisseur, in terms of the wealth and novelty of the data as well as the innovation of the argument. But it's also intended as a story which can be enjoyed by a much wider group than merely that of professional academics. I've long been a believer in what Eric Hobsbawm once described as 'the intelligent and educated citizen',[13] and I've written this book with such a reader firmly in mind. So the book contains the scholarly apparatus of Bibliography and Notes and References for those who are keen to pursue matters further on particular points; but *Irish*

Freedom can also be read without reference to such pages – as an historical tale for the general reader.

The perspective of the author possibly requires some comment as well. To write the history of nationalism necessarily demands an attempt at imaginative empathy with the vast range of people involved in the story being told. But it need not mean that one shares the assumptions of those under scrutiny. Non-Protestants can study the history of the Protestant Reformation, just as non-Nazis can write authoritatively about the tortured subject of Nazism; the same is true, I believe, across the range of human experience. This book about Irish nationalism is written by someone who is not, in fact, a nationalist of any variety or nation. (In writing it, I've often been reminded of George Bernard Shaw's spiky observation, 'As an Irishman I could pretend to patriotism neither for the country I had abandoned nor the country that had ruined it.'[14]) Some people write about Irish nationalism as fellow-believers in the nationalist religion; others write with a venomous hostility towards their subject of study. By contrast, I'm writing as someone born and long-resident in Ireland, who wants to explore and explain a compelling and important subject in ways which are fair to all concerned, whether they are nationalist or not: the intention is to provide empathy and balance, and to evaluate rather than solely to celebrate or condemn.

So the book aims to explain Irish nationalism rather than merely to describe it; and it tells the reader what shelf after shelf of research books and articles on Irish nationalists have unveiled; it narrates an historical tale using rich, varied data on often obscure yet important events and people; and – above all – it aims to stimulate debate on a major topic. My previous books have dealt with exponents of an aggressive, twentieth-century version of Irish nationalism, focusing as they have on the IRA.[15] In contrast, this book considers a much broader range of Irish nationalists, involving earlier periods of nationalist experience and examining all shades of nationalism in Ireland, constitutional as well as revolutionary. Over such a wide range, I can't expect readers always to agree with my arguments; indeed, one of my hopes is that this book may provoke fruitful disagreement, debate and reflection concerning Irish and wider nationalist politics. If readers are entertained by what the book reveals about intriguing aspects of the past, and if they consider some of what I argue to be stimulating, then I'll be more than satisfied with that.

3

Before starting to tell the Irish story, we need a brief statement of what nationalism actually is, of why and when it emerged, of what drives and lies behind it, and of why it has so dominated the world. And even before this, it's necessary to set out a clear understanding of some other key terms if we are to avoid unhelpful vagueness. The word **nation** is derived from Latin; more particularly, it comes ultimately from the verb *nascor*, meaning to be born, to descend from, to spring from. So its initial sense involved actual ties of blood and birth, and yet it has lastingly implied a much wider set of attachments and much more extended ties of belonging (already signified in the Latin word *natio* – a nation, people or race). Dictionaries record perceived modern meaning of the word 'nation' ('A distinct race or people, characterized by common descent, language, or history, usually organized as a separate political state and occupying a definite territory'), and also something of the word's changing historical usage ('family, kindred, clan', 1584; 'the whole people of a country', 1602).[16] But in addition to the list of supposedly shared features which this kind of community possesses (descent, territory, history, culture, language, and so on), there are in the nation the crucially linked dimensions of consciousness and scale. If people do not think themselves a nation – or do so only in tiny numbers – then it is doubtful that a nation exists. As one leading scholar of the subject has pragmatically put it, 'any sufficiently large body of people whose members regard themselves as members of a "nation", will be treated as such'.[17]

National relates to, or is distinctively characteristic of, the nation (hence national identity, national character); while **nationality** suggests either the fact of belonging to a nation, or something of the national character, identity, consciousness or feeling consequent upon this fact. **Patriotism** has a distinctive Irish meaning which we will address later in the book, but as a general term it may perhaps be taken to refer to affection or love for one's nation, and a measure of loyalty to it.[18]

What of **nationalism** itself, its origins and development and dynamics? The true definition and explanation of nationalism lie in a particular interweaving of the politics of community, struggle and power. And if we ask what, at root, makes people into nationalists and makes nationalists of so many people, then the crucial place to start is with the necessity and appeal of **community**.

For nationalism to have been so persistently and popularly powerful, it must have resonated with key instincts, needs, drives and dimensions of being human; and this relation between nationalism and humans' deepest needs, though rarely spelled out in more traditional histories of nationalism, is essential to understanding the subject, and to explaining why nationalist versions of community so appeal. It's not that it is necessary or more natural for humans to be nationalists, but rather that nationalism has been able powerfully to respond to many of the deepest needs and instincts of humanity, and that our recognition of this is crucial to explaining nationalism's pervasiveness and durability. Scientific research makes clear that humans are sociable by nature: we're not equally predisposed towards the solitary and the interactive, but have a biological drive towards group aggregation. A wealth of research now points us towards again believing in human nature, and when we consequently ask what humans want or need, we find deep and dominant instincts towards survival, security, protection and safety. Our survival instinct is inbuilt, and one attraction of community clearly lies in what it can offer in the realm of protection, the provision of necessary means of existence, and so on. But inbuilt also is our instinct towards belonging, and in particular towards belonging to stable and coherent communities. The latter meet our practical needs (for food production, and for those things such as economic exchange which require cooperative action), but they also promise to satisfy our need for meaningful definition of who we are: something essential if life is to be tolerable, purposeful and fulfilling. Belonging, bonding and attachment within effective and durable social groups (especially groups which we perceive to be special and distinctive) lie at the heart of what it is to be human. For practical and psychological reasons, therefore, community – of precisely the kind which is associated with nationalism – appears to suit human nature.

In this it reflects the central fact that nationalism simultaneously meets emotional, psychological and material or practical needs. For this to be the case, there needs to be an agreed loyalty to national community, and this in turn requires that there be shared means of communication between members of the group: things that provide the basis for agreement, coherence, trust and interaction. These can take various forms, and they are often enough practical as well as of emotional or psychological value. *Territory*, the nationalists' homeland, might be one such element. Nationalist community tends to involve attachment to our own special place, to a land which we work, on whose resources we rely, and from whose distinctive features we derive emotional and practical sustenance. To the centrality of place might be added the vital communal feature of *people* themselves. Again, there are practical dimensions (community with those around us is required for our survival), but the ennobling of our own people also allows for enhanced self-worth, fulfilment, purpose and meaning. Our people – those whom we know, and those in the greater, imagined community – are a special group. And nationalists often take this further with extended notions of communal *descent*. To some degree, this aspect of national community is an invention: nations are not, in fact, neatly sealed racial groups of shared descent. Yet nor are shared blood-ties irrelevant: the people to whom you are born do often play a vital part in your sense of national community; it's also true that there will often enough be a greater degree of blood-relatedness between yourself and your own national community than there will be with, for example, the people of a distant nation. Thus myths of shared national descent intensify attachment in ways which are partly, but only partly, fictionally based.

The broad set of languages which we can call *culture* provides further definition of what it is to be a nationalist and explanation of why national community so appeals. Culture can involve actual shared language, but also the languages of religion or music or sport or diet or value, which allow for shared interaction and trust and meaning within a national group. And the key feature here is our own national culture's perceived specialness. Our music and sport are not just random examples of wider patterns but rather – so we as nationalists will think – they are unique and indeed superior. Just as we associate with special people, so we do so by means of distinctive culture. And this helps explain the appeal of the community: if this is uniquely dignified and durable, and I am a part of this, then to affirm my national culture is to affirm and ennoble myself.

National community relies on a sense of *history* in very many cases: this group is a lasting one, we believe, gaining worth through its historic achievements and legacies, and acquiring purpose and direction through its imagined future. There may often be a simplification involved in the national histories which communities imagine around themselves. But the sharing of such myths allows for notions of greatness, of enriched identity in asking who we are, of intense purpose in terms of a past decline to be arrested if future glory is to be achieved. We know that the human mind is oriented towards narrative interpretations of important things around us, and towards drawing moral sense from them. Hence the appeal of historical stories which contain lessons and morals, simplified and anachronistic though these stories may be. The national community tends also to have, therefore, an *ethical* dimension. Our group is not merely typical in what it embodies, but is characterized rather by superior moral claims, values, purposes and obligations. Nations are righteous communities. And it's considered by nationalists to be right that all humanity be divided into nations: this is the true moral order for the world.

A darker feature of nationalist community – but again one which both defines and explains its appeal – is to be found in the idea of *exclusiveness*. Nations are self-defining, self-aware groups. But what you are implies and requires a category of what you are not. If my national culture, history and so on define who is within my community, then they also define who is outside, beyond and excluded from it. And this too can appeal to many people: in telling a tale of good versus evil, in providing comfort and moral certainty at the same time. This exclusivism – the politics of 'in-group' and 'out-group' – varies from nationalism to nationalism, and from period to period within any given national community. But its hostile, negative and often aggressive presence is frequently felt, offering boundaries of meaning with potentially awful implications.

National communities do not all require all these features – shared attachments to territory, people, descent, culture, history, ethics, and exclusivism – but they do require some of them, and the emotional and practical logic within each of these features helps to explain the existence, durability and pervasiveness of such communal groups. Yet nationalism involves more than membership of such self-conscious community. It also involves **struggle**: activity, movement, collective mobilization, sometimes a programmatic striving for goals, and certainly a commitment to necessary change. So what do nationalists struggle for? This can, of course, vary vastly. Communal agendas of struggle can be directed towards gaining or preserving the sovereign independence of your national community; towards the achievement of secession from a larger political unit, or independence from an imperial power; towards maintaining national political or cultural survival, or achieving economic advantage for your community; towards winning freedom in political terms, or the right to cultural expression for the national community; and very much else.

Why do nationalists so struggle? Again, often overlapping or coexisting motivations can be detected: self-preservation, the advancement of material or economic interests in a practically beneficial way, the desire for prestige or dignity or meaning, a reaction to threats (actual or perceived), an urge to avenge past wrongs, a need to put right a relative group grievance. In all of this, nationalist struggle involves the rectification of what is wrong: the replacing of an unfortunate 'is' with a desired 'ought to be'; and in all of this, what we see is an individual engagement with the organized pursuit of communal goals, and the way in which communal advantage benefits that individual nationalist in powerful ways. And how do nationalists pursue such struggle? Through violence (in wars of national liberation, expansion or annexation); through party or electoral political process; through cultural campaigns, movements and initiatives; through the embedding of national ideas in frequent rituals and routines, and in the emblems built into national life and place – there are very many means of communal, national mobilization around varied goals.

But nationalism is not merely about community in struggle, but also and centrally about questions of **power**. Power is what is so frequently sought by nationalists; and the deployment of power in pursuit of nationalist objectives defines – and again, I think, helps to explain – nationalist activity. It might even be suggested that, at root, nationalism is really a politics *of* power. For nationalists tend to assume the nation to be the appropriate source of political power or authority, and tend to seek power for their own distinctive national community. The legitimacy of national power involves the alluring prospect of those in power in your community being – in key ways – just like yourself, coming from your own national group and reflecting and representing the interests and values which constitute you as an individual. This often involves power over the state: while state and nation should not be confused with each other, they do exist in frequently close relationship. The most common goal of nationalists at their historic high points of communal struggle tends to be the pursuit of state power for the nation. National freedoms are thought to be best – indeed, only – achieved, protected and guaranteed by possession of state power, and by its constant defence against threats internal and external alike. So we find the mismatch between state and nation (occasions where members of one national community find themselves in a state ruled by another) to be the most powerful generator of nationalist movements in history – not least, of course, in Ireland.

Nationalist power also focuses on the vital notion of sovereignty. One of the central ideas of nationalism is that political sovereignty is a right held by the nation, that the national community should possess full sovereignty over itself as a free, independent and self-governing unit. Why should this so appeal as a legitimizing principle of power? The answer lies in the linkage made within nationalism between equality, sovereignty and freedom. The ideas of John Locke (1632–1704) were foundational here, given his decisive argument that legitimate political authority rested on the consent of the governed. But upon this Lockeian foundation came an even more important layer of argument, drawn from the innovative ideas of Jean-Jacques Rousseau (1712–78) and his interweaving of popular sovereignty, equality and freedom. Within the nation, all people share equally in the sovereign power which makes and legitimizes decisions for the group. Thus any law (whether or not, in practice, it might limit one's daily liberty in some way) derives ultimately from one's own authority: and one of the central ideas and attractions of nationalism is that by sharing equally in the power which governs us in this way, we are made truly free. As nationalists, we give consent to our national rulers and to their possession of sovereign power: and such individual attachment to the idea of popular national sovereignty seems to make a certain sense because we, as individuals within the national community, have an equal share in the sovereignty through which decisions are made for us. As such, we are supposedly liberated.

So state power and sovereignty rely on communal consent and in practice on the idea of self-determination, the power of a population to decide its own government and politics. In nationalist thought, the collective will of the community expresses itself in legitimizing the nation as the proper and free political unit: for nationalists, indeed, self-determination is a central political right. (Over and over in our Irish story, we'll hear this term deployed.) Again, the appeal of this idea to so many people is easy to explain. If you self-determine yourselves as a group (sharing those features of community which we have discussed, and which make us who we are), then those ruling over you not only represent and reflect you, but are ultimately answerable to you as an individual who is typical of your national group. How should individuals protect their own interests, liberties and rights? To the nationalist, the answer lies in a theory of self-determination which seeks to group people into bonded national communities, each possessing and consenting to and legitimating its own way of life.

If power is, therefore, the objective and the explanation of so much nationalist struggle, then power too lies at the heart of what it is that nationalists actually do, in their day-to-day and year-to-year activities. Power is deployed by nationalist communities in their pursuit, achievement and maintenance of objectives; power is used as leverage in nationalist campaigns for the righting of wrongs, for the winning or defending of freedom or culture; power can be wielded in violent, propagandist, intimidatory, administrative, verbal, literary, state, sub-state and many other forms of persuasion and coercion. This involves mobilization rather than merely individual acts; and the attraction of wielding such power helps to explain the durable appeal of nationalism as part of one's way of life.

So community, struggle and power offer the interwoven definition and explanation of nationalism and its extraordinary dominance. But can these aspects of human life not be expressed and enjoyed and pursued through other means than the national? Can we not find community in our family or village, pursue struggle at the purely local level of campaigning, wield power through our prominent role in job or business? To some extent, clearly we can and we do. But the particular interweaving of community, struggle and power in the form of nationalism offers far grander opportunities than are available through these other routes. The family cannot offer the scale of interaction to provide for our necessary exchange or safety; even a powerful job will not allow for access to the kind of serious power available through nationalism; and the expression of sub-national cultural enthusiasm will not allow for such large-scale, durable, all-inclusive possibilities as will the national. This last is perhaps the crucial point. For nationalism has an absorptive quality, which allows it to subsume and incorporate and gain further strength from other areas of our life in ways which seem to strengthen them too. The family offers comfort and meaning and belonging, but is protected by the power of the national community; the interests of the business are defended and furthered by the nation; sporting enthusiasm or musical pride gain distinction and exaltation through their national dimensions. While feminism, socialism, or religion can all appeal very powerfully, none can absorb the nation in the way that nationalism can absorb them. Women as well as men can be in the nation; all classes can be and are repeatedly claimed to be in the national community; and religions cannot offer equally meaningful power, as neither the local religious community nor the single world-rule of one Church or faith offer the kind of feasible power that a national group can and often does hold.

And the question is less why people group themselves according to identity or allegiance, but rather why – of all the available and competing forms of group identification – the national has so predominated over others. The answer is that, despite its many failings, nationalism has seemed to offer a richer and more varied set of possibilities here than its rivals, and has seemed to present a more capacious and effective world-view. The individual and the local; the rational and the visceral or emotional; the economic and the material as well as the psychological and the spiritual; the cultural and the political – nationalism has seemed to offer so many varied possibilities at once that it has devoured or eclipsed its rivals.

I don't write this as a nationalist, but in an attempt to explain the durability, pervasiveness and power of nationalism as the world's most significant political force. And central to the appeal of nationalism – and to what its adherents persistently, ostensibly and often enough genuinely see as its essential feature – is the associated idea of freedom: freedom pursued, achieved and maintained. Nationalists pursue freedom in the sense of political independence for their nation; in the sense of liberty of cultural expression; in their linking together of popular sovereignty, equality and freedom; in the pursuit of freedom from economic burdens upon the national community; and so on throughout history. As we'll see later in this book, the story is, in practice, much more complicated than this might sound: nationalists can constrict as well as liberate. But freedom has been a recurring melody within the nationalist symphony.

Another important aspect of our subject concerns the question of when nations and nationalism arose. Some hold that nations are ancient, perennial, or even primordial in the sense of existing from the very beginning of humanity. There are those who see the nation as, effectively, a timeless entity, unchanging in its distinctive and special glory. More modestly, some think that nations and even nationalisms can certainly be detected in the pre-modern period. But another school of thought considers that nations and nationalisms are, in fact, very modern creations: that nations have been produced by nationalists in the period from the eighteenth century onwards, to meet specifically and uniquely modern needs and conditions. On this latter reading, nationalism is a response to, and even a function of, modern developments such as industrialization. In pre-modern times, the needs of communities could be met at local level: kin and village provided all the necessary connections and interaction for societies which existed in static and small-scale form. When technological change occurred, however, there was a need for greater mobility (to meet the needs of industrialization, for example, and to allow for the growth of urban centres and communities which required economic and other interaction over larger units of space and population). How could kin association, or entirely local shared culture, provide for the needs of such modern communities, which required shared languages and values and assumptions in order to work effectively? They couldn't, so the modernist argument runs, and therefore nationalism was born. What was the unit for the newly created shared culture which allowed people to move about over larger areas and yet still fit into society and operate well within it? The nation. According to this view, nationalism and the nation were not only dependent on modern conditions (the capacity for travel, communication, or knowledge about things beyond your locality, and so on) but were specifically created to meet the needs of the technologically-expanded modern world.

It might be best to accept neither of these stark positions (the perennial/primordial on the one hand and the modernist on the other) entirely on their own terms, and some scholars have now sought ways of achieving something of a compromise between them. Each of the two positions has much in its favour, but each also has conspicuous faults. Nations clearly are not timeless in the sense of being unchanging, and the kind of nation imagined in, say, the nineteenth century would have been unimaginable in many of its aspects to a person from the medieval period. On the other hand, it's equally clear that some nations did – in admittedly primitive form – exist prior to the process of industrialization so stressed by some modernists.

So it might be better to suggest the following. Nationalists do create and re-create nations in the modern period, but in doing so they tend to use pre-modern ingredients: these ingredients are inherited rather than chosen from a limitless pool; they are not infinitely malleable; and their interaction with one another, and indeed their success, depend in part upon qualities which are inherited and defined by pre-modern layers of experience in each nation. Nations may be invented, but not all inventions work or become popular: successful nationalisms build on prior foundations which, to some degree, determine the shape and appearance of each nation in question. Nationalists work with pre-modern inheritance and understanding, and their nationalisms gain strength from – just as they are constricted by – their particular historical long-rootedness. So continuity as well as discontinuity is part of the story. Pre-existing, pre-modern attachments are important rather than trivial, although there was something new and vital in the eighteenth-century forging of a connection between equality, popular sovereignty and freedom within the context of the nation. After this connection had been forged, modern nationalism emerged – but it was a force which drew on prior historical momentum. Nationalism and the nation should be seen as modern phenomena which emerged in the eighteenth century, but which built upon important foundations in the form of an earlier proto-nation (first, primitive, ancestral).

So ultimately the two questions (What is nationalism? Why does it so dominate human history?) are crucially linked in explanation, and this book argues that such explanation lies in understanding the particular nationalist linkage between community, struggle and power. Community suits human nature and our deepest human instincts: we want survival, self-protection, safety and security and we possess a group instinct; social by nature, we want to belong to a stable, coherent and effective community which will meet psychological needs (regarding purpose, self-esteem, meaning) as well as material and practical ones. The shared features of nationalist community (drawn variously from territory, people, descent, culture, history, ethical superiority and exclusivism) are important here as possible means of communication. And such national community offers rewards that are superior to – more capacious and powerful than – rival versions of group identity. Yet this community identification is only part of the nationalist story and explanation. Collective struggle is also vital, whether for sovereignty, unity, independence, material benefits, cultural status, or group and individual advancement – and, in all of this, for freedom. Each of these goals has its obvious appeal, but there can be allure also in the rewards of struggle as such. And this collective mobilization turns on questions of power: power as a goal (the establishment, legitimation, possession and consolidation of power, often in the form of a state which is sovereign and self-determining), and also power as something by means of which you secure and guarantee the goods which you pursue as a nationalist.

This general explanation accounts for nationalism in general, rather than enabling us to understand the intricacies of how, where, why and when it came into particular people's lives in any one place. In order to do that, we need to test our theory of nationalism against the history of our particular – in this case, Irish – nation. More precisely, we need to look through the combined lenses of community, struggle and power at the detailed story of nation and nationalism in Ireland.

PART ONE

IRELAND BEFORE 1800

ONE
'A WILD AND INHOSPITABLE PEOPLE'?
PRE-1700 IRELAND

1

> Ireland is situated in the North Atlantic, between the degrees
> fifty-one and a half and fifty-five and a half north, and five
> and a quarter and ten and a third west longitude from
> Greenwich. It is the last land usually seen by ships leaving
> the Old World, and the first by those who arrive there from
> the northern ports of America.... Who were the first
> inhabitants of this island, it is impossible to say, but we
> know it was inhabited at a very early period of the world's
> lifetime – probably as early as the time when Solomon, the
> Wise, sat in Jerusalem on the throne of his father David.
>
> Thomas D'Arcy McGee[1]

Ireland's ancient distinctiveness has been much celebrated by modern
Irish nationalists. But how far back into Ireland's compelling history
can we meaningfully talk of an Irish 'nation', 'nationality' or even
'nationalism'? Most books on Irish nationalism simply avoid examining
this question; perhaps understandably, they concentrate instead on the
modern period. Yet the issue of when an Irish nation emerged is a
vital one and we can't explain and understand Irish nationalism
without looking closely at the pre-modern era. If, for example, there
was nothing in pre-modern times that we would recognize as a nation,
then modern Irish nationalists during the past 200 years or more have
been again and again deluding themselves, and much Irish nationalist
argument and assumption will turn out to have been ill-founded. But
if, on the other hand, there do indeed turn out to have been national

continuities between the modern era and an older, earlier Ireland, then we can only properly understand why modern Irish nationalism emerged and developed precisely as it did, through an examination of those more distant times.

A small island on the edge of western Europe, Ireland occupies a total area of 32,595 square miles; at its greatest length it is only 302 miles, and at its greatest width only 171. Around 10,000 years ago the first people arrived here, nomadic hunters who spread to different parts of the island and who represented its earliest human habitation. One of the last places in western Europe to be inhabited, Ireland was to acquire numerous names: 'Ériú' is the Old Irish origin of the modern 'Éire' and of the first part of the English 'Ireland'; the Latin term 'Hibernia' also gained currency (being used by observers such as the English monk-historian Bede, author of the great *Ecclesiastical History* (c. 731), and relating to the wintry qualities of the island).

And Ireland also acquired many interwoven layers of population. Different civilizations and peoples and groups were, from the earliest history of old Ireland, written into the story of its inhabitants; so notions of a monochrome race, of any supposed racial 'purity' or homogeneity, are deeply misplaced. Since ancient times the Irish gene pool has been profoundly mixed, and recognition of this hybridity is important if we are to assess later claims regarding true or authentic or pure Irishness. There was no single, original Gaelic or Irish race, just as there were no discernible natives in the sense of an original people than whom all others and their descendants are less truly Irish. The mixing of populations makes nonsense of any such claims. (Indeed, the word 'native' – if retained – should probably be kept merely as a term for those who have been born in Ireland. This would have the merit of reflecting the word's actual meaning, and it would have the further attractions of being universally fair to people of any descent and of avoiding misleading assumptions about race and authenticity.)

Even in the Iron Age, the people of Ireland were genetically very mixed, and the Irish population has been heterogeneous or kaleido-scopic in terms of race or ethnic origin for as long as we can trace it. Waves and waves of incomers produced a long-mixed, intermingled Irish population, with hybridity and mongrelism of descent being the result. This was true from the earliest peopling of the island ('Prehistoric Ireland was a considerable racial mix'[2]), a racial mixture having been established even by around 100 CE. It was possibly sources relating to this period which formed the basis for one of our earliest accounts (and maps) of Ireland: that produced in the mid-second century by the Alexandrian Greek geographer Ptolemy. Even his version of Ireland and its people, however, predates the emergence in the fourth century of a sufficient body of contemporary written evidence for Ireland truly to enter the historical period. So much of our very earliest Irish story is, of necessity, vague and patchy. An important example of this concerns the idea – so vital to later nationalist thinking – of the Irish Celts, for the Celtic myth has long held a central, popular place within Irish self-image and identity (and in much modern self-presentation and marketing, as even the perusal of an Irish airport bookstore will confirm).

Important Irish nationalists have often embedded their vision of Ireland's distinctive identity within a Celtic setting, at times making the Celt and Celticism definitive of authentic Irishness. The great Fenian Michael Davitt (1846–1906), for instance, dedicated his *Fall of Feudalism in Ireland* (1904) 'To the Celtic peasantry of Ireland and their kinsfolk beyond the seas', and frequently depicted the Irish as Celtic.[3] Other prominent figures have also written the Celts firmly into the Irish national story, stressing the supposedly long-term continuity, tradition and unity of the Irish people or 'race' right back to earliest times;[4] and there exist still many books on the shelf proclaiming the view that the Irish were Celts.[5]

But did the Celts actually exist in Ireland? Written evidence cannot answer the question, but current archaeological evidence suggests that we should, perhaps, abandon the notion of early Ireland (or, indeed, early Britain) being inhabited by Celts at all. As far as ancient Ireland was concerned, 'the Celts, as popularly conceived, did not really exist'.[6] People in Ireland did not call themselves Celts or Celtic until the eighteenth century, nor did anybody else use those labels to describe them until this much later period. From then onwards, the terms have had profound meaning for many Irish people; but to assume that such meaning is built on actually-existing ancient Irish Celts is ahistorical. There appears to have been no Celtic invasion of, or mass-migration of Celts to, Ireland; contrary to the image still so widely popular today, it appears that Celtic Ireland did not actually exist.[7]

This should not lead us to dismiss the power or attractiveness of Celtic identity for many modern people, in legitimating later national identities through supposed ancient lineages: pride, self-consciousness, authenticity and distinctiveness have all been strengthened by the idea of the ancient Celts in Ireland. And the culture (the striking jewellery, for example) supposedly explained by a Celtic population, might be considered just as alluring if one understands it as involving cultural influence and exchange rather than Celtic invasion or migration. But it's important to be clear about what actually happened in the past rather than merely to project on to it those things which we might find more comforting. If no racial or ethnic group in Ireland in the ancient or medieval period was known, or identified itself, as Celtic, then we should not pretend that they did so, and 'the Celts' is a title which should therefore be rejected for Irish people from these centuries.

Unlike much of Britain, Ireland was never subjected to Roman rule or occupation. The conquest and control of the island do seem to have been considered (and considered feasible) by some;[8] but although such an invasion might have been planned in the first century CE, much of the fascination of medieval Ireland arises from the fact that – unusually, among modern western European nations – it was a place which the Roman empire did not in fact encompass. In contrast to Britain, which was part of that empire until the early fifth century CE, Ireland developed within a more detached context. Relations between the neighbouring islands were important even in this early period: though it had not directly experienced Roman colonization, Ireland did come under the influence of Roman culture (tools and the wine trade provide good examples), an early example of the way in which physical proximity between Ireland and Britain again and again helped to determine developments on the smaller island.

2

Nature has placed the two islands of Britain and Ireland in such close neighbourhood that it was inevitable that their destinies should be interwoven in various ways ... Ireland, lying to the west of the greater island, has by geography and history been made to feel the impact of it from early times.

Edmund Curtis[9]

Indeed, how could it have been otherwise? Ireland and her larger neighbour had known a long history of interaction before the famous English invasion of the twelfth century, and expansion often involved movement in the opposite direction to that later incursion. During the fourth and fifth centuries, for example, there was considerable movement between the two islands, and Irish colonists took over significant parts of Wales and Scotland; English and Welsh forts were commonly built to protect people from the raids of Irish pirates. So Irish attacks on Britain, Irish migrations to Wales, England and Scotland, and Irish settlements on the larger island all complicate the often-assumed pattern of timeless English bullying.

Other connections beyond the island included trade (extensively with Britain, but also with Spain and Gaul): in the sixth and seventh centuries CE goods, texts and people all moved back and forward between early Ireland, Britain and mainland Europe. At this time Irish learning, art and skilled craftsmanship seem to have been highly impressive, and Irish culture to have been of significance and influence within Europe. In Ireland itself the early medieval period saw mixed patterns of agriculture (arable as well as livestock, with much emphasis on crop cultivation). Woodland was widely prevalent, and was vital for heating, building and other purposes. Apparently low levels of early Irish population (probably between half-a-million and a million around the eighth century) allowed for impressive levels of prosperity; for those at the higher end of the stratified social world there was plenty of meat, milk, butter, cheese, honey and even beer. So Bede's opulent-sounding eighth-century observations might not have been entirely wide of the mark: 'Ireland is the largest island after Britain, and lies to the west ... The island abounds in milk and honey, and there is no lack of vines, fish, and birds, while deer and goats are widely hunted.'[10]

Early Ireland was socially stratified and distinctly hierarchical: an inegalitarian society within which status was of the highest significance.[11] Around the eighth century there was a broad division of society into kings, aristocrats and those beneath them, with slaves operating at the base of the pyramid; slaves were reasonably common in early Ireland, some of them having been acquired by force in raids such as those on western Britain in the fourth and fifth centuries. There appears to have been much stability in the medieval Irish order: during the fifth- to seventh-century period, for example, the broad patterns of Irish social structure seem not to have changed dramatically. But one crucial change which did occur during this early period – and which was to have the most profound effect on the later development of Irish nationalism – was the establishment within Ireland of Christianity. This involved a very lengthy process. We do not know precisely when Christianity first came to the island, though it might possibly have been during the fourth century; by midway through the fifth, it had established some foundations; and by the second half of the sixth century the conversion of Ireland to Christianity had in significant measure been achieved. This had not been a smooth, easy, uniform or inevitable process. In 431 CE Palladius was sent by Pope Celestine I as the first bishop to the Irish Christians,[12] so already by that date there were Christians in Ireland; there are definite signs that as early as the fourth century a sizeable Christian community had existed here. Palladius apparently made some progress in his Irish mission, and during the fifth and sixth centuries other churchmen came to Ireland to Christianize the place further.

But some Irish kings were recalcitrant in their attitude towards the new faith; much pagan belief continued long into medieval Irish life, and even in the seventh century it seems that complete Christian control of the island was not secure. Moreover, although the sources for the sixth and seventh centuries show Ireland to have been firmly Christianized, those sources originate mostly with Christian authors and so need to be considered carefully in light of the intentions, biases and preferences of those who produced them.

Yet the broad pattern remains: in early Ireland Christianity did come to replace prior cults and practices and beliefs. By the time of the eighth century the Catholic Church in Ireland was well established and respected: it provided rites and served numerous other important functions for the Irish people (baptism, Mass, preaching). And the people came to maintain the Church and therefore effectively paid its clergy. Famously, great monasteries (not to mention important nunneries) were established. During the sixth century Clonmacnois, Clonard and Bangor emerged and, although one should not over-emphasize the role of the monastic within the early Irish Church, these developments do reflect the establishment within Ireland of ecclesiastical authority, of Church wealth, and of a sturdy version of Latin Christianity. As with all profound religious movements, this Catholic Christianization of Ireland clearly had a deep effect on society at large: one of the striking things about the early-Irish Church is the degree to which it was not cut off in quietistic fashion from society, but rather interwoven with it in terms of authority, revenue acquisition, arbitration and so forth.[13] In many ways Church and society had become one.

So Ireland came to lie firmly within medieval Christian civilization, a distinctive part of a wider culture and interacting fruitfully with it. The early-Irish Church considered study and learning to be of great importance, a fact reflected in justly celebrated works such as the gloriously illuminated Books of Kells (a Latin copy of the Gospels completed around 800 CE) and Durrow (an even earlier decorated copy of the Gospels). And celebrated figures also arose. Colum Cille (Columba the Elder, 521/2–97) was a significant monastic influence in the early-Irish Church, and the founder in the late sixth century of the monastery at Durrow from which the famous Gospels manuscript emerged. Columbanus (Columba the Younger, 543–615), a Leinster-born monk trained in the County Down monastery of Bangor, typified another important dimension of early Irish Christianity, that of the *peregrinus* – one who chose to leave home and to live instead as an exile. Columbanus left Ireland in 587 and worked for years in mainland Europe, just as many other Irish churchmen during the medieval period appeared across European lands.

It's interesting to consider how different Irish history and Irish nationalism might have been had Christianity *not* come to Ireland, and it is also worth identifying one of the sharpest ironies of the process by means of which it actually did so. For one of the crucial features which determined the early arrival and establishment of the new faith in Ireland was the island's proximity to Britain. Catholic Christianity – so vital a force in the development and character of Irish nationalism, and so long to be a centrally-defining feature of anti-British politics in Ireland – came to Ireland largely through British influence: 'the principal context of the conversion of Ireland was the relationship between Ireland and Britain';[14] 'It was probably from south Wales that Christianity first came to Ireland.'[15] The main base for Christian missionaries who came to Ireland was Britain, the fact that Christianity was dominant in the larger island by the late fifth century therefore helping to explain Ireland's conversion. And those Irish who had gone to Scotland, Wales and England had often maintained contacts with their homeland, thereby providing an important route through which Christianity travelled so powerfully across the sea to Ireland. Yet again, Irish raids on Britain gathered many slaves there, and thus brought large numbers of Christians to Ireland, further reinforcing the likelihood of the new religion spreading and establishing firm roots. So those later Irish nationalists who so celebrated Ireland's Catholicism celebrated something which owed a great deal to British proximity and influence.

Exemplifying much of this was Ireland's most famous Christian of all: St Patrick. The nation's patron saint, a legendary figure celebrated throughout the world each year on 17 March, Patrick had achieved mythical status from as early as the seventh century. But if he has been the Irish nation's hero, then he was also, in literal terms, a 'west Brit'. Apparently, his original name was Maewyn Succat: he was born in the west of Roman Britain (probably in Wales) around 416 and was captured while still a teenager by Irish raiders who enslaved him and took him to Ireland, where he spent about six years in captivity. After subsequently escaping, he went back to Britain but then returned again to Ireland where, as a bishop, he preached the Christian Gospel to the as yet unconverted – and where he spent the remainder of his life.

It has been thought that Patrick's arrival in Ireland as a missionary bishop occurred around 432 CE and that he died in the late fifth century. But, in truth, little is certain concerning this Irish national saint. Patrick the Briton did indeed work in Ireland and he did endeavour to convert the Irish to Christianity, probably in the early/ mid-fifth century. He does appear to have founded a Church in Ireland. But since the only serious information on Patrick comes from his own writings (to the modern historian, a depressingly thin and unreliable source-foundation), we cannot be confident of too much. Many of the dates of his career remain uncertain. It's possible that two or more people's experiences have been welded together to produce the career later celebrated as Patrick's; and while we do know that there was a Patrician mission to Ireland, we cannot be at all sure about how influential it actually was.

Yet Patrick does reflect key features of the Irish conversion, both in the influence of missionary faith and effort, and also in the importance of British proximity. In assessing the conversion of Ireland, we should also acknowledge the intrinsic features of the faith which came to dominate. And we should situate this religious transmission within the contemporary political context to whose moulding it made such a significant contribution. At the top of Ireland's social and political hierarchy sat the king, but patterns of medieval Irish kingship were complex and changing. In the fifth century, there existed a large number of kingdoms (probably over 100) and so the Irish kingdom was small and the personal quality of the king's rule facilitated by his being able to be intimate with his people. The resilient pattern of such small-scale rule meant that petty, rival kingdoms covered Ireland for much of the medieval period. These many kingdoms were not all equal with one another, but rather existed at various levels of importance. A lower-order king ruled over a *tuath* (a people; more specifically, the lay people of a small kingdom), and had no king beneath him. On the next rung up stood the king who enjoyed a position as overlord of several other kings. Above him again lay the king of a province. There was, in early Christian Ireland at least, no unified Irish kingdom covering the whole of the island. Communication and movement were too difficult for this to have become meaningful, kings had no standing army in this period, and obviously no police or other force which could implement rule in anything like a modern fashion. So the Irish political reality was messy during the seventh and eighth centuries, as competing dynasties jostled and struggled with one another.

It was not that kings lacked ambition or even a measure of real power: churchmen and ecclesiastical theorists helped to forge early-

Irish notions of kingship, drawing on biblical sources and example; and by the eighth century Irish kings did have a certain legislative, judicial and revenue-raising authority. This might involve more promulgation than enforcement, but it contributed to stability and order none the less. Yet it was provincial kings who were the key players at this point, and this reflects the lack of an effective high kingship or supreme Irish kingship for the early Christian era. By the late seventh century there did exist a sense of the concept of kingly rule over the whole of the island. But in practice such territorial control was too difficult and remained as yet unrealized: even as late as the eighth century the Irish law tracts do not recognize a high king of Ireland, a king exercising authority over all of the Irish island.

Such a high kingship would have implied a practical Irish unity which, at this stage at least, remained elusive. But there is evidence from early Ireland (at least by the seventh century) of a consciousness that such all-island rule might at least be possible, and during ensuing centuries strenuous efforts were made to establish it in practice. In later nationalist imaginations, the romance of this pursuit was often associated with the hill of Tara in County Meath, around twenty miles to the north-west of Dublin and regarded by some as having been the seat of Irish high kings. Even by the seventh century Tara was held to be very significant as a seat of kingship, and possibly to have implied more than ordinary provincial power. Yet none of this means that seventh-century kings actually lived or based themselves there, and at this stage any all-Ireland kingship simply did not operate in practice.

Medieval Irish political shape was affected from the late eighth century onwards by the intrusion of Vikings, groups of highly mobile warrior-pirates pursuing plunder. Initial Viking raids in Ireland, Britain and France occurred around the same time (the end of the eighth century). The Ostmen, as they called themselves, first raided Ireland in the mid-790s; by 823 they had circumnavigated the entire Irish coastline. Between the mid-790s and 807 Viking attacks were hit-and-run assaults on the coast and islands; after the latter date these (mostly Norse) raiders engaged in more activity on the Irish mainland itself. In 837 Viking fleets first travelled on Irish inland waterways; by the 830s the raids of the Ostmen had intensified in frequency and had extended in range to include much inland activity, which included the taking of captives. The raiders first wintered in Dublin in the 840s, during which

decade we find the first recorded Viking–Irish alliances – a phenomenon which was soon to become quite common. Viking settlements
became established (Dublin, Waterford, Wexford and Cork among
them), and much intermarriage took place – hybridity yet again. A
second Irish Viking phase occurred in the early tenth century, roughly
from 914 to the 930s, while from the mid-tenth century onwards the
Ostmen made a powerful impact on Ireland as traders.

How important was the Viking effect on Ireland? Was it the case
that, with the aggressive arrival of the Ostmen, there emerged among
the Irish some form of incipient and responsive national identity or
self-awareness? It is possible that the Ostmen helped to sharpen self-
image on the island, and yet several qualifications should probably be
made. For one thing, it is now far from clear exactly how decisive or
devastating the impact of the Vikings actually was, and how significant
a fault-line their appearance truly represents in Irish history. There was
much continuity between pre- and post-Viking Ireland, and earlier
assumptions about the inauguration of a new Irish era have now been
questioned. Moreover, it was simply not the case that the Irish united
against the Viking newcomers. A more common pattern was for some
Irish leaders to fight with the Ostmen against other Irish kings. Thus
the famous battle of Clontarf in 1014 (an inspiration to later figures,
such as 1916 rebel Thomas MacDonagh, who used its memory to try
to inspire his own men before the Easter Rising[16]) was not a contest
between the Irish and the Vikings to see who would prevail in Ireland,
nor a battle to free Ireland from the Ostmen, but rather a clash
between rival Irish forces, one of which enjoyed Viking support in the
conflict. And the considerable extent of intermarriage and intermingling between Ostmen and Irish continues to suggest a pattern of
hybrid layering rather than of sharply defined cultural division.

By the time of the second Viking wave, however, there had emerged
a more serious attempt to establish power across the island. During
the ninth and tenth centuries political leaders were at times able to
exercise comparatively extensive authority,[17] and a telling example here
was Brian Bóruma, king of Munster, who had by the late tenth century
acquired great power throughout much of the Irish south. Political
fragmentation remained, and any notion of established permanency or
continuity of power was absent. But Brian had managed to set up a
form of Irish overlordship by the start of the eleventh century and he

aimed to present himself as a kind of emperor of the Irish. Although he failed to realize this ambition, he did make some progress towards setting up a kingship of Ireland, in terms of receiving submission from other Irish kings. Had Brian survived the battle of Clontarf, then possibly his overlordship might have been consolidated; as it was, Bóruma was killed in that battle north of Dublin on Good Friday 1014. His forces won the day against the combined Ostmen and Leinstermen (the latter challenging Brian's authority over them), and his death occurred at a point when it had seemed possible that he might make the kingship of Ireland something of a practical reality. Brian's descendants remained kings of Munster after Clontarf, but they did not achieve the Irish supremacy which he had pursued: so the impressive power which he had managed to acquire failed, in the end, to outlive him.

Not that subsequent Irish kings lacked ambition. Turlough O Brien had, by the time of his death in 1086, managed to establish authority across much of Ireland. But even this striking achievement did not extend right across the island, nor did it involve the establishment of continuous, settled power. Rather, it was a form of royal authority which had to be established and reasserted and maintained through repeated invasions of subordinate kingdoms.

The complex pattern of twelfth-century power struggles between rival kings reflected Ireland's essentially monarchical conceptions of political power; and it involved, ultimately, the pursuit of a genuine kingship of Ireland. This was echoed by the establishment during that century of a new national structure in the Irish Church. This in turn clearly had implications for the imagining, and the achievement, of meaningful political unity, so interwoven had the ecclesiastical and the political realms become. So this establishment of a national Church was highly significant, and it was a Church established under the primacy of Armagh ('Armagh, the seat of the blessed Patrick and the special see of the primacy of the whole of Ireland', as one medieval observer put it[18]). Twelfth-century kings themselves could create laws, impose taxes, grant land and depose some kings while installing others. They had far greater resources and forces at their disposal than had their Irish predecessors, and so a figure such as Turlough O Connor, king of Connacht from 1106, was able subsequently to make the kingship of Ireland more of a reality than had previously been the case.

3

> It is obvious to the meanest intelligence how far back I could
> look for the origin of Fenianism. If the English had not come
> to Ireland, and if they had not stayed there and done all the
> evil so many of them now allow they have been doing all
> along, then there would have been no Fenianism. And here
> ... I could easily go back to Strongbow.
>
> John O'Leary[19]

These words of the nineteenth-century Fenian John O'Leary
(1830–1907) reflect the lasting role which the famous twelfth-century
English invasion of Ireland was to play in Irish nationalist thinking. It
became a very familiar argument. Ireland should rightfully be free,
united and independent; from the twelfth century onwards it was
enslaved by evil England; the subsequent history of the Irish was the
history of struggle to free themselves from this oppressive embrace.
And such arguments flourished well beyond the nineteenth century.
As late as the year 2000 I myself was unambiguously informed – by an
ex-IRA gun-smuggler in his New York apartment – that Irish history
could easily be explained: 'The Brits – they're the problem, and will
be. They have been since 1169, and will be until such time as they
leave.'[20]

But while Strongbow and his invader-comrades have therefore
possessed much posthumous relevance for varying shades of Irish
nationalist, the first place to start is an attempt to understand the
English invasion in the context of its own times. The twelfth century
was not the beginning of interaction – even of aggressive, invasive
interaction – between the two neighbouring islands. In terms of
Church, trade and learning, and also in terms of settlement, migration
and raiding, Ireland and Britain already possessed by the time we reach
the 1160s a very long, mutual history – some of it positive, some more
distasteful. The English invasion was part of a process of lengthy
interaction which, given the two islands' proximity, should hardly
surprise us.

Nor was it really an 'English' invasion at all. During the late twelfth and early thirteenth centuries Ireland was colonized by an international group which had earlier conquered England and parts of Wales and Scotland, such processes of colonization then being the norm in contemporary Europe. Those who invaded and settled in Ireland in the twelfth century were not all English but rather came from a mixture of backgrounds. The people who came to Ireland as part of this Anglo-Norman endeavour spoke Norman-French and were themselves of hybrid ethnicity, for there had already been intermingling between the English and Welsh and the Normans who had settled in England and Wales. So those who arrived in Ireland in May 1169 were a striking racial mixture: Anglo-Norman lords from Wales, and their hybrid followers, through whose veins flowed a mixture of English, French, Welsh and Flemish blood.

Even the king of England at the time, Henry II, is perhaps not best understood in terms of his English dimension. Being the English monarch was only one of his roles, and not really the central one either. England was but one of the territories which Henry and his successors possessed, his dispersed power stretching into mainland Europe; he spent less than half of his reign as English king actually in England.

Moreover, the invasion was less a case of an English king planning and initiating a westward, colonial expansion than of a king who was almost adventitiously drawn into an Irish excursion. The Anglo-Norman invasion of Ireland arose not primarily from English ambition, but rather from a shift in the provincial power-balance within Ireland itself. Dermot Mac Murrough, king of Leinster since at least 1132, was in 1166 deposed, dispossessed and forced from his Leinster kingdom, having run out of allies after many rivalrous conflicts during the previous three decades. At the start of August in that latter year he set sail for Bristol to look for help; the following summer, 1167, he came back to Ireland with a small band from Wales and with their aid began to win back part of his kingdom. During 1169 and 1170 small groups of Anglo-Normans also arrived in Ireland from Wales in response to Dermot's appeal, and they enjoyed speedy military success. The main body of Dermot's allies landed in May 1169 in County Wexford (which they rapidly took). For when Mac Murrough had approached Henry II for help in 1166, the king had not been willing to become actively involved himself; rather, he had accepted Dermot's offer of allegiance and had agreed to allow people from his kingdom to come to Dermot's aid.

None of this should really surprise us. It was common for a figure such as Dermot, keen to regain his kingdom, to seek out help from a powerful ruling neighbour and from neighbouring forces; for those who answered his call (like the adventurer Robert Fitz Stephen, who led the force which arrived in May 1169), Ireland offered opportunities for material reward and the augmentation of individual power. Among those with whom Dermot came into alliance was Richard Fitz Gilbert de Clare (Strongbow), whom he had met in Wales in 1166–7. Strongbow arrived in Ireland in August 1170, landing near Waterford with a strong force by contemporary standards (probably in the hundreds, and so effectively an invading army). With Dermot he went to Dublin, which duly fell to these invading forces in September.

From 1169 to 1171 the Anglo-Normans conquered Leinster and beyond, and with Dermot's death in the latter year Strongbow himself became king of Leinster. His power-base was now established and his ambitions ranged far beyond that kingdom alone: Ireland presented a chance to expand his own authority beyond that which he enjoyed in England and Wales. But he had to beware of offending Henry II; and it was with a view to curbing his own potentially over-powerful subjects, rather than in the role of a malevolently expansive English imperialist, that in October 1171 Henry himself arrived in Ireland, near Waterford, with a sizeable army. Indeed, it appears that there had been some prior appeals to the king from the Irish themselves, and again this helps to paint a more detailed picture of the contemporary nature of the twelfth-century colonization. An Irish power-struggle had prompted an Irish invitation for Anglo-Norman intervention; when those responding to that call threatened to become more mighty than the monarch wished his barons to be, the king – with some Irish support – arrived in person to establish his own firm authority over his barons.

Certainly, Henry prepared carefully for his Irish sojourn and an extensive expedition ensued. And it could be pointed out that when Irish kings submitted to him and to his formidable army, they had little realistic choice but to recognize his authority in this way. Henry remained in Ireland during 1171–2, leaving from Wexford on 17 April in the latter year. No Irish figure or force had been in a position to mobilize serious opposition or resistance, and Henry's involvement in Ireland, whatever its origins, did have momentous significance. He established the lordship of Ireland, which survived for four centuries until Ireland became a kingdom in the sixteenth century, during the reign of Henry VIII.

Henry II's own lordship did not extend in practice throughout Ireland, however, and we should not think in terms of modern-style, pervasive and penetrative authority. The king and his successors were in fact hesitant and ambivalent, rather than aggressively expansive, in their subsequent dealings with Ireland. But most Irish kings *had* submitted to Henry II when he arrived in Ireland, tending to see him as a check upon his own Anglo-Norman subjects' power here; indeed, the rush to submit to the king in part resulted from a sense that Henry's comparatively distant authority might be preferable to the more imminent power of a rival Anglo-Norman around the corner. The king offered protection from these Anglo-Normans, and the Irish figure claiming high-king status – Rory O'Connor – would in any case have sought to demand allegiance from the other Irish kings. So the choice was one between allegiances, and a willingness to associate with the invader in many cases became the norm.

While some in Ireland clearly thought the English arrival far from entirely negative, there was at least some resistance and hostility to the incursion, and this occurred from early on. Though the Irish were themselves divided, friction did develop between Anglo-Norman leaders and those Gaelic kings who did not come under effective control. It is often, and understandably, remarked that this process of colonization was therefore that of an incomplete conquest. But is this the most meaningful way of framing the episode? It's true that the invaders only managed to gain genuine control of part of the island (colonial dominance, broadly speaking, being stronger in eastern and southern-central Ireland than elsewhere), and that Irish lords therefore remained in power in large parts of the country, with pre-invasion traditions remaining vibrant. But it could be argued also that, in the context of the times, a complete conquest was in fact an unrealistic prospect altogether: the notion that it could have happened (or even that there was a great will that it should) might be misplaced, since the material and other resources for a genuine, all-pervasive Irish conquest probably did not exist at that time. In any case, from the Anglo-Norman perspective, as long as local rulers did not grow utterly out of control in a threatening way, then formal, full conquest was not necessary. Provided that Irish rulers broadly accepted royal authority and the personal form of allegiance that this involved, then (the unlikely) prospect of full, complete conquest was not really needed. A flexible relationship of authority would probably suffice.

So in a period during which colonization was far from uncommon (with many other countries in Europe and the Middle East conquered by the Normans from the eleventh to the thirteenth century), the newcomers added their own contribution to the hybridity of Irish population, culture and politics. Had there been no invasion, then clearly Irish history would not necessarily have been a benign story of fairness and freedom, as seems sometimes to have been implied in later Irish nationalist rhetoric. But it is clear that, together with the influence of the Catholic Church, the political relationship with England proved the greatest lasting influence determining the shape of Irish nationalism through the centuries.

In the twelfth century itself, we can learn something of how that relationship worked through the tendentious yet invaluable writings of prolific author Giraldus de Barri: Giraldus Cambrensis, or Gerald of Wales (1146–1223). A Paris-trained cleric of Anglo-Norman-Welsh descent, Gerald was born in Pembrokeshire[21] and he was a member of one of the leading Norman families which participated in the twelfth-century Irish invasion and settlement: the Barry family were part of the Geraldine clan which played a significant part in the enterprise, and Robert Fitz Stephen (who had led those arriving in Wexford in May 1169) was himself Gerald's uncle. Gerald was a royal clerk in the service of Henry II, and he came to be an important chronicler of Ireland and of the invasion. He first visited Ireland in the early 1180s and his *History and Topography of Ireland* was produced after that visit: appearing in 1188, this is the first major survey of Ireland by a foreigner who had actually visited the country and gathered their data first-hand. And, indeed, Gerald was to be a frequent visitor to Ireland. In 1184 he joined Henry II's entourage and in 1185 he was sent to Ireland by Henry with the king's son John, landing at Waterford on 25 April 1185.

In 1199 Gerald paid a third visit to Ireland, and then a fourth commenced in 1204 (when his Irish sojourn lasted for around two years). So Gerald's writings on Ireland – his *History and Topography* and also his *Expugnatio Hibernica* – represent highly important sources for those wishing to learn of the late medieval period. His accounts were, of course, loaded with the biases that one would expect from a twelfth-/thirteenth-century chronicler (someone who, like his contemporaries, saw history writing as involving a moral dimension, and as a means of guiding and inspiring appropriate human activity) and from a man who was related by blood and allegiance to the invaders and their king. Gerald's sympathies obviously lie with the twelfth-century conquerors of Ireland, and he celebrates their deeds and mission, while morally condemning a pre-Norman Ireland which he presents as barbaric and unChristian.[22] The latter claims helped to legitimate Henry's own, papally-sanctioned invasion in the 1170s, and Gerald in his writings emphatically set out to offer justification for the Irish conquest: 'The kings of Britain have a right to Ireland,' he claimed; and he perceived the justness of this royal claim to lie partly in history, but also in more immediate events such as 'the spontaneous surrender and protestation of fealty of the Irish chiefs', and 'the favour of the confirmation of the claim by the Pope'. And all this was reinforced by the vividness of Gerald's unflattering presentation of the Irish: 'They are a wild and inhospitable people. They live on beasts only, and live like beasts ... a barbarous people, literally barbarous ... a filthy people, wallowing in vice.'[23]

It might be true that in 1155 Pope Adrian IV had legally sanctioned the prospect of Henry's invading Ireland, ostensibly with the goals of extirpating vice and moral impropriety here, of reforming the Church and reinforcing Irish Christianity; the relevant papal document (*Laudabiliter*) sanctioned an invasion on the grounds that it would facilitate Irish religious reform and the extension of the Christian faith and the Catholic Church. But while the king had therefore sought and obtained a papal licence to invade and take control of Ireland, his invasion had not immediately followed and it was in the end occasioned by the later – and indeed the Irish – events of subsequent decades. The papal sanction does, however, point up another irony in the pre-history of Irish nationalism: Henry's conquest of Ireland possessed formal papal legitimation; he himself received support from many higher clergy when he arrived in Ireland (the bishops and archbishops thinking him the best foundation upon which to build Church reform); and thus the twelfth-century English invasion – so lamented by later, ardently Catholic Irish nationalists – at the time of its occurrence enjoyed conspicuous Catholic blessing.

Once the Anglo-Normans had arrived in Ireland, however, they faced the problem that the island was not run centrally in any unified way. Influence and power tended to be patchy and irregular and, to some extent, this pattern was to continue. The invaders did not manage to gain effective control of the whole of Ireland and so what emerged was in practice a world of two communities: part of the population was beholden to the English king, while significant sections remained beyond meaningful control and were run by Gaelic lords. Admittedly, this two-culture image was blurred in places, the English in Ireland and the Irish in Ireland (as they might respectively be termed) becoming on occasions so intermingled through marriage and cultural merging that by the late-medieval period the division between the two was far from everywhere discrete.

During the late twelfth and the thirteenth centuries Ireland was a place through which English kings could reward their loyal followers, a territory over much of which the monarch could provide justice and order and protection, and an island which kings expected to contribute to royal resources. Henry II's son John assumed the title lord of Ireland; when John became king of England (over which he reigned from 1199 to 1216), the English king thus became, henceforth, simultaneously the lord of Ireland. Lordship signified domination and submission, but it was also understood that obligations applied to both parties in this relationship: obedience and service travelled one way, aid and favour and patronage and protection the other. And lordship, *dominium*, was very much a personal bond (the term colony being much less common at the time, though lordship and colony were both used in the medieval era itself).

In 1185 John – by then lord of Ireland but not yet king of England – visited Ireland for the first time, to assume the lordship in person; his next visit was in 1210, this time as king. On the latter occasion he landed near Waterford in June and stayed in Ireland for the rest of the summer. He appears to have strengthened English law and custom on the island (managing to have the barons agree in principle that the laws and customs of England should be adhered to in Ireland as well), though he also seems to have had some rather awkward dealings with provincial Irish kings. He was enthusiastically received in Dublin, and John's reign as king in England was influential as far as Ireland was concerned, since there was during this reign a higher level of royal engagement with Ireland than was customary during the Middle Ages. His visit in itself reflected this (after John's 1210 sojourn in Ireland, the next royal expedition there did not occur until 1394–5), and reinforced the royal rule by proxy and by allegiance which was the medieval pattern for post-conquest Ireland.

But such allegiance to the lordship rested mainly among the Anglo-Norman (and other) arrivistes; prior Irish inhabitants tended not to give such loyalty and existed, in many cases, in a Gaelic Ireland which was beyond the lordship's reach. So the power of royal authority in Ireland failed to match that of royal authority in contemporary England, and English ways and institutions and models were far from uniformly embedded in practice. For one thing, medieval power was at its strongest over regions which were frequently visited, or resided in, by the monarch: yet, as noted, Ireland was not visited by a king during the entire 1210–1394 period. So while there was a royal preference that law in Ireland should be identical to that in England, and while English legislation was formally transmitted to Ireland, this legal equivalence never uniformly became the case in reality.

This pattern of patchily enforced colonization was long to continue, not least because late-medieval English monarchs were preoccupied with much else besides Ireland. The Statutes of Kilkenny, enacted in the Irish parliament in 1366, were largely a codification of existing laws, and an attempt to ensure that the English of Ireland and the lands that they had conquered should indeed remain English. These Kilkenny Statutes lamented the increasing Gaelicization of Ireland's English colony and were intended to reverse such a trend. They proscribed marriage between the English and the Irish, and proscribed also the admission of the Irish of Ireland to governmental office or to ecclesiastical posts within English areas of the island; they commanded that the English in Ireland should speak only English among themselves, and furthermore that they should not use the Irish versions of their names. The Statutes of 1366 said much more than just that the Englishness of the English in Ireland should be preserved from corrupting Gaelic influences, but it is for this that they tend to be remembered. And the legislation really set out an ideal standard for which the English in Ireland were supposed to aim. In practice, relations between the English and Irish cultures in Ireland remained considerably more fluid than a cold reading of this legislation would suggest: the Irish and English communities frequently blurred into one another where they interacted persistently and where close and fairly harmonious dealings could emerge between the two groups.

In the fourteenth century, then, the king of England was lord of Ireland also, and concerns for English security unsurprisingly played a part in how the monarch viewed this Irish lordship. By mid-century, English political authority grew from London and Dublin while a self-consciously Gaelic society in Ireland closely coexisted, and an English population in Ireland possessed a complex identity (to some degree, one which lay between English authority and Gaelic society).

If during the fourteenth century there was some measure of retreat on the part of colonial power in Ireland (with local rulers being the most conspicuous winners), then during the fifteenth century the now famous English Pale reflected contemporary political and cultural realities in Ireland. This fortified line marked out and signified the area around Dublin within which English rule truly functioned. Beyond this boundary, as long as the nominal authority of the king was respected, practical power was of necessity left to rest with locally powerful magnates. At the end of the fifteenth century this English Pale – the area within which English law, custom, language and culture flourished in Ireland – was a region which had shrunk to a comparatively small area around Dublin itself.

And the late-medieval period witnessed developments which might suggest the emergence of something like a proto-national conscious-ness in Ireland. In 1381 Irish clergy protested to the English king that they should properly not be bound by statutes from an English parlia-ment within which they were not represented. In 1460 an Irish parliament meeting in Drogheda declared that 'the land of Ireland is and at all times hath been corporate of itself'[24] and was bound only by its own legislation. If this marked a declaration that Ireland was bound by Irish legislation alone rather than by English statutes, then could this 1460 parliament be seen as having effectively declared a form of parlia-mentary Irish independence? The picture is probably much less simple than that. The gesture of 1460 certainly did not necessarily involve disowning loyalty to the king. Moreover, in fifteenth-century Ireland the parliament was comparatively limited in power and function:

> The fifteenth-century Irish parliament was above all an administrative board, with only minor, and local, legislative functions before 1494. It was important and successful precisely because it was an instrument of royal government, and as such it helped to extend royal control rather than to promote separatist tendencies.[25]

4

> The contrast in religious outcome between England and the other Tudor kingdom of Ireland could hardly be greater: in Ireland, official Protestantism became the elite sect and Roman Catholicism the popular religion, in a result unique in the whole Reformation. In no other polity where a major monarchy made a long-term commitment to the establishment of Protestantism was there such failure.
>
> Diarmaid MacCulloch[26]

Though rarely treated in detail in studies of modern Irish nationalism, the Reformation is one of those episodes without which nationalism, as it has actually existed in Ireland, is simply incomprehensible. Around 1300 the influence of English royal government had affected roughly two-thirds of Ireland, but by the mid-fifteenth century such influence had been cut back to cover less than half of the island; given the lack of resources or men necessary for implementing policy systematically, English state power in Ireland was restricted and authority was, at best, vicariously extended via local gentry and nobles over much of the country. Areas too far from Dublin could not be more than distantly supervised.

So when Henry VII inaugurated the Tudor regime in 1485, he inherited in Ireland a dual and potentially troublesome possession. The English and the Gaelic worlds in Ireland did interact, but they were also in many ways markedly different from each other. Within this two-culture situation, the English community in Ireland seems to have seen itself as just that, an English political community which resided in Ireland rather than in England.

Could Ireland represent a threat to English royal security? In 1487 the royal pretender Lambert Simnel appeared in Dublin and was accepted by the Earl of Kildare, Lord Deputy of Ireland, as being the Earl of Warwick. As such, he was crowned king of England in the Irish city, thereby reinforcing something of the more negative strategic reality of Irish proximity to England (a persistent theme in the history of Anglo-Irish relations and, later, in that of Irish nationalism). In 1491 another impostor, Perkin Warbeck, appeared in Cork, further underlining the potential for danger.

In September 1494 Henry VII appointed his four-year-old son, Prince Henry, as Lieutenant of Ireland, and Sir Edward Poynings as Deputy-Lieutenant. The following month, Poynings landed at Howth, with around 400 men, and when his parliament met at Drogheda in December it passed the famous Poynings' Law (in reality, one of many laws passed by this parliamentary gathering). Ireland had possessed its own parliament since 1264; Poynings' 1494 legislation was intended to mean that a Lord Deputy in Ireland would not be able to use parliament for purposes other than those approved of by the king himself. The new law stated that no Irish parliament could properly be held without the king's prior consent, approval and licence, and without the king, his lieutenant and his council approving any intended legislation in advance. If no bill could be introduced save those approved in advance by the king and his council in England, then it was hoped that no Irish parliament would in future give apparent legitimacy to a pretender to the English throne. So the motivation behind Poynings' Law was essentially the pursuit of security rather than that of imperial subjugation. Initially intended as a means of limiting the independent power of the Lord Deputy, in practice and in time the new law had the effect of limiting the legislative independence of the Irish parliament: it meant that bills tended to be initiated by the king, with the Irish parliament increasingly becoming a mere instrument of royal will, and indeed meeting much less frequently than before.

Such, then, was the context as we enter sixteenth-century Ireland – a century labelled by one of its historians as a period of 'incomplete

conquest'.[27] The early part of this century was the period of King
Henry VIII's rule (1509–47) and of the Reformation which lastingly
divided European Christianity into Protestant and Catholic. The theological feud famously involving Martin Luther in the early sixteenth
century erupted into a major fissure in European history, as during the
1520s the Protestant Reformation spread powerfully through much of
Europe. The religious ideas of the new faith (a theology of all-
embracing human sin, of human incapacity to fulfil God's law, of God-
given salvation with free redemption and forgiveness through faith in
Christ, of the centrality of Scripture and the superiority of this Word
of God over the words of the Church or of mere men) helped to ignite
religious, social and political upheaval, as religious thinking and
motivation interwove with social and political concerns.

    In England, the Protestant Reformation first emerged less because
of the attractions of theological innovation than because of the king's
political and personal exigency. Luther did early on attract a cult in
England, but it was not this which stimulated Henry VIII's break from
Rome and England's Reformation by royal command. Unable to obtain
papal annulment of his first marriage (and keen to embark upon his
second), the king broke from the authority of Rome, and so the
legislative Reformation of the 1530s laid the foundation for the
conversion of formal English religion to Protestantism. The reign of
Edward VI (1547–53) saw a more full-blooded shift towards Protestant
faith and doctrine, and while Mary's reign (1553–8) witnessed an
attempted Catholic restoration in Tudor lands, the lengthy rule of her
successor Elizabeth I (1558–1603) saw England become, in effect, a
Protestant nation. 'The middle decades of the century saw the Mass
adjusted, translated, abolished, reinstituted, then abolished again – this
time, as it turned out, more permanently – in 1559.'[28] This Reformation was a gradual, jagged and complex process, marked by much
continuity as well as great shifts: most parishes, for example, did not
change their vicar during these tumultuous, mid-century years. Just as
there had been a certain vibrancy to pre-Reformation Catholic faith
and devotion and practice, so too Catholicism lived on in many minds
and hearts after the English Reformation and there was a tenacity to
post-Reformation English Catholicism. In some places Catholics continued to be Catholics, remaining defiant enough to 'continue in this
Catholic profession', as one recusant put it in Oxford in 1581.[29]

But the broad pattern remains that, by 1603, England had formally and overwhelmingly become Protestant.[30] It was not, of course, the case that in England all people became deeply reformed in their thinking even after Elizabeth's reign. But a situation in which the Church had become Protestant and the people substantially so, represented a marked and decisive achievement. Politically driven at first, complicated and messy in its evolution, the English Reformation had none the less worked.

Not so in Ireland, which remained largely Catholic. Henry VIII was declared king of the realm of Ireland in 1541, Ireland thereby changing by legislation from a lordship to a separate kingdom, albeit one which belonged to the English monarch. But Henry did not intend to absorb Ireland into the English nation, and there continued a recognition of a sense of Irish difference and hostility as far as the Gaelic Irish were concerned (a government report of 1515 referred to the latter as 'the king's Irish enemies',[31] and state papers from 1534 show the 'defence of Ireland' still to have been an anxiety[32]). But as material and spiritual power changed from Catholic to Protestant hands during the sixteenth century in England, so too a Protestant Reformation was exported to Ireland – where it fell on stony ground. In May 1536 the Irish Reformation parliament met and enacted the key statutes of the Henrician Reformation as had been passed in England, the 1536 Act of Supremacy declaring Henry to be supreme head of the Church of Ireland. But declarative statutes could only represent the start of what needed to be a wider and longer process of actually implementing change on the ground – a process which did not occur in Ireland.

Although there were committed, indigenous Irish Reformists and a Protestant state Church of Ireland did emerge, very many of the sixteenth-century Irish retained their loyalty to the Pope and strongly resisted attempts to make them comply with what now became the state religion. The newly Protestant state Church took over in Ireland, as it did in England, the ecclesiastical economic and physical infrastructure. But an alternative, Catholic Church continued to flourish, and the majority of the Irish population remained loyal to it and rejected the new religion. The Edwardian and Elizabethan periods did witness attempts to consolidate Protestantism in Ireland, but Catholicism remained strikingly and resolutely resistant, and by the end of the 1560s Irish Protestantism was clearly struggling; from 1590 onwards it was obvious that Ireland's Protestant Reformation was sinking every-where.[33] Indeed, in time, the Counter-Reformation would triumph in Ireland over the Reformation. And in this, Ireland deviated from what became the usual post-Reformation European experience, that of *cuius regio eius religio*: according to this pattern the religion of the state's rulers (the princes) became the religion of the people; in Ireland, by contrast, the state was now Protestant but most people emphatically were not.

This was not an inevitable occurrence,[34] but it was one which had huge importance for the later development of Irish nationalism, in ways which could not have been anticipated at the time. Had the Protestant Reformation succeeded in Ireland, it is perfectly possible that the history of Irish nationalism – of separatism and rebellions, of culturally-inspired movements for independence – would have been almost entirely different. For from the sixteenth century onwards political or ethnic division between English power and any Irish who opposed it was a division made more deep and impermeable because it was reinforced, if not defined, by religion. Irish Catholicism would now for centuries be identified with a certain resistance to English power, while Protestantism was associated with that power itself. If the English nation emerged as a Protestant nation, then its Irish rival undoubtedly grew strong as a Catholic community. As a result, the character of Irish nationalism, and the gulf which divided it from accommodation within the British embrace, are both in part explained, one of the key features differentiating Irish from Welsh or Scottish relations with England being the pervasiveness of a different Irish religious faith. As with other places,[35] organized religion helped to shape the nation in Ireland, and in embryonic form began to do so from at least the early-modern period. For while modern observers, living in an age less firmly Christian than those which preceded it, might consider religion to be a surface emblem or badge of deeper realities and allegiances,[36] this was not how earlier ages saw things at all. To those who embodied the emergent Catholic Irish identity in the sixteenth century – and also to those who later, for example, made up the ranks of nineteenth- and early-twentieth-century Irish nationalists – Catholic belief, experience and culture were indissolubly part of one's sense of proto-nationality. This was one legacy of the failure in the sixteenth century of the attempted Protestant Reformation in Ireland:

that the state-sponsored Reformation failed to win over indigenous Ireland had the most profound impact on the shape of later Irish nationalism. Tudor authorities had recognized that the conversion of Ireland to Protestantism would be a good way of ensuring political loyalty;[37] the converse, of course, was also true.

But why did it fail? Why did state and Church become Protestant while most of the people remained Catholic? Four main reasons might be suggested: a lack of will, a lack of power and resources, a lack of sufficient guile, and a distinctive religious setting against which to work.

Tudor rulers displayed a marked ambivalence towards their Protestant project in Ireland. It was not a particular priority for Henry VIII, who was unwilling to commit the kind of energy, time and resources which would have been necessary for the implementation of the Irish Reformation. Similarly, during Edward VI's reign, the enforcement of the Reformation in Ireland did not rate particularly highly on the royal political agenda. Indeed, the pattern of Tudor attitude towards the Irish mission was that of intermittent engagement: the importance of Ireland came and went from royal vision, and there was a rather low-priority, unsustained approach. There was not, for example, sufficient commitment to the financing of the necessary educational aspects of the Reformation in Ireland, or a willingness to commit to the scale of repression that would have been necessary for ensuring conformity to the new faith. Lack of will on the part of the English royal administration partly explains slack implementation.[38]

Reinforcing this, however, is the question of whether effective power and resources existed in any case for the imposition of the Protestant faith in meaningful terms. As noted, royal control in Ireland was far from secure or uniform or robust. In contrast, for example, with Wales (where the Reformation was a great success), Ireland had not been thoroughly subjugated in the medieval period, and it remained a rather alien place to sixteenth-century English eyes. Thus Tudor monarchs were only effective rulers over a part of the island (their effectiveness being at its strongest in the east). If the Dublin administration was only rigorously powerful in a limited part of the island, was the state really in a strong enough position to impose change as significant as that involved in the attempted Reformation? The fragility of Henrician Irish government was underscored when in 1534 much of the country

was able to rise against the king and in the name of loyalty to the
Pope; and even in 1590 the resources available to the Dublin authorities
for the implementation of reform were very limited.

So, in contrast with the extent and depth of Tudor power in Wales,
the state's power in Ireland was just too limited. Governmental
resources had long been inadequate, a position which had not been
changed during the early years of Henry VIII's reign. As a consequence,
the demands made on those supposedly implementing the Protestant
Reformation in Ireland far outstripped the resources which were
available to them; and this reality was deepened by the weakness of the
Irish Church in terms of poor finances, lack of clergy, and ruined
buildings. Broadly speaking, effectiveness in the implementation of the
Tudor Reformation correlated directly to the value of ecclesiastical
livings and the smallness of parishes. Where benefices were rich, better-
qualified clergy tended to be found and the process of Reformation
was facilitated as a consequence; in most of Ireland, however, livings
tended to be poor and clerical talent rather sparsely evident. And
where parishes were small, conversion and religious control were rather
easier; with widely dispersed patterns of settlement, Ireland was characterized by comparatively large parish size.[39]

A third explanation for the failure of the Irish Reformation concerns
the lack of guile, craft and subtlety involved in the attempted Protestant
implementation. Numerous mistakes were made. Rather than dealing
with the relevant Irish elites (the chiefs in Irish society) as allies, the
Tudor regime increasingly relied instead on the policy of plantation or
settlement. Not surprisingly, this helped to make Protestantism (along
with those who bore it with them as incoming planters) seem alien,
hostile, foreign and negative rather than welcome, beneficial, friendly
and useful. Again, Wales provides a useful point of comparison. There,
the Tudors (who had Welsh origins and who could be meaningfully
presented as Welsh) played local cultural forces to their advantage
rather than treating them – as in Ireland – as enemies. In contrast to
their Irish counterparts, elites in Wales came to think that their power
would be enhanced by the Protestant Reformation and by the associated Tudor changes in government; they therefore held their interests
to lie with rather than against religious Reform. Irish experience was
very different, with the attempted Reformation relying too heavily on
compulsion rather than persuasion or cooption. The frequent use of

English Protestant preachers and of English or Scottish settlers as carriers of the new faith reinforced the imposed, foreign quality of the Protestant religion. Old English (as the English in Ireland could now be labelled, to distinguish them from newer arrivistes) and Gaelic Irish together shared a Catholic faith, and both saw the Reforming newcomers and officials – the New English – as people who would take power away from them. In a situation within which royal power relied on local elites for its strength and as the agents of any change, this was fatal to the Tudor regime's Protestant Irish endeavour.

Thus politics and religion became decisively interwoven. The sought-after religious changes of the sixteenth century were seen by many as part of a broader Tudor revolution or reform of government, one which in Ireland was perceived as a threat to the autonomy and power of local elites. Certainly by the 1570s, those most conspicuously trying to implement the Reformation in Ireland were strongly associated in the popular mind with a rather unwelcome military and political English programme: the Reformation came to be seen as an English, foreign imposition. The consequent non-cooperation of the lay Irish elite with this attempted process of Reformation was one of the key factors explaining the failure of that undertaking (not least because of the problems of clerical talent and parish size alluded to above). The power of the English state in Ireland became associated with the arriving Protestant community here, while Catholicism united those of varying ethnic backgrounds who had – whether as Old English or Gaelic Irish – been linked by a shared Catholicism with those whom they ruled. What appeal was there to these crucial elites in welcoming a religion which undermined that bond, and which brought with it the prospect of diminished political clout? Rather than implement the Reformation, as the state would have required, Irish lay elites helped lead the resistance to it, a feature of profound importance in a society so characterized by great social deference.

In contrast to Protestantism, therefore, Catholicism came to seem native and indigenous. This was something of an irony, given both the role which English proximity had played in making Ireland Catholic, and the particular ways in which this had been expressed: a Catholic establishment such as the Dominican Black Abbey in Kilkenny – set up in the thirteenth century by William Marshal the younger, Earl of Pembroke – had been founded and had flourished precisely as a result of pre-Reformation English involvement in Ireland.[40] In many ways, the Irish Catholicism which came, after the Reformation, to express deeply anti-English politics, had been something of an English creation in Ireland.

To a degree, all this set the pattern of later Irish nationalist history, with the newly arrived New English seeing their interests and advantage to be tied in with state power and the state religion, and with opponents of state power becoming deeply identified with Catholicism. Indeed, for opponents of the Protestant Reformation in Ireland – whether Gaelic Irish or the Old English who had found Catholicism a useful means of dealing with others on the island – Catholicism now came to be seen as essential to the definition of true Irishness, an emblem which was to last for centuries into the history of Irish nationalism.

Across much of Europe, the intersection of lay elite interest with the Reformers' message constituted the essence of the Protestant movement's success, and yet in Ireland from early on this vital link was lost. By the time of Edward VI's reign in mid-century there was a mingling of military coercion with attempted religious change, but this combination of liturgical innovation and aggressive rough-handling only reinforced for many Irish Catholics the impression that the new ideas were alien and hostile. Tellingly, Mary's Catholic reign produced no martyr in Ireland: 'There was little need to prosecute heretics in Ireland as there were so few ... In Ireland no heretics were burned and nothing disturbed the return of Catholic worship.'[41] Too many of the sixteenth-century Irish elite remained Catholic recusants, and pervasive Catholic influence persisted. One Protestant zealot was able to proclaim in 1580 that Ireland 'does swarm with Jesuits, seminaries, and massing priests, yes, the friars and these do keep such continual and daily buzzing in the poor people's ears that they are not only led from all duty and obedience of their prince, but also drawn from God by superstitious idolatry'.[42]

In other ways too the lack of guile in Tudor Reformation strategy in Ireland can be identified. Attempts to spread Protestantism in Gaelic came too late and were too feeble to be effective (and yet again the very different story in Wales stands in marked contrast, with vernacular religious communication proving central to it). The Reformation required popular evangelism, relying as it did on the spreading of the word through sermons, new doctrines and – most vitally of all – the Bible. Sermons and liturgy in Irish needed to reach the large Gaelic-speaking population, but a catechism in Irish did not appear until 1571, while a New Testament (the central text for the Protestant Reformers) did not emerge in Irish until 1603. Trinity College, Dublin (founded in 1592) did not deliver the anticipated Irish-speaking ministry, and in Ireland the Reformation movement evangelized in the English language – a profound mistake, since evangelism through English to a largely Irish-speaking audience predictably proved very difficult, and only tended to reinforce the idea that Protestantism was alien. Indeed, in Ireland it was subsequent Counter-Reformation Catholicism, rather than Reformation Protestantism, which was conducted in the language of most of the people, and which came to be seen as their natural religion.

A fourth reason for the failure of Tudor Protestantism in Ireland lay with certain distinctive features of the religious situation which preceded the Reformation here. In Ireland, but not in England or Wales, by the time the Reformers tried to convert the Irish to Protestantism there was a very strong, reform-oriented culture among Irish Franciscans, Dominicans and Augustinians. The reform movement in these three Orders was known as the Observant movement (since its supporters wanted a stricter observance of the Rule prescribed for friars), and – again in contrast to Wales – it was strong in late-fifteenth- and early-sixteenth-century Ireland, and those involved with it represented an influential, spiritual elite which enjoyed considerable moral authority and high reputation among the laity, not least in Gaelic Ireland. Moreover, they used the vernacular in their evangelism, thereby reinforcing the impression (indeed, the reality) that theirs was the faith of the people. Religion in this form was difficult to displace, uproot, dislodge. For the Observants were a powerful spiritual elite, widely dispersed, extremely energetic, numerous and deeply rooted among the laity. Determinedly opposed to the Protestant Reformation in Ireland, these formidable friars represented a strong barrier against its progress in Ireland. Observants were, in some cases, flatly recalcitrant; and they were respected by, among others, many within those very Irish elites which the Reformation so badly required on its side. Moreover, if the supposed corruption and presumed need for reform within the old Church represented one possible line of argument for the Reformers, this vibrant and popular Catholic reform movement stood bulkily in the way, and made Irish Catholicism a more difficult target for the Protestant Reformers effectively to hit. And if in Gaelic Ireland the clergy and people were closely tied together, there was also no substantial tradition of religious dissent in Ireland, no native tradition of heresy such as English Lollardy upon which the new religion could build.

So although it would be wrong to suggest that the Protestant Reformation in Ireland was inevitably doomed, there were strong reasons which help to explain its substantial failure. Across sixteenth-century Europe the religious changes associated with the Reformation had a deep impact on the contours of politics, and so it was also in Ireland, albeit in a different way from the norm. Later in Ireland the cause of the Catholic religion and the cause of Ireland the nation would increasingly become interwoven with one another, in ways which it has taken a very long time to begin to unravel. Indeed in this early-modern period it would be wrong to try to disentangle the religious from the political too neatly: to contemporaries, religious beliefs and ideas necessarily had implications for political and civil developments. (At its starkest, one might remember that hostility towards Elizabeth I could be – and was – justified by people on grounds of papal hostility towards the queen. Religion and politics represented interwoven parts of the same world rather than embodying discrete forces.)

And this religious-political process of the Irish non-Reformation had complexities within it.[43] It is true that the failure of the Irish Reformation made Ireland and its subsequent nationalism more mark-edly different from Britain and more difficult to assimilate or absorb within a British framework. But it is also true that, in part, the Reformation failed in Ireland precisely because of prior differences here from the conditions which obtained in England. The failure of the Reformation made Ireland and its later nationalism different; but prior Irish difference had also contributed to the failure of the Reformation.

5

The memory of the black curse of Cromwell lives among the
people. He remains in Ireland as the great exemplar of
inhuman cruelties.

Alice Stopford Green[44]

The late sixteenth century was still marked by English anxiety concerning the security of the Crown's interests and authority in Ireland. Even in the 1590s the English presence in Ireland was, in essence, military. What was to be done? One answer combined political security with religious purpose, and is usefully epitomized in the arguments of the London-born, Cambridge-educated English poet Edmund Spenser (c.1552–99), who spent time in Ireland towards the end of the century (acquiring a large estate in County Cork), and who favoured a rather Draconian approach to the completing of the conquest of Ireland. Religious reform and political subjugation were as one here, as reflected in Spenser's allegorical epic *The Faerie Queene* (1590–96). This stressed the benefits of violence when deployed for truly worthy causes, and indeed emphasized that the righteous must be prepared so to use violence against evil. Force had proved historically necessary in order that civility should defeat barbarism, and Spenser presented a single British world as having been created – through conquest – out of the varied materials of England, Scotland and Wales. Within this portrait, England had an historic and religious mission to defend civility and genuine Christianity, and to do so through the production of a unitary state within the islands of Britain and Ireland. For Spenser, therefore, English Crown authority and religious motivation were intermingled to such a degree, that any attempt on our part mechanically to disentangle them would distort the contemporary view in anachronistic ways. As portrayed by somebody like Edmund Spenser, state interests and the interests of true religion were simply inseparable.

The cause of true religion was certainly at the heart of Spenserian plans for Ireland and for its reform: Protestantism should, he thought, be the end-goal and justification for political schemes in early-modern

Irish strategy, and it is within this setting that we should understand the politics of the early-modern Plantation of Ireland. A Tudor scheme for the reform of the troubling neighbour-island, Plantation became concerted policy under the first of the Stuart monarchs, James I (who ruled during the years 1603–25). It involved the colonization of Irish land by settlers planted here from England and Scotland. For the settlers, new opportunities were available in the new land; for the authorities, the colonies would offer many supposed benefits: security against foreign attack, control of the local population, defence of royal interests, the stimulation of economic development, and – perhaps above all – an exemplary model of civility and true (Protestant) religion which would have a transforming effect on the barbarous Irish.

For the ultimate purpose of, and justification for, Irish Plantation was the Christian one of spreading true religion: dark Catholic influence would be replaced by Protestant light and civility. Indeed, many Planters themselves reached the conclusion that their role would never be fulfilled without the undermining of the Catholic Church's influence around them in Ireland. Whatever its lasting and much-condemned later political consequences, at the time this was emphatically a religious project, a thoroughly Protestant mission. The bringing of true religion to the inhabitants of Ireland would, of itself, be of spiritual value and benefit; religious considerations and motivations were central and decisive, not marginal and incidental, to the Plantation of Ireland in the sixteenth and seventeenth centuries.

As one might expect, this Plantation process was extremely jagged and patchy. In 1571 Sir Thomas Smith undertook to colonize an area in County Down in the north of Ireland; in practice, by the time the body of incomers arrived in 1572, it involved far fewer people than had been hoped, and comparatively little came of the scheme. In the 1580s an attempt was made to set up through Plantation a new society in Munster (civilized settlers being intended to dominate and to be emulated by their surrounding inhabitants), and in the 1590s the government held that military conquest and Plantation were much needed in order to reform and civilize Ireland.

If it worked as intended, then Plantation would make Ireland British.[45] Some Plantation projects were informal, others (such as Munster and Ulster) more formal Crown projects. By the mid-seventeenth century over 20,000 English people had settled in Munster, and around 15,000 English and Scots in Ulster (the latter being from the start a British rather than merely English undertaking). But it is important to remember that not all those of British background in Ireland owe their Irish residence to the Plantations: as we've already seen, the process of migration between the two islands was much more long-term and ongoing than that.

Yet Plantation did produce a large English/British interest in Ireland, a significant body of Irish Protestants who were tied through religion and politics to English power. And the consequences of this for the later development of Irish nationalism and its ambitions were profound. This was to be particularly the case in Ulster, where in 1610 a major Plantation scheme was launched. Land in Counties Donegal, Armagh, Cavan, Fermanagh, Londonderry and Tyrone was divided into variously sized plots and granted to the incomers, who then lived in newly established Protestant clusters. The Ulster model involved the Plantation community as the explicit, distinct focus for the establishment of a British Ireland: they would be self-contained communities set apart from the dislocated Irish, the latter being excluded. Not all Plantation fitted this pattern, however. Under the early-seventeenth-century Leitrim scheme it was intended that the Irish inhabitants be more integrally involved in the newly established Protestant community: with much of the prior population thus incorporated, a new social order could be created.

In Leitrim, as elsewhere, schooling and the Church were both seen as crucial to the process of an anglicizing civilization. (The architectural design of British society in seventeenth-century Ireland had as one of its central supports the Church of Ireland.) And from 1620 to 1641 Leitrim did witness a great transformation as a result of colonization schemes. The Gaelic social order there was replaced and usurped, with much dislocation of the Irish population as a consequence.

Did Plantation work in bringing Ireland to a supposedly proper order, in making Ireland British? State-sponsored Plantations in Ireland had been one instrument of policy from the mid-sixteenth century onwards, and Plantation schemes remained an important strand of British method in Ireland until the mid-seventeenth century. But security and conquest did not result as had been hoped, and it is the vulnerability and partiality of outcome which are perhaps most striking. As early as 1598 the Munster settlement was overthrown by people aiming to expel the English from that southern province; and although English authority was quickly restored, the episode demonstrated the fragility of English interests in and control over Ireland. Plantation did succeed in paying off debts to courtiers and royal servants through the grant of Irish land, and it did establish significant areas of British, Protestant settlement and loyalty and power. But the attempted conquest of Gaelic Ireland remained elusive even into the seventeenth century; the early-seventeenth-century Plantations simply had not led to full or effective English control over Ireland. The experiment in making Ireland British had not worked out as fully as its framers had intended, and dark consequences were to flow from this merely partial success.

The vulnerability of the British in Ireland was famously and bloodily made evident in 1641, when settlers were attacked in a famous rising. The assaults began in Ulster in October, and although they have been seen by some as a rebellion against the Ulster Plantation, their roots were rather more complex: some of those involved had been beneficiaries of the Plantation, and now feared for their interests amid the turbulence of 1640s politico-religious convulsions. Gaelic Irish rebels and the Old English forged an alliance in revolt. Sectarian massacres did occur, with more than 4,000 settlers being killed. The rising spread southwards from Ulster and across much of the island, and although inflated figures long circulated about the extent of killing, the actual violence was frightening enough; and the insurrection did involve vengeful violence practised by Catholics upon Protestants. The year 1641 was to enter the political memory bank of later Irish Protestants ('It would be hard to overestimate the significance of the breakdown in Ulster society in 1641 for future relations between the communities on this island. The memory of Irish attacks on English and Scottish settlers in 1641 . . . contributed to that sense of insecurity characteristic of the Protestant community in Ulster. . . . The fear of betrayal, the sense of being under siege, and the dread of massacre – the legacy of their seventeenth-century experience – are etched deeply in the historical consciousness of the Ulster Protestant community'[46]); and the events of 1641 forcibly strengthened religious division as the key, contemporary fault-line in Irish political life. Protestants' sense of vulnerability was accentuated, as was their notion that all Irish Catholics (Gaelic or Old English) were united against them. For all its variation across Ireland, and its exaggeration in subsequent polemic, 1641 helped to guarantee religious anxiety and hatred in that most sealed of bonds, the bloody episode of violence.

That dreadful year also marked the beginning of an effective Irish civil war which spanned the 1640s and beyond. The civil wars on the neighbouring island provide a crucial context here, as did the 1618–48 Thirty Years War in mainland Europe. In 1642 Irish Catholic forces demanded the establishment of a civil administration more to their taste, and the result was that now the forces of state and settler faced the Confederate Catholics of Ireland, who established their head-quarters at Kilkenny. These were not anti-royalists (they in fact declared themselves for the king – Charles I – and for Catholicism, as well as for their country), but they did create at least theoretical administrative structures of their own, having formed an assembly in 1642 at Kilkenny (hence their alternative name, the Confederation of Kilkenny); this body had the aim of protecting and furthering their interests and of administering Catholic-controlled parts of Ireland.

The Catholic representatives who met in 1642 were an occasionally uneasy coalition of Gaelic Irish and Old English, and they marked an interesting stage in Irish political development. It was to God, Ireland and the king that they proclaimed loyalty (their seal of office carried the words *Pro Deo, Rege et Patria, Hibernia Unanimis* – 'For God, King and Fatherland, Ireland United'), and so the Confederate royalist cause both reinforces and complicates ideas of an emerging proto-national politics. Ireland was clearly envisioned in united terms and its per-ceived interests were to be pursued through administrative representa-tion;[47] and yet it was Catholicism which provided much of what bound them together, and it was to an English king that they proclaimed devotion. Religion was the crucial factor here: much divided the Confederate Catholics (different origins, different social classes and interests, provincial rivalries, personal antagonisms), but they shared their Catholicism and a commitment to uphold their right to practise that Catholicism freely. And while their actual achievements in terms of effective government should not be downplayed, there was here a proto-nation rather than a nationalist movement proper: the mid-seventeenth-century political elite did defend the Irish kingdom's supposed constitutional privileges against Westminster, but the Confederates did not claim sovereignty – so crucial a feature of nationalism as such.

The proto-nation of the 1640s, however, was emphatically a Catholic one. The end of the 1640s and the start of the next decade saw the immediate failure of this Irish Catholic struggle, and the period has become associated in later nationalist memory with, above all, the name of one man. Oliver Cromwell (1599–1658) presented himself as a liberator of Ireland, his military campaigning here during 1649–50 involving, in his eyes at least, an emancipation from Catholicism, barbarism and royalism alike. In the wake of Charles I's defeat in the English Civil War, and his execution in 1649, Cromwell incorporated the kingdoms of Ireland and Scotland into a Commonwealth with England. His role as an English political leader represents his main historical importance; but his Irish career – as Lord Lieutenant and military leader – has earned him almost unrivalled opprobrium within the Irish nationalist imagination. Although only in Ireland for a matter of months, Cromwell is seen as emblematic of the suppression of Irish Catholic and royalist forces and interests in the 1650s, and his name is popularly associated with the confiscation of much Catholic land. (Under the post-Civil War Commonwealth regime most Irish Catholic landowners – whether Old Irish or Old English – were dispossessed of land by law, some receiving smaller holdings in Connacht in recompense. After this point, Protestants owned the bulk of the land in Ireland.)

As indicated by the quotation at the head of this section, from later nationalist historian Alice Stopford Green (1847–1929), Cromwell has entered Irish nationalist memory as epitomizing English cruelty and oppression. It is easy enough to see why this has been the case. The 1640s and 1650s witnessed strenuous efforts to secure and to anglicize Ireland, and Cromwellian forces did massacre Catholics and confiscate lands. Cromwellian policy in Ireland amounted to more than the bloodily famous events of Drogheda and Wexford;[48] but those sieges (Cromwell storming Drogheda on 11 September 1649 and Wexford on 11 October), did involve notorious massacres. The brutality of Cromwell's army was unexceptional by contemporary standards, but it has easily and understandably become etched into a long Irish nationalist memory of grievance against England (albeit, in this case, against an English republican).

So Cromwellian violence in Ireland will not and should not be forgotten. But nor can it be properly understood except against contemporary contexts and attitudes. Here it is vital to recognize not only Cromwell's own personal and profound Protestant faith, but more importantly the international and political setting of the period. Political violence between Protestant and Catholic abounded in early- and mid-seventeenth-century Europe. So mid-century Cromwellian violence has to be understood against not only the massacres of Irish Protestants by Irish Catholics in 1641 (recent, vivid events in which Cromwell saw collective Irish Catholic complicity, and for which Drogheda and Wexford represented a kind of reprisal), but also the slaughter of thousands of Protestants by Catholics in Magdeburg in 1631. Contemporary Protestant fears and anxieties do not make Cromwellian violence any less horrific in terms of its human costs; but they do help us to avoid the frequently anachronistic and isolationist approach often adopted by those who condemn them as yet another example of perennial English barbarity towards Ireland. The early-modern period was one filled with religious violence, carried out by both Catholics and Protestants, and by people whose beliefs in religious truth and in eternal salvation and damnation informed their acts. Irish Protestants' awareness of wider European (as well as specifically Irish Catholic) violence was the context for their own sense of vulnerability and for their own violent acts.[49] And Protestant anxiety would be even more striking in the late-seventeenth-century context: at the end of the sixteenth century around half of Europe had been in Protestant control; 100 years later, only around a fifth remained in Protestant hands. Protestantism seemed in international retreat, and Catholics and Protestants alike in Ireland could see themselves as part of an international war against the other.

In this sense, the later nationalist (and anti-nationalist) focus of memory on episodes of earlier conflict might be seen to reflect central elements of the struggles of the pre-nationalist era. It is widely recognized that history – whether remembered or misremembered – tends to play a major role in nationalist imagination.[50] And in Ireland, modern attention to the battles of the Boyne (1690) or Aughrim (1691) alerts us to the strongly religious dimension to pre-nationalist div-isions. The Restoration of the monarchy in 1660 had confirmed Irish Protestants in owning the land which they had acquired or confiscated; when Catholic James II came to the throne in 1685, many Catholics (resentful of their Irish lot) consequently looked to him for support. James fell out with the English parliament and fled to France in 1688, to the protection of his cousin Louis XIV; in England he was succeeded by Protestants William and Mary, who were hostile to Louis's ambitions. The Boyne and Aughrim followed James's attempt to win his throne back and to do so from Ireland, and the Catholic-Jacobite-versus-Protestant-Williamite character of these battles reflected the realities of pre-nationalist political and religious divisions in Ireland.

It has become fashionable in recent years for scholars to present the modern Irish conflict between nationalism and unionism as an ethnic one, within which religion plays merely a surface role as a kind of badge, an easily exchangeable emblem of something deeper and more genuinely causal. For later periods, there may be something valuable in such an analysis. But for the seventeenth century it would be utterly mistaken to downplay the centrality of religious commitment or the power of religious belief to govern the direction of political change. For it was less ethnic descent than religious attachment which defined battle lines in these years. Whether Old English (essentially descended from the Anglo-Normans) or Gaelic Irish (with older Irish roots), it was possible to be united as a Catholic political family. Landowners who were Catholic and Gaelic, and landowners who were Catholic and Old English, could unite together in fear of what the Protestant administration in Dublin might do to them. And this political pattern would have been unimaginable without the failure of the Irish Prot-estant Reformation.

So the Catholic population – on which foundation later Irish nationalism would be built – was not ethnically homogeneous but it was united in its Catholicism: 'Unlike the populations of other colonies in the Atlantic world, the population of Ireland by the late seventeenth century resolutely resisted simple categorization into colonized and colonizer. Religion, not national origins or even date of arrival, was to be the great divide.'[51] Among other things, this demolishes any neat sense that Irish nationalism-versus-unionism involved a native-versus-settler division: not only were many modern Irish unionists not descended from the Plantation, but many of the supposed nationalist 'natives' were themselves drawn from comparatively recent waves of Irish immigration. In any case, can people born in a country, and possessing ancestors there who date back very many years, really be delegitimized as inauthentic settlers? Would this be an argument to deploy against Americans with Irish, or Polish, or German, or Italian ancestry, or against Pakistanis or West Indians in contemporary England?

TWO

'RATIONAL IDEAS OF LIBERTY AND EQUALITY': THE EIGHTEENTH CENTURY

1

I think I can hardly overrate the malignity of the principles
of Protestant ascendancy, as they affect Ireland.

Edmund Burke, 26 May 1795[1]

Visitors and visionary writers: what might they tell us about the
question of Irish nationalism in an eighteenth-century context? Founding Methodist John Wesley (a frequent visitor to Ireland, making forty-
two trips in total) was emphatic about the distinctiveness which
separated Ulster from the rest of the island in the 1750s:

No sooner did we enter Ulster than we observed the difference.
The ground was cultivated just as in England; and the cottages not
only neat, but with doors, chimneys and windows. Newry, the first
town we came to (allowing for the size), is built much after the
manner of Liverpool.[2]

As someone who travelled four or five thousand miles a year, and who
met a great number of people as he did so, Wesley was perhaps a
valuable enough itinerant observer. And although he had been educated at Charterhouse and Oxford, this Church of England cleric did
possess an Irish dimension. In 1750 alone he travelled very extensively
here; it was a place he greatly loved; and there were other contextual
connections too. Wesley had read, and appears to have met, Jonathan
Swift (1667–1745), that Irish literary giant so ubiquitously familiar
throughout the English-reading world. Dublin-born and educated at

Trinity College, Dublin (TCD), Swift was – among other things – a strikingly talented popular author, writing frequently for a general rather than for a specialist audience. A friend of Voltaire (who was a great admirer of Swift's *Gulliver's Travels*) and a cousin of the poet John Dryden, Swift swaggered through literary and political arguments: satirical, aggressive and wittily raging.

His politics are complex and much contested, the great writer being read by some as a friend to liberty and a liberal, by others emphatically as a Tory, a conservative.[3] Yet the key question for us here concerns Swift's Irish dimension, and more particularly whether he might be seen as some kind of Irish proto-nationalist. He lived in Ireland for most of his life (though not, it should be noted, entirely happily); and he devoted much attention to Irish issues, writing over sixty pamphlets about them. Conspicuous among his Irish writings are his wonderful series of pseudonymous pamphlets, *The Drapier's Letters to the People of Ireland*. In the summer of 1722 the English government had granted a patent to the English ironmonger/manufacturer William Wood, authorizing him to coin over £100,000 worth of copper halfpence for Ireland. The ensuing dispute over 'Wood's Halfpence' was a profound one, a serious conflict between the eighteenth-century Irish and English establishments. And it was this copper coinage controversy which provided the occasion for Swift's *Drapier's Letters*. There was great Irish resentment over Wood's patent: the scheme was produced in London without any recourse to the Dublin parliament or to Irish opinion, and so nobody in Ireland had been consulted about whether this new coinage scheme was a necessary or beneficial development; worse still, the coins were to be minted in England, and the terms of the patent were perceived by many to be too favourable to Wood himself.

The dispute was primarily an economic one (in which aspect it might perhaps be seen to prefigure a theme so common in later nationalist campaigns in many places[4]): the Irish Protestant elite did not dispute the king's right to grant a patent, but rather whether the flooding of Ireland with these coins at this time would have a damaging effect on the Irish currency regime and economy. Swift clearly thought that it would: 'I should never have done if I were to tell you all the miseries that we shall undergo if we be so foolish and wicked as to take this cursed coyn.'[5] His *Drapier's Letters*, the original of which were first published in 1724, were written for a wide audience and they did indeed help to mobilize resentful and furious Irish opinion to the extent that the Whig government in London had to withdraw the patent. So in the early 1720s the English administration in Ireland had been unable to implement its policy in Ireland: the managers who ran the Irish parliament had refused to cooperate in the implementation of Wood's patent, and without the cooperation of local political elites English government could not be carried on effectively. In all of this, Swift's pamphleteering had played a significant part.

Though it was Ireland's economic well-being rather than her constitutional position which was central to this controversy, *The Drapier's Letters* did promote the idea of greater Irish legislative independence (drawing significantly here on the arguments of the Dublin-born political writer William Molyneux (1656–98)).[6] Swift contended that Ireland, like England, had a right to be governed by laws of its own creation. If the real enemy of Swift's polemic was less Wood himself than the English government, then it was also true that Swift clearly thought Ireland had a right to enjoy some legislative independence from that London regime. The people of Ireland had as much right to freedom as those of England, and yet they were currently being denied such liberty.

> Were not the people of Ireland born as free as those of England? How have they forfeited their freedom? Is not their parliament as fair a representative of the people as that of England? ... Are they not subjects of the same king? Does not the same sun shine on them? And have they not the same God for their protector? Am I a free-man in England, and do I become a slave in six hours by crossing the channel?[7]

In all this we can hear pre-echoes of that sense of affronted dignity which was to lie at the heart of later nationalism and which does so much to explain its motivating power.[8] But great care is required in assessing any supposed nationalism on Swift's own part. Seen by some as a kind of national champion, expressing Irish resentment at features of England's treatment of the smaller island, he was in fact ambivalent about the island of his birth, articulately defending its rights while often enough despairing of its actual condition. Much that Swift believed would certainly sit awkwardly with later Irish nationalist assumption. He held that people were obliged to offer obedience and allegiance to the sovereign monarch and his or her legislature. He was profoundly conservative and hierarchical in social terms, and seems to have been hostile to the Irish language (which he considered to be barbaric). He referred to himself as an Englishman born in Ireland; and while we can acknowledge his resentment towards England in many matters, we would also have to note how far he resented Ireland too (seeing his residence there as an exile: writing from Loughgall in County Armagh in 1722, Swift reflected, 'My comfort is, that the people, the churches and the plantations make me think I am in England.'[9])

Swift did argue – and very eloquently – for certain liberties for the Irish. But the Irish he had in mind were not the mass of the (Catholic) people, whom he held not to share equally in sovereignty and authority. Rather, Swift had in mind the middle-class and elite Protestants of Ireland: this – an emphatically Protestant Irish kingdom – was his nation, and it was one which had very little to do with nationalist conceptions of community as they were developed by later generations. Swift was wary of the idea that the people as a whole should exercise practical power: this seemed to him very dangerous. There might, he acknowledged, be a power of last resort in the people, but this was really a power to be exerted only in the gravest of emergencies.

So while Swift's *Drapier's Letters*, for example, address the supposed English mismanagement of affairs relating to the Irish Protestant people, it was not the case that Swift was greatly concerned with the Catholic majority and their own grievances. Indeed, one of the vital foundations for Swift's politics was an Irish institution which played spectacularly little part in the development of modern Irish nationalism: the Church of Ireland. Swift, who became Dean of St Patrick's in Dublin in 1713, was personally and professionally committed to this established Church, seeing it as a defence against unbelief and anarchic chaos. He believed not only that government was of divine institution, but also that his own Anglican Church protected social morality and behaviour and well-being, and that it consequently deserved to hold a position of leadership within society. Conforming to the established religion was presented positively in *Gulliver's Travels* (Swift's marvellous tale of the supposed voyages of Cambridge-educated Lemuel

Gulliver, originally published in 1726 and mostly written from 1721 to 1725).

Jonathan Swift fiercely defended the power and privilege of the Established Church in Ireland, and he could be sharply critical alike of Rome and of Dissent. He thought that when the state–Church relationship was spoiled then the country would necessarily suffer. So Swift's mission to defend the Church of Ireland – its rights and its privileges and position – was, in his view, a mission also to defend the welfare of Ireland itself. The Church of Ireland was, to him, the true national Church, an institution whose welfare was central rather than incidental to his country's well-being.

So if it was Protestant Ireland for which this Protestant clergyman really spoke, then it is also the case that Swift's deepest loyalty was to his Church, and that his patriotism was more a case of loyalty to a Church and to an idea of Church–state relations than to any modern conception of the nation. Just as his vicious, witty satires upon individual and systemic corruption reflected his Christian conviction about the fallenness of humanity and his deep pessimism about its condition, so too his politics were at root religious. Swift's Irishness is vital to understanding the man. But while he did display a concern for defending Ireland's political rights and economic well-being, he protested against English injustice without embracing cultures and identities which would form the basis of Irish nationalism. Indeed, the central loyalty he possessed was to an institution – the Church of Ireland – against which Irish nationalism was firmly to set its face.

If Swift's Irishness has recently come under a powerful spotlight,[10] then the same is true of other great eighteenth-century figures; and here again important questions are raised concerning the possibility of early hints of Irish nationalism. A striking example is offered by the case of the dramatist and politician Richard Brinsley Sheridan (c. 1751–1816). Dublin-born and Harrow-educated, Sheridan was the author of celebrated plays such as The Rivals (1775) and The School for Scandal (1777). And he was also a political figure of some weight: in 1780 he became MP for Stafford, and he was appointed Under-Secretary for Foreign Affairs in 1782 and Secretary to the Treasury in 1783. He was never in Ireland from the time of his youthful departure in 1759 until his death in 1816. Yet, despite this, his Irishness has come to be greatly stressed in recent years.[11] He certainly thought of himself as Irish and he remained mentally focused upon the place: his Irishness, his Irish nationality, were very important to him, and a strong case could be made to the effect that he remained committedly Irish despite his lengthy absence from the island itself.

This had political dimensions, for Sheridan the ironic playwright was someone who could use words as political weapons. A talented public man of letters, he was politically prominent in England also: he was associated with schemes for parliamentary reform (being an enthusiast for broadening the franchise, and for annually elected parliaments), and he was explicit in his commitment to the idea of preserving public liberty. But while he became a key figure in the cause of democratic reform in English politics, his political ideas had an Irish angle too. In the mid-1770s he attacked those who lived in England while simultaneously owning Irish land. More importantly, he displayed a keenness for a measure of Irish independence, and opposed too strict an Irish subordination to laws made in London. Sheridan's father was a Grattanite in politics – a follower of the Patriot hero Henry Grattan (1746–1820), that champion of Irish parliamentary rights and liberties, forever associated with the cause of Irish legislative independence. And both Sheridan and his brother Charles had been influenced by the thinking of John Locke: Richard himself was keen to defend the idea of Ireland's sovereign independence, while Charles in 1779 published a pamphlet asserting that since government derived its authority and power from the community that had established it, so British government in Ireland lacked lawful power.

Another later nationalist theme prefigured in Sheridan's arguments concerns the condition and grievances of the Irish Catholic majority, for whom the celebrated playwright (though Protestant himself) showed a limited measure of sympathy. In the poet Thomas Moore's phrasing, Sheridan was 'far too sagacious and liberal not to be deeply impressed with the justice of the claims advanced by the Catholics'; 'On the general question ... of the misgovernment of Ireland, and the disabilities of the Catholics, as forming its most prominent feature, his zeal was always forthcoming and ardent.'[12] Sheridan certainly refused to enter into contemporary anti-Catholic prejudice, and in this attitude he resembled his rival, the great Edmund Burke (c. 1730–97). Sheridan and Burke were both middle-class Irish Protestants with Gaelic dimensions to their background, and both men flourished in contemporary

England in truly extraordinary careers. They parted political company on central matters – including the French Revolution, which Sheridan welcomed and which Burke famously denounced. But while Sheridan attacked Burke's position on the Revolution and the two men became enemies as a result of their divergence over this epochal event, their careers and ideas do both highlight vital and similar themes concerning the later history of nationalist Ireland.

Burke was (probably) Dublin-born, and he was educated at TCD from 1744 to 1748. An Anglican Whig constitutionalist, he made a very successful career in England (elected to the London parliament in 1765, he remained an MP until the 1790s); he emerged as a prominent orator and political statesman; and he deserves to be recognized as easily the most significant political thinker that Ireland has ever produced. His politics tend, understandably, to be seen through the unavoidable lens of his classic anti-Revolutionary text, *Reflections on the Revolution in France*, initially published on 1 November 1790. Hostile to Rousseau, Burke had denounced the French Revolution in a speech of February 1790. It was not that he was a great celebrant of the pre-Revolutionary monarchy in France; but he did hold that the basis of an ancient constitution had still existed there, a foundation on which a suitably limited monarchy could have been built. To him, the Revolution was an unnecessary and a profoundly negative innovation: it was an historically backward move towards irrationality and violence, an atavistic shift in the opposite historical direction from those modern, rational, libertarian values to which he himself subscribed.

Burke's famous intervention in the French Revolution debate reflected much within his influential philosophy. He was instinctively hostile towards the revolutionary in any case ('The dislike I feel to revolutions'; 'a revolution will be the very last resource of the thinking and the good'); and in the French experiment he perceived further evidence to reinforce his historically-conditioned scepticism about the feasibility of absolute equality ('those who attempt to level, never equalize'). He detected a sharp contrast between high-minded schemes for change and their actual outcomes ('very plausible schemes, with very pleasing commencements, have often shameful and lamentable conclusions'),[13] and he disliked using abstract theories to deal with practical political problems.

In response to the Revolution, Burke saw himself defending hierarchy and property against a particular revolutionary assault; but he also thought of himself as defending that ground which existed between the despotism of the masses and the despotism of the monarch. In seeking to occupy a middle ground, this great parliamentarian preferred a system containing checks and balances, and a structure comprising social hierarchy, law, prescription, tradition and precedent. These last points were vital ones for his thought and argument. He stressed the value of tested and old opinions and practices, he looked for guidance from the wisdom embodied in the past, and he privileged historically acquired experience over revolutionary theorizing. Political principles, he thought, should be assessed not in terms of their abstract appeal but rather in terms of their practical working-out against the actual circumstances which would determine their effect. One should begin with concrete experience and build arguments from there, rather than commence with broad abstraction; for Burke, history rather than philosophy was the true place to start if one wanted to understand politics.

Eloquent and intellectually forceful, Edmund Burke offered a strong case for political caution and for an historically minded conservatism. His hostility to French events – towards the Revolution and its sympathizers – reflected his deep mistrust of attempts to re-create human society without due regard for tradition and history. His anti-Revolutionary philippic famously prompted the radical Thomas Paine (1737–1809) to reply with his *Rights of Man* (1791–2), in which reason and revolutionary possibility were interwoven and enthusiastically celebrated. And it is telling that Burke was engaged in hostile argument with Paine, the great 1790s hero of radical Ireland. As with Burke's hostility towards Rousseau, so also his anti-Paineite position set him against the tide of the emerging nationalist Ireland at the end of the eighteenth century.

Burke's Irish dimension is very important ('I never can forget that I am an Irishman'[14]), and this has long been noted.[15] Ireland had formed him: he spent his first two decades here, was educated at TCD, and was sharply influenced by his Irish connections and relations. His mother (Mary Nagle) was a County Cork Catholic and, when young, Burke had spent lengthy periods with her family. Thus, to his Quaker schooling and Church of Ireland baptism and upbringing was added a Catholic layer: Burke's experience of and sympathy with his Catholic relations in Munster, his part-education in a Catholic school, and his mother's (and possibly his father's earlier[16]) Catholicism, all helped to prompt in him a concern with the relationship between Catholics and the state in Ireland.

The post-French Revolutionary Burke was anxious lest what had happened in France might spread also to England, and his latter-day Irish concerns were pertinent here. Could Catholic disaffection provide the foundation upon which a pernicious French alliance and revolutionary movement could be built in his native land? Could Ireland in the 1790s be the means by which the French attacked and undermined England? He feared as much. In his view, the Irish Penal Laws (under which Catholics suffered various disabilities, and which had been at their strength at the time of his own quasi-Catholic childhood) divided Christians negatively, and presented Catholic Ireland with an unwelcome choice between submitting to oppression or leaning towards rebellion; if only they were treated as full and equal citizens, they would fall under the influence of their natural – and naturally conservative – social leaders, and social harmony and order would be safer. Burke considered religion to be one of the great unifying bonds in a properly ordered society, yet in late-eighteenth-century Ireland he found a confessional state in which the denominational allegiance of the elite was shared by only a minority of the people. So Irish Catholics were cut off from their natural conservatism through their exclusion from the state; and this was a theme which pressed itself upon Burke all the more sharply owing to his own Catholic connections within Penal Law Ireland.

From the start of his political career Burke had supported the cause of Catholic relief, having early developed an antipathy towards the way in which Ireland's Protestant Ascendancy – the ruling Church of Ireland elite – treated the majority of the Irish population; indeed, he was significantly involved in practical measures to dismantle the relevant legislation. He could not stand indifference to human misfortune, he hated slavery, and he loathed the abuse of power (whether in America, India, France, or wherever): these attitudes provide the background to understanding the importance of his conception of Ireland as a place in which the ruling elite both abused their authority and lacked appropriate bonds of affection to the majority over whom they ruled. Burke had long hated the Penal Laws (on grounds of injustice, and also because they directly affected his own family); in the 1760s he argued forcefully about these laws that 'The happiness or misery of multitudes can never be a thing indifferent. A law against the majority of the people, is in substance a law against the people itself'; 'Now as a law directed against the mass of the nation has not the nature of a reasonable institution, so neither has it the authority.'[17] In 1792 he described the Penal Laws as representing a system 'as well fitted for the oppression, impoverishment and degradation of a people, and the debasement, in them, of human nature itself, as ever proceeded from the perverted ingenuity of man'.[18]

In the 1790s Burke supported Catholic enfranchisement and Catholics' right to be admitted to parliament; he was very pleased with the 1793 Catholic Relief Act (which enfranchised Catholics and in Burke's view restored them to their position of loyalty); and he wanted to see Catholics united in support of the system rather than excluded from and dangerous to it. Paradoxically, therefore, Burke became known as a defender of the old order in France, but a critic of it in Ireland; an opponent of dramatic change in England but an enthusiast for it in the land of his birth. Yet his view was that these stances grew out of a consistent set of principles. Concerned with social cohesion, order, justice and fairness, he felt that the Protestant elite in Ireland, and the system under which they flourished, were socially damaging and dangerously exclusive. Most of Burke's writings on Ireland involve an assault on the failings of the Protestant Ascendancy here: Ireland had been divided, he thought, by unjust, sectarian discrimination which required redress. The English constitution – which Burke considered worthy of great respect – had in Ireland resulted in oppression and injustice. Reform was required if the state was to protect itself.

So Burke's particular Irishness bequeathed to him a profound sympathy with the Irish Catholics' plight and a desire to advance their interests in line with his philosophy of social cohesion. He was an early enthusiast for what was to become one of the lasting arguments driving modern Irish nationalism forward: the case for redress of Catholic grievance and for the advancement of Catholic power in Ireland. In the politics of his day in Ireland, Burke was on the Catholic side against the Protestant Ascendancy. Indeed, he was frequently to be cited later by Irish nationalists: nineteenth-century Young Ireland militant John Mitchel invoked him in order to strengthen his criticisms of the Penal Laws in Ireland;[19] nationalist historian Alice Stopford Green deployed him in her attack on English and Anglo-Irish oppression of Irish Catholics;[20] W. B. Yeats was a frequent celebrant;[21] Irish nationalist leader John Redmond's nephew, in advocating Home Rule, enlisted the great eighteenth-century writer in support of his case.[22]

But can Burke himself be read as proto-national? Certainly, the youthful Burke was not indifferent to the claims of Irish distinctiveness. *The Reformer* of 1748 was a weekly paper which he edited and largely wrote himself while a student at TCD, and it was critical of Irish people for being too indulgent of English culture to the detriment of their own. There was here a certain sense of something like a cultural national identity, and of the dangers represented by English influence over Ireland.

Yet, in so much else, it is hard to square the great philosopher's ideas with a later Irish nationalist politics: 'Though he continued throughout life to take an active interest in the affairs of his native country, there is nothing national, let alone nationalist, about the policies he advocated for Ireland.'[23] Burke was not an enthusiast for Irish legislative independence, which he felt would strengthen the Protestant elite (of which he was so critical) and thereby damage Catholic Irish interests. And while he had a deep and lasting concern for Irish interests, he rejected the notion of any supposed exclusiveness of Irishness and Englishness from one another. An enthusiast for an organic British empire, Burke saw Ireland and Britain as parts of the same great dominion and thought that this was exactly as it should be. To him, Irish interests and British interests were complementary, and what helped one helped the other. Unlike Molyneux, Burke held that Ireland had indeed been originally conquered by England. But, unlike later Irish nationalists, he did not want Ireland removed from the constitutional, imperial connection with Britain. That connection was to everybody's benefit. It is, therefore, far from surprising that in the more recent period it has been modern-day unionists rather than nationalists who have most loudly trumpeted the ideas of Ireland's greatest political philosopher.[24] For Burke's concern that Catholic disaffection be addressed was a concern to preserve order and the integrity of the Irish–English connection, rather than to subvert them. Were Catholics offered a choice between oppression and rebellion, then the state faced grave danger; but, should Catholic disaffection be assuaged, then order could be maintained and the harmony of England's relationship with Ireland rendered more secure in the dangerous context of the 1790s. Burke identified with the cause of Irish Catholics sincerely and effectively but, unlike the later nationalist tradition, he did not link this cause or grievance with separatism. Quite the reverse.

From all this, one can see an Irish dimension to contemporary English political debates. Indeed, the two were frequently enough integrated. One of Burke's most able assailants, William Hazlitt (1778–1830), was himself of partly Irish background. Hazlitt detested Burke's politics, accused him of a lack of integrity, and espoused Whiggish rather than Tory ideas. But, as with Burke and Swift and Sheridan, Hazlitt's own Irishness has now been highlighted as helping to explain his politics.[25] And in the careers of these talented figures one can see, not nationalism, but an outlining of some of the debates and themes which were certainly to feed into it: Irish economic and political interest against English influence, Irish dignity and autonomy, Catholic grievance, and – as John Wesley sharply noted – Ulster difference.

2

Whoever takes the trouble of inquiring, will find, all the English Parlements, who have presumed to impose laws upon Ireland, without the consent of the People, were of the slavish and corrupt stamp ... and the Irish Parlements, at the same time, were not much better.

Charles Lucas, 1748[26]

Anglo-Irish tensions, and Irish divisions. In 1720 the British Declaratory Act stated Ireland to be subordinate to the imperial Crown of Great Britain, and to the power of the Westminster parliament. Thus the kingdom of Ireland was subordinated and bound to the Crown, under the authority of the king, and bound by the laws passed by the London parliament. To some later Irish nationalists, this has been the key point to stress: namely, Ireland's (as they would see it, wrongful) subjugation by her bullying neighbour. And yet there has been much sharp debate about whether eighteenth-century Ireland can best in fact be read as a colony,[27] or whether instead it is best understood as a more normal contemporary society, typical within the European ancien régime – a place ruled over by a pre-industrial, landed elite, and within which vertical ties of obligation, patronage and acquiescent deference were more significant than horizontal ties of shared economic standing or identity.[28] (It is worth stressing, for instance, that despite the Declaratory Act Westminster tended not, in practice, to use its legislative powers with regard to Ireland.)

Certainly, eighteenth-century Irish Protestants were clear that they did not live in a colony. In mid-century, the kingdom of Ireland contained about 400,000 Protestants; only a fraction of these were landowners, although much popular opinion has long assumed a conflation of 'Protestant' and 'landowner' for this period.[29] The reality was much more complicated, and the eighteenth-century Irish mixture of populations was very varied across the island. Ulster had a Protestant majority, while the Protestant minority in Leinster represented a larger proportion of that province's population than did the Protestant minorities in either Connacht to the west or Munster to the south. Irish Protestants felt (often rightly) that they were less well-off than their English equivalents. And eighteenth-century Protestant Ireland was marked by an anxiety born of minority status. This was much more marked in the latter part of the century, especially after the French Revolution. But the logic of numerical vulnerability meant that Protestant fear about Catholicism, though shared by English Protestants, had a very different quality in the Irish setting. The 1730s population in Ireland was over 2 million; of these, over 70 per cent were Catholic, and the fact that Irish Catholics outnumbered Protestants by three to one is vital to understanding the emergent shape of Irish political conflict.

Knowing that the end of the century would bring catastrophic and violent crisis, it is tempting to see the preceding years as ones necessarily pointing in that direction. But this would perhaps be misleading. The early eighteenth century was characterized by comparative stability, and for much of the century the contemporary bonds of patronage and deference did work tolerably well; this was not a society physically held down, suppressed, or repressed by force. If the many acquiesced in deferring to the few, then this was merely how society consensually functioned, and class differentiation did not necessarily carry with it sharp hostility between society's various social classes.

The central difficulty in ruling early-eighteenth-century Ireland in fact concerned the relationship between Ireland's political elite and English ministers;[30] in this sense, the politics of the masses were not seen as crucial to the business of governance (unless they were perceived as a pressing threat to order, stability and security). The eighteenth-century electoral system left little space for genuine popular participation. The Irish parliament had come into being in the medieval period, had only begun regular meetings in the late seventeenth century, and had then met on an annual basis from 1785 onwards. Comprising a House of Lords and a House of Commons, the Dublin parliament (as in Great Britain and continental Europe) involved religious restrictions: Catholics could not vote in elections nor be elected. Religiously and socially exclusive though it was, politics in this period was not, perhaps, quite as sexually monopolistic as might be assumed: women frequently attended parliamentary debates, exerted political influence (not least over MPs), canvassed for parliamentary candidates and participated significantly in late-eighteenth-century Irish Patriotism.

Land and religion formed the architecture of political life: landownership was the basis for private wealth and contemporary influence, while religion defined ideas, beliefs and identities in Ireland as elsewhere in Europe. The Kilkenny-born philosopher and Anglican cleric George Berkeley (1685–1753) recognized the significance of religious influence, and argued in the 1730s that Irish-speaking missionaries could play a key role in converting the Irish from Catholicism, thereby uniting the people of the island in one shared religion. (In 1731 around two-thirds of the Irish population was Irish-speaking, a proportion which had dropped to around 50 per cent by 1799.) In fact, however, religious division endured and remained central to the politics of the eighteenth century: 'The remembrance of past conflicts between Catholic and Protestant directly impinged upon relationships between the respective communities in Ireland.'[31]

If religion related to conflict, then it also defined the Irish Patriotism so characteristic of these years. Eighteenth-century Irish Protestants frequently became Irish Patriots, identifying the Irish nation with Protestant Ireland, and struggling for the defence and promotion of their own interests as against the power and influence of England. And religion clarified the nature of Britishness itself too. England, Ireland, Wales and Scotland had shared a monarch since 1603, Great Britain coming into being in 1707 with the union of the parliaments of England and Scotland, and religion was clearly a unifying force within this emergent Britishness. While Protestantism should not be seen as monolithic, it remains the case that the Catholicism of most Irish people constituted one barrier to their full absorption into the British family. Protestantism defined and united people in explicit contradistinction to Catholics, and the implications for Ireland here were crucial. For British Protestants, it was Irish Catholicism which was significant in marking the Irish out as different. And this attitude existed in the context of an international anxiety: anti-Catholicism was not merely a case of British hostility to Catholic Ireland, but to an Ireland most of whose population shared a Catholicism which was a genuinely threatening international force and imperial danger. While the various non-English parts of the British state all held on to their separate self-definitions (partly as a compensatory way of preserving self-image, identity and respect against the potential threat of being smothered by England), in the Irish Catholic case there was a more deeply powerful barrier to British absorption. The failed Reformation continued to exert historical force.

All of this came to matter more with the increasing importance during the eighteenth century of a forceful public opinion, and it is within this framework that the Volunteer movement was to carry such weight. This paramilitary, or part-time military, group was established in 1778, originally with a view to maintaining order and defending Ireland from possible French invasion during the absence of regular troops owing to the American Revolution. Numbers were impressive (around 40,000 having been mustered by late 1779), and membership was broadly middle-class. The Volunteers came to embody a newly emerging politics of the respectable classes: beyond the realm of parliament the Volunteers could exert pressure for political causes, and they dramatically managed to do so. The year 1779 saw a campaign for free trade (granted in 1780), while the early 1780s saw the Volunteers campaign in support of Irish legislative independence from England. The Volunteer Convention of 1782 at Dungannon marked the start of what turned out to be a successful move for such autonomy.

Within the Irish House of Commons figures such as the leading Patriot Henry Grattan – Dublin-born, TCD-educated, and himself a prominent Volunteer – led this campaign. But extra-parliamentary Volunteer pressure was crucial in coercing the concession in 1782 of an end to the formal, legal subordination of the Irish to the English parliament: the Declaratory Act (which had claimed the right of the English House of Commons to legislate for Ireland) was repealed, and Poynings' Law amended, so the Irish parliament had at least the appearance of equality with London, and the achievement of legislative independence of a sort.

Patriotism itself represented a new awareness among eighteenth-century Irish Protestants of Irishness and a pursuit of Irish interests. The idea of political subordination to England came to seem less tolerable, with Patriots opposing undue English control of Irish affairs, defending Irish interests versus Westminster power, enthusing over true citizenship, responsibility, political philanthropy, a sense of the public interest, and actions in the best interest of the 'common weal' or community. Here we see, perhaps for the first time in Ireland, something resembling modern nationalism in key respects. There was a notion here of popular sovereignty, of the importance for proper authority of some mandate from the people, of a stark defence of Irish interests against foreign (English) interference and power. This Protestant proto-nationalism involved a definite national identity, together with a sense of Irishness defined in terms of place, clear boundaries, history and indeed an argument based on supposedly inherited historical rights. Here was the Lockeian idea of the people being able to refashion politics, should current rulers be considered tyrannical. Admittedly, there were limits to this creed in comparison with later nationalism, since those involved represented only about a tenth of the population. Irish Protestants didn't see their Catholic neighbours (or indeed those from the Presbyterian community) as part of the nation. But if the Patriot nation was Protestant, it still possessed clearer elements of nationalism than prior political groupings had done in Ireland. Patriots argued that Ireland was a separate kingdom from England, deserving to be governed in accordance with its own laws;

and in the sense of community, of organized struggle, and of conceptions of the importance of political power, we do see here a proto-
nationalism.

So in figures such as Grattan or Henry Flood (1732–91), both
Patriots in the Dublin House of Commons in the 1770s, we witness an
important development. In parliament itself, the Patriot was one
opposed to corruption of the political system (through unfair taxation,
for example, or the abuse of the liberties of the subject). Patriots were
ostensibly committed to public rather than to individual interests,
possessed a love of their country, and showed a desire to seek the
enhancement of the common good (whether through parliamentary
reform or economic improvement). And liberty lay at the heart of the
Patriot argument.

The new arrangement of 1782 has come to be forever associated
with Henry Grattan ('Henry Grattan is the only Irish historical figure
to enjoy the accolade of having a phase of Irish parliamentary history
named after him'[32]); he had embraced the cause of Irish legislative
independence in 1780, and showed himself capable of articulating
(as in a famous speech in the Irish House of Commons on 16 April
1782) a case in favour of the British parliament relinquishing its
legislative jurisdiction over Ireland. In time 'Grattan's Parliament'
came to possess powerful symbolic importance for many later Irish
nationalists who pursued autonomy from Britain ('Nothing short of
1782 can or ought to satisfy Ireland', as the important nineteenth-
century nationalist W. J. O'Neill Daunt put it in 1870[33]). That
Grattanite era came to be seen by some as something of a golden
age of prosperity and freedom; but the degree to which 1782 itself
represented a watershed should not be overstated. Prior to this date,
potential interference by London in Irish legislation was not frequent;
and much control still remained with the British government even
after legislative independence. The constitutional revolution of 1782
was markedly limited when judged by modern standards. Over half of
the 300 seats in the Irish House of Commons were the property
of fewer than 100 individuals; Crown patronage virtually ensured a
majority in the House. It was, moreover, an entirely Protestant parliament, with Catholics unable to sit in or vote for it; it therefore failed
to resolve the problematic relationship between the governing Ascendancy on one hand, and the bulk of the people on the other. Grattan

himself had not sought to weaken the Anglo-Irish connection, but rather to establish constitutional equality with Britain for the Irish Protestant kingdom – under the Crown. For 1782 involved an exclusively Protestant conception of the Irish people or nation; whatever its celebrated status among later Catholic nationalists, legislative independence of this era was not something in which Catholics could share.

Yet some among the Volunteers did hold strongly to the view that Dissenters and Catholics should unite to pursue reformist politics. And in the immediate aftermath of the constitutional concessions of 1782, a campaign began for parliamentary reform: the aims included more frequent elections and an increase in the number of MPs (though not, initially, the facilitation of Catholic involvement within the formal political world).

If the struggle for power on behalf of an Irish community was at the heart of Grattanite and Volunteer politics – and it's reasonable to suggest that it was – then this was a very different kind of communal power struggle from that which later came to embody nationalist Irish politics. More closely tied, perhaps, to the basis of what later emerged as Irish nationalism was the politics of Catholic reform, and here we face the vital historical phenomenon of the Penal or Popery Laws. Mid-eighteenth-century Irish Catholics (even those who offered objections to the manner of contemporary politics) often tended not to be hostile to or subversive of the government itself. But the issue of redress of Catholic grievances – the Catholic question – emerged in the eighteenth century as a central feature of Irish politics, and one which has yet to reach final resolution even in the twenty-first century.

The Penal Laws were a rather muddled and complex set of anti-Catholic restrictions which had been enacted by the Irish parliament in piecemeal fashion (rather than as part of any systematically conceived body of coherent legislation; for this and other reasons, comparisons between the Irish Penal Laws and the twentieth-century South African apartheid system are utterly misconceived). Yet, while not representing a unified project, the Popery Laws did reflect some broad themes and objectives. The motivation behind the laws involved a mixture of Protestant piety, self-defence, revenge and self-interest. Were these laws supposed to produce Catholic conversion to Protestantism? To some degree, yes. But by at least the mid-eighteenth century, Irish Protestants knew that their Catholic neighbours were

not going to be separated from their Catholic Church (and many Irish
Anglicans had shown very limited interest in actually converting
Catholic neighbours in any case). More realistically, the Popery Laws
were intended to restrict the political power of Catholics, who repre-
sented such a numerical and international threat: the protection of
Protestant establishment interests was paramount.

So, from the 1690s through to the 1720s, a series of laws curtailed
Catholic activity over a range of political and other areas of life. The
extent of Catholic landownership was restricted, no Catholic being
able legally to inherit land from a Protestant or to buy an interest in
land save for a lease of not more than thirty-one years; on his death,
the Catholic's land had to be equally divided up among his sons. Discriminatory legislation was also directed against the Catholic clergy
(limiting their legal number on the ground), against Catholics possessing weapons, and against Catholics holding office in local or central
government, or being members of parliament.

Rather like anti-Catholic discrimination in Northern Ireland after
1921, the Penal Laws of the eighteenth century have acquired a
grotesque popular reputation. Like all persistent myths, this one reflects
a reality (that of power and discrimination). But some clarity and
qualification are also required. Neither the will nor the resources
existed for the implementation of the Penal Code, so anti-Catholic
legislation often had, in practice, a comparatively limited impact.[34]
Catholic priests in early-eighteenth-century Ireland remained here
despite the laws against them: there were apparently nearly 1,500 on
the island in 1731. Restrictions on actual Catholic worship fairly soon
ceased to operate. Moreover, the Penal Laws could, of course, be
crossed, if Catholics turned from their Church to embrace the established religion: by 1771 at least 4,000 Irish Catholics had indeed done
precisely this. And if Catholics did convert in this way, then that didn't
necessarily weaken Catholicism and the Catholic interest in Ireland:
it might simply mean that there now existed a body within the elite,
sympathetic to Catholic interest while yet holding some real power.

For contemporary power rested above all in land, and it seems that
a significant minority of landowners still remained effectively Catholic,
and that the Catholic landowning tradition was much stronger and
more consistent than has sometimes been thought. It should also be
recognized that the Popery Laws were the kind of legislation common

in other societies at that time (including Italy, England, Spain and France). Religious discrimination was the norm (and, indeed, the persecution by Catholics of Protestants elsewhere in Europe was one justification used in defence of the Popery Laws in Ireland). What was exceptional in the Irish case was that the majority rather than the minority suffered under these formal disabilities.[35]

So while there was some distance between what the law prescribed and what happened on the ground, this legislation did carry enormous political and symbolic weight. To the majority of the Irish population, law seemed frequently enough to be hostile rather than protective, exclusive rather than inclusive. The legacy of this for later conceptions of state authority in Ireland was profound. Respect for law among the majority of the Irish population was undermined and corroded, since the law was so clearly directed against their community: many Catholics came to see the law in Ireland as Protestant and British law, as law which preserved the unjust ascendancy of others over oneself and one's community.

What else – apart from their usefulness to later nationalist propagandists – was the effect of the Penal Laws? Paradoxically, they tended to strengthen the bond between Catholic people and Church through the shared identity of perceivedly wrongful exclusion. In a society in which everyone believed in God, and in which religious division was crucial, such grievance solidified community and provided a foundation stone on which nationalist strivings for power could eventually be built. And perhaps the key point about the Penal Laws was less that they debarred people from otherwise attainable democratic freedoms (which the nature of contemporary social structure would in many cases have denied them anyway, for reasons relating to class), but rather that they debarred some Catholics from taking what would otherwise have been their place in the chain of vertical hierarchy, deference and patronage. Had there been no Penal Laws, then some Irish Catholics would have been located in the upper realm of authority. But the reality of landed wealth would have remained a vital barrier to modern-style equality, and it would not have been the case that Catholics suddenly became – in our modern sense – free and equal.

Agitation against the Popery Laws gained momentum in the late eighteenth century – indeed, there came to be a clear sense that these laws were going to be repealed. In 1756 a Catholic Association was formed and, following this, in 1760 a Catholic Committee was established in order to campaign against the Penal legislation (initially without much to show for its energetic efforts). Concessions to Catholics had begun in 1750 when they were admitted to the lower grades of the army. The 1770s then saw a relaxation of certain laws regarding property, and Relief Acts subsequently undid much of the structure of Penal disability: measures which passed through parliament in 1778, 1782 and 1793 removed many of the disabilities suffered by Catholics. Yet, despite the fact that most of the discriminatory measures against Catholics had been abrogated by 1793, the issue of full Catholic civil equality was to become a defining one for the last decade of Irish eighteenth-century politics, and for the movement which many see as the first truly modern expression of Irish nationalism: the Society of United Irishmen.

3

By their exclusion from the two houses of parliament, the whole body of the Catholic gentry of Ireland, a high-spirited race of men, are insulted and disgraced, thrown down from the level of their fortune and their talents and branded with a mark of subjugation ... The denial of the right to sit and vote in parliament is now, undoubtedly, the chief grievance of the Catholics of Ireland.

Theobald Wolfe Tone[36]

The Irish political system in the 1790s was affected by British influence at virtually all levels. Proximity to Britain has always been a vital context for understanding the evolution of Irish nationalism, and this crucial decade – during which modern Irish nationalism was forged – offers no exception. In the late eighteenth century, Irish government was effectively a wing of British government: the leading players in the Irish administration (the Lord Lieutenant, the Chief Secretary, the Under-Secretaries) were all responsible to and appointed by the government in Britain. During the 1790s, however, both the Irish political relationship with England and political relations within Ireland itself were to be challenged by the Society of United Irishmen, founded in Belfast in October 1791 and in Dublin the following month. Initially, the Society was an advanced, constitutional reform group. By 1798 it had evolved into a revolutionary body, looking for French help in producing a separatist rebellion; but in 1791 the United Irishmen were an open, constitutional Society with a primarily propagandist function, directed towards political reform. Largely middle-class in composition, the new radical Society saw Ireland's problems as arising from the fact that the authorities had strayed from the proper principles of representative government. They pursued the achievement of civil rights for Catholics (still denied the vote and the right to be elected to the House of Commons) and also parliamentary reform, and they sought these goals through a union of Irish people of different Christian denominations. Indeed, if political equality and parliamentary reform were to be achieved, then the United Irishmen held that they would only be so achieved if members of Ireland's rival confessional groups (Protestant, Catholic and Dissenter) came together in their pursuit.

The Belfast group which first founded the Society was Presbyterian; once set up, however, the group invited a man of Church of Ireland background – Theobald Wolfe Tone (1763–98) – to become involved. Tone was not the most important source of United Irish ideas (the Belfast Presbyterian William Drennan (1754–1820), who circulated a paper in 1791 outlining an initial plan for such a Society, perhaps deserves that description rather better). But Tone was destined to become easily the most famous member of the Belfast group, and it was he who drafted its 1791 *Declaration and Resolutions of the Society of United Irishmen of Belfast*. This expressed the 'heavy grievance' that there was no national government in Ireland, and demanded as a counterbalance an equal representation in parliament of all the people: a union of all Irish people was required in order to preserve liberties, and reform of parliament was urgently required. Once parliament had been reformed and rendered representative, then the political evil of English influence could be remedied. The *Declaration* also claimed that this was an age in which 'all government is acknowledged to originate from the people'.[37]

Thus the initial United Irish argument involved a sense of popular

community and also of the struggle for appropriately representative
power to be established on their behalf. English government ruled
Ireland and was corrupt, serving as it did the interests of another
country. Reform was therefore needed, hence the urgency of struggle:
in 1794 the United Irishmen in Dublin agreed a plan advocating the
payment of MPs, the holding of annual parliaments, and the establishment of universal male suffrage. Uniting the people, combating English
influence, reforming the political realm: these were the early aims of
the United Irishmen, and they pursued them with propagandist skill
and ingenuity. Following the Society's 1791 formation, its newspaper
the *Northern Star* was published in Belfast from 1792 to 1797 (financed
and edited by Samuel Neilson). And the United Irishmen utilized not
only newspapers but also poetry, ballads and pamphlets. Like many
later Irish nationalists, they were literary in their style (and in their
influences here they relied heavily on English example – not for the
last time in the Irish nationalist story, Irish radicals drew imaginative
strength from the literature and culture of their enemy).

But if they were brilliant publicists, their identity as a group was to
alter greatly from the mid-1790s onwards. In March 1793 the Volunteers were banned, and this represented a blow to the United Irishmen,
who had thought that a revival of the Volunteers could help to effect
political change as had been the case earlier in 1782. In May 1794 the
Dublin Society of United Irishmen was itself suppressed, and this
helped further to push the movement in that clandestine, conspiratorial, insurrectionist direction which some in the movement had
already sought. New, secret structures were recognized in a revised
constitution adopted on 10 May 1795, and by mid-1795 the United
Irishmen were reconstituting themselves as a secret, revolutionary
society, especially in Ulster.

Another key change was that from the mid-1790s onwards the
nature of the United Irishmen became increasingly defined by a
support-base tied to Catholic communalism and Defenderism. The
Defenders were a Catholic Irish secret society, a politico-social movement. Agrarian, sectarian, anti-English and anti-settler, the Defenders
had their origins in the sectarian animosity between Catholic and
Protestant in the Armagh of the 1780s, and the leaderships of the
United Irishmen and the Defenders had been in contact with each
other since 1792. The Defenders themselves embodied much that was

later to become important within sections of militant Irish nationalist politics: they were a communal would-be defence force of aggressive stamp, anti-Protestant, and sharply revanchist and violent in tone. Defenderism involved intimidation and it reflected the logic of Catholic–Protestant division in contemporary Ireland; yet from the mid-1790s onwards this sectarian body and the United Irishmen increasingly blurred together, with the two movements in some places effectively merging and with a wider alliance between them being forged. In Armagh, for example, the Defenders became incorporated into the United Irish movement but without shedding the sectarian logic which had impelled and motivated them. And during the mid-1790s the United Irishmen were recruiting heavily and successfully among the Defenders in much of Ulster. So alongside the oft-quoted and appealing anti-sectarian rhetoric of the United Irishmen should be set the much less alluring politics of Defender-style intimidation and threats (directed against jurors and witnesses, for instance).

In part, this reflected the great difference between the early United Irish movement and what it later became. William Drennan himself was tried for seditious libel in 1794 and, though acquitted, he subsequently had nothing more to do with the United Irish organization. As the decade progressed, it was towards baneful violence that Irish politics moved. Sometimes hailed by later nationalists as a great moment at which Ireland's various factions united to fight as one, the end of the eighteenth century might more appropriately be read as one of the most terrible examples of Irish division and bloody revenge.

Partly under Wolfe Tone's own inspiration, the United Irishmen had increasingly moved towards revolutionary conspiracy and in the direction of a French-backed, separatist rebellion. By December 1796 a large French military/naval force had reached Bantry Bay, in County Cork, with Tone himself on board and with a view to supporting the United Irishmen. No landing was attempted (there had been a disastrously disruptive storm), but anxiety about an Irish rising had long existed among the authorities. William Pitt had expressed such fears emphatically in 1792, in regard to the problem of Catholic disaffection in Ireland. And such worries became more sharply focused with the beginning of war against Revolutionary France early in 1793: now dissent on either island was something to be suppressed as quickly as possible. In January 1796 the Attorney General presented to the Irish

House of Commons in Dublin a bill 'for the more effectually preventing of insurrections, tumults, and riots, by persons stiling themselves
Defenders, and other disorderly persons'.[38] The government arrested
many United Irish leaders in March 1798, and when the rebels soon
afterwards attempted to establish an Irish republic in place of British
rule in Ireland, their efforts were patchy, bloody and unsuccessful.

There had long been something of a military flavour to United Irish
organization (even during its more constitutional period in the early
1790s);[39] but when in 1798 the Risings did occur they tended to be
poorly organized, ineffective and brutally suppressed – once the rebellion had erupted, the authorities used Draconian methods in order to
deal with it. The first serious outbreak of rebellious struggle occurred
on 26 May 1798, and was mainly based in Wicklow and Wexford –
areas in which the United Irishmen had not been notably at their
strongest, and so a strange setting for the Rising if one were to see it
as a purely United Irish rebellion. In fact, the leadership and motivation of the Rising were more complex than that. But during the
spring and summer of 1798 there were eruptions also in Antrim, Down
and Mayo, and the year saw maybe 50,000 rebels face around 76,000
soldiers of the Crown. Up to 30,000 people were killed, despite the
comparative brevity of the conflict. The fighting in Antrim and Down
lasted barely a week, the Ulster rebellion turning out to be something
of a fiasco; in south Leinster the fighting lasted slightly longer than six
weeks, with some rebel success being achieved in Wexford and parts of
Wicklow. So the Rising of the 1798 insurgents was patchy, some places
(such as County Kilkenny, for example) being notably quiet.

According to French military thinking, Ireland had long been seen
as England's weak link, her vulnerable Achilles' heel. But in 1798
French help arrived too late. As we saw at the start of this book, Tone
himself was on the French military expedition which reached the Irish
coast in October 1798 (at which point he was captured). But, despite
its popular association in the modern mind with Wolfe Tone, and
despite being seen by many later observers as a neatly United Irish
episode, the 1798 Rising did not in fact follow the pattern set down by
the leadership of that movement. Things happened in an ad hoc and
rather localized fashion, and they frequently took on a sectarian
dimension as a result (as one would expect, given the painful sharpness
of sectarian tensions in 1790s Wexford and Wicklow, for example).

Certainly, not everyone killed by the forces of the Crown in that terrible year was a member of the United Irishmen, and there was some mismatch between United Irish strength and the intensity of rebel violence.[40] Part of the rebels' failure lay in the authorities' counter-measures. From the start, the United Irishmen had been riddled with government informers (a theme which was to recur in later Irish republican conspiracies). Though informer networks were irregular and far from neatly coordinated,[41] they did help to provide the authorities with detailed knowledge about United Irish member-ship and activities (though the government knew far less about the Defenders).

Yet if 1798 was not an entirely United Irish rebellion, the 1790s have come to be seen as their decade. In particular, the United Irishmen have assumed a uniquely important place within Irish nation-alist thinking, and this is for obvious reasons: not only was there a major rebellion here against English rule in Ireland, and an apparent moment of truly revolutionary possibility, but also – unlike any other Irish nationalist moment – the United Irishmen involved significant numbers of Irish non-Catholics. Most of the northern United Irishmen were Presbyterians, and – though not a Christian – the most famous United Irishman of all, Theobald Wolfe Tone, did come from a Church of Ireland background. The many Presbyterians involved in the con-spiracy seem to offer an answer to those who critically proclaim that Irish nationalism has merely been a form of political Catholicism, a narrow and sectarian movement. Indeed, to some later nationalists, the United Irish movement has carried more powerful implications still: the 1790s – when significant numbers of non-Catholics allied in a nationalist campaign – are seen as the norm from which virtually all subsequent Protestants in Ireland have deviated as a result of elite manipulation, false consciousness, or sheer badness. In such light, modern unionism is sometimes read as artificial, deviant and misguided.

And yet the United Irishmen failed spectacularly. Their rebellion was incoherent and bloodily suppressed. Even those who are broadly sympathetic to the Society openly acknowledge that their attempt to end sectarian division in Ireland was unsuccessful, and that it was founded on an exaggerated sense of their capabilities: 'the United Irishmen overestimated their ability to transcend the inherited politics of religion in Ireland'.[42] Not for the last time in Irish nationalist history, a movement which sincerely sought to harmonize those from different religious backgrounds in fact exacerbated division between them: Ireland in 1800 was far more bloodily divided than it had been a decade earlier. The rebellion should not be read purely as a sectarian episode,[43] but some of the violence in 1798 did take on a hideously sectarian quality. Most notoriously, in Wexford on 5 June over 100 Protestant children, women and men were burned to death by the rebels in a barn at Scullabogue.[44] For in Wexford sectarian resentments (partly focusing on conflicts over land and recent settlements) played an important part in the story of 1798: fears and hatreds, vendettas and score-settling, the vengeful targeting of neighbours – all of this was a part of the tale and accompanied the ideological idealism which is more commonly associated with the 1790s. Indeed, it is hard to imagine that any challenge to the Protestant Ascendancy and state in late-eighteenth-century Ireland would have been seen as lacking a sectarian dimension, a fact given greater sharpness by beleaguered Protestants' fear of Catholicism in Ireland but also beyond it.

Moreover, there is something peculiarly simplistic about citing non-Catholic United Irishmen as some kind of proof that Irish Protestants should be nationalist. Should the large numbers of Catholics who were *opposed* to the rebellion be seen as proof that Irish Catholics should forever be loyal to the English Crown? Loyal Catholics there emphatically were. In May 1798 over 2,000 of them signed an Address to the Lord Lieutenant which could hardly have been more explicit.

> May it please your Excellency,
> We, the undersigned, His Majesty's most dutiful and loyal subjects, Roman Catholics of Ireland, think it necessary at this moment publicly to declare our firm attachment to His Majesty's Royal Person, and to the Constitution under which we have the happiness to live. We feel, in common with the rest of His Majesty's subjects, the danger to which both are exposed from an implacable and enterprising enemy, menacing invasion from abroad, and from the machinations of evil and disaffected men conspiring treason within this His Majesty's kingdom. . . . Allow us then to assure your Excellency, that we contemplate with horror the evils of every description, which the conduct of the French Republic has produced on every nation hitherto weak enough to be deluded by its

promises of liberty and offers of fraternity. We anticipate similar misfortunes as awaiting this His Majesty's kingdom in the deprecated event of successful invasion.[45]

And there was significant, practical Catholic support – for example in north Cork – for the Crown forces during the 1798 rebellion itself.[46]

Was it naive of the United Irishmen to have assumed that lasting sectarian division within Irish society could be overcome as they had imagined? Scholarly views differ greatly here. Some authorities hold that the 1790s were indeed a moment at which sectarian futures could have been be avoided, and that the decade represented a 'window of opportunity', 'a window which beckoned to the still unattained prospect of a non-sectarian, democratic and inclusive politics adequately representing the Irish people in all their inherited complexities'.[47] Others have been much colder in their analysis ('Was the United Irish project bound to fail? The short answer must be yes'[48]), and there is much on which to base such scepticism. At the very least, there was a great tension between Defenderist, sectarian Catholic politics and the initial United Irish ambition to transcend such dynamics. And since the two movements effectively merged in many places, the Defenders' revanchism and rural violence must be read as a central part of the United Irish story too. As with so much later Irish nationalism, the politics of the United Irishmen contained both a communal religious dimension (what else would one expect in a period when religion was so central to people's understanding of public as well as private affairs?) and also a professedly inclusive, non-sectarian aspiration which deserves to be taken seriously.

Nor was it merely the case that the United Irishmen failed to erase sectarianism (or even that they tended in practice to deepen it: as their most comprehensive and authoritative chronicler has pithily put it, 'The legacy of the United Irishmen, however interpreted, has proved as divisive for later generations as the practice of this so-called union did in the 1790s'[49]). Examination of the roots of their ideas also points in a less ecumenical direction than casual observers often assume. Certainly, as far as eighteenth-century Presbyterian radicals were concerned, the crucial context for the granting of political emancipation to Catholics was not a desire to embrace Catholicism, but rather the conviction that Catholicism was on the wane. The non-Presbyterian

Tone was himself hostile enough to the Catholic Church, and eighteenth-century Irish Protestants in general assumed that their own religion was (of course) politically superior to Catholicism. Liberty was firmly identified with Protestantism, while Catholicism was seen as tyrannical. If individual Catholics were considered able now to embrace liberty, then this was as a result of their becoming, in fact, less Catholic.

And this is one aspect of the French Revolution's importance for the origins of United Irish thinking. To reform-oriented Irish Protestants, the Revolution in France seemed to hold out the prospect of Catholics themselves dismantling oppression and freeing themselves from the papal yoke. This was held to have momentous implications for Irish politics. It was not a matter of ecumenical toleration or secularism in any modern sense, but rather a working-out of the perceived weakening of the Catholic Church. For, whatever they were, the United Irishmen were not ecumenical or secular. Presbyterian radicalism was profoundly biblical, theological and deeply religious, and this era involved not so much secularism-versus-sectarianism, but rather competition between different versions of Christianity and their relationships to politics. It is the very persistence of religious attachment which is striking among the radicals: one of the few things the United Irishmen did not like about their radical hero Tom Paine was that he attacked Christianity. (This was very clear in the case of Thomas Russell (1767–1803), whose desire for a new and better world sprang directly from his devout, millennialist Christianity, and who was in fact deeply hostile to the secularly-minded Paine's *Age of Reason*.[50])

So religious outlook and political ambition were interwoven for many people in this first Irish nationalist movement. The supposed demise of Catholicism – signalled by the French Revolution – would allow Protestants to treat Catholics as free equals. It would also provide sufficient safety for Irish Presbyterians to allow them to attack the privileged position of Irish Anglicans without fear. If Catholics in France could attack the Church and free themselves from it, if Popery were indeed dying, then there was less reason to object to the extension to Irish Catholics of civil equality: they could, it turned out after all, be free of their superstition and their authoritarian Church. France showed that Catholics could exercise citizenship rights in an appropriate and non-tyrannical manner. If French, and therefore Irish, Catholics could demonstrate political maturity, and could show that they genuinely loved liberty, then there was no need to fear their political emancipation.

In this sense, it is the conflict between Catholics and non-Catholics – in religious terms – which is striking. And it is important to note that its most authoritative historian has flintily described late-eighteenth-century Irish Presbyterian radicalism as 'the continuation of the war against popery by other means'.[51] Indeed, it was in those areas where Catholics were the minority that Presbyterians were most likely to join the United Irishmen: where Catholics predominated, and where the political implications of Catholicism were therefore very different, Presbyterian involvement was much less in evidence. So we should not, perhaps, be surprised to find anti-sectarian political rhetoric accompanied in this decade by so much practical evidence of sectarian division, and indeed by its intensification. For even the advanced non-Catholic radicals were, in key ways, anti-Catholic, just as United Irish Defenders were often anti-Protestant, and zealous for redress of long-held Catholic grievance and the replacement of a Protestant ascendancy with a Catholic one. Welcome to modern Ireland.

And, in a sense, to Irish nationalism. For in tracing the origins and nature of United Irish political thinking, we can see the emergence of a recognizably modern nationalist philosophy. It was, of course, one born from a specific context. Part of this related to the American and French Revolutions, and to the sense of expansive possibility thus encouraged; in Thomas Paine's words, 'From what we now see, nothing of reform in the political world ought to be held improbable. It is an age of revolutions, in which everything may be looked for.'[52] The American Revolution resonated partly because of the personal connections between Ireland (especially the Irish Presbyterian community) and the rebellious colonists; if the writings of Irish Protestant patriots such as Jonathan Swift and Henry Flood were frequently quoted in Revolutionary American pamphlets, then the reverse influence was also telling. And the political lesson from Ireland's emigrant relatives seemed a clear one: if colonies such as the American could assert and win independence from England, then were not possibilities open also for Ireland?

If the personal and ideological links between Ireland – especially Ulster – and America were strong, then the impact of that other great eighteenth-century Revolution, the French, was even more significant. When the ancien régime fell in 1789, radicals in many countries were inspired with the hope that the world could be dramatically changed, and Ireland was no exception. In the new era produced by the French Revolution, some Irish radicals were to turn into republican revolutionaries themselves and the terms of politics would become transformed. Wolfe Tone certainly thought the influence of the French Revolution decisive in arousing the Irish people from political torpor, and expressed the view that the Revolution in France soon 'became the test of every man's political creed' in Ireland, the nation being 'fairly divided into two great parties, the Aristocrats and the Democrats (epithets borrowed from France)'.[53]

So, in crucial ways, the French Revolution helped to bring nationalism to Ireland. Not only did the implications of a more defensive, retreating Catholicism play on the imagination of Presbyterian Irish radicals, but in broader fashion too the ideas and consequences of the French upheaval helped to create nationalist Ireland. The old order in France had been founded on dynastic sovereignty and on noble privilege; the post-Revolutionary French world was one characterized by much wider popular participation in and power over politics: the popular, communal struggle for power had decisively arrived. And so the central lesson of the French Revolution, as it evolved over ensuing decades, was that regimes would not be seen as legitimate unless they somehow managed to involve popular participation. This issue – the interweaving of political legitimacy with public opinion – was vital in forging Irish nationalism: for the ideas upon which this shift rested were ideas which now spread to and dominated and defined Irish debate.

These ideas might best be seen through the lenses of Paine, Rousseau and Locke. Late-eighteenth-century Irish radicals enthused over Thomas Paine's *Rights of Man* more than they did over any other contemporary publication. Written in response to Burke's *Reflections on the Revolution in France*, Paine's work not only related to the ideas of a leading Irish ideologue, but was extensively distributed and highly popular in Ireland; it made an especially deep and lasting impression in Belfast, but cheap editions were also widely circulated in Dublin (where it first appeared in March 1791).

The United Irishmen themselves were supportive of and enthusiastic about Tom Paine: in June 1792 he was proposed for and granted honorary membership of the Dublin Society, while in the previous year – in reference to *Rights of Man* – Martha McTier had tellingly commented to her brother William Drennan that 'I never liked kings and Paine has said of them what I always suspected.'[54] Thomas Russell was influenced by Paine's thinking; and Wolfe Tone – that great distiller of others' ideas – was himself greatly influenced by Paine, whom he met (they discussed Edmund Burke), and whose work he avidly read in the 1790s. Tone himself frequently referred to Paine in his own writings, considering him 'vain beyond all belief, but he has reason to be vain, and for my part I forgive him. He has done wonders for the cause of liberty, both in America and Europe, and I believe him to be conscientiously an honest man.'[55] Paine was indeed very important, for Irish radicals had been dismayed by Burke's famous attack on the Revolution. When *Rights of Man* appeared in many editions in Ireland, sold well there and had extracts published in numerous newspapers, this reflected the fact that radical Ireland had found their antidote to Edmund Burke. That Paine then became a supporter of Irish radical causes further deepened the extent to which he and his book had greatly strengthened Irish radical politics.

Paine's ideas helped to form the philosophy of this first major Irish nationalist movement. Paine saw his treatise as an explicit defence of true 'principles of freedom'; but with Paine we see clearly not just the politics of 'nations' (to which he frequently referred), but also the distinctively novel politics of modern nationalism. For here – as with Rousseau, to whom we will come in a moment – was the crucial intersection of equality, sovereignty and freedom, and the explicit expression of democracy through the nation. Paine stressed that the rights of choosing governors and framing governments resided not 'in this or in that person, or in this or in that description of persons', but rather that it resided 'in the whole: that it is a right resident in the nation'. The nation functioned as an egalitarian, communal unit, its sovereignty and freedom residing equally in all of its people: 'Every citizen is a member of the sovereignty.'[56] It was important, therefore, that national sovereignty was so prominent in *Rights of Man*, because Paine's understanding and popularizing of that concept helped to define the nationalist component to United Irish thinking.

But Paine was important not just in terms of his etching of French

Revolutionary ideas on to an Irish canvas. His American experience (on which he drew in his writings) also gave him resonance in Ireland. Ulster Presbyterians, in particular, were receptive to ideas which connected with their American relatives and which carried parallels with their own politics: if Paine espoused reason against ignorance, and liberty-versus-tyranny, then – given the American example – was it necessary that London embodied the more blessed of these conflicting ideas? Many Irish Presbyterians had read the celebratory reflections on the new American dispensation of Dissenting minister Richard Price, who had prompted Burke's *Reflections*. Now they also enjoyed the resonant case put by one who had responded in turn to Burke.

The United Irishmen embodied the idea that, once parliament was reformed, laws would be made by the people and the people would therefore be free. This central tenet of modern nationalism was powerfully disseminated to Ireland – resonantly, accessibly and dramatically – by Tom Paine: when they deployed extracts and slogans from Paine in their propaganda, the United Irishmen showed themselves to be nationalists.

These ideas had not originated with Paine; rather, he was the particularly important route by means of which they conquered radical Ireland. Deeper sources for the root nationalist ideals of popular sovereignty, liberty and equality might be found in Rousseau and Locke, each of whom also had a direct impact on the transmission to Ireland of these electrifying notions. Rousseau might have had far fewer Irish readers than Paine, but the latter had drawn explicitly on the former, and Rousseau himself was also directly influential over key United Irish figures (William Drennan was among them, and Thomas Russell had also read Rousseau). *The Social Contract*, first published in 1762, was well known in Ireland in the late eighteenth century. Rousseau undoubtedly had considerable impact in Dublin, and much more extensively than this there existed a notable eighteenth-century interest in his ideas and recognition of his genius: in far-reaching late-eighteenth-century periodicals in Ireland there was keen engagement in debate involving Rousseau's work.

And behind Rousseau lay Locke, whose ideas had justified and organized the thinking behind the American Revolution and had also resonated with those of the theorists of the French Revolution. Locke therefore enjoyed a profound, indirect impact on radical Ireland in this period, but he also had a direct effect, his Irish readers including Theobald Wolfe Tone and Robert Emmet. Both men had been educated at TCD, where Locke was greatly venerated in the late eighteenth century and very prominent on the curriculum. The influence of Locke on late-eighteenth-century Ireland and Irish political debates, indeed, cannot be disputed,[57] and he in particular appealed to radicals here – especially in the 1790s. The United Irishmen distilled and publicized Locke's arguments in their pamphleteering; their paper, the *Northern Star*, cited him; and if the idea of popular sovereignty was central to the thinking of people like Tone, then this reflected the direct route by means of which modern nationalist ideas had reached Ireland. Locke had been one of the main influences on Paine's ideas, and Locke himself was widely read (by, for example, northern Irish radical activists in the 1790s). And Locke was seen as directly relevant to the conflict with Britain, as well as to the justification of people's right to armed resistance against oppression.

If their absorption of Lockeian teaching helps to establish the United Irishmen as marking the emergence in Ireland of nationalist politics, then it is also important to note that these radicals, often seen as Ireland's first real republicans, reflected influences and assumptions rooted deeply in their own period alone. It is also important to note that the term 'republican' possessed for the United Irishmen a set of meanings which would have been entirely lost on most modern republicans in, for example, the late-twentieth-century IRA. The United Irish movement drew heavily on classical republicanism, or civic humanism, a tradition of ideas inspired by readings of ancient Greece and Rome, and which involved a highly specific notion of 'republican'. To a civic humanist such as the Irish Presbyterian philosopher Francis Hutcheson (1694–1746) – a great friend of William Drennan's father – politics was to be seen in terms of the opposition between corruption and virtue: man was inherently political, and citizenship required the individual to participate in public, civil affairs in order that the common good be maintained. This was very much the politics of the Enlightenment era, replete with classical references, great confidence in the human capacity to improve our condition, and a profound sense of the importance of public honour. It exerted a great influence on United Irish thinking: Hutcheson's central notion regarding 'the greatest happiness of the greatest number' was William

Drennan's aim in forging the idea of the United Irishmen, and many
of Hutcheson's political ideas were directly echoed in United Irish
arguments (he was an enthusiast for a popularly elected assembly as a
barrier against tyranny, for the reform of political representation, and
for frequent and balloted elections).[58] To Hutcheson, political authority
should properly be founded on the consent of the people, an idea so
central to the emergence of modern nationalist thinking.

Other contemporary influences upon the United Irishmen – such
as Freemasonry – would also have raised eyebrows among the members
of a twentieth-century IRA Active Service Unit, and among many
other modern-day celebrants of the United Irishmen. And other
distortions of their historic importance have at times emerged. One
involves what might be termed the socialization of the United Irishmen. A strong tradition within left-wing Irish republicanism has sought
to portray the United Irishmen, and Wolfe Tone in particular, as
proto-socialists, as ideological ancestors of the nationalist class-warriors
of the twentieth century. The brilliant 1916 rebel James Connolly, for
example, claimed that, 'Tone built up his hopes upon a successful
prosecution of a class war';[59] later, Connolly's most talented socialist-
republican successor, IRA novelist and agitator Peadar O'Donnell
(1893–1986), presented Tone in similar terms, as someone who 'saw
the poor as the freedom force of the nation'.[60]

Such readings of Tone were anachronistic (and fit a pattern very
familiar to historians: 'The most usual ideological abuse of history is
based on anachronism rather than lies'[61]). Much of the Connolly–
O'Donnell leftist reading rested on a key statement by Tone himself,
written in Paris in 1796: 'Our independence must be had at all hazards,
if the men of property will not support us, they must fall: we can
support ourselves by the aid of that numerous and respectable class of
the community, the men of no property.'[62] Did this not indicate that
Tone – like Connolly and O'Donnell – saw Ireland's struggle for
independence as rooted in the conflict between the Irish working class
and their class opponents? Probably not. For in the eighteenth century
the term 'property' was used primarily to refer to landed property, and
Tone's resonant phrase ('the men of no property') should almost
certainly be understood in this light, to signify the middle class. There
was a sense of class conflict in Tone's thinking, but it was not between
the working and the other classes, but between the middle class[63] and

the landed aristocracy (an utterly different conflict from that enthused over by James Connolly and Peadar O'Donnell). Although some – like Thomas Russell – did have a profound sympathy for the poor and a genuinely democratic instinct, the United Irishmen were no proto-socialists, were not keen to undermine the security of private property, and did not exemplify socially revolutionary politics. Tone himself was not a modern-style democrat (exhibiting instead rather elitist attitudes towards the masses), and while there was a mass politicization of the lower orders in the 1790s, this should not lead us to assume any radicalization in terms which genuinely resembled later socialist politics.

A similar point might be made with regard to the United Irishmen and women. There were impressively far-sighted figures involved here: the radical Presbyterian Mary Anne McCracken – born in Belfast in 1776 and living to ninety-six years of age – argued forcefully with her brother (Henry Joy McCracken) that demands for the rights of man should be extended to women. A Society of United Irishwomen seems to have been established in Belfast by 1796, though women such as McCracken herself would have preferred not separate societies, but rather female admission to the main political bodies. It was not the case, however, that the United Irishmen in general embraced the issue of women and politics in a public sense: exhibiting the late-eighteenth-century notion of appropriately separate roles and spheres for the two sexes, the United Irishmen were reluctant to admit women into the political process. Women did make a contribution to the 1798 rebellion – and people such as Mary Anne McCracken were lucid in their attachment to 'rational ideas of liberty and equality'[64] – but they had been effectively excluded from the programme of the United Irishmen and, for the most part, women in 1790s radical Ireland played a supporting part in the drama. Yet their arguments and fire should be recorded. As one might expect, McCracken herself could express the passionate radical excitement of the time as powerfully as any man, as in her March 1797 declaration:

> Let us not be terrified or dismayed, but repose with unlimited confidence where we can never be deceived. If the complete Union of Ireland should demand the blood of some of her best Patriots to cement, if they will not sink [from] their duty, but meet their fate

equally unappalled, whether it be on the scaffold or in the field convinced that in the end the cause of Union and of truth must prevail.[65]

There were to be nationalist heroines from this period – Anne Devlin (1780–1851) famous among them for her role in turn-of-the-century patriotic adventures. But, for the most part, nationalist Ireland at its eighteenth-century emergence was – for good or ill – emphatically run by the boys.

4

It would be a manifest exaggeration to call him [Theobald Wolfe Tone] a great man, but he had many of the qualities of mind and character by which, under favourable conditions, greatness has been achieved, and he rises far above the dreary level of commonplace which Irish conspiracy in general presents. . . . His judgment of men and things was keen, lucid and masculine, and he was alike prompt in decision and brave in action.

W. E. H. Lecky[66]

Celebrated by many as the first true Irish republicans, what kind of portrait did the United Irishmen paint? They did focus on issues which became central to later nationalist politics in Ireland: popular sovereignty, autonomy from England, redress of Catholic grievance, attempted reform followed by aggressive militarism, alliance with England's foreign enemies, and so on. But in other ways, too, they typified much that was to follow in the nationalist story. Pursuing a unity among Irish people, they prompted developments which left Ireland more bloodily divided than they had found it. Famous for espousing an inclusive ideology, on close inspection their ideas and actions could evince also a profoundly sectarian communalism. (And – ironically, given their intended transcendence of denominational division – the United Irishmen would come to be remembered in distinctively Catholic manner.[67]) Ultimately keen to separate Ireland from England, their rebellion of 1798 in fact contributed to the establishment of an Act of Union between Great Britain and Ireland – a Union which was to last for over a century.

So while the radical politics of the 1790s have outlived many other episodes in terms of their supposed legacy and importance, this process might involve a more ambiguous inheritance than is sometimes assumed. One set of radical republicans argued 200 years after the 1798 upheaval that 'The United Irishmen and the great rebellion of 1798 are not mere history – something that happened in the dim and distant past. The dramatic events of those times ... made an impact on Irish political affairs that has endured ever since.... In this bicentenary year, the issues raised by the 1798 rebellion are still very much alive.'[68] Yet it is far from certain that those issues were ones most clearly seen through the lenses of celebratory radical republican nationalism.

Much of this can be helpfully considered through examination of the most famous and compelling United Irishman of all, Theobald Wolfe Tone – 'the most lovable as well as the most talented of Irish nationalists'.[69] Tone's legendary status in the Irish nationalist tradition is such that he requires special analysis, even if his later fame has rather exaggerated his contemporary importance. Contrary to some later assumption, Tone did not lead the 1798 Rising; nor was he as significant as William Drennan in creating the ideas of the initial United Irish Society; nor did his career last as long as that of Thomas Russell, who was there from the foundation of the United Irishmen in 1791 right through to their final gesture of 1803. But Theobald Wolfe Tone did become a nationalist hero in Ireland of almost unrivalled stature. He was an inspiration to vast numbers of later nationalists, Thomas Davis, Patrick Pearse, Ernie O'Malley, Harry Boland and Frank Gallagher all among them.[70] As another eminent nationalist, Sean O'Faoláin, was to put it, Tone became 'the great prototype on which all later would-be revolutionaries instinctively modelled themselves'.[71] A much later generation of radicals in the 1960s celebrated Tone in their (similarly) vain attempt to undo Irish sectarian division:[72] as in the 1790s, however, the sought-after transcendence of sectarianism was lost amid often sectarian conflict as the northern troubles arose in the late twentieth century.

Tone's influence was certainly lasting and profound. One of the

1916 Easter rebels (and subsequently a very influential Irish nationalist politician himself), Sean MacEntee, later argued that, 'To give anything like an adequate conspectus of the events which led up to 1916, it would be necessary to recount almost a century and a half of Irish history. In particular,' he continued, 'one would need to elaborate on the importance of Theobald Wolfe Tone; for, from his teachings stem many of the characteristics of modern Ireland. Without Tone there might not have been a rising and almost certainly not a Republic of Ireland. He was among the most perspicacious of our patriots.'[73] Even more cautious and careful appraisals – such as that offered by the Burkean nineteenth-century Irish historian W. E. H. Lecky, quoted above – have contained some striking regard for Tone. And great claims have continued to be made: for Hubert Butler, Tone 'was the father of Irish republicanism and also I think of Irish nationalism';[74] Tone's most accomplished biographer records him as having become 'the recognized founder of Irish republican nationalism'.[75]

And it is not hard to see why Tone has attracted such lasting celebrity as the supposed founding father of republican Ireland. Energetic, dynamic, lively, quick-minded and engaging, Tone remains one of the most alluring and attractive of Irish political figures. Observers have sometimes commented upon his accessibility ('Other leaders ... had nothing to do with living. Tone was the first human note; "drunk again", in his diary meant much: it brought him down to mortal level'[76]); but it is also his swashbuckling swagger and his love of romantic, adventurous soldiership which have endured. Tone himself claimed that he possessed 'a wild spirit of adventure', and that he had long enjoyed 'the untamable desire' to become a soldier, finally indulged in the 1790s.[77] A Dublin-born, middle-class Protestant, Wolfe Tone was a TCD-trained lawyer, and though he referred to 'the sincere dislike' he held towards the legal profession,[78] he was more positive about Trinity itself: 'I preserve, and ever shall, a most sincere affection for the University of Dublin'.[79] (Indeed, Tone was an early exemplar of a tradition that we will repeatedly encounter in this book, that of Trinity College Irish nationalism.) Bored by the law, Tone loved the idea of being a soldier and he enjoyed a lifelong passion for the military and for its attendant excitements: in his own words, he possessed 'a romantic spirit of adventure'.[80]

Tone's beguiling autobiographical writings show him to have been the most convivial of Irish revolutionary heroes, and his youthful tragedy – taking his own life after his capture in 1798 – has surely reinforced his appeal. (Again, Tone is here an early version of a repeated pattern – stretching from Robert Emmet through Kevin Barry to Bobby Sands – of the doomed young Irish republican.) But while he has inspired and pre-echoed later Irish nationalists, it is only as an eighteenth-century man that we will properly understand Theobald Wolfe Tone. Like the other United Irishmen, he drew many of his ideas from the well of contemporary influences (a fact reflected in his quotation from figures such as Voltaire). He emerged to prominence in relation to that most eighteenth-century of Irish political issues, the question of Catholic reform. Like Edmund Burke (whom he only once actually met), Tone had a mother who had converted from Catholicism to Protestantism, and indeed Tone's early 1790s arguments had a distinctly Burkean ring to them. His 1791 pamphlet, *An Argument on Behalf of the Catholics of Ireland*, argued the case for emancipation of Catholics, and for there being common political interests between members of Ireland's different Christian denominations. Tone held not only that parliamentary reform was urgently required, but that it would only be just and effective if it encompassed the extension of the franchise to Catholics: reform needed to embrace Irishmen from all religious families.

Selling quickly in thousands, Tone's *Argument* became an immediate success, a political bestseller. It reflected ideas currently in circulation (Tone probably being more of a talented popularizer of others' ideas than a particularly original thinker himself), and it was specifically aimed at Ulster Dissenters who were politically radical but still wary of Catholics. In 1792 Tone was appointed agent to the Catholic Committee (replacing Edmund Burke's son Richard), and in the following year the Committee dissolved itself, confident in what it had achieved and in the imminence of the remaining changes being made.

Tone thus began the 1790s not merely as one who filled the shoes of Burke's son, but as one whose arguments fitted Burke's own preferred pattern. In 1793 Tone was making the emphatically Burkean case that it was not Catholic reform which posed a danger to the connection between Ireland and Britain, but rather opposition to Catholic reform. If Catholics were denied the possibility of loyal liberty, and were presented instead with a choice between slavery and resistance, then here lay the true danger to the British connection. The crucial thing to understand about Wolfe Tone is his shift from an espousal of Burkean reform to a stance which, by 1798, embodied precisely the kind of revolutionary politics which Burke had so feared. For by the end of his life, Tone had transformed himself into a revolutionary who was keen to bring French-inspired rebellion to Ireland.

There were, it is true, many continuities in his thinking. It's perhaps best, for example, to see him as having been a comparatively early, but initially reluctant, Irish separatist. On 9 July 1791 Tone had expressed the view: 'My unalterable opinion is that the bane of Irish prosperity is the influence of England. I believe that influence will ever be exerted while the connexion between the countries continues.'[81] (He had recognized in Swift the idea of English influence being the bane of Irish political life.) In 1793 he expressed his sense that while parliamentary reform offered the remedy for the problem of British influence over Irish politics, his own personal preference might lie with Irish independence:

> but Ireland being connected as she is, I for one do not wish to break that connection, provided it can be, as I am sure it can, preserved consistently with the honour, the interests, and the happiness of Ireland. If I were, on the other hand, satisfied that it could not be so preserved, I would hold it a sacred duty to endeavour, by all possible means, to break it . . . [82]

Tone's practical politics did gradually evolve, however, and the dating of his separatism has been the subject of keen historiographical argument.[83] Until 1795, public espousal of full Irish separation from England was very rare indeed. Yet by 1796 Irish radicalism had become more separatist and more republican, and by this year, at least, Tone was indeed a separatist republican himself. By this stage, republican liberty and freedom from England were necessarily connected to each other in his thinking, and his anti-Englishness had grown starkly clear. (Tone's journal for 26 November 1796 declared, 'The truth is, I hate the very name of England; I hated her before my exile; I hate her since, and I will hate her always!'[84])

Echoes of this anglophobia can be heard in the views of many subsequent enthusiasts for Tone's legacy. Moreover, argument has raged over whether Tone's main argument should be seen as his case for uniting Irish people of differing religious background, or his separatist zeal to undo the connection with an England which caused Irish political ills.[85] But two points seem clear enough. First, Tone had considered that these two goals – unity of the people and aggressively won separation from England – could be harmoniously combined; second, the 1790s forcibly suggested that, in reality, they could not. The aggressive pursuit of Irish separatism – then as later – tended in practice to reinforce Irish sectarian division, and to render unity ever less attainable.

Theobald Wolfe Tone's most famous passage, from his 1790s *Memoirs*, is rousing and understandably much repeated. In 1796 in Paris he reflected back on the 1790s; and whether or not these views accurately reflected Tone's actual priorities from 1791 onwards, they none the less became lastingly enshrined in the Irish nationalist imagination among the most celebrated of declarations:

> To subvert the tyranny of our execrable government, to break the connection with England, the never-failing source of all our political evils, and to assert the independence of my country – these were my objects. To unite the whole people of Ireland, to abolish the memory of all past dissensions, and to substitute the common name of Irishman in place of the denominations of Protestant, Catholic and Dissenter – these were my means.

But even Tone's immediately ensuing passage located such rhetoric within a more limited and realistic political framework:

> To effectuate these great objects, I reviewed the three great sects. The Protestants I despaired of from the outset, for obvious reasons. Already in possession, by an unjust monopoly, of the whole power and patronage of the country, it was not to be supposed they would ever concur in measures, the certain tendency of which must be to lessen their influence as a party, how much soever the nation might gain. To the Catholics I thought it unnecessary to address myself, because, that, as no change could make their political situation worse, I reckoned upon their support to a certainty; besides, they had already begun to manifest a strong sense of their wrongs and oppressions; and, finally, I well knew that, however it might be disguised or suppressed, there existed in the breast of every Irish

Catholic an inextirpable abhorrence of the English name and
power. There remained only the Dissenters, whom I knew to be
patriotic and enlightened . . .[86]

For it was the Dissenters (the Presbyterians) on whom Tone really
focused. This partly reflected the tremendous vibrancy of 1790s Belfast
politics (although some of those who were intellectually influential
within 1790s Belfast – people such as William Bruce (1757–1841) and
Henry Joy (1754–1835) – themselves grew disillusioned with the
radicalizing of the reform movement and, unlike Tone, evinced a
scepticism about whether French invasion would produce lasting Irish
liberation. More moderate figures such as these had initially welcomed
the French Revolution, but were to oppose the eventual 1798 insurrection, and became supporters of the Act of Union which more firmly
linked Ireland to Britain.[87]).

Tone himself greatly enjoyed Belfast and celebrated its politics,
within which he identified the Presbyterians as especially important:
'The Dissenters of the north, and more especially of the town of
Belfast, are, from the genius of their religion, and from the superior
diffusion of political information among them, sincere and enlightened
republicans.'[88] As noted, however, the fissure between Dissenter and
Protestant (the latter term, in the eighteenth century, referring to
members of the established Church of Ireland), was compounded by
divisions within the Catholic community (many fighting in the Crown
forces as well as many others for the rebels), and by bloody violence in
1798 between Catholics and non-Catholics. In Tone's own case, it was
the conflict between England and France which set the framework; and
these two great nations, engaged in wars with each other around the
world, saw their conflict in its Irish form devour Wolfe Tone. Captured
in 1798 and denied a firing-squad death, Tone was instead sentenced
to death by hanging. To prevent this, he cut his own throat on 15
November 1798, dying four days later, aged thirty-five. The nineteenth
century saw the emergence of great celebration of this most eighteenth-
century of rebels. As so often, fame was built on a combination of
striking literary record and the enthusiastic work done by celebrants of
later generations (initially, in this case, Tone's son William, whose
influential edited version of his father's writings appeared in 1826).

To some nineteenth-century eyes, Tone embodied a shift in political approach, Young Irelander Thomas D'Arcy McGee looking back and asserting: 'We must not look, therefore, to see the Tones and Emmets continuing in the constitutional line of public conduct marked out by Burke in the one kingdom, and Grattan in the other. The new age was revolutionary, and the new men were filled with the spirit of the age.'[89] There is much in this. But it is also true that Tone in many ways clashed with what later nationalists in Ireland would come to assume. The United Irishmen did make some attempts to promote the study (if not the revival) of the Irish language, but Tone himself was not keen on it, possessing little of later nationalists' enthusiasm for romantic Gaelic celebration. A hero for Catholic nationalists of many later periods, Tone himself disliked Catholic (especially Irish Catholic) priests, considered the Catholic Church to be an enslaving institution hostile to liberty, and was profoundly anti-papal in outlook. A non-Christian founder of a tradition adhered to for the most part by Christians, he was also a socially snobbish elitist celebrated by later egalitarians, as well as a critic of America (which he hated and thought extremely vulgar) yet the hero of a militant Irish nationalism which was lastingly to thrive in that country.

Modern claims on Tone may at times have threatened to obscure the reality of the contemporary man, but it remains undeniable that Tone did in other ways resonate with what was to follow. His focus on popular sovereignty lay at the heart of modern nationalism, and he epitomized much else that was to lie at the core of nationalist Irish politics. A parliamentary reformer who eventually turned to rebellion, he thereby embodied the two major traditions in Irish nationalist agitation. He argued for redress of Catholic grievance, and also for Ireland to occupy her true position of esteem among the nations of the earth, valuing her honour and integrity (just as nationalists of other nations have so frequently stressed such values themselves[90]). He unsuccessfully sought to establish interdenominational unity, and he focused sharply upon the defining question of national government: as early as 1791 he had considered it a misfortune that Ireland possessed no such government, since to derive government from another country involved being governed by a nation which would pursue its own interests more firmly and consistently than those of Ireland. In all of this, Tone saw himself as a lover of liberty, a committed opponent of tyranny: 'Liberty is the vital principle of man: he that is prepared to live is prepared for freedom.'[91] And in all of this he was clearly a nationalist.

5

Nationalism is a phenomenon which came into being in Europe around the eighteenth century.

Montserrat Guibernau[92]

Much of the old orthodoxy regarding eighteenth-century Ireland has now been reconsidered in scholarly analysis:[93] stark assumptions concerning the supposedly appalling oppression of Catholics, the antagonism between aristocracy and peasantry, the idea of English misrule as the cause of Irish economic problems,[94] or even the colonial quality of the Irish–English relationship itself – all of these have been questioned to some degree. But how far had this newly-assessed century produced a modern-style nationalism? Most theorists of nationalism have tended to see the phenomenon as a creature of the period which began around the late eighteenth century,[95] and there is reason to hold that this dating makes sense for Ireland also. In the United Irishmen we do have a politics of self-conscious national community, clearly bounded according to territory and also to people (the unity of whom was repeatedly raised up, celebrated and pursued); there was a cultural-national dimension to United Irish politics, a sense of history, and belief that one held an ethically superior stance within an historic struggle for democracy; there was fierce exclusivism here also, whether in anglophobic relation to England, or in terms of local sectarian definition of in-group and out-group within Ireland. Likewise, there was a clear politics of organized communal struggle – reformist, propagandist, revolutionary, programmatic – and of a struggle focused on the goals of liberty, political independence and power. The state and sovereignty were central to the endeavour. Power was certainly wielded (through word and violent threat and deed), and alterations in the mechanisms of power were central to United Irish ambition:

political power structures required reform, while ultimately English power had to be replaced by Irish power. Here also were an attachment to the idea of restoring proper purity and virtue to the political realm, and a commitment to popular sovereignty, equality and freedom in a movement which had been directly and indirectly influenced by the vital ideas of Locke and Rousseau. In the earlier part of the century there had evolved an increasing assertion of Irish rights as befitted a separate kingdom; but with the late-eighteenth-century United Irishmen, Irish nationalism was born.

This nationalism built on earlier ethnic foundations (as with those United Irishmen who did encourage the study of the Irish language, for example), fitting the wider pattern of a modern nationalism which draws from pre-modern strength: 'while national identity is mainly a modern phenomenon, pre-modern ethnic communities and identities are widespread and processes of national formation and representation are found in all epochs'.[96] But it was emphatically a modern politics, and with its striking intersection of equality, sovereignty and liberty it represented something new. The 1790s were a crucial decade in the emergence of modern Ireland: popular republicanism, separatism, loyalism and Orangeism were all born then. And so too was nationalist Ireland.

PART TWO

THE NINETEENTH-CENTURY DRAMA

THREE

CATHOLIC REFORM AND CULTURAL NATIONALISM, 1800–1850

<hr>

1

> Indeed, the domestic habits of no nation in Europe were less
> known to the English than those of their sister country, till
> within these few years.
>
> Maria Edgeworth (1800)[1]

English-born and English-educated, the novelist Maria Edgeworth
(1767–1849) came from a family which moved to their Irish estate in
1782; her father was an improving landlord and Edgeworth herself
lived in County Longford until her death in 1849. Her Irish residence
therefore straddled what in many ways has been the defining event
with which Irish nationalism has so long been challenged, and against
which so many have in their various ways struggled. For on 1 August
1800 (in the Irish Parliament) and earlier on 2 July (in the British),
royal assent was given to the Act of Union, which duly became
operative on 1 January 1801. And so, on this latter date, the United
Kingdom of Great Britain and Ireland came into existence. Under
this new arrangement there was to be one parliament in London,
with 100 seats in its House of Commons for members from Irish
constituencies. The government of Ireland under the Union would
continue to rest in the Lord Lieutenant, the Chief Secretary and the
Irish Privy Council: the Lord Lieutenant and Chief Secretary were
both political appointments, with the latter being the chief government spokesman on Ireland in parliament.

The Act of Union became lastingly one of the most important
contexts for Irish nationalism: for much Irish nationalist political

history (and as the basis of virtually all Irish nationalist political argument) the Union was crucial. It lasted for well over a century, and within its framework there evolved the modern politics of nationalist Ireland.

Why had the Act been introduced? As so often, we need to look at concentric circles of context: Irish circumstances, exigencies and immediate politics; British political attitudes and imperatives; and tensions on the European continent which framed British perceptions of need. It seemed to London by 1800 that the existence of Ireland as a separate kingdom – subordinate though it was – none the less represented a threat to the security of the British state. Prime Minister William Pitt had long been considering an Act of Union between Ireland and England; on hearing news of the 1798 Rising, he decided that Union would follow as soon as the rebellion had been defeated.

But while the outbreak of rebellion in May 1798 thus forced Pitt to look closely at Ireland, he had far from neglected the neighbouring island during previous years and a Union between the two kingdoms had indeed been long considered in British high-political circles. Pitt himself favoured a full legislative Union as the only workable solution to the problems of the English–Irish relationship, and as the best way forward for the interests of the empire – the latter being a subject of central importance for him. He thought that an independent Irish legislature would not work either for the peace of Ireland or for the security of Britain. The uniting of the parliaments would, he hoped, build a new security. If, eventually, within the context of a Union Catholics could be included in parliament through civil emancipation, then their support could further help to strengthen the state and the empire.

So Union in 1800 was not merely a spontaneous reaction to rebellion, but rather a longer-term response grounded in London's view of Irish, British and imperial needs (and legislative union had been entertained by some in Britain and Ireland throughout the eighteenth century, as one political alternative). The 1798 rebellion enabled Pitt to make his preference into policy, rather than creating that preference in the first place. If Ireland could be securely incorporated into the British–Irish relationship within a strong United Kingdom, then this would strengthen the very heart of the empire: it would not be merely a case of subjugating Ireland to Britain, but rather of centralizing Ireland at the very core of a stronger empire: Ireland was to be brought to the centre of imperial power, and the Act of Union was intended to consolidate the British state.[2]

The specifically Irish context was also vital, in particular the 1782 constitutional revolution and what had followed it. Patriot Henry Grattan had insisted on the repeal of the 1720 Declaratory Act (which had stated the British parliament's right to pass laws binding on Ireland) and the modifying of the 1494 Poynings' Law (which had stated that the British and Irish Privy Councils could change or kill off proposed Irish bills); when these two changes had been made, the situation was one in which mechanisms for London's control over Ireland had been removed, and not satisfactorily replaced from a governmental point of view. Irish legislative power was still comparatively limited, but the sense within Ireland of an embryonic political independence of mind has to be considered. Grattan's own thinking was founded on the idea that Ireland was a sister kingdom to Britain, subject to the same monarch but essentially equal in status. From a London perspective, such a stance left the link between Ireland and Britain too weak to be reliable as things stood.

The years 1798–1800 made it clear that Ireland could represent the weak link in British defences, and the Union offered a way of doing something about this Achilles' heel. So the 1798 Rising might have been the immediate prompt for Union; but behind this lay not only the fears generated by the French Revolutionary contagion, but in Ireland specifically the dangerous setting produced by the abuse of Protestant power and the extent of Catholic disaffection. The Union, it was hoped, could simultaneously improve British and imperial security and also the relations between religious groupings in Ireland itself. In Pitt's view, at least, losing the Irish parliament but incorporating the Irish people would strengthen and secure the empire, and this was the central purpose of the Act of Union.

But if it were to work, the Union had to attain support from an Irish majority, and therefore the delicate question of Catholic emancipation was central. Attempts were strenuously made to win over various different Irish interests to the Union, and there was a significant body of Catholic Irish support for the measure prior to its introduction (although, tellingly, the great future leader of nationalist Ireland, Daniel O'Connell, organized a meeting of Dublin Catholics in

1800 to oppose the Union). It was clear that Catholics would have preferred equality without a Union to equality with one: within a Union, Catholics would be a minority; without a Union – but with equality having been granted – they would achieve ascendancy.

The Catholic leadership in Ireland seemed to think (and seems to have been allowed to assume) that Emancipation would shortly follow Union, and that Union was therefore the best route towards the freeing of Irish Catholics from their continuing status of civil inequality. It remains far from clear what the larger Catholic population thought in the run-up to the Union: general indifference to the passing of the measure appears to have been widespread enough. But in the immediate pre-Union period there was a complex Irish political pattern, characterized by pro-Union pro-Catholics as well as pro-Union anti-Catholics, and by anti-Union pro-Catholics as well as anti-Union anti-Catholics. For the authorities, the relation between Union and Catholic Emancipation went right to the heart of the issue which has so lastingly troubled British rulers of Ireland: the dilemma of how best to address the central Irish nationalist communal grievance, that of Catholic reform within the United Kingdom. If one thought Irish Catholics potentially loyal and accommodated members of the state, then logic pointed towards magnanimity, equal incorporation and toleration. Yet if one thought the opposite – that Catholic Ireland represented a non-assimilable community – then the logic of equality might seem far less sure. (And this has remained a central dilemma for unionism in its dealings with nationalism even into the most modern periods.) This problem around the time of the introduction of the Union was sharpened by the task of trying to satisfy Catholic claims while avoiding the simultaneous exacerbation of Protestant fears (again, a difficulty which was to prove of long duration for those running Ireland from London).

As things actually emerged during the nineteenth century, the Union was undoubtedly weakened by the authorities' failure to accompany it at once with Catholic Emancipation. The early years of the Union saw the lingering of the communal grievance of Catholic disability – one of so many continuities across the 1800 divide – and this fed disaffection in ways which stimulated the growth of a powerful new form of Irish nationalism.

In the main, this was to take a constitutional and reformist path during the nineteenth century. But the earliest years of the Union did witness what was to become a famous example of more aggressive nationalist insurrectionism, in the form of Robert Emmet's rebellion of 1803. It has been argued that the Irish national ideal which most effectively survived into the nineteenth century was an 'insurrectionary separatist one' rather than a more conciliatory model,[3] and Emmet might seem to offer blazing endorsement of this view. He had been born in Dublin on 4 March 1778: the Emmets were a well-established Irish Protestant family, sympathetic to Catholic Emancipation and to advanced political ideas. Although Emmet's father (Dr Robert Emmet) was state physician for Ireland, he none the less held the views of an Irish patriot, and Robert Emmet junior inherited both his name and something of his radicalism from his father. Emmet was a student at Trinity College, Dublin from October 1793 onwards (providing yet another example of TCD nationalism, Trinity students indeed being heavily implicated in preparations for a United Irish rebellion).

One of the first books Emmet read in the year of his accession to Trinity was John Locke's *Two Treatises of Government*. More specifically, the late-eighteenth-century Locke was the Locke of the second Treatise, *The Essay on Civil Government*, and it was this essay, the second Treatise, which Emmet definitely read. Again, therefore, we can trace one of the direct routes by which the ideas at the heart of modern nationalism reached Irish minds. (It's worth noticing also that as a child Emmet had been familiar with the writings on liberty of United Irishman William Drennan.)

A rather gentle, epicene character, Emmet might be seen as the classic late-eighteenth-century bourgeois revolutionary. In the 1790s he wrote poetry, some of it reflecting his political reading of the unequal politics of the Anglo-Irish relationship (although it should be noted that he seemed content at this stage with the idea that, injustice once removed, Irish–English union might be acceptable). Yet Emmet was emphatically to become a rebel. Tied tightly into the network of revolutionary life (his brother Thomas Addis Emmet (1764–1827) was a good friend of Tone and of Thomas Russell), Robert Emmet was involved in restructuring the United Irish movement after the disaster of 1798, and in preparing for a new insurrection. There remained among the rebels in the years at the turn of the century an expectation of a French arrival in Ireland, and a keen anticipation that England's enemy would help to make Ireland's rebels strong.

When it occurred, Emmet's rebellion represented something of a leftover from 1798, built on plans made in the wake of that defeat. Although Emmet (like many a later Irish nationalist rebel) was passionate about military tactics, his July 1803 rebellion descended into something of a drunken riot and was easily enough suppressed. Plans for the rebellion were secretive, precise and yet severely flawed: the capture of Dublin had been central to the scheme, but Emmet had anticipated more rebels joining him in his adventure than turned out to be the case in practice. The rebellion did surprise the government and caught them cold (and the severity and scope of the subsequent crackdown reflected the seriousness with which the Dublin and London authorities took it[4]); but the endeavour was undone partly through the rebels' own disintegration. And with the failure of Emmet's rebellion, the United Irish conspiracy was over.

The 1803 rebels' aims were encapsulated in their Proclamation, addressed to the 'People of Ireland': 'We war not against property, – we war against no religious sect . . . we war against English dominion.'[5] Independence was to be wrested from England by the Irish people's own hands: the rebels were fighting to grab due liberty for their nation. Community, struggle and power.

Emmet himself escaped from Dublin after the rebellion; he was arrested in August 1803 and his subsequent trial for high treason on Monday, 19 September was to become a focal point for Irish nationalist memory. The rebel having been found guilty and sentenced to death, it was Emmet's trial speech which formed the basis for his status as a legendary Irish nationalist hero: 'the man dies, but his memory lives', proclaimed Emmet in court, and his utterance helped to ensure the accuracy of this prediction.

> I have but a few more words to say – I am going to my cold and silent grave: my lamp of life is nearly extinguished: my race is run: the grave opens to receive me, and I sink into its bosom! I have but one request to ask at my departure from this world, it is the charity of its silence! – let no man write my epitaph . . . when my country takes her place among the nations of the earth, then and not till then – let my epitaph be written.[6]

Judged by many to have been a brilliant dock speech (despite some argument about the precise details of what he actually said), Emmet's oratory helped to ensure his posthumous standing. Hanged and beheaded in Dublin on 20 September 1803, having displayed dignity and composure as he went to his death, Emmet inspired many (including Shelley, who wrote him an elegiac tribute, 'On Robert Emmet's Tomb').

The legend of Robert Emmet which emerged soon after his death was one which proved very durable. The noble-minded, sympathetic hero of 1803 was, perhaps, easier to mould into legendary shape because comparatively little was actually known for certain about him: awkward reality could not spoil the pure myth. The Irish nationalist memory of Emmet had a distinctly Catholic quality to it,[7] and there were to emerge seemingly endless references to the man in the writings and statements of later Irish nationalists.[8] In 1896 Alice Milligan and Ethna Carbery's separatist paper *Shan Van Vocht* celebrated him as 'the most beloved of our patriot-martyrs': 'He gave up his life freely and nobly in the flower of his youth, when life's sweetest joys were his to claim, therefore is it that his name has a power beyond that of any other to inspire the young men of Ireland to noble deeds.'[9] The high priest of 1916, Patrick Pearse himself, took great inspiration from Emmet, and drew comfort from the apparently redemptive quality of Emmet's nationalist death.

Even in the twenty-first century, Emmet's memory lives on in the minds of militant republican zealots. On 20 September 2003 in Dublin the dissident Irish republican party Republican Sinn Féin (RSF) commemorated the 200th anniversary of Emmet's execution (at the exactly appropriate time and date). The oration was given by Seán Ó Brádaigh, and exemplified classic nationalist themes: sentimental inspiration from history, the celebration of uncompromising struggle, a definition of the nation through the supposed inclusion of the whole community and through definition against an immoral and illegitimate enemy in England:

There is something special about Robert Emmet, something exceptional and even lovable, that has made him 'the darling of Erin', for the last two hundred years. He has inspired scores of biographies and hundreds of songs. Thousands of boys are named after him. . . . It was on this very day, September 20, 1803, at this very spot in front of St Catherine's Church and at this very hour that young Emmet died for Ireland on England's gallows tree. Emmet deserves our respect, our admiration and our gratitude. Were it not for him, and countless other patriots, the Irish nation would long ago have faded away and disappeared in the mists of history. His memory endures and his deeds and words have inspired many who came after him, chief among them Patrick Pearse. . . . We of Republican Sinn Féin, who have gathered here today, hold true to Tone's and Emmet's teaching and purpose – to break the connection with England and establish an independent Irish republic, uniting Protestant, Catholic and Dissenter under the common name of Irishman. Tone and Emmet, Pearse and Connolly, saw Ireland as one nation of thirty-two counties. They regarded English rule in Ireland as an illegality. Now, two hundred years later, Republican Sinn Féin adheres to the same judgement.[10]

This was all as Emmet had hoped: 'When my spirit shall have joined those bands of martyred heroes who have shed their blood on the scaffold and in the field in defence of their country, this is my hope, that my memory and name may serve to animate those who survive me.'[11] One way of reading this is that, while his rebellion was a failure, his memory managed to achieve triumph. Only twenty-five years old at his death, Emmet was an idealistic, tragic young hero, brave and even characterized by a doomed romance. Yet it is also worth questioning what, precisely, his heroic standing has achieved. Neither Patrick Pearse nor Republican Sinn Fein managed to achieve Irish republican independence, their militancy proving more a matter of intense commitment than of practical fruitfulness.

Yet the romantic and rather sentimentalized celebration of Robert Emmet retains great allure for some (as do the cases of other romantic heroes from this era such as Thomas Russell: passionate, highly emotional and instinctively extreme, this handsome, charismatic, energetic, charming man was another major leader of 1803 and was convicted of high treason and executed – hanged and beheaded – at Downpatrick). Emmet's own dramatic death and memorable trial speech provided the foundation for a still-vibrant cult. Visual images – the noble, idealistic poses of popular depictions such as that by Edmond Fitzpatrick and others[12] – reinforce this kind of memory. But in truth the notion that Irish freedom could be won and Irish differences resolved through violence remains as questionable now as it was in 1803. Over twenty people were executed after Emmet's rebellion, and around fifty had died in Dublin on the night of the insurrection itself. Did the sentimental memory of Emmet really outweigh such losses?

The failure of Emmet's rebellion showed the end of any serious danger from United Irish-style insurrectionism to British rule in Ireland. But other forms of violence (agrarian, communal) were to remain a problem for the authorities: agrarian violence could be practised in order to defend existing patterns of land usage and occupation, or to prevent what were considered excessive demands in terms of rent. Of course, early-nineteenth-century rural unrest was not unique to Ireland, being experienced also in England, Scotland and Wales. But it remained a serious problem here: the typical threatening letter, or the shot fired into your house, might not represent the worst form of violence, but they were frightening enough if you were the one on the receiving end of them. The term Whiteboy[13] continued in use in the early nineteenth century, deployed in reference to those protesting about agrarian grievance. And there could be other distinctively Irish features of such violence. For such crime and disorder in Ireland embodied a double challenge to British government in the nineteenth century. There was the basic challenge as to whether government could maintain order properly, but also the deeper challenge as to whether British government in Ireland was legal and legitimate anyway.

Here, the legacy of the Penal Laws was of possible significance, in having established in many Irish Catholic minds the sense that law was hostile to their community rather than representative or protective of it. And if there remained among some a contemptuous attitude towards English law in Ireland, then this was further compounded by sectarian division. Absenteeism and sectarian fracture produced in Ireland barriers between landlords and their tenants, with the result that Irish magistrates were often in the localities rather isolated representatives of a law and a government which were not respected by the population. Military detachments were frequently required in order to back up the magistrate locally in dealing with rural disorder and agrarian violence. Thus the mechanisms of power and order were frayed in a world in which many still considered the law to be against them, and to be a punitive rather than protective phenomenon.

Was this Irish-British relationship, then, colonial? This has been a highly-charged subject of debate, since one's conclusion here has had profound relevance even to modern conflicts such as the Northern Ireland troubles. (As David Lloyd has pointed out, 'To assert that Ireland is and has been a colony is certainly to deny the legitimacy of British government in Northern Ireland and no less to question the state and governmental structures that have been institutionalized in the postcolonial Free State and Republic of Ireland.'[14]) And so debate has raged about Ireland's relationship to empire, colonialism and the place of Irish people and their suffering within the wider hierarchies of oppression.[15] Many − from a variety of very different perspectives − have sustained the view that Irish history has had a central colonial dimension,[16] and that this lasted definingly into the Union period.[17]

Indeed, some very prominent writers have placed Ireland firmly within this colonial framework. Yet this has not been without complications. Edward Said, one of the most significant of all post-colonialist scholars, clearly set his own understanding of Ireland within the context of imperial and colonial power. Yet he defined imperialism as 'the practice, the theory, and the attitudes of a dominating metropolitan centre ruling a distant territory',[18] which would seem an odd context in which to place the British–Irish relationship. Rather strangely including Ireland in a list of 'distant lands' which Europe sought to rule, he overlooked the more pertinent fact of so many Irish people's role in European imperialism over non-European peoples. For geographical proximity between Britain and Ireland had produced a cultural and physical intermingling which set these islands' relationship apart from any other British colonial experience. Irish nationalists themselves during the nineteenth century tended not to describe the Irish–British relationship as a colonial one. Indeed, many Irish nationalists not only distinguished Ireland's place from that of British colonies, but were enthusiastic enough about that British colonial project in any case (Young Irelander William Smith O'Brien being a striking example). Irish people experienced the British empire as colonized and also as colonist ('After 1800, the Irish of all descriptions entered enthusiastically into the business of empire'.[19]) Certainly for the period of the Union, there was an ambiguity to the situation: in some ways Ireland was seen as an integral part of the United Kingdom, in others as a place apart. And the term quasi-colonial probably better describes the ambiguity of the experience than does any more stark depiction.[20]

Whether colonially defined or not, if Irish community were to express itself in national terms then it required both imaginative and organizational force. At TCD one of Robert Emmet's closest friends had been Thomas Moore (1779–1852), who adored the martyr of 1803: 'Were I to number indeed the men among all I have ever known, who appeared to me to combine in the greatest degree pure moral worth with intellectual power, I should, among the highest of the few, place Robert Emmet.'[21] Moore himself was crucial to forging the Emmet legend; but he was also a strong force in moulding and sustaining the modern nationalist imagination in Ireland, and was one of the colossal figures within nationalist Irish culture. Born in Dublin, he was a TCD-educated Catholic poet who built an extraordinary reputation and success in the nineteenth century – especially in England. In 1799 Moore had gone to London where his *Odes to Anacreon* brought him success; then followed a collection of erotic verse published under the pseudonym Thomas Little.

But it was his sentimental, delicately enchanting *Irish Melodies* which really established his importance. The first of these appeared in 1807 and the *Irish Melodies* as a whole were written in eight parts between that year and 1834. Dublin composer John Stevenson (1761–1833) provided musical arrangements for the first seven sets, and the *Melodies* made Moore into a great popular success. Although his music is still available today,[22] Moore has now largely slipped from modern Irish nationalist culture (and indeed from wider historical memory: he didn't even merit an entry in the excellent 1998 *Oxford Companion to Irish History*[23]). Through much of the nineteenth century, however, he was celebrated as Ireland's national poet, and his hugely popular songs were a key medium for the spread and intensification of Irish nationalist feeling. There were over a hundred *Melodies* in all, about a third of which had an Irish political content to them (and in some ways Moore might be seen as having continued the United Irish tradition for politically-charged verse).

Dedicated to Emmet, some of the *Melodies* referred directly to him and it was through Moore's songs that many people were later to encounter the martyred hero of 1803. If Irish republican mythology has often featured the sincere, brave, noble-minded victim of a cruelly unjust Britain, then Moore's sentimental, melancholic depiction of the tragic-romantic Emmet fitted the bill perfectly and lastingly. Translated into several languages, Moore's *Melodies* helped to internationalize Emmet's political struggle (just as Emmet himself had sought to internationalize Ireland's own).

More broadly, Moore's songs came to represent a key influence on Irish nationalist consciousness and tradition, a widely resonant cultural event within the transmission of Irish nationalism.

DEAR HARP OF MY COUNTRY

> Dear Harp of my Country! in darkness I found thee;
> The cold chain of silence had hung o'er thee long,
> When proudly, my own Island Harp! I unbound thee,
> And gave all thy chords to light, freedom, and song!
> The warm lay of love and the light note of gladness
> Have waken'd thy fondest, thy liveliest thrill;
> But, so oft hast thou echoed the deep sigh of sadness,
> That even in thy mirth it will steal from thee still.
>
> Dear Harp of my Country! farewell to thy numbers,
> This sweet wreath of song is the last we shall twine;
> Go, sleep, with the sunshine of Fame on thy slumbers,
> Till touch'd by some hand less unworthy than mine.
> If the pulse of the patriot, soldier, or lover,
> Have throbb'd at our lay, 't is thy glory alone;
> I was *but* as the wind, passing heedlessly over,
> And all the wild sweetness I waked was thy own.[24]

Irish literary nationalism may have had its origins in the United Irishmen of the 1790s, but its development was sharply and lastingly defined by this immensely influential popular song-writer. In particular, it is worth noting the prominence within Moore's work of those who had resisted past oppression. Moore was certainly an Irish nationalist; but his politics were probably more in tune with the United Irish vision of the nation (with which he had sympathized) than with the Catholic nationalism which came to dominate in the nineteenth century in Ireland. A Catholic married to a Protestant (the actress Bessy Dyke), Moore was more emblematic of the diverse, liberal-leaning, pluralistic national vision of the early 1790s than of the kind of national politics over whose triumph Daniel O'Connell was magisterially to preside.

But Moore – the 'colossus of Irish songwriting'[25] – was none the less a grand success, a major Irish writer in the English language and one greatly admired by the composer Berlioz and the poet Byron (the latter being a good friend of Moore, and the subject of his own fascination[26]). Romantic and sentimental Irish nationalism had found its greatly talented voice, a voice which could, at times, offer 'savage indictment of English perfidy and policy'.[27]

2

Ireland has never produced a greater man than O'Connell.

Michael Davitt[28]

But the most powerful, stentorian voice of all belonged to somebody else. Daniel O'Connell (1775–1847) is arguably the most important politician in the entire history of Irish nationalism. He was born on 6 August 1775 in County Kerry, to a wealthy Catholic family, and he became a hard-working and very able barrister: while Irish Protestants were to shun his nationalist politics, many of them were keen enough to employ him as a lawyer. Indeed, O'Connell's skills as a lawyer – quickly mastering a topic in detail, deciding on a precise course of action, and then arguing eloquently and persuasively in pursuit of a clearly established aim – were to serve him well as a politician too. A highly talented speaker and organizer, by the time of his death in Genoa on 15 May 1847 O'Connell ('The Liberator') had introduced effective mass-nationalist politics to Ireland and had done much to define its lasting quality. For early-nineteenth-century Irish politics were dominated by two issues – the political, constitutional relationship between Ireland and Britain; and the rights of Catholics – and on both these questions O'Connell's became the most important voice for decades.

Chronologically, the Catholic question came first in his career. The Dublin parliament had passed Catholic relief measures during the 1770s, 1780s and 1790s, allowing for Catholic ownership of land and for Catholics to vote. But there still remained the important issue of allowing access for Catholics to those positions from which they remained excluded by penal legislation, including the right to sit in parliament, to hold senior government office, to be a judge, or to be a King's Counsel. This question of Catholic Emancipation was, through O'Connell in the 1820s, to force itself unstoppably on to the British political stage. There was an early-nineteenth-century expectation that parliament existed partly to redress legitimate grievances: in this sense the Catholic question was to be dealt with within a very British framework. But the extra-parliamentary context – that of mass mobilization in Ireland and the apparent threat of political violence here – distinguished this from normal Westminster business.

In 1823 O'Connell founded the Catholic Association, to campaign for Emancipation and to advance Catholic interests. Prior to this he had been engaged in often frustrating efforts to push for the redress of Irish Catholic grievance, but from 1824 onwards his momentum was inexorable. Initially, subscriptions to the Association were one guinea a year (reflecting its social membership); in February 1824, however, O'Connell proposed a new category – that of associate member – comprising people who would pay a minimum subscription of one penny per month. This, the Catholic Rent, not only raised revenue, but also transformed the Association from a comparatively small to a mass-political movement. It would no longer be possible to claim that it represented only an elite, since it now included very many of the poorer classes; indeed, the Catholic Association has some right to be considered the first truly popular, mass-democratic organization in the modern world.

The idea of a scheme such as the penny-a-month plan was not itself novel, but it was newly implemented and made to work by O'Connell in the 1820s. Many thousands of people could now, for the first time, meaningfully be involved in the communal struggle of the Catholic Irish nation, as the penny-a-month scheme both widened and deepened the agitation for Emancipation.

At local level hundreds of thousands were involved and, with meetings and discussions, the effective mass movement of communal nationalist struggle had arrived. Crucial to this process was the fact of the Catholic Church throwing its weight behind O'Connell's Catholic Rent, allowing it to become successful in otherwise impossible fashion. The message was declared Sunday by Sunday at Mass, the priests were vital in spreading the necessary message (O'Connell deliberately leaving much power in priestly hands within the Association movement), and the enemies of O'Connell were presented as the traditional opponents of Catholicism in Ireland.

The most powerful popular movement yet to have emerged in British (let alone Irish) political life, O'Connell's Catholic Association dominated contemporary politics, forcing the hand of parliament and ultimately achieving major reform. And it was an Irish Prime Minister in London who was to ensure the passage of the sought-after legislation. For in January 1828 the Duke of Wellington became Prime Minister (with Robert Peel as Chief Secretary for Ireland), and the Catholic issue greeted him as a pressing concern. Enjoying huge national and international prestige and reputation, Wellington was to prove a hard-working Prime Minister. Born in 1769 to an Anglo-Irish family, he had left the island in 1794 and had only returned for any significant period in 1807–8 (during the period when, as Sir Arthur Wellesley, he was Chief Secretary for Ireland from 1807 to 1809). But Wellington crisply recognized something of Irish realities: as early as 1824 he had prophesied armed conflict in Ireland, and by 1825 he had recognized that the Catholic question would require some movement to be made in London. The fear was that even if the Catholic Association were to be suppressed, there would be a serious risk of violence and indeed the danger that something more militant might replace O'Connell's movement if Catholic grievances remained unresolved.

These anxieties had become yet more pressing with O'Connell's by-election victory in County Clare in June 1828. Here, O'Connell resoundingly triumphed in a contest prompted by the sitting member (Vesey Fitzgerald) having become President of the Board of Trade, and therefore needing to seek re-election. Catholic priests were absolutely vital in mobilizing for the Clare poll, and O'Connell's emphatic victory meant that his and his priests' Catholic cause in Ireland had either to be met with concession or with harsh coercion. Wellington decided that the latter was too dangerous, and that Emancipation should come sooner rather than later. During 1828–9 his administration therefore crafted a measure which granted Catholics the right of holding (almost all) political office and of becoming Members of Parliament.

In February 1829 the decision to grant Catholic relief was announced to parliament, and in the following month the relief bill was placed before the House of Commons. A significant proportion of both Houses and of the wider British public were opposed to the measure, but the bill none the less received royal assent in April 1829.

Of course, the removal of Catholic disabilities was not the same thing as full equality: the Church of Ireland was still the Established Church there, enjoying a privileged position within the state. But when the Catholic Relief Act became law on 13 April 1829, rendering Catholics in Ireland and Britain eligible to sit in parliament and to hold most (but not all) offices of state, a revolutionary change had been effected. Wellington had been driven more by a pragmatic sense of expediency than by any doctrinal conviction. He did believe that it would be wrong to exclude Catholics from the political governance of a country which was predominantly Catholic; but it was primarily the fear of civil war which had decided his mind on the necessity of Emancipation. The king (George IV) was opposed to concession, as were many others; but the Prime Minister enjoyed some considerable influence over George and struggled to persuade him that anything other than allowing such Catholic reform would risk destabilization and civil war in Ireland.

So two great Irishmen had, between them, forced Catholic Emancipation on to the statute book. Fearing the threat of mass unrest, Wellington forced Catholic relief through the British system against much opposition; but the pressure had been masterfully applied by Daniel O'Connell, whose very impressive Catholic Association had mobilized Irish nationalist opinion and thereby exerted irresistible leverage upon London to grant Emancipation. In the view of the great nineteenth-century Irish historian W. E. H. Lecky, the successful nationalist struggle for Catholic Emancipation 'had demonstrated clearly the coercive power which might be exercised over parliament by organized popular agitation'.[29] Quite so. But the enduring Catholic question had soured relations between the British state in Ireland and

Irish Catholics during the first three decades of the Union and, to some degree, this set a pattern from which it proved difficult to escape. The fact that Catholic Emancipation had been postponed until 1829, and that it was only then dragged unwillingly through a form of mass coercion, had dire effects on relations between Catholics and Protestants in Ireland (whose conflicting interests were magnified by Emancipation), and also between and Irish Catholics and the British state.

The campaign for Emancipation was, at root, a communal struggle for power: 'the power of Catholics not only to influence events but to direct them; not only to establish their rightful place in the Irish nation, but to be the Irish nation'.[30] But Emancipation did not resolve all problems in Irish political life. Relations between central and local government in mid-nineteenth-century Ireland were weak and problematic and this compounded problems of day-to-day administration and governance here. It had long been the view of the Whigs in England that the Irish Protestant landlord class had failed in their duties, and that much of the problem which existed in Ireland was down to their failure. In England the local landed gentry acted as the state's effective agents; in Ireland this did not happen to the same degree of effectiveness, partly due to the lack of integration between the landed and the people, occasioned by religious difference. One aspect of Ireland's nineteenth-century administrative difficulty was that English Whig, Liberal governments rejected traditional structures of local Irish administration as being preserves of a failed Protestant ascendancy, without creating alternatives which could have commanded the confidence and support of the majority of Irish people.[31]

Nineteenth-century Ireland existed in a quasi-colonial condition: in many ways, it differed from British colonies (enjoying direct representation in the House of Commons, for example); in others, however, it differed from the rest of the United Kingdom (in having, for instance, an Irish administration at Dublin Castle). Certainly there were deep Irish religious divisions, and central difficulties there with the Union. Catholics had been in some cases supporters in Ireland of the Union in 1800; by the 1840s they had become the strong foundation on which anti-Union politics were built. In 1800 Protestants in Ireland had been the principal opponents of Union; by the 1840s *they* were its defenders and advocates. When O'Connell campaigned for Repeal of the Union, virtually no Irish Protestants backed him (despite his deliberate efforts, at times, to win them over). By mid-century, therefore, the enduring sectarian geography of modern Ireland had been mapped out.

For the champion of Catholic liberty had from 1830 onwards effectively commenced his campaign for the Repeal of the Union (a Union which, as we saw, he had openly opposed at its birth in 1800). Catholic Emancipation, among its other achievements, had allowed O'Connell himself to develop a parliamentary career, and this had been something which the leader of Irish nationalism had been very keen to do. He emerged as a rather effective, eloquent and diligent British parliamentarian. After the 1832 general election, he became leader of a group of Irish MPs who were – ostensibly, at least – committed to achieving Repeal. But what did Repeal actually mean? In some ways – rather like the later Irish nationalist phrases 'Home Rule' and 'The Republic' – the word was important less in referring to a specific set of constitutional proposals than as an emblem of an idea: that of greater autonomy and freedom for Ireland from England. O'Connell himself stated his objective to be that Ireland should be governed by the monarch, Lords and Commons of Ireland: Repeal, he asserted, would leave the monarchical link intact, and it in no sense involved rejection of the Crown. What was supposedly envisaged was not complete separation from Britain or anything like it, but rather an Irish parliament to deal with Irish politics, within what would effec- tively be a federal system linking together the constituent nations of the neighbouring islands.

But was Repeal feasible, and did O'Connell believe it to be so? The answer to both questions is probably negative. British governmental and political opinion were firmly keen to uphold the Union, seeing Repeal as the first step towards Ireland leaving the empire. So O'Connell's second crusade differed here from his first, Emancipatory mission. And he knew this. Aware that Repeal was unlikely to be granted, he also understood that a strong campaign on its behalf could represent a useful lever by means of which to extract reforms from Westminster for Ireland. This, surely, was the essence of O'Connell's nationalist politics of Repeal,[32] and it was the politics of coercive bargaining, practised by a deep and brilliant pragmatist. O'Connell first moved Repeal in the House of Commons in 1834, knowing it to be a non-starter in the House; he founded, in 1840, the Loyal National Repeal Association; but he happily left the precise nature of the Repeal in question relatively vague. Less woolly, however, was his cooperation during the 1830s with the Whigs, by means of which he secured reforms and concessions for Ireland.

In 1841 the Tories returned to power and the political context therefore shifted. Repeal agitation underwent a crescendo towards 1843, during which huge (or 'monster') meetings were held across much of Ireland – large gatherings at many of which O'Connell himself was present. In October 1843 Prime Minister Robert Peel banned the monster meeting which had been called for Clontarf, just north of Dublin. Peel was prepared to use force; and so, fearing unrest and violence, O'Connell duly called off the meeting. This Clontarf decision highlights one of the crucial aspects of Daniel O'Connell's brand of nationalism: his deep commitment to non-violent agitation. He was not a pacifist, believing there to be such a thing as a just war. But he was consistently hostile to revolution, political violence and conspiracy. Though frequently deploying martial imagery in his speeches, O'Connell was sharply opposed to the practice of rebellious, insurrectionary or communal violence in practice. As a lawyer, he revered the law and wanted it obeyed and adhered to: illegal violence was the enemy of the kind of ordered Irish democracy whose creation he so keenly sought. He sharply disapproved of the methods used in the 1798 Rising; and he abhorred Emmet's rebellion five years later, saying of Emmet himself that, 'A man who could coolly prepare so much bloodshed, so many murders, and such horrors of every kind has ceased to be an object of compassion.'[33] O'Connell persistently called on the Irish Catholic population to turn their back on secret societies. The Repeal Association founded in 1840 was established firmly on the basis of the principle of moral force and of non-violent politics: the Association's constitution explicitly rejected the use of violence and the breaking of the law. Under O'Connell's lawful leadership the Repeal Association was to be emphatically constitutional and peaceful; those who broke the law were considered enemies of Ireland.

The issue of O'Connell's attitude towards political violence came to a climax in 1846 in a famous debate involving a wing of his Repeal movement, the Young Irelanders (whom we will consider in detail in a moment). In January 1846 the Repeal Association had unanimously committed itself to exclusively peaceful, legal, constitutional methods in its pursuit of legislative independence for Ireland. But O'Connell remained anxious to establish the principle of moral force beyond question and so in July of the same year he introduced the Peace Resolutions, which reaffirmed the Repeal Association's commitment to non-violence, to moral force and constitutionalism ('peaceable means alone should be used, to the exclusion of all others save those that are peaceable, legal and constitutional'[34]). O'Connell placed these Resolutions before the General Committee of the Association in order to guard the principle – so vital to him – of the superiority of moral over physical force. In a sense he was only attempting to secure what had always been there at the heart of the Association – the commitment to exclusively peaceful and legal methods of Irish nationalist struggle – but the initiative started a keen debate which possesses resonances even today. For while O'Connell insisted that the Association declare for his purely non-violent principles, some Young Irelanders seemed to praise both moral and physical force, while some (like John Mitchel and Thomas Francis Meagher) made plain that they had no objection in principle to the use of violence in pursuit of what they considered to be beneficial political change. The Peace Resolutions were overwhelmingly carried, but the issue remained a vital one: it was not so much that Young Ireland were keen at this stage definitely to take up arms; rather, they did not want to rule it out for the future, in case at a later period they might (as some of them did in the later 1840s) come to think such violence politically necessary.

The debate about whether unequivocally to accept the principle of non-violence has continued within Irish nationalism into the twenty-first century, and the legacy of O'Connell is clear enough. Nationalist Ireland's greatest leader eschewed the revolutionary path and chose to work within the legal framework of the British constitution. A reader of Edmund Burke, the Liberator could rightly defend his stance both in terms of his achievement (most spectacularly, Catholic Emancipation itself), and also by posing the counterfactual question: what kind of Ireland would have been produced had he led his vast following down a violent path? The Union would almost certainly not have been undone by force, and the scale of bloodshed and Irish division would have been on a disastrously huge scale.

Yet the O'Connellite approach did, perhaps, have a slightly more complex, ambiguous relationship to violence than is sometimes assumed. For the great nationalist leader not only engaged in the rhetorical deployment of violence (through his martial imagery),[35] but more importantly relied on the idea that violence was a possibility were his nationalist demands not met. He did not threaten violence, and he consistently denounced its use in impressive, noble fashion. But he did play on the idea that there existed, behind him, the danger of profound Irish civil disorder were his legitimately expressed demands not conceded.

And this is perhaps the essence of O'Connell's brilliance: the subtle combination of legal, parliamentary politics with extra-parliamentary mass mobilization.[36] He could be markedly conciliatory. His implied stance towards British politicians was that, should fairness be displayed on Irish questions, then Ireland and Britain could be harmoniously reconciled. Again, when the recently crowned King George IV visited Ireland in 1821, O'Connell was publicly and effusively loyal to his monarch, seeing nothing inconsistent about an Irish nationalist being loyal to the Crown, as worn by someone who was also king or queen of Ireland. But while he taught loyalty to the Crown and sincerely wanted his followers to be respectably behaved, orderly and law-abiding, there was yet about O'Connellite politics the muscular application of extra-parliamentary pressure. The Liberator roused mass passions in Ireland in ways that were ominous for the British government, and he was sharply aware of the value which these mass passions had for him. Through such large-scale popular mobilization he could apply pressure on London which, though itself within the law, could not really be resisted without the result being serious violence.

In the end, O'Connell's politics of moral force were, arguably, more effective in outcome than more aggressive tactics would have been. And behind O'Connell's combination of the parliamentary and the extra-parliamentary lay that most valuable of political skills, pragmatism. It is here that O'Connell's oft-mentioned Benthamite[37] tendencies are important, for he sought to assess a strategy's usefulness by considering how far it would maximize the achievement of practical benefit. One should not exaggerate the influence which Bentham had over O'Connell (the latter's Catholicism did produce difficulties in the two men's political relationship, Bentham being disappointed when religion entered politics in the manner that it did so decisively with O'Connell).

But O'Connell's liberalism was similar in many ways to that of the great utilitarian. Both men sought the production of the maximum feasible benefit for the maximum possible number; and in other ways too their careers and attitudes echoed each other's – both men had trained as lawyers, for both men legal reform was crucial to their politics, both men deeply loathed slavery, and both exhibited flexible pragmatism.

One feature of this pragmatism was the recognition by O'Connell of the necessity and nature of the British framework as one of his theatres of operation. The kind of change which O'Connell sought, and the kind of ordered, democratic Ireland which he desired, were best attained essentially within the British parliamentary world. And while he exerted great and effective pressure from beyond Westminster, his politics reflected his understanding of the contemporary culture of political change: in Britain (as, for that matter, in Germany) in the early nineteenth century, politics were conducted most effectively through broadly reformist rather than revolutionary methods. O'Connell's evolutionary, non-violent approach suited the zeitgeist, and his achievements were maximized as a consequence of this. So, as with most of the great leaders of nationalist Ireland (Charles Stewart Parnell, Eamon de Valera and John Hume among them), O'Connell's career was centred for the most part on democratic and non-violent politics rather than violent revolutionism. Much later, Sean O'Faoláin presented O'Connell as, among other things, a distiller of some of Thomas Paine's ideas for an Irish context; and he also highlighted the central point about the great leader: 'What he gave us is hard to tell. Much good, much bad, but one thing was priceless – the principle of life as a democracy.'[38]

If democracy, and a preference for moral rather than physical force, lay at the heart of O'Connell's brand of nationalism, then so too did Catholicism. Religious community and belief and experience were intricately interwoven into what it meant to be Irish, and here O'Connell was the high priest of Catholic politics. For while his mobilization democratized Irish nationalism, his politics also Catholicized it to such a degree that Catholicism became a crucially defining characteristic of Irish nationalism under the Union. Emancipation, clearly, was a Catholic issue, both as a goal and in terms of the Church's integral role in organizing the agitation towards it. But the Catholic Church came also to endorse the later Repeal campaign, and

O'Connell's Catholicism was, throughout his career, crucial to his identity and that of his movement.

It is true that he sometimes stressed the inclusiveness of his vision of Irish identity ('I include all – Protestant, Presbyterian, and Catholic'[39]), and that he hoped to be able to win over significant Protestant support to his Repeal banner. But he had no meaningful success in this regard and, tellingly, he was profoundly unfamiliar with Ulster realities; Ulster, of course, had been the setting for important, cross-class Protestant opposition to Catholic Emancipation.[40] So the division of mainstream Irish nationalism from Protestant Ulster politics had long, pre-partition, roots, even into the politics of one of Ireland's greatest nationalist leaders. In a sense, O'Connell here fitted a pattern with which later generations would become familiar. Rhetorically non-sectarian, in practice he tended to identify Irish nationalism with Catholic interests, community, organization and identity. And this was partly why, in contrast with his Young Ireland associates, he could remain the true leader of mass nationalism in Ireland. In his alliance with the Catholic clergy, in his individual Catholic devotion and his deference towards the Church, in his role as the winner of a great victory for Catholicism – in all of this he was able to draw on organizational and attitudinal reservoirs which would otherwise have been unavailable to him. The French Revolution had delivered a shocking blow to Catholicism; but in the nineteenth century the Church grew strong again and gained in an international confidence[41] which provided the broader framework for O'Connellite Irish nationalism.

So O'Connell led a mass movement which expressed essentially Catholic grievances, and he combined a rhetorical inclusiveness with a lack of understanding regarding the depth and seriousness of anti-nationalism in Ireland. At times, he seemed explicit enough about the Catholicism of nationalist Ireland ('The Catholic people of Ireland are a nation'[42]) and this should be set against the effective Protestantism (or perhaps Anglicanism) so central to contemporary Britishness.

For the broad map was already sketched out: could Catholic nationalist Ireland be accommodated within a United Kingdom whose dominant player – England – was so emphatically Protestant? The Union had begun with a major Catholic grievance, and this pattern was followed during much of the ensuing century, despite the Emancipation of

1829. With Daniel O'Connell, Irish nationalism became Catholic nationalism and it has never quite shed this identity.

If moral force and Catholicism were the central pillars of O'Connell's building, then what of language? Unlike his Young Ireland comrades, O'Connell was not a Romantic cultural nationalist. He took a typically pragmatic, utilitarian view towards the Irish language itself, a language which he could speak but in the preservation or revival of which he showed no striking interest. Asked in 1833 whether the use of Irish among the peasantry was diminishing, he tellingly responded:

> Yes, and I am sufficiently utilitarian not to regret its gradual abandonment. A diversity of tongues is no benefit ... It would be of vast advantage to mankind if all the inhabitants of the earth spoke the same language. Therefore, although the Irish language is connected with many recollections that twine around the hearts of Irishmen, yet the superior utility of the English tongue, as the medium of all modern communication, is so great, that I can witness without a sigh the gradual disuse of Irish.[43]

But while O'Connell did not share Young Ireland's German-style Romantic nationalism, part of his mass appeal did lie in his Gaelic origins and in the communal, cultural authenticity which these seemed to bestow. (Here, again, we can see the way in which modern nationalism drew strength from pre-modern roots; and the same could be said of the Catholicism discussed above.[44])

O'Connell's appeal transcended narrow class boundaries and – again, in ways which would be replicated in later Irish nationalist movements – O'Connell himself eschewed class division within the national movement. He firmly respected the rights of property and (himself a landlord) he was keen on preserving the existing social order rather than disturbing or overturning it. He never developed a distinctive or precise policy on the land question, and he generally relegated social or economic questions behind constitutional and religious ones. Indeed, his political victories sometimes reinforced class stratification: at the same time as Catholic Emancipation was introduced in 1829, so too was a measure which disenfranchised the forty-shilling freeholders in Ireland and set up instead a ten-pound franchise.

Yet, if not a social radical, he was a great innovator in terms of establishing the practical mass mobilization of nationalist Ireland. It was not just that, under O'Connell, the first truly mass-nationalist movement emerged in Ireland. It was also that O'Connell himself was so central to the organization, administration and management of this mobilizing process. He understood the intricate dynamics of local power in Ireland, and his role in the large – 'monster' – meetings was uniquely important. O'Connell not only held very large and innovative gatherings (which could number hundreds of thousands at a time), but he was extremely gifted also in the public theatre of political performance; he had shown himself able, as one authority on Irish nationalism has aptly put it, to rouse the peasantry through a combination of 'magnificent oratory' and 'shameless flattery'.[45] A fluent and highly skilful orator in both Irish and English (and, incidentally, one who on occasion deployed his beloved Thomas Moore's words in his own rhetoric), O'Connell himself directly helped to bring about a truly mass, national Irish sentiment: extensive, organized and systematically coordinated. And in addition to his establishment of a mass nationalism which took on the British state in Ireland, O'Connell also made a strong stand on wider questions of liberty and equality. He argued strenuously against black slavery and was likewise a champion of Jewish emancipation; hatred for racial or colour-based prejudice ran deep within his thinking.

So, while his party and his movement did not survive for long after him, his political style offered a pattern which many were to follow in crucial ways. O'Connell pioneered a socially conservative, mass nationalism based on Catholic Ireland, committed to moral rather than physical force, pragmatic rather than romantic in orientation, and libertarian in much of its spirit.

George Hayter's 1834 oil portrait of Daniel O'Connell[46] shows a dignified, rosy-faced, confident and respectable parliamentarian, and each of these impressions is valid. O'Connell was to become understandably celebrated by Irish nationalists themselves, as a heady cult was developed – both during and after his lifetime. Extraordinary celebrations engulfed Dublin in August 1875 to mark the centenary of the great man's birth, with Lord O'Hagan – who had known O'Connell – delivering a celebratory oration.[47] And O'Connell powerfully exemplifies many of the broader themes of the politics of nationalism. His was an emphatically modern mass movement, but one which drew on longstanding cultural traditions and attachments and assumptions (about the Gael, for instance, or Catholicism). Here was a nationalism which reflected deep communal (especially Catholic) bonds, and which was systematically organized in struggles for power, for greater autonomy, and for the refashioning of the state. Boundaries and exclusions were now more clearly marked out in the emerging map of sectarian Ireland, while under O'Connell's extraordinary leadership nationalist struggle reached new levels of programmatic organization (in the Catholic Association, for example, or the Repeal Association). Mobilization to redress grievance represented a communal struggle for liberty: as O'Connell drew on pre-existing senses of the national community, he led successive, novel struggles which were emphatically in pursuit of freedom – from Catholic disabilities, or through the achievement of greater Irish autonomy. And power was the essence of the project: mass-mobilized power was the leverage mechanism used to achieve reform or concession; and communal access to power was the goal of the movement for Catholic Emancipation.

O'Connellite nationalism could combine the allure of the nation's greater good with the attractions of more sectional, and even personal, gain (O'Connell himself energetically pursued public office for his family, friends and supporters, a process which appealed on numerous – personal as well as political – levels). And here, in O'Connellite struggle, was nationalism becoming powerful through its intersection with an emergent democracy, a democracy indeed to which it helped to give birth. Popular power and cultural power were both markedly evident: at Repeal meetings it was made clear both that 'the people' were the genuine source of true political power, and that the Catholic Church and faith held a special place within the Irish nationalist community as it struggled.[48]

3

> To lose your native tongue, and learn that of an alien, is the
> worst badge of conquest – it is the chain on the soul.
>
>   Thomas Davis[49]

If Daniel O'Connell was something of a Benthamite utilitarian,[50] then
a group of his colleagues in the 1840s Repeal campaign was to embody
a rival brand of nationalism, one that was heavily influenced by
European Romanticism. On 15 October 1842 there appeared the first
edition of what was quickly to become an influential new newspaper,
The Nation; it was around this paper that the Young Ireland movement
initially revolved. At first, *The Nation* was very much a part of
O'Connell's Repeal movement, an important mouthpiece for that
agitational campaign. Changing realities of communication are important here (as so often in explaining nationalism[51]): mid-nineteenth-
century levels of literacy were higher among Irish Protestants than
among Irish Catholics, but at this stage roughly half of those over five
years old claimed to be able to read (while by the time of the 1861
Census over half of the Irish Catholic population could do so). *The
Nation* contained news, poetry, political and social analysis, and even
some literary criticism. Under the editorship of the experienced and
ardently religious Catholic journalist, Monaghan-born Charles Gavan
Duffy (1816–1903), the paper became a speedy, popular success
(striking evidence again of the point stressed by scholars such as Karl
Deutsch, that nationalism depended on a communications revolution
in areas such as literacy and the mass media: it was not that such
changes made mass nationalism inevitable; but – without such developments – mass nationalism was unimaginable[52]). Duffy himself presented the Irish national movement, on the eve of the appearance of
The Nation, as having been 'torpid and lethargic'. Certainly, the arrival
of the new paper injected fresh energy into Irish nationalism: 'It was
said a new soul had come into Ireland with *The Nation*, and it made
itself felt in every fibre of the national character.'[53] The 1840s birth of

The Nation, indeed, resonated powerfully with many people, including the County Tipperary Young Irelander-turned-Fenian, Michael Doheny (1805–63):

> The publication of *The Nation* was really an epoch which marked a wonderful change, and from that day forth self-reliance and self-respect began to take the place of grateful, but stultified, obedience and blind trust. The change became more marked as the publication proceeded. In speech, article, song and essay, the spell of Davis' extraordinary genius and embracing love was felt. Historic memories, forgotten stories, fragments of tradition ... supplied him substance and spirit wherewith to mould and animate nationality. Native art, valour, virtue and glory seemed to grow under his pen. All that had a tendency to elevate and ennoble he rescued from the past to infuse into the future.[54]

Along with Duffy, the other two men crucial to the founding of this influential newspaper were Thomas Davis and John Blake Dillon; and these three were the initial leaders of what became known as Young – in contrast to O'Connell's 'Old' – Ireland. The Protestant Thomas Davis (1814–45) had been born in County Cork and educated at TCD; he joined O'Connell's Repeal Association in 1841. John Blake Dillon (1814–66) was the son of a County Mayo Catholic shopkeeper and, like Davis, had a TCD education and had joined the Repeal Association in 1841. Under the guidance of this famous triumvirate, Young Ireland represented a diverse (rather than tightly organized) group of Repealers, working with Daniel O'Connell in the early 1840s and then subsequently diverging from his politics. They were romantic, cultural nationalists, rhetorical and poetic: a classic mid-nineteenth-century European grouping.

As with so much else in the Young Ireland world, so too in regard to the central question of Ireland's political relationship with Britain there was a range of stances adopted by different figures and at various times within the movement. The temptation to read earlier nationalist preferences through later (for example, separatist) lenses would be a mistake here. Simple Repeal of the Union itself would, in theory, involve full independence for Ireland except for the retention of the Crown link. But – like O'Connell himself – Thomas Davis was very much prepared to tolerate federalism, and this offered Ireland a more limited form of self-government, and the retention of Irish MPs at the London House of Commons (which would legislate on imperial and foreign matters). If federalism offered a useful compromise between imperial involvement and Irish self-government, then others came – by the latter part of the decade, at least – to espouse a more emphatic version of Irish freedom. In 1848 the *Irish Felon*, coedited by James Fintan Lalor (1807–49) and John Martin (1812–75), proclaimed that 'Nearly six millions of the people of Ireland are understood to be advocates of national independence';[55] and by the late 1840s John Mitchel was advocating a republican form of politics.

Yet in 1846 *The Nation* claimed that it had never supported a policy of total separation from Britain; and the paper carried varying views regarding its preferences in terms of Ireland's relationship with the British empire.[56] Differences also manifested themselves in terms of political strategy. Thomas Davis suggested, as early as 1844, that Repeal MPs might refuse to take their seats at Westminster and sit instead as a body in Ireland (a prefiguring of later Sinn Féin tactics). In the years after Davis's death in 1845, however, some within the group came increasingly to favour more aggressive, violent approaches to the national struggle.

Much was cloudy and ambiguous, therefore, in the politics of Young Ireland in the 1840s, and it is best to consider them as a patriotic group espousing various versions of a political case for increased Irish autonomy from Britain.

In any case, the truly central feature of the Young Ireland movement was not so much its formal-political programme as its argument regarding culture and Irish nationality. Culture has been one of the most important aspects of the community lying at the heart of nationalism, and Ireland provides no exception to this pattern. The Irish national idea beloved of Davis, in particular, was that of building a nation which transcended religious and ethnic difference; the means to achieve this, he believed, lay readily to hand in culture. And here we see one of the clearest of all Irish examples of the pattern identified by so many theorists of nationalism:[57] the emphasis on the unifying potential of shared and distinctive history, language, music and art; and the clarity provided by excluding what lies beyond these elements of culture – in this case, that which was English. Cultural enthusiasm would engender emotional attachment to the nation, thus generating individual and communal meaning simultaneously and feverishly; culture and history would produce a politics of inclusiveness which would unite the Irish people on Irish territory, claim for them the moral high ground, and distinguish them from the British of the neighbouring island. So for Thomas Davis, a shared culture – history, language, music, art – would allow for the creation of a non-sectarian, inclusive definition of Irish nationality (so important, among other things, if people of Davis's own religion and ethnically-mixed back- ground were to be included[58]); and this nationality would stand in marked distinction from that which was English.

Davis was a figure of profound and lasting importance for Irish nationalist thought, his youthful death (he was only thirty) robbing Ireland of one of its most powerfully enthusiastic nationalist imagin- ations. He was firmly convinced of the necessity of combating the anglicization of Ireland (Young Ireland could be profoundly anglopho- bic in many of its expressed sentiments). He was appalled at the contemporary erosion of distinctively Irish culture, and horrified by what he took to be modernity's destruction of this unique past. In Carlylean fashion, Davis lamented the destructive effects of 'mechanical civilization':

> Scattered through the country in MS, are hundreds of books wherein the laws and achievements, the genealogies and pos- sessions, the creeds, and manners and poetry of these our prede- cessors in Ireland are set down. Their music lives in the traditional airs of every valley. Yet mechanical civilization, more cruel than time, is trying to exterminate them, and, therefore, it becomes us all who do not wish to lose the heritage of centuries, nor to feel ourselves living among nameless ruins, when we might have an ancestral home – it becomes all who love learning, poetry, or music, or are curious of human progress, to aid in or originate a series of efforts to save all that remains of the past.[59]

So Irish history – authentic, distinctive and inspiring – lay at the centre of the Young Ireland conception of the nation (just as history has done so often in the minds of nationally-minded zealots elsewhere[60]). On what now seem to be rather shaky foundations, Davis celebrated very much the idea of the Celt (it was as 'The Celt' that he signed his first verse offerings in The Nation).

More broadly, the Young Irelanders did much to cultivate appropriate heroes from the past. Davis enthused over Jonathan Swift as a great Protestant patriotic model (in an attempt to show that there was historical depth to the idea of Irish unity against England), and he also invoked those other Protestant celebrities, Tone and Emmet; it was another TCD-educated Protestant, John Kells Ingram (1823–1907) (a County Donegal-born poet who later became something of a conservative), who immortally framed such rebels by writing 'The Memory of the Dead' (which was published in *The Nation* in 1843):

> Who fears to speak of Ninety-Eight?
> Who blushes at the name?
> When cowards mock the patriots' fate,
> Who hangs his head in shame?[61]

The Young Irelanders were a very literary species of nationalist, poems and ballads featuring prominently in their attempted intensification of national enthusiasm, attachment and sentiment. Many of these romantic intellectuals themselves wrote poetry. The Catholic poet, Dublin-born James Clarence Mangan (1803–49), exemplifies the last of these. He was greatly influenced by German Romanticism, as in his translation of the Bonn history professor E. M. Arndt, under the title 'Our Fatherland' (1844):

> Fatherland, and Fatherland!
> This *is* to be the eternal song!
> The poet's heart, the patriot's hand,
> Must ever war with fraud and wrong!
>
> . . .
>
> Fatherland, and Fatherland!
> We poets have no nobler song![62]

And his sentimental verse also involved translation from the Irish, as in 'A Cry for Ireland' (published in *The Nation* in October 1846):

> Oh, my land! . . . oh, my love!
> What a woe, . . . and how deep,
> Is thy death to my long-mourning soul!
> God alone, . . . God above,
> Can awake . . . thee from sleep,
> Can release thee from bondage and dole![63]

Language itself formed a major part of Young Ireland's cultural struggle. Though not himself a fluent Irish-speaker, Thomas Davis wanted the language to be cherished, valued, taught, preserved and – where possible – gradually extended. It was not that there should be a forcible language reversal, with Irish replacing English, but rather that Davis exhibited a Fichtean[64] emphasis upon the importance of a separate national language for a separate nation.

> The language, which grows up with a people, is conformed to their organs, descriptive of their climate, constitution, and manners, mingled inseparably with their history and their soil, fitted beyond any other language to express their prevalent thoughts in the most natural and efficient way. To impose another language on such a people is to send their history adrift among the accidents of translation ... A people without a language of its own is only half a nation.[65]

So, as with many mainland European nationalists in the nineteenth century, the notion of a distinct language was important to Ireland's romantic cultural nationalists also. In contemporary context, this mattered profoundly: the great Italian nationalist Giuseppe Mazzini (1805–72) was among those who thought that its lack of a national language and of a special historic destiny or mission suggested that Ireland was not a genuine nation after all.

If history and language were central to Young Ireland's conception of culture, then so too was music; the idea that the character or spirit of a people was bound up closely with their poetry and music had been evident among the United Irishmen of the 1790s, but in the Young Irelanders it achieved a crescendo. 'No enemy speaks slightingly of Irish music,' Davis proudly proclaimed, 'and no friend need fear to boast of it. It is without a rival.'[66] As so often with revivalist cultural nationalisms, Davis's arguments here were more prescriptive than they were accurately descriptive. He did not celebrate Irish composers as such, but rather those who produced what he considered deliberately Irish national music, music which spoke to his notion of Ireland's passionate heart. If true Ireland were to be celebrated and preserved, then music such as Moore's, or other explicitly national tunes, were required in order to generate and sustain romantic Irish national sentiment.

But isn't this a rather narrow, constricting view? There were, for example, highly prominent and successful Irish musicians whose cultural achievements did not suit Davisite thinking; were these people not authentically Irish? What of Michael William Balfe (1808–70) and Waterford-born William Vincent Wallace (1812–65), two of the three leading composers of romantic opera for Victorian London? Wallace's implausibly jolly, Meyerbeer-influenced *Maritana*[67] was a remarkable success when it opened at Drury Lane in November 1845.[68] (Wallace's own life echoed his rather bizarre operatic plots: a well-travelled emigrant, he apparently complemented his musical career with periods as a sheep-farmer and whale-hunter; and having deserted his first wife in Australia, he bigamously engaged in a second marriage in America.) *Maritana*, together with Balfe's *Bohemian Girl* and Julius Benedict's *Lily of Killarney* (two Irish composers, and a third opera with an Irish setting), formed a trio of highly popular works ironically known as the English Ring – though they bore no relation in musical or intellectual significance to Wagner's great tetralogy. Davis sneered at composers such as Balfe,[69] and although the music over which Davis himself enthused was itself firmly sub-Wagnerian, his own arguments did carry echoes, at least, of that great composer's conception of distinctively national art, purged of foreign impurities, and furthering the greatness of one's glorious nation. Art should be explicitly national: 'National art is conversant with national subjects. We have Irish artists,' Davis lamented, 'but no Irish, no national art.'[70] Yet alternative views might be sustained. The prodigiously talented pianist and composer John Field (1782–1837) hardly fitted Davis's ideal for Irish music but, cosmopolitan though he was, he surely left us an important Irish artistic legacy. Dublin-born, he moved to England where he studied under an Italian (Muzio Clementi) who took him around Europe; Field settled for years in Russia, and pioneered a musical form (the piano nocturne) which influenced and was made world-famous by a Pole (Frédéric Chopin). Were the remarkable talents and music of this Irish pianist and composer, whose achievements impressed not merely Clementi and Chopin, but also Haydn and Schumann, not worthy of being claimed as equally Irish art?

As with so many nationalists elsewhere, therefore, the Young Irelanders expressed a paradoxical politics: they echoed the cries of increasingly ubiquitous nationalists across the world, while at the same time stressing the uniqueness – indeed, the superiority – of their own particular culture.[71] This latter aspect helps to explain the sense of high morality evident in the writings and assumptions of the Young Irelanders: there was, in their view, an ethical responsibility on people to preserve and celebrate a heritage as special and sacred as the national tradition.

And, despite its rather unappealing ethical snobbery, there is undoubtedly an infectious enthusiasm in this Davisite attempt to create a new sense of Irishness through the celebration of authentic culture. Davis sought that all should enthuse over Ireland's shared and glorious past, and achieve freedom by immersion in a heritage which overflowed with the unique and irreplaceable riches of Irish literature, language, art and music. Even if one were to deride him for his political naivety, one might remain impressed by the sincerity of Davis's zeal. But could culture produce the desired result? It did offer one way around the problem that an appeal to ethnicity would not produce unity. This was certainly true in Ireland, which had been ethnically hybrid since prehistory. And it was a common enough problem elsewhere also. In Italy, for example, there was no pre-existing, unified ethnic group corresponding to the nation created in the late nineteenth century; there, it was nationalists who had the task of creating ethnicity, rather than ethnicity creating the nationalists' nation.[72]

Yet in Ireland there were problems with the cultural route too. The things identified by Davis as forces which would unite those who lived in Ireland, possessed often enough within them the potential also to divide. It was all very well to celebrate – as Davis, for example, did – martial exploits from Irish history. But mid-nineteenth-century Irish people would not all identify with the same side in those past battles and wars. Indeed, whether one celebrated anti-English rebellion, Gaelic culture and language, or grievance largely associated with the downtrodden Catholic population, it was as likely that one would reinforce divisions within Ireland as that one would produce a clear fissure between Ireland and England.

For the very intimacy of the two islands produced both the sense of urgency behind Young Ireland's cultural mission and the central obstacle to its advance. Britain did threaten the kind of culture so enthralling to Davis, but the centuries of cultural and actual cross-migration between the islands had also produced in Ireland a significant population to whom Gaelic, anti-English, Catholic-soaked politics would simply not appeal.

None the less, the Young Irelanders were zealous and eloquent in their campaign. Naturally enough (and, once again, echoing nationalists elsewhere), they placed education at the centre of their work, believing in its power as a vehicle for political change, and for creating a public opinion after their own idealistic image. William Smith O'Brien (1803–64), himself educated at Harrow and at Trinity College, Cambridge, was lastingly enthusiastic about education; writing youthfully to his mother in 1819, he referred to his 'love of reading and getting knowledge'.[73] And education could take varied forms – from reading rooms to newspapers to ballads to formal institutions – and reflected the Davisite desire that one should wholly absorb oneself in authentic Irishness:

> to make our spirit lasting and wise as it is bold – to make our liberty an inheritance for our children, and a charter for our prosperity, we must study as well as strive, and learn as well as feel ... We must give our children in schools the best knowledge of science, art, and literary elements possible. And at home they should see and hear as much of national pictures, music, poetry, and military science as possible.[74]

Education was essential to the forging of the good national citizen.[75] More pointedly, if a nation were to be built across the confessional divide, then educational structures assumed huge significance. Denominationally separate education – the Irish norm – was disastrous for those who sought to produce a shared communal identity and purpose. Davis himself clearly favoured an inclusive, comprehensive definition of Irish nationality – something to which he did much to draw the Catholic Charles Gavan Duffy as well – and among the Young Irelanders there was a marked interest in the notion of non-denominational education. Figures such as William Smith O'Brien firmly favoured denominationally mixed education as the basis for a newly pluralistic Ireland, and this issue reached something of a crescendo with the Colleges Bill of 1845, introduced by the government of Prime Minister Robert Peel. This proposed the setting up of three non-denominational colleges (in Belfast, Galway and Cork), within which there would be no religious provision and within which, therefore, it was hoped that non-denominational university education would be made available. Peel had been keen, in particular, to provide the Catholic middle class with the opportunity for a good university education, and they would now – he hoped – be able to side-step the Protestant Trinity College in Dublin.

Young Ireland (who broadly favoured interdenominational university education) offered support to the idea: here, perhaps, was the crucible in which to mix the new Ireland that they desired. But the Colleges Bill prompted a famous and major division between Young and Old Ireland, with O'Connell opposing what he presented as Godless colleges. Despite O'Connell's (and the Catholic hierarchy's) opposition, the Bill was passed, establishing the Queen's Colleges of Belfast, Galway and Cork (the origins of the respective modern universities in each city). But by the 1850s Catholics were prohibited by their Church from entering these new Colleges except for purely professional qualifications.

This sharp disagreement between Young Ireland and O'Connell was a telling one. Up until 1844 the Liberator was supposed to be a supporter of mixed education; but his correspondence with the Catholic clergy showed not only his deep hostility towards Peel's proposed mixed Colleges, but also that – long before Peel's Bill – he held a far from hostile view towards the idea that education should indeed come under Church control. Young Ireland itself was by no means absolute in its support for mixed education: several of its key figures (Duffy and John Mitchel among them) came to endorse the orthodox Catholic stance on education, and it is arguable that only Davis among the prominent Young Irelanders was heading towards a genuinely secularist position on Irish education. But if one were committed to an inclusive nationality, then mixed education was logical, even necessary, and Young Ireland's greater enthusiasm for the 1845 Bill reflected their political approach. In contrast, if – like O'Connell – one recognized that the foundation for successful mass nationalism in nineteenth-century Ireland rested on the Catholic population, then a more sectarian pragmatism might ensue.

For some within the Young Ireland orbit, national struggle had an economic dimension. Thomas Davis himself aspired towards industrial protectionism and peasant proprietorship (both of which notions later became central to Sinn Féinish economic thought). But the key figure in Young Ireland economics was undoubtedly James Fintan Lalor. Though not himself of peasant background, Lalor came to advocate the establishment of a kind of peasant proprietorship as a replacement for the existing tenant–landlord system of ownership. Wrongly celebrated by some later nationalists as a socialist or an exponent of land nationalization, Lalor in fact had a different ambition. Getting rid of the aristocracy was his mission: aristocratic lands should, he argued, be forfeit to the people, with small farmers thereafter embodying an effective peasant proprietorship.

To Lalor, land was centrally vital to the understanding of necessary political change. The land, he declared in January 1847, was an issue 'beside which Repeal dwarfs down into a petty parish question'.[76] To him, Repeal of the Union had to be linked to some issue which (unlike Repeal) could mobilize and invigorate a national movement: this he identified in the politics of the land: the reassertion of Irish liberty would be achieved through a struggle towards the reconquest of Irish land. He did not consider the landlord class to be truly part of Ireland's authentic community ('I never recognized the landowners as an element, or as part and portion of the people'[77]). Landowners did not hold their land with the assent of the people, and to change this economic structure would be to transform the Irish nation. In a letter to John Mitchel in June 1847, Lalor resoundingly set out his position:

> My object is to repeal the conquest – not any part or portion but the whole and entire conquest of seven hundred years – a thing much more easily done than to repeal the union. That the absolute (allodial) ownership of the lands of Ireland is vested of right in the people of Ireland – that they, and none but they, are the first landowners and lords paramount as well as the lawmakers of this island – that all titles to land are invalid not conferred or confirmed by them – and that no man has a right to hold one foot of Irish soil otherwise than by grant of tenancy and fee from them . . . these are my principles.[78]

In January 1847 Lalor had outlined his theory of 'moral insurrection'. This was founded on the notion that nobody had the right to assume jurisdiction or authority over anyone else without the latter's consent, and that any attempt to assume such authority without consent need not compel obedience but might legitimately be resisted. This, Lalor saw as the foundation for national politics: 'every distinct community or nation of men is owner of itself; and can never of right be bound to submit to be governed by another people'. So it was legitimate to resist usurped authority, and this Lalor advocated in the Irish case.[79]

According to the later judgment of Sinn Féin founder Arthur Griffith, Lalor was 'a land reformer rather than a nationalist'.[80] But Lalor in fact exemplified much that lay at the heart of Irish and wider nationalism: a sharp sense of authentic community, together with commitment to a struggle which would wield and ultimately achieve meaningful power for that national community. True independence, he argued, was rooted in economics and in the overthrow of the aristocracy. While he tended to focus on economic issues, he was a firm believer in the people as the true source of sovereignty (one of the essential elements, as we have seen, of nationalist thinking). Indeed, he produced one of the most celebrated of all Irish national declarations of sovereignty, and it had an earthy economics at its heart:

Ireland her own – Ireland her own, and all therein, from the sod to the sky. The soil of Ireland for the people of Ireland, to have and to hold from God alone who gave it – to have and to hold to them and their heirs for ever, without suit or service, faith or fealty, rent or render, to any power under Heaven.[81]

Though not truly a physical-force zealot, Lalor was also to express his nationalism through gestural violence: on 16 September 1849 he was among those leading a rebellion in Tipperary and Waterford. The previous year had also seen what is exaggeratedly referred to as the Young Ireland Rising, in truth a militarily disastrous rebellion led by William Smith O'Brien. That had, of course, been a year of European risings elsewhere: January 1848 had seen revolts in Sicily and Naples; February 1848 witnessed revolution in Paris; revolution also broke out in Venice on 17 March and in Milan the following day; March 1848 also saw uprisings in Munich, Budapest, Cracow and Berlin, while in June a Prague rising was crushed. Some Irish spirits were raised by all this. John Mitchel's *United Irishman* celebrated the Sicilian revolt, for example, as a justified and successful venture:

Since the 13th of January Sicily has been in insurrection against the royal authority. The people have long been endeavouring to obtain for themselves a representative system of government, and various other reforms equally urgent. Becoming at length exasperated, they have broken out in open revolt, and have already been almost entirely successful.[82]

But the Irish version of such rebellion was small-scale: even nationalist zealot Michael Davitt was to refer to the episode as 'the ridiculously small revolution of 1848'.[83] Yet although the rebellion was a profound failure, with negligible support, it did come to carry weight in Irish nationalist tradition and therefore deserves some reflection. Later militants (such as Patrick Pearse) were sharply conscious of there having been a traditional flame of defiance passed on in successive generations; if nothing else, the skirmish of 1848 served a purpose here for some.

It also reflected the submerged militancy within what was generally a far from violent Young Ireland style of nationalism. As their argument with O'Connell had demonstrated, some within Young Ireland – including that 'most unlikely revolutionary',[84] the rather diffident gentleman-nationalist William Smith O'Brien – had wished not to rule out the possibility of pursuing their aims through force (though in O'Brien's case it was, ideally, through the organized threat of force, rather than its use, that Repeal should be won). Rhetorically, Young Ireland had celebrated military exploits in the past; and even the rather pacific Thomas Davis could deploy rhetorical notions of the efficacy of force, as in his ballad, 'Our Parliament', which looked back to the eighteenth century:

> 'Twas once in College Green, boys,
> Our Parliament, our Parliament,
> But its blessings might be seen, boys,
> Where'er you went, where'er you went.
> 'Twas won by armèd men, boys,
> The Volunteers, the Volunteers;
> We were united then, boys,
> And had no fears, and had no fears.[85]

Rebellion also provided – as so often in later years – a new stage on which nationalism could be performed: that of imprisonment. John

Mitchel, William Smith O'Brien and the Waterford-born Thomas Francis Meagher (1823–67) were all arrested on 21 March 1848; and in the latter half of 1848 two sets of trials took place: some people were indicted for treason (those who had acted in the Rising), while others were charged with treason felony (for supporting or exhorting rebellion). After the 1848 Rising, the authorities were keen to avoid the danger of making hero-martyrs out of the rebel prisoners. The latter were, in fact, treated rather well: death sentences were commuted to life transportation, and treason prisoners were sent to the Australian convict penal colony of Van Diemen's Land in 1849.

For the elite members of the movement, indeed, post-rebellion imprisonment was often a rather gentlemanly affair: if imprisonment represented a key stage on which Irish nationalists could play their parts, then for some it proved to be elegantly draped. Irish prisoners sent into exile in these years did not necessarily experience an arduous journey. John Martin and Kevin O'Doherty were well fed and obtained wine and brandy from the captain of the ship; indeed, one authoritative scholar has described their journey as possessing 'all the qualities of a pleasure cruise', while radical Young Ireland Martin himself acknowledged during the journey that 'probably we both drink and smoke too much'.[86] For these were gentlemen-convicts. The state was punishing them in a way that was considered appropriate to their station and, here as so often in Irish nationalist history, class helped to determine different tones of experience.

For some, indeed, incarceration was framed in celebratory optimism (Thomas Francis Meagher writing poetically in Clonmel Jail in 1848, 'I love, I love these grey old walls!'[87]). But 1848 none the less embodied a militant strand in Irish nationalism which was to prove extremely durable and significant. Its lasting emblem was John Mitchel (1815–75), that most inveterate opponent of Britain ('the open enemy of British tyranny in Ireland';[88] 'the breath of my nostrils is rebellion against that accursed Empire'[89]). Mitchel was born near Dungiven in County Derry on 3 November 1815. His father was a Unitarian minister (and had had a limited involvement with the United Irishmen), while his maternal grandfather had actually been a United Irishman; carrying these flames, Mitchel himself came to express the most defiant of Irish nationalist attitudes. While he was a child the family moved to Derry city and then (in 1823) to Newry in County

Down. In 1830, aged fifteen, the bookish John Mitchel (he loved Shakespeare, Scott and Dickens) entered TCD: though still living in Newry, he took his degree in 1834, at the age of eighteen. Having trained as a solicitor, he practised in the early 1840s at Banbridge, County Down (and was thus a link in a very significant chain of Irish lawyer-nationalists).

In the spring of 1843 Mitchel had become a member of the Repeal Association; two years later, he joined the staff of *The Nation*. He knew Davis and Duffy, working closely with the latter on the newspaper. But the large-scale tragedy of Ireland's 1840s Famine transformed him. He mistakenly took the British government's actions during the Famine to be genocidal and as a response he grew more extreme in his politics (to the extent that even Duffy became greatly alarmed). Mitchel separated company from *The Nation* and in early 1848 he set up (as proprietor and editor) the *United Irishman* as a deliberately revolutionary organ. (Besides Mitchel himself, contributors to the *United Irishman* included James Clarence Mangan, Thomas Devin Reilly and John Martin.) In the event, this aggressive nationalist weekly paper lasted only three-and-a-half months, until Mitchel's arrest for treason felony in May 1848.

While in 1846 Mitchel had thought the constitutional route to legislative independence to be a viable one, by the later 1840s he had come to view violence as necessary for breaking the link with England, and this was a view which lived on for some time in his thinking. He came to see constitutional nationalism as deeply incoherent. Writing to his sister from the United States in August 1855, Mitchel declared himself a revolutionary still: 'Don't understand me to mean that I have given up revolutionary projects. Quite the contrary.'[90]

That rare being, an Ulster Protestant Irish republican, Mitchel displayed a Mazzinian hostility towards compromise: once he had engaged with something, he tended to do so to an extreme. As a prisoner, he was well treated during his captivity; but his powerful *Jail Journal* was to become a lasting source of sustenance to very many militant nationalists. It certainly exemplified its author's deep anglophobia: 'The English government never yet observed any single treaty which it was convenient for them to break'; 'no British statesman ever officially tells the truth, or assigns to any act its real motive'.[91]

Aggressive legacies were left by such fiery spirits. Mitchel himself was to become a celebrated figure for many later nationalists; Constance Markievicz, herself in jail as a republican militant in 1919, felt inspired by his writings: 'I love Mitchel. Some of his phrases simply bring the tears to my eyes. He always rings true to me.'[92] And other legacies were also left by aggressive mid-century nationalists. The 1848 Young Ireland rebel Terence Bellew McManus (1811–61) was transported in 1848; but he fled from Van Diemen's Land in the early 1850s, going to San Francisco where he was warmly welcomed by members of the Irish community, who gave a public dinner and ball in his honour. He settled in the city and died there in 1861. Yet his funeral was to mark another stage in his nationalist career. McManus's coffined body was taken by the Fenians during 1861 through several US cities to New York and then to Ireland where – on 10 November 1861 – a huge Fenian-organized funeral was held in Dublin ('not a mere funeral, but a semi-political demonstration was designed'[93]).

Other old boys of the class of 1848 had later careers of a different stamp. Thomas D'Arcy McGee (whom we met at the start of this book, escaping from a Donegal beach), had travelled to the United States. He had, in fact, first emigrated to the States as a teenager, and had then returned to Ireland where he duly participated in the 1848 Rising. Now, he settled in Buffalo, New York, where he ran a newspaper called the New Celt. In 1857 he was invited by Irish businessmen to Montreal, where he ran a paper entitled the New Era, and in Canada he was elected to the House of Assembly and became a leading politician. So the youthful Young Ireland rebel became a leading Canadian nationalist politician; in doing so he moved from revolution to constitutionalism and reversed the supposedly paradigmatic shift (made by people such as Theobald Wolfe Tone or Patrick Pearse) from reformism to latter-day rebellion. D'Arcy McGee's different trajectory brought him to a pro-welfarist style of thinking. He held that, for Canada, immigration offered great opportunities for wealth-production, and that politicians should focus due attention on immigration and employment policy: the social state should look to protect and advance the welfare of immigrants, who were a source of wealth and strength to the country. Financial assistance should, in his view, be provided for immigrants on their Canadian arrival, if needed. In Canada, therefore, McGee came to believe in parliamentary reform and in the paternal responsibility of a social state. A social visionary, he thus emerged as an exponent of conciliation and compromise; and he further held that Canada should be seen as a colonial model for the Empire, calling on England to treat Ireland as she did his adopted Canada.

D'Arcy McGee's career offers one view of the internationalization of Young Ireland. Other international contexts are vital also to our understanding of this episode in Irish nationalist history. In many ways they fitted the romantic zeitgeist of mid-nineteenth-century Europe. Thomas Davis's German-influenced conception of nationality, celebrating the uniqueness and superiority of an Irish culture purged of foreign contamination, might not have generated the kind of cultural masterwork produced by Richard Wagner, but it did (as we have already hinted) echo Wagnerian styles of thought, the great composer's hostility towards the Jews or the French being the equivalent of Young Ireland's anglophobia.[94] As with other mid-century European nationalists (Wagner himself among them), there was with Irish nationalists a simultaneous desire for the glorification of one's own nation, its culture and achievements, and a definition of that nation in ways which effectively excluded incompatible groups.

Ireland's 1848 rebellion echoed mainland European turbulence, and comparative reflection on what lay behind the latter suggests further echoes still. The Sicilian-born Francesco Crispi (1818–1901), for example, was an 1848 revolutionary who later became a prominent nineteenth-century Italian statesman (an authoritarian figure whom Mussolini would greatly admire). Crispi exhibited a deeply romantic nationalist philosophy, of the kind which swept Europe in the early to mid-century (and evident in the writings of Scott, Carlyle, Hugo and Leopardi). In place of narrow materialism, restraint and respectability, Romanticism offered an intensity of emotion, an emphasis on liberty, and a stress on the productive value of sacrifice and suffering. Crispi (who never lost his religious faith) was devoted to the spiritual rather than material foundation of the Italian nation; in this, as in his concern with education as part of the nationalist mission, he can be seen as a fellow-spirit of Ireland's 1840s romantics.[95]

Crispi was a friend of both Mazzini and Giuseppe Garibaldi (1807–82), those giants of Italian nationalism, and the national movements and national ideas evolving in Ireland and Italy in the 1830s and 1840s had much in common. To Mazzini, nationalism was a religious, sacred calling which transcended grubby materialist concerns and interests. He believed not only in God but also in the forward progress of humanity under God's guidance: indeed, in Mazzini's thinking, God's hand had drawn the natural map of nations and God had a special role and mission for each distinctive nation. In all this there were Irish echoes, and one can see many similarities between Mazzini's Young Italy society (founded in the 1830s) and Ireland's mid-century Young Ireland romantics.

So where late-eighteenth-century Irish nationalism had drawn on contemporary zeal for reason and the ideas of the Enlightenment, its mid-nineteenth-century descendant drank at the well of Romanticism (indeed, representing a kind of emotional rejection of the Enlightenment). Some, like James Clarence Mangan, were absorbed in Schiller and Goethe. But a more vital influence still was the writer and historian Thomas Carlyle (1795–1881). The Presbyterian Scot could be disparaging enough about the Irish, but he identified the cause of what he felt to be their wretchedness in centuries of English injustice towards the neighbouring island: 'We English pay, even now, the bitter smart of long centuries of injustice to our neighbour island. Injustice, doubt it not, abounds; or Ireland would not be miserable.'[96] And Carlyle was a great influence, certainly, on Young Ireland. Davis, Lalor, Mitchel and Duffy were all somewhat under his spell, and clear resonances can be detected between their thinking and his ideas. In both cases, history was seen as of primary importance. Again, for Carlyle, the spiritual determined the material rather than the other way round, and this spiritual understanding of humanity produced in him not only a keenness for emotion, but also a preference for what he termed 'Dynamics' (relating to 'the primary, unmodified forces and energies of man, the mysterious springs of Love, and Fear, and Wonder, of Enthusiasm, Poetry, Religion'), as against 'Mechanics' (relating to more finite and rationally measurable qualities).[97] Here are pre-echoes of Davis's lament about the effects of 'mechanical civilization' (Carlyle firmly denounced industrialization and its social consequences). So, too, Carlyle's assertion that 'The wisdom, the heroic worth of our forefathers, which we have lost, we can recover'[98] is echoed in Davis's arguments about the necessity of saving all that remained of the past. And in all this the Young Irelanders were very much creatures of their time: the 1840s were also the decade when, for example, another Carlylean intellectual – Henry David Thoreau – was pursuing his own solitary crusade against materialism, commercialism, modernity and the mechanical, in his cabin at Walden Pond, Massachusetts.[99]

Again, John Mitchel (who actually knew the Scottish-born, London-based thinker) shared many of Carlyle's assumptions, in his preference for the heroic over the utilitarian, for example, or his notion that industrial man had lost his soul. Carlyle's Irish influence might seem ironic, perhaps, given that Oliver Cromwell was one of his heroes. But his poetic, spiritual approach, his utopian scepticism about the rational and the material, and his conviction that 'injustice breeds injustice'[100] all found willing ears in Young Ireland. His influence might not, perhaps, be considered entirely benign by early-twenty-first-century observers: Carlyle was deeply authoritarian in his thinking, more than slightly anti-democratic, and prone to a racial reading of history with which many would now be uneasy. But he remains one of the most important of outside influences upon the development of Irish nationalist ideas. Although Carlyle pulled back from too sharp an attack on Jeremy Bentham himself, his philosophy was markedly contrary to Benthamite utilitarianism. And if Bentham was O'Connell's philosophical anchor, then Carlyle served a similar role for the Liberator's allies and adversaries in Young Ireland.

One final international detail needs to be noted, not least because it sits awkwardly with much later assumption about the overlap between militant nationalism and socially progressive sympathy. As mentioned, Daniel O'Connell – that socially and politically conservative leader of Catholic Irish nationalism – was committedly enthusiastic about the cause of freedom, including that of American blacks. In stark – and still rather jarring – contrast, John Mitchel not only strongly supported the slave-owning American South in the Civil War there, but explicitly enthused over slavery itself. Writing to his sister from Washington, DC, in 1859, Mitchel clarified just how zealously he in fact favoured slavery:

We are rapidly advancing here to the accomplishment of our great measure – the revival of the African slave-trade. Wm. O'Brien [William Smith O'Brien, who had recently visited Mitchel in America], though he seems well content with the institution of slavery, hesitates as yet about the actual importation. He will be properly indoctrinated however. At present he is on a visit with a large sugar planter in Louisiana (an Irishman from Tipperary) who works about 150 negroes, and wants plenty more from Ashantee.[101]

The Young Ireland years embodied the profound attractions of emotionally entwining oneself with one's imagined nation. As a later nationalist, Arthur Griffith, was to put it regarding Thomas Francis Meagher's patriotic epiphany during the 1840s, 'Meagher found himself when he found his country.'[102] And this Young Ireland episode involved many of the classic themes of nationalism. Here was a romantic conception of land and territory, a zeal for integrating the whole people, an intense focus upon the importance of culture and history, an ethical righteousness of attitude, and an exclusivist anglophobia. Here was struggle against an old (for some, the oldest[103]) nation, against whose power and influence one set oneself. The struggle involved some practicalities (Lalor on the land, for example), but also an attachment to quasi-egalitarian popular sovereignty, so often the motor force for nationalist politics: Lalor and Martin's *Irish Felon* (the successor to the *United Irishman*) proudly proclaimed 'LIBERTY-EQUALITY-FRATERNITY' on its mid-nineteenth-century front page.

Young Ireland was not successful in terms either of achieving Repeal of the Union, or of making a reality of their sought-after inclusive Irishness of all religious denominations: their inability to attract serious Protestant support was a deep and crippling problem for them and for what they stood for. And, as one later authority was to lament, even late-twentieth-century Ireland still lacked some of the Young Irelanders' planned-for developments: 'Davis urged the unity of Protestants and Catholics – they seem more disunited now than in the 1840s when he was writing – and pressed for undenominational education, which still does not exist below university level in Ireland.'[104] Young Ireland did not espouse a coherent or programmatically-defined cause. Yet this might, perhaps, be their real strength and legacy as far as later nationalism was concerned. The very diversity of Young Ireland's arguments yielded a rich harvest for different kinds of later nationalist to reap: 'Every cause or opinion found justification in its ideological stockpile. Republicans and dual monarchists, physical-force men and pacifists, socialists and capitalists, could all claim plausibly to be the inheritors of the authentic Young Ireland tradition.'[105] There were also some personal chains linking the Young Irelanders with the later-nineteenth-century politics of Home Rule, for example: Young Irelander John Blake Dillon was the father of Irish Parliamentary Party figure John Dillon; Young Irelander John Martin lived on to become a Home Ruler, as – more strikingly – did John Mitchel and Charles Gavan Duffy.[106] Drawing on Ireland's past, the Young Irelanders themselves became a part of later nationalism's inspirational, historical inheritance.

4

Land in Ireland *is* Life. Just in the proportion that our people contrive to keep or to gain some foot-hold on the soil, in that proportion exactly they will live and not die. All social, all industrial, all national questions resolve themselves now into *this* – how many Irish cultivators can keep root in the earth during the present year – so that the storm and blight, the famine, and the black flood of pauperism may not sweep them off, away into destruction and outer darkness? Not to the individual farmer only is this a life-and-death question, but to society and to the nation. With the ruin of the tillers of the soil, *all* is ruined.

United Irishman, 19 February 1848

In 1843 in America an unfamiliar blight was noted on the potato crop. Within two years it had spread to Europe and it was first noted in Ireland in late August 1845. This fungus-created potato blight (the fungal disease was *Phytophthora infestans*) was to set off a series of events which would prove momentous for the history of Irish nationalism. Following the arrival of the blight, most of Ireland's potato crop was consequently lost, and for several years its impact was devastating. Crisis loomed, with the disease spreading speedily and widely throughout Ireland: the blight was to appear in every county. Structurally, the problem was the extremely high dependence of the Irish poor on the potato: easy to grow (even on poor land), potatoes were the staple diet of over half of the Irish population, and so the dangers were clear enough. As successive crops failed, people had less on which to fall back, the previous crop's failure having already thinned their resources. Thus the Famine arrived in Ireland. Its effects were at their worst in 1847, the consequences of starvation being compounded by those of disease.

The government introduced soup kitchens briefly in 1847 (private soup kitchens had already had some effect); but, although millions received soup, the government's relief measures were still not dealing with the true extent of the problem. There was much philanthropic donation – in Ireland, Britain and beyond – and without this the effects of the Famine upon its victims would have been more terrible still. (It's often noted that a Providentialist kind of Christian belief may have hampered British governmental reactions to the Famine; it's much less often pointed out that evangelical Christian commitment to charity played a very significant part in stimulating what relief there actually was.)

But the human cost of the crisis was enormous. Much of the potato crop failed in 1848, and the blight was evident also during 1849–51. Emigration was one strategy for survival: there had been many Irish departures before this calamity, but their scale during and after the Famine was far greater. And, while pre-Famine emigrants mostly headed for Britain, Famine emigration increasingly involved moving to the United States. As emigrants frequently sent money back to Ireland, they facilitated further emigration and thus helped to produce Irish communities in the USA.

In 1841 the Irish population lay at around 8.3 million; in 1851 it numbered only around 6.5 million. Between 1846 and 1851 around a million people from the then population of over 8 million died; the main cause of death was not starvation but rather the range of diseases following on from malnutrition (cholera, typhus, dysentery); between death and emigration, the Irish population fell by around 2 million between 1845 and 1851.

Understandably, the Famine – and the appalling disintegration of life which it involved – eclipsed constitutional nationalist arguments in mid-century Ireland. O'Connell died in 1847, and in any case the struggles of contemporary nationalist politics were not greatly intensified, for the reason that the Repeal demand seemed irrelevant to the tragedy. There was no serious rebellion during the Famine: crime did increase significantly during the Famine period, but this rise involved mainly non-violent crime (theft) rather than violent acts; communal acts of violence in the form of rebellious or insurrectionist action on any serious scale did not take place.

There were some in Young Ireland circles who saw the Famine less as a natural disaster than as a stage in the process of a government policy to replace people with livestock on the land. But the impact of the Famine on Irish nationalism was far more marked after the event than it was tangibly evident during it. For the appalling scale of the episode was to become written firmly and enduringly into Irish nationalist narratives of British oppression. Some writer-observers have agreed. Cecil Woodham-Smith's influential account, for example, attributed pre-Famine Irish poverty, suffering and misery virtually to a sole, British cause ('the system under which land had come to be occupied and owned in Ireland, a system produced by centuries of successive conquests, rebellions, confiscations and punitive legisla- tion'.[107]) In such readings, British iniquity lay at the heart of the Famine morality tale. 'In the long and troubled history of England and Ireland no issue has provoked so much anger or so embittered relations between the two countries as the indisputable fact that huge quantities of food were exported from Ireland to England throughout the period when the people of Ireland were dying of starvation.'[108] But, as Woodham-Smith herself candidly observed, issues were in some ways more complicated: first, vast amounts of food (wheat as well as corn) were imported into Ireland during this same period (far more being imported than exported at the Famine's worst point, in fact); second, the worst-hit areas were ones in which corn tended not to be grown, and so it would have had to be distributed – a process for which no proper provision existed; and, third, those in need of the corn might well not have been able to do much with it, having become used only to potato-cooking: in Woodham-Smith's words, 'There was no means of distributing home-grown food, no knowledge of how to use it and in addition the small Irish farmer was compelled by economic necessity to sell what he grew. He dared not eat it.'[109]

It seems clear enough that the British government neither caused the Famine nor acted with genocidal intent during it (though some still find solace in asserting the contrary). Indeed, no government action in that period could have averted large-scale excess mortality during the Famine. Yet, had more been spent (or had money been spent more efficiently), many lives could surely have been saved. So the subject of British government thought and action during the Famine remains a serious question for students of Irish nationalism. It has become acceptable (even necessary) in British high-political circles to adopt an apologetic stance regarding this episode in British–Irish relations. Does this make historical sense? Could things have been dramatically different? Crop failure in itself was not new to Ireland; there had been partial potato crop failures (mostly in the west) in the 1830s and in 1842. But the usual pattern was for localized rather than general failure, or for failure in one year only: the 1840s experience was, therefore, tragically different in duration and in scope from anything previously encountered.

How did the British response really measure up? The Prime Minister at the onset of the blight, Robert Peel, had already had a lengthy involvement with Ireland. His first parliamentary seat, in 1809, had been for Cashel in County Tipperary; between 1812 and 1818 he had been Chief Secretary for Ireland, during which time he had in 1814 founded a permanent police force there, and (from 1816 to 1818) been involved in the alleviation of Irish food shortages; again, as Home Secretary in 1822 he had been in charge of relief provision during the crisis of subsistence caused by the crop failure of that year. Perhaps something of this first-hand experience yielded results: nobody died as a result of the crisis during the year following Ireland's initial potato failure of 1845. Some have disputed the extent to which the lack of excess mortality in this period was due directly to Peel's actions; the public works programme which he initiated in the early stages of the problem depended significantly on local initiative. But we should note what was in fact done. Peel's short-term relief measures involved the purchase of £100,000 worth of Indian corn, which was to be slowly released on to the market in order to keep prices down. Local relief committees (comprising clergy, landlords and large farmers) were formed throughout the country: these bodies raised large amounts of money through voluntary subscription, oversaw public relief works (to provide employment during times of scarcity) and purchased and resold corn from government depots. Extra employment was created by making new roads and walls, many of the latter still serving as a silent and moving epitaph to this mid-nineteenth-century tragedy.

Broadly, Peel's aim in regard to Ireland had been to win over Irish Catholics while remaining firmly committed to maintaining order. His record, judged by the potentially dreadful context of the Famine, should not be judged too harshly. With Peel's departure from the premiership in 1846, a Whig government returned to power until 1852, and it was this which presided over the most calamitous period of Irish Famine. For after 1846 the authorities opted emphatically for public works as the appropriate way in which to deal with Famine-related distress. Much was again done. The 1846–7 public works programme at its height employed over 700,000 people, thereby supporting 3.5 million – around half of the Irish population; in the winter of 1847 the government also did decide to provide some food. But, since disease and starvation were to kill such vast numbers, this broadly non-interventionist policy clearly did not work. The public works programme foundered partly because its administrators did not take full account of price fluctuations, and partly because there was in any case a four-week delay between changes in price and adjustments to money wages; an adequate wage was all too often simply not forthcoming.[110] Moreover, committed as they were to free trade, the Whigs opted (for the most part) not to continue Peel's strategy of exporting food to Ireland; instead, and controversially for some later observers, they chose to let market forces deal with food supply. For under the Whigs the two key figures dealing with Irish Famine relief were Sir Charles Wood (the Chancellor of the Exchequer) and Charles Trevelyan (Permanent Secretary at the Treasury). Government expenditure required Treasury sanction, and so the views of Trevelyan assumed huge importance for mid-century Ireland. It was not that the Whigs were unanimous: they were in fact divided between a comparatively interventionist, flexible approach on the one hand and a policy of minimal intervention on the other. But it was the latter that was advocated by Wood and Trevelyan, and it was this approach which prevailed. So ideological constraints prevented potentially more effective action, as the economics of laissez-faire dictated a preference for non-interference with the market.

In the pre-Famine era, the attitude of the London government had tended towards that of looking for the modernization of Ireland and its agriculture; some have raised the issue of whether such background decisively conditioned the way in which the government responded to the Famine in practice, with the authorities perhaps seeing the latter as an opportunity for such modernization. Certainly, by the 1840s, some in British political circles thought the Irish economy deeply in need of modernization, but there are limits to the justifiable extent of condemnation of British officials: even Cecil Woodham-Smith openly acknowledged Trevelyan's conscientiousness, scrupulousness and integrity.

And, inadequate though they were, the measures introduced by the government should be noted. In 1847 the Destitute Poor (Ireland) Act introduced the idea of setting up soup kitchens throughout Famine Ireland, and around this time Alexis Soyer (1810–58), the Paris-trained, celebrated French chef at London's Reform Club, and arguably the most famous contemporary chef in Europe, was enthusing over the potential for soup kitchens as a means for addressing the problems of the poor. Soyer now turned his thinking towards Ireland. Accustomed as he was to working in opulent surroundings (a previous Irish connection had been a dinner given at the Reform Club in 1844 by some friends of Daniel O'Connell, at which the Liberator's famously proscribed 1843 Clontarf monster meeting had been honoured in one of Soyer's most ingenious creations, 'Le Soufflé Monstre à la Clontarf'), Soyer also showed a persistent interest in charitable cookery and during the Famine he ran a major soup kitchen in Dublin. He had made a cheap soup recipe designed for the London poor, claiming that this could, almost single-handedly, provide the nutrition that a person needed. So the Reform Club was persuaded to allow its star chef leave of absence in order to set up his Dublin kitchen and, in 1847, at the authorities' instigation, the celebrity chef went to the Irish capital to oversee the mass distribution of his soup to the Irish needy.

He left for Ireland in February 1847 and stayed there until 11 April. On Monday, 5 April 1847 his soup kitchen opened in Dublin. The people were provided with hot, palatable and comparatively nutritious soup and bread; over a million rations were distributed. Soyer's Dublin kitchen produced good food for large numbers at great speed and the response there was positive and overwhelming. This experiment did not suffice, but it does demonstrate that some efforts were made, even during the much-maligned period of Whig government, to deal with Irish need. It is also worth reflecting on some of the thoughts of this particular benign agent, as they did highlight the structural difficulty underlying the Irish Famine. While in Ireland during his almost seven-week sojourn, Soyer was horrified to note that fish was being used as fertilizer for potatoes, rather than as food, simply because people in Ireland 'know how to cook potatoes to perfection and are totally ignorant of the way to cook fish ... the country produces plenty of vegetable and animal substances, and the waters washing your magnificent shores teem with life ... They only require to be properly employed to supply the wants of every one, with good, nourishing and palatable food.'[111] Soyer thought that the poor should eat as well as possible, and put considerable effort into making this a reality; but he also thought that, as in France, so also peasants in Ireland should be able to produce good food from the good ingredients around them.

None of this undermines the case of those Irish nationalists who have argued that – even in the context of the mid-nineteenth century – more could have been done to alleviate appalling Irish suffering. It is entirely understandable that the Famine should have become etched into communal national memory: a scar caused by a tragedy involving people, territory and assumed enemy-oppressor; a horror written into nationalist communal history, and calling out for some form of subsequent redress. But the key question is not, of course, what a twenty-first-century state would do (and our own pitiable record in the modern world in dealing with contemporary famine should lead to some humility: pious condemnation of past societies might seem hypocritical from any of us who live in opulently wealthy societies, in a world in which millions still starve). Rather, the issue is what was realistic in the contemporary circumstances of the Irish Famine. The fact that large-scale rations could be distributed shows that the state enjoyed the capacity to provide high levels of support, and the fact that the state had on previous occasions of crop failure responded in interventionist mode suggests that some Irish pain and loss were clearly avoidable in these dreadful years. The Famine did, after all, occur within an extraordinarily wealthy state.

And this was a point which some contemporaries themselves emphatically stressed. 'When we are involved in a crisis such as the civilized world has never yet seen,' an editorial in the Catholic nationalist daily newspaper the *Freeman's Journal* asserted on 5 April 1847, and no age of the world has, perhaps, equalled in the deadly fruits which the national calamity has hitherto produced – when subjects of the most powerful monarchy upon earth, and within one day's reach of its mighty and flourishing capital, are putrefying in their wretched hovels, or in their half-buried state, the prey of ravens, swine and dogs – with fever pressing hard on the still surviving victims, and pestilence coming up on the summer wind to sweep away the wretched refuse of our wasted population – when all these things occur to the mind, who will say that we have not cause to revive our sorrows, and lift up our voice against the policy which aggravated our disasters, and assimilated our people with the beasts that perish?

Such reflections led to an anger at British orthodoxy: 'We lose all patience with that mental perversity which sees in the famine, and its consequences, the inevitable order of things – the incontrollable march of destiny which willed the death of half-a-million of innocent beings.'[112]

But for Irish nationalists the key question must be whether an Irish government would have acted in such a way as to prevent the Famine, and here matters are more difficult. Later generations of nationalists have, understandably, used the Famine as a way of denouncing the evils of the Union with Britain. But the alternative to Union was some form of Irish nationalist administration, and contemporary alternatives, rather than anachronistic and hindsight-driven remedies, should be our focus. So what did the dominant Irish nationalists at the time say and do? There was debate at the time concerning Whig policies in Ireland, and there certainly were voices offered in criticism of such policy: but not coherently so from the Irish Members of Parliament, who were divided in their response. So it was not the case that there was a unified alternative policy-in-waiting from those with political authority and sanction within Irish nationalism. Parliamentary criticism of the Whigs came more from English than from Irish MPs, a challenge to the assumption sometimes casually held that an Irish government would automatically have solved or ameliorated the Famine problem.

So British culpability might have to be offset with a recognition of the probable deficiencies of any likely Irish nationalist response. Would a Dublin-based government have averted the crisis or dealt with it more effectively, given the identity of the classes and interests which would have been in such power at that time? Would an Irish government have been kinder, or much more efficient? Some scholars have judged the British response to 1840s Irish famine to have been deeply inadequate,[113] and there is much in this kind of case.[114] But the Irish nationalist political elite failed to offer an adequately coherent opposition to government policy; this hardly suggests the inevitability that an Irish administration would have averted the Famine or triumphed over the crisis.

Was the Famine a fault-line in the history of Irish nationalism? And is it true, as the constitutional nationalist Stephen Gwynn suggested, that 'Ireland before the great famine is one picture; Ireland after it, another'?[115] There is no doubt about the Famine's central role in many Irish nationalist self-presentations (Charles Gavan Duffy: 'The condition of Ireland at the opening of the year 1847 is one of the most painful chapters in the annals of mankind'[116]). But what were its legacies in terms of nationalist Ireland? How did the Famine rewrite nationalist senses of history and community?

One element concerned the legacy of embittered and anglophobic emigrants. Emigration long remained an emotive topic and one which fuelled Irish nationalist argument ('The history of emigration, even unwritten as it is, is full of sadness and misery,' observed the *Freeman's Journal* in 1874: 'Every mail brings us some tale of woe on shipboard or on land'[117]). But the Famine changed the dynamics of the Irish–British political relationship by helping to establish an irate Irish–American nationalist population of significant weight. By the late 1860s there were an estimated 2 million people in the United States who had been born in Ireland. And many of the Famine emigrants carried with them an anger at the circumstances of their leaving and a dual conviction, first, that they were exiles rather than emigrants and, second, that Britain was to blame for their plight. Here was built a reservoir upon which later Irish nationalism could draw: the Famine had produced a newly large and angry transatlantic Irish nationalism, and provided a basis for lastingly rage-filled revanchism.

The Famine also had an effect on one of the cultural elements of nationalist Ireland, by eroding Irish language-speaking communities. Irish-speaking areas were very hard hit, many of those who died or emigrated having come from such places; and English was subsequently to be the language of the Irish – even of Irish nationalists. A third effect on the evolution of Irish nationalism involved Catholicism, and the strengthening of the Catholic Church's position in the aftermath of the tragedy. The bond between hard-hit people and their consoling Church grew closer, and divisions between Catholicism and the main Protestant Churches in Ireland deepened: the Protestant proselytism associated with some Famine relief (however sincere in its contemporary motivation) helped to leave a legacy of anger and division. And so post-Famine nationalism was more deeply Catholic, and so it long effectively remained.

Fourthly, the Famine-induced loss of population and prompting of many evictions led to shifts in agricultural arrangements, with the enlargement of many farms. The death or emigration of many landholders led to a farm pattern of fewer, on average larger, units: the number of farms of under fifteen acres fell spectacularly in some areas of the country. As Karl Marx observed in the 1860s, there was a 'centralization' of farms smaller than fifteen acres, with the number of larger holdings increasing.[118]

In the post-Famine period, indeed, insecurity concerning land together with this culture of consolidation produced the ironic phenomenon of late-nineteenth-century land-nationalist argument: many holding late-nineteenth-century land in Ireland had benefited unsentimentally from the Famine by consolidating and enlarging their farms; and these people were often at the heart of a vibrant nationalism which drew strength, among other things, from anti-British grievance regarding that very Famine. For the majority of those who survived it, the Famine indeed produced economic benefits; average Irish incomes rose dramatically in the late nineteenth and early twentieth centuries, and there was marked improvement too across various other measures of living standard (including life-span, height, and birth weight).[119] Post-Famine Irish nationalists had in many cases done well out of the Famine. The great Michael Collins's own father was one such Famine survivor, who benefited from the agricultural prosperity which followed the appalling tragedy;[120] and the revolutionary Collins was among those who argued that the British had manufactured the Great Famine.

As with modern-day famine, life for the non-suffering proceeded in familiar form during the Irish catastrophe. Sheridan's comedy *The School for Scandal* was performed at Dublin's Theatre Royal in the week during which Soyer's soup kitchen opened in the same city; again, John Mitchel bitterly claimed of Dublin in 1847 that 'that city had never before been so gay and luxurious ... the theatres and concert-rooms had never been filled with such brilliant throngs'.[121] But the later Irish nationalist memory of the Famine, however selective or ill-informed, did contribute to the generation of an angrier and more geographically dispersed communal, national struggle. Given the scale of the tragedy, this is hardly surprising.

FOUR
FENIANS AND PARLIAMENTARY NATIONALISM,
1850–1900

1

> The worst about the Irish is that they become corruptible as
> soon as they stop being peasants and turn bourgeois. True,
> this is the case with most peasant nations. But in Ireland it
> is particularly bad.
>
> Frederick Engels[1]

When I was at Oxford in the 1980s, there was a wonderful Marxist
bookshop in the covered market in the city. Like Marxism itself, that shop
is now defunct. But, with its shelves of Russian-published editions of
Marx, Engels, Lenin and others, that little bookshop represented an
enthralling space for a left-wing history student. At the heart of the
intellectual capital of capitalist England, here on these shelves was an
alternative philosophy of history and politics, one which still at that stage
considered the future to be in its possession. One of the many books that
I bought in that shop was a volume of the extensive writings of Marx and
Engels on *Ireland and the Irish Question*. To a Belfast-born son of a Belfast
mother, this book held a compelling quality, and I read and re-read it
during my time at Oxford (its margins repeatedly annotated and its spine
practically broken, as I look at it here on my desk twenty years later).

Karl Marx (1818–83) considered 'the solution of the Irish question
as the solution of the English, and the English as the solution of the
European'.[2] Ireland was pivotal. 'If England is the bulwark of landlordism and European capitalism,' Marx wrote in 1870,

> the only point where one can hit official England really hard is
> Ireland. In the first place, Ireland is the bulwark of English

landlordism. If it fell in Ireland it would fall in England. In Ireland this is a hundred times easier since the economic struggle there is concentrated exclusively on landed property, since this struggle is at the same time national, and since the people there are more revolutionary and exasperated than in England.[3]

Here we have the essence of the classical Marxist line on Ireland, and the clue to its still enduring appeal even now for some people. Ireland was capitalist England's Achilles' heel, the revolutionary starting point for the journey to international freedom. If the aristocracy could be defeated in Ireland, then there would be a domino effect in the neighbouring island: Ireland was England's 'weakest point. Ireland lost, the British "Empire" is gone, and the class war in England, till now somnolent and chronic, will assume acute forms'.[4] And, with Ireland free, the conflict between the English and Irish working classes in England itself – a conflict which Marx held to be damaging to revolutionary prospects there – would necessarily diminish.

This Marxist interpretation has attracted many over the years, not merely for reasons of hard-edged leftist ambition, but also because it rests on an appealingly romantic vision of the Irish as the Marxists' greatest ally. While the English subjugated all others, wrote Marx's great comrade Frederick Engels (1820–95), 'Only with the Irish the English could not cope. The reason for this is the enormous resilience of the Irish race.'[5] A similar view lies behind Engels' despair in 1843 over what he saw as Daniel O'Connell's wasted revolutionary opportunity:

> two hundred thousand people always surround him! How much could have been done if a sensible man possessed O'Connell's popularity or if O'Connell had a little more understanding and a little less egoism and vanity! Two hundred thousand men – and what men! People who have nothing to lose, two-thirds of whom are clothed in rags, genuine proletarians and sansculottes and, moreover, Irishmen, wild, headstrong, fanatical Gaels. One who has never seen Irishmen cannot know them. Give me two hundred thousand Irishmen and I will overthrow the entire British monarchy.[6]

Marx and Engels' reflections on Ireland and nationalism are important, but not because Marxism ever had any serious chance of dominating Irish politics. Their arguments matter for other reasons. First, Marxist ideas have at times influenced sections of Irish nationalist movements in ways which have had a significant impact on their struggle, even if these ideas have not led Irish nationalism as a whole to turn to the left. The 1916 rebel James Connolly didn't get the Ireland that he wanted, nor did IRA leaders Peadar O'Donnell in the 1920s or Cathal Goulding in the 1960s, and nor did the leftists within the Provisional IRA in the late twentieth century. But, in each case, Irish politics was affected by important initiatives which had been prompted by Marxist nationalists: whether in revolutionary stimulus during the First World War (Connolly), land agitation in the 1920s Irish Free State (O'Donnell), the initiation of northern civil rights agitation in the 1960s (Goulding and his left-thinking allies such as Roy Johnston), or murderous revolutionary violence from the 1970s onwards (the Provos). Marx's ideas helped to create a strain of revolutionary republicanism which in turn jolted Irish politics in powerful – if not quite the desired – fashion.

Second, Marx and his comrades might have reached an unpersuasive answer to the question of why nationalism is as it is (very few would now share anything like Marx's form of economic determinism); but the Marxists did at least ask some of the right questions. They tried to get to the roots of nationalism – the 'why?' as well as the 'what?' – and in doing so their searching intellects pointed towards highly important problems. If you were going to understand the dynamics of Irish nationalism, for example, you had to look to social and economic realities. In 1888 Engels crisply set out arguably the central Marxist thesis on history, namely 'that in every historical epoch, the prevailing mode of economic production and exchange, and the social organization necessarily following from it, form the basis upon which is built up, and from which alone can be explained, the political and intellectual history of that epoch'.[7] As Connolly and others later recognized, this meant that one had to understand material, social relationships if one wanted to explain the workings of nationalism in Ireland; even for those of us who do not share Marx's and Connolly's leftist faith, it remains true that nationalism can only be explained properly if one takes account of social and economic forces.

It wasn't that Marx was devoted to nationalism as such: class, rather than nation, was the vector of historical change and, in his view, ultimately the workers' identity would transcend loyalty to mere nation.[8] So, in the end, Marxism was an ideology subversive of nationalist faith; as that great theorist of nationalism Ernest Gellner pithily put it, 'Marxism contained the anticipation of the decline of nationalism.'[9] But Marx did think it necessary that the workers should move, stage by historical stage, into the future; and one such stage involved nationalism: 'the proletariat must first of all acquire political supremacy, must rise to be the leading class of the nation, must constitute itself *the* nation'.[10] Eventually, once class antagonisms had evaporated, so too conflict between nations would dissolve and become irrelevant. True revolution could not be produced in one nation alone; but nor could revolution be achieved without working-class organization within the national framework. Thus it was that Marx favoured Polish and Irish nationalism, as well as the unification of Italy and of Germany. While nationalism could reflect the interests of the dominant class within the nation, it could also in some cases be a necessary step towards the emancipation of the working class itself, and this was certainly what Marx and Engels (and many left-wing Irish nationalists after them) thought in relation to Ireland.

Devoting a reasonable amount of thought to Ireland, these two great Victorians held that Irish nationalism was a necessary and progressive force, and they duly offered it their support. Marx might not have offered as systematic an analysis of nationalism itself as his later supporters might have liked; but his broad thinking on the subject was pretty clear. Marx and Engels distinguished between those they considered historical nations (of which Ireland was one), and those that involved less significant national communities. Great nations were to be supported; national independence could in some cases be the necessary pre-condition for appropriate social development; some nations could be dismissed (including numerous East European peoples) but there were, Marx thought, cases where the national cause deserved his support, such as Poland (where it might damage Tsarist power) or Ireland (where it might weaken capitalist England). Where national development would hasten the historical development of class struggle, then nations were progressive; where not, theirs was a reactionary cause.

If history was effectively determined by class struggle ('The history of all hitherto existing society is the history of class struggles'[11]), then this was also how one had to understand nationalism. Economic conditions would explain political instincts (touring Ireland in 1856, Engels noted particularly 'a total absence of any industry at all'[12]), and in the Irish case the national cause was understood in relation to its supposed furtherance of the eventual emancipation of oppressed social classes. Marx and Engels could be dismissive of nationalist Ireland at times, in practice. Although Engels had some personal links to that revolutionary Irish republican organization, the Fenians, he and Marx could be very critical of what they considered to be counter-productively bloody Fenian actions;[13] in general, Marx tended to oppose the use of revolutionary terror, thinking it a sign of political immaturity to attempt to achieve by terror things for which the mass of the people were, as yet, unready.

But Engels and Marx did consider there to be a role in the emergence of English revolution for the cause of Irish freedom; and even for Irish emigrants to England. Engels noted in the 1840s that socialism had had little success in Ireland. However, he also observed that Irish immigration to England had 'degraded the English workers' and 'aggravated the hardship of their lot'; as a consequence, Irish immigrants had played their part in accentuating the gulf between bourgeoisie and working class in England and had thereby 'hastened the approaching crisis' there – a crisis which would, in Engels' view, have a necessarily violent resolution: 'all hope of a peaceful solution of the social question for England must be abandoned. The only possible solution is a violent revolution, which cannot fail to take place.'[14]

There is much that Marx and Engels clearly got wrong regarding Ireland and nationalism. They underestimated the seriousness of Irish (namely, unionist) opposition to nationalist advance, and they overstated Ireland's importance for the development of English radicalism. More broadly, their thesis that class rather than nation represented the ultimate motor-force of world history almost certainly distorted the respective significance of these two phenomena. Economic developments (industrialization, for example) did play a key part in the emergence of nationalism in the modern period,[15] and to this extent Marx and Engels' economic determinism was sound enough. But they exaggerated and simplified this process. Nations and nationalism were not merely consequences of economic change or class relations: they were built on sturdier, broader foundations, and offered rich psychological, cultural, political, and communal-egalitarian rewards, as well as economic appeal for many classes; and this broader quality allowed nationalism, ultimately, to devour Marxism itself.[16] But Marx's reflections point towards the crucial fact that – in our interpretation of the Ireland of his own day, for example – we must recognize that nationalism could be significantly driven and defined by economic questions (such as that concerning the land).

Marx was not, of course, the only major Victorian intellectual to engage with Ireland and with its nationalist politics. The liberal sage John Stuart Mill (1806–73), whom Marx knew, himself turned his formidable mind in an Irish direction, and again philosophical observations drew attention to material realities. 'Once at least in every generation the question, "What is to be done with Ireland?" rises again to perplex the councils and trouble the conscience of the British nation.'[17] True enough. And, as we shall see, Mill could sharply identify some of the key issues at play in contemporary nationalist Ireland, such as the attitude towards a cultivator's rights regarding land. Indeed, Mill earned the respect of some Irish nationalists, Home Ruler Justin McCarthy among them. McCarthy (who in turn knew Mill) described himself as 'a devoted admirer of Mr Mill's writings, and of his personal and public character', and observed of the great man that, 'The manner in which he had treated the Irish land question in one of his books had won for him the admiration of all Irish nationalists.'[18]

And Mill's liberal thinking highlighted some of the deeper issues which we need to consider when assessing Irish nationalism's communal struggles for power. In 1859, for example, Mill identified one of the key, persistent challenges facing national communities as they pursued and exercised power: that of protecting individual freedom. In contrast to those who argued that the 'nation did not need to be protected against its own will', Mill judged that, in reality,

> The 'people' who exercise the power are not always the same people with those over whom it is exercised; and the 'self-government' spoken of is not the government of each by himself, but of each by all the rest ... the people, consequently, *may* desire to oppress a part of their number, and precautions are as much needed against this as against any other abuse of power.

'There is a limit' – Mill continued – 'to the legitimate interference of collective opinion with individual independence; and to find that limit, and maintain it against encroachment, is as indispensable to a good condition of human affairs as protection against political despotism.'[19]

Mill's laudable stress on individuality was, of course, tied to his conception of freedom: he favoured the idea of the sovereign and free individual, and held that liberty should be absolute except where that liberty did harm to others. But if liberty was absolutely necessary, and individual liberty a central feature of life as it should be lived, then could such freedom be achieved and guaranteed through nationalism as it worked in practice? It wasn't that liberalism did not concentrate also on the rights and interests of communities as well as those of individuals; indeed, for it to be effective, it had to do so. It is rather that Mill's thinking highlighted what was to be one of the persistent tensions within Irish, as other, nationalist movements which ostensibly worked for freedom: the tension between individual liberty and community action.

As his words suggested, the reconciliation of liberty with community – especially, perhaps, in charged contexts of tense, bitter struggles for power – would prove difficult and painful. Mill was concerned with 'the nature and limits of the power which can be legitimately exercised by society over the individual', asserting the central principle

> that the sole end for which mankind are warranted, individually or collectively, in interfering with the liberty of action of any of their number is self-protection. That the only purpose for which power can be rightfully exercised over any member of a civilized community, against his will, is to prevent harm to others. . . . The only freedom which deserves the name is that of pursuing our own good in our own way, so long as we do not attempt to deprive others of theirs or impede their efforts to obtain it.[20]

But if the limitation of someone's liberty cannot be sanctioned unless that limitation prevents harm to other people, then who is to make and monitor such decisions in the context, for example, of rural or political conflict such as that which was to prevail in Ireland in the decades after Mill's 1859 essay? In late-nineteenth-century (as in more recent) Irish nationalist history, this was to be a major question, and arguably one which was imperfectly answered in practice – especially when the context was that of aggressive, violent nationalism.

2

What is distinctive of Fenianism? Actually, it originates from the Irish Americans. They are the initiators and leaders. But in Ireland the movement took root (and is still really rooted) only in the mass of the people, the lower orders. That is what *characterizes* it.

Karl Marx[21]

The word 'Fenian' referred to the warriors of ancient Ireland, and was to describe the famous revolutionary movement founded in March 1858 – on St Patrick's Day, in Dublin – by the 1848 veteran James Stephens. This conspiracy of bearded rebels could not initially settle on a name, being known variously by comradely, secret-society titles such as 'The Organization', 'The Brotherhood' or 'The Society'. The term 'Fenian' itself originated with the parallel branch of the group in America, headed by Stephens's friend John O'Mahony, but it came to be used to describe the Irish movement too (and the labels Irish Republican Brotherhood (IRB) and Irish Revolutionary Brotherhood were also to be deployed).

Whatever its title, the new movement had its roots in the now large Irish immigrant community in the United States, following the collapse of the 1840s Young Ireland movement (to the aggressive wing of which Fenianism might be seen as a sequel). Exemplifying our point about the impact of the Famine on exile Irish nationalism, the Fenians drew strength from 'the Irish men and women of America who pray, hope and labour for the disenthralment of their race and the redemption of their native land',[22] as the organization's own New York weekly journal put it.

Fenianism involved a commitment to popular politicization,[23] yet also to secrecy of method and to the establishment of a democratic and independent Irish republic. In essence, this freedom from Britain was to be achieved by violent struggle: constitutional politics (at least of the British parliamentary variety) was largely despised and rejected. The Fenian oath acknowledged the Almighty, and involved allegiance to an Irish republic whose independence and integrity were to be defended. Strong on the supposed sentiment and feeling of the Irish people, and on their own vanguard representation of this, the Fenians were deeply defiant regarding Ireland's distinctive and proud culture: 'At the present day there is probably no people on earth who are more pronounced in their opinions, more faithful to their traditions, or more mindful of the marked peculiarities which go to make up national character, than the Irish people.' The community's national culture was irrepressible: 'notwithstanding the fact that the English policy has, especially during the past decade, been of a character to completely denationalize the Irish, it has been utterly powerless to damp those ardent national characteristics which belong to the Celtic race'.[24]

But it was their commitment to separatist violence which distinguished Fenian nationalists most significantly. In the late 1860s the authorities themselves took the movement very seriously. For arms had been smuggled, an insurrection was attempted, and violent, fatal acts were initiated. The Fenians themselves had at times declared great confidence in the imminent achievement of their aims, in February 1866 proclaiming that 'Fenianism seems to be sprouting up everywhere', and declaring it evident that 'England is loosening her iron grasp on Ireland'.[25] (Again and again in the Irish nationalist story we meet nationalists' notion of history as progress, and of an inevitable, inexorable movement of history in a nationalist direction.) Such verbal buoyancy was not, however, to be matched in the realm of martial achievement. The Fenians had originally intended to hold a Rising in 1865, when Fenian strength and revolutionary potential were probably at their greatest. But in late 1865 the government struck: well informed about Fenian activities, they managed to suppress the IRB paper, the *Irish People*, and to arrest key leaders.

In 1867 the Fenians did attempt a Rising: in February there were weak military efforts in England and Ireland; early in the following month a more significant Rising was initiated, its two main focal points being Dublin and Cork, though there was also lesser activity in other places, including Limerick, Tipperary, Waterford and Clare. 'Clonmel, Thursday night [7 March 1867]. It has been currently reported here that the Fenians have assembled in large numbers in the Devil's Bit Mountains, which must be anything but comfortable quarters in this terrible weather.' 'Ennis, Wednesday [6 March 1867]. I have some startling news to send you. The Fenian epidemic has at last broken out amongst us in a very active shape.' 'Dundalk, Thursday morning [7 March 1867]. All the hills about here, as well as the Carlingford Mountains, exhibited bonfires, or, perhaps, signal fires, last night.'[26]

The Fenian aim had been to hold out for Irish–American reinforcements. Skirmishes did dribble on for some weeks, yet in truth the Fenian Rising was quelled easily enough. There was only a handful of deaths, and there had been poor organization and no great mass sympathy for the insurrectionary gesture. Effectively, the Rising had been defeated before it began: leaders had been rounded up; American help was insufficient; arms were too short in supply (large-scale arming of Fenians only really taking place after March 1867); clerical denunciation had had an effect on wider sympathy (the Catholic Church being no friend to such secret societies); and – not for the last time in Irish rebel history – the authorities knew much of what was afoot through a network of informers (and had, for example, heavily protected Dublin in anticipation of the rebellion).

But Fenian violence continued after the Rising, and bloodily so. Leading Fenian Brother Colonel Richard O'Sullivan Burke was arrested in London in December 1867 and placed on remand in the city's Clerkenwell Prison, there to await his trial. On the afternoon of Friday, 13 December, an explosion destroyed a prison wall in a Fenian attempt to rescue Burke. The blast destroyed houses, killed twelve people and injured many more (including some badly burned children). And it failed as an escape attempt. The aim had been to blow up the wall of the Clerkenwell House of Detention with a view to liberating Burke; the prison wall that had been attacked was the one enclosing the yard where the prisoners took their exercise. But Burke was not freed by this bungled, fatal effort; and the two men and one woman who set the explosion were afterwards arrested.

The far from sympathetic *Irish Times* condemned the London explosion as a 'diabolical Fenian outrage',[27] an editorial in the paper arguing:

The Clerkenwell outrage surpasses in reckless and fiendish cruelty anything that has been perpetrated for many years. To explode a barrel of gunpowder in a densely crowded neighbourhood – to

maim and blind and hurl to sudden destruction innocent, unconscious victims – to deal the felon stroke of murder and of life-long
mutilations worse than death on men, women, and children who,
even in a state of open war would have been sacred amid the fury
of battle – this is a crime the turpitude of which cannot be
expressed in words.[28]

In terms of its ostensible goal, Fenian nationalism clearly failed: the
republic was not established. But the Brotherhood had enjoyed significant levels of support in Ireland and also in Britain and the United
States, its apparent simplicity of goal and method possessing some real
allure. It had involved some of the most zealous figures in militant
nationalism, and saw them engage in an international conspiracy.
Founder and chief of the Irish Fenians, Kilkenny-born James Stephens
(1824–1901), had fled to Paris after the 1848 imbroglio, and had found
there that his ideas were reinforced by the insurrectionist revolutionism
then modish in that city (yet another example of the historical
intersection between Irish nationalism and wider international currents
and trends). Others, such as John O'Mahony (1816–77) and Michael
Doheny, were also in Paris, that mid-century city of revolutionary
culture.

Stephens himself could be somewhat demanding of obedience from
his revolutionary comrades, possessing a rather dictatorial and author-
itarian attitude and style. But he did initiate some major developments.
In the summer of 1863 he had decided to launch an IRB paper, the
first issue of the *Irish People* appearing on 28 November that year: a
Fenian mouthpiece to be jointly edited by County Tipperary romantic
Irish nationalist Charles Joseph Kickham (1828–82), Dublin-born
Protestant and TCD-educated former Young Irelander Thomas Clarke
Luby (1821–1901), and Tipperary-born John O'Leary – who soon
assumed overall editorial responsibility for the paper.

Stephens was celebrated by the American Fenian newspaper as a
cultivated, literary, educated man – 'one of the most polished gentlemen of the present day'[29] – but O'Leary and Kickham are at least as
telling in terms of the nature of Fenian nationalism and legacies.
O'Leary was, again, TCD-educated, and – though apparently not a
sworn member of the Brotherhood – he endured imprisonment for his
Fenian associations and left an intriguing literary legacy in the form of

his *Recollections of Fenians and Fenianism*, dedicated to his great friend Thomas Clarke Luby.

O'Leary was a great admirer of Theobald Wolfe Tone, and in becoming a Young Irelander he had been won to the cause through reading the poems and essays of Thomas Davis. He had been 'converted to nationalism by the poems of Davis',[30] as his friend and acolyte W. B. Yeats (1865–1939) later put it; in O'Leary's own words, 'for all that is Irish in me, and, above all, for the inspiration that made me Irish, the fountain and the origin must always be sought in Davis'.[31] Yeats's father, the painter John Butler Yeats (1839–1922), captured the old Fenian O'Leary in a 1904 portrait[32] which reflects the dignity and line-worn face of its subject's long commitment. For nationalist zealot O'Leary emphatically was. Having been captured for the faith by Davis, O'Leary then read *The Nation* very closely. And, in a style which Patrick Pearse would make more famous early in the next century, O'Leary identified a chain of nationalist figures in an attempt to make history work for the contemporary cause:

> To my mind, Theobald Wolfe Tone and Thomas Davis – the example of the one mainly transmitted to us through the teaching of the other – had much more to do with Fenianism than any famine or failure. . . . Fenianism is the direct and, I think, inevitable outcome of '48, as '48 was the equally inevitable, if more indirect, outcome of '98, and the immediate origin of the movement is undoubtedly to be found among the '48 refugees in America.[33]

O'Leary's thinking points us to some of the social realities of Fenianism. He expressed a marked preference for the artisan class ('it is in this class I have always found the best Irishmen'[34]) over the middle class; for he held that you couldn't often make rebels out of middle-class material, since risk in rebellion is more immediate and sure than is material reward. And he highlights also some of the intellectual influences still present in nationalist Irish minds (he had, for example, been greatly influenced by Carlyle, recalling of his student days that he remembered 'taking in regularly the *Latter-Day Pamphlets* of Carlyle, of whom I had long been an ardent reader and admirer'[35]).

For his part, Charles Kickham also tellingly leads us to key features of a certain kind of nationalism and nationalist trajectory. He was firmly attached to a particular place, locality and people – as so often in our story, the actual as well as the imagined community formed a vital part of his nationalism. Kickham's uncle had been an agent for the newly established *Nation* in October 1842: a copy was sent weekly to Kickham's father and the paper was read aloud in his home when he was young. So, through family connections, the *Nation*'s romantic nationalism was an influence on the boy from early on and helped to frame his thinking. And yet Kickham's roots – genealogically and intellectually – were hybrid. He came, apparently, from a family originating with an English settler of the Cromwellian era; and he was very well read in Shakespeare, Tennyson, Defoe, Dickens (his favourite author) and Eliot, and greatly influenced by such English classics.

A talented political propagandist, Kickham had supported O'Connell's Repeal campaign and he long retained vivid memories of attending an O'Connellite monster meeting in September 1845. But as a keen admirer of Thomas Davis, Kickham was sympathetic to Young Ireland. And, indeed, his politics became sharply aggressive early on: he grew hostile to the parliamentary method of nationalist approach, and even as early as 1848 he was inclined towards physical-force separatist politics; he was certainly and emphatically of that disposition by the mid-1850s, when he exhibited a keenness for openly defiant nationalist politics.

Kickham became a local Fenian leader and was arrested in 1865. By this stage he had had a brief American sojourn in 1863, during which his intimate witnessing of Irish emigration had greatly moved him, as he saw at close hand the personal sorrow of many emigrants and the political tragedy of Ireland losing so many of its people. (And emigration unavoidably showed itself at local level to nineteenth-century nationalists. Donegal weaver and tailor Charles McGlinchey (1861–1954) recalled of his Inishowen locality that, 'All during my time people kept going to America and there's not a family in the parish but has somebody belonging to them in the States.'[36]) After his arrest, Kickham was sentenced to fourteen years of penal servitude for his supposedly traitorous intentions as a Fenian.

While in prison in Woking in Surrey, he had to live intimately with those criminal prisoners alongside whom he was incarcerated, and he deeply resented having to mix in company which often included brutal criminals such as murderers, or people guilty of sexual offences. The Fenians tended to be treated like their fellow-prisoners, and this formed one of their complaints about prison: that they were not treated differently from (and better than) ordinary convicts. Prison could be ghastly enough. Active County Cork Fenian and proudly Catholic product of a Christian Brothers' education, John Sarsfield Casey (1846–96), was imprisoned in the 1860s in foul conditions: 'I jumped up and found, to my disgust, that my clothes were swarming with fleas and bugs. I almost vomited, cast off my clothes, shook them and then cast off the bedclothes. It was literally alive with all sorts of vermin; the sheet and blankets were stained with vomit, blood, etc.' Yet Casey's revolutionary commitment enabled him to read such experiences in the light of a tradition of nationalist martyrdom and imprisonment, alluding favourably to Emmet and Mitchel.[37] For prison struggle was to become an important feature of the Fenian repertoire; not for the last time in Irish nationalist history, aggressively-minded prisoners sought recognition of their political commitment, while the prison authorities wanted to break the republicans' spirit.

Kickham's own imprisonment (of almost three years and four months) ended when he was released in 1869. He and some other pardoned Fenians reached Dublin on 6 March to be greeted by a large and enthusiastic crowd. He emerged from jail with undimmed political zeal, and with prison having made him famous: arrest, trial, publicity and release had combined to make him a celebrated Fenian. And he was convinced that the IRB should engage in armed rebellion whenever the chance emerged, favouring not terrorist assassination but rather disciplined, military, honourable, regular rebellion.

Kickham remained a romantic exponent of nationalist sentiment rather than of crisply defined and hard-headed political ideology (surely the essence of much powerful Irish nationalism: sentiment, emotion, strong feeling and an intensity of enthusiasm). His novel, *Knocknagow*, might be entertainingly fluent rather than creatively original, but it reflected Kickham's view that literary output could be important in the process of regenerating the nation and national feeling (and *Knocknagow* was indeed to become something of a classic of Irish nationalist fiction). Kickham also exhibited the ethical self-righteousness so common in nationalist zealotry: for he tended to equate what he took to be wrong political strategies with morally wrong motivation; like many nationalists, he considered bad politics to be interwoven with bad morality, and that those who opposed you politically could be seen as somewhat immoral and therefore discredited.

So in O'Leary and Kickham we can hear many of the strains of our nationalist music: attachment to people and place (Kickham's family and local loyalty), and to history (O'Leary and Tone); celebration of distinctive culture (reflected in both men's adoration of Thomas Davis); the satisfying moralization of politics (in Kickham's notions of honourable warfare, and of the inferior ethics of those who disagreed with him); the pursuit of Irish autonomy through various means of struggle (violent, literary, prison-centred), each in its own fashion highly rewarding. (Even violence could have its attractions: leading Fenian John Devoy (1842–1928) was a romantic Irish nationalist very keen on adventure, whose career included a stint in the French Foreign Legion.) Fenianism embodied the central nationalist idea of ridding your country of foreign (in this case, British) influence, and its pursuit of legitimate Irish government and independence drew strength from the visceral, exclusivist appeal of anglophobia. Who was to blame for Ireland's historical suffering? The answer came with a political and emotional charge ('the Irish Catholic political hatred', as Yeats crisply phrased it[38]), and this lay behind the Fenians' serious attempt to overthrow British power in Ireland.

The Fenians identified nationalism as the route to liberty ('The first grand, indispensable step toward Freedom is Nationality'[39]), and their separatism was revolutionist in spirit. If you were going to end the foreign oppression of your community and your culture, then uncompromising struggle should be directed towards an uncompromised separatist goal. Thus it was that there was an anti-parliamentary strain within Fenian thinking, a denunciation of parliamentary politics as corrupt, self-serving, demoralizing and ineffective. In part, this reflected the failure and ineffectiveness of the most recent decade of constitutional nationalist parliamentary politics, that of the 1850s Irish parliamentary party: 'The Fenian movement in the sixties ... owed much of its appeal to the widespread disgust with constitutional agitation that followed the collapse of the party of the fifties.'[40]

The Fenians would, instead, pursue violence – and not always only against the British. On 22 February 1864 the Cork journalist, politician and nationalist propagandist Alexander Martin Sullivan (1829–84) and others called a nationalist public meeting at the Rotunda in Dublin.

Sullivan's paper, *The Nation*, was hostile to Fenianism, and Fenian James Stephens did not want to see the kind of broader objectives which Sullivan might foster flourishing among Irish nationalists. And so hundreds of Fenians attended the Rotunda meeting, Sullivan and his supporters fleeing the hall in fear of this intra-nationalist intimidation. Nationalism was not always a story of freedom, as the tumultuous scenes that night clearly showed: 'In the body of the hall the vast mass of human beings swayed to and fro, cheering and shouting in the most excited manner.' Speakers were interrupted, fights broke out ('sticks were raised and blows struck'), the platform was stormed and utter confusion ensued. The Fenian platform-stormers 'indulged in much disorder and violence extending even to the breaking of several of the seats. For a considerable time the Round Room of the Rotunda was the scene of a carnival of uproar and disorder.'[41]

There could be a measure of blurring, at times, between the constitutional and the physical-force strands of nationalist struggle: 'social interaction between republicans and MPs was not unusual'.[42] By 1875 at least two people from the IRB Supreme Council (Joseph Biggar and Frank Hugh O'Donnell) were also MPs. But, in essence, Fenianism involved the belief of someone like Charles Kickham, that Irish freedom could only be achieved by people who were uncorrupted by a connection with British parliamentary institutions; his idea was of a revolutionary movement pure of such sullying influences.

In part, this reflected a notion which we meet frequently enough in nationalist Ireland, that the struggle is not just a means to an end, but also definitive in itself of the character of the nation. Fenians saw constitutional politics as involving the degradation of national virility, strength and manhood. The kind of methods you used demonstrated the kind of nation you were; so effete parliamentary compromise was unacceptable. In contrast, masculine violence demonstrated that Ireland was developing the moral qualities which made it worthy of its independence. And here we come to one of the deepest characteristics and – for some – one of the great attractions of the Fenian path, namely its attitudinal quality. As one leading historian has put it, 'the real importance of Fenianism lay less in its ideas than in its attitude . . . it embodied an inspirational sense of character-building, a posture of self-respect, and the repudiation of servility. The Fenian, even without an actual rebellion, was a mental revolutionary.'[43] Strongly opposed to deference, the Fenians prefigured something of the defiance of the twentieth-century IRA style of politics. The Cookstown-born Fenian James Mullin (1846–1920) attributed his republicanism to his mother, who had impressed him with 'the meanness of bowing the head and bending the knee to any man or set of men made from the same clay as myself and set above me by accident only. This creed was confirmed by an early perusal of Paine's *Rights of Man*.'[44] In the Fenians, one saw the defiantly aggressive politics of nationalist grievance, involving pride and a marked hostility to servility or submissiveness. The Fenians were not asking for what England might give, but demanding what was rightfully theirs, and were prepared to take it by force for their nation.

Here we detect echoes of many other nationalisms, with pride, self-respect and dignity lying at their heart, and with national honour and glory contrasted with the negative image of a hated national enemy and opponent.[45] Another theme familiar from the nationalist litera-ture,[46] and clearly evident in the Fenian case, is the social dimension to their cause and appeal. They were emphatically and dangerously a revolutionary movement. But their appeal was also, in part, recrea-tional, especially in the mid-1860s.[47] Drilling and marching themselves represented a kind of social activity; meeting in pubs and for sports gatherings, even more so. Most Fenians did not take up a gun in conflict; but very many did go drinking together, or attended the races as a group of comrades. And public houses were centres for Fenian socialization and recruitment alike; we should not see the social as competing with the political: pastime and revolutionism were entwined together.

For, despite James Stephens's conspiratorial instincts, Fenianism developed in Ireland something of a very public social quality, with visible demonstrations and gestures rather than revolutionary secrecy often enough being the norm. There was a conviviality to Fenianism, and this was very much on view: in marching, enjoying picnics, hold-ing public meetings, and so on; in the 1863–5 period, the attraction of pastime was arguably indeed 'the key to the mass appeal of Fenianism'.[48]

The social aspect of the Fenians' nationalism is also of importance in terms of their background: over half of the Dublin Fenians were artisans, and in general the skilled working class and lower middle class filled the ranks of the movement. And it did include female activists. The Ladies' Committee was founded in 1865, mainly by wives or relatives of male Fenians (including Mary Jane O'Donovan Rossa, Letitia Luby, and Ellen and Mary O'Leary); for six years this group raised money to support the families of incarcerated Fenians; and Fenian women also involved themselves in the smuggling of arms into Ireland. Does social composition give a guide to material motivation? Did lower-middle-class frustration play its part in leading people towards Fenian anger? Perhaps. But, in terms of goals, Fenian priorities remained firmly focused on the achievement of national independence, with all else secondary to this aim. Fenianism could, in places, be anti-landlord and anti-grazier; the growth in Fenian membership in parts of Connacht and Ulster related to small-farmer ambition for the ownership and redistribution of land. But the movement had no coherent social programme: great differences of view existed between its various leaders. And even where there was an economic argument, it tended to reinforce the primacy of separatism (as in the Fenian case that the land problem could not be solved within a UK framework, but only once independence had been won).

Winning independence by means of a violent secret society was not, of course, to the taste of the powerful Irish Catholic Church, whose clergy condemned and clashed with Fenianism frequently and significantly. But Fenian attitudes towards the Church and Catholicism were far from simple. The movement might be characterized as somewhat anti-clerical and yet still basically Catholic, the dispute being over the appropriate role for the clergy in politics and political life. This was fiercely contested territory. Charles Kickham, a practising Catholic, was keen to defend Fenians against Catholic clerical onslaught. It wasn't that he opposed Ireland being Catholic; indeed, he was delighted that it largely was so. But he stood up against clerical condemnation of Fenianism and could not imagine, in his own case, a clash between his Catholic faith and his Irish nationalist religion. He simply saw no conflict between them; and so he argued against listening to what he took to be a bad political lead from the priests.

In practice, the fact that most Fenians were loyal Catholics ruled out the prospect of the movement becoming full-bloodedly anti-clerical or secular. Instead, the line had to be that there was not necessarily a clash between being a good Catholic and a good Fenian simultaneously.

For his part, James Stephens was more fully anti-clerical in the continental European sense, instinctively hostile as he was to the priest being influential in politics. The more typical Kickham took a different view, having no objection to priestly involvement in politics – as long as priestly views accorded with his own. His only problem was when (as in the 1860s) the priests had, in his view, got it wrong politically. You should follow priests in spiritual matters, but not listen to them if they told you to do, politically, what you didn't want to do.

In the event, Fenianism survived Catholic clerical attacks robustly enough, with Kickham in particular playing a leading role in offering resolute defence against priestly onslaught. As so often, the Irish Church was unable mechanically to crush unwelcome nationalist politics among its flock. Some Fenians could be critical enough of their clergy, as with John O'Leary's mordant observation that 'I, however, personally think that priests are, as a rule, on a lower level of culture than lawyers, doctors, and others of the so-called educated classes.'[49] In practice, most Fenians simply remained devout Catholics and ignored political condemnation from the pulpit, a pattern which was to remain prominent in militant nationalist politics well into the twentieth century in Ireland.[50]

As with the Young Irelanders who had so inspired them, so also with the Fenians, political achievement lay less in contemporary victories than in the bequeathing of a rich legacy to later nationalist generations. As with the Young Irelanders, again, some of this involved literary legacies (O'Leary, Kickham, Davitt and others leaving influential accounts to feed the imagination of their political children and grandchildren). And they left also a legacy of martyrs: iconic dead heroes who saved the movement from ridicule for its military failure, and who contributed to the rich history available to future generations of Irish nationalists. On 18 September 1867 there was an attempt to rescue Thomas Kelly and Timothy Deasy, Fenians who had recently been captured in Manchester. In this rescue raid on the prison van which was taking the men from court to jail, a police officer (Sergeant Charles Brett) was killed. Kelly and Deasy escaped, and were not recaptured. But people were captured and charged for their part in the raid itself: five men were found guilty of murdering the policeman. Of these, one was pardoned and one had his sentence commuted to life imprisonment; the other three (William Allen,

Michael Larkin and Michael O'Brien) were executed on Saturday, 23 November 1867.

The three men showed bravery at their death, there was great sympathy among Irish nationalists for them, and they became political martyrs. Icons of republican resistance to British rule, more for their deaths than for their aggression itself, Allen, Larkin and O'Brien thus played a part in igniting and fuelling strong nationalist sentiment.

As so often in the history of modern Irish nationalism, the cultivated martyrdom of the Manchester three had a keenly Catholic quality to it: Masses – and there were a great many of them – for the souls of the Manchester martyrs were not religiously neutral acts. Not all, of course, celebrated. In the wake of the execution of Allen, Larkin and O'Brien, the *Irish Times* editorial argued that:

> The Fenian conspirators have now had fearful proof that assassination, under any circumstances, will not be treated as a political offence, but as an outrage upon national law. The three condemned men and their friends claimed immunity because the death of Brett was caused by an effort to rescue political prisoners. The law makes no such distinction, but rigidly exacts from the man proved to be guilty of the wilful death of another the penalty for murder.[51]

But the Fenians did, through their martyrs as through ballads, popular literature and attitudinal gesture, keep alive an alternative, aggressive nationalism in the late nineteenth century: in maintaining the language and rituals of separatism, they provided a human link through which a later generation of revolutionary zealots could be inspired. This could be seen again and again in Irish localities. On St Patrick's Day in 1874 in Lurgan a large number of police and soldiers had been present as a procession of St Patrick's Day celebrants marched into the town, with people carrying banners bearing likenesses of Allen, Larkin and O'Brien (as well as of Tone and Robert Emmet); the procession was attacked by an Orange party, and riotous violence ensued, the soldiers and police having forcibly to clear people off the streets; there were scenes of 'the greatest tumult and excitement. The soldiers remained in the streets to a late hour';[52] and militant nationalism fought prominently on. Later observers might not think that romantic intensity or Fenian extremism were necessarily a more truly Irish, more appropriate, or more beneficial phenomenon than restrained and patient moderation; but there were those who held that only aggressive struggle would suffice.

In contrast, constitutional nationalism involved a more conciliatory emphasis and strategy. A figure such as Isaac Butt (1813–79) – that 'fluent, convivial, and more than slightly dissipated'[53] founder of the movement for Irish Home Rule (political autonomy from Britain) – believed in the British empire which the Irish had done so much to build, and was very hostile to Irish separatism. As a Donegal Protestant Irish Tory, Butt had opposed Daniel O'Connell over Repeal in the early 1840s. But the Famine and the inspiration of Young Ireland between them helped to make a nationalist of him, and he played a major (if now rather occluded) role in stimulating the constitutional nationalist struggle into life, and setting in motion a viable national-constitutional politics. He was a tenacious politician, and a greatly talented man: the authoritative leader of Irish nationalism in the mid-1870s, he had been TCD-educated and was a brilliant lawyer who, after the 1848 Rising, defended William Smith O'Brien and Thomas Francis Meagher. He resembled that more famous, later Home Ruler Charles Stewart Parnell in being a socially conservative parliamentary politician, and in failing to achieve the Home Rule which he sought; indeed, Isaac Butt's was in some ways a failed career (all of the Irish legislation brought in the 1875 session by Butt and his colleagues in the House of Commons was either defeated or withdrawn, for example). But it was Butt who, in 1870, founded the Home Government Association upon whose foundations his more celebrated successor, Parnell, was to build, and the early-1870s emergence of Butt's Home Rule movement is one of the less loudly trumpeted fault-lines in modern Irish nationalism. The Home Government Association was superseded in November 1873 by the Home Rule League and its British sister organization, the Home Rule Confederation.

And then on 3 March 1874 a gathering of Irish Home Rule MPs, meeting in Dublin, set up a Home Rule Party. The aim was to form and consolidate a genuine party for Home Rule in the London House of Commons, a party which would pursue the restoration of an Irish legislature. The culture of Home Rule nationalism was striking and impressive at this stage. The moderate nationalist newspaper, the *Freeman's Journal*, observed that the 3 March gathering was 'characterized by that display of mutual consideration, moderation, and goodwill so necessary for success in the struggle for the restoration of our native legislature'. The resolutions adopted by the Home Rule MPs 'breathe that spirit of dignified moderation, of calm and self-contented earnestness, which is well calculated to convince the judgment of the English people that their interests and the interests of the empire will be as much served by the concession of Home Rule as those of Ireland herself'.[54] Looking back through the bloodstained lenses of modern Irish perspective, there is much to be celebrated here in this persuasively moderate style of nationalist struggle.

3

> I am pledged to obtain for Ireland the right of national self-government.
>
> Charles Stewart Parnell[55]

A cricket-loving, Protestant country gentleman with an anglicized accent, he was the forceful leader of Gaelic, Catholic Irish nationalists in their late-nineteenth-century struggle against England. An elitist, social conservative who sought political change through parliamentary methods, he led the masses in an explosive land struggle and in doing so formed an alliance with revolutionary Fenianism. Born in 1846, Charles Stewart Parnell was the dominant presence (during his life) within Irish nationalist politics and (after his death in 1891) he exerted a similar influence within nationalist Ireland's ensuing mythology.

He came from County Wicklow and enjoyed a distinguished family background, and an undistinguished 1860s career as a student at Magdalene College, Cambridge. Always sharply conscious of his social position and its implications, this Wicklow landowner was a proud man: argumentative and strong-minded, individualistic and markedly superstitious. He was a highly intense person of considerable emotional force, and a man characterized by extraordinary strength of purpose once engaged upon a mission.

His illustrious family was alluded to by his supporters during the early years of his political career, and family background is essential to understanding the man's impact on nationalist Ireland. Parnell was descended from a possible Cromwellian, who had arrived in Ireland at the time of the Restoration. His great-great-great-grandfather's brother, the TCD-educated poet Thomas Parnell (1679–1718), had known Jonathan Swift ('O Swift! If fame be life . . . /Thou canst not wholly die. Thy works will shine/To future times, and life in fame be thine');[56] and his father, John Henry Parnell (1811–59), was a Wicklow country gentleman, educated at Eton and Trinity College, Cambridge. If Parnell's specific background – that of the County Wicklow Anglo-Irish Protestant ascendancy – is vital to understanding his nationalism,[57] then figures such as his father, grandfather and great-grandfather feature prominently: John Henry Parnell was both social elitist and liberal in his political outlook; Parnell's grandfather, William Parnell (1780–1821), was a landlord, an MP and a man committed to both the recognition of Catholic civil rights and the improvement of Irish rural conditions; his great-grandfather, Sir John Parnell, was an anti-Union Patriot. In all of this there are discernible pre-echoes of (and possibly influences over) the career of the most famous of the Parnells. A friend of Thomas Moore, William Parnell saw it as natural for the landed gentry to lead rather than to clash with the peasantry, with the mass of the Irish nation. Parnell surely read the writings of his grandfather and, like him, was a landlord pragmatically involved in politics, sympathetic to the improvement of the Irish land system and of governmental representation alike.

So the oft-mentioned influence of Parnell's mother upon his politics, in directing him towards anglophobia, has probably been exaggerated. (Her profound social snobbery might have been a more telling area of influence or reinforcing example.) In truth Delia Parnell's own nationalism and her political activity have at times been exaggerated: her thinking on politics appears frequently to have been vague and confused (more than one observer even doubted her sanity). Certainly, she doesn't seem to have been especially sharp or influential in her own right, in political terms, and it is not at all clear that her political views played a key role in the development of young Charles's thinking.

Yet the combined influence of his family – towards land reform, parliamentary engagement and the redress of Catholic grievance – does seem to have framed his development. And there was nothing unusual in itself about Parnell entering politics nor, given some of his family ancestors, about his doing so in the paradoxical way that he did (as a Protestant landlord leading a Catholic peasant movement). Indeed, it might be argued that his entry into politics, and his stance when he did so, were logical enough given his background. He was at something of a loose end before his immersion in political life, was a far from affluent or fully occupied landlord, and opted for politics as a natural enough progression.

But there was nothing ordinary about his rise to political significance. Entering the House of Commons in 1875 as Home Rule MP for Meath, he came to dominate Irish nationalist politics at Westminster and to force nationalist Ireland's concerns upon the agenda of London politicians. And Parnell's nationalism involved far more than parliamentary assertion. He sustained what one leading Irish historian has called 'a brilliant but artificial alliance',[58] and this temporary welding together of disparate forces – land movement, parliamentary party, Fenians, Catholic Church – embodies one of the most powerful examples of nationalist Irish mobilization and communal struggle. The question is less why Parnell adopted the politics that he did (important though that question is) than why so many Irish people, with such different goals and backgrounds, decided in the late nineteenth century to pursue their goals within the framework of his nationalism. Why did it make sense for people to pursue land-related goals, or religious devotion, as part of a nationalist movement? To understand this, we need to consider in turn the four main parts of Parnell's political world, and then to ascertain the combined dynamics which unified and drove them.

First, the land, one of the most deep-rooted and evocative features of the Irish nationalist community's grievance and struggle. The image of the vulnerable, evicted tenant has long remained a powerful one within Irish nationalist history, and – despite the fact that evictions were less frequent than is sometimes assumed – the sense of suffering and of a need for redress certainly screams out again and again from the sources available for the late nineteenth century. At the start of 1882 reports of ongoing evictions in Carrowmenagh, Inishowen, in County Donegal were presented by the *Derry Journal* in poignant terms: 'the families turned out numbered in the aggregate between forty and fifty individuals, including one centenarian and a good many children'; 'In all the sad record of Ireland's story there is no word which carries a more painful suggestiveness than eviction.... The history of any country can produce no picture more darkened by wrong and sorrow than the scene of an Irish eviction.' The Carrow-menagh evictions took place in the necessary presence of soldiers and police officers, and the Scottish landlord ('little known personally in the place') was as sure of his case as were the tenants: 'How the case stands between agent and people is not easily put in words. Both are intensely impressed with the feeling of being in the right'; 'It is stated on part of the owner that the rents have not been raised for many years, but the people hold that this proves nothing for the landlord, as all along the rent was too much.'[59]

More 'painful performances' were in evidence in the same period (early 1882) elsewhere in Ireland, including County Fermanagh evictions for non-payment of rent or costs, carried out under military supervision: 'It was a sad spectacle to see the old blind man, carrying a weak little child, beseeching the bailiff to accept bail for the amount of the decree unpaid'; but 'the law took its course' and the eviction was effected.[60] Again in Fermanagh, the grievances felt by tenants against landlords were clear from the case of a Mrs Barrett, evicted in January 1882 from land belonging to a Colonel J. G. Irvine:

> Mrs Barrett, and her four little orphan children, were not – it is alleged – thrown out for non-payment of rent, but because she refused to sign an estate office document depriving her of any claims to compensation. She made a strong appeal to Colonel Irvine to allow her and her little helpless family to remain in the house, every stone and brick of which were built by her father, and that she was prepared to pay him whatever rent he thought fair.

But the eviction went ahead. 'As Mrs Barrett is the representative of one of the oldest families on the estate, her neighbours are naturally indignant at Colonel Irvine for making her the object of such treatment.'[61] Anger led to outrage in the land-related struggle: there were armed attacks on landlords and on those tenants who had taken farms from which people had been evicted;[62] often enough, private and personal disputes fed into such outrages, as agrarian and individual rivalries combined.

But if we are to understand the nature of this poignancy and viciousness, we have to see the central issues at stake, and these were both practical (security and survival on the land, day-to-day) and theoretical. For power over the land, legal rights in relation to land, and ultimately the question of the ownership of one's land, were vital issues to determine if one were indeed to attain security for oneself and one's family. And here we come to the struggle between landlord and tenant, between those who owned and those who worked Ireland's land. Tenants focused on what became known as the three Fs: fair levels of rent, fixity or security of tenure over the land, and free sale (allowing the tenant to sell their interest in the property – effectively, to sell their tenancy). But beyond these lay, ultimately, the issue of who rightfully had a claim to owning the land which tenants worked. John Stuart Mill had sharply identified the central question here, with his observation that: 'it is not the right of the rent-receiver, but the right of the cultivator, with which the idea of property is connected in the Irish popular mind'.[63]

Landholding might be represented in law as though Irish realities echoed those in England, but in truth this was not the case. A history of dispossession and of religiously defined communal division rendered the Irish case profoundly different. In Ireland, relations between landlord and tenant were not those of people bound together in community, but of people divided (especially by religion). This was a point which had been sharply noted by Fintan Lalor: 'The feelings that exist in England between landlord and tenant, coming down from old times, and handed on as an heirloom from generation to generation ... are here unknown.'[64] So landlords and tenants in Ireland held divergent views on the legitimacy of landownership: for many tenants, it was they who truly held a right of property, and many tended to treat the land as if it were indeed their own. So behind a question such as fair rent was an ulterior conception that the tenants had a right to the land in any case, without any rent being paid: rent only earned them what they thought should rightfully be theirs in the first place, and the illegitimacy of the very system of landlordism – rather than the important question of rent-levels alone – lay at the heart of peasant politics on the land. Ultimately, in the eyes of many Irish tenants, the only fair rent was no rent at all.

This issue concerning the legitimacy of landownership underlies the Irish nationalism of this late-nineteenth-century period,[65] and it was reflected in extensive debates about how to deal with Irish struggles over land. Various views were zealously espoused. In 1869 the Scottish-born Liberal agriculturalist and commentator James Caird (1816–92) intriguingly offered one perspective on how to solve the Irish land problem. Having visited Famine-hit Ireland in 1849, and now again twenty years later, Caird had obtained views from people in each Irish province and had become deeply engaged with his subject. 'Ireland, in 1869, presents a strange spectacle. The landlord's rents are well paid, the tenant farmers are prosperous, the labourers never had higher wages; yet there is a general feeling of uneasiness and discontent.' For the farmers wanted to secure their land: 'The demand which the farmers and their political advisers make, is "fixity of tenure", a phrase which may extend to a substantial transfer of the ultimate right of property, or may be modified to a reasonable security against precarious possession.' Caird identified the precariousness of yearly tenure, and the lack of compensation for tenants' improvements, as key problems. On eviction, he argued, a tenant should be entitled to the value of any improvements he had made; and tenancy arrangements should be altered to allow for the presumption of longer land tenure. Should the law be made more just in this fashion, Caird suggested, then the likelihood of agrarian crime as a means of redress would be significantly reduced. Here were arguments central to the land debate, and here also was a shrewd recognition both of the clash between community morality and law, and of the unity of community in such a struggle: 'although a great part of the tenantry are satisfied with their present position when under good landlords, of whom there are very many in Ireland, yet their feelings, as a body, go with those of their own class who are not so fortunately circumstanced'.[66]

By 1870 another pamphleteer argued strenuously for 'compensation for tenants' improvements', and held that,

It is now universally admitted that land legislation for Ireland is inevitable. The promises of the government, the universal cry of Irish tenants for redress of wrongs, the present condition of Irish agriculture, and the unsatisfactory relation of landlord and tenant, warrant the supposition that the settlement, or attempted settlement, of the Irish land question cannot be longer delayed.[67]

Again, Marcus Keane (land agent to the Marquis of Conyngham) wrote from County Clare in 1868 to the effect that, 'as land agent of several large estates, as well as a landed proprietor', his personal interests were firmly 'on the side of the landlord class'. Notwithstanding this, he had become a forceful advocate of tenant right; thirty years of 'experience and observation' regarding the land question had brought him to the view that justice and expediency demanded significant land reform. He argued that 'compensation for occupation right (which every good landlord has practically acknowledged) should be made a statutable right', and that 'tenancies from year to year, save in exceptional cases, should be practically abolished, and leases for thirty years be substituted'.[68] Landlords, tenants and whole population would benefit, Keane claimed, from such changes.

Contrary positions were also held. A pamphlet published in 1868 by the barrister R. M. Heron, for example, challenged the notion that the English conquest had generated modern Irish problems. In addressing 'the anomalous social condition of Ireland in the nineteenth century' – the poverty of Irish people so close to wealthy England – Heron wanted to challenge what he saw as current orthodoxy: the idea that Ireland's problems originated in 'the long series of wrongs inflicted for centuries by the English government'. This theory, he argued,

> is just one of those favourite popular cries which mislead the judgment away from a calm and critical examination of facts and causes. Has it ever occurred to those who raise this cry to ask, – What was the condition of Ireland when the conquest was effected in the reign of Henry II? The people were without industry or organization. The society, as compared with that of contemporary states, was of the rudest and most primitive character . . . From the loose way in which wrongs are imputed to England by national prejudice and foreign sympathy, one would be inclined to infer that the conclusion was that the conquest of Strongbow had destroyed Irish civilization. It would be much nearer the truth to say that this very conquest of Ireland was the first step in its acquaintance with modern civilization. It was the bringing of the island within the pale; subjecting the people to the laws and customs of feudality, the habits of subordination and labour, and the influence of commercial relations.

Regarding Irish land problems in the nineteenth century, Heron referred to 'the incapacity of the tenant class, and the indifference of landlords to enterprise'.[69] Similarly sceptical of English guilt towards Ireland was the Duke of Argyll, who in 1893 published the anti-Gladstonian *Irish Nationalism: An Appeal to History*: in this he argued that Irish problems were rooted, less in historical English malevolence or interference, than in disadvantages and difficulties and responsibilities which were located in Ireland itself. These disadvantages included geographical position (which had isolated Ireland from beneficial currents), geology (with an Irish lack of great mineral resources), neglect of educational development, and patterns of landholding. Like Gladstone himself, Argyll turned for sanction to Edmund Burke ('the greatest Irishman who has ever lived, except perhaps two others – Bishop Berkeley and the Duke of Wellington'), quoting the lines:

> what grievance has Ireland, as Ireland, to complain of with regard to Great Britain; unless the protection of the most powerful country upon earth – giving all her privileges, without exception, in common to Ireland, and reserving to herself only the painful pre-eminence of tenfold burdens, be a matter of complaint. The subject, as a subject, is as free in Ireland, as he is in England. As a member of the empire, an Irishman has every privilege of a natural-born Englishman, in every part of it, in every occupation, and in every branch of commerce.

Argyll concluded his argument with more words from Burke: 'I must speak the truth. I must say that all the evils of Ireland originate within itself.'[70]

The broad issues variously considered by Caird, Keane, Heron and Argyll went to the heart of the politics of Irish land in the late nineteenth century. How did one address tenants' concerns regarding the precarious possession of their holding, or the compensation due to them for their investment in the land? To what extent were the problems of Irish land conflict the fault of Britain, and to what degree did they more simply rest with inappropriate tenant and landlord behaviour in Ireland itself? And how far was there a clash between existing law and reasonable justice? Could one hold that contemporary legality was neither fair nor binding on the tenantry, based as such law was on usurpation, historical injustice and abuse of power wrought by England in Ireland?

Into all of this strode Parnell. Relations between landlords and tenants in his own county, Wicklow, were generally good, as were Parnell's relations with his own tenants. But while Wicklow had traditionally been blessed with comparatively good landlords and prosperous tenants, deep problems existed across much of the rest of the island. Parnell himself made his position clear early enough. In an address to the electors of County Dublin in 1874 he proclaimed firmly: 'I believe security for his tenure and the fruits of his industry to be equally necessary to do justice to the tenant and to promote the prosperity of the whole community.'[71] In the following year he declared that, 'Without fixity of tenure and fair rents the tenants would never be happy, nor would the country be prosperous.'[72] Beyond this Parnell held that the tenant, as well as the landlord, had property rights which deserved recognition and protection: he favoured tenant purchase as the solution to the Irish land problem, with the person who farmed the soil doing so as its owner. The politics of land, then, represented one of the most forceful instances of economically-driven nationalism in modern Ireland.

After 1870 it was indeed on the tenant farmers, rather than on the landlords, that British parliamentary attention primarily focused (and in the last thirty years of the century it was the tenant farmer who emerged as the dominating socio-political force in nationalist Ireland). In 1870 itself Gladstone's First Land Act made a significant concession to tenant concern by giving legal status to tenant right, or the Ulster custom, where it already existed: this custom involved the right of a departing tenant to sell his interest in the land, including the value of any improvements made during that tenant's occupancy.[73]

William Ewart Gladstone (1809–98) had been concerned with the economic situation in Ireland long before he became Prime Minister in 1868. But the 1870 measure only represented a limited part of what Irish tenants felt to be necessary. Matters were intensified with a late-1870s agricultural depression and crisis caused by the combined effect of poor weather, poor harvests, comparatively poor prices and increased agricultural competition from Australia and the United States. The west was especially badly affected and, while the whole rural economy suffered, tillage was particularly hard hit. The year 1879 was a dreadful one for Irish agriculture, marked by a severely cold winter, disease among animals, and drastically falling cattle prices. Tenants frequently now fell into arrears with their rent and some duly went bankrupt; with some landlords seeking to exact usual rents from their tenants despite the agricultural crisis (and prosecuting and evicting some of their tenantry), agrarian agitation was produced. One specific instance could be found near Irishtown in County Mayo, where tenants were pressed for arrears of rent and lay under the threat of eviction. In March 1879 County Mayo-born radical nationalist Michael Davitt became aware of the case and embarked on a dramatic initiative. Together with the separatist James Daly, Davitt organized a meeting which was attended by thousands at Irishtown in April: rents were consequently lowered in the area, and a fire of agitation had been sparked into vigorous life. In August 1879 Davitt set up the National Land League of Mayo with a view to undoing the existing land laws of Ireland, and indeed to getting rid of evictions and of the rents which many farmers considered to be an unacceptable demand in the context of agricultural crisis and low prices. Agrarian agitation thus emerged in Ireland's western counties directly from this 1879 crisis and hardship.

Davitt himself had joined the IRB as a nineteen-year-old in 1865 – having come from a family with a tradition of being 'agin the government'[74] – and he was a Fenian who was keen on doing away with landlordism: he came to favour land nationalization as the answer to rural Ireland's question (an idea which never gained much ground in Irish minds during this period, any more than similar ideas would catch on in Ireland when in later generations they were espoused by figures such as James Connolly or Peadar O'Donnell). But while Davitt's agitation never brought about such revolution, it did transform modern Irish nationalism, and his association with Parnell is the key to understanding this. (The two men had first met shortly after Davitt's release in December 1877 from Dartmoor, where he had been incarcerated for treason–felony.)

For after the 1877–9 agricultural adversity facing peasant Ireland, and the terrible 1879 harvest, the impetus for a wider land movement was created. In 1879, therefore, the Irish National Land League was founded by Davitt in Dublin, with the proud Parnell as its President. In response to a circular from Parnell himself, a meeting was held at the Imperial Hotel on Wednesday, 21 October: 'the objects of the League are, first, to bring about a reduction of rack-rents; second, to facilitate the obtaining of the ownership of the soil by the occupiers.'[75]

And so, with the 1879 fusing of the forces for land agitation and nationalist political advance, a New Departure in Irish politics had been initiated.

Certainly, for Michael Davitt, the League was a means of preventing mass evictions of tenants, and ultimately of doing away with landlordism itself. But if Davitt was the League's founding father, Parnell was its President and its dominant spirit. The Land League initiated a campaign of agrarian protest against what were thought to be unfair rents; when rent levels were not lowered, rent was often refused and the struggle took on a new character. Evictions were opposed – legally and illegally – and ostracism and force were used against those who took on land which had previously been occupied by now-evicted tenants. Bailiffs serving writs were also targeted, as were landlords themselves, farmers who were paying (or thought to be paying) rent, and farmers who refused to join the League. Threatened and actual violence reflected and intensified the fact that the 1879–82 Land War involved much bitterness, and the Land League's agitation undoubtedly had practical effect – helping, for example, to prompt the crucially significant 1881 Land Act. This (Gladstone's Second Land Act) endorsed the three Fs long pursued by Irish tenant farmers, providing for fixity or security of tenure, free sale of a tenant's interest in a property, and fair rents (decreeing that special land courts should determine rent levels).[76]

But beyond the three Fs lay the goal of replacing landlordism itself with a system of peasant proprietorship. The 1885 Ashbourne Act empowered a Land Commission to advance money to tenants for the purchase of their holdings, and to purchase whole estates for resale; an Amendment Act of 1888 increased the limit of advances allowed. The 1891 Balfour Act made the Land Commission permanent, while the Wyndham Act of 1903 furthered the process of the purchase and subsequent resale of estates to occupying tenants. Thus occurred the effective establishment of peasant ownership in Ireland: far from Davitt's land nationalization, here was a reinforcement of small-scale land possession which bolstered rural conservatism and private ownership for many decades to come, helping to define a socially conservative Irish nationalism in the process.

So one key strand of Parnell's nationalism lay in his leadership of a land agitation which had been born of agricultural crisis, which focused on specific mid-term demands, and which eventually revolutionized Irish landholding culture (albeit in a socially conservative fashion). Davitt himself was clear about the extent and the practical nature of what had been done. The Land League episode, in his view, undoubtedly constituted a 'revolution',[77] and he was explicit and emphatic about what he saw as the League's practical results and achievements: it was with a list of such achievements (Land Acts, the conversion of British politicians to the politics of Home Rule, and so on), that he began his own famous book on the League.[78] This was no foggily romantic nationalist campaign, but a practical, exigency-driven and goal-oriented nationalist struggle. An Irish nationalist meeting in Glasgow on Wednesday, 31 December 1884 heard MP William Redmond (1861–1917) ask, 'Why should they support Mr Parnell and the Irish Parliamentary Party? Because' – he said –

> that party, led by that man, had completely revolutionized the Irish people and Ireland ... They had dealt with the land question, but they were not going to be satisfied with the Land Act. Landlordism was not a thing the Irish people were going to forgive in a hurry, for it was an institution whose hands were stained absolutely with the blood of the Irish people for generations gone ... The Irish Parliamentary Party intended to break up the landlord clique, and that they meant to do by buying them up with British money and so get them out of Ireland.[79]

And here was the Parnellite paradox: why was a socially conservative Protestant country gentleman leading a radical, Catholic, anti-landlord mobilization? Even though in the mid-1870s there still existed a significant landowning presence among Irish Home Rule politicians, the spectacle of a landlord enthusing over tenant right remains a striking one (and many within Parnell's own class in Wicklow indeed considered him to have acted as a political traitor, duly treating him as such; to be the head of one community could in practice lead to ostracism from the other).

The explanation[80] behind this paradox lies at the heart of Parnell's own view of the relation between the land and Irish nationalism. Solving the land question would, in his view, favourably determine the kind of nationalism which flourished in Ireland. Parnell thought that if one could solve the conflict between landlords and tenants over land, then one would facilitate the landlords' participation in the national movement as its natural leaders: as such, they would be able properly to fulfil their duties in their natural role as responsive leaders of the Irish people. As Parnell himself put it in 1879: 'if you had the land question settled on a permanent basis you would remove the great reason that now exists to prevent the large and influential class of Irish landlords falling in with the demand for self-government'.[81] So, while Fenians tended to argue that self-rule needed to be achieved before problems such as the land could be resolved, Parnell argued essentially the opposite. In his view, the land question could indeed be effectively answered within a UK parliamentary framework. This done, the conflict between landlords and peasants over rent would be over, and the landlords would be able to take the place which Parnell the landlord held to be natural for them at the head of the Irish national movement.

The first part of this process did indeed come to pass, with the British state effectively lending Irish peasants the money with which to buy their farms from their landlords; this was the most important feature of Westminster land legislation in the late nineteenth and early twentieth centuries, producing a culture of owner-occupancy throughout much of Ireland.

The second part of the trick – that the landlords should take their place at the head of the national movement – did not succeed. But if we are to understand Parnell's own conception of the nature of Irish nationalist politics we must recognize both the centrality of land to his vision, and what this implied about his nationalism. Two points are vital. First, his was an essentially conservative politics. He sought to ensure that social hierarchy was preserved rather than subverted. And although he presided over a revolutionary shift in Irish landownership, it was a socially conservative change which occurred: contrary to Davitt's more genuinely revolutionary aspirations towards land nationalization, Parnell's policy in effect produced the most conservative kind of nationalists imaginable, in the form of small-farm owners committed to private property. Second, Parnell's politics recognized what the Fenians tended to miss, namely that divisions within the Irish nation, among the people of the island, were as important as conflicts between Ireland and Britain for the definition of the nature of Irish nationalism. Solve the tension between landlord and peasant (code in many cases for Protestant and Catholic respectively), and you would remove one of the debilitating conflicts within nationalist Ireland.

In this sense Parnell's was a conciliatory form of politics, and his radicalism was a socially conservative one: he opposed Davitt's land nationalization and wanted to transform rather than to eliminate his own landlord class, stressing that they should receive a fair price for the land which they would have to sell. Parnell's argument on the land had been to some extent prefigured by John Mitchel's thinking in the 1840s: Mitchel had thought that the Irish movement should be fully national, that therefore the landed classes should be a part of it, and that the tenure question had thus to be solved in a way which was acceptable simultaneously to landlords and occupiers.[82] But it was under Parnell's light that this argument became practically pursued in terms of mass agitation and communal mobilization.

During this economic crisis and Land War of 1879–82, women made very significant contributions. The Ladies' Land League (LLL) is the usual focus here, and it is indeed important. Started in America in 1880, in 1881 it was established in Ireland too. The guiding spirits were Parnell's sisters, Anna and Fanny. In the summer of 1880 it had been Fanny Parnell (1849–82) who had had the initial idea from which the LLL sprang: the notion was that if the talents of women were harnessed, then the land movement would be energized in a new and powerful way. Just like many men, so too Fanny Parnell saw the land movement within a nationalist frame: in the 1860s she had displayed Fenian sympathies, her nationalist commitment was deep and lasting, and central to her nationalist politics was a staunch commitment to the Land League and its crusade. Indeed, for her the land agitation was the central struggle; whether nationalists should adopt constitutional or violent methods was of less importance to her (she had some close links with Irish-American Fenians). A true Irish nationalist celebrity, Fanny Parnell was, by the time of her death, a genuinely national figure. Like Fanny, Anna Parnell (1852–1911) was ardent and courageous in her support for the Irish land cause and, again like Fanny, she wrote poetry. (Fanny Parnell's 'Hold the Harvest!' (1879) gained a certain celebrity: 'Now are you men, or are you kine, ye tillers of the soil?/Would you be free, or evermore the rich man's cattle toil?/The shadow on the dial hangs that points the fatal hour –/Now hold your own! or, branded slaves, forever cringe and cower.'[83])

It was Anna Parnell who, in January 1881, actually founded the LLL, and she and other women tirelessly engaged in public meetings (at which Anna frequently spoke), in organizational work, in the struggle against evictions, and in support of those who had indeed been put off their land. When in October 1881 the government dissolved the Irish National Land League (declaring it illegal and arresting its leaders) the LLL took over the land agitation and defiantly kept it going. In addition to its respectable leadership, many peasant women joined the LLL. So while the Ladies' League involved female leadership, and highly visible, celebrated figures, it also reflected a wider female involvement in nationalist mobilization.

And indeed women's involvement in the Land War went far beyond the LLL. From the beginning of the struggle many women actively participated at local level. For women were involved in the male-dominated Land League itself: there were limitations on their role (they would be among the crowd at Land League meetings, while the speakers on the platform would be men); but they did act in repossession of land from which people had been evicted, and some were imprisoned as a consequence of such activity. Women took part in boycotts, they protested against evictions, and their role as actors in the communal land agitation was important.

If land was the first element in Parnellite nationalism, then Home Rule was the interrelated second. A solution to the land conflict would, in Parnell's view, remove one obstacle to appropriate and harmonious national progress. And that progress involved the struggle for self-government for Ireland.

Parnell and his political party pursued what they considered to be a properly representative Irish assembly, one which would enjoy limited legislative autonomy from Britain. Such autonomy – Home Rule for Ireland – would, as Parnell himself put it in 1890, 'enable us to take part in the government of our own country' and 'enable us to develop the long neglected resources of our country'.[84] In such a view, an Irish parliament was essential to Irish freedom and to proper government alike. Ageing Parnellite eccentric The O'Gorman Mahon (1800–91) declared in 1874 that he was committed to bringing about Home Rule for Ireland, 'believing, as I do, that in her native Parliament alone can she hope to attain that freedom which as a nation she is entitled to demand and assert'.[85]

Parnell presented the case in terms of the restoration of an old parliament, and as the embodiment of government through due consent rather than through coercion and corruption. As MP for Meath (1875–80) and for Cork city (1880–91), he acted on London's parliamentary stage, and did so with impressively dramatic effect. He had, of course, inherited a politically distinctive family tradition here, with Irish patriotic parliamentarians among his ancestors: more specifically, this legacy appears to have involved a strong emphasis upon representative, responsive, consensual government – something of which one can hear clear echoes in his demand for a Dublin parliament. Initially making little obvious parliamentary mark, during 1877–8 he came to prominence through a campaign of obstruction in the House of Commons: with a small group of Irish MPs he adopted a policy of systematically delaying English and Scottish legislation introduced into the House, by means of deliberately lengthy and irrelevant speeches (these speeches, in Gladstone's rather acidic words, 'sometimes rising to the level of mediocrity, and more often grovelling amidst mere trash in unbounded profusion'[86]).

But parliament was his stage in more serious manner also. Not only was this to be his chosen means of answering the land question, it was also both the method and the goal of his Home Rule ambitions and it was on parliament that much of his power rested. In 1874 Home Rulers won sixty seats in the House of Commons; from 1880 onwards Parnell became Chairman of the Irish Parliamentary Party, and his creation of a disciplined, independent Irish parliamentary grouping enabled him to pursue Home Rule by constitutional means, and to force the issue on to the British high-political agenda. In 1882 he dissolved the Land League; this was then replaced by the very different Irish National League, established in October 1882 for the primary purpose of pursuing Irish national self-government (and with the secondary aim of supporting the reform of the Irish land system).

Parnell's parliamentary focus both reflected European and UK realities, and involved a particular political alliance in England. During the nineteenth century organized political parties became, across much of Europe, the main vehicle for political expression, argument and change; and the establishment of this liberal-democratic norm had the most profound (and almost certainly benign) consequences for the nature of Irish nationalist struggle. The notion of parliaments and of organized party politics, of bargaining centrally through parliamentary means, came to define much – if not most – modern nationalist practice in Ireland. And, as so often, this was an ironic by-product of that very Union with Britain against which nationalists in Ireland so frequently campaigned.

More specifically, Parnell himself aimed to hold a House of Commons balance of power between the two main UK parties; after the 1885 General Election this goal was realized. So, not for the last time, Irish politicians at Westminster craftily used their numerical usefulness in order to magnify their political significance. Having established his and his Party's importance in England, Parnell was able to advance the cause of Home Rule through his alliance with Gladstonian liberalism. Unlike the Tories, post-1882 Liberals were prepared to accept the substance of the Irish nationalist case: namely, that the real issue in Irish politics concerned legitimate, historically rooted, communal grievance in the realms of politics and economics. Gladstone was the vital figure here. Building on the broad Liberal acceptance of an Irish nationalist framework, he was happy to support the cause of Home Rule (to which he was effectively converted in 1885). He had long been concerned with Irish problems: when he came to power in 1868 he did so as one explicitly committed to dealing with them. After his adoption of Home Rule, however, his engagement was more momentous for the evolution of nationalist Irish history. In February 1886 Gladstone replaced the Conservative Salisbury as Prime Minister and prepared a Home Rule Bill for Ireland. In June this (Gladstone's first) Government of Ireland Bill was defeated in the House of Commons by 343 votes to 313. The July 1886 General Election (following Gladstone's resignation) returned Salisbury to power. But, after his 1892 General Election victory, Gladstone introduced his second Government of Ireland Bill in February 1893, this time seeing it defeated in the House of Lords in September of the same year.

Gladstone's imperial preference was for self-government and so his Irish policy fitted into a wider pattern. Conciliation rather than coercion was his approach in relation to South Africa and to India, and so again Ireland matched other parts of his thinking. And Gladstone did not see Home Rule as undoing, but rather as balancing and strengthening, the Union. He sought, not Irish independence, but rather that the empire should be more flexibly and much better run.

The Irish would, in his view, be enabled through Home Rule to run Ireland for their own advantage within the British empire.

So British parliamentary alliances and British political thinking provided the context for Parnellite Home Rule nationalism, just as Irish nationalist argument provided the ideological framework within which English Liberals engaged with Irish politics. Gladstone himself approached the politics of Ireland with a species of crusading enthusiasm, and his Christianity was a vital influence here. If Aristotle and Burke were major influences upon the great man,[87] then so too was his commitment to the politics of Christian conscience and responsibility: his early evangelical influences were overlaid with a later High Church orientation, but throughout he was motivated towards what he considered the appropriately just, Christian path. And it was an intentionally conservative path. From Burke, whom he frequently read, Gladstone had derived a pragmatic approach towards historically-minded, gradual change, holding that reform should come through organic rather than revolutionary historical shifts. Thus both Gladstone and Parnell – the two leaders whose political relationship in these years did so much to define Irish nationalism – were essentially conservative in their approach.

Other intriguing influences might perhaps have played a part in fine-tuning Gladstone's Irish politics. He knew the Clontarf-born and TCD-educated Home Ruler, theatre-manager and writer Bram Stoker (1847–1912), and he read Stoker's novel *The Snake's Pass* shortly after it was published in 1890. Stoker was a devoted admirer of Gladstone, and had sent him a copy of the novel, which the two men were promptly to discuss and which Gladstone apparently liked: 'Mr Gladstone was then full of Irish matters,' Stoker recalled, and had been especially intrigued by the oppressive role of the gombeen man (usurer, money-lender) in rural Irish society; the great man had spoken 'very kindly and very searchingly' of *The Snake's Pass*.[88] And this latter tale would indeed have echoed – and surely reinforced – some of Gladstone's conceptions of Ireland, for the novel tells of a wealthy English gentleman who falls in love in the west of Ireland with a poor woman of vulnerable, rural background who has fallen victim to the villainy of a grasping gombeen man. This money-lender has, in the words of one character, 'made the law an engine of oppression'.[89] So here we have Gladstone enjoying a tale of a beautiful but troubled land, romantic

1. Theobald Wolfe Tone.
The father of Irish republicans,
Tone cut his own throat after being
sentenced to death for his part in
the Rebellion of 1798.

2. The United Irish Patriots of 1798. Left to right: William Corbet (1779–1842),
Michael Dwyer (1771–1826), Robert Emmet (1778–1803), Thomas Addis Emmet
(1764–1827), Lord Edward Fitzgerald (1763–98), James Hope (1764–1846?),
William Jackson (1737?–95), Henry Joy MacCracken (1767–98), William James
Macneven (Macnevin) (1763–1841), Samuel Neilson (1761–1803), Arthur O'Connor
(1763–1852), Archibald Hamilton Rowan (1751–1834), Thomas Russell (1767–1803),
Henry Sheares (1753–98), John Sheares (1766–98), James Napper Tandy (1740–1803),
Matthew Teeling (died 1798), Theobald Wolfe Tone (1763–98).

3. *Above.* 'United Irishmen in Training', James Gillray's satirical depiction of Wolfe Tone's supporters, 1798.

4. *Left.* Henry Grattan (1746–1820). The leader of the Patriot Party, who secured legislative independence for Ireland in 1782 and opposed union with England in 1800. Engraving from an original painting by Alexander Pope.

5. *Above*. 'The Holy War – A Vision'. A satirical cartoon, published in 1826, depicting the struggle for Catholic Emancipation in Ireland, which shows the Pope engaged in debate with the English clergy and the Duke of York.

6. *Right*. Daniel O'Connell, *c.*1820. Popularly known as 'the Liberator', O'Connell founded the Catholic Association in 1823 to fight for emancipation. Elected to Parliament in 1828, he only took his seat after the Emancipation Act was forced through by Wellington's government in 1829.

7. *Above.* A contemporary cartoon showing O'Connell taking his seat, while the Duke of Wellington and Sir Robert Peel, the Home Secretary, look on.

8. *Left.* In 1843, O'Connell, now keen to see the Union between England and Ireland repealed, began organising what *The Times* called monster meetings throughout the country. The first was at Trim, County Meath, which attracted a crowd of over one hundred thousand. It was estimated that three-quarters of a million people assembled on the Hill of Tara to hear the Liberator speak.

9. The Fenian attack on the prison van containing Thomas Kelly and Timothy Deasy in Manchester in September 1867. For their part in this fatal raid, William Allen, Michael Larkin and Michael O'Brien were executed in November that year.

10. Howard Helmick's *Reading the News: The Proclamation of the Land League*. Founded by Michael Davitt (1846–1906) in 1879 and with Charles Stewart Parnell as President: 'the objects of the League are, first, to bring about a reduction of rack-rents; second, to facilitate the obtaining of the ownership of the soil by the occupiers.'

11. Charles Stewart Parnell (1846–91), Home Ruler,
Member of Parliament and 'the uncrowned king of Ireland',
as seen by 'Spy' in *Vanity Fair*, September 1880.

12. Irish Home Rulers in the House of Commons in 1881.
Inset is Michael Davitt.

13. The Royal Irish Constabulary protecting a government reporter at a meeting of Parnell's supporters in 1886.

and beguiling in its depiction, and yet requiring the urgent adjustment of social wrongs and suffering in its countryside; into this exotic but unjust world steps the decent, powerful Englishman, and the story ends benignly: with the villain dead, the English gentleman and the beautiful Irish peasant happily marry. If only the story of Home Rule had ended in such fairy-tale fashion.

For Home Rulers themselves, the benefits of the proposed auton-omy would include far greater economic prosperity, as argued, for example, by Cork-born journalist Justin McCarthy (1830–1912; an admirer of Gladstone and, as it happened, also a friend of Bram Stoker). Elected MP for County Longford in 1879, in the following year McCarthy became Vice-Chairman of the Irish Parliamentary Party, assuming the position of Chairman in 1890. Long-resident in England, he campaigned there for Home Rule and among his argu-ments were the economic: 'Our capital under a Home Rule govern-ment,' he told the House of Commons in 1886, 'would be induced to flow, for we should have industry and trade. We would bring all the resources of the country into play, as to Irish fisheries, piers, harbours, canals, navigation, roads.' A Home Rule parliament would not, he said, be 'a parliament of politicians, but one of earnest, energetic, practical men, anxious to restore the prosperity of their country'.[90]

Despite the centrality of parliament to Parnell's political career, he was in two senses a politician whose ambition stretched beyond Westminster. First, and most clearly, his deployment of parliamentary leverage was with a view to the establishment of a different, Irish parliament. By the end of the nineteenth century Ireland was, if anything, *over*-represented in the House of Commons; but in Parnellite thinking this was not the point, since his criticism of Westminster government of Ireland was that the London parliament was not – indeed, could not be – sufficiently responsive to those who were to be governed in Ireland itself, and that those in Westminster could not have the confidence or trust of the Irish whom they currently sought to govern. A Dublin parliament was required if truly representative Irish politics were to be established. Second, while Parnell sought to express Irish nationalist grievance and to seek redress of that grievance through Westminster, his application of pressure there depended also on extra-parliamentary muscle. Nineteenth-century Irish nationalism involved the attempt to bargain with the powerful, and the existence of a mass, popular movement beyond the walls of parliament undoubtedly helped here.

As so often, therefore, Parnell inhabited ambiguous territory: he was a parliamentarian who deployed the implied threat of extra-parliamentary muscle, a London politician who relied on Irish-based power, and someone who sought to use Westminster legislation in order to remove Ireland from the jurisdiction of that very parliament.

Although he was ultimately unable to deliver Home Rule, Gladstone did achieve a significant degree of popularity among Irish nationalists for a time. In June 1887 he was even presented with an inscribed shield, a hurley and a match ball by the Cork County Executive of the IRB-dominated Gaelic Athletic Association (GAA). This last gesture held some significance given that the third element of Parnellite nationalism did involve the politics of force, and here the IRB were crucial. Michael Davitt had tried to recruit Parnell into the IRB in 1878, and it is possible that Parnell did actually take the IRB oath in 1882 in Dublin.[91] If so, then this reflects the extent to which Parnell the parliamentarian was prepared to go in order to try to persuade separatists that they could indeed rely upon him. Here again we meet the ambiguity of Parnellite nationalism. Fenians tended to be convinced of the futility of constitutionalism, and yet here was the great constitutional leader playing to their ears. In early 1882, under the so-called 'Kilmainham Treaty', Parnell was released from prison[92] on the understanding that he backed law and order and that he opposed agrarian violence; and yet it seems that he might have taken the IRB oath immediately upon his release from jail. No simple notion of there being a clear-cut division between constitutionalism and physical force within Irish nationalism can survive such ambiguity.

Yet there were none the less rival centres of gravity for those respectively enthusing over aggressive or parliamentary politics. Parnell might hint at shared goals – as with his famous, *Job*-like statement in Cork in January 1885, that 'no man has the right to fix the boundary to the march of a nation. No man has the right to say to his country, "Thus far shalt thou go and no further," and we have never attempted to fix the *ne plus ultra* to the progress of Ireland's nationhood, and we never shall.' On the central question of 'national self-government for Ireland', therefore, Parnell hinted that theirs was but part of a potentially longer struggle: 'while we struggle today for that which may seem possible for us with our combination, we must struggle for it with the proud consciousness that we shall not do anything to hinder or prevent better men who may come after us from gaining better things than those for which we now contend'.[93]

But his preferred methods were less vicious than those of his Fenian allies, and his underlying thinking diverged from theirs. Those who practised Irish nationalist violence justified their actions in part by the claim that English rule in Ireland was not only illegitimate but was also itself sustained by violent rather than constitutional methods; in 1885 Michael Davitt himself suggested that 'England's rule of Ireland is government by physical force, and not by constitutional methods',[94] a central, legitimizing idea for republican violence of later generations too.

Such views could legitimate cruel and awful acts. Distance might lend a certain romance to the actions of nationalist secret societies, but their intimidation and brutality have involved often thuggish means of establishing communal control over neighbours or opponents. The 1882 Phoenix Park murders embodied a famously gruesome example: on 6 May the Fenian offshoot, the Invincibles, killed the recently appointed Liberal Chief Secretary for Ireland, Lord Frederick Cavendish (together with his Under-Secretary Thomas Burke) outside the Vice-Regal Lodge in Dublin. Public and political opinion in Ireland and Britain was understandably horrified by such brutality (the men had been 'hacked to death by twelve-inch long surgical knives'[95]), especially when it had been deployed against people recognizably interwoven with many lives: Burke was the son of a Galway Catholic (his brother Augustus was a very able painter); Cavendish had been married to one of Gladstone's nieces.

Given such horror, and Parnell's flirtation with aggressive Fenianism, it might seem strange that the fourth element in his nationalist alliance should be the Catholic Church and community. Yet, Protestant though he was, and anti-Fenian though the Catholic establishment tended to be, this Catholic dimension to Parnell's politics was of profound significance. He himself demonstrated a sharp awareness of the need to have the Catholic Church on his side, and was most careful not to alienate the clergy. After some early mistrust, by the early 1880s better relations had been established between this Protestant landlord and the Irish Catholic Church which lay at the heart of nationalist Irish community: he was prepared to endorse with some enthusiasm the idea of denominational education; Catholic priests became integral to his movement; and Catholic clerical backing was very important to him during much of his career.

And other key nationalists of this period similarly recognized and identified the importance of Catholicism to nationalist politics. Michael Davitt in the mid-1880s affirmed the centrality, within the Irish nationalist struggle, of forcing the English to allow 'the Catholics of Ireland religious equality'.[96] In a letter of 1874, Home Ruler The O'Gorman Mahon asserted his Catholic loyalty against suggestions of an unCatholic attitude on his part: 'I yield to no man living in regard and reverence for the visible Head of the Church [the Pope] to which I have the happiness to belong.' Mahon had stated that he was an Irishman first, but now tellingly added: 'who can point the difference between an Irishman and a Catholic?'[97] O'Connellite and subsequent Home Ruler William Joseph O'Neill Daunt (1807–94) as a young man had converted to Catholicism, considered it the only true religious faith, and thought of the Catholic Church as unambiguously the Church of the Irish people.[98] Even John Mitchel, though himself not a Catholic, explicitly identified Catholic grievances and the non-freedom of Catholics in Ireland as central to his conception of what the Irish nationalist struggle was about.[99]

Such attitudes were crisply mirrored by Catholic clerical support for late-nineteenth-century nationalism in Ireland. Many clergy became involved in the 1879–82 Land War; admittedly, there was some anxiety concerning the revolutionary potential of the Land League, yet this tended to reinforce a priestly sense that it was necessary to become involved, and that priests should themselves direct the movement along appropriate channels. Catholic bishops were initially far from enthusiastic about Home Rule itself, but they later came to endorse it; indeed, from 1881 onwards the Catholic Church was crucially and integrally part of the Parnellite advance. This had organizational implications, and it also counted heavily in terms of local clerical guidance as to how the flock should vote.

And it is at local level that the interweaving of organized Catholicism and nationalist struggle becomes most clear. An October 1879 land demonstration at Gort, County Galway, provides a typical example. Reflecting grave concern for the tenants and poor of the district, this large, open-air gathering in the heaviest of rain was an emphatically nationalist event and it was presided over by Catholic priests. On a platform in the market square (adorned with banners proclaiming messages such as 'No Evictions'), the Chair of the meeting – the Very Rev. Shannon – was the fulcrum of the event: 'You know,' he said, 'that the object of this meeting is, first, to press upon the landlords to give a reduction of their rents according to the great depreciation in prices both of agricultural produce and also of stock of every description.'[100] At such events, the priest expressed the politics of nationalist Ireland.

Clearly, Irish Catholicism was far from monolithic regarding political issues. At high-clerical level this was reflected, for example, in the tussle between the ultramontane Archbishop of Dublin, Paul Cullen (1803–78: a sharp opponent of Fenianism and of much Irish nationalist mobilization) and the more obviously patriotic Archbishop of Tuam, John MacHale (1791–1881). Equally clear, however, was the integral significance of Catholicism for any powerful political movement in late-nineteenth-century nationalist Ireland. It was less that priests exerted mechanical influence over the people in terms of political decisions (though this plainly did occur on occasions) than that the influence of Catholic teaching and thinking was so pervasive as to require no such crude application of power at particular moments.[101] Catholicism was one of the central languages of cultural communication and meaning within nationalist Ireland.

This was evident again and again at local level, especially perhaps where the struggle was most instistent. Irish nationalist (and special correspondent for the *Daily News* in Donegal) Jeremiah MacVeagh noted in a pamphlet on Gweedore that at the end of the 1880s there the peasants' 'lives are a continual struggle and their habitations a disgrace to civilization'; the 'miserable hovels' in which they lived 'absolutely defy description'. When in 1887 there was a heavy fall in the value of produce, tenants claimed a corresponding rent reduction but were refused this by their landlords. In 1888 the peasants therefore combined together under the leadership of the local Catholic priest and withheld rent from the landlord, until he should see fit to treat them more fairly. In 1889 evictions ensued, accounts of which, said MacVeagh:

read like those of a country in a state of insurrection; for what with roads cut at intervals, and bridges blown up, and fierce resistance, the January evictions proved very sensational. At three houses in particular, such fierce resistance was offered that an order was given to the military to fire on the defenders, and the houses are since landmarks in the locality, being known respectively as Doogan's Fort, O'Donnell's Fort, and Curran's Fort.

But at the very onset of the tenants' struggle the person leading them was the celebrated Father MacFadden, parish priest of Gweedore; and at the January 1888 Falcarragh meeting which had inaugurated the communal campaign, another priest who was deeply involved (Father Stephens) warned the tenants 'of the desperate struggle on which they were entering, and implored of them not to enter the combination unless they were prepared to stand faithfully by each other'.[102] Priest-led communal struggle.

The late-nineteenth-century Irish Catholic Church was zealous to gain complete control over education (primary, secondary, university) as far as it pertained to Catholics, and it enjoyed considerable success in this endeavour. The bishops were wary of letting even the Catholic laity have too great a say in Catholic education, and they were especially keen to reduce the influence of the British state over the education of Catholics. Clerical control over the community's education can be identified strikingly in the case of the Christian Brothers' Schools which were to have a profound impact upon the development of later Irish nationalism. In 1875 the Christian Brothers taught around 32,000 boys in nearly 300 Irish schools; this number declined to below 26,000 boys by 1918. But during the late nineteenth century the Brothers markedly increased their profile in secondary-level school teaching.

And it is important to stress, in partial explanation, that Catholic priests of course came from that nationalist community over which they presided: they were open to a similar mixture of formative influences, as were their parishioners, and it was this very fact of their being so harmonious with their people which made their political role so resonant and explicable within nationalist community. The nineteenth-century Church – like newspapers in more recent times – had to echo as well as fine-tune and direct popular thought on political questions, or else risk losing the sympathy of its audience.

Thus there was a seamlessness, to contemporaries, about the joining together of Irish Catholicism and Irish nationalism: the two phenomena were not separate pieces clumsily welded to each other (and, by implication, separable from each other); rather, they enjoyed a unified form. Again and again the sources for the study of nineteenth-century Ireland proclaim this identification, as nationalists of that period themselves saw it. St Patrick's Day (17 March), long established as a national day in celebration of Ireland's patron saint and of Irishness alike, provided many examples. In March 1885 the Dublin-published, nationalist *Freeman's Journal* presented the Catholic and the national as intricately interwoven, an editorial observing that 'St Patrick's Day comes round again tomorrow, and the preparations which are seen on all sides for its approach tell pleasantly how the old sentiment lives for the great National Festival. The customary religious ceremonies of the day will be observed throughout the Catholic Church.'[103] Two days later the paper made the matter even more explicit, in its reflections on the previous day's St Patrick's Day or 'National Festival': 'Yesterday the National Festival of the Irish race ... was celebrated in a manner that evidenced the strength of the enduring sentiment which binds Faith and Fatherland together in one sacred cause.' At a crowded, twelve-noon High Mass at the Catholic Cathedral in Marlborough Street, Dublin, a panegyric on St Patrick had been given by a Redemptorist Father, whose sermon had proclaimed that:

> St Patrick at his death left Ireland an island of saints and doctors, and so she continued for three hundred years till the sacrilegious murderer, Henry II, with his hands red with the blood of the murdered St Thomas of Canterbury, came to her shores and ... succeeded in reducing the country to slavery. Then came Henry VIII, who, after making England an apostate from the Catholic faith, commanded the Irish people to give up that same faith. But they refused to do so, and against the cruel, relentless and fiendish persecutions of Henry and those who followed him, they waged a brave and sacred fight, which had received the blessing and material assistance of the Holy Father. The Irish people passed through the ordeals of fire, the scaffold and hellish torture with their faith unshaken, and it was as strong in their breasts today as it had been in the days of the saint who first bestowed it on them. Ireland was

still in bondage, but he felt that the day was near at hand when she would be released from that bondage ... he believed that the time of Ireland's redemption was near at hand. He saw indications of that in the unswerving adherence of the people to the faith, and in the spirit of nationality – true nationality – which animated them and in the close connection between religion and patriotism. He appealed to them to continue to unite faith and fatherland, priests and people; and if they wished to bring about the redemption of their country, let them one and all be true sons of that religious faith which St Patrick planted in their midst.[104]

The preacher, the Rev. Hall, here outlined the kind of case which unsurprisingly caused alarm among Irish unionists: if the Irish people were really defined by their Catholicism and their opposition to England, then what place would there be for non-Catholics who preferred the Union?

Eleven years earlier a similar theme had been trumpeted. According to the *Freeman's Journal*, on St Patrick's Day 1874

a monster meeting of the Catholics of Belfast was held in the Ulster Hall, under the auspices of the Ulster Catholic Association. The Most Rev. Dr Dorrian presided, and a large number of Catholic and national toasts were spoken to by his Lordship and a number of Catholic clergymen and laymen. The hall was decorated with banners and the majority of the gentlemen present wore regalias. As a grand national entertainment it was a great success.[105]

As a means of communication, identification, sincere commitment and ennobling self-image, Catholic faith and supremacism offered rich rewards in this period; a confident, triumphalist, internationally powerful and ambitious Catholicism had as its local manifestation in Ireland a well-organized and life-enhancing communal culture. And such communal bonds had a deeply anti-English quality:

Ireland has never been behindhand in testifying devotion to the Holy See. In times of peril to the faith and of severest persecution of Catholics Ireland remained loyal, and resisted alike the corrupting overtures and the cruel menaces by which England strove to break the ties which bound the children of St Patrick to the chair of St Peter.[106]

For nation had, in a sense, become religion – a pattern evident in the writings of people like the important nationalist politician A. M. Sullivan.[107]

And so the struggle for Catholic faith and meaning and redress of grievance gained sharpness and national flavour because of the English enemy against whom this struggle was directed. There was an effective fusion of the Catholic and the national, and an associated notion that anti-Catholicism implied anti-Irishness. To very many Irish nationalists in this era, the disentangling of nationalism and religious faith would have been unimaginable: God and Ireland were not understandable without each other; they were inseparable. A later, less godly age might find this difficult to grasp, but we should recognize and respect the fact that this was how Irish nationalists saw the world at that time; for example, in late-nineteenth-century County Donegal – seen as epitomizing in its western reaches the authentic purity of Gaelic Ireland – Catholic clergy and laity alike preached a nationalist message which united Catholicism, nationality, locality and Gaelicism.[108]

Nationalism's exclusivist quality offers one of its most disagreeable yet resilient features: knowing what you are not can represent one of the more satisfying aspects of believing in what you are (while also, of course, playing to some of our uglier and more dangerous instincts). In late-nineteenth-century nationalist Ireland, Catholicism offered some valuable yet simultaneously disturbing resources here. If the nation was Catholic, then what of the non-Catholics on the island? And the notion that the Irish people in these years were being forged into a Catholic people was one not only sought by ecclesiastics at the time, but also upheld by some later scholars who have studied the period. Historian Emmet Larkin's suggestion, for example, that the 1850–75 period had witnessed a devotional revolution 'that had made pious and practising Catholics of the Irish people *as a people*',[109] can only be taken seriously if one assumes either that Irish Protestants were not Irish, or that they did not exist. Similarly, the assertion by historian Brendan Bradshaw that 'Down the centuries until their final emancipation in 1829 the Irish remained committed to Roman Catholicism, and so it continues to this day'[110] – a claim published in 2002 – would seem to rule Protestants out of Irishness altogether.

Parnellism, therefore, embodied a powerful interweaving of com-

munity, struggle and power. Why was it that people expressed their
economic, or their religious, or their political, or their cultural aspirations through nationalism? Because nationalism alone allowed them to
express all these things at the same time, and in ways which – through
their interweaving in such a powerful movement – gave greater
strength to each of these aspects of their lives. Practical, land-based
concerns were paramount. In the grotesque shadow of the Famine –
still very much a memory to many people alive at the time of the Land
War – and in the context of late-1870s agricultural crisis and
depression, it was entirely understandable that rural Irish people were
preoccupied with questions of agricultural reform, redress and ownership; community impulse was focused on practical needs, struggles and
the means of survival, and so national community had material
foundations, and land issues were the basis for its mobilization. But
the matter went beyond this too: as Catholics, nationalists could gain
daily meaning for their lives from their consoling, triumphant Christian community; and the priests were involved in the struggles over
land also, and gave those struggles greater force (against an enemy,
whether landlord or British state, which was effectively non-Catholic[111]
and which lay beyond your self-conscious boundaries). So the materi-
ality of nationalism was interwoven with psychological and spiritual
Catholic threads, and grew all the stronger as a consequence. Again,
the practical urgency of land-based struggle was reinforced by a
nationalist sense that communal history vindicated your collective
action: the land that you worked, and on which you sought necessary
security, was land wrongly held by historical usurpers, from whom you
now sought to wrest it back.

How were necessary change and security going to be achieved?
Well, collective, programmatic nationalist struggle offered a realistic
mechanism of power. Where the spiritual authorities, or the local
community, could only labour in vain, a nationwide movement with
access to political power could plausibly offer the prospect of changing landed realities; through national-scale leverage, change could
indeed be brought about, as power was deployed against the powerful
within the state, and Westminster legislation was won by parliamentary and extra-parliamentary pressure. With changes in the scale of
possible communication (marked mid-nineteenth-century railway
building, and the expansion of the network during the 1850s and

1860s; increasing urbanization, literacy, newspaper culture, road net-works, postal and telegraph services), mass-nationalist struggle and community enjoyed a real prospect of successful mobilization; it even offered the possibility of establishing attractively representative Irish political power under Home Rule. Redress of grievance concerning economy and state; communal survival; the achievement of political power – all could be brought within reach by means of nationalist struggle. In that scientifically-identified process by which more suc-cessful ideas ultimately triumph because it makes more lasting success for humans to keep on imitating them, mind-to-mind,[112] nationalism understandably flourished because it made such powerful sense of so much in people's material and imaginative lives – effectively and simultaneously.

The intertwining of religious, economic and political struggles – and the dignity and pride brought by such struggle in itself – can be seen in the case of somebody such as Michael Davitt. An interview with him in Portland Jail at the start of 1882 reported that 'He has to wear the convict garb, but this is about his only disability, beyond being shut off from the knowledge of what is going on outside, and, as the uniform is worn in the cause of Ireland, he is proud of it and not ashamed.'[113] A later interview (in London) had Davitt saying:

> The Irish question has ever been, and is still, briefly this – Our struggle since the conquest of Ireland has been for the rights of religion, the use of the land for the maintenance of our people, and for the privilege of ruling ourselves. You [the English] have resisted us by every exercise of power and statecraft on all and each of these, our fundamental rights as a nation, and our most cherished aspirations as a race.

Pride, religion, land, political autonomy, freedom: and great confidence in the prospect of victory: 'Dublin Castle and Irish landlordism must go the way which the penal laws went, and no earthly power can arrest their fall.'[114]

Nationalism could kill the hated system of Irish landlordism, and produce instead the material and psychological security of peasant landownership ('to think of a thing as your own makes an inexpressible difference, so far as pleasure is concerned'[115]). At the same time, it strengthened ties of community, as a self-conscious group was

mobilized: the nationalist struggle included both the practice (meetings, demonstrations, boycotts, violence) and the pursuit of power;
and strong ties of local and more expansive neighbourliness and shared
community were evident within the Land War.[116]

For the key thing is not to ask why Parnell thought as he did in
regard to the land, or why he became a Home Rule politician
(important though those questions undoubtedly are). The truly
important questions to ask are why people expressed their attitudes
towards the land within a nationalist framework (which was not
inevitable and should not be taken for granted), and why land,
Home Rule, Fenianism and Catholicism variously interwove as they
did for so many people in ways that made Parnell's nationalism
resonate so powerfully. And the essence of the answer lies in the
interlinking of community, struggle and power. When Parnell linked
the politics of land with the parliamentary struggle for political
autonomy, and enlisted the support of the Church and the Fenians
in doing so, he offered people an irresistible combination: as the
community (which they as individuals proudly imagined themselves
to be), they could combine to campaign powerfully for pressing
and important freedoms. And self-definition and pride were reinforced by the boundary between self and opponent: Catholic Ireland
fought against Protestants, while rural Ireland fought against urban
England.[117]

So the Land League, properly understood, was not merely a movement campaigning for the alteration of land-tenure legislation or for
personal gain (getting ownership of a farm, or expanding one's
acreage). As nationalism, it was also a force which refused to accept
the system of landlordism itself, a system upon which British rule in
much of Ireland was held to rest. And a measure such as the 1881
Land Act, though intended as a compromise between two positions,
came to be seen by many Irish nationalists as a weapon to be used in
furthering their own cause at the expense of enemies whom they
sought to defeat. Land agitation, as a part of nationalist strategy, was
among other things something which undermined the credibility,
legitimacy and effectiveness of British rule and of British institutions
in Ireland. So the pursuit of personal gain and communal prestige and
power, the material and the spiritual, the local and the imagined-
national, were all tied together. This is why a development such as the

1879 New Departure, with its merging of the politics of land and of nationalism, was such a telling episode.

And, ultimately, Parnellism involved that individual freedom which was derived from sharing sovereignty in national community. 'I am a native of Ireland,' proclaimed Michael Davitt,

> a country rich in almost everything which makes a nation great – a fertile soil, an industrious and a virtuous people; but lacking this one thing . . . Liberty. My country is ruled by another – by England. And that rule is maintained by a garrison of anti-Irish landlords and a horde of unsympathetic officials.[118]

In place of such a non-autonomous arrangement, Home Rule offered a more dignified kind of future; and the struggle itself involved a building of greater self-esteem: 'The essence of what [Parnell] did can be summed up in a single sentence. *He gave his people back their self-respect.*'[119] Tied in with this is the respect of those who knew him – those like Justin McCarthy, who had first met Parnell in 1876 and was to become one of his followers: 'Among those whom Parnell really knew I can only say that I am convinced that there never was anything in his conduct or his manner which showed him in any other character than that for which nature and training had fitted him – the character of a gentleman.'[120]

Parnell's struggle was famously interrupted by the manner in which his personal life intruded upon his political career: the great leader having been cited as co-respondent in a divorce case in 1889, the IPP split during the following year.[121] Among his legacies, therefore, was factional bitterness. An anti-Parnellite demonstration in County Armagh in March 1891 was publicized with the announcement not only that speakers would include Michael Davitt, but explicitly that the gathering was to be held 'to protest against the unpatriotic and shameful action of Mr Parnell and his followers in their efforts to bring ruin and disgrace on our country'; 'Come in your thousands,' the large advertising poster appealed, 'and show by your numbers that south Armagh is still true to Ireland and the Irish Parliamentary Party.'[122]

Yet subsequent nationalists did fight over the legacy of this opportunistic, flawed and magisterial chief. Some pointed to his more militant moments and claimed him for aggressive separatism; others focused on his constitutionalism and rather ignored his more aggressive mode of struggle. A Parnellite cult, myth and shadow prevailed for years, and part of his appeal did lie in his defiant, non-deferential attitude. For all his hierarchical instinct and his parliamentary commitment, even his parliamentary style itself was associated with obstructionist transgression. His was a constitutional politics, but one with a hard edge and an aggressive, unyielding spirit. One legacy which he could not leave, of course, was an Irish Home Rule parliament – which eluded him – and neither could he point the way all that helpfully in terms of nationalist response to unionist Ireland. Like Gladstone, Parnell underestimated the depth and extent of Ulster unionist opposition to Home Rule, and he had no adequately sensitive answer to the question which this posed for Irish nationalism. That there was vast popular support for unionism in Ulster had been all too obvious for years, the evidence being there for any nationalists willing to open their eyes (in the form, for example, of mass unionist meetings and demonstrations[123]). Yet Parnell remained naive about the prospect of a Dublin parliament resolving the differences between northern Protestants and the Catholic Irish nation. And the very logic behind Home Rule itself could, with appropriate irony, be the ultimate problem for Irish nationalists in Ulster: if Irish nationalists could secede from the UK on the principle of self-determination, then why should Ulster unionists not secede from a Home Rule Ireland, invoking that very same principle?

4

Ireland after the seventeenth century was not a colony, but a
sister-kingdom and then, after 1800, an integral part of the
British polity, inextricably linked with British politics, and,
as always, exposed to British cultural influence. This made
Irish political, social and economic development a concern
of England in the way that the affairs of a remote dependency
were not.

D. G. Boyce[124]

In County Mayo in 1898 the United Irish League (UIL) was founded
by the maverick nationalist MP William O'Brien (1852–1928). This
organization aimed to redistribute grass-ranch land to western small
farmers and to set the politics of the smallholder against the grazier
(material struggle once again feeding and explaining nationalist mobilization). O'Brien himself was a County Cork Catholic whose nationalist
parents had been supporters of Young Ireland nationalism; a youthful
Fenian, he eventually came to think the revolutionary extremism of
the Fenians to be futile, and his lengthy political career was concerned above all with the land. Again, however, the material and
the religious are interwoven in our story. O'Brien hero-worshipped
Thomas William Croke (1824–1902; the Catholic Archbishop of Cashel
during 1875–1902), and the UIL was strongly supported by the Ancient
Order of Hibernians (AOH), an organization deeply 'devoted to Faith
and Fatherland' and a nationalist group which was 'essentially a
Catholic Society, being formed ... for the defence of the Faith in
Ireland'.[125]

At local level, Catholic priests were influentially involved in the UIL
and were key to its leadership and direction. So, while the League
sought the compulsory purchase of tenanted land, wanted to see the
division of grazing land among smallholders, targeted landlords and
graziers alike in their agitation, and in time became effectively a wing
of the Irish Party (John Redmond was AOH President from 1900, Joe
Devlin its General Secretary from 1905), there was simultaneously here

a politics of Catholic community in struggle. On 21 January 1899 a meeting was held in Donegal town under the auspices of the UIL: a large crowd of nationalists gathered, together with a significant number of Catholic clergy, one of whom (the Right Rev. Monsignor McFadden) chaired the meeting. From the platform, McFadden declared (to great cheers from the crowd) that, 'He would stand on every such platform until the time came when they would have a platform and parliament of their own in College Green.' They would 'fight on unceasingly until was achieved that which was the right and privilege of every nation and every people, the right of making their own laws in their own country. (Great cheering)'. So a priest was presiding over a land-oriented meeting, and proclaiming the central nationalist message of the freedom embodied in the sovereign right to make one's own laws as a national community.

The statements made and the resolutions read at this meeting sharply emphasized the degree to which this was a politics centred on the attainment of national power for an expressly Catholic community: McFadden himself was explicit that theirs was a struggle of 'the priests and people' together, while one resolution declared that 'as self-government is the natural and inalienable right of all civilized nations we hereby pledge ourselves to continue our best efforts in the cause of Home Rule till the aspirations and labours of the Irish people be crowned by success by having restored to them their parliament in College Green, and thus putting an end to misgovernment and oppression'.[126]

The UIL thus favoured the sale of the land to the people, the restoration of evicted tenants to their holdings, and also the establishment of Catholic university education, and the cause of the Irish language. Here was a very clear example of the central argument of this book: a nationalist movement based on a clear definition of community (Catholic, land-working, Irish-linguistic), engaged in struggle as a nationalist organization with a specific programme (regarding land, autonomy, education), aiming at power in the form of an Irish Home Rule parliament, and clearly aware of its explicit or implied enemies (graziers, landlords, non-Catholics).

One vital feature of all this was culture. *Pace* Yeats, the 1890s was in fact a period of the utmost political energy in organized forms. Yet there was, it is true, a conspicuous cultural nationalist flourish at the end of the century, a cultural politics of relative group-worth. Language was central here. Some held that an anglicizing tide was washing away truly Irish culture, and that Irish-language restoration was an essential bulwark against this process. The language represented supposedly traditional, authentic Ireland, and declinist zealots felt the need to produce revival in order to protect a cultural nation which might otherwise simply die.

From the mid-eighteenth century onwards the Irish language had certainly faced the problem of decline; still, at the start of the nineteenth century around half of the Irish population was monolingually Irish-speaking, and it was this century of the Famine which was to witness Irish language collapse. By the mid-nineteenth century only 5 per cent of the people were monolingual Irish-speakers; at the start of the twentieth, the figure was under 1 per cent. Irish was in danger of dying out, English simply the language most useful in dealing with business, state or emigration. And so, just as the mid-nineteenth-century Young Irelanders had been stimulated to national struggle by their fear of anglicization, so too the later part of the century saw cultural struggle in the face of dangerous decline. In 1877 in Dublin the Society for the Preservation of the Irish Language was formed; its leaders were George Sigerson and Thomas O'Neill Russell, and the Society published Irish texts at a low price. In 1878 the Society for the Propagation of the Irish Language was founded and, far more significantly, the Gaelic League was established in 1893, with the TCD-educated Douglas Hyde (1860–1949) as its President. Hyde had been fascinated by the Irish language since his youth, and (from a Church of Ireland background) he serves as a reminder that Gaelic enthusiasm was not necessarily a Catholic preserve. The League ran language classes and social events (as so often in nationalism, the social dimension swiftly became an important part of a movement's appeal), and it hoped to revive Irish as both a spoken and literary language.

The notion that such a mission could long remain non-political seems naive and, despite the important pioneering work done by Protestant preservationist zealots, it was to be as a weapon in the hands of Catholic Irish nationalists that the language would become most piercing. Here we're back again both to the importance of distinctive culture as a means of communication, and also to the politics of exclusivism (in this case, exclusivism of an emphatically non-English variety; but it might be noted also that around the turn of the twentieth century certain Gaelic League figures displayed a clear anti-Jewishness also[127]). The absorption of linguistic revivalism into Irish nationalist enthusiasm is the key point. Gaelic League organizer Alice Milligan's Belfast-based *Shan van Vocht* ('Poor Old Woman') was founded in 1896 as a nationalist literary magazine. Edited by the Omagh-born Milligan (1865–1953), this 'national monthly magazine' (as it described itself) had Anna Johnson (pseudonym: Ethna Carbery; 1866–1902) as its secretary. The epigraph under the paper's title gives a flavour of the publication – 'Yes, Ireland shall be free/From the centre to the sea,/ And hurrah for liberty/Says the Shan Van Vocht' – and the magazine enthused over the Irish language. An article by Edith Dickson in February 1896 ('Our National Language') argued in Davisite fashion that

> The first and greatest reason why the Irish should preserve their language is just the simple reason that it is their own. A nation that has lost her language has lost part of her birthright, and a large part of her nationality: it is impossible that any language should suit a nation as well as her own tongue, in no other language can her poets clothe their ideas as well.

What was to be done?

> Well, every one can begin the work by starting at once to learn Irish. . . . But the way really to restore the Gaelic tongue is to teach the children. By teaching the children English it was crushed and in the same way it must be raised. In every district where a little Irish is spoken it should be taught in the National schools, and then it would soon spread to other districts. Prizes also should be offered for proficiency in Irish, and for Irish poems, with a view to creating a modern living literature – the pure expression of the Celtic genius in the Celtic tongue.[128]

While such women were espousing the cause of the language, other cultural-nationalist celebrants were focusing on manly sports. During the 1870s there was a growth in the number of organized athletic meetings in Ireland, although by the late 1870s some enthusiasts were anxious about the state of athletics in Dublin itself, with some clubs disintegrating and financial problems causing difficulty. But in the provinces there was still a growth in athletic meetings and an eagerness for traditional sports (such as weight-throwing and jumping events). The markedly nationalist National Athletics Sports of Mayo was set up by an IRB man in 1879 (with Parnell as one of the new group's patrons). But some zealots felt the need for a national body to oversee athletics on a national (and Irish nationalist) basis. It was held to be important that distinctively Irish national sports should not die out and be eclipsed by their English rivals. So on 1 November 1884 the Gaelic Athletic Association (GAA) was formed, with County Clare's Michael Cusack (1847–1906) its key founder. Charles Stewart Parnell, Michael Davitt and Archbishop Croke of Cashel were all invited to become patrons (which they promptly did), thereby underlining at the outset the nationalistic complexion of the new sporting venture; four of the seven-member committee which founded the GAA were Fenians.

For the early GAA was dominated and run by nationalists,[129] whether of Parnellite or more aggressive hue. At its inception the GAA had sought and achieved the blessing of Home Rule nationalist leaders; and within a very short time the organization was effectively being run by the Fenians[130] (a development far from welcome to many Catholic priests). So the GAA was both a nationalist and a sporting body, its appeal gaining from this dual quality. The rule prohibiting Royal Irish Constabulary (RIC) members from membership of the GAA (and, indeed, from participation in tournaments), represented an attempt to limit police surveillance of IRB members. For the IRB had moved very quickly indeed to assume control of this venture. Before even the second annual convention of the GAA in 1886, Maurice Davin (1842–1927), an athlete and first President of the GAA, was the only non-IRB member of its Executive – and even he had imbibed strong nationalist influences from his childhood, supported Home Rule, and had (possibly) been a youthful Fenian himself.

Davin was illuminating as a keen cultural nationalist, with an Irish-language interest to complement his sporting zeal; he also thought that, in political matters, the GAA should simply take its lead from Archbishop Croke. So Irish nationalist politics and GAA cultural nationalism remained intricately yet strongly interwoven, especially at local level: the sense was reinforced that 'the people' meant the Irish nationalist people; and that meant, in effect, Catholics. The Association had a fractious first few years, as power battles were fought out tenaciously. But it experienced great early successes: a mere year-and-a-half after its foundation the GAA possessed in the region of 50,000 individual members. Ironically promoting Irish athletic ideals and practice on the model of Victorian English manliness,[131] the GAA was keen both on a revitalization of distinctively Irish sports and also on the crucial question of access to sport, especially for the working classes and with a view to promoting a patriotically conceived physical fitness. The need was for a non-class-biased national fitness project; and so nationalism was expressed through sport in this organized, communal way: spectator and participant alike identified with the nation, a nation strengthened in its well-being by such activities.

And just as a nationalist such as Thomas Francis Meagher was a keen advocate of hurling, so again Davin, Cusack and others among the GAA's early enthusiasts were themselves sympathetic to the Gaelic League venture, and supported the League when it was established in 1893. There emerged at local level considerable cooperation between the GAA and the Gaelic League. Nationalism could apparently do it all.

As we have seen, any notion of a pure Gaelic race, or of Gaelic original Irishness, was deeply unhistorical. The Goidels, who seem to have imposed their Gaelic culture over part of the island, were themselves far from its first inhabitants, but merely one among a successful group of incomers; and the notion of the Gael as the original and legitimate Irish figure is historically unsustainable. But, though hybridity and mongrelism were the historical reality, there were clearly comforts in notions of being more truly Irish than others (specifically, more so than Protestant incomers from the time of the Reformation onwards). As with so many nationalisms elsewhere, the Irish myth of shared descent allowed for a feel-good communal celebration of what were partly reinvented old behaviours. And, as with so many nationalisms, what was comfortingly assumed to be the case took on more political weight than what had actually happened in the distant, hybrid past.

But distorted self-images form part of all powerful nationalist self-images (including the British as well as the Irish, it might be noted). For some, the truly Irish would reject all things British: rejecting the monarch, as in the 1897 protests against Queen Victoria's Jubilee; opposing the empire; supporting the Boers in the Boer War;[132] and celebrating the 1798 centenary with commemorations (as organizing secretary of the 1798 centenary celebrations in Ulster, Alice Milligan invited her friend, and former Fenian activist, John O'Leary to Belfast). And yet many Irish nationalists (Home Rulers prominent among them) were not necessarily anti-imperial, feeling that, once Home Rule were to be granted, the Irish could then live comfortably enough with the empire. And, despite what some separatist rhetoric might suggest, the British monarchy had actually been rather popular in nineteenth-century Ireland, with most nineteenth-century nationalists themselves being monarchists of one brand or another.[133] Indeed, nineteenth-century Irish nationalist thought itself ranged from a desire for outright independence from England, through autonomy with some kind of English link, to reform within the United Kingdom. Many in nationalist Ireland were happy enough with some royal connection, the monarchy even being seen by some as a possible bridge which could reconcile Irish autonomy with the British connection. Royal visits to Ireland tended to be greeted by large-scale popular enthusiasm, a matter of annoyance to some Irish nationalists; when Queen Victoria visited Ireland in 1900, she was favourably received by most.[134] And ambivalence surely coloured the British–Irish relationship during the Queen's long period on the throne: some saw Irishness and Britishness as antagonistic, some as complementary, and there was complexity also in the gaze directed from Britain towards Ireland: 'Victoria's personal ambivalence towards the Irish – alternating between a matronly enthusiasm for their participation in royal visits and British wars and an increasingly personalized antagonism towards any manifestation of Irish nationalism – was shared by many of her British subjects.'[135]

More quietly than royal visits, other developments were proceeding: the Local Government Act of 1898 furthered the development of democratic responsibility which was to lie at the heart of nationalism's ultimate appeal. Under this legislation, Irish County Councils and Rural and Urban District Councils assumed fiscal and administrative responsibilities, and Ireland thus witnessed a great expansion of local democracy, and of representative local self-government (in which Catholic nationalists came to play a prominent part). The early years of the next century were to see such transitions writ large in the Revolutionary era.

PART THREE

THE LONG TWENTIETH CENTURY

FIVE

WORLD WARS AND REVOLUTIONS, 1900–1945

1

Nobody in Ireland of any intelligence likes nationalism any more than a man with a broken arm likes having it set. A healthy nation is as unconscious of its nationality as a healthy man of his bones. But if you break a nation's nationality it will think of nothing else but getting it set again. It will listen to no reformer, to no philosopher, to no preacher, until the demand of the nationalist is granted. It will attend to no business, however vital, except the business of unification and liberation. That is why everything is in abeyance in Ireland pending the achievement of Home Rule.

George Bernard Shaw (1906)[1]

Is Shaw's mischievous argument persuasive? Is it right to see Irish nationalism in his quasi-Freudian terms, and the nationalist movement as 'the agonizing symptom of a suppressed natural function'?[2] We'll return to this question a little later, but one thing to note at this stage is that Shaw's argument hints that, as far as nationalism is concerned, the twentieth century in Ireland has effectively been a long one. It is customary for historians in general to suggest the opposite.[3] In broader terms this might make sense, but for the historian of Irish nationalism it is probably better to see the twentieth century as involving questions and answers which extend from the late-nineteenth-century Home Rule dilemma to the disintegration of the Provisional IRA's violent separatism at the beginning of the twenty-first century. How was autonomy for nationalist Ireland going to be pursued (through parliament, through guns?) and resolved (through full separation, by means of Home Rule?); how were British–Irish linkages, and in particular Ulster unionist convictions, to be recognized and then balanced with nationalist ambitions? It would be unwise to suggest, even yet, that we have reached final answers to these questions. But it is clear that these late-nineteenth-century issues have cast a shadow into the twenty-first century.

They were – and remain – questions of interrelated culture, religion, politics and economics, and we need to think about each in turn as they operated in the early years of twentieth-century Ireland.

The Irish nationalist historian Alice Stopford Green provides a fascinating version of one style of cultural-historical argument, exhibiting as she does a spiritual reading of Irish nationality, and a notion of a nation spiritually bound together. Green argued that as early as the era of the Roman empire, the Irish had seen themselves as 'one race ... united in one culture, and belonging to one country', and characterized by a culture that was 'liberal', 'democratic and national'.[4] Such anachronistic views have been forcefully undermined by modern scholarship,[5] as has her notion that the nineteenth century in Ireland was one in which 'A hundred years of ceaseless agitation, from the first tragedy of Robert Emmet's abortive rising in 1803, proclaimed the undying opposition of Irishmen' to the Union.[6] In Green's rather stark view, the Union simply could not work to Irish advantage; in her eyes, no good could come of Irish people taking their affairs to an English parliament.

But while her arguments might look narrow and jejune to modern readers, they do lead us to some questions which were central to pre-First World War debates about culture and Irish nationalism. Green was personally integrated into the nationalist community: Roger Casement was a friend, as was the cocaine-using[7] Erskine Childers, and Green played a role in the nationalist gun-running of 1914. Her politics were conventional enough in terms of the emphasis which she placed on the sovereignty of the Irish people, and the crucial importance of the attainment of self-government. But, as noted, she also interwove into this nationalism a thread of cultural assertion: one race, one nation, one culture.

Various themes were played on this melody by pre-1914 Irish nationalists. These included the magnificent Yeatsian variation, with its emphasis on a Protestant-inclusive understanding of national dignity. William Butler Yeats delighted in what ancestrally tied him into Irish history, and he was determined in his own life that he would write himself and his people into the Irish nationalist story.[8] To such ends, he helped found the Irish Literary (subsequently the Abbey) Theatre, a project with nationalist idealism and imagination at its core. His close friend (another Protestant Irish nationalist) Augusta Gregory (1852–1932) was deeply involved with him in this enterprise. Like Yeats, Gregory was keen to give greater dignity to Ireland. And she defended a third Protestant nationalist, John Millington Synge (1871–1909) in one of Ireland's most famous cultural set-pieces. Synge's *Playboy of the Western World* was first performed at the Abbey Theatre in 1907 to some hostile reaction from certain nationalists who considered it to mock western Irish peasants, and to involve morally inappropriate behaviour. (As Yeats himself noted of the *Playboy*: 'It is never played before any Irish audience for the first time without something or other being flung at the players. In New York a currant cake and a watch were flung, the owner of the watch claiming it at the stage door afterwards.'[9]) Synge came from a distinguished and talented family: he was himself an accomplished musician, while his cousin Edward Millington Synge (1860–1913) produced some very striking watercolours and etchings of Brittany in the early years of the century. And J. M. Synge was one of a powerful set of Protestant nationalists in Ireland: firmly not of the Irish-Ireland, Gaelic League variety, such figures offered lastingly intriguing versions of the nationalist self-image. The late nineteenth century had witnessed the growing political marginality of Protestant Ireland, and so vulnerability provided the context for the Yeatsian style of Protestant script: if a national self was to be imagined, then the talent and distinctiveness of Protestant Ireland would have to be there.

But the epicene, Protestant nationalism of W. B. Yeats did not appeal to all. For one thing, figures such as Waterford-born David Patrick Moran (1869–1936) – the high priest of Irish-Ireland and founder-editor of *The Leader* from 1900 – asked how the Abbey Theatre's plays could possibly be truly national and authentically Irish if they were performed in English. Moran was a talented if myopic zealot, a cultural nationalist of formidable journalistic skill, and one who sought a Gaelic cultural risorgimento. It wasn't that Moran shared nothing with Yeats: both espoused a nationalism which was passionate and anti-materialistic (Yeats having argued at the end of the nineteenth century the dubious view that 'Ireland is leading the way in a war on materialism'[10]). But for Moran anti-materialism, anti-Englishness and pro-Catholicism were unavoidably interwoven, and it was Gaelic Ireland which must dominate and define Ireland in the new century.

In 1898 Moran had returned to Ireland from England to be horrified by the extent of the influence wielded here by British mass culture. In *The Leader* Moran argued that the Irish language was the key to true Irishness and, unlike Yeats, Moran held a comparatively propagandist view of art, judging it by its value to the national cause rather than according to any intrinsic or independent artistic merit. His vision seems unappetizing now (he was sharply anti-Jewish, for example) but in his controversial fashion he outlined much that was to be central to nationalist Ireland's cultural argument in the twentieth century. The Gael was the key element of Irishness, the binding spirit of the nation; so in saving the Gaelic past one was preserving the authentic and true Ireland, resurrecting a former civilization of glorious quality, and establishing continuity with a legitimating and a validating Ireland of history: 'the foundation of Ireland is the Gael, and the Gael must be the element that absorbs'.[11] Moran's argument reflected the picture painted by scholars of nationalism such as Elie Kedourie in his own (disapproving) portrait of nationalism, regarding the supposedly natural and distinctive expression of each people through their language and nationality:

> I have no desire to add to the existing definitions of that which we call a nation. But if we regard countries as several collections of human energies, then one is differentiated from another by certain general characteristics affecting the manner in which these energies are put forth. A characteristic way of expressing thought, a distinct language, is usually the most prominent mark of a nation.[12]

As so often elsewhere in nationalist histories,[13] such cultural nationalists in Ireland thought in terms of the contemporary awakening of an historically embedded culture, and saw the struggle for such cultural revival as necessary to the nation's survival. The flaws of an anglicized present could be judged, arraigned and condemned against the standard of an imagined Gaelic past – a past supposedly pristine, harmonious, distinctive and dignified. It was a politics of decline (not unfamiliar among nationalists and patriots across much of the world[14]). The present was unsatisfying and the villain – in this case, England – was repeatedly identified; the people had lapsed from the true faith but could be reconverted by cultural-nationalist preachers. At root, what made Ireland (and therefore yourself as an Irish person) special and distinctive? One obvious answer lay in the reservoir of a Gaelic ethnic past which differentiated you from your powerful English neighbour: as so often with nationalism, much of its power was derived from its capacity to distinguish you from assumedly less elevated rivals (hence the elegantly phrased arguments of one eminent historian that, 'in modern Ireland culture has been a divisive rather than a reconciling influence'[15]).

But if enjoyment and celebration of this unique culture also allowed for convivial sociability, then all the better. Hence much of the appeal of the Gaelic League, whose activities undoubtedly did possess considerable social as well as ideological appeal, and whose activities flourished in the early twentieth century: the League's annual income rose from about £1,000 in 1901 to roughly seven times that amount by 1904. If English civilization threatened to destroy the distinctively authentic Ireland, if the Irish language – the very symbol of Irish culture – was endangered, then extreme campaigning was required. Gaelic Leaguer and frequent contributor to *The Leader* Arthur Clery (1879–1932) captured something of the urgency of the Irish-Ireland case when he described the work of Moran's paper as a kind of 'moral surgery'; a nation was 'founded on language, habits, customs, tradition, and common history',[16] all of which must be cherished if it was to live. (Yet again, this is a pattern of argument very familiar from elsewhere, including the striking example of Germany.[17])

If such definitions established what was authentically Irish, then, of course, they equally set out what was inauthentic and unIrish; if genuine Ireland was Gaelic, then non-Gaelic streams were of less importance. And a second shared means of cultural communication for Irish nationalists of this period was unquestionably religion. Notwithstanding the important contribution of eccentric Irish Protestants such as Yeats or Gregory, the main current of nationalism was driven by Catholicism. If England was non-Gaelic, then it was also non-Catholic, and very many Irish nationalists in the early twentieth century identified the nation's Catholicism as central and definitive.

In part, this related to the influence of priests over the education and thinking of nationalist Ireland. An outstanding emblem of such priestly influence lay in the writings of Canon Patrick Augustine Sheehan (1852–1913), Catholic parish priest of Doneraile (a small town in County Cork) from 1894 onwards. Sheehan began to write novels in the 1890s, a Catholic clergyman battling stridently in fiction for his Church and against what he took to be the malign influence of social modernization upon Catholic Ireland. He was a writer of the Irish literary revival, but one who was keen to combat the influence of Protestant authors. An Irish-Irelander, a keen cultural protectionist, he wrote primarily because he feared that the Catholic Church might not possess necessary influence in the new Ireland that was then appearing.

Sheehan thought that his Church should dominate Irish cultural life, and that Catholicism lay at the heart of Irish nationality; he very sharply opposed any idea of a secular state. So while his view of Irish history had partly been drawn from Thomas Moore and Thomas Davis (and while he could on occasion express the hope that 'the barriers of racial and sectarian prejudices may be broken down'[18]), Sheehan's own nationalism was emphatically Catholic-nationalist. He saw colonialism in Ireland as having been anti-Catholic, and he interpreted the subsequent struggles against Britain as struggles for the faith (a lasting perception for many Irish nationalists, as it turned out). Wanting the Catholic Church to hold a dominant position in Ireland, he really wrote for Irish Catholics and his works were hugely popular: over 100,000 copies had been sold prior to his death in October 1913, and he can lay claim to having been one of the most influential writers of his era.

Widely read and important, it remains unclear precisely how influential, in any mechanical sense, such writers were. Was Sheehan's posthumously published novel, *The Graves at Kilmorna*, influential in any decisive way over nationalist thought and action? This tale of zealous, earnest patriots involved in the 1867 Fenian rebellion does tend to celebrate Fenian rather than parliamentary politics, presenting constitutional nationalism in grim, negative terms. Constitutionalism is depicted as corrupt (a view now rather disputed by modern scholarship[19]), while there is a keen representation of pastoral patriotism

('It is a beautiful view ... and ours is the most lovely country on the face of the earth',[20] one of the central Fenians declares, early on in the novel). A rather poignant tale – both of the central characters are killed – Sheehan's *Graves at Kilmorna* reflects its author's hostility to what he saw as the selfish, materialist betrayal of true Irish nationalist ideals.

And Catholic nationalism prevailed in powerful fashion across many sections of the people. Though initially founded in New York, the Ancient Order of Hibernians in the early years of the twentieth century became a major Catholic Irish nationalist benevolent society. Membership stood at 10,000 in 1905, but at a much more imposing 60,000 by 1909. Enthusing over a Faith and Fatherland style of politics, the AOH was a kind of Catholic Irish freemasonry, a nationalist version of Orangeism, perhaps. Protecting Catholic interests, opposing English abuses of power, for a time supporting the UIL, the AOH offered social outlets and support, offering comradeship in business and seeking preferential job opportunities for Catholics (discrimination?).

The vital point here – especially in our own day, when the explicitly Catholic quality of Irish nationalism has begun to be soft-pedalled – is to grasp just how far such people identified Irish nationalism and indeed Ireland itself with Catholicism. In 1910 AOH National President Joseph Devlin (1871–1934) argued that

> From the time of its foundation down to the present, the history of the Order is, to a large extent, the history of the Irish nation in its three hundred years' struggle for religious and political freedom. Wherever the banner of hope was raised for Ireland, there the members of the Order were to be found rallying beneath its folds. As they have been, so they remain – ever loyal to the Church, ever faithful to the fatherland.[21]

For this militant lay Catholic organization, Irish nationality remained tightly interwoven with the cultural language of Catholicism.

Such was the narrow sectarianism of the AOH, indeed, that even some other Irish nationalists themselves became anxious. In 1911 the IRB's separatist paper *Irish Freedom* declared the Hibernians' 'narrowing down of nationalism to the members of one creed' to be a 'fatal' development in Irish political life. With direct reference to the AOH, it continued: 'that the driving power of the official Nationalists should be supplied by an organization of which no Protestant, however good a patriot, can be a member, is in direct opposition to the policy and traditions of Irish nationalism'.[22] But, whatever the separatists behind *Irish Freedom* may have thought, the policy and traditions of mainstream nationalism were indeed moving down an Hibernian-style route. In part, this reflected the deep sectarian competition and rivalry in pre-First World War Ireland. It is sometimes assumed by Irish nationalists that sectarianism is really a unionist phenomenon, that it was produced by partition, and that it happens basically in Northern Ireland. But pre-partition Ireland witnessed widespread and mutual sectarian aggression, and it would be difficult to understand the nature of Irish nationalism without acknowledging this fact.

Power rested then disproportionately with Protestant Ireland, and many nationalists saw unionism as a culture of ascendancy and discrimination. At the start of 1899 the weekly *Donegal Vindicator* (a Ballyshannon-published paper with circulation in Donegal, Fermanagh, Leitrim, Tyrone and Sligo) reported on the clash of cultures between Fermanagh unionists and nationalists, referring to what it considered the unjust 'perpetuation of unionist supremacy' and openly referring to 'unionist foes'.[23] But the *Donegal Vindicator* was also explicit both that those who wrote for it did so emphatically 'as Catholic journalists' and also that there existed in contemporary Ireland a recognized and sharp competition of communal identities and interests between Donegal Catholics and Donegal Protestants.[24] For pre-partition Irish nationalism involved a struggle for freedom which was focused on existing discrimination against your community, and which involved a desire to create in its place a rival world of mutual protection, advancement and favour for your own people. Why was it so appealing to imagine a state run by and representing your own side? Partly because this would provide the power necessary to promote your own interests and advantage, and the power needed to redress the imbalances which currently favoured the other side. What Protestants were condemned for sustaining was to be replaced by nationalist success. Thus emerged the religio-communal struggle for power, and for the capacity to distribute the resources of the state, which so defined Irish nationalism.

Each religious community had anxiety about the threat posed by the other, and so sought ascendancy for itself. Ultimately, this would involve state power; but it was manifest also in competitive, Protestant-versus-Catholic sectarian civil societies (hence the significance of the AOH). As so often elsewhere,[25] nationalist mobilization in Ireland was given strength by a sense of practical grievance (insufficient jobs or wealth) experienced by the individual as a representative part of a wider community: such grievance was experienced by individuals self-consciously thinking as part of a disadvantaged or threatened group. Self-determination mattered to Irish nationalists, in part, because it legitimated the coming to power of a Catholic Ireland which had suffered practical injustice in the past, and which wanted to redress this situation. And religion was no mere surface element here. Unionists did see nationalism as a clerically-led culture seeking its own ascendancy and likely to deploy power intolerantly (were they mistaken?); for their part, many Irish nationalists did hold a firm view about the specifically Catholic mission which God had ordained for the Irish nation (within but also beyond Ireland itself).

Very practical anxiety about job and other opportunities thus drove nationalism forward. It helped inspire D. P. Moran to find evidence of Protestant discrimination against Catholics; it prompted Catholic nationalists to establish and join organizations which would act as guardians against discrimination and which would assert Catholic interests. And neither side tended to listen to the other; so the gap grew wider and more ugly between Protestants (who were understandably fearful of Catholic assertiveness), and Catholics (who understandably organized self-protection and struggled for communal advancement). This involved business, but also education, there existing a strong sense at the end of the nineteenth century that Catholics in Ireland were oppressed because there was not a Catholic university:[26]

> we are sorry to say that a grave injustice continues to be inflicted on our country by the government acting on the promptings of a stupid and unjust bigotry, by the denial of Catholic University education. The Catholic taxpayers of Ireland are in an overwhelming majority, and yet they are denied their natural birthright in this respect.[27]

These religious divisions involved undeniably political activity. And so, as we've hinted, the stimulating Yeatsian argument about a post-Parnellite death of politics (set out in the 1920s) holds continuing fascination but, in truth, little empirical reality:

The modern literature of Ireland, and indeed all that stir of thought which prepared for the Anglo-Irish war, began when Parnell fell from power in 1891. A disillusioned and embittered Ireland turned from parliamentary politics; an event was conceived; and the race began, as I think, to be troubled by that event's long gestation.[28]

Yeats was surely right that culture played a role in fostering nationalism, and he perceptively identified the romantic, poetic quality to much post-Parnellite nationalism in Ireland. But he was here typically writing himself very centrally into Irish history, dubiously implying that his own theatrical and literary efforts and circle had helped to create modern Irish nationalism and revolution. In reality, while culture did provide one political arena, more conventional political battles were also fought, and more orthodox political plans laid.

For politics had continued to flourish after Parnell, and the most powerfully significant strand had remained parliamentary nationalism.[29] From Parnell's death through to the 1916 Easter Rising, constitutional politics dominated the field within nationalist Ireland; the key player here was County Wexford-born John Redmond (1856–1918), now somewhat back in vogue with historians after far too long a period of comparative obscurity.[30] An MP successively for New Ross, North Wexford, and then Waterford city, Redmond became leader of the Irish party's Parnellite faction after the great leader's death; the obvious successor to the lost chief, from 1900 until his own demise in 1918, Redmond was Chairman and leader of a reunited IPP.

During these years this TCD-educated barrister impressively pursued the politics of Home Rule. What did that politics involve? In a July 1883 lecture Redmond had stressed that it was 'of the utmost importance that the case of Ireland for Home Rule should be stated calmly, dispassionately and logically', and he had attempted to do precisely that.

What do I mean by Home Rule? I mean by Home Rule the restoration to Ireland of representative government, and I define representative government to mean government in accordance with the constitutionally expressed will of a majority of the people, and carried out by a ministry constitutionally responsible to those whom they govern. In other words, I mean that the internal affairs of Ireland shall be regulated by an Irish parliament – that all

Imperial affairs, and all that relates to the colonies, foreign states
and common interests of the Empire, shall continue to be regulated
by the Imperial parliament as at present constituted. The idea at
the bottom of this proposal is the desirability of finding some
middle course between separation on the one hand, and over-
centralization of government on the other.[31]

In a sense this was classic self-determining nationalism: representative government for the national majority; and in these terms Home
Rule might be seen, as one of Dublin-born novelist Eimar O'Duffy's
literary creations succinctly put it, as 'common sense and practical
politics'.[32] And this judgment has been echoed by some of the leading
authorities on Irish nationalism: 'The logical and reasonable solution
to the Irish problem was Home Rule for all Ireland with special
safeguards, and even a degree of internal autonomy for parts of north-
east Ulster.'[33]

It is important that Redmond saw the nationalist demand not so
much as an innovation, but rather as a matter of struggling to restore
what had properly once been. This was to be a common and powerful
theme in nationalist assertion (in Ireland as elsewhere, regarding ethnic
culture as well as political structures[34]): Redmond's own nephew also
presented Home Rule as 'a "Restoration"' – or, more intriguingly, as
'the restoration' to Ireland of 'the British Constitution as represented
by a National Parliament'.[35]

And yet it was very much because of present wishes and needs that
this past arrangement was to be pursued. In 1912 the Nationalist MP
Jeremiah MacVeagh set out what Home Rule meant, and why Ireland
should possess it.

Home Rule means self-government, but does *not* mean separation.
Home Rule means that the Irish people should govern themselves,
through an Executive responsible to a Parliament, in all purely Irish
affairs. But an Irish Parliament would have nothing to say regarding
the Crown, the army, the navy, treaties, peace or war, foreign or
colonial affairs, coinage, religious liberty or personal freedom.
These matters would be dealt with by the Imperial Parliament.

And, yet again, the foundation of nationalist argument rested on
democratic conception. There were, MacVeagh stated, many reasons

why Ireland should have Home Rule: 'but one of the best of all democratic reasons is – *because she wants it*'.[36]

By the time these words were written, it seemed that she would indeed get it. The Parliament Act of 1911 meant that London's House of Lords could delay, but not prevent, legislation passed by the House of Commons. If the Commons favoured Home Rule, then the Lords couldn't now stop it indefinitely from becoming enacted. This seemed to some Irish nationalists to offer encouragement, and to provide yet more need for nationalist commitment and organization. The Lurgan Branch of the United Irish League, inviting people to join their number, made precisely these points, as well as setting out lucidly the essence of the nationalist crusade of that period:

> This year, 1911, has opened propitiously for the cause of our beloved land. The struggle of the past one hundred and ten years has been waged for the single purpose of regaining our national freedom, so that Ireland might be free to govern herself by her own parliament, with a responsible executive. That purpose is now within our grasp. The sole obstacle to its attainment, hitherto, has been the House of Lords; and the power of the House of Lords will, within the next few months, be broken by the people's representatives in the House of Commons. Still, there is necessity for a strong organization in the country behind Mr Redmond and his loyal colleagues, if we are to see our hopes successful within the life of the present parliament, and it is the imperative duty of every true son of Ireland to enrol in the national ranks for the final effort to set the crown on our work. Is there an Irishman worthy of the name who would stand aside at so eventful a time in our national life?[37]

Here was a typical Home Rule attitude, combining confident expectation that the measure would be delivered, eagerness to organize for a final push to achieve this, and blindness (even in Lurgan) to the fact that Irish unionists rather than London politicians were the main obstacle to Home Rule's advance: for the vast majority of Irish Protestants were as hostile to Home Rule in 1911 as they had been in the 1890s.

In this era of repeated governmental initiatives to resolve the supposed problem of Ireland, the Third Home Rule (Government of

Ireland) Bill came before the London House of Commons on 11 April 1912. It proposed a bicameral Dublin parliament, the House of Commons to comprise 164 members, the Senate only forty; the Bill stressed the supremacy of the Westminster parliament over that envisaged for Dublin, and provided for forty-two Irish members of the London House of Commons. Most early-twentieth-century Irish Catholics expected a self-governing Ireland to emerge through Home Rule, a matter of particular significance for that educated elite which anticipated that it would lead this newly autonomous Ireland.

But what of those Irish people who opposed this anticipated future? Opposition among unionists ran deep, and it involved religious, political, economic and cultural objections. As C. S. Lewis's pious, whiskey-drinking, Ulster Protestant father had expressed it in 1882, 'I believe the cause of Irish agitation [for Home Rule] to be on the one hand the Roman Catholic religion and on the other the weakness and vacillation and the party selfishness of English ministers.'[38] Many Irish nationalists underestimated the depth of such feeling, and early-twentieth-century nationalists tended to be rather dismissive of, ignorant of, and arrogant and naive towards their supposedly fellow-nationals. True, some – like Ulster Protestant liberal Home Ruler Joseph Johnston (1890–1972) – did bother to offer extended arguments in an effort to persuade unionists to accept the nationalist plan: in 1913 Johnston (a Fellow of TCD) argued that unionists should not use force to oppose Home Rule, claiming that 'the evils ensuing from the acceptance of the Home Rule Bill by Ulster are exaggerated beyond all reasonable limits'.[39]

But would his fellow-Protestants be persuaded? The scale of organized unionist resistance suggested otherwise. On Saturday, 23 September 1911 a huge unionist, anti-Home Rule meeting in the north was addressed by the formidable Edward Carson (1854–1935). Nationalists might not take such gestures and associated arguments as seriously as perhaps they should have. In an editorial, the nationalist *Irish News* was briskly dismissive of Carson's 23 September speech: 'merely a monotonous repetition of the old, out-worn platitudes that have served the purposes of gentlemen like him since the first quarter of the nineteenth century'.[40] But was such a view realistic?

Arguably, it was naive to underestimate the seriousness of the obstacle which unionism represented, and closer consideration of

Carson himself would perhaps have been rewarding. Dublin-born and TCD-educated, the melancholic Carson had a deeply impressive career: an extremely successful barrister, Solicitor-General for Ireland in 1892, and subsequently Solicitor-General for England, he was knighted and was an undoubted establishment success in England; Carsonite unionism existed much closer to the centre of British political life than some of its successors, being able to enlist the eager support of major political players and of weighty cultural figures also (including Rudyard Kipling and Edward Elgar). Unionist leader from 1910 to 1921 (entering the House of Lords in the latter year), Edward Carson now lies buried in Belfast's St Anne's Cathedral, where fewer pilgrims greet his tomb than seek out that of his TCD contemporary Oscar Wilde (1854–1900). Carson disliked the foppish writer, and as it turned out he helped to catapult Wilde into decline when cross-examining him at the Old Bailey in 1895 during Wilde's ill-advised prosecution of the Marquess of Queensberry for libel. Just as Carson had helped to destroy nationalist Wilde's career and life, so he later sought to crush Home Rule also.

For it was Carson's politics which formed the backbone of his career. He devoted his life to the defence of the Union between Ireland and Britain, and he sought to prevent disorder, chaos and anarchy. In the late 1880s he had become counsel to the Attorney-General for Ireland, and he appeared for the Crown against Irish nationalists in circumstances which at times required great personal courage. Added to his bravery was a sharp sense of the importance of political theatre, and he brought this to his leadership of unionist resistance to Home Rule. A moody and rather neurotic creature, Carson (and with him James Craig) led a brilliant campaign, and the weight of unionist feeling during the Home Rule Crisis remains striking. On 28 September 1912 – 'Ulster Day' – 237,368 men signed a Solemn League and Covenant pledging themselves to oppose the Home Rule conspiracy; 234,046 women signed a similar 'declaration'.

Such pledges were given teeth when the Ulster Volunteer Force (UVF) was formed in January 1913, to coordinate paramilitary force in defence of unionists' position within the United Kingdom. The idea that it would be necessary for unionists to oppose Home Rule by creating a citizen army had been present in 1886 and 1893; now it had come to fruition and by the end of the year the UVF had built something like a state within a state. Their drilling made clear to those who would see it the substance of unionist resistance, and this was reinforced by the appointment of a provisional government which could protect unionists from the perceived evils of the Home Rule nightmare.

It was convenient, perhaps, for nationalists (including, for example, people such as later IRA man Dan Breen) to present such activity as having been mere bluff. But it is clear that Carson himself was not bluffing during these turbulent days, and it's hard for any serious observer to consider that his thousands of followers were doing so either.[41] For the student of Irish nationalism, this is a vital point. We cannot assess the quality of nationalist argument unless we are clear about whether nationalists have got their reading of unionism correct. Were unionists illegitimate, self-deluding, and a mere paper obstacle to nationalist advance? Were their arguments specious or not? If unionist commitment turns out on close inspection to be sincere and durable, and their arguments open to rational defence, then a major part of Irish nationalist thinking – the notion of the inevitability and moral superiority of an all-island, non-British Ireland – collapses.

So should unionists have done what their opponents demanded, and effectively become nationalists? Much modern opinion tends to be instinctively unsympathetic to unionism. Yet it is difficult to see why its central arguments should be so casually dismissed. Nationalists in Ireland (like nationalists elsewhere) understandably resort to self-determination in justifying their desire for autonomy from Britain. But if it was morally wrong to oppose nationalist demands for such self-government, why should unionists be denied a similar right (and they were explicit at the time about their objection to Home Rule being grounded firmly in this right to self-determination)? It seems fatuous simply to say that Ireland should be a single unit for self-determination because it is one island: should similar arguments deny the Scots or the Welsh their right to nationhood? And, on the Irish island itself, the geographical pattern of confessional-political allegiance made this a problem very difficult to solve. There was too large and concentrated a Catholic nationalism across much of Ireland for the UK state easily to absorb; but there was too solid a unionist bloc in the north-east of Ireland for nationalists to deal with either. Nor did the nine-county province of Ulster offer any neat solution. In 1911, Ulster had a

Protestant majority, but only a slim one (56–44 per cent); Counties Antrim and Down possessed significant Protestant majorities (80/20 per cent, and 68/32 per cent, respectively), while Armagh and Londonderry more narrowly favoured Protestants (55/45 per cent, and 54/46 per cent, respectively); the other five counties all had varying degrees of Catholic majority (Donegal 82/18 per cent, Cavan 79/21 per cent, Monaghan 75/25 per cent, Fermanagh 56/44 per cent, and Tyrone 55/45 per cent). The numbers game would not, therefore, yield any neatly satisfactory partition.

In any case, was Carsonite unionism really based on unreasonable or incomprehensible claims? Some contemporaries argued that Ireland comprised not one nation, but two; yet even if one were sceptical about such a thesis, it remains true that unionists did not fit into the Irish nation as it tended to be defined by Irish nationalists (Catholic, Gaelic, anglophobic, even separatist) and it seems peculiar that we should expect them simply to have acquiesced in their expulsion from the state of their choice.[42]

Unionists could claim as much moral sanction from democratic legitimacy as could their nationalist rivals. Beyond that, there is the issue of culture, religion and economics. Edward Carson certainly believed deeply that Ireland could only be truly prosperous and happy within the United Kingdom, and many other unionists held that nationalist Ireland was culturally isolationist, economically backward, would-be tyrannical, Romish in religion, and constricting of Protestant, British liberties. Was this unionist view sustainable, or were their undoubtedly sincere fears exaggerated? Some of the arguments of pre-partition (and some of the actions of post-independence) nationalists regarding the Irish language suggest that unionist cultural anxiety was not entirely fanciful. As to economics, Belfast had enjoyed a staggeringly successful Victorian economy, and the notion that unionism was progressive, dynamic and energetically forward-looking grew partly from this fact. There's much evidence to suggest that late-nineteenth- and early-twentieth-century Belfast fitted more appropriately within a British than an Irish framework, when considered in terms of economic development and experience. Industrialization made Belfast resemble Glasgow, Manchester or Bristol far more than it did Dublin, Cork or Galway,[43] and unionists unsurprisingly identified their economic interests with the Union and with the world's leading empire.

Against them, they perceived a tyrannical, coercive, priest-dominated nationalist movement, and their religious rights as citizens lay at the heart of their unionism. Were there grounds for concern, for unionists who faced the prospect of being a permanent minority in a Home Rule Ireland? Developments such as the Catholic Church's 1908 *Ne Temere* decree (which stipulated that marriages between a Catholic and a non-Catholic were only valid if conducted according to the rites of the Catholic Church, and that the children of such marriages had to be brought up as Catholics) clearly did little to assuage anxiety. And the emphatic Catholicism of the independent Ireland which did emerge in the 1920s might suggest that unionist thinking was not entirely without some factual basis.

None of this is to say that unionists were essentially right, and nationalists wrong. But it is to stress that there was nothing inherently irrational about unionists seeking to protect their cultural, economic, religious and political interests within a state of their choice. After all, this was precisely the case that contemporary nationalists so forcefully made for themselves.

And some heterodox nationalists recognized as much. Irish-Irelander and Moranite Arthur Clery held that the unionists of Ulster did indeed form a separate nation, that they were therefore entitled to self-determination, and that the areas in which they predominated should be retained by Britain rather than included in a Home Rule Ireland. Clery effectively faced something here which many of his nationalist contemporaries comfortably avoided, and he was in practice that rare thing: a candidly partitionist Irish nationalist. In his own words, 'you can no more talk Protestant Ulster into Irishry than Ireland can be argued into Englishry'; Ulster Protestants 'form a sort of anti-Ireland within our Ireland ... they do not happen to be Irishmen, and have no desire to become such'. Ulster Protestants, Clery suggested, were not part of the Irish nation and should therefore be excluded from Home Rule – to which he sharply recognized them to be a central obstacle. What he recommended was that unionists should have their own 'Home Rule within Home Rule', with those areas of Ulster Protestant predominance simply remaining within the United Kingdom.[44] This would leave as few people as possible in Ireland within a polity to which they were hostile.[45]

Clery's arguments were rare in nationalist Ireland, and the years surrounding the Third Home Rule Bill witnessed increasing aggression and the growing polarization of Ireland's rival political communities. Ironically, indeed, the UVF mobilization was welcomed by some Irish nationalists as showing the appropriate paramilitary way forward. Scholar-nationalist Eoin MacNeill (who could be seen as the founder of early-Irish history as a modern academic discipline, and who still enjoys some respect as a scholar – 'the greatest historian of early medieval Ireland', as one modern authority has labelled him[46]) also played a significant part in the founding of the Irish Volunteers, a nationalist militia established in Dublin in November 1913 in defence of the Home Rule struggle. To some degree prompted by and modelled on the Ulster Volunteers, these Irish Volunteers exemplified a trend which was frequently enough to be evident in the history of nationalist Ireland: that of one ethno-national gesture of aggression kick-starting organized paramilitarism on the other side (a similar pattern was to be evident, for example, in 1960s Northern Ireland). And so 1913–14 witnessed an extraordinary para-militarization of Irish politics, at least in terms of dressing, parading and training as soldiers. From 1914 onwards the clerically-dominated AOH encouraged its members to join the Volunteers, although it was not entirely a Catholic affair. Protestants had armed the UVF already, and now different Protestants again brought guns to Ireland in July 1914, this time in pursuit of the Irish nationalist cause: for Roger Casement (1864–1916) planned and funded, and Erskine Childers (1870–1922) then executed, the importation of weapons and ammunition for the Irish Volunteers at Howth.

And the strand of aggressive nationalism ran deep. In 1910 the IRB gained some momentum with the establishment of the separatist paper *Irish Freedom*. The editorial of the first issue, written by Bulmer Hobson (1883–1969), made its classic nationalist stance very clear:

> We believe that free political institutions are an absolute essential for the future security and development of the Irish people, and, therefore, we seek to establish free political institutions in this country, and in this we wish not to be the organ of any party, but the organ of an uncompromising National idea ... We stand, not for an Irish Party, but for National tradition – the tradition of Wolfe Tone and Robert Emmet, of John Mitchel and John O'Leary. Like them, we believe in and would work for the independence of

Ireland – and we use the term with no reservation, stated or implied; we stand for the complete and total separation of Ireland from England and the establishment of an Irish government, untrammelled and uncontrolled by any other government in the world. Like them, we stand for an Irish Republic.[47]

Freedom, state power, national tradition, independence, heroes from history, territorial integrity and complete sovereignty: here was a full-blooded nationalism indeed.

Hobson has suffered a long historiographical eclipse, but he is a figure of genuine importance for the history of Irish nationalism: 'Though Hobson was later to be almost written out of the nationalist story, he played a leading part – perhaps the leading part – in the mobilization of a credible Irish liberation movement in the decade before 1916.'[48] Ulster-born and Quaker-educated, he had become interested early in life in the Gaelic League, through the writings of Alice Milligan and Ethna Carbery in the Shan Van Vocht. Joining the League in 1901, he became an IRB man in 1904 and then in the following year co-founded the Dungannon Clubs with the Belfast man who had sworn him into the Brotherhood, Denis McCullough (1883–1968). The Dungannon Clubs were intended to promote republicanism, and in early 1906 they established branches in much of Ireland. That summer they held open-air meetings and – in tune with this advanced nationalism – Hobson in time duly became a leading Irish Volunteer and organizer of the Howth gun-running. But the important thing to note is that IRB activists worked zealously, whether through cultural organizations or conspiratorial pseudo-militarism, to set fuses burning towards a nationalist explosion which, eventually, was to change Ireland in 1916.

One casualty of that explosion was to be the Irish Nationalist Party. Home Rule had been enacted (the Bill having passed through the House of Commons on 25 May 1914, to become law on 18 September), but was postponed at the start of the First World War. IPP leader John Redmond supported Britain in the war, arguing in September 1914 that the Irish Volunteers themselves should fight for Britain in the conflict. Initially, he carried a majority of Irish nationalist opinion with him in this, and his policy was not perhaps without some sense. A short war was anticipated, and the eventual extension of the conflict transformed the outcome of Redmond's calculation. For he had thought that common service, sacrifice and suffering in the wartime British Army would unite nationalist and unionist with beneficial results for Ireland's future and create the basis for Irish unity (as a later novelist would have it, 'Gordie had joined the Irish Volunteers that drilled to fight the Ulster Volunteers that drilled to fight Home Rule. But then the war came and they all joined up and were drilling together now to fight the Hun'[49]). Before condemning Redmond too hastily, we should remember that in mid-1914 it was the common view among very many in Europe that war made sense. So might a shorter war, or a more sympathetic attitude towards Irish nationalists during it, have allowed for Redmond's dream to be fulfilled, and for Home Rule to soothe that long-turbulent relationship between Irish nationalism and the British state?[50]

Perhaps, and the conciliatory dimension to Redmond's politics should be respected. He was not oblivious to Protestant Ireland (his mother had been Protestant), and his essentially moderate nationalism possessed many qualities which were lacking in more aggressive, rival brands of struggle. It wasn't that Redmond was entirely divorced from more sharp-edged approaches: there was an energizing, rhetorical aggression to some of his speeches, and during the 1890s Redmondites and Fenians worked together to a significant degree. Once again, therefore, the dividing line between physical-force and constitutional nationalisms in Ireland was a far from crisp one: in rhetoric and agitation, Redmondite nationalists had a Fenian tinge to their politics in these years, just as the Fenians had a Redmondite (for example, electoral) dimension to their own approach.[51] As late as 1909 at least a quarter of Irish nationalist MPs were former Fenians, and most of them retained pride in this background rather than disavowing their former allegiance. Indeed, for some late-nineteenth-century parliamentarians, the constitutional and physical-force allegiances had been simultaneous. John O'Connor Power, returned in a May 1874 by-election as MP for County Mayo, was during the mid-1870s simultaneously both a Member of Parliament and a leading IRB man (with a ballot paper in this hand . . .). Joseph Gillis Biggar, MP for County Cavan 1874–85, and for West Cavan 1885–90, was again both a parliamentarian and a Fenian.

Yet there do remain some key differences between Redmondism

and the more aggressive species of Irish nationalism which replaced it in Sinn Féinish form after the 1916 Easter Rising. Far more than the Sinn Féiners, John Redmond did retain a sense of the importance of trying to reconcile rival creeds in Ireland; his nationalism was far less exclusivist than were some rival versions (including the one which was shortly to prevail). Like the later Social Democratic and Labour Party (SDLP) in Northern Ireland, Redmond clearly recognized the signifi- cance of Ireland's internal division, rather than focusing energy purely upon a conflict between Ireland and Britain. He not only held a benign view that Home Rule would inaugurate a period of good relations in Ireland, but was also markedly hostile to the idea of coercing people into an autonomously nationalist Ireland against their will (a rather noble view, in light of the violent atrocities later practised without success but at terrible cost by successive Irish Republican Armies). Redmond possessed a reasonably broad definition of the Irish nation and of who was in it (he himself came from a family descended from a twelfth-century Anglo-Norman invader); and he sought to persuade his fellow-nationalists to avoid bigotry in their outlook (once again, a stance not casually to be dismissed, given the obstinacy and intolerance shown by many subsequent Irish nationalists).

We should not, of course, exaggerate the degree to which Redmond- ism had resolved all contemporary difficulties. Like so many Irish nationalists, he too tended to skim over the problem of unionist Ulster, emphatic as he was in his own mind that Ireland was one nation, not two. As he had put it in a Dublin lecture in 1886, 'I assert that there are no two nations in Ireland today, that all the people of this land – Catholic, and Protestant, and Presbyterian – of Celtic, or Norman, or Saxon extraction – are all children of one nation bound together not only by common interests, but by common traditions, memories and history.'[52] (This was a classic nationalist formulation; compare the definition of the nation offered by leading scholar of nationalism Anthony Smith: 'a named human population sharing an historic territory, common myths and historical memories'.[53])

1916-and-all-that destroyed Redmondism: he and his Home Rulers were subsequently long eclipsed in nationalist politics and memory, having been punished for that worst of all political errors – being on the losing side of history. But constitutional nationalism was strong until late in that losing day. Prior to his martyred apotheosis, rebel leader James Connolly had only been able to garner a pathetic handful of votes from nationalist Ireland, and by contrast Redmondism did reflect the instincts of a lengthily powerful national opinion in Ireland. From the 1870s until the First World War, Home Rule dominated Irish nationalist thinking and expectation, and most Irish nationalists were very happy to endorse the kind of constitutional compromise with Britain which Home Rule embodied. Despite his historiographical rehabilitation, Redmond still lacks popular renown on anything like the scale of Ireland's most famous nationalist leaders, whether consti-tutional (O'Connell, Parnell, de Valera, Hume) or more aggressive (Tone, Emmet, Mitchel, Connolly, Collins, Adams); and I doubt very much whether this will change. But his Home Rule near-miss and his eclipse are tantalizing none the less. One observer suggested in May 1918 that, 'Had England granted Ireland colonial freedom on entering this war, John Redmond might be yet alive, ruling Ireland as her first Premier.'[54] In the end, Redmond's version of nationalism – relatively inclusive, consensual, tolerant and firmly democratic – was eschewed for some years by nationalist Ireland. Much, perhaps, was lost as a result.

So: culture, religion, politics – and (of course) economics. The years 1900–03 witnessed a great movement for the abolition of landlordism, and this carried with it strong nationalist themes. Land hunger and land possession were to remain longstanding features of Irish political life and of Irish nationalism. In regard to the west, there had emerged agreement among many nationalists by the end of the nineteenth century that land redistribution was the only answer: untenanted, grazing land – once distributed – was seen as providing the solution to small farmers' problems. So between 1891 and 1921 the western small farmers and farm labourers engaged in a struggle for more land, and did so through nationalist movements (the UIL from 1898 to 1919, and also Sinn Féin after 1905). By the time of Irish independence in the early 1920s, the situation had indeed been transformed by land reforms: many people had shifted from being tenants to being land-owners, and much grazing land had been redistributed.[55] And the struggle over land would long persist. John B. Keane's famous play, The Field, sees a character killed in order to prevent him from outbidding a local farmer for a local plot of land, one of the killers proclaiming that 'Land is all that matters. Own your own land.'[56] But the key thing here is the date: for the play is set, not in the struggles of the late nineteenth or early twentieth centuries, but rather in 1965. The notion of intimidatory, communally-sanctioned violence in pursuit of Irish land is something still imaginable, therefore, in the era of Bob Dylan.

The late-nineteenth- and early-twentieth-century Land Acts had seen the British state facilitate tenants' transition into peasant proprietors, and this defined much Irish nationalist self-image for generations. The idea of the countryside emerged as paradigmatic within the Irish nationalist imagination (an Irish example of the much wider tradition of landscape being imagined in powerful, cultural ways[57]). Here, in this Irish celebration of the arcadian, was a nationalist attachment to particular place (*my* field, *my* farm, *my* townland); a place now possessed after specific struggle; a territory which had been acquired from particular enemies beyond clearly delineated religious, ethnic and political boundaries; and a territory which, in its rural aspect, distinguished Irishness in cultural terms from its far more urbanized British neighbour. So the hard-headed economics of owning your own land were interwoven with a practical and emotional attachment to specific, communally-defining geographical place.

Some economic arguments went beyond this, of course. Many nationalists casually assumed that the regeneration and revitalization of the nation would produce an economic betterment for all classes and for all members of the nation. 'Sinn Féin means the end of empty talk and humbug, and the beginning of genuine national work,' as one Sinn Féiner put it in 1908: 'it means more wealth, more employment and better wages for the people; it heralds the dawn of a new era rich with promise for our long suffering country.'[58] Nationalism would be the best of all things for all people. Socialist republicans who pointed out some rather less benign aspects of nationalists' intra-communal class relations, tended not to win many supporters.[59] And the dominant allure of nationalism lay in the fact that it could bind culture, religion, politics and economics together in ways that made practical and imaginative sense to so many people so much of the time. William O'Brien's All-For-Ireland League (AFIL) was launched in 1910, with a view to combating landlordism (economics) but endorsing also a scheme of limited all-Ireland devolution (politics); and it was Canon Sheehan (that emphatically Catholic cultural nationalist) who wrote the AFIL manifesto. Again, D. P. Moran thought a true Ireland to be Gaelic – but Catholic also; and he for a time sought an industrialized Ireland free from English political power. And his cultural-nationalist *Leader* did much to highlight anti-Catholic discrimination – a mission which possessed interwoven religious, economic and political dimensions.

Yet again, the cultural Gaelic League was effectively to become a part of the broader Sinn Féin political movement, and the post-1916 republican militants went through their name-changes as a reflection of this fact. (John or Jacky Whelan became Sean O'Faoláin, Charles Burgess became Cathal Brugha, Owen Duffy became Eoin O'Duffy, Ernest Malley became Earnán O Máille or Ernie O'Malley, Peter O'Donnell became Peadar O'Donnell, and so on. Zealous Irish nationalists required Irish names; 'What's the use of fighting the English for centuries if we're going to call our children Ronald?' as a celebrated memoirist later phrased it.[60]) And if Gaelic culture (with its ancient historic roots) became a politicized, separatist phenomenon, then it is also worth noting that the Catholic clergy had been prominent in supporting Gaelic cultural nationalism, and indeed that they themselves had frequently implied that Gaelicism and Catholicism were in some way overlapping with each other

In October 1900 Inghinidhe na hÉireann (Daughters of Ireland) was founded by nationalist heroine Maud Gonne and others (including Anna Johnson): the group was committed to pursuing Irish independence, but also to encouraging the study of Gaelic, and of Irish literature, history, music and art; and to combating the influence of vulgar English culture in Ireland. So this enthusiastic nationalist network combined, again, various elements of nationalism and of what made it appealing – culture, history, sovereignty; distinctive community, and the struggle for power to protect and realize it.

Or, again, we might consider the Cork-born cultural nationalist and teacher Daniel Corkery (1878–1964). His *Hidden Ireland* (1924), 'a study of some of the Munster Gaelic poets of the eighteenth century', was an evocation of a lost world of authentic Irishness, and a striking example of the way in which modern nationalism was informed and defined by historically embedded, long-distant past cultures: 'Reading those re-discovered poets day after day, I was more and more struck with the extent to which the modes of medieval literature survived in them.'[61] Corkery wanted to preserve what he considered to be an endangered Irish culture and an endangered national identity. He was an integral part of early-twentieth-century nationalist community and argument, characterized by powerful friendships and beliefs alike. He was a great friend of doomed republicans Tomas MacCurtain and Terence MacSwiney;[62] there was close comradeship here, as well as a sense of moral superiority (Corkery wrote of 'the majesty of [Mac-Swiney's] moral stature',[63] and in contrast he distrusted the Irish Parliamentary Party). And Corkery jaggedly moved towards an endorsement of Sinn Féinism, and from moral-force to physical-force nationalism, before becoming in time a supporter of Fianna Fáil.[64] People, culture, history, ethics; militant struggle; and formal political mobilization. And all of this was set in a far from parochial context. Corkery celebrated Irish culture, but also exhorted Irish writers to learn from Russian literature. Again, he had among his books Rabindranath Tagore's *Nationalism* (which had emerged out of lectures given by the Bengali poet in Japan and the United States during 1916–17[65]). Tagore might have been sceptical about nationalism, but here were Irish nationalists (Corkery, but also Yeats and IRA men Peadar O'Donnell and Ernie O'Malley) reading his works.

Far more important an influence on nationalist thinking was the journalist Arthur Griffith (1871–1922) and here too we can see the linkages between different melodies which tied the nationalistic music together and made it so powerful. Born in Dublin to working-class Catholic parents, Griffith was educated by the Christian Brothers and – a Parnellite by devotion – had sympathized in his early years with the Irish Party, only to become disillusioned. Griffith was an extraordinarily able propagandist, the founder of that self-reliant nationalist movement Sinn Féin, and a long-dominant influence on Irish nationalist thought. He was very heavily influenced by cultural nationalist Thomas Davis; and Griffith himself was not a separatist in the strict sense of the word – certainly not a doctrinaire republican. His famous *Resurrection of Hungary*, first published in the pages of his *United Irishman* in 1904, but subsequently brought out in various editions, represented one blueprint for gaining Irish independence, using what Griffith imagined to be the Hungarian route (namely along dual-monarchist, Austro-Hungarian lines). Some are deeply sceptical about how accurate this Irish–Hungarian comparison actually was, but it clearly showed Griffith – one of the most important of all Irish nationalists – to be content with some link between Ireland and Britain and, indeed, between his country and the British Crown.

Yet Griffith forcefully pursued greater political autonomy for Ireland, and cultural and economic autonomy too. In 1900 he and another ex-CBS boy, William Rooney (1873–1901), founded the de-anglicizing Cumann na nGaedheal, and the founder of Sinn Féin ('Ourselves') also favoured economic autarky as the basis for a newly strong (and newly industrialized) Irish economy. There were powerful combinations here, in the celebration of distinctive Irishness, the confidence in new possibility, and the self-reliant dignity which was to be taken from an interwoven Catholic, Gaelic, autonomous and economically vibrant Irish future. But there were, perhaps, more dubious aspects to all of this too. Would more nationalist and autonomous government necessarily be better government, and would it in fact produce the kind of economic revitalization which somebody such as Arthur Griffith envisaged? Was a Catholic Gaelic zealot necessarily more Irish than, say, a Protestant with little attachment to the ideas and images of the Gael, and – if so – precisely why was this the case? And were Griffithite ideas of Irish specialness entirely benign? Griffith himself clearly wanted Ireland to be recognized as dignified and glorious, but he also saw some peoples as inherently superior to others and (like D. P. Moran) he demonstrated, for example, a disagreeable anti-Jewishness.[66]

2

I went out to fight for Ireland's freedom and it doesn't matter what happens to me. I did what I thought was right and I stand by it.

Constance Markievicz, at her 1916 Court Martial in Dublin[67]

The next act in our drama – the 1916 Easter Rising – gave centre-stage prominence to nationalists of more republican, separatist and aggressive stamp than Arthur Griffith (who was not a 1916 rebel). There had been serious planning for a rebellion against British rule during 1915–16, while longer-term preparation by zealots such as the old Fenian Tom Clarke (1857–1916) predated even this. By early 1916 plans were at an advanced stage, and the ensuing narrative of the Easter rebellion has often been told.[68] An inner circle within the IRB leadership (together with Marxist James Connolly's small Irish Citizen Army (ICA)) conspired to plan the episode, working with Irish Volunteers such as Patrick Pearse and Thomas MacDonagh. The Volunteers' official leader, Eoin MacNeill, was kept out of the loop (and in the event tried to prevent the rebellion through a counter-manding order, cancelling the planned Volunteer mobilization for Sunday, 23 April). By the time that the actual rebellion commenced, therefore, there was no realistic prospect of success, and notions of a general rising were certainly disappointed (partly because of the failure to acquire the anticipated weaponry from Germany). But on 24 April 1916 – Easter Monday – around 1,200 rebels took over buildings in Dublin, much to the surprise and astonishment of the British authorities in Ireland; a rebel proclamation was read, and fighting ensued until the insurgent surrender on 29 April. Less significant action occurred elsewhere (Galway and Wexford included). Overall, 450 people (mostly civilians) were killed and more than 2,600 wounded.

What was the popular response? Versions vary, and initial reactions were certainly mixed. After he and his fellow-rebels had surrendered and been taken prisoner by the British in Dublin, Sean MacEntee's recollection was that they 'were marched through the streets. The city was quiet and almost deserted as we trudged along. Here and there at some few windows were a few onlookers; most of them, so far as one could judge, sympathetic.'[69] Curiosity and fear were probably as common. (And looting was a popular response as well: 'The "under-world" of the city quickly realized their opportunity, and first tackled the shops in Lower Sackville Street. The windows were smashed and hordes of people crowded into the shops, returning with bundles of wearing-apparel of all descriptions.'[70])

But the aftermath of the rebellion – with sixteen leading figures being executed – was to produce an emotional high temperature, and a deepening of sympathy for the rebels. The executions have long been condemned ('England in her stupid attempt to suppress the rebellion of 1916 created not one Robert Emmet but sixteen to be forever worshipped on Ireland's altar of liberty'[71]), but in wartime what would one expect? Was this really so Draconian a state reaction? Yet in the end there can be no doubt that the crankish eccentricity of Pearse and his comrades – so unrepresentative of public political opinion on Easter Monday 1916 – came with the wartime help of the British authorities to embody a seemingly inevitable Irish nationalist orthodoxy.

For some this came to be seen as a moment of epiphany. Coincidentally in Dublin during the rebellion, Maire Comerford returned home to County Wexford, her life having been changed: 'my only thought was to get back somehow and join the Movement'.[72] And those with grander imaginations also adopted this epochal moment. By 1916 W. B. Yeats had distanced himself from the politics of Patrick Pearse; yet Yeats's most famous 1916 poem – for all of its undoubted ambiguity – remains one of the most striking evocations of that dramatic episode:

> I write it out in a verse –
> MacDonagh and MacBride
> And Connolly and Pearse
> Now and in time to be,
> Wherever green is worn,
> Are changed, changed utterly:
> A terrible beauty is born.[73]

The rebels quickly became Irish national saints, and yet they were in some ways a strange crew to achieve such sanctification, given the attitudes which (rightly or wrongly) then and later prevailed in nationalist Ireland. The indefatigable radical James Connolly (1868–1916) had had very little success in persuading the Irish people to adopt his Marxist republicanism while he had lived; and the Ireland which has emerged in the near-century after his death would surely have caused him great grief. Station and statue commemorate this anti-partitionist, Marxist, republican insurgent in Dublin; and yet the country of which Dublin is the capital is a partitioned country, firmly capitalist, and one which has decisively turned its back on the politics of physical-force republicanism. The pillars of Connolly's thought have all fallen down around the emblems which still salute his memory.

Others too among this talented 1916 leadership appear strange saints when set against the assumptions (laudable or otherwise) of most people in nationalist Ireland. School headmaster Patrick Pearse celebrated the beauty of young boys' bodies in an obsessive, eroticizing manner with which many would be rather uneasy. (Would you be happy if the headmaster at your son's school wrote lines such as these in a poem addressed to a young boy: 'I forgive you, child/Of the soft red mouth'; 'Raise your comely head/Till I kiss your mouth'; 'There is a fragrance in your kiss/That I have not found yet/In the kisses of women'?[74]) And while Pearse almost certainly did not act on his rather unself-conscious homosexual instincts, the same cannot be said of another key figure from the Easter episode, the great humanitarian Roger Casement, who was one of the most fascinating members of this complex class of 1916. Putting together Casement's various diaries can produce intriguing reading: on 24 June 1910, for example, he and Arthur Conan Doyle together attended in London a performance of *The Speckled Band*, a dramatized version of a Conan Doyle Sherlock Holmes story from the 1890s; after the performance, Casement paid two men to have sex with him in the early hours of the morning.[75]

'Marxist' and 'homosexual' have not been among the most common terms used by modern Irish nationalists to describe themselves; yet Connolly, Pearse and Casement were three of the founding fathers of 1916. And, when examined closely, one can see that they and their colleagues were indeed a remarkable group of zealots. The Edinburgh-born Connolly came to Ireland in 1896, in which year he founded (in a Dublin pub) a rather bohemian Irish Socialist Republican Party (ISRP). This remained a politically marginal group, never possessing more than eighty active members (among them, Alice Milligan's brother Ernest). Karl Marx's daughter Eleanor supported the ISRP, and this party's Programme of 1896 was explicit about the Marx-inspired state socialism which it envisaged:

OBJECT

Establishment of an Irish Socialist Republic based upon the public ownership by the Irish people of the land, and instruments of production, distribution and exchange. Agriculture to be adminis-tered as a public function, under boards of management elected by the agricultural population and responsible to them and to the nation at large. All other forms of labour necessary to the well-being of the community to be conducted on the same principles.[76]

The ISRP wanted an end to capitalism but also to British rule over Ireland; but these long-haired, card-playing, stout-drinking revolutionaries were deeply unsuccessful when competing in elections.[77] And it is not, perhaps, all that hard to see why. Connolly saw Irish nationalism as a phenomenon to be explained by class conflict as it evolved through history, and he considered the working class to be the agent of social and national liberation alike: 'only the Irish working class remain as the incorruptible inheritors of the fight for freedom in Ireland'.[78] Britain ruled Ireland for economic advantage; this was secured through capitalism, which Britain would therefore maintain as long as she ruled Ireland; those in Ireland who were oppressed by capitalism possessed a social impulse towards its (and therefore Britain's) overthrow in Ireland; those in Ireland who benefited from capitalism had material reasons for backing some kind of British connection. The social and the national were thus unavoidably interwoven: 'The cause of labour is the cause of Ireland, the cause of Ireland is the cause of labour. They cannot be dissevered.' 'Who are the Irish?' Connolly asked in 1916, answering: 'the Irish working class, the only secure foundation upon which a free nation can be reared'.[79]

But while Connolly thus defined the national community in terms of class, most Irish people simply refused to follow him, preferring a more inclusive vision of their nation. And Connolly's preference for state ownership of the means of production sat awkwardly within a nationalist community which had come to be dominated by post-Famine peasant proprietors. Again, his Irish nationalism was anathema to most Irish Protestants, whose class interests – in so far as they did determine national allegiance – tended to tie them to the United Kingdom rather than to Irish separatism. Actually existing Protestant workers undermined Connollyite orthodoxy, as he himself rather mournfully noted in 1913:

According to all socialist theories north-east Ulster, being the most developed industrially, ought to be the quarter in which class lines of cleavage, politically and industrially, should be the most pronounced and class rebellion the most common. As a cold matter of fact, it is the happy hunting ground of the slave-driver and the home of the least rebellious slaves in the industrial world.[80]

But things were hardly better when Connolly turned to Catholic Ireland. Karl Marx had been committed to a harsh critique of religion; and Vladimir Lenin (1870–1924) might see socialism as in battle against 'the fog of religion', defiantly proclaiming that 'Marxism is materialism' and that the ideology was 'relentlessly hostile to religion'.[81] But such positions were simply not feasible for James Connolly, a revolutionary whose effective constituency was Catholic Ireland and who was himself a Catholic.[82] Connolly tried to argue that his Marxism was harmonious with Christian teaching,[83] but Catholic Ireland simply didn't believe him.

It was because of these huge obstacles in his socialist republican path that Connolly sided in 1916 with bourgeois rebels, in conditions which his earlier self would have rejected. His one-time hopes for syndicalism had been destroyed with the defeat of the strikers following the Dublin lock-out of 1913.[84] The British government appeared to be threatening partition as a response to armed unionist action, and so maybe violent gesture would be required to prevent this unwelcome rupturing of the national territory. Above all, the working class had let Connolly down by failing to heed his words, and so he became involved in a rebellion which showed little trace of class conflict as its defining ideology, but which instead exhibited an inclusive, cross-class approach to the nation.[85] Hailed by some as an inspired political high point, Connolly's 1916 gesture actually reflected the dead end which his Marxist republicanism had encountered. And his experience helps to illuminate one of the great political questions of the modern era: why has nationalism so eclipsed and obscured socialism in modern history? This question has been addressed by many scholars of nationalism,[86] but the Connolly case study presents helpful answers.

For it can clearly be explained why, like many other Marxist revolutionaries, Connolly discovered to his cost that nationalism cut through and transcended class loyalty: it was a far more capacious vehicle for communal struggle towards power. Connolly's theory of the nation had an in- and an out-group – but far more (the non-working class) were excluded by him than were excluded from the struggle by cross-class nationalists. Connolly's nation represented one strand within the people; those free from Marxist thinking could include in their imagined community everyone living on the island, now and in the past and in the future. Connolly, the fabulously impressive auto-didact, could set an example of considerable dignity; but other nationalists could summon resources of Church and ethno-cultural heritage which were open to all potential nationalists (effectively, the Catholic Ireland of the time), and nationalism could appeal to those who owned (or still wanted to own) their land in their own private hands. If you wanted to build a mass movement, you needed to provide goals which would satisfy material and emotional needs, and everyone could see a self-determining, sovereign national state as their own; in contrast, the Marxist could only hope to mobilize a part of the non-Marxist's potential nation. So the community was more far-reaching in scale, and the struggle for power more feasible, if one abandoned class struggle. And – in 1916, however briefly – even Connolly himself effectively had to do precisely this.

He clearly hoped that his Marxist vision might yet come to fruition eventually, and in this sense he never abandoned his leftist faith. But the irony of his execution in 1916 was that his role in the rebellion both gave life to his memory and also helped to bury what had been distinctive about his nationalism, namely its class-struggling, Marxist dimension. Ultimately, Connolly's 1916 gesture contributed towards the strengthening of non-Marxist Irish nationalism. He had not been the first to proclaim the gospel of Irish socialism (nor even that of Irish socialist republicanism[87]). But he was remarkably lucid and courageous in its exposition, and the manner of his 1916 death made him easily Ireland's most famous republican socialist. His moment of final triumph, however, was produced because of the failure of his argument to persuade any but a tiny number of Irish people that he was right.

Was Roger Casement more typical? Hardly, despite the fact that he – like Connolly – has been treated to far more studies than even Irish prime ministers have tended to enjoy.[88] Even leaving aside the embarrassment which Irish nationalists have so often experienced (why?) regarding his Ortonesque homosexuality (Casement's sexual diaries having detailed what one scholar has referred to as 'a terse and, at times, explicit record of encounters with rent boys'[89]), Casement was unusual in the republican ranks. This was true in terms of his religious journey. As we will see, the Rising was a Catholic affair. Yet the Casements were an Ulster Protestant landowning family, although Roger's mother had been originally Catholic. Casement himself had been baptized Protestant, and then rebaptized as a Catholic at his sometime Catholic mother's request, while a child; but he did not spend his life as a practising Catholic.

Unusually tortuous though his religious and sexual lives were, Casement was a deeply important figure in the story of 1916. He had been highly significant in the increasing belligerence of republican planning and capacity. He had, for example, addressed a major AOH National Convention in July 1914 in Norfolk, Virginia, appealing for arms for the Irish Volunteers – an appeal to which AOH delegates responded sympathetically. (The US AOH was very supportive of the 1916 rebellion, and had contributed money to the Volunteers.) Indeed, Casement had raised significant amounts of money to purchase rifles for the Volunteers and had, of course, helped plan and fund the importation of weapons and ammunition for the Irish Volunteers at Howth in July 1914. During the First World War, Casement attempted in Germany to recruit an Irish Brigade from among captured Irish (British Army) soldiers and, vainly, to persuade Germany to send a force to Ireland. So while he arrived in Ireland in 1916 with the intention of trying to postpone the Easter rebellion (he landed from a German submarine on Friday, 21 April and was subsequently captured and taken to England to stand trial), he had none the less been instrumental in producing the militancy which lay behind the famous rebellion.

The compelling eccentricity of Casement's case was reinforced during his last days. He was hanged in London in August 1916, for treason; but between his conviction and his execution the British authorities had used the diaries which apparently detailed his homosexual activities, in order to undermine the momentum behind calls for a reprieve. Many people had been engaged in such calls, including his old theatre-going companion Arthur Conan Doyle, who decently contributed £700 towards Casement's defence and organized a reprieve petition on his friend's behalf. W. B. Yeats also sought clemency for Casement (though the great poet apparently claimed that he had signed Casement's reprieve appeal purely 'to please Maud Gonne, who nagged him into it'[90]). And Yeats had taken an admirably relaxed

attitude towards the question of Casement's sexuality itself ('If Casement were homo-sexual, what matter!'[91]), though he also appeared to
endorse in public poetry the thesis that Casement's homosexual diaries
were a British forgery ('They turned a trick by forgery/And blackened
his good name'[92]).

Casement's career had been significant long before he turned his
energies towards organizing nationalist arms shipments into Ireland in
1914 and 1916. He had been an impressive crusader for the rights of
people exploited by imperial injustice, and his Conradian travels and
ambiguities make him ever-intriguing (appropriately, perhaps, he had
met and liked Conrad himself). Casement was deeply humanitarian,
and deeply self-regarding also; possessed of great enthusiasm, energy,
self-important vanity and a striking tendency towards unreality, his
fervour and his impracticality both shout out from the records of his
life. He was charming and markedly anglophobic and romantic and
greatly proud of his impending 1916 martyrdom:

> Think of the long succession of the dead who have died for Ireland
> – and it is a great death. . . . It is a glorious death for Ireland's sake
> with Allen, Larkin and O'Brien, and Robert Emmet – and the men
> of '98 and [Presbyterian United Irishman] William Orr – all for
> the same cause – all in the same way. Surely it is the most glorious
> cause in history.[93]

Casement probably was, as he himself later claimed, an Irish separatist
long before his 1916 adventure. The youthful Roger had been a keen
admirer of Parnell, and it is clear that the teenage Casement had
possessed distinct Irish nationalist sympathies; he became a great
admirer (and enthusiastic reader) of the militant John Mitchel, he
wrote for Plunkett and MacDonagh's *Irish Review*, and before the war
he had keenly worked in the hope of an English defeat by Germany in
the world conflict which he rightly sensed to be imminent.

But the most iconic of this great triumvirate of 1916 nationalists
was the Rising's high priest, Patrick Pearse, and his life and views did
rather more fully echo the central themes of Easter Rising nationalism
as the subsequent faithful were to interpret them.[94] Born in Dublin in
1879, and educated by the Christian Brothers and at the Catholic
University College, Dublin (UCD), Pearse displayed an almost Yeatsian
sense of the importance of how people would see things afterwards; in

his 1916 gesture, he showed an equally Yeatsian knack of decisively moulding that later understanding. He was a remarkable, confused and lastingly compelling man. Having joined the Gaelic League in the 1890s, he became editor of its newspaper *An Claidheamh Soluis* in 1903. Like so many nationalists elsewhere, Pearse recognized the central importance of education, and took a pioneering and direct role in this himself. For in 1908 he set up a Dublin school – St Enda's – of which he was the headmaster and the guiding cult-leader. More than thirty past or present St Enda's boys were in the General Post Office (GPO) with Pearse in Easter Week 1916. And Pearse had indeed seen his school as – in part – an experiment in the cultivation of national identity. St Enda's was explicitly Irish nationalist: it was bilingual, Irish-Ireland in emphasis, and also child-centred and modern-looking in its educational orientation. The aim was to fashion a new generation of boys, one which would embody true Irish national identity: education, for Pearse, was at the heart of the national question and of national regeneration, and his Irish-speaking endeavour here drew partly on the strong influence wielded upon him by the ideas of D. P. Moran. But there was more to it than that: Pearse had also been affected by the educational ideas of Maria Montessori and by the epic music dramas of Richard Wagner.

His boyish adventure at St Enda's also suited the zeitgeist reflected in Boy Scout success in England (the Boy Scouts, like Pearse's school, were established in 1908), and both were symptoms of a wider trend towards building the youthful virility supposedly appropriate to a strong nation. It is in this context that Pearse's views of children and Ireland should be framed (Baden-Powell himself had written to Pearse in 1909 inviting him to set up an Irish branch of the Boy Scouts, an approach declined by the future 1916 rebel). Ironically enough, Pearse's emphatically Irish school involved his adaptation of certain of the methods of English public schools, and he saw St Enda's as their worthy Irish match.[95] Yet again, therefore, we see here the tendency within nationalism to emulate that national enemy against which one reacts and sets oneself.[96]

In Pearse we can recognize the capacity of nationalism to express much widely varied human aspiration. Pearse the spiritually-oriented cultural nationalist and devoted Catholic found that his imagined Ireland and his struggle for its forward march could fill his life.

Political autonomy was vital here, if such progress were to be cemented and protected, and Pearse the Home Ruler became Pearse the separatist rebel. For the spiritual and intellectual independence of the nation – as well as its formal-political liberty – were crucial to his argument. He insisted on what he called 'the spiritual fact of nationality',[97] and indeed on a spiritual reading of the Irish nation which would have pleased those scholars favouring a perennialist view of nationalism: for over a thousand years, Pearse argued, the Irish mind had seen its national freedom exist in unchanging form. For much of Pearse's case sounds like a very classic nationalism: to him, the nation was unproblematically united (*pace* James Connolly, it was harmoniously class-inclusive rather than defined by class conflict); it was organic, and possessed of an absolute right to freedom. Pearse aspired to a lost culture which was not, factually, his own (not a native speaker of Irish, he only started to learn it when he joined the Gaelic League). He revelled in nationalist heroes, especially dead ones, modelling himself to some extent on Robert Emmet (as W. B. Yeats clearly recognized), and devoting his last sermons to the inhabitants of nationalist Ireland's Valhalla – Tone, Davis, Lalor and Mitchel among them. The rural west was more authentic than the urbanized east of Ireland, and nationalist zealotry was absolute in its commitment: 'We have the strength and the peace of mind of those who never compromise.'[98]

Again, echoing much patriotic argument elsewhere,[99] Pearse's political analysis was declinist: a great nation had, through the malign intervention and complicity of various villains, fallen from its proper condition; it now required remedy and redemption which the declinist prophet could facilitate. Decline could be reversed, though drastic and brave action might be required, and this explains Pearse's view of 1916 as a moment of national salvation. Central to his 1916 action was his conviction that recent constitutional nationalism had demonstrably failed ('There has been nothing more terrible in Irish history than the failure of the last generation'[100]). Material interests and grubby compromises had led the nation into decline; for Pearse, it seemed that the Irish people had entered into a Faustian agreement with Britain. This had yielded shiny advantages (selfish, material gratification) at the cost of a loss of soul; Irish nationalists of the previous generation were, quite simply, Faust to Britain's corrupting Mephistopheles. So something new was required, a different kind of struggle: pure, decisive, and appropriate to a nationality which was holy rather than worldly. The redemptive effort of Easter was the result.

But what were the character and results of Easter 1916 itself? It was very much a First World War event, from Pearse's Rupert Brooke-style poetic patriotism to the republicans' seizing of wartime opportunity. Genuinely serious planning for the Rising commenced after the start of the war, and James Connolly and others were clear about the different kind of struggle made necessary and possible by this great and awful conflict: 'We believe in constitutional action in normal times; we believe in revolutionary action in exceptional times,' he wrote at the end of 1915; 'These are exceptional times.'[101] In these exceptional First World War times, violent insurrection was needed, and success against a distracted enemy was just conceivable. When better to take on the world's dominant power? When better for the conquered nation to reassert itself?

Like many others on the left, Connolly had found himself profoundly disappointed by the failure of international socialism to resist and prevent the World War; far from uniting as a class, the workers of each country had volunteered in huge numbers to kill one another in the name of their respective nations. Some redemptive gesture on behalf of the Irish working class was required, and Connolly and his ICA would offer the required sacrifice. And might wartime Ireland just offer enough opportunity for republican success? Home Rule had, frustratingly for nationalists, been postponed, and Redmond's support for the British rested on doubly dubious assumptions: of a short war, and a more helpful attitude than he was actually to receive from the British War Office. So nationalist Ireland did not commit itself to the war with the same depth of zeal as did other parts of the United Kingdom (recruiting was particularly unpopular in agricultural Ireland, and enlistment rates were far from impressive).

Moreover, the British response to the Rising was determined by wartime exigency and context too. As already suggested, the famous executions and their equally famous role in deepening Irish nationalist disaffection from the British were hardly, in fact, all that surprising. In the terrible context of the First World War, what could such a state be expected to have done? Across many areas of British life, wartime decisions had been taken to use illiberal methods in ultimate defence of a liberal way of life.[102] And, given the harshness judged necessary to deal with troops at the front itself, could a state really have decided to allow armed insurrectionists to be punished much more gently? (In some ways it is the extraordinary tolerance displayed during the war by the UK state which is surprising, allowing, for example, paramilitary groups openly to march in its cities.)

Fittingly for such a wartime event, the Rising was emphatically aggressive. In this round of the Irish nationalist boxing match against heavyweight England, it was an Irish punch that was thrown first. Behind this, it is worth noting the prior aggression of some of those involved in republican politics. One of the seven signatories to the rebel Proclamation, County Leitrim's Seán MacDiarmada,[103] had – along with his feisty mentor and co-signatory Tom Clarke – been instrumental in forging the rebellion. And he had been espousing republican violence long before 1916, arguing in favour of physical force from 1909 onwards. Another rebel, Constance Markievicz, had also been arguing from an early, pre-war period, in favour of preparing for republican violence. And anti-English violence was sought by some republicans in the most vicious of forms: during the World War, in 1915, another future rebel, Michael Collins, argued 'that every English-owned vessel, no matter what or whom it is carrying, ought to be torpedoed by Germany'.[104] There was, therefore, something of a celebration of violence among some key players in republican Ireland, (Yeats recalled Maud Gonne as having celebrated the intrinsic merits of war in the late nineteenth century). So, while the war provided the opportunity and the momentum towards an actual fight, the violent, aggressive instinct had been there at the core for some time.

But if it was wartime aggressive, the Rising was also dramatic and poetic-intellectual in its inspiration: 'The revolt was staged consciously as a drama by its principal actors. It is not without significance that Pearse, Plunkett and MacDonagh had all directed plays in their time.'[105] Those many theorists of nationalism who have seen intellectual van-guardism as vital to the fostering of nationalist movement[106] would feel no surprise at events in Dublin in April 1916. Here was the teacher-poet Pearse, the autodidactic scholar-writer Connolly, together with their rather literary fellow-leaders, fighting as they imagined themselves into the leadership of their nation. One of the exe-cuted heroes of the Rising was Thomas MacDonagh, whose poetic-sentimental instincts were typical. There was a rather dreamy quality to MacDonagh's mind, as exemplified by one of his early poems, 'Of a Poet Patriot':

> His songs were a little phrase
> Of eternal song,
> Drowned in the harping of lays
> More loud and long.
>
> His deed was a single word,
> Called out alone
> In a night when no echo stirred
> To laughter or moan.
>
> But his songs new souls shall thrill,
> The loud harps dumb,
> And his deed the echoes fill
> When the dawn is come.[107]

Maud Gonne's close friend Ella Young, who knew Pearse and Mac-Donagh and who was in Dublin during the 1916 rebellion, referred to it as 'a poet's Rising',[108] and there is much to support this view.

Yet, ultimately, it was a political event. The rebel 'Proclamation of the Republic' embodies the key themes which lie at the heart of nationalism itself. The community is clearly, emphatically identified: its people ('Irishmen and Irishwomen', 'the people of Ireland', 'cherishing all the children of the nation equally'), its culture ('In the name of God'), its assumption of descent ('the dead generations'; 'In every generation'), its history (the 'old tradition of nationhood'), its ethics (the guarantees offered, the allegiance claimed, and the noble manner of the struggle – without the dishonour of 'cowardice, inhumanity, or rapine'). The community was engaged in dramatic struggle: this was the politics of 'arms', of a struggle 'organized' by revolutionary and military organizations. And the national struggle was clearly for a particular kind of power: popular ownership of Ireland being 'sovereign', the rebels proclaimed 'the Irish republic as a sovereign independent state', favouring independent government based on representative self-determination ('representative of the whole people of Ireland'). And through it all the declared goal was that of Irish 'freedom'.[109]

In practice things were not, of course (or ever), so neat. Patriots such as the 1916 rebels could suggest that their free Ireland would rest on democratic self-determination and it is clear that a reasonable case can be made to the effect that the nation can be (and often has been) the solid ground upon which democracy can be (and often has been) constructed.[110] Yet 1916 in Ireland was, at best, a case of democracy after the event, of a non- or pre-mandated gesture by a vanguard elite which rather arrogantly identified its own will with the best interests of the people. As one scholar put it many years ago with regard to the leaders of the Rising, 'In 1916, half-a-dozen men decided what the nation should want.'[111] For there was a deep solipsism – a conviction that self was the only really existing thing – at the heart of rebel politics in the self-selecting world of 1916. Self and nation were conflated, others' views were invalidated, dismissed or ignored, and the outlook of many of the actually existing Irish people was simply excluded.

Solipsism was to remain part of the republican mental-political attitude for some time,[112] as was another feature of the character of 1916, its marked Catholicism: 'The devout Catholicism of the leaders and men of 1916, from Connolly to Pearse, was one of the most striking aspects of their personalities. And it was not only that they were all Catholics . . . they also thought in terms of the special nature of the Irish Catholic people.'[113] This Catholicism was evident during the week itself: the rebels recited the Rosary in the General Post Office (GPO) during the Rising, and were attended by Catholic priests. The leaders of the Rising were also attended by priests prior to their executions, even Connolly the Marxist and Casement the Protestant. For his part, Casement took instruction and became received into the Catholic Church during his last days, appearing to suggest in his final reflections an identification between Irishness and Catholicism. (At his death, Casement apparently exclaimed, 'For God and Kathleen ni Houlihane'.[114]) The Rising represented a moving and excluding inter-twining of religion with politics, in an expressly Catholic version. And, in death, this continued: there was very much a Catholic quality (what else would one expect?) to the celebration and remembrance of Easter Week, the rebels enjoying a nationalist apotheosis which involved them being lifted up in a Catholic martyrology. The rebels had hoped to produce a national resurrection ('We die that the Irish nation may live,' as Sean MacDiarmada put it, writing from his prison cell in 1916 on the day before his execution[115]); but the Catholic religious dimensions of Irish nationalism were interwoven with the rebellion also.

In time, the cost of this was to be felt in north-east Ireland where the largest concentration of Protestants lived. Even as early as May 1916 a British Cabinet Memorandum was noting the stark difference between Ulster and the rest: 'Throughout Leinster popular sympathy for the rebels is growing'; in Connacht 'among all sections of nationalists hopes are generally expressed that the dupes of the revolution will be dealt with leniently'; in Munster 'general sympathy among all nationalists is becoming intensified in favour of the rebels arrested or sentenced'; but 'public opinion generally throughout Ulster remains opposed to the rebellion'.[116]

For the rebel mind tended not to address the problem of unionism or Ulster at all seriously. This was true of Pearse,[117] as indeed of Casement, whose own myopia concerning Ulster was perhaps less forgivable given his family background. He claimed to have 'aimed at winning the Ulster Volunteers [the UVF] to the cause of a united Ireland. We aimed at uniting all Irishmen in a natural and national bond of cohesion based on mutual self-respect.'[118] But such views were far from realistic, and some of Casement's own writings display a harsh lack of sympathy or understanding for Irish politics different from his own. Shortly before the First World War he wrote, in reference to Ulster unionists, that, 'Sometimes the only thing to bring a boy to his senses is to hide him – and I think "Ulster" wants a sound hiding at the hands of her that owns her – Ireland's hands. Failing that – I pray for the Germans and their coming. A Protestant power to teach these Protestants their place in Irish life is what is needed.'[119] Here Casement clearly didn't respect the validity of any Ulster unionist case, and rather thought unionists largely to be dupes.

For his part, James Connolly admitted that his theory failed to match Ulster realities and, while some might wish to sustain the view that unionist Ulster (generation after generation) was filled merely with willing dupes who were washed in false consciousness, in reality neither this nor any neat anti-imperialist self-righteousness quite stands up to serious scrutiny. Neither Casement nor Connolly was, for example, anti-imperialist when it came to Germany. Casement knew the far from sweet workings of German imperialism better than most, yet initially gave strong support to Germany in the war; Connolly thought Germany a comparatively progressive power, intrinsically deserving of his support. So the anti-imperialistic 1916 rebels were for a time very pro-German (and, in that sense, pro-imperialist) in their sentiments.

The Rising was also characterized by the power of activist minority energy to change history – albeit not quite in the activists' anticipated direction. (Neither Connolly's Marxism nor Pearse's anti-materialism was to characterize the state built upon the separatist foundations of 1916, as even the most casual observer of modern Dublin would have to admit.) But the small – actual, not imagined – community of activist nationalist zealots who lit the fuse did alter the Irish story. At local level during 1914–16 there had already been frequent indifference to the war among Irish nationalists; but the degree of disaffection from Britain was decisively changed by the events surrounding Easter 1916. Clarke and MacDiarmada are significant here within this passionate clique which helped to change the Irish story. MacDiarmada, apparently an AOH man for a time, was also an IRB and Sinn Féin organizer in pre-Rising days, his galvanism helping to prompt the revolutionary moment of 1916. (In this sense, the often dismissed mislabelling of the Rising as a Sinn Féin rebellion is not quite as entirely off-target as is sometimes assumed: true, the party did not organize the Rising, but at individual level some Sinn Féiners' zeal did greatly help to contribute to the event; Michael Collins himself had long been a Sinn Féiner.) The eager MacDiarmada was, in some ways, the classic hectic activist: as a young man he had read voraciously in Irish culture and history; he was rather preoccupied with Robert Emmet and 1803; he was committedly anti-parliamentarian; and – intriguingly for our argument about how the key ideas of nationalism reached Ireland – he also had Paine's *Rights of Man* in his book collection.

This point regarding activists is surely crucial to understanding how nationalism induces historical change. The ideas of the rebels might be simplistic (many of Pearse's own political ideas being, in the words of one candid authority, 'vague and half-baked'[120]); yet there was a very serious intent and effect involved here, and its underlying rationale should not be casually dismissed. How was change to be brought about? What power was to be deployed in order to achieve nationalist goals? Nationalist Lennox Robinson's play *Patriots*, first produced at the Abbey Theatre four years before the Rising, in April 1912, featured the character James Nugent, a militant Irish revolutionary nationalist recently released from jail after a lengthy sentence. Nugent voiced something of the essence of physical-force enthusiasm, stressing that change, at root, always came from aggressive action: 'Parliament may have passed some good bills in its time, but it passed a devilish lot of bad ones too. And it's not the fellows at Westminster we have to thank for the good ones; it was some man in Ireland who maimed a bullock or shot a landlord that did the work.'[121]

With the redemptive Easter gesture itself, even the romantic, sacrificial and sentimental layers of memory should not occlude the bloody reality and consequences of the episode. For one thing, not all of those involved in republican militancy sought a glorious defeat (Casement and Hobson, for example, wanted a successful rising or for there not to be one, while at least some of those who planned the rebellion itself did so with the aim of military success). And might this have happened to a greater degree – had the arms actually been landed, for example, or had MacNeill's countermanding efforts not intervened?

In the event, even the militarily defeated rebellion did have a very practical political effect. The IRB's official position was that war against England should follow upon, rather than stimulate, popular sanction. But the fanaticism and eccentric vision of the Pearseans reversed this understanding of struggle and democracy. Without sanction, you acted and people then retrospectively endorsed your gesture. The inspiring directness, courage and simplicity – reinforced by the execution ending – did, after all, produce a conversion moment: 'Then came like a thunderclap the 1916 Rising.'[122] So this became the defining birth of a new period, to be endlessly saluted or interpreted by scholars, novelists, musicians. To the many historical accounts[123] should be added many novels,[124] as well as the still-enchanting music of Hibernophile composer (and pseudonymous Irish nationalist poet) Arnold Bax.[125]

But even such elegiac music cannot eclipse the destructive and divisive dimensions of the Easter Rising. Some people had a good rebellion: future leading republican Harry Boland (1887–1922) emerged from the fight unscathed, and apparently didn't kill anybody; but many others were not so fortunate. And to the many dead and maimed, we must also add further victims of this burst of Irish political violence. For the most emphatic achievement of 1916 was to destroy a constitutional, parliamentary, conciliatory version of nationalism (a nationalism founded on the principles of compromise, trust, toleration, and opposition to political violence or coercion). Trust, in particular, was destroyed, the bloodshed of 1916 driving Ireland's two political communities, nationalist and unionist, much further apart.

Among the legacies of Pearse, Connolly, Casement and their comrades, then, was an intensification both of violence and, through this, of Irish division in these crucible years. So Eoin MacNeill, the much-condemned formal Volunteer leader who tried to put off what he feared would be a disaster, perhaps deserves rehabilitation. Like many from this period, he self-Gaelicized (John MacNeill adopting 'Eoin' during the early days of the Gaelic League); unlike many, he was pivotal in the foundation of both the Gaelic League and the Irish Volunteers. Fascinated by what he called 'the living Irish language',[126] MacNeill had seen the League as crucial to historic Ireland, to its essential nature and distinctiveness. He was a man of great integrity as well as high intelligence, and he believed deeply in the separateness of Ireland from England; but he held that the extent to which this separateness could be realized in practice depended upon a rational assessment of what history at any given moment allowed. So to see him as an other-worldly, naive creature who was outmanoeuvred by pragmatist rebels would be a simplification – and even perhaps a reversal of reality. The Volunteer leader is often held to have been out of step with pressing 1916 realities, but is this actually true? Might it not be that MacNeill rightly sensed that too imminently militant a revolutionism might be unhelpfully destructive for Ireland? Such moderate conservatism of approach surely has much to recommend it, when set against some of the competing versions of Irish nationalism at the time and, particularly, when set against the consequences of its more aggressive and brutal rivals. Usually dismissed, the eminent scholar-nationalist from the Glens of Antrim might have been right all along.

So George Bernard Shaw might be judged to have been accurate in suggesting that the power of nationalism arose from a sense of broken nationality – from the denial of appropriate cultural respect, necessary self-government and so on. But it was Home Rule that he identified as the remedy – and this too was in turn to be broken by those who engineered 1916. There were indeed problems with British political legitimacy in Ireland, and these lay behind, and were intensified by,

Easter Week. But the era of consensus was also a victim of those bloody, pseudo-sacred days.

After the Rising, over 2,500 people were deported to England: they were held in various prisons for a few weeks, during which time around 650 were released and allowed to return home, and there then remained 1,863 men in custody. Frongoch in north Wales was an internment camp for German prisoners of war: it was duly vacated and now housed most of the Irish 1916 prisoners. Numbers were not huge. By the end of July 1916 only 600 remained there, others having been released. The alumni of this republican prison-university included impressive names (future Revolutionary leaders Richard Mulcahy and Michael Collins prominent among them), and it is true that Frongoch witnessed some organizational tightening. There were formalized military staffs among the prisoners, who smuggled military manuals into the camp for the training of the Volunteers: discipline, military training, organization and comradeship. But it should not be assumed that Frongoch was decisive in producing subsequent revolution: it might have accelerated some aspects of the advance, but is it really sustainable to think, for example, that greater dispersal of post-rebellion prisoners would have prevented the later growth of republican Ireland?

Either way, they soon were released. Frongoch internees were set free in December 1916, as were other Irish prisoners who were being held in Reading Jail. Nor did post-Rising prisoners necessarily think their treatment to have been inordinately harsh. In May 1916 Constance Markievicz wrote to her sister Eva from Mountjoy Jail in Dublin: 'Now darling, don't worry about me for I'm not too bad at all, and it's only a mean spirit that grudges paying the price. Everybody is quite kind, and though this is not exactly a bed of roses, still many rebels have had much worse to bear . . . when I think of what the Fenians suffered . . . I realize that I am extremely lucky.'[127]

Markievicz (1868–1927) was an eccentric figure within Irish nationalism (from the well-known Gore-Booth family – the eldest child of Henry Gore-Booth – she had rebelled against her privileged background, having trained at London's Slade School of Art). But she was significant enough, founding the nationalist youth organization Fianna Eireann in 1909 and playing a reasonably prominent role in 1916 itself; and she tellingly exemplified the powerful cocktail of authenticist

elitism, egalitarianism and self-righteousness which typified so many
of her revolutionary crowd. From 1918 to 1921 she was in prison
(Holloway, Cork, Mountjoy) and clearly exhibited both the radical
anti-snobbery and the elitist arrogance of the revolutionary. Regarding
King George V's visit to Dublin in 1911, for example, she wrote to her
brother: 'we are all praying that King George will not come again for
many a long day. Even if I were not a nationalist I should object to
kings' visits, for they but bring out the worst qualities of people. All
sorts of snobbery is developed.' But her subsequent comments reflected
her own hostility to the morally vulgar as well as to British power in
Ireland. During the king's sojourn, she wrote:

> The town filled with drunken and immoral soldiers and sailors,
> their pockets full of money. Utterly undisciplined and bent on
> amusing themselves, these fellows in their gay uniforms with their
> talk of foreign lands have no difficulty in making themselves
> popular and corrupting boys and girls alike. One gets so furious at
> this sort of thing being forced on a city against its will, and one
> wonders so why a king comes at all, if – to do so safely – he has to
> bring an army and a navy from England, and police from the
> country. The town was like a place that had been recently captured,
> and was in the hands of an army.[128]

The post-Rising era saw heterogeneous Irish nationalists group
together under the umbrella of Sinn Féin, the perhaps ironic beneficiaries of the Easter gesture and its aftermath. There were by-election
victories in 1917 (February in North Roscommon; May – very narrowly
– in South Longford; and July in East Clare, where Eamon de Valera
(1882–1975) triumphed in the by-election occasioned by the First
World War death of John Redmond's brave brother William). And
there was much momentum behind the republican cause now. When
County Kerry Volunteer Thomas Ashe (1885–1917) died as a result of
force-feeding while on hunger strike in jail, the resultant funeral
testified to the mood of the era. Many thousands thronged the Dublin
streets, and thousands more took part in the funeral procession from
the City Hall to Glasnevin, where the interment took place:

> For hours before the removal of the remains from the City Hall,
> where they had been lying in state, crowds gathered outside that

building, and the assembling of contingents in this and adjacent
thoroughfares was watched with the greatest interest by thousands
of sightseers, who not alone lined the streets, but were congregated
in windows and on every possible vantage point.[129]

In time, the effects of 1916 were to see the IPP effectively replaced
by Sinn Féin as the dominant voice of the nationalist Irish community.
But what did this mean in practice? There was, as one might expect,
some considerable continuity. The leading scholar of this political shift,
David Fitzpatrick, has sharply noted that 'the spirit of the constitutional movement did not die with the body'; 'many of the converts
from constitutionalism to Sinn Féin carried their old political habits
and assumptions with them'.[130] (Though *Dracula* had been written by
a Home Ruler – Bram Stoker – it was Sinn Féin which drew strength
through political vampirism in these years.) At leadership level, certainly, there was much continuity between the IPP and new Sinn Féin,
which helps to explain the smoothness of the shift from one party's
hegemony to that of the other. The 1916 episode redounded to the
benefit of Sinn Féin, and many of the released 1916 internees were
significant in reorganizing the party in these days. By late 1917 the new
nationalism was on a surge (late-war economic conditions in Ireland,
with unemployment and rising food prices, favoured anti-British
causes during 1917–18); and in these days many younger Catholic
clergy strongly supported Sinn Féin, an important feature of the latter's
growth in 1917–18.

So the party which Arthur Griffith had founded, and which had
significantly grown in terms of branches from 1905 to 1909 but had
then gone into something of a decline, now blossomed again. Strengthened by the post-Rising sympathy for more direct, militant politics,
the Sinn Féiners attacked the IPP's stance and record: Nationalist Party
MPs were accused of being self-serving, and of having agreed, for
example, to the increased taxation of Ireland. And this shift – like the
Rising itself – was a First World War episode. The Nationalist Party's
approach to the war had become discredited as that conflict dragged
bloodily on ('No one now thought it was a good notion to kit up
against the Kaiser and go to Flanders'[131]). Furthermore, the fact that
Home Rule was on the Statute Book seemed ever less impressive as
these terrible trench years continued.

The more impatient politics of Sinn Féin matched the nationalist mood and, indeed, it was a specifically wartime issue which cemented the Sinn Féin foundations. In British desperation in the spring of 1918 it was decided to extend conscription to Ireland – a deeply unpopular move among nationalists here, and one which greatly helped to intensify Irish nationalist sentiment. Though conscription was never implemented in practice in Ireland, the nationalist community here engaged in energetic and sharply focused struggle against its threat, an anti-conscription pledge being taken by huge numbers within Catholic Ireland.

Even militant republicans who celebrated the 1916 tradition were themselves to acknowledge the decisive importance of the conscription threat in 1918. In the words of Donegal-born Eithne Coyle, who became a leading Cumann na mBan republican,

> The news of the Easter Week insurrection came to us in Donegal like a flash of light; a flash that was short-lived, but it drove us into the organizations, that up to that time, scarcely existed in our part. The Volunteers were organized for the first time. The threat of conscription came, and I remember well we all wrote our names down against it in the porch of our church. That would be April 1918, when we signed the pledge.[132]

Another Donegal-born republican was even more emphatic: 'I was still teaching when 1916 came. Its ripples were scarcely felt in the Rosses [County Donegal]. It might have passed and been forgotten had not England pushed the people together with her threat of conscription.'[133] Intelligent observers beyond the militant family also considered the conscription crisis to have been decisive in intensifying nationalist anger and politics, constitutional nationalist Stephen Gwynn (1864–1950) among them.[134] The crisis around possible conscription helped to kill off British legitimacy in Catholic Ireland – an ironic achievement for a measure which was never operationalized.

And it was emphatically Sinn Féin and the Volunteers who emerged victorious as the leaders within mainstream Irish nationalism. People signed the anti-conscription pledge, whether Nationalist, Sinn Féin or Labour in affiliation, but it was Sinn Féinism which represented the angry disaffection most aptly. In this, they benefited from religious blessing too. The Catholic clergy were very much to the forefront in the anti-conscription campaign, and links in this struggle were particularly strong between the Catholic Church and Sinn Féin.

The December 1918 UK General Election provided the stage on which to perform their victorious act. Of 105 seats, Sinn Féin – impressively and dramatically – won a total of 73, the IPP only 6, and Unionists 26. Some people still exaggerate the reality of the voting here, suggesting far larger margins of Sinn Féin victory than were the case.[135] In fact, Sinn Féin won 48 per cent of the vote in December 1918, and 59 per cent of the seats in contested constituencies; the IPP held around a third of votes cast in the election. But there can be no doubt of the scale or importance of Sinn Féin's triumph (or of IPP collapse: the Party had held sixty-eight seats at the time of parliament's dissolution). In 1918 there was vote-rigging in favour of republicans and also some intimidation and violence, but these cannot in themselves account for such a clear margin of victory within nationalist Ireland. Sinn Féin – as often with more radical-sounding parties – had a strength of backing among the young, and this benefited them as there had been a recent extension of the franchise to younger voters. (The Representation of the People Act, operative for the first time in the December 1918 election, allowed for men aged twenty-one and over, and women over thirty, to vote; the young and the female contained many Sinn Féin supporters. Not for the last time, UK reform unwittingly furthered the cause of militant anti-British nationalism in Ireland.)

What had people actually voted for? Not necessarily the republic sought by separatists (Sinn Féin had actually been rather ambiguous, rather than doctrinally committed, on that point). But Sinn Féin unquestionably were committed to the furtherance of the cause of Irish self-determination, and this was stressed by many, including the fiery IRA man Dan Breen, who considered Sinn Féin's December 1918 victory to have been 'the greatest manifestation of self-determination recorded in history. On the principles proclaimed by Britain and her allies, our claim to complete independence was unanswerable.'[136] One might dispute this judgment, but there is no disputing the centrality of self-determination and sovereign power to Sinn Féin's nationalist argument. In 1907 in Dundalk the Dungannon Clubs had merged with Griffith and Rooney's creation, Cumann na nGaedheal, to produce the Sinn Féin League, whose objective was 'regaining the sovereign independence of Ireland'.[137] In the event, revolutionary Sinn Féin was to be a coalition of divergent, competing interests and views, held together by a vague but powerfully alluring goal – Irish independence. They denied the legitimacy of British rule in Ireland, and of the institutions in which such illegitimate power was vested. So they had fought the 1918 election on an abstentionist basis: their struggle was for votes, not for the right to sit in a parliament whose power they refused to recognize.

Already, there were signs of division within this broad nationalist family. (What else would one expect with such a major movement?) By 1917 militant figures like the ever-feuding 1916 veterans Cathal Brugha and Michael Collins had already come greatly to distrust Griffith's Sinn Féin; and it is important to note also that the post-Rising Volunteers were flourishing. By the end of 1917 their morale was strong and their organization robust, and the April–May 1918 threat of conscription had led to a marked increase in Volunteer activity. This tended to mean parades and training, as well as recruitment: during 1917–18 most Volunteer action involved what one historian has termed acts of 'public defiance'.[138] Killing came later.

3

> To each one of us in the movement, the Republic seemed
> the Ireland of his desire. To some, the vision glowed of a
> liberal, progressive state on friendly terms with the rest of
> the world; others dreamed of a pious island, fortress of
> Catholic and Gaelic traditions in a decadent and anarchic
> age; many hoped for state socialism, some for a great release
> of individual art and enterprise. By tacit consent, such
> differences were not discussed. What importance had they,
> compared with the aim which united us – to free Ireland
> from alien control?
>
> Dorothy Macardle, on the 1919–21 period[139]

The Irish Revolution and its legacies embodied what have been
identified as the two main problems associated with the phenomenon
of nationalism: 'state break-up' and 'control of the state by the majority
nation'.[140] Irish nationalist violence destabilized British Ireland and
broke up the existing UK state in aggressive fashion; and each of the
two consequently emerging states – independent Ireland and Northern
Ireland – came to characterize both the benefits and the dramatic
disadvantages of states controlled by national majorities and biased in
their favour.

The first stage of this process – the war between republican Ireland
and British Ireland during 1919–21 – has been given many names: the
Anglo-Irish War, the War of Independence, the Troubles, the Tan
War. None of these descriptions quite works. This conflict was emphatically not one between England and Ireland; at the very least, it
involved Britain rather than merely England, and in any case there was
far too much conflict between Irish people themselves for 'Anglo-Irish'
to be adequate as a description. The 'War of Independence' label fails
also, given the far from fully independent outcome of 1921 (although
'War *for* Independence' might be more fitting). The 'Troubles' is far
too vague a term, and the 'Tan War' simply too narrow (focusing
more attention than they deserve upon the sartorially motley Black

and Tans – British ex-servicemen recruited to reinforce the Royal Irish Constabulary (RIC) in their anti-IRA struggle in 1920).

However it is labelled, the 1919–21 conflict is one whose broad narrative is well known (though even aspects of the basic story can still be fought over in sharp-edged exchange).[141] It involved impressive propagandist politics, with Sinn Féin coming to represent an alternative source of political legitimacy for many in nationalist Ireland. A rival parliament – Dáil Éireann – was established in Dublin in 1919,[142] and a Declaration of Independence and a Democratic Programme were both issued. These reflected the centrality to republican nationalism of our central nationalist themes. The Irish people were 'by right a free people', stated the Declaration of Independence; they had been wrongly ruled by England but were now committed to the 'complete independence' of the Irish republic, incorporating enthusiasm for 'the people's will, with equal right and equal opportunity for every citizen'; the new parliament celebrated its representative quality, and represented indeed 'the ancient Irish people'; only law produced by egalitarian, representative, sovereign power was legitimate ('the elected representatives of the Irish people alone have power to make laws binding on the people of Ireland'). The Democratic Programme reinforced such themes, reiterating 'the right of the people of Ireland to the ownership of Ireland and to the unfettered control of Irish destinies to be indefeasible'; the country was 'to be ruled in accordance with the principles of Liberty, Equality and Justice for all, which alone can secure permanence of government in the willing adhesion of the people'; the nation had a supervening ethical claim upon all its members ('the duty of every man and woman to give allegiance and service to the commonwealth'); and all of its territory and people were subject to its sovereign authority.[143] Here was a celebration of the supposed achievements of nationalist struggle: territory, united and ancient people, culture (for there were religious and Gaelic gestures too); ethics, enemies, and egalitarian notions of sovereign law-making in the newly independent, self-determining and representatively governed state – this was the classic nationalist mix of community, struggle and power.

Accompanying this political initiative through Dáil Éireann, though really semi-detached in origin and direction, was an IRA (Irish Republican Army) struggle against the forces and representatives of the British state in Ireland. During 1917–18 there had been much overlap between the respective memberships of Sinn Féin and the Volunteers (the latter to become the IRA). As the IRA became more violent, however, there came to be more of a distinction between the two wings of the republican movement: the Dáil did not publicly take responsibility for IRA activities until 1921, and even some of the IRA's most committed soldiers acknowledged that many nationalists did not support the killing and maiming which the republican army practised.[144]

There is no doubt that republicans were the aggressors in this war, whether in the fatal attack of January 1919 in which the IRA killed two RIC men in County Tipperary (and which is usually held to have inaugurated the conflict), or in the killings of police officers in Dublin in late 1919 and early 1920. But there then developed a cyclical pattern of vicious violence: republican, state and loyalist brutality marred life across much of Ireland in gruesome, repellent and vengeful fashion, according to 'the runaway tit-for-tat logic'[145] of this reprisal-fuelled and ugly war.

Prior to 1920 most IRA operations involved drilling and marching, and violence itself remained rare during 1919. In January 1920, however, IRA GHQ formally sanctioned attacks on RIC barracks and this might be seen to mark the real start of the War for Independence, since it implied a more systematic approach to the republican struggle. During 1920 violence escalated, and there emerged IRA flying columns – effectively, mobile guerrillas. The police became increasingly ostracized – a deliberate republican strategy – and found it harder and harder to gain information about the IRA from the community. Reprisals by state forces tended to rebound against the authorities, further deepening popular disaffection. Not for the last time in British Ireland, military measures taken to repress IRA violence often led to increased rather than diminished republican sympathy among the Catholic nationalist population.[146]

A famous day such as Bloody Sunday (21 November 1920) illustrates something of the darkness of these times. IRA men killed over a dozen people (most of them British Intelligence agents) in Dublin in the morning; in the afternoon, British forces killed twelve civilians at Croke Park, also in the capital, at a Gaelic football match. In the evening, two Dublin IRA men (Dick McKee and Peadar Clancy) were arrested and killed by Crown forces. Dispute has raged (and rages still) concerning who fired first at Croke Park. It is possible that IRA men in the crowd in or around the Park did fire first; or did the RIC and Auxiliaries simply raid Croke Park in reprisal for the IRA's killings that morning? Those morning killings reflect another important aspect of this nationalist war, namely the intelligence conflict. The idea that the IRA unambiguously outwitted and outmanoeuvred British intelligence in Ireland during these years has now been tellingly questioned.[147] But it remains fairly clear that the IRA had considerable success in thwarting British rule during 1919–21: through paramilitary action, intelligence work, political gesture, and the provocation of state clumsiness. By early 1921 significant sections of the Irish nationalist population were sympathetic enough to the IRA rebels to make British government of nationalist Ireland impossible in normal ways.

In the summer of 1921 stalemate had been reached and a truce was declared (coming into effect on 11 July): this marked the prelude to fraught negotiations and a troubled peace, as we shall see. At this stage, no decisive or knock-out blow had been delivered (or looked likely to be delivered) by either side; this conflict was not going to end through military victory.[148] The IRA could not simply be defeated, but they had their own deep problems too. One was a shortage of firepower, a difficulty for the IRA across much of Ireland in mid-1921 and a major problem for republicans throughout the 1919–21 conflict. One eminent IRA man from the comparatively active county of Longford was himself frankly to acknowledge that, 'Even at the best of times we had arms for only a fraction of the available men';[149] another prominent revolutionary observed, 'In May and June 1921 ammunition for the men on active service had all but run out. It was almost impossible to secure supplies.'[150]

The 1919–21 Irish War for Independence has often been described and narrated. But actually explaining it, in terms of the dynamics of nationalism, is a different task, and one which is probably best attempted through careful consideration of politics, violence, religion, social forces, intellectual influences and broader cultural setting.

It was emphatically a political war, and focused on the nationalist struggle for self-determination, sovereignty and state power. Harry Boland, one of the most significant of republicans in this conflict, was lucid about what he sought: 'a free and independent Ireland – not a paltry Home Rule or Colony but Ireland absolutely sovereign'.[151]

Another famous republican revolutionary, Liam Mellows, had stated in January 1918 that he was aiming to 'free my country from the tyrannous domination of England'.[152] The Dáil established in January 1919, comprising the available Sinn Féin MPs who had just been elected, was one which embodied a republican alternative legitimacy; and this parliament espoused self-determination and Irish freedom.

This was a struggle for popular sovereignty (republican activist Maire Comerford referring to these heady years as 'the people's revolution'[153]), and for a legitimacy based on the idea of the national community having its own representative rulers. Sinn Féin saw itself as a movement which represented the nation (with all that that implied for those who stood outside or against it, of course); but by May 1921 – when elections for a devolved parliament returned 105 Sinn Féin MPs unopposed for the twenty-six counties of southern Ireland – there might seem to have been considerable weight behind this republican self-image. This was, to republican eyes at least, a nationalist struggle for liberation, the goal being self-determination and political autonomy for the Irish people as a nation. Sinn Féin's English organization was entitled the Irish Self-Determination League; 'We here in Ireland are fighting in our own way, the only way open to us – for the principle of self-determination,' leading republican Eamon de Valera had asserted in 1918;[154] and it was on self-determination and sovereignty that de Valera himself later focused so much in the dealings with the British in 1921. His great opponent in the 1921–2 split over the Anglo-Irish Treaty, Michael Collins, also concentrated on the importance of sovereignty and of popular will, just as these questions had likewise been important to Sinn Féin in 1917: 'Sinn Féin aims at securing the international recognition of Ireland as an independent Irish republic. Having achieved that status, the Irish people may, by referendum, freely choose their own form of government.'[155]

To republicans, this was merely democracy. As in 1916, however, the truth was probably more complex. There clearly were great difficulties with British legitimacy in Ireland in 1919, and even more deep problems by 1921. So much is clear. But it is far from clear either that republicans were keen to follow (or even to clarify) precisely what the actually existing Irish people wanted, or to define the national community flexibly enough to accommodate Ireland's full population. The IRA could hold that they embodied the national will, but who determined that this was the case? The IRA could assert that the more separatist you were, the more truly Irish you could be thought to be; but again, what if an Irish person disagreed? The answer could be brusque, and brutal enough to raise some doubts about the practical implications of republican democracy and community: 'The people of this country would have to give allegiance to it or if they wanted to support the Empire they would have to clear out and support the Empire elsewhere.'[156] History, as republicans rather simplistically read it, was an ancient story of Irish separateness from England: pre-Norman Ireland had been politically and culturally united and free, and modern-day nationalists were merely setting things in their proper and historically rightful order.[157]

Was this approach entirely persuasive? It has been widely recognized that nationalism – a creed involving a sense of absolute values, and of truths which lie beyond compromise – has on occasions conflicted with democratic politics,[158] and there was certainly a strain of this in early-twentieth-century IRA nationalism. Liam Lynch (later to be IRA Chief of Staff) typically clarified where power was to lie in his own preferred view: 'the army has to hew the way for politics to follow'.[159] For the 1919–21 nationalist struggle was a bloody, insurrectionary one. The IRA label was certainly in use as early as late 1916; during 1919–21 the Volunteers had firmly become known by this name. And it was as soldiers that these people saw themselves.[160] Violence was seen as necessary for the achievement of change. How were the British to be made to agree to Irish national self-determination and freedom? Through the coercive argument of violence rather than the futile deployment of constitutional, moral or purely parliamentary pressure.

Ireland could be made ungovernable through killings, through attacking and often enough destroying RIC barracks, or by intimidating people and persuading them to boycott British Ireland (and republican intimidation had been evident even as early as late 1916). Violence magnified the importance of your nationalist struggle, and it demanded attention and response. It prevented your opponent from ignoring you or imposing their own solution upon you. It helped you to gain and maintain control over your own community; and it prompted the state into delegitimizing itself through counter-productive violence, since it was difficult for the state to deploy forces against the IRA without also (dis)affecting the wider population. People who would not engage in

IRA violence might be turned against the British state by Crown-force harshness, as is implied in northern nationalist Joseph Devlin's words, written from the very House of Commons itself in 1920: 'The most that can be done is to keep before the people of this country the policy of reprisals, and in that we are fairly successful. Now the English people are beginning to realize what is going on in Ireland in the name of law and order.'[161]

But the attractions of violence went beyond the mere matter of getting from point A to point B in nationalist struggle. Violence was considered to be of value in itself, in terms of what it reflected about a nation which deserved its freedom; in terms of the careers and roles which it gave to many young men; and in terms of the attitudinal defiance which it inculcated. Dignity, pride and self-respect were all embodied in IRA resistance and defiance. And – once the bloody cycle had begun – violence also satisfied the desire for revenge, for hitting back.

Was this brutality legitimate? Yes, said the republicans, and this has been the traditional nationalist view. Again, however, some qualifications might perhaps be mentioned. It was not the case that IRA violence was legitimated through popular mandate (it simply was not), nor even that it was particularly popular among the wider nationalist population: 'The use of violence by Volunteers was not popular, either within the movement or with the population.'[162] Most of those who had been in the Volunteers were themselves (understandably) reluctant to become involved in violence, and the more intense that violent struggle became, the smaller was the group of people who enthusiastically supported it (a correction of the all-too-frequent assumption that modern Irish politics has demonstrated a tendency towards widespread enthusiasm for violence as a way of sorting out differences).

Nor was IRA violence legitimate because of Dáil sanction – the soldiers were as sceptical about the politicians as the Dáil was wary of the gunmen. No. Violence was legitimated because, for a small group of zealots, it offered political and other rewards in terms of a powerful expression of nationalist struggle. You could claim, as republicans did, that violence was directed against an 'army of occupation in Ireland'.[163] But this denied the complexity of a situation in which many of the RIC were not only Irish Catholic, but Irish nationalist in sympathy. Moreover, much IRA violence was not directed against armed enemies at all. Sometimes remembered heroically, this 1919–21 war was not, for the most part, a war of combat courage, and it often enough involved the targeting of vulnerable people in vicious ways.[164] Most casualties (whether IRA, military, RIC or civilian) did not occur in combat, but rather when the victim was defenceless, and often when they were alone. This was a vicious and brutal conflict, with a cruel quality to it. Most of the victims of the violence during 1916–23 as a whole were civilians, members of no fighting group; most of the violence was directed at non-combatants, rather than taking place in military exchanges and battles between warring armies. In some cases, indeed, the violence seems merely to have been directed against out-groups, those beyond the republican community, whether vagrants, homosexuals, strangers or Protestants.[165]

If the violence was targeted beyond the community, then its roots lay very much in actual, small, bonded communities of local activists and initiators. As in 1916, activists could change the world (and, as in 1916, not entirely in the way that they had hoped). For the most part, the lengthy shelf of memoirs produced by IRA ex-revolutionaries showed them, rather like one of George Bernard Shaw's characters, to have had hands more accustomed to the sword than to the pen. But these are revealing tales none the less and they tend to reinforce the importance of local, small-scale intimacy in the groups which produced IRA violence. This was true within the radicalization process, as the group of mates drilling together was arrested, imprisoned for minor offences and perhaps treated rather roughly; as they duly became more cohesive through the camaraderie and shared kudos of incarceration, and then, on release, as they attempted to procure weapons; as they thereby engaged in further friction with a now hostile state, with life lost and the cycle of vengeful attacks having been initiated – and escalating week by week.

Small groups of zealots could provoke a Draconian state response, as violence generated counter-violence. Conviction and zealotry among the vanguard produced the Revolution, and local loyalties to friends or inspiring leaders could determine the pace of the struggle. So the nation responded very variably to the call to arms in 1919–21. Southern counties (especially Cork, Kerry, Tipperary and Limerick) were the most active and intense, though Dublin city was very energetic also.[166] Local cycles of bloody escalation often determined the pace of the war, which was far more a set of local conflicts than it was one war directed centrally by GHQ in Dublin (which was not really able to exercise too tight a rein on autonomous local IRA units: 'Whatever success the IRA had outside Dublin was largely dependent on local initiative'[167]).

Republicans might see this as a case of good (or bad) local leadership, but for historians it points also to the politics of contingency. A particular group of eager militants could help to produce their own war; and people would often join the movement because of some fortuitous local development (such as a by-election: the 1917 South Longford contest seems to have been one such mobilizing moment, galvanizing many in that locality). So while Irish nationalism is partly a story of large, impersonal, structural forces – the economics of the Union after 1800, the technological changes which made Britain the world's dominant empire, and so on – it was here also a story of decisive, local, small-scale or even individual initiative and influence, personal choice and action.[168]

Clearly, those personal and small-group choices made sense within a broader communal context, and foundational to this was Catholic Christianity. The revolutionaries were virtually all Catholic, and unless we think this a coincidence (which is not really a serious proposition), then we have to hold that Catholicism was central to their struggle in some way. 'Non-Catholic guerrillas were almost non-existent. . . . A survey of 917 prisoners convicted under the Defence of the Realm Act in 1917–19, for example, produced one declared "agnostic" and no Protestants.'[169]

Twenty-first-century Irish republicanism and Irish society have grown more secular and so it's easy to lose sight of precisely how far such change has represented a rebalancing within the internal weighting of republican ideology. As elsewhere, the balance between the various cultural items on the nationalist menu can change; in Ireland (as, for example, in Croatia) religion used to play a far more explicitly significant role in nation-building than is at present the case,[170] and it would be unfair to the nationalists of the past to dismiss this central part of their life and thought and action.

The 1919–21 IRA were emphatically Catholic revolutionaries who assumed God to be active on their side: whether Terence ('Terry always to his friends'[171]) MacSwiney in 1920,[172] or Frank Gallagher writing about 1920;[173] whether the 'devout Catholic' Cathal Brugha,[174] or eminent republican Richard Mulcahy whose own world view was shaped more powerfully by Catholicism than by anything else.[175] Leading republican Eoin O'Duffy had been raised in devoutly pious fashion: Holy Water and the Rosary accompanied him into the Revolution, and Catholicism was central to his ideology as an Irish nationalist;[176] many other IRA men attested to their committed Catholicism during Revolutionary days: 'Attendance at Mass was of course dangerous, but I doubt if we ever missed Mass on a Sunday from the time the [East Clare IRA Flying] Column was formed.'[177]

God was on your side, He had a distinctive mission for Ireland the nation, and He demanded a certain spiritualism of outlook: 'one feels that one is always fighting for God and Ireland, for the spread of our spirituality such as it is, to counteract the agnosticism and materialism of our own and other countries'.[178] Such hostility towards materialism was very evident ('we are not a materialistic nation!'[179]), as was a sense that the communal should prevail over the individual. This was a group which self-consciously emphasized spirituality and sacrifice and the efficacy of suffering,[180] and which adhered to what it considered a superior morality of nationalism: the nation called to you and deserved your loyalty, but this had an ethical, religious dimension to it amid a moralization of politics. (And the foreign was, as so often, held to be associated with immorality.)

Many of the Revolutionaries were to carry their Catholic understanding of Irish freedom with them for many years (the ever-committed Mary MacSwiney could insouciantly write in 1935 that, as far as Irish republicans were concerned, a 'social programme in accordance with Catholic principles is quite good enough for anyone'; she hoped that the IRA would imminently 'declare that they stand for no programme which is inconsistent with Catholic principles'.[181]) And lasting Catholic belief and self-image were pervasive partly because of educational and other influence over the Revolutionary generation. Priests had been key influences over their intellectual, philosophical, educational and moral foundation, and this at times had a markedly patriotic flavour. If the IRA had been largely educated by the Catholic Church, then in particular the teaching of the Christian Brothers seems to have had an impact on the thinking of many who were to become activists.[182] So IRA men had frequently been profoundly influenced by patriotic and Catholic teachers, many indeed ascribing their induction into republican thinking to the impact of such local figures. Just as education can be one of those means of inculcating national awareness and allegiance in established states,[183] so too in the alternative culture of the Christian Brothers' Schools (CBS), a new nation was being encouraged to grow. And while the CBS were teaching Richard Mulcahy, Ernie O'Malley and others, less direct influences – such as the popular novels we encountered from the pen of Canon Sheehan – also helped to reinforce a sense of pride in a specifically Catholic Irish nationalism.

It was not that the Church as such backed the militant cause; the clergy were less keenly supportive of the IRA during 1919–21 than they had been of Sinn Féin during 1917–18, for example. Though far from monolithic, the Church itself tended to oppose the IRA's use of violence. Nor was it a question of the IRA fighting against formal religious persecution. Even the fiery IRA leader Tom Barry openly acknowledged that, in the early twentieth century, 'there were no disabilities for Catholics in Ireland, instead they were perfectly free to practise their Faith'. But Barry did take for granted the uniform Catholic piety of his IRA ('In the years of the 1920–23 struggle we continued saying our prayers, attending Mass and receiving the Sacraments when and where possible'); and his reading of the long-term struggle betweeen Ireland and England through the centuries was one which focused on a fusion of denominational-religious and ethnic-communal suffering ('the destruction of the Catholic religion', 'confiscation of lands and properties of the Gael').[184] There was nothing inevitable about Gaelic and Catholic experience being fused so closely; but by the time of the Irish Revolution this was precisely what had occurred in the minds of the Revolutionaries themselves.

And such identification clearly had consequences for those not Catholic (or, indeed, not ethnically Gaelic). The confessionalization of Irish republicanism had strengthened it as a communal force: all were bound by the same rituals, faith, habit, core belief, and by the sense that nationalism involved a struggle to redress wrongs against Catholic Ireland. The Catholicism of nationalist Irishness was inextricably interwoven into it. And this had obvious advantages also in terms of what you were not; in Ernie O'Malley's typically candid recollection, there was 'a pitying commiseration' for those not of the true faith.[185]

In-group and out-group. If the Catholic community had suffered, then at whose hands had they done so? Protestant Britain, and Protestants – landlords and others – in Ireland. If Catholic Ireland defined itself as the nation, then historically the process had also worked the other way, as a Protestant Britain had effectively defined itself in exclusive ways too. Thus it was that the 1919–21 IRA (and their enemies) on occasions exhibited an ugly sectarianism of word and deed.[186]

Some nationalists from the Revolutionary generation turned to a deeper religious life when their Revolutionary ardour had cooled. Sean O'Faoláin was one such deeply Catholic nationalist intellectual, who moved in a kind of Wagnerian shift from youthful romantic nationalist enthusiasm, through disaffection and disenchantment, towards post-Revolutionary, European-influenced Catholicism and artistic expression. But regardless of personal religious odyssey, the point remains that the IRA of the War for Independence were not only overwhelmingly Catholic in number, but also formed a self-consciously Irish Catholic community of nationalists: faith and fatherland were united. In the view of someone like Terry MacSwiney, religion and nationalism simply could not be separated: nationalism was divinely ordained, and the committed nationalist was a better Catholic as a direct result of that commitment.

But the great strength of nationalism – and the key to understanding why it has driven the lives of so many people – is that it can make sense of so much more than one aspect of life. Nationalism allowed for the IRA and their community to pursue self-determination, sovereignty and political freedom in ways which emancipated every individual, and in ways enriched and strengthened by Catholic identification and grievance and commitment. But it also, simultaneously, made sense of a variety of social backgrounds and material conditions and hopes. Nationalist motivation clearly cannot be understood without acknowledging people's ostensible purpose and motive; but neither can it adequately be accounted for purely in this way. There are some causes which lie unrecognized by nationalists themselves but which are, none the less, decisive. (It is here that people such as the theorist of nationalism Ernest Gellner were so wonderfully right, in identifying developments such as technological or economic change as motive forces behind the emergence of modern nationalism, despite the fact that most nationalists were themselves oblivious to such influences.[187])

In terms of the 1919–21 IRA, social background and status provide a setting for such layered explanation. Much excellent work has now been done by historians concerning the social profile of the Revolutionaries.[188] Who were the IRA? Well, they tended to be young, male, Catholic (in background, certainly, but often enough also in devoted practice), probably unmarried, drawn from a variety of social classes within the Catholic community (though less likely to come from either stark end of the social scale); and they very probably had relatives or family connections in parts of the republican movement.

Many possible backgrounds, therefore, could lead to IRA membership. Contrary to some republican self-portraits, the IRA was not in this period an army of, for or drawn from the poor: it drew people from all sections of the Catholic community. Shop assistants and clerks might have been disproportionately represented, as were artisans and skilled tradesmen, but the IRA did gather members from all sections of Catholic life. So any crude economic determinism must be rejected. But this does not mean that economic or material motivation and context play no part in explaining why people joined the alternative army. *Pace* the Marxists, to look to class explanation need not mean looking to the left. There were indeed class tensions in these years, and they did affect the republican commitment of some.[189] Yet if there was a class conflict at the heart of republican nationalism, then it was not anti-capitalist class conflict waged by the working class upon their social oppressors, but rather something of a battle within the middle class. An emerging Catholic lower-middle class was coming into its own and seeking to gain greater opportunity and power than it held in a world which was currently – in its view – overdetermined by a Protestant or a Catholic upper-middle-class establishment. In searching for a new Ireland, such upwardly mobile Revolutionaries were not seeking to do away with capitalism or class order or respectability, but rather to inherit the reins over them all.

This could relate to what one leading scholar has termed 'status resentment'[190] among the rebels, and here one can see the role played in nationalist motivation by the interweaving of self-esteem, the 'desire for recognition',[191] and material opportunity. The Revolutionary elite of 1919–21 included some who were angry at what they took to be a lack of appropriate opportunities for themselves, and a lack of adequate respect for their culture, community and dignity. The existing status system didn't satisfy; creating a state run by your own kind would solve the problem. And when independent Ireland emerged, there was indeed a move towards discriminating in favour of your own, once your nationalist friends were in positions powerful enough to help with this.[192]

Here, the individual's driving motivation – always the ultimately crucial vector for historical change and explanation – was tied in with the collective community. The individual's dignity, respect, status and self-regard could best be furthered – and made most sense – within a communal movement for group power. The mismatch between *my* ability and opportunity was to be rectified by communal action, and *my* own disadvantage was to be seen as a representative example of the nation's oppression. If there were indeed blocked mobility or relative deprivation, then one experienced it and remedied it as part of the group. Such patterns are not, of course, unique to Ireland, the discontentment of the educated unemployed or under-employed being recognized as a widespread phenomenon within the rise of nationalist movements.[193] As in many other nationalist settings, the anger of a self-perceivedly, relatively disadvantaged group – a social group aspiring to greater opportunity and power – played its part in producing nationalist momentum.

This relates to the undoubted drive and professional ambition of some of the Revolutionaries.[194] And it explains also the attitudinal revolutionism of the IRA, their profound hostility to deference and to marks of servility ('I made the men manoeuvre in demesne land to rid them of their inherent respect for the owners'[195]); violence could liberate from slave-mindedness. Here again was another function of violent action, in this case violence as defiance: the only nations worthy of independence were those willing and able to grab it for themselves, rather than those which asked meekly for it to be handed to them. Violence would reflect and further inculcate appropriate Irish defiance, rather than deference, regarding Britain. And, of course, in explaining the nationalist enthusiasm of these years, we need to remember that nationalism could legitimize the furtherance of very practical goals, such as the forcible acquisition of land:

Beside usual widespread revolutionary action of [the] Sinn Féin party, an agrarian movement of a highly organized, lawless and dangerous character is being developed in western counties of Ireland, and may well extend throughout the country. Entry is made with overwhelming numbers on the land of well-to-do and law-abiding farmers and land owners, areas of land devoted to pasture are marked out, declared to be seized in the name of the Irish Republic, and sub-divided between participators in the crime.[196]

Other social forces also played their part. The curtailment of emigration during the First World War kept at home some of what might, economically, be thought of as the surplus population, and this on occasions helped add to the ranks of the post-war disaffected (as was, very occasionally, recognized by the more perceptive republicans themselves). Again, intergenerational influences or conflicts could play their part, in various ways. At times family tradition helped to inspire republican commitment. Dublin-born Harry Boland – President of the IRB, and American Envoy of the Irish republicans during the War for Independence – provides an example. His father had been a GAA man and an IRB figure of some significance, while an uncle was in the Fenians also; when Harry himself had joined the IRB in 1904 in Dublin, he had done so along with his brother Gerald, and the two brothers were jointly to enlist in the Volunteers at their 1913 foundation. For others, however, IRA activity was a way of rebelling against parents – against their politics, their authority, or even the dullness of quotidian life at home. Being in the IRA meant emancipation from boredom and from home itself: 'If it was nothing else, it was a brief escape from tedium and frustration to go out the country roads on summer evenings, slouching along in knee breeches and gaiters, hands in the pockets of one's trench-coat and hat pulled over one's right eye';[197] some young men were socially 'discontented', they were unhappy with subordination to their elders, and so the 'wise domination of age, to some hard and harsh in the soul as the cancer of foreign rule, made volunteering an adventure and a relief'.[198]

And when they volunteered as IRA men, they often enough did so as a group of bonded comrades together, local young men in an actual as much as an imagined community. The great theorist of nationalism Benedict Anderson was, of course, right to stress that nations demand imagined, faceless communities of loyalty;[199] but these would be meaningless – in terms, at least, of passionate commitment – without the politics also of actual, known, bonded, smaller communities. The power of IRA nationalism lay partly in its combination of a grandly ennobling imagined Ireland, with the local mates and family of your village or town. Both were part of the story. Personal connections, allegiances, loyalties and inspiration were vital (as vital as political ideology, at times); actual comradeship was nationalist community. In jail in the early 1920s that member of the republican aristocracy Sean MacBride (1904–88) observed that he had 'developed during the time I was with [Eamon de Valera] a tremendous respect and love for him'.[200] Around figures such as Michael Collins, similar cults of devotion were to grow as the revolutionary adventure progressed. For this was very much an adventure. The world of Erskine Childers's 1903 novel presaged, in its 'pent-up patriotism' and its adventurous 'crazy chivalry',[201] much that was to feature in the Irish Revolution in which Childers – like many others – was to lose his life.

And these were very much boys on an adventure. There were female activists, and important ones,[202] but the prevailing assumption in the republican club was that it was primarily a boys' own affair; while in the IRA, for example, one man noted that 'I associated exclusively with boys and men.'[203] The IRA itself was exclusively male, and while the wider republican movement contained many female members, their roles tended to be sexually determined and limited by the contemporary views of the era. Cumann na mBan (the Irishwomen's Council) was founded in April 1914 in Dublin, committed to organization in furtherance of the cause of Irish nationalism, and to assisting and raising cash for the arming and equipping of a group of Irish*men* for the defence of Ireland; many joined, but their role was a secondary one to male struggle. As a President of Cumann na mBan, Eithne Coyle, herself put it, 'We were more or less auxiliaries to the men, to the fighting men of the country.'[204] Just as women had played a largely auxiliary role in 1916, so now Cumann na mBan supported the IRA: through first aid, cooking, making flags and sewing badges on to Volunteer uniforms; through taking despatches and ferrying arms and ammunition; through storing and transporting weapons (a much easier task for women to do effectively in those years); and through scouting locations for IRA attacks. Cumann na mBan cooked the food and washed and mended the clothes for the IRA; and this sharp gender division of labour continued into the next phase also of the national liberation movement, an IRA report from October 1922 commenting that Cumann na mBan were 'providing comforts for prisoners as far as their resources allow'.[205]

Another aspect of the social base of nationalism which helps to explain its appeal is the drive which some republicans possessed towards the production of a better, idealistically conceived future society. Ireland free would be materially and socially more prosperous and successful. Such imagined futures were varied, competing and often terribly vague. As ex-republican Francis Stuart caustically phrased it, there were 'practically as many visions of what the Republic entailed as there were people. And most of them completely unrealistic.'[206]

Some thought the new, post-British social order would involve the improvement of everybody's social welfare; others – a small but articulate minority – espoused a leftist future. The left could identify a conservative such as Arthur Griffith as deeply hostile to their own Connollyite instincts.[207] There were those, like Donegal IRA man and future novelist Peadar O'Donnell, who saw the IRA in class-defined terms ('Out of the ranks of workers and peasants the Irish Republican Army grew ... The workers became the insurrectionary nation'[208]), and who thought of the struggle against Britain as driven by class conflict within Ireland against capitalism; and there were those whose organizational links led leftward (Constance Markievicz, for example, was in comradely international contact with Russian zealots[209]). But, as with the great Connolly himself, such left-wingers were to make little Marxist impression on the thinking of the republican movement as a whole.

The years 1919–21 emphatically did not produce a Marxist social revolution in Ireland; nor did more than a small fraction of the IRA wish such a revolution to occur. But for many of those involved in the War for Independence there was a sense of some – probably vague – social-millenarian dimension to the republican dream. For some, the oppressed classes would liberate a nation in which they themselves would see social freedom dawn; for most, it was held that all classes would benefit from national freedom, that class harmony would somehow prevail in the new Ireland. In the important international question of why nationalism has tended to prevail over socialism, one obvious answer (evident again here in the Irish case of 1919–21) is that the former can appeal to all classes, the latter only to a segment of the nation. The IRA and their friends in 1919–21 were very much a cross-class movement, and their nationalism derived strength from that.

For Marxists such as Peadar O'Donnell, intellectual frameworks involved a combination of Marx, Connolly, and Irish nationalists such as Fintan Lalor. What were the intellectual influences upon the movement as a whole? Some – the Catholic-inflected ideas of Canon Sheehan, for example – have already been mentioned. And, as so often elsewhere in nationalist movements,[210] there was a role to be played by the intellect and intellectuals in forging the Revolutionaries' nation. Some of the reading was predictable enough, and no less powerful for that. Tom Barry took inspiration from his avid reading of 'the stories of past Irish history', those of heroes Theobald Wolfe Tone, Robert Emmet and John Mitchel among them.[211] Here, reading reinforced a rather simplistic historical view, and one which offered comforting republican self-justification: 'we had been slaves for 700 years. 'Twas time that that was ended!'[212] Sean O'Faolain read Terence MacSwiney, Patrick Pearse, Tom Clarke, John Mitchel and Theobald Wolfe Tone; Ernie O'Malley buried himself deep in Theobald Wolfe Tone; and Michael Collins (1890–1922) – 'the most gifted, ruthless and powerful Irish politician of the twentieth century', as his most recent biographer has styled him – apparently loved reading Irish history.[213]

So the intelligentsia of the Revolution were strengthened by Ireland's strong literary republican tradition: here was a reservoir of powerful ideas and arguments, and one which could water the wider movement indirectly. And, as one would expect, many intellectual and literary influences reflected Ireland's linguistic and physical proximity to Britain: these were paradoxically very British rebels, in some respects. Harry Boland loved Byron and Kipling; Peadar O'Donnell enjoyed Wodehouse, Shakespeare and Dickens. County Limerick's famous IRA son, Frank Ryan (1902–44), grew up surrounded by Shakespeare and Dickens; young Terry MacSwiney loved Dickens and Shakespeare also, as well as Tone and Mitchel; Sean O'Faoláin loved Shelley, Dickens, Arnold, Browning, Hardy and Scott; while Ernie O'Malley[214] wallowed in Chaucer, Shakespeare, Milton, Dickens, John Buchan – and even the *Times Literary Supplement*. This was not a new phenomenon. In his youth Eoin MacNeill had read widely in Scott and Shakespeare, an absorption which long stayed with him; Roger Casement had loved Keats, Shelley and Tennyson. Before them, the United Irishmen had been greatly influenced by British literary culture, just as the Fenians after them had quoted Shelley in exposition of their own Irish republican argument.[215] So, too, in re-creating the mental world of the early-twentieth-century IRA, we cannot avoid recognizing the degree to which they were soaked in British literature, part of the paradoxical broader process identified by George Boyce whereby Irish nationalism 'bears the ineradicable influence of England'.[216] (And those who have stressed that nationalism often involves a mixture of resentment, influence and emulation between enemies, might find rich evidence among this Revolutionary Irish generation.[217])

Nor was this irrelevant to the nature and appeal of these young people's republicanism. These were Shelleyan Revolutionaries (fittingly, Shelley himself had not only visited Ireland, but had also espoused the cause of Irish freedom), and Shelleyan Irish republicanism was the theme for these heady days. Such Romanticism celebrated youth, welcomed the apotheosis of heroic death, despised the dull, the mundane and the quotidian, and condemned the existing, imperfect world. There was here a spiritual and imaginative restlessness, a politics of dissatisfaction and yearning, and a definite zeal for adventure. IRA nationalism did arise from political conditions and conflicts, and it did possess a formal ideology and programme. But it also involved an intoxicating, communal atmosphere, and could involve the ecstasy of yearning, and the associated exaltation of glorious struggle. One might consider these attitudes disturbingly naive and deeply unrealistic (as is likely to be the case when one calmly reflects on utopian struggle); but their sentimental force and their intensity were part of the republican world, and that which made the IRA dream unrealistic also made it so appealing – namely, its Romantic, millenarian quality.

The Revolutionaries were stronger on spiritual, literary or moral ground than they were in terms of the economic, the scientific or even – in any detailed sense – the political. But while this lack of practicality rather hampered them in some ways, it presented one obvious strength: vague emotion was more alluring than more coldly measured assessment. Ethical self-righteousness and a religious sense of nationality allowed for powerful emotion to outflank reason on occasion: 'I rarely thought; I felt.'[218] As Sean O'Faoláin put it in relation to Irish rebels

and patriotic attitudes, it was the 'emotional' rather than the 'intellectual', and 'sentiment rather than thought', which tended to prevail.[219]
Elsewhere, considering the rebel Constance Markievicz, O'Faoláin was
led 'to wonder if revolutionary movements ever move towards defined
ends, whether all such movements are not in the main movements of
emotion rather than of thought, movements arising out of a dissatisfaction with things as they are but without any clear or detailed notion
as to what will produce satisfaction in the end'.[220]

Romantic Ireland was evident also in the profound imagination of
place, in the attachment to particular territory and the imbuing of its
physicality with patriotic significance. The literary rebels expressed this
most powerfully,[221] their imagined nation involving romanticized conceptions of the place in which the community lived, and of the manner
in which place distinctively moulded the people. Here, the intellectual
and the literary lead us to the broader appeal of revolutionary culture.
If IRA members in these days did see themselves, in Frank Gallagher's
words, as 'the manifestation of an ancient nation's immortality',[222]
then that ancient nation was authentic if culturally bounded in
particular ways. What made you distinctive, different from and
superior to the British? What helped to suggest that Irishness and
Britishness were mutually exclusive of each other? In part, the Ireland
of the Gael.

For, if the Catholic Church had been one key formative influence
over this generation, then another had been the Gaelic League. Both
could appeal across lines of class division, and both defined community
in ways which allowed for meaningful – and meaning-bestowing –
languages of culture and communication and sameness. In pre-
independence Ireland linguistic revivalism had created an alternative
self-image – distinct and unEnglish – on which the Revolutionaries
could build. The socializing dimension of organizations like the Gaelic
League should be recognized, but these do not on their own explain
the phenomenon. (Many associations could offer social life; why
choose this one?) It was not that the rebels were necessarily especially
fluent in Irish (often enough they were not), nor that their cultural
inheritance was entirely non-English (it wasn't). In fact, this was precisely the point. It was the very ambiguous standing of Irish Catholics'
culture – part-British, but not entirely comfortable in the United
Kingdom; part-Gaelic, but not entirely so – that made Gaelic zealotry

and boundary-drawing so appealing. Why am I different and special? If I am in doubt about the answer, then a partly reinvented Gaelic self can emphatically and satisfyingly answer that question. Hence the appeal of the kind of ethnic myth-celebration characteristic of someone like Sinn Féin propagandist Aodh de Blacam (1890–1951):

> The sole bond of Irish nationality is – and always was – the native Gaelic culture, and whatever the changing details may be, the underlying motive of every strong national movement can be traced to *the restoration of Gaelicism*. Movements and causes in Ireland may always be observed to succeed or fail in proportion as they approximate to Gaelic tradition.[223]

*

Why, therefore, would someone become a republican nationalist during 1919–21? We all might require security, social connections, dignity, prestige, and so on: why did so many choose the nationalist route to achieving them? Nationalist community could make ennobling sense of physical surroundings (through romantic, patriotic interpretation of territory and landscape); it could offer a powerful image of how the individual fitted in with the wider people, a people who enjoyed the communality of supposedly shared descent, aged history and proud culture (Gaelic, Catholic); it involved a commanding ethical ground, whether in terms of the duty that all owed to the greater nation, or of the sense that Ireland and her cause were characterized by a moral superiority over her enemies; it offered a clear sense of what you were not (British, non-Catholic, non-Gaelic) and allowed for expressions of this (whether through self-definition, or more physical acts of boycott or even violence). This version of community offered a powerful combination of dignity and honour, reinforced by its long historical roots.

And the community could engage in alluring struggle, whether as a means of achieving redress of grievance (political, economic, social, cultural) or as something which was inherently ennobling in itself. Here was a politics of double exasperation: at the injustices experienced under British rule in Ireland, and at the supposed failure of orthodox means of political redress. Struggle, once begun, had its own appeal: that of hitting back, or of enjoying the power and momentum of

Revolution itself. And, ultimately, struggle was a most compelling form of power: power shared equally by all in the sovereign, self-determining people, newly emancipated to govern their own lives; power to allocate resources yourself, for the benefit of your own community and under the authority of those like you; power in a new state, legitimized by nationalist popular sovereignty and independence. As such, the object of struggle was very modern; and yet it drew (as in its Catholic or Gaelic aspects) on far older lineages of strength and meaning.

Not everybody, of course, fitted all of these aspects. But many could be drawn to quite a few of these features of nationalism and it was nationalism's superior capacity to offer so much simultaneously, and to do so with such power, that made it forceful. You could define yourself as distinctive, make sense of the land and people around you, act in comradeship and adventure with your mates, draw on the prestige of a noble history and culture, hope for power and for economic or other rewards, gain revenge on enemies – and all at the same time. The appeal of the GAA and of Sinn Féin and of the IRA and of the Gaelic League; of enjoying power with your friends and over your enemies; of achieving prestige and influence as a professional Revolutionary; of participating in secret society adventure (Gerald Boland on the IRB: 'I thought I was a great fellow to belong to an Oath Bound Secret Society whose object was to establish an Irish Republic'[224]) – in the careers of so many Revolutionaries, one can see this powerful combination played out.[225] And, looking back on 1919–21, many of these Revolutionaries saw the years as glory days, as heady high points of individual and communal-national life: these later came to be seen by many as the days of unity, belief and commitment, and of an attractive simplicity of political goal and argument. The Revolution might have been prompted by contingent factors, whether the First World War (the context for 1916, and for the conscription crisis), or British clumsiness at times (as W. B. Yeats put it in 1920, 'England is always doing the right thing at the wrong time'[226]). But it seemed no less momentous for that.

4

For to feel oneself a martyr, as everybody knows, is a pleasurable thing.

Erskine Childers[227]

Much nationalist rhetoric stresses the unity of the nation. But what happens when the fractures within national communities become unbearable, whether along class or regional or religious lines? The republican movement of 1919–21 had been heterogeneous in its political and social views, but it had remained comparatively united; when these Irish nationalists were offered a deal in 1921, however, their community was rent in two.

The Anglo-Irish Treaty (more properly, the Articles of Agreement for a Treaty between Great Britain and Ireland), signed in December 1921, was the outcome of the War for Independence, and it gave more than many Irish nationalists had expected to see in the immediate future. It bestowed on the newly created Irish Free State (of twenty-six counties) the same constitutional status as the Dominions of Canada and New Zealand – not the Republic of republican dreams, it is true, but not a negligible measure of sovereign autonomy either. Free State Members of Parliament would have to swear an oath which declared them 'faithful' to the British monarch, and there were other crucial limitations to the new measure of Irish freedom: British forces were to have access to certain Irish harbour facilities, for example, and the six counties of the north-east (Antrim, Londonderry, Tyrone, Fermanagh, Armagh and Down) were to be excluded from the Irish Free State.

The story of Irish nationalism has long been one of divisive as well as unifying politics, and the dramatic Dublin Dáil debate over the 1921 Treaty nicely epitomizes this feature of the tale. For here was a striking example of that all too common phenomenon: elite-nationalist competition and disagreement over how to define the nation, and how to further its interests in relation to the state (a phenomenon widely studied by theorists of other nationalisms and considered central to their development).[228] Pro-Treaty arguments centred on recognizing the significance of what had been achieved, the lack of any better alternatives in practice, and the need for mature pragmatism rather than dreamy, unrealistic idealism. (At times pro-Treatyites seemed to echo the Wildean sentiment that 'Ideals are dangerous things. Realities are better. They wound, but they're better.'[229]) Michael Collins – the buoyant, ebullient, egotistical, ferociously hard-working Michael Collins, veteran of the 1916 GPO, Revolutionary networking genius, and the ultimate republican insider – argued strenuously in defence of the Treaty which he and others had negotiated with the British. He claimed, almost certainly rightly, that the Treaty was the best deal then available. He also argued that the alternative to it was a renewed war, from which Irish nationalists were not going to get a better outcome. The Treaty, Collins said, 'gives us freedom, not the ultimate freedom that all nations desire and develop to, but the freedom to achieve it';[230] 'After a national struggle sustained through many centuries,' Collins claimed in 1922, 'we have today in Ireland a native government deriving its authority solely from the Irish people, and acknowledged by England and the other nations of the world'; the 'substance of freedom' had been attained.[231]

If nationalists were to show themselves capable of self-government, then democratic order – the establishment and maintenance of which was the key issue for any state – had to be shown to be achievable. And was absolute and utter independence from Britain necessarily in tune anyway with the historic Irish nationalist sense of how self-determination could best be reflected? The Act of Union had lasted for nearly 125 years, during which lengthy period most Irish Catholics had clearly been happy with something less than full secession from England; the idea that the Union had been persistently opposed or hated by the majority of the nationalist population seems unrealistic, when set against detailed readings of actual historical experience.

But anti-Treatyites were having none of this. Mary MacSwiney (whose brother Terry had become one of the republican martyrs) saw the issue as simply 'between right and wrong'. 'Search your souls tonight,' she told the Dáil in December 1921, 'and in the face of every martyr that ever died for Ireland take an oath in your own hearts now that you will do what is right no matter what influences have been brought to bear on you.'[232] For such enthusiasts, millenarian hopes were not to be calmly dashed in the form of this tepid compromise deal. An oath of fidelity to the British Crown? Was this the dream for which the republican faithful had fought and killed and died?

Anti-Treaty Irish nationalism was convinced of its own credentials with regard to the central matters of sovereignty and self-determination; in 1923 IRA Chief of Staff Frank Aiken reaffirmed the importance of the 'fundamental principle that the Republic of Ireland is a single sovereign nation whose citizens are entitled to frame their own destiny'.[233] Ireland possessed an absolute right to national self-determination, and so anti-Treaty arguments were often cast in high-moralistic terms. As so often with nationalist thinking elsewhere, decisions could be built up less from practical questions than from matters of apparent morality. If Britain was offering a choice between Treaty and renewed war, then this next stage in the conflict would not be a civil war, but a continuation of the Irish war against Britain. And such ideas resonated with the longstanding Irish nationalist assumption that the old enemy, for selfish reasons, fomented avoidable Irish disagreement. If some Irish people were dupes for such a scheme then, once again, here was a familiar theme from nationalist history: the notion of betrayal. Conveniently, nationalist opportunity could be seen to have been thwarted at decisive moments by the foolish and treacherous behaviour of the compromisers (a much later deal, in Belfast in 1998, would offer another example in due course).

In truth, however, the argument over the 1921 Treaty reflected a very real series of powerful tensions: between what Revolutionary propaganda had claimed to have been achieved (the establishment of the true Republic), and what had in fact been brought about; between unyielding principle, and the principle of political pragmatism; and between the will of a vanguardist elite which held that it alone knew the true nature of popular interest, and the clearly-pro-Treatyite will of most actual Irish people.

For majority opinion in nationalist Ireland was emphatically pro-Treaty. The June 1922 Free State General Election represented a decisive defeat for anti-Treatyite politics: 58 pro-Treaty candidates were elected, as against 36 from the anti-Treaty camp. The others elected were, in no case, anti-Treatyite in their stance: 17 Labour, 7 Farmers' Party, 10 Independents; even more emphatically, no anti-Treaty candidate headed the poll in any contested constituency. Each pro-Treaty candidate won, on average, 5,174 votes, as against the anti-

Treaty average of only 3,372 votes. First-preference votes demonstrated the large margin of anti-Treatyite defeat, even among the famous names: Mary MacSwiney came only fourth in Cork Borough, and Constance Markievicz fifth in Dublin South; in Kildare–Wicklow the anti-Treatyites Erskine Childers and Robert Barton could only muster 3,354 first preferences between them, whereas the pro-Treatyite who headed the poll won 9,170 votes himself alone.[234] The Dáil had narrowly voted in favour of the Treaty (on 7 January 1922, by sixty-four votes to fifty-seven); the nationalist community as a whole was far more clearly in favour of the 1921 deal with Britain.

So the pro-Treaty authorities in the new state could emphasize, justly enough, the support of 'the will of the people'[235] as far as the Treaty was concerned; it is now fairly clear that theirs was the more democratic of the rival positions in 1922–3;[236] and they could argue that they were fighting – just as during 1919–21 – for the right of the Irish people to decide how and by whom they would be governed. In contrast to the latter-day British regime in Ireland, and in contrast now to the anti-Treatyite republicans, the Irish government enjoyed legitimacy in the eyes of the majority of the community. This allowed for them to suppress their IRA opponents without losing popular backing (again, in marked contrast with British experience during 1919–21). Legitimacy and popular sovereignty were the key components of this more effective nationalism. The 1922 Constitution which defined the political foundations of the Irish Free State clearly stated that: 'All powers of government and all authority legislative, executive, and judicial in Ireland, are derived from the people of Ireland and the same shall be exercised in the Irish Free State (Saorstát Eireann) through the organizations established by or under, and in accord with, this Constitution.'[237] So self-determination – the European mode in this early-1920s context – was reflected in Ireland in a workable compromise. Responsive, representative Irish nationalist government had been established, albeit on less exalted terrain than some IRA zealots had anticipated.

And this battle for nationalist legitimacy was waged, as before, across rather than between social classes. Leftist republicans, and some later observers, have suggested that the early-1920s Civil War was a class war. But research has now shown clearly that anti-Treaty republicanism was not, in fact, a war of the poor against more privileged classes, a war of the haves against the have-nots.[238] The violence of 1922–3 between pro- and anti-Treatyite forces within Irish nationalism did not follow the pattern of social disadvantage or of social disruption and labour conflict (much as anti-Treatyite Peadar O'Donnell and others might have liked it to have done so), and class background did not adequately explain people's attitudes during the Civil War.

It was certainly not a war of left versus right, even O'Donnell himself later admitting that the anti-Treatyites had been as socially conservative as their Free State opponents and that there would have been little difference, as far as the social system was concerned, even had his own side won. Marxists have sometimes sneered at the early-1920s focus on what they have taken to be mere symbols (painting the letter boxes green, and so forth) rather than the material, class substance of contemporary politics. But this seems unfair, and it misses the centrality to nationalism of precisely those symbolic dimensions of life which do bestow genuine meaning, pride, prestige and definition upon nationalists the world over. In Free State Ireland as elsewhere, nationalism had everything to do with symbols.

And amid all this, once again, was the issue of community. Was the will of the actual people to decide the issue, and were local, personal loyalties to override the broader national will? People seem often enough to have chosen a Civil War side because of individual ties to those whom they followed, admired, remembered or honoured. Frank O'Connor opposed the Treaty because Daniel Corkery had decided against it; many followed Michael Collins in the other direction. As the nation divided, new actual communities were built more tightly, in rival relation to one another, and these often focused on love, friendship and intimate loyalty.

When the Treaty debate was followed by Civil War bloodshed (extending from 28 June 1922 until 30 April 1923),[239] there were many personal tragedies. Harry Boland – the ultimate comrade, so committed to club-like community – was killed by Free State forces, dying as an anti-Treatyite in the early, summer days of this 1922 war between nationalist brothers. He was only thirty-five years of age. That same summer – on 22 August 1922 – Boland's great friend Michael Collins was killed in an anti-Treaty ambush in County Cork (though Collins himself had not, it seems, been the particular target of the attack). Cathal Brugha died, having been shot in Dublin in July 1922 in the early days of the Civil War; Liam Mellows (1892–1922) and others were executed by the new regime in prison in December 1922; Erskine Childers, whom Frank O'Connor considered to have been 'one of the great romantic figures of the period',[240] had been executed the previous month. And blood was still being spilled beyond the republican family. On 22 June 1922 Field Marshal Sir Henry Wilson (military adviser to the new Northern Ireland government) was killed in London by Irish republicans. The killers were Reginald Dunne and Joseph O'Sullivan. Both were ex-British soldiers, both London-born Catholics; and both were members of the London IRA and the IRB. Apparently acting on their own initiative, they appear to have thought (wrongly, it now seems) that killing Wilson would in some way further the cause of Irish independence and the position of Belfast Catholics. Mistakenly thinking that Wilson was responsible for Catholic deaths in Belfast, they took it upon themselves to kill him.

The Civil War was won swiftly enough by the Free Staters, with their superior numbers and resources and popular legitimacy. But there was poignancy in the tragic conflict, despite its comparative brevity. There was sadness, for example, in the attempts of people such as Harry Boland to maintain nationalist unity after the Treaty, and to reconcile what was now a very fractious band of brothers. There were grisly acts of violence on both sides, and there were martyrs newly minted. Boland himself had a cult constructed around him following his death in 1922; the same was true, to a more marked extent, with the great Michael Collins. Rival Valhallas filled up quickly, as both republicans and Free Staters built their collections of dead heroes and thereby sought to further their rival causes.[241] National community had broken into competing communities – fighting over vital questions concerning the nature and legitimacy of Irish state governance, sovereignty and self-determination – and this division long remained very painful within nationalist Ireland.

Of course, very many Irish people simply took no side, and stood detached from the Civil War conflict, with the result that large parts of Ireland experienced very little violence. As everywhere else, people could exist neutrally or at some remove from the ethno-national groups around them and claiming them.[242] Not so, however, the Irish Catholic Church, which firmly committed itself to the new Free State order. In October 1922 the Irish Catholic hierarchy declared clearly in favour of the Free State and ordered a general excommunication of (and deprival of the Holy Sacrament to) any IRA member carrying on the struggle against the newly established political authorities. This caused some personal pain, and much anger, among anti-Treaty republicans; in Mountjoy Jail, republicans were annoyed by the chaplains' refusal of absolution to the prisoners ('the immediate reaction to it was that scores of men ceased attending Mass'[243]), and also at the Church's refusal to allow the dead bodies of prisoners into churches, and the further refusal of priests to ask for the congregation's prayers for the republican Roll of Honour. And yet – as with the Fenians before them – many anti-Treatyites simply held that the Church had got its politics wrong. They remained Catholics, retained a sense that their faith was central to their nation, and yet maintained their republican commitment.

But what of the 1922–3 Civil War and that part of Ireland where Catholicism could not be assumed? One thing that the Irish nationalist debate on the 1921 Treaty was emphatically not about was the partitioning of the island into two states: only a tiny fraction of the Treaty debate in the Dáil concerned partition, and pro- and anti-Treatyite attitudes were not, in fact, all that different regarding the north; the Civil War fighting, meanwhile, was most intense in the south-west of Ireland, the region furthest away from unionist Ulster. The Government of Ireland Act of 1920 had effectively partitioned Ireland, establishing the basis for a six-county north and a twenty-six-county south, each possessing its own executive and its own bicameral parliament; and this arrangement came into effect in May 1921. By the spring of 1914 some form of partition had been accepted as a part of any forthcoming Irish settlement; by 1920 a devolved parliament for Northern Ireland had been provided for, and the Belfast parliament was duly inaugurated by King George V in June 1921. The May 1921 elections for this body had seen unionists win forty out of fifty-two seats, a reflection of the fact that the six-county northern state had been established as a majority-unionist entity.

But why had Ireland been partitioned, and what did this mean for Irish nationalism?

There was certainly a long separateness about the politics and culture of parts of Ulster. This was true economically, Belfast having been Ireland's only nineteenth-century industrialized city. Ulster had done best under the Union in economic terms, and so it was unsurprising that it should so strongly reject separation from the empire which fed it. It was not that Ulster was purely industrial and the rest of Ireland simply agricultural. But it was true that the concentrated industrialism of eastern Ulster stood out from the economy of the rest of the island (and this was starkly true in the linen industry and in ship-building). So the failure of most of nineteenth-century Ireland to industrialize (a failure which economic historians are now more reluctant to attribute to the union with Great Britain)[244] helped to generate twentieth-century partition. This was compounded by religious division, the pattern of settlement having left a far more concentrated Protestant population in the north-east than was the case across the rest of the island. In 1924 the Irish nationalist Stephen Gwynn candidly stated the confessional reality which lay behind the recent partition: 'it is only the exceptional Protestant or the exceptional Catholic who belongs to a culture and shares an outlook not generally associated in Ireland with his creed'.[245]

As it turned out, the new northern state was born in violence. The Belfast war of the early 1920s was bloody and vicious and a conflict from which no side emerges with glory. Even those who rightly highlight the atrocities committed against northern Catholics can recognize that there was no 1920s monopoly on northern viciousness: 'At this time Catholics and Protestants were as bad as each other in terms of murder ... it would be unreasonable to try and suggest that it was only Roman Catholics which [sic] suffered during this horrific period in our city's history. There were atrocities carried out by Catholics.'[246] The victims were mostly civilians, innocent and vulnerable targets on both sides. IRA actions, loyalist violence, violence by state forces – all played their part. On 18 July 1920 Ulster-born RIC officer Gerald Smyth was killed by the IRA in Cork; on 21 July thousands of Catholics and socialists (the perceivedly disloyal) were driven from their work at the Belfast shipyards; on 22 August 1920 the IRA killed RIC man Oswald Swanzy as he left church in Lisburn; fatal sectarian conflicts then ensued in Belfast and elsewhere. Thus while the roots of partition lay before 1920, the contingent interaction of events in the Revolutionary years themselves produced avoidable levels of carnage.

Many northern Protestants thought the IRA in the south to be engaged in what might now be termed the ethnic cleansing of Protestants there, and their fears were heightened as a consequence; nationalists in the north became ever more anxious and vulnerable in turn; and violence ensued. One side's violence brought forth reaction, and so the process developed in bloody escalation. Both sides were guilty of some hideous violence (intimidation, shootings, expulsions from workplace or residence), and the numbers killed in Belfast alone during 1920–22 reached nearly 500. For while the existence of different ethnicities within the same state need not always produce violence, such a situation can be an inflammable mixture, and so it was to prove in twentieth-century Ireland, pre- and post-partition. This was partly due to the unfortunate pattern of population numbers and locations. Rival groups (nationalist and unionist) were too extensively intermingled to allow for neat partition (despite the ingenious suggestions of some regarding possible alternative boundaries[247]), and in Northern Ireland itself was created a minority situation about as bad as could be designed. Effectively, there had been too large and powerful an Irish nationalist minority within the United Kingdom of Great Britain and Ireland; too large and concentrated an Ulster unionist minority within Ireland for Irish nationalists easily to deal with; and now too large and growing and intermingled an Irish nationalist minority within Northern Ireland. So everybody felt threatened, and nobody felt able to show the magnanimity required for lasting and final compromise. Here was the nightmarish map of Irish minorities, ever receding into smaller numbers without ever being solved: minorities which could not comfortably be absorbed or ignored or coerced.

The gravity of this problem for Irish nationalism can hardly be overstated. Yet nationalist responses to the problem of unionism and of partition were notoriously feeble.[248] To most Irish nationalists, Ireland's unity seemed natural and axiomatic, religious and economic differences were considered no great problem, and the fault for any Irish division was seen as firmly British in origin (just as the task of resolving it was likewise judged to be a British responsibility). So Harry Boland could casually proclaim in 1919 that 'Ulster belongs to Ireland, every inch of it. Not as much as would "sod a lark" can be claimed by England';[249] while the nationalist *Irish News* in the north was firmly set against partition from the start, as were Nationalist politicians whose message was carried in the paper at the time of the dividing of Ireland:

'The historic unity of Ireland is to be violated with results disastrous to the peace and prosperity alike of the North and South.'[250] To nationalists, partition was crazy and artificial, Northern Ireland a factitious and illegitimate entity, and the problem could be dismissed or ignored; 'Nationalist leaders rarely faced up to the mutual fear that existed between Catholic and Protestant and tended to define the problem out of existence.'[251] Partition was assumed to be temporary[252] (great hope was placed in the ill-fated Boundary Commission set up under the 1921 Treaty), and yet nationalist actions were tellingly ineffective. In 1920 nationalists set up the Belfast Boycott Committee, which sought during the early 1920s to use a commercial boycott of Ulster as a way of preventing further intimidation or expulsion of Catholic workers in Belfast (and ultimately as a means of persuading unionists that they should no longer oppose Irish unity). Predictably, perhaps, the boycott had little positive effect in practice,[253] and certainly did nothing to lead to the re-employment of Catholics or to unionist enthusiasm for Irish unification.

And was the nationalist assumption about the daftness and temporary nature of partition well grounded? If nationalism derived strength from ideas of self-determination, culture, history, ethics, exclusivism and so on, then why should unionism not engage in a similar process? 'Nationalists are in the habit of referring to the "artificial partition" of the island. In principle, there is nothing artificial about the partition: it is a result of history, traditions and demography. When Catholics decided to secede from the United Kingdom, Protestants seceded from the secession.'[254] Nationalists have tended to see partition as a mutilation of naturally united territory; but there are alternative interpretations which require to be taken very seriously (in the words of a later unionist politician, David Trimble: 'Partition was inevitable. It was a response to the social reality of two Irish nations'[255]).

For all of the imperfections of the line drawn in the 1920s to divide nationalist south from unionist north – and for all of the problems encountered in Northern Ireland during the twentieth century – the real and lasting problem for nationalist Ireland has been to come up with a better alternative to such flawed partition. And the problem of unionist Ulster highlights some of the key aspects of the 1916–23 Irish Revolution, as far as our understanding of Irish nationalist history is concerned. For the very essence of nationalism was what undid it in

Ulster. What united nationalist people (shared culture, descent, history), what allowed them to draw boundaries of exclusion and inclusion, what gave them their ethical superiority (a sense of historic grievance), all backfired when it came to unionism, and all tended to tear apart the notion of an integral Irish territory and people. If you celebrated Gaelicism, nationalist ethnic homogeneity, Catholicism, the validity of suffering at Protestant or British hands, then unionists were excluded, and could produce their own rival brand of community no less valid or strong than one's own. If one claimed the right of self-determination, of belonging to a state run by people like oneself; if one sought the freedom offered by egalitarian popular sovereignty, then unionists could simply replace autonomous Ireland with the claims of a legitimate UK state. And nationalist struggle – whether Home Rule parliamentary or Revolutionary republican – exacerbated these divisions.

So the Irish Revolution – celebrated by republicans as a struggle between Ireland and Britain – turns out also to have been a struggle between Irish people themselves: nationalist-versus-unionist; republican-versus-Home Ruler; pro-Treaty-versus-anti-Treaty; IRA man-versus-RIC man. Roger Casement's friend Arthur Conan Doyle had early on depicted the situation which had arisen by August 1914 as 'a devil's brew of Irish civil war',[256] and maybe he was right here to recognize something of the intra-Irish dimensions of the conflict. Irish nationalism involved all these various conflicts in these bloody and divisive years. As scholars have shown,[257] it is overly simplifying – indeed, profoundly distorting – to see the violence of the Irish Revolution as purely or essentially a case of Ireland-against-Britain, or as something entirely heroic. Sentimental ballads and celebratory imagination still linger (regarding James Connolly, for example: 'For inside that grim building stood a brave Irish soldier/Whose life for his country was forced to lay down. . . . There was many a sad heart in old Ireland that morning/When they murdered James Connolly, the Irish rebel';[258] or IRA martyr Kevin Barry (1902–20): 'In Mountjoy Jail one Monday morning/High upon the gallows tree/Kevin Barry gave his young life/ For the cause of liberty/Just a lad of eighteen summers/Yet no one can deny/As he walked to death that morning/Proud he held his head on high';[259] or the great Michael Collins himself: 'Friends and comrades standing by/In their grief they wondered why/Michael, in their hour of need you had to go'[260]). But, for all of the attractions of such a response, the heroic is not the only framework in which to place these figures and their exploits. The number of those wounded or killed during the 1916–23 Revolution was over 10,000, and the IRA was responsible for well over half of the attributable casualties of these troubled years.[261] As noted, most of the Revolution's victims were not killed or wounded in combat: they were civilians, non-combatants, and effectively defenceless. And the outcome was hardly that of republican dreams: Irish unity was not won, and nor was full independence; social justice was not achieved, nor economic improvement quickly built.

5

There are no people in the world more long-suffering than the Irish farmer; ages of poverty and ill-treatment have hardened him to suffering, even to the point of starvation.

Maurice Moore, 1931[262]

Veteran Irish nationalist Maurice Moore here focused attention on one of the problems which faced newly independent Ireland, a problem which has troubled many emergent nationalist states all around the world: how does one deal with the fact that, when national freedom arrives, social problems and inequalities and disappointments remain? Moore himself was involved in promoting a 1920s campaign built around the issue of land annuities money paid by the Free State to Britain (money which Irish farmers handed over in effective repayment of the advances made to them under the 1891 and 1909 Land Acts, and which had facilitated their participation in the process of land purchase). Some farmers found that the payments were impossible to make, and republican zealots such as the IRA's Peadar O'Donnell sought to build a community campaign against the annuities, and against paying the annuity arrears which had developed in some areas in Ireland. As editor of the IRA's newspaper, *An Phoblacht*, O'Donnell was able to publicize the issue, and his argument was that these payments embodied the sharp and unjust end of British power as it had been wielded in Ireland. Were the true Irish people ('the remnants of the Gaelic stock') to be evicted from their land and lives by an ostensibly nationalist Irish regime in the 1920s Free State, because they couldn't pay to Britain the money with which they had bought back land that had rightfully been theirs all along?

> Can these homes stamped unmistakably with the personality of these Gaelic folk – and they are yet a vital, unbroken set of people – be razed because tribute to Britain is not being paid? The national conscience will be tried out in these cases, and if the nation does not cry halt, then indeed we have fallen very low, very low.[263]

O'Donnell the revolutionary was here trying to use a sharp-edged issue of pressing urgency – rural poverty – as the means of stirring nationalist struggle against Britain, and against the arrangements on which the Free State was itself based.

Others also picked up the land annuities issue, and in the event 1916 veteran Eamon de Valera's Fianna Fáil party was to utilize the matter as part of its successful campaign for election to power in 1932. But de Valera's approach – to reduce the payments, but to retain them rather than paying the money to London – reflected that leader's more moderate, and far-from-O'Donnellite, political and economic approach.

For the politics of independent Ireland were reflected in its parties' respective economic approaches. To some degree, economics did help to determine political choice. The fact that the Free State remained a country of peasant proprietors, for example, effectively closed the door to any land nationalization of the kind instinctively preferred by someone like Peadar O'Donnell: in 1870 only 3 per cent of land-occupiers had owned their holdings; by 1929 only 3 per cent did not; and those who had fought a struggle in order to own their land were not now about to hand over the deeds of ownership to the state. In this sense, the practicality of economic life was predictably reflected in the pattern of nationalist politics. But, in other ways, politics could also determine economics.[264] Fianna Fáil's espousal of native economic ownership and self-sufficiency made little economic, but considerable political, sense. There wasn't enough native capital or expertise to allow for Irish ownership and successful self-sufficiency at the same time;[265] but it was still politically attractive to stress Sinn Féinish self-reliance and pride through such policies, and they were maintained to electoral advantage by de Valera's party during the 1930s and 1940s.

Political and economic instincts echoed one another, and were mutually reinforcing. The pro-Treaty politicians of the Cumann na nGaedheal party adopted a politics which tolerated strong links with Britain (defending the 1921 Treaty left them little choice); and Cumann na nGaedheal also tended, economically, to favour large rather than small farmers, and therefore to lean towards the economy of export to England (on which large-farm cattle-rearing was founded). For their part, Fianna Fáil – a party which arose from the anti-Treaty position – favoured a politics of severing political links with Britain, and also enthused over an economics of protectionism and self-sufficiency which, again, pointed towards separation from the neighbouring island. De Valera's party seemed to offer greater political autonomy and also more economic freedom (and both these developments would supposedly produce material benefits). Once again, nationalism offered everything.

Yet in practice, of course, it didn't. Not only did self-sufficiency elude the new Ireland, but what economic stability there was rested on the continuation of large-scale emigration. Pre-independence nationalist thinkers such as Arthur Griffith had claimed that the English stifling of Irish economic development had prevented the kind of population growth which would have occurred had autonomy and protectionism prevailed. But having an autonomous and protectionist state did not, in fact, prevent emigration, or solve Irish economic problems. Nationalist promises were, at best, only partly fulfilled.

And if the economic policies of nationalist Ireland excluded the emigrant, then they also reinforced the exclusion from nationalist thinking of unionists in the island's north-east. In their different ways, and with their different audiences, Cumann na nGaedheal and Fianna Fáil both played the rural card in defining their nationalism. But this was possible only if one ignored the very different position north of the border (which, of course, they largely did). The difference between north and south – in 1926, for example – was crucial, agricultural and manufacturing sectors of the economy playing very different roles in the two jurisdictions. Almost 35 per cent of the workforce in Northern

Ireland were engaged in manufacturing, while under 10 per cent were so engaged in the nationalist Free State; nearly two-thirds of Ireland's manufacturing employment was in the north. The industrialization characteristic of Northern Ireland – and the implications of this for employees, in terms of access to British and imperial markets – had profound consequences for an Irish nationalist community which still at this stage identified the idealized nation with rural imagery, and which was still wedded to a rurally-oriented economics.

In cultural as well as economic terms, the establishment of the Irish Free State in 1922 provided great challenges. It was one thing to denounce the oppression under which one's culture had suffered at British hands; it was quite another now to build a state for which one was responsible and answerable. As elsewhere, maintaining unity was a high priority, and this was far from easy in 1920s independent Ireland. One couldn't celebrate the unity of the whole island, as it was partitioned; nor was there an obvious unity in a state born out of fratricidal Civil War among nationalists. But there were things upon which pro- and anti-Treatyite could agree, and here partition was in fact a blessing. For all shades of nationalism in the south were Catholic, and all thought Gaelicism appropriate; and so the removal from the new state of non-Catholic, non-Gaelic northerners made life considerably easier as distinctively Irish nationalist culture was built into the daily fabric of the new state.[266] Cultural nationalism, and Catholic culture, were no longer now an alternative politics, but became state orthodoxy: Gaelicism and Catholicism, indeed, became the twin emblems of the new nationalist state.

It was not that Gaelic zealotry necessarily had an easy time in the 1920s: the Gaelic League had had 819 branches in 1922, and only 139 in 1924. But there was a sense in the Free State that the regime was in tune with a set of religious and cultural ideas which harmonized popular sentiment. Sinn Féin had long argued that Irish should be introduced into schools as a compulsory subject, and when Irish nationalists inherited the state in the 1920s they implemented this idea; it was decided that all teachers should know the Irish language by the time they left teacher-training college, and there was a systematic attempt to regenerate Irish through the education system. In the event, this policy failed to restore Irish as a meaningful first language of everyday use. (And this was unsurprising, given the context: by the end of the 1920s, as one authority on Irish nationalism has pointed out, 'the infant classes of over ninety per cent of primary schools were being instructed wholly or partially through Irish, a language most of them never heard in the home, by a teaching force many of whose members were but poorly equipped and supported for the task'.[267]) But the very effort itself reflects the fact of ongoing nationalist cultural struggle even once political independence had been won. The rewards of this should not be ignored, in terms of pride in distinctive culture, the attempted reinvigoration of ancient language, and so on. But nor should we ignore its more negative effects. The language policy did not enhance educational standards in the new Ireland (and there were great problems, for example, with the development of Irish science under the new dispensation).[268] Moreover, the broader cultural conservatism of the new state now looks rather narrow in conception and implementation. As interwar Ireland became a Catholic nationalist state, it was not just that the 1920s governments expressed their loyalty to the Pope, but also that society was fashioned according to Catholic enthusiasms and views. In a sense, this merely reflected the democracy of a Catholic nationalist state. But proscriptive legislation – regarding, for example, divorce and contraception and films and books[269] – produced a deeply conservative society. 'Political life in the newly independent Irish Free State, even in the immediate aftermath of a revolution, reflected in obvious ways the essential conservatism of the predominantly rural Irish electorate.'[270]

On St Patrick's Day each year, all government ministers would attend an Irish language Catholic Mass in Dublin's Pro-Cathedral, nationalist gesture here fusing together state, religion and cultural expression. And in the new Ireland the Church keenly guarded its control over education, wanting to maintain as near as possible a monopoly on primary and secondary education and thereby giving it a tremendous moulding influence over all shades of thinking among the young. So Catholic influence was less a matter of mechanical control over policy decisions (though this did occur on occasions) than a matter of pervasive impact on all levels of thinking. And the influence of such clerical influence on Irish politics was lastingly significant, in terms of how nationalist politicians in independent Ireland carried out their political duties: 'At least up to the 1950s many politicians, including ministers, clearly thought they owed some kind of duty of obedience to the Catholic hierarchy in the carrying out of these duties.'[271] Down at least to the 1970s, nobody seeking serious political support in independent Ireland would have challenged the identification of the Irish nation with Catholicism.

The Catholic flavour of the new state underlined the problem with the supposed unity of the country: while the absence of Catholic laws would not have led northern unionists to leap at the prospect of Irish unity, the introduction of such a Catholic set of rules undoubtedly reinforced (and in their own view vindicated) unionist anti-nationalism in Ireland.[272] The emphatically Catholic 1929 centenary celebrations for Catholic Emancipation (and the 1932 Eucharistic Congress too) demonstrated Irish nationalist pride in the Catholic identity of the new order, and such pride should not be dismissed or scorned. Independent Ireland's most significant nationalist, Eamon de Valera, repeatedly made clear that he thought Ireland a Catholic nation.[273] Likewise, the enthusiasm for all things Gaelic could translate into an exclusivism regarding rival cultures (the Gaelic League in the 1930s was holding meetings to protest against 'the wave of jazz which is sweeping through the country to the detriment of national music and dances'[274]). For many people, such were the rewards – and such was the point – of nationalism. Once you possessed your own state, you expected people to fashion it in your own chosen cultural image.

But there were those – as ever – among the former Revolutionaries who considered this narrow world something of a disappointment. For some, after the Revolution, the failure of political rebellion to achieve its millenarian goal led to effective disenchantment with politics itself; for others, intellectual energy led towards post-revolutionary bohemianism, and to a celebrity status accorded by more conventional readers to the exciting gunman-writer; and for many, the writings of the post-Revolutionary period involved a fascinatingly dual kind of subversion: the subverting of the imperialistic British regime against which they had fought; but also the subversion of elements of the Irish republican myth itself. This is a pattern evident in the writings of people as diverse as Frank O'Connor, Ernie O'Malley and Brendan Behan. By the time we reach the 1930s and 1940s, former Revolutionaries such as Sean O'Faoláin and Ernie O'Malley were certainly lamenting the narrowness and the intellectual constriction evident in the particular kind of Gaelic, Catholic state which their Revolution had in fact produced. Ireland was, in O'Faolain's pungent phrase, 'the worst country in the world for intellectuals'.[275] (Most of O'Faolain's own fiction was banned in independent Ireland.)

So emigration could, for some, be less a sad experience than a marvellous and emancipating opportunity; 'It is always pleasant to leave this country,' observed one of Samuel Beckett's fictional characters from the 1930s,[276] Beckett himself being a conspicuous emigrant from Ireland and a critic of the Free State's proscription of books and contraceptives. Kafka once described a European's first days in America as a kind of rebirth; for many Irish emigrants this was to prove true, and there were freedoms also to be found in Australia, Britain and Canada. This had, as we have seen, long roots: during the period of the Union around 5 million people had left Ireland for America. Then as now, when people left the young independent Ireland, experiences in the States were very varied. For some, a mixture of emigrant rage and consolidated national identity in the foreign setting, produced an enthusiasm for nationalist causes. Just as Irish-American anger had been fuelled by the Famine, so too there was an anglophobic spirit among many twentieth-century emigrants. Organized channels for such rage were created and sustained: the secret and militant Clan na Gael in 1867, for example, and in more recent times the Friends of Irish Freedom (established in New York in 1916, although Clan influence was exerted through this body too). The Friends epitomized numerous strands within Irish-American nationalism, centrally that of a commitment to independence for the home country: as they put it themselves, they were pledged 'To encourage and assist any movement that will tend to bring about the national independence of Ireland'.[277] So the politics of nationalist Ireland lived on in the diaspora. And deep-rooted emigration did not merely involve America. There had been around 14,000 Irish immigrants to London alone during 1851–61; 7,000 during 1861–71; 19,000 during 1871–81; and 20,000 during 1881–91. The Irish in England perhaps displayed less striking upward mobility than some other immigrant groups,[278] although it is also true that middle-class emigration to England in the nineteenth century had been important and had produced some great achievements and achievers (Wilde, Yeats and Shaw among them[279]).

As noted regarding the phenomenon of Famine emigration, those who left Ireland (along with their descendants) could make a distinctive contribution to the Irish nationalist community, and to the development of Irish nationalism itself. This had been the case with Fenianism, and again it had been so during the Revolution. In 1919 the United States had contained many emissaries, political propagandists, gun-runners and fund-raisers from the war at home in Ireland; again, the American Association for the Recognition of the Irish Republic, founded by de Valera in 1920, played a key role in arousing public support in the States for the Irish republican cause. The 1920s and 1930s IRA depended significantly on US support for their financial backing as they continued to dispute the legitimacy of the (in their view, insufficiently) independent Irish state. But most Irish Americans had supported the 1921 Treaty, and in any case emigrant Irish nationalism had dynamics of its own, not necessarily focused primarily on Ireland. St Patrick's Day came to be more intensely celebrated by the diaspora than in Ireland itself. March 17 street parades – surely the definitive St Patrick's Day event – were apparently a North American innovation; even by the 1840s there were organizations in place across much of the United States to coordinate such parades; and by the late nineteenth century St Patrick's Day also reflected tensions within the Irish-American community, between an identification with the presumed political needs of Irish struggle and the American priorities of group identity, interest and expression of the Irish community abroad.[280]

At home, Revolution quickly gave way to comparative political quiescence (itself a fact unimaginable had not partition and emigration between them taken away so many potential dissenters from the new order). And, notwithstanding Oscar Wilde's quip that democracy merely means 'the bludgeoning of the people by the people for the people',[281] we are now – looking back from the early twenty-first century at rival twentieth-century styles of politics such as fascism or communism – in a better position to recognize the enduring qualities of democratic political life. In independent Ireland, the establishment of stable democracy was certainly very impressive, and it should not be taken for granted. Passing from the brutally fratricidal Civil War of the 1920s to a bloodless and dignified change of government between the rival factions a decade later represents one of Irish nationalism's most striking political successes.

But why did Ireland fare so much better than many other

post-revolutionary states in achieving – and so very quickly – a stable democratic political system? For parliamentary authority was supreme and was widely recognized as such, elections were decisive in terms of who would govern the state, and rival political organization was allowed. In part, Irish nationalist success here rested ironically on British legacies. Irish political parties had grown up under the Union, in the context of British parliamentary democracy. From O'Connell through Parnell and Redmond, the expected form of political expression had been overwhelmingly that of democractic parliamentary politics. Nineteenth-century Ireland had become deeply imbued with a belief in constitutional, democractic politics on the British model, the latter being the only one of which Irish nationalists had had direct experience. By the time of emergent independence in 1922, therefore, nationalist Ireland had been sending their representatives to the London parliament for many decades, and had come to assume the value of this kind of politics (if not of this particular venue); parliamentary democracy was Irish nationalists' expectation, democratic assumptions concerning majority rule and open politics having become the Irish norm.

Similarly, there was a British institutional legacy, as the administrative infrastructure behind democratic governance (the civil service, for example) was adopted by the new regime. Having acquired their own, non-British state, Irish nationalists substantially did things in a manner which was modelled on the British way. Behind all this was another key explanatory factor in relation to Ireland's relatively smooth shift to independent democratic stability. For the British context under the Union had been one which had furthered the development of a vibrant civil society,[282] and this greatly strengthened the likelihood of democratic politics surviving. Admittedly, there were rival civil societies, Protestant and Catholic. But the existence of such cultures none the less helped to provide the foundation for strong and resilient democracy. Institutions, bodies and organizations independent of the state bonded people together in a coherent way, and – pre-independence – they had helped to inculcate in people a sense of constitutional practice (electing people within organizations, holding people accountable for their leadership, and so on). So the diffusion to Ireland of British constitutional values and assumptions via civil society had produced a strong associational life in the nineteenth century (trade unions, the

GAA), and this had further helped to naturalize democratic practices and assumptions.[283] The effect had been all the more marked, since civil society had been built up around ideas (Catholic, Gaelic) which were distinctive to Irish nationalism, and which were shared across the Civil War divide.

Again, if urbanization and educational sophistication strengthen the likelihood of democratic political survival, then the British legacy to Ireland was beneficial. For the idea that independent Ireland was in a kind of Third-Worldist state at its birth is simply unsustainable:[284] it was, in fact, already relatively urbanized and educated by 1921, and at the time of independence was a European economy (sharing far more in common with other European economies than with the kind of economy characteristic of twentieth-century, post-colonial, emerging states in Africa). In all of this, therefore, there is a sweet irony, the democratic success of the anti-British nationalists' new Irish state depending significantly on the benign legacy left by an opponent so long denounced as appallingly evil.

But, whatever the objective conditions inherited in 1921, there was simply no certainty of the survival of Irish democracy. The conditions of inheritance might have been favourable, but the choices and actions of the Irish nationalist political elite would now prove decisive. Here, it was crucial that the 1920s regime – that of the pro-Treaty Cumann na nGaedheal party – showed itself committed to democracy and, indeed, to the nationalist state rather than to the self-interest of party.[285] As scholars have begun to note,[286] the unglamorous pro-Treatyites consolidated national independence and stability in quiet but profound ways. By the time that the anti-Treatyites of Fianna Fáil took power in 1932, strong democratic foundations had certainly been laid. And so the celebrated Revolutionary turbulence of 1916–23 – the famous story of rebellions and killings and imprisonment and adventure and millenarian dreams – turns out on close inspection to have been an aberration from the normal, milder path of Irish nationalism. The Revolution was a deviation, necessary or otherwise, from a familiar and stable path of constitutional democracy in Ireland.

And, ironically, it was the anti-Treatyite Eamon de Valera who was to prove Michael Collins' pro-Treaty arguments to have been right all along: de Valera's party, Fianna Fáil, was to show that the 1921 Treaty did indeed provide the freedom to achieve freedom, just as Collins had claimed. This helped to ensure the survival of democratic Ireland, and of the self-determined freedom which was so central to Irish nationalism. Founded in 1926 as a break-away from the purist anti-Treaty republican tradition, the Fianna Fáil party quickly came to dominate that wing of Irish political life. De Valera's decision to go into parliament in 1927 validated the institutions of the Free State, a trend reinforced further when the party won the 1932 General Election. That election had witnessed a very high turnout, and one of the key points about Fianna Fáil in these years was their capacity to attract disaffected republicans into the Free State constitutional arena, with the promise that power would allow for that arena to be politically purified. In the 1923 Free State general election, only 58.7 per cent of the electorate had voted, and anti-Treaty republicans had won the support of only 27.4 per cent of those who had done so. By the time of the 1938 General Election, 75.7 per cent of people voted, with Fianna Fáil winning 51.9 per cent of the vote. Disillusioned anti-Treatyites were being drawn back by de Valera into constitutional political struggle, and Fianna Fáil were helping to legitimize the independent Irish state as a consequence.

Once in power, these new republicans undid those disagreeable parts of the 1921 settlement which they could do something about. The oath of fidelity to the British Crown (required of those entering the Dublin parliament), the office of Governor-General, British access to Irish naval facilities, the right of appeal to the British Privy Council, the payment of land annuities to Britain, the 1922 Constitution itself – all were dismantled as de Valera's constitutional crusade vindicated the arguments of his old Civil War adversaries.

Crucial to this onward march was a sharp and attractive sense of national community. There were, of course, personal bonds (the new cabinet of 1932 had been prisoners and rebels together a decade earlier in the Civil War). But beyond this there was a powerful Fianna Fáil definition of a distinctive and dignified nationalist Ireland, with symbol, history, Gaelic ethnicity and culture, and Catholicism all being woven together.[287] De Valera himself stressed the need for non-antagonism within the nation (as so often within nationalism, solidarity was greatly valued): he wanted to prize 'the national interest as a whole', he said in 1926, and to avoid the 'clashing' of the various sections within the national community.[288] If non-antagonism within the nation was crucial, then so too were pride and self-respect. Like Daniel O'Connell before him, de Valera himself was vital here to the appeal of Fianna Fáil nationalism, with his cult of personality and his unique public demeanour. Hieratic in manner, the party leader exuded a quality sharply identified by Sean O'Faoláin: 'For whatever else may be said of him [de Valera], nobody will deny that one of his greatest qualities – and it contributes greatly to his influence – is dignity.'[289]

Fianna Fáil's nationalist community also involved actual priests. De Valera was explicit about his party's adherence to Catholic principles, and Fianna Fáil made it clear that they were committed to an Irishness interwoven with Catholicism. The new 1937 Constitution emerged as an emphatically Catholic document, de Valera having taken strong Catholic-clerical advice in drafting it. And its depiction of community was, fittingly, very conservative: as some female republicans themselves sharply noted,[290] de Valera's Constitution was inimical to the equal treatment of women ('the state recognizes that by her life within the home, woman gives to the state a support without which the common good cannot be achieved'; 'The state shall, therefore, endeavour to ensure that mothers shall not be obliged by economic necessity to engage in labour to the neglect of their duties in the home').[291]

This bilingual 1937 Constitution reflected the vision of community celebrated by Fianna Fáil, and also demonstrated the importance to such nationalism of the politics of power. Old republican diehards such as Sean MacBride certainly felt that the 1937 Constitution altered the realities of the nationalist map: 'When the new Constitution was adopted (1937) I felt there was no more need for the IRA and we should put all the energy we had into starting a republican party, and by political means we would be able to achieve reunification and an Irish republic.'[292] And the Constitution did point to the interweaving of community with power: integral territory was claimed ('The national territory consists of the whole island of Ireland, its islands and the territorial seas'), while state sovereignty was tied in with cultural uniqueness: 'The Irish nation hereby affirms its inalienable, indefeasible, and sovereign right to choose its own form of government, to determine its relations with other nations, and to develop its life, political, economic and cultural, in accordance with its own genius and traditions.'[293]

The struggle to maintain such freedom was very much part of

Fianna Fáil's politics, and organized struggle was something at which the party excelled. Their basic unit, the cumann (the local branch or association), was the backbone of the new party as it grew in the 1920s and 1930s, and de Valera himself went on a countrywide promotional tour soon after Fianna Fáil's foundation. Their newspaper *The Nation* was followed in 1931 with the *Irish Press* – a crucial communicative medium of which Frank Gallagher was editor-in-chief, and de Valera himself controlling editor. As the struggle against the Treaty was pursued, as sovereignty was strengthened, as economic and cultural battles were fought, this paper helped to consolidate and transmit a specifically Fianna Fáilite vision of nationalism.

And, once again, the appeal of the struggle was that it tied so much together at once. The promise of more jobs or land, or better housing, did appeal in themselves; but they also formed part of an economic policy which stressed self-reliant Irish dignity, and greater independence from the old British enemy. Thus Fianna Fáil's advocacy during the late 1920s and the 1930s of economic protection for much of the Irish economy was presented as both politically and economically attractive. De Valera's party was focused on political power in a direct sense (and from its 1926 inception the party was well organized, pragmatically oriented, and sharply committed towards electoral political success); but it was also a party whose winning of a parliamentary majority would consolidate freedom from Britain (cultural, political, economic), and who would guard such freedom according to the central nationalist principle of self-determining majority rule. Once the latter had been achieved, nothing – whether the risk of seriously pursuing Irish unity, or the moral imperative to engage in an anti-Nazi war after 1939 – could be allowed to get in the way.

This involved both an overlap with, and a repudiation of, the party's Revolutionary past. Irish (as other) nationalists showed a sharp sense of the importance of history (in its early years, republicans Frank Aiken, Ernie O'Malley and Peadar O'Donnell were all subscribers to the professional, scholarly journal *Irish Historical Studies*). And a figure such as Ernie O'Malley, who had himself helped in the groundwork for establishing the *Irish Press*, could be seen to hold and sustain a nationalist world-view on which de Valera constitutionally built. A book like O'Malley's 1936 IRA memoir, *On Another Man's Wound* (no less than other republican literary outpourings such as Liam O'Flaherty's Dostoyevskian 1937 novel, *Famine*), presented versions of nationalist memory which could be seen as legitimating struggle against England. Here was English or Protestant villainy and tyranny, and Irish and Catholic communal victimhood; here the defenceless had taken violent action in order to liberate themselves. Both with militant pasts, O'Malley and O'Flaherty liked each other's books, and one can easily enough see why: each presented English rule as tyranny, and each made communal claims to national Irish victimhood. So *Famine* depicts the awfulness of Famine suffering, but presents it as originating in English and Protestant Irish villainy, and as resulting from English tyranny. 'It's the people against the tyrants,' one of the characters proclaims, and rebellious violence is presented as understandable and legitimate within such narrowly conceived politics. But while literary depictions such as O'Flaherty's presented nineteenth-century Ireland as having been ruled purely by coercion ('Under a tyranny, the only active forces of government are those of coercion') and requiring violence as a necessary response,[294] the reality of the Union was, in fact, far more complex. Even most committed Irish nationalists from that period themselves saw the English–Irish relationship as more subtly nuanced, and eschewed revolutionary violence.

The nationalist family shared many of these memories, but once in power in their own state, politicians could turn against former comrades should the latter persist in obstreperous behaviour. Militant republicans such as the IRA had welcomed Fianna Fáil's 1932 election victory (as it expelled their old enemies, the pro-Treaty Cumann na nGaedheal party, from authority); but they were in fact welcoming their nemesis into power, and the IRA's relationship with Fianna Fáil soon cooled. The IRA came to hold the view that de Valera's party would inevitably let down its republican supporters and their expectations, and that this would then allow the IRA themselves space for some forward movement. In reality, the opposite was nearer to the truth, as Fianna Fáil deepened and broadened its support. Here, as so often in the Irish nationalist story, we are again far from the myth that extremes always dominate Irish politics. It was the constitutional, gradualist pragmatism of de Valera, rather than the vanguardist violence of the IRA, which appealed to more and more Irish nationalists.

'There were a lot of people that thought he was going slowly, but he was going somewhere,' as one old Cumann na mBan zealot ruefully put it in later years, 'and they were happy with it.'[295]

And Fianna Fáil did hold very different views, now, from the IRA. The state which they now controlled was, in their newly acquired Weberian view, the sole monopolist on the legitimate use of force within independent Ireland's territory; and so the IRA had to be dealt with firmly. In the summer of 1936 the organization was proscribed, its Chief of Staff (Moss Twomey) having already been arrested. As early as January 1934 the IRA's *An Phoblacht* had been referring to 'Fianna Fáil's anti-republican campaign' and to de Valera's 'puppet state'; the 'mask', said the paper, 'is off'.[296] Indeed it was. A meeting of the government on 23 June 1939 introduced an Order suppressing the IRA ('It is hereby declared that the organization styling itself the Irish Republican Army (also the IRA and Oglaigh na hEireann) is an unlawful organization and ought, in the public interest, to be suppressed'[297]). Present at this meeting with de Valera himself were former republican Revolutionaries turned government ministers, such as Frank Aiken (Defence), Sean Lemass (Industry and Commerce), Tom Derrig (Education) and Sean MacEntee (Finance).

And yet extra-constitutional republicans – those who continued to think independent Ireland to be insufficiently independent – were themselves explicable (both in terms of their enthusiasms and ultimately their failure) within the framework of our thesis on nationalism. Militant republicans in these interwar years stuck firmly to their Rousseauan nationalist ideals, interweaving sovereignty, equality and freedom ('the Irish people is by right a free people', committed 'to secure and maintain its complete independence . . . and to constitute a national policy based upon the people's will, with equal rights and equal opportunity for every citizen'[298]); again, the interrelated politics of equality, sovereignty, freedom, unity and state legitimacy were emphatically endorsed in the IRA's 1925 Constitution;[299] and militant republicans' desire to reintegrate the whole Irish territory was complemented by a focus on both the imagined, Gaelic nation of ancient vintage, and the actual republican community (there were, for example, many cries for the release of republican prisoners, not least from the ever-strident Maud Gonne[300]). Culture was clearly there, both in republicans' Catholicism (the IRA in these years recited the Rosary at commemorations, and tended to salute Catholic churches while they were on parade; for its own part, late-1920s Sinn Féin was explicit in its Catholic allegiance), and in their formal endorsement of the Irish language. Moral superiority was also evident (as the IRA Army Council put it in October 1938, 'The [Irish Republican] Army is above political parties'[301]); and so too was exclusivism directed against those judged to be imperialist in Ireland.

Yet when it came to the politics of power, militant republicans were undone by those constitutional nationalists whose struggle involved more realistic notions of progress. The IRA could dream of military methods bringing success (Chief of Staff Moss Twomey in 1929 described the Irish separatist problem as being 'essentially military in character'[302]), and it could offer certain psychological rewards: one of the killers of Cumann na nGaedheal politician Kevin O'Higgins in 1927 recalled that he and his fellow-killers were, at the time of the murder, 'just taken over and incensed with hatred'[303] towards their old political enemy and now victim. But, ultimately, violence was no rival to a nationalism which could combine Irish community with self-determined, legitimized, sovereign power over an actually functioning independent Irish state. If militant republicans were anti-partitionist, comradely, ethnically-rooted, cultural and historical nationalists, with a sense of moral superiority and an implicit exclusivism, then so too were Fianna Fáilers. And the latter had engaged in a struggle which recognized the realities of power (electoral, bureaucratic) and something of its limitations (regarding the implications of British strength and unionist opposition, for example).

So hard-line republicans could sneer at de Valera's new-found majoritarianism, but it was this which had undermined the IRA in independent Ireland. It was solipsistic of republicans to confuse their own diminishing cult with the nation, when de Valera could point to huge levels of popular endorsement for his own communal struggle. Thus militant republicans could only represent an irritation to the state in these years, rather than a serious threat to its survival: in mid-1924 IRA membership appears to have stood at around 15,000; by late 1936 the number was below 4,000.

Was there more mileage, perhaps, in a truly radical nationalism, a left-wing rival to de Valera's Catholic conservatism? There was certainly nothing unusual about a left-wing, anti-fascist nationalism in interwar

Europe, and Ireland had its own variety of passionate crusaders, among them the ever-ebullient Peadar O'Donnell, the bellicose Frank Ryan, and the gloomily thoughtful George Gilmore (1898–1985). For these figures and their comrades, hard-left politics offered the only viable future: 'Abroad and in England communism is growing extraordinarily,' observed the eighty-one-year-old aristocratic radical Charlotte Despard in 1926. 'We mean to try and start a group here. So far as society is concerned that is the only hope for this tormented world.'[304] (Despard became an executive member of the Workers' Party of Ireland, within which James Connolly's son Roddy was prominent.)

Like Marx himself, Irish nationalists of the socialist republican type saw in poverty the subversive and revolutionary potential for the overthrow of the old social order. With the international depression of 1929 and subsequent years, was there not life in such a nationalism in Ireland? Its exponents certainly made an energetic and impressively committed case, and spawned organizations such as the IRA offshoots Saor Eire (1931) and the Republican Congress (1934). They saw James Connolly as the crucial figure on whom to focus in Irish history,[305] and it was Connolly's spirit which drove left-republican groups in this period. As Sheila Humphreys (a Cumann na mBan woman who joined the Republican Congress) observed, 'Connolly's socialism started the Congress. Definitely.'[306] Connolly's daughter Nora was herself intensely involved in the early days of this 1930s Republican Congress ('I went everywhere organizing it'[307]), and it was a Connollyite nationalism which such people committedly espoused. Britain had colonized Ireland for economic benefit; such benefit was achieved through the capitalist system; as long as British links and control were maintained, therefore, capitalism would be sustained in Ireland; so those in Ireland who flourished under capitalism would support the British connection; by contrast, those Irish people whom the capitalist system oppressed had a social imperative to sever the British link, and it was in this anti-capitalist group – rather than in capitalist Ireland – that true republicanism could be found. Pro-capitalist Fianna Fáil, it therefore followed, could not be true republicans. 'Fianna Fáil cannot possibly unite the country,' Peadar O'Donnell proclaimed in 1934.[308] Comrade Gilmore amplified the theme: 'It is becoming every day more apparent that the middle class leadership of Fianna Fáil, in pursuance of its policy of protecting capitalism in Ireland, is not attempting to sever the connection with the British empire but is negotiating with a view to altering the form of association.'[309]

There was great ingenuity in this kind of argument, and it could make sense of people's surroundings powerfully enough. Peadar O'Donnell's Donegal background had impressed him both with the evils of social hardship and injustice and with the possibilities that such problems could be remedied through the communal toughness of those with whom he had grown up: as so often with nationalists, O'Donnell's thinking was built on his distinctive local origins and observations (a clear example of the widely relevant point that one can only truly understand the genesis and nature of nationalists' ideas by setting them in the particularities of their local time and place).[310]

But Irish socialist republicanism failed during the 1920s and 1930s to achieve the revolution that its able adherents so keenly sought. By the late 1940s and early 1950s, when he was editing the literary and social periodical *The Bell*, Peadar O'Donnell himself was finding that 'the young men who formerly came to him with manifestoes now only wanted a fiver'.[311] In the early 1930s the Irish state had been very anxious about republican-leftist menace, and O'Donnell and his friends had been pursued using the powers created by the capacious 1931 Constitution (Amendment No. 17) Act.[312] Yet 1930s left-republican public meetings were marginal enough affairs in practice, and could be easily mocked by less than sympathetic observers.[313] Even some republican comrades who liked him did not take O'Donnell's own socialism too seriously: as Cumann na mBan's Patsy O'Hagan put it, 'I liked Peadar. I did not pay great attention to some of his theories but I loved his droll humour; he was so offhand and gay.'[314]

With the late-1930s collapse of the Republican Congress, the death of this generation of socialist republican projects was clear. Why had they failed? There are still very able scholars who hold to the view that a radical socialist Irish future was a possibility in the early years of the twentieth century.[315] But close examination of the evidence suggests that there were very high walls for the left to overcome in terms of Irish communal definition. If one turned to the Church, or to Gaelic ethnicity, or to patterns of landownership, then the leftist version of nationalism faced great difficulties when competing with more conservative and inclusive forms of politics in nationalist Ireland. The sharp hostility of Catholic voices towards Marxism and socialism is clear from the strident pages of a publication such as the *Catholic Mind*: 'wherever the Catholic Church is a strong force, and simultaneously, the socialists are a strong force, we see the two in violent antagonism'; 'Communism is a graver danger than any existing organization';[316] and this helps to explain why more Church-friendly forms of nationalism could flourish.

With the republican socialist cult of the interwar years in Ireland the broader question, of why nation so often trumps class, can be addressed in another useful case study. All classes were welcome in the nation, while left-republicans effectively appealed only to the anti-capitalist working classes: 'We believe that a republic of a united Ireland will never be achieved except through a struggle which uproots capitalism on its way.'[317] For Fianna Fáil, but not for socialist republicans, all the resources of nationalist imagination and community were available (territory, people, ethnic descent, culture, history and so on); and for Fianna Fáil, but not for marginal revolutionary leftists, the machinery of the sovereign state – for all its imperfections – offered a popularly sanctioned way of moving things forward in attractively practical ways. In the 1930s, of course, many people on both left and right thought liberal democracy to be doomed; but they were profoundly wrong.[318] The nationalism which endorsed liberal democracy – and which gained from its engagement with self-determining states as the workable framework for such democracy – was the nationalism which was historically to triumph.

The survival of democracy in interwar Ireland is as impressive as was its creation, when one considers the fate of so many democrats in Europe in these years. Irish nationalism too was to engage with the world's darker contemporary forces, and it did so in varying, compelling ways. In the 1930s the pro-Treatyite wing of Irish nationalism spawned a quasi-fascist movement – the Blueshirts – which long remained effectively forgotten, but which a newer generation of scholars has thankfully now restored to our memory of nationalist Ireland's past.[319] The Army Comrades' Association (ACA) had been established in the early 1930s, an organization of ex-Free State army people committed to guarding one another's welfare; but the ACA were to grow more ambitious. They presented themselves as defenders of free speech against IRA thuggery, and in March 1933 started wearing the blue shirt; May 1933 saw them begin to use the straight-arm salute, while in July the eccentric ex-Revolutionary Eoin O'Duffy (1890–1944) took over leadership of the group, which now adopted the title National Guard. In September 1933 these Blueshirts merged with the Centre Party and Cumann na nGaedheal to form the Fine Gael (initially, the United Ireland) party.

O'Duffy's Blueshirts clashed violently with republicans, and they were banned and ultimately crushed by de Valera's legitimate state. But it's important to stress that they were themselves an Irish nationalist movement,[320] and one which reflected key ideas of community, struggle and power. The Blueshirts were enthusiasts for Gaelic Ireland; they sought to protect the economic interests of cattle-farmers in an era when de Valera's policies threatened these people's rural livelihoods (indeed, O'Duffy and others claimed to have inherited Parnell and Davitt's tradition of agrarian nationalism); they deeply identified Catholicism with Irish patriotism (Blueshirt intellectuals such as James Hogan, Professor of History at University College, Cork, or Michael Tierney, Professor of Greek at UCD, looked to Catholic Europe for their inspiration. Son-in-law of Eoin MacNeill, Tierney wrote for the Blueshirt paper *United Ireland* and he was emphatically a Catholic nationalist intellectual: deeply influenced by papal thinking, he sought the regeneration of Ireland as a Christian society, and favoured a corporate and vocational system as the alternative to failed democracy); the Blueshirts' cultural emphasis mixed the ludicrous with the impressive (W. B. Yeats flirted with the Blueshirts during 1933–4, even being prepared to write songs for the unfortunate movement); they claimed the whole of Ireland's territory and people, strongly advocating an irredentist anti-partitionism; they offered an escape for some from the boredom of rural 1930s Ireland (just as the IRA had done in the Revolution, and the Fenians before this in the nineteenth century). And the Blueshirt struggle was organized and – for a time – it was formidable enough (in 1933 the ACA had claimed to possess around 100,000 members): it focused on sovereignty, unity, independence, material benefits and cultural status, as well as on group and individual advancement. O'Duffy and his colleagues sought and exerted power, and all of this (as in their anti-communism and their commitment to the muscular protection of the right to free speech) was cast as a politics of freedom.

Yet they were also a quasi-fascistic group. Some scholars have downplayed this, presenting the Blueshirts as having possessed few of the essential characteristics of fascist movements ('The Blueshirts are frequently described as fascists. They were not. . . . The Blueshirts deviated widely from the standard fascist model'[321]). Yet there were clearly fascist elements to Blueshirtism (the shirt, the salute, the mass rallies, the deployment of violence, the key ideas of some leading figures), and it's probably best to see the movement as one in which there existed a tension between a more fascistic leadership and a restraining rank-and-file: 'There was definitely a strand of fascist thought, policy, and admiration in the Blueshirt psyche, but this was successfully muffled and marginalized'; 'In terms of being a fascist movement the Blueshirts as a whole undoubtedly fall wide of the mark: this despite the obvious commitment to fascism by O'Duffy and other organizers and ideologues.'[322]

O'Duffy himself clearly displayed anti-democratic and fascistic views; indeed, after his resignation as President of Fine Gael, his fascist ideas came to be more obvious (just as Fine Gael's politics became more traditional after O'Duffy's departure). Yet, while he himself was heavily involved with European fascist organizations, O'Duffy's Blueshirt movement not only engaged with continental political struggles (as in its disastrous trip to Spain to fight for Franco), but also reflected some of the difficulties which pro-Treatyite nationalists in independent Ireland were facing in the early 1930s. Out of power since 1932, and facing a powerful adversary in Eamon de Valera, the Blueshirts represented some pro-Treatyites' unhappiness with Fianna Fáil Ireland. Their sense of community and community interests pushed them towards engaging in a politics which was both Irish nationalist and quasi-fascistic. The Blueshirts were not fascist in the German or Italian manner, but their fascistic qualities represented, sadly, one of the routes down which nationalist struggle and disaffection in Ireland could lead in this period.

It might be embarrassing to acknowledge that nationalist Ireland backed fascism in Spain during 1936–9, and that it largely stood aside in the Second World War fight against Hitler, but this was the essential reality, and its explanation is evident enough. A conservative Catholic nationalism had been dominant in Revolutionary Ireland, and so the struggle in Spain – interpreted by many as one involving godless communism versus the Faith – was easy enough to read. Thus the ex-

IRA and Republican Congress man Frank Ryan took only a small-scale band to fight against Franco, while Eoin O'Duffy's crusade reflected nationalist Ireland's broad, Francoist instincts. When hundreds of O'Duffyite volunteers set off from the Irish west coast in December 1936, there were bands, hymn-singing crowds and crusade-blessing priests to send them off resoundingly. The Irish Francoists made a rather inglorious show of themselves when they actually got to Spain: there was friction with the Spanish, as well as discontentment, poor discipline, bad leadership and low morale. But the predominantly rural O'Duffyites who went to fight in Spain included many ex-IRA men, and they represented a part of Irish nationalist – indeed, Irish republican – history. For many of the Irish Brigade who fought for Franco it was anti-communism, rather than any zeal for fascism, which predominated as a motivation. And this anti-communism mingled with a profound Catholic piety. Motives also included a desire for adventure, for employment, even for travel. But enthusiasm for the Catholic faith – and for its necessary defence in Spain – was a powerful and decisive motivation for many of O'Duffy's followers to the Spanish conflict; and for many of these people Catholic faith and Irish nationalist sympathy were interwoven. For some, indeed, the struggle in Spain was of a piece with the Irish Revolutionary war recently fought to free Ireland from Britain.

The less numerous and less typical anti-Francoites also, of course, embodied an Irish nationalist response. Among those Irish republicans who went to fight against fascism in Spain was County Tyrone poet and Connollyite left-republican Charlie Donnelly (1914–37) – a romantic figure in his literary tastes (which included Keats and Shelley), his lifestyle (in poverty in 1930s London he preferred a book and a packet of cigarettes to a meal), and finally in the manner of his youthful Spanish death, aged just twenty-two, while fighting against Franco. But three times as many Irishmen fought for Franco as fought against him, despite a public preference now for remembering Frank Ryan rather than Eoin O'Duffy as the typical Irish nationalist enthusiast in this struggle. In December 1936 about eighty International Brigade Volunteers, led by Ryan, left Ireland to fight against Franco in Spain: but they had had to sneak out of Ireland more quietly than O'Duffy, knowing that Irish opinion was essentially hostile to their mission. Frank Ryan's own courage should not be ignored, nor should we just disregard his view that fighting against fascism linked Irish nationalism with wider struggles for freedom. But uncomfortable facts remain: most within nationalist Ireland leaned to the right in the Spanish struggle, and Ryan's own peculiar journey was to lead him to side with England's enemy, Nazi Germany, during the Second World War.

While Ryan himself explicitly stated a preference for a Nazi rather than an Allied victory in the latter conflict,[323] others within nationalist Irish republicanism went further in their alliance with the Nazis. In 1939 Sean O'Faolain lamented what he called 'the curse of nationalist opinion in Ireland': 'that it lacks independence: it automatically looks to see what Great Britain is doing in any given situation, and without a thought it does the opposite'.[324] In the context of a struggle such as the Second World War, this knee-jerk anglophobia could lead into dangerous waters. Eire, as the southern state was now known, adopted a neutral stance in the war, but the IRA took a pro-German (at times, anti-Jewish) approach. The army was committed to aiding the German war effort, and their leader Sean Russell (1893–1940), in Germany in 1940 as a guest of the Nazis, urged his hosts to use the IRA to attack British forces in Northern Ireland as part of a broader German attack on Britain. Russell's own contacts with Nazi Germany dated from the mid-1930s, and the logic of this emerged when the Second World War IRA identified Irish 'freedom' and Ireland's 'absolute independence' with Nazi victory.[325]

The IRA's association with the Nazis had little practical effect (its threat to Irish neutrality was greater than its military weight). But, given that some Irish nationalists have identified their own communal suffering (at the hands of Britain and of Northern Irish unionists) with that of the victims of Nazism, there is some irony – and no little disgrace – in the fact that the IRA colluded with Hitler at a time when unionists (such as future Northern Ireland Prime Ministers Terence O'Neill and James Chichester-Clark) and future victims of republican violence (such as Lord Mountbatten and Airey Neave) were fighting against him.

Nor was it just the ongoing IRA which displayed such instincts. Many Irish nationalists (including Maud Gonne and Dan Breen) were sympathetic to the Nazis, and numerous other Irish nationalists were clearly anti-Jewish in their thinking in this period. Northern nationalist

politician Malachy Conlon had distasteful views of this kind – and nor
was he a trivial figure. He was comfortably elected as Nationalist MP
for South Armagh in 1945, having expressed deeply anti-Jewish views,
and he was crucial to the establishment and running of the nationalist
Anti-Partition League (APL).[326] This is not to suggest either that Irish
nationalist suffering at British and unionist hands was trivial (it
wasn't), nor that Irish nationalists all favoured fascism (they didn't).
But the notion that Irish nationalists have necessarily been progressive
on issues concerning justice and freedom is one which needs to be
qualified significantly. It might be a comforting aspect of many
nationalist traditions to assume a position of ethical superiority; in
most cases, that of Irish nationalism among them, this can only be
maintained by ignoring the messy complexity of historical experience.

6

Irish nationalists in the province of Ulster entered the
twentieth century optimistic about their political future. Like
nationalists throughout the island, they were relying on the
Irish Parliamentary Party in alliance with British Liberals to
deliver a substantial form of self-government for the island
as a whole. The opposition of Irish unionism and particularly
of Ulster unionists to Home Rule tended to be dismissed as
a mixture of bigotry and the defence of vested interest.

Henry Patterson[327]

In Northern Ireland itself, nationalists faced some very different issues
of community, struggle and power from those which faced their
southern counterparts. As the minority in the six-county northern
state which had been set up in the 1920s, they could not realistically
hope for power, and it was this which tied together their struggle for
fair treatment with their preference for an all-island polity in which
they would form part of the majority population within the state.
Many nationalists at the time of partition had assumed the division of
Ireland to be a temporary one, and so nationalists in the north initially

boycotted the new state and its institutions. Nationalist politicians didn't take their seats in the Northern Ireland parliament until 1926; the Royal Ulster Constabulary (RUC) never gained its intended full quota of Catholic members (though it might be worth recording that in 1923 the force was 21 per cent Catholic); nationalist leaders refused to participate in the 1921–2 Lynn Committee (which reviewed education provision) and the 1922–3 Leech Commission (reviewing local government boundaries).

On each side of this clash between national communities (northern nationalist and Ulster unionist), understandable decisions worsened the political context. Unionists were insecure, facing a hostile nationalist state to the south, a third of the Northern Ireland population whose tradition was equally hostile to unionism, and a London government of dubious reliability. They therefore prized loyalty to the state (in modern Ireland, of course, deeply interwoven with confessional background), and allowed Catholic disadvantage to fester in ways which did indeed make Catholics more firmly nationalist and potentially more threatening. Nationalists opted not to participate in shaping the new state, and so the state was moulded in ways even more unfavourable to them (in terms, for instance, of electoral boundaries as redrawn by the Leech Committee).

James Craig (Northern Ireland's unionist Prime Minister from 1921 until his death in 1940), presided over a regime which, in the end, lacked the magnanimity towards nationalists which might perhaps have strengthened the security of the state:

> His government responded well to the military and external political challenges faced by the new state: but the demands of achieving long-term stability within a divided society as well as long-term prosperity within an area of rapid economic decline proved to be beyond the intellectual or imaginative capacity of the new regime.[328]

Yet the context for Craig's defensiveness and partial failure was, in significant measure, one determined by Irish nationalism also. IRA violence in the founding years of Northern Ireland heightened unionist anxiety, as did the increasing Catholicization and Gaelicization of independent Ireland once de Valera came to power in 1932, and the understandable sense among northern nationalists themselves that the new northern state was neither fair nor legitimate. All of this was worsened by intercommunal violence. IRA attacks on Protestants and on the security forces, or republican raids and robberies, were matched by loyalist violence against Catholics (from which the RUC did not protect them sufficiently, and for which the police themselves appear on occasion to have been responsible[329]).

So there was, from the start in Northern Ireland, a lack of communal confidence on either side of the confessional–political divide. For most nationalists, there was a sense of the properness of a united Ireland and the illegitimacy of the six-county state in the north (a sense reflected in the *Irish News* day by day, and also in many Catholic clerical pronouncements).

When in December 1925 a London–Belfast–Dublin agreement confirmed the Irish border which was then in existence, northern nationalists faced the less than agreeable prospect of being a minority in someone else's state. Yet what could be done to change the situation? In January 1933 Hanna Sheehy-Skeffington, assistant editor of the republican paper *An Phoblacht*, was sentenced to one month's imprisonment in Northern Ireland, having been arrested earlier in the month in Newry while addressing a public meeting. The charge against her was that that of entering County Armagh in defiance of a 1926 Exclusion Order which the Northern Irish authorities had served upon her. In court in Armagh Sheehy-Skeffington was gloriously defiant: 'I recognize no partition. I recognize it as no crime to be in my own country. I would be ashamed of my own name and my murdered husband's name if I did. [Her husband was the writer Francis Sheehy-Skeffington, who had been killed in 1916, having tried to prevent looting during the Rising.] ... Long live the Republic!'[330] This gives a picture of arduous and defiant struggle. Yet too much harshness should not, perhaps, be read automatically into such episodes. The prisoner's sister, Mrs T. M. Kettle, had expressed anxiety about Sheehy-Skeffington's treatment in prison. But when the writer Rosamund Jacob visited her on 17 January the emerging picture was not too discouraging: even the Dublin authorities conceded that 'Mrs Kettle's fears as to the prison treatment of her sister do not appear to be substantiated' by what Jacob had reported. According to Rosamund Jacob, indeed, the prison governor 'was very agreeable, and seemed willing to do what he could for her [Sheehy-Skeffington]'.[331]

There were violent actions by the IRA in the north in the interwar era. But the republican army represented a minority of the nationalist minority (most of whom supported the constitutional Nationalist Party). The northern IRA tended to be drawn from the less than wealthy classes (as the IRA's Belfast OC rather plaintively put it in 1934, 'The bulk of our members are unemployed.... We have 460 men in Belfast but only about 150 working'[332]), but they were unable to offer either thorough defence against sectarian attack or any prospect of undoing partition by means of the gun.

Yet violence was not the only means of national struggle, and one should not assume too casually that there was no energy (or even efficacy) to northern nationalist political action. Patrick O'Neill (Nationalist MP for Mourne Division, County Down) was in the 1920s actively engaged in supporting local concerns and interests (such as the issue of harbour development in Killough, County Down, and the promotion of the local fishing industry),[333] and not without some success. Even from early days, nationalist politicians and their lobbying constituents were far from passive, and nationalist politics had in it more vigour than casual assumption sometimes suggests.

In any case, while state power was denied them, nationalists could still build community definition and meaning, and emphatically did so. The Catholic hierarchy reinforced the idea that partition was unnatural, and that the northern state was artificial rather than legitimate; and they became important leaders of their community. Moreover, nationalist political leaders in the north displayed deeply Catholic influences and ideas, a reflection of the importance of distinctive dimensions to communal politics. The prominent Joe Devlin – Nationalist MP for Belfast West from 1921 to 1929, and for Belfast Central (Stormont) between 1929 and 1934 – was both a sentimental Irish nationalist (very keen, among other things, on Thomas Moore's *Melodies*) and a deeply Catholic patriot. At the death of this Belfast-born, CBS-educated politician and AOH leader in 1934, the understandable tributes demonstrated, amid other things, the deeply Catholic nature of Devlin's and his community's politics. A memorial leaflet from 1934 carried numerous quotations in honour of the recently deceased nationalist leader: southern nationalist politician W. T. Cosgrave observed that Devlin 'was a gifted statesman, an eloquent orator, a devoted Catholic. We have lost a true patriot'; a Christian Brother described Devlin as having been 'our most famous Belfast pupil. He was proud of being a Christian Brothers' boy. We were proud of Joe. He was always obedient to the laws of God and of His Church.' The same souvenir leaflet outlined 'Prayers to Obtain a Good Death: Every night say three "Hail Mary's", and "O Mary, I am thine, save me". Jesus, Mary, and Joseph, I give you my heart and my soul. Jesus, Mary, and Joseph, assist me now and in my last agony. Jesus, Mary, and Joseph, may I breathe forth my soul in peace with you.' The leaflet also noted that 'All profit on these leaflets goes for Masses for his [Devlin's] soul. Each nationalist and Catholic should get one.'[334]

SIX

COLD WARS AND REVOLUTIONARIES, 1945–2005

1

> We had the Republic of our will and vision from 1916 to 1923, but it struggled unsuccessfully for recognition and a stable place in the international scheme. What we have today is substantial: a status and a Constitution: a freely-working, democratic state.
>
> Dorothy Macardle (1946)[1]

Some old nationalist Irish Revolutionaries felt proud of what had been achieved through their communal struggle for power. Dorothy Macardle, quoted above, stressed what had been won by 1946 for independent Ireland, in terms of status, formal institutions and democracy – in some ways, the essence of nationalism itself. But many were less celebratory of what had been done since the establishment of independence for the twenty-six counties, and it sometimes seemed as though time had become rather frozen in that Revolutionary moment itself, a quarter of a century earlier; in the summer of 1946, when Welsh poet Dylan Thomas visited Ireland, his sojourn in Dublin was memorable for 'peaty porter' and for the 'endless blarney of politics never later than 1922'.[2]

But how *did* Irish nationalism work in mid-century independent Ireland? In addition to what Macardle rightly identified as major achievements (and they were undoubtedly very impressive), there were also certain narrow, cold and restrictive aspects to the faith as it had worked out in practice. The distinguished American academic John V. Kelleher noted crisply of censorship in mid-century independent Ireland that 'Every Irish author of any standing is represented on the list of banned books . . . Since the [1929 Censorship] Act went into effect, about 1,500 books have been proscribed, including just about every Irish novel worth reading.'[3] Again, the Irish-speaking, Aran sweater-wearing world of Hugo Hamilton's mid-century childhood suggests a Catholic Irish nationalism which involved much narrowness ('It's forbidden to speak in English in our house' – a proscription enforced through violence against the children; 'My father said we could only play with children who could speak Irish') and pretence (including parental denial regarding a relative who had been in the British navy).[4]

For there was a double-edged quality, as so often, to the powerful and rewarding themes within nationalism. The Irish language emancipated, and simultaneously it could also constrict. So too with the celebration of rural Irish beauty, a marked feature of many Irish Revolutionaries' imagined Ireland, seen through lenses of patriotic intensity. As so often,[5] topography and patriotism continued to interact after the Revolution, the romantic, rural, Arcadian view of Ireland being sustained by the new state. But there were less glorious aspects here as well. That rural Ireland long remained prominent in Irish nationalists' proud imagination should come as no surprise. Even as austere an observer as the Austrian philosopher Ludwig Wittgenstein was deeply taken by the rustic beauty of the place in the 1930s and 1940s, and made a positive comparison between unspoilt rural Ireland and a decaying urban England. In Wittgenstein's own record, Cambridge represented a 'disintegrating and putrefying English civilization'; by contrast, travelling in County Wicklow in 1947, he apparently kept remarking to himself, 'what a really beautiful country this is'.[6] But Wittgenstein's view of rural Ireland turned out, in practice, much less positively. In the late 1940s he stayed in an isolated cottage in Connemara in the west of the country; the local man (Tommy Mulkerrins) who was paid by the owners of the cottage to look after their property did not entirely impress the distinguished philosophical visitor. The Mulkerrins family, Wittgenstein claimed, were ill-disposed to do any work: Tommy's mother, though a seamstress, dressed in rags; and although Tommy himself was a passable carpenter, every chair in their cottage had a broken leg. Mulkerrins was recorded in the philosopher's diary as being 'unreliable'. And if Wittgenstein was rather shocked by the Irish locals, then the reverse was also true. His immediate neighbours in Connemara thought him utterly insane, refused to interact with him, and even forbade him to walk on their land because they feared that this mad philosopher would frighten their sheep.

Irish nationalists themselves sometimes evinced a Wittgensteinian ambivalence about Irish Arcadia. Ernie O'Malley and his American wife, Helen, sought bucolic fulfilment in mid-century Mayo, only to have their genuine love of rural Ireland offset by marked frustrations. 'You have to be very self-supporting to live in the Irish countryside,' O'Malley wrote in 1940, 'I mean intellectually self-supporting. There is no art, no library worth a small curse, no one who writes or paints near to you: very few people who read.' His wife was even more scathing, writing in 1943 that 'I don't believe life in medieval Russia could be any harder than it is in Ireland in 1943. . . . I well understand why the average person of any ability leaves.'[7] When Irish-American director John Ford made his saccharine west-of-Ireland film *The Quiet Man*, he enlisted ex-IRA man O'Malley as a kind of technical adviser (he was on set with John Wayne and Maureen O'Hara during each day's filming in Mayo in the summer of 1951). But the contrast between the idealized west of the film – amiable, romantic and harmless, even in its violence – could hardly be more starkly different from mid-century Ireland as Ford's technical adviser had actually experienced it: O'Malley's life had by 1952 (the year of *The Quiet Man*'s release) already involved an ugly divorce, following his wife's kidnapping of two of their three children, and some far from harmless violence and domestic unpleasantness.[8] Indeed, Ford's famous film is also in sharp contrast to the more brutal Maurice Walsh short story on which it was based: the buffoonish, fairly even-handed central fight of the film is very different from the cruel, one-sided beating of the original story.[9] (A similarly vicious, one-sided fight occurs also in County Kerry-born Walsh's novel, *The Key Above the Door*[10].)

The Quiet Man could successfully soften and romanticize Irish reality, but only for those whose blinkers allowed them to see a part, rather than the whole, of the national picture. In any case, the role of the rural in Ireland's nationalism was unavoidably to change, from a celebration of self to an appealing escape from urban reality. By mid-century, the process was in full force by means of which independent Ireland would move towards becoming a far less rural society: the percentage of people engaged in agriculture fell from 52 per cent in 1926 to 36 per cent in 1961 (and to a mere 15 per cent by 1986).[11] This did not rule out a celebratory, escapist value to Arcadian nationalism, but it did significantly diminish the political power, and alter the role, of the rural in nationalist politics.

Yet invocations of supposedly paradigmatic rusticity continued, as did a Catholic complexion to southern society. Though not mirror-images of each other, Ireland's two states – north and south – were both based on a majority culture which defined the confessional minority as less prominent and orthodox:

The partition of Ireland created two states embodying rival ideologies and representing two hostile peoples. Roman Catholic nationalists acquired effective control over twenty-six counties in the Irish Free State, while Protestant Unionists secured the six counties of Northern Ireland. . . . The subsequent maintenance of local power by the dominant majority in each state was not softened by respect for the freedom of individuals or dissident minorities.[12]

And this situation continued for many years, creating both smugness and a hierarchy of communities in each jurisdiction. In late-1940s Dublin, the visiting Wittgenstein was, again, less than impressed by orthodox Irish realities: 'I would much prefer to see a child educated by a decent Protestant pastor than by a greasy Roman Catholic priest. When I look at the faces of the clergy here in Dublin, it seems to me that the Protestant ministers look less smug than the Roman priests.'[13] More weightily, the narrowness of independent Ireland as experienced by Protestants, and the reasons for the southern state not appealing to northern unionists, were both acknowledged even by Irish contemporaries with nationalist and republican sympathies: 'no northerner can possibly like such features of southern life, as at present constituted, as its pervasive clerical control; its censorship; its Gaelic revival; its isolationist economic policy'; 'whatever pious aspirations or resolutions may be found in the Constitution of Eire about religious tolerance it is a matter of common knowledge to those who care to enquire, or even observe, that the Protestant in the south has as little chance of getting his fair share of public appointments as the Catholic in the north'.[14]

For, north and south, people (disingenuously? ignorantly?) said that it was not Protestants (or Catholics) whom they opposed, but disloyal imperialists (or disloyal nationalists). In fact, the connection in modern Ireland between confessional tradition and political outlook was so strong and deeply rooted in ethnic pasts that to draw any such distinction was in many cases implausible. The loyalty to Britain which Irish Protestants felt was to a Protestant Britain, and to a Britishness which had historically drawn much definition and strength from that Protestantism; the Irish nationalism to which many nationalists felt such profound allegiance was a nationalism which had involved the fighting of frequently Catholic causes, for the redress of Catholic grievances, and such struggles had therefore had a markedly Catholic quality. To imagine that there was no causal link between someone's religious background and their politics was to misunderstand the nature of modern Irish politics.

So the independent Ireland built by nationalists by the middle of the twentieth century could be narrow enough at times. Yet it wasn't the case that nationalist Ireland had no international, outward-looking dimensions, even at intellectual level. Dorothy Macardle, author of the classic republican text *The Irish Republic*, was clearly familiar with the work of Freud;[15] ex-IRA novelist Peadar O'Donnell had fashioned his thinking under the powerful influence of Karl Marx's writings; while Ernie O'Malley spent his melancholic post-Revolutionary days reading, among others, Franz Kafka and Isaiah Berlin. And all three figures – together with other nationalists in their circle – exhibited a marked bohemianism.

In other ways, too, mid-century nationalism had international dimensions. Entering the United Nations in 1955, Ireland achieved a disproportionately conspicuous role there, both through the energy and talent of delegates such as Frank Aiken, Frederick Boland and Conor Cruise O'Brien, and also through the nature of its chosen causes (including opposition to South African apartheid, and the promotion of African and Asian decolonization); 'From the mid-1950s until the mid-1960s the Irish delegation, led by an extraordinary team of talented, dedicated diplomats, occupied a prominent place in the [UN] General Assembly.'[16] And emigration (old and new) also involved Irish nationalism in international settings in the mid-twentieth century. In 1940–41 there were 678,000 Irish-born people living in the United States and 86,000 in Canada;[17] and while many of these were nationalist neither in background nor in emigrant activity, others undoubtedly were. These included the feisty Michael Flannery (1902–94), who was born in Tipperary, joined the IRA in 1917, took part in the 1919–21 War for Independence, opposing the 1921 Treaty, and then emigrated to the States where he was subsequently based. Flannery gained relative notoriety for his actions during a later stage of nationalist Irish violence, but it's worth noting also his mid-century agitation, during the IRA's border campaign of 1956, since it again interweaves community with militant struggle: 'During that period, I was elected President of the Gaelic Athletic Association (GAA) in New York. During my term as always, the Association continued to help by passing resolutions and promoting field days to raise money to help the fight in Ireland.'[18]

Emigration, of course, involved a very varied pattern, in terms of region of origin and destination, motivation for departure, social class and emigrant experience: 'Irish diaspora nationalism was never a uniform ideology. It found expression in only some areas of Irish settlement, and its manifestations often depended on local conditions.'[19] And emigration offered an argument for nationalist Ireland to adopt back home too. At the start of 1955 it was reported in the *Dungannon Observer* ('largest circulation of any paper in County Tyrone'), that the National Vice-President of the Ancient Order of Hibernians, J. G. Lennon, had spoken in Cookstown about the tragedy and causes of Irish emigration: 'It was a regrettable feature of life in Ireland that year after year the country was forced to export the best of her people to create better nations than she was able to create for herself.' This, he continued, 'was due to foreign interference and oppression'.[20]

Party politicians who had made a career of wrestling against such interference and oppression fought on in a variety of ways in these mid-century years. In July 1946 former 1930s IRA Chief of Staff Sean MacBride founded Clann na Poblachta ('Party of the Republic'), basing the new group on republicans and republican sympathies, and managing to win 13 per cent of the vote at Eire's 1948 General Election. The Clann[21] aimed – not without some early success – to gather in disaffected republican voters who were disappointed with Fianna Fáil, and MacBride's party joined the interparty government formed in Dublin in 1948, with Fine Gael's John A. Costello (1891–1976) as Taoiseach (Prime Minister). This was a peculiar and hybrid coalition, comprising Fine Gael, the Labour Party, National Labour, Clann na Poblachta and the populist agrarian party Clann na Talmhan; here, among other things, pro- and anti-Treaty politicians attempted to build harmonious government, although the experiment lasted only until 1951.

In December 1948 this interparty regime passed the Republic of Ireland Act, thereby publicly renaming the state (which became the Republic of Ireland in April 1949). Also significant in revealing important preoccupations within mid-century nationalism was the controversy over the Mother-and-Child scheme. In 1950–51 the Waterford-born Minister for Health, maverick Clann na Poblachta talent Noel Browne (1915–97), pushed on with a free medical care scheme for mothers and for children under sixteen, with medical provision to be made available to the whole population without a means test. This met opposition from the Irish Medical Association (doctors not wanting to lose fee-paying patients), and also from the Catholic Church. The latter held Browne's scheme to be hostile to Catholic social teaching, arguing that the state should not intervene in matters in which a lower body – here, the family – could provide what was necessary. The Church was anxious about the prospect of pregnant women being educated in regard to motherhood – at least by someone other than the Church itself – and feared that doctors' advice to Catholic patients could, in some future cases, involve information about birth control or even abortion. The bishops' intervention in the Mother-and-Child episode was decisive. Browne stood firm, but Costello (as Taoiseach) and MacBride (Browne's party leader) helped to force their Minister's resignation in 1951. This, together with rather fawning declarations of obedience to Church teaching, reinforced for some the idea that this 1950s episode reflected a simple Church–state clash, with the Church the easy victor. Such readings were amplified by Browne himself, whose argument was that Irish independence had merely cloaked a new (this time, Catholic-clerical) oppression:

> In 1922, finally liberated from colonial oppression, we were totally inexperienced in the exercise of power in a popular democracy. In the majority, an embittered, illiterate peasant people, unprepared for the sophisticated complexities of our new freedom and taking the easy option, we shed the oppressive restrictions of British

imperial power to slide, willingly, into the secure, welcoming, anti-democratic, totalitarian cocoon within the competing imperialism of Rome rule.[22]

Such words indicate Browne's capacity for seeing matters in clear – perhaps overly clear – terms: his political actions could be naive and clumsy, he seems to have been a difficult colleague, and there was certainly more to this episode than just a state-versus-Church encounter. Yet that latter clash was also part of this story, and it was a telling one about the state of nationalist politics at the time. The Catholic Church had decisively intervened to stifle a government scheme on a vital issue – for these Mother-and-Child plans were dropped – and the government showed itself keen to stress its obedience to the clerical authorities' teaching. Nor was this case isolated from broader government policy: the interparty government had sent Pope Pius XII a message of 'respectful homage' which declared their desire 'to repose at the feet of Your Holiness the assurance of our filial loyalty and devotion as well as our firm resolve to be guided in all our work by the teachings of Christ and to strive for the attainment of social order in Ireland based on Christian principles'.[23] Those principles were clearly to be seen through Catholic lenses, and in some senses this merely reflected the realities of an overwhelmingly Catholic state, in which population and politicians alike had imbibed Catholic values. As de Valera had himself pointed out in defence of his Catholic Constitution of 1937, 'ninety-three per cent of the people in this part of Ireland and seventy-five per cent of the people in Ireland as a whole' were Catholic in allegiance and philosophy.[24] Yet the Church's influence in an episode such as the Mother-and-Child imbroglio – or, again, Archbishop of Dublin John Charles McQuaid's influence over a subsequent Taoiseach (Sean Lemass) on other issues[25] – demonstrated that shared Catholicism involved not just a very meaningful language of community for nationalist Ireland, but on some occasions a perceived need for restriction of the range of the movement and freedom available to nationalist politicians.

Fianna Fáil briefly held power again from 1951 to 1954, before a second interparty government (this time comprising Fine Gael, Labour, and Clann na Talmhan) held the reins between 1954 and 1957. But it was Fianna Fáil which dominated independent Ireland's nationalist political life, holding power consecutively from 1932 until 1948, and then again not only from 1951 to 1954, but also from 1957 until 1973. During that last phase, some important modifications of nationalist orthodoxy were made, and a crucial figure here was Sean Lemass (1899–1971) – 'as hard-headed a man as there is in Ireland',[26] in Sean O'Faoláin's flinty phrase. Lemass's career in some ways epitomizes the trajectory of much modern Irish nationalism in the twentieth century. Educated by the Christian Brothers, a participant in the 1916 Rising, active in both the War for Independence and the Civil War (in the latter as an anti-Treatyite), he was then a founder member of Fianna Fáil in 1926 as republicanism wandered towards constitutionalism. When it did so, Lemass the ex-prisoner and ex-IRA man became Lemass the cabinet minister (taking on the post of Minister for Industry and Commerce in 1932). A protectionist in this political phase, by the time of his becoming Taoiseach in 1959 he had become convinced of the necessity for great change in the direction of economic nationalism, and he duly presided over the opening up of the Irish economy during his tenure of office until 1966. Pragmatic and opportunistic in his nationalism – a kind of lightweight Daniel O'Connell – he made possible the development of Irish economic life by enabling it to shift from protectionism towards free trade, and he had the courage to recognize that his earlier Sinn Féinist thinking had (in economic terms, at least) been disastrous.

Thus Lemass – and crucial colleagues such as Minister of Finance James Ryan and brilliant civil servant T. K. Whitaker – altered the central economics of nationalist Ireland. The 1958 Programme for Economic Expansion mapped a path away from protectionism and towards a recognition of the importance both of foreign capital as a necessary basis for growth, and also of the export market. And Lemass's regime – he was Taoiseach until 1966 – did help stimulate growth and reduce levels of emigration, and he sought to reintegrate the Republic's economy with that of the United Kingdom (an Anglo-Irish Free Trade Agreement was signed in 1965).

So this canny Fianna Fáil politician undid the protectionism which he had helped to install in the 1930s, his policies encouraging necessary foreign investment in Ireland's economy. He made some changes also in another key area of Irish nationalism, that of its approach to the lost counties of Northern Ireland. His position here was rather ambiguous: at times he questioned, in traditional patriotic rhetoric, the permanence and legitimacy of the northern state ('The fact that partition – although it has lasted for almost forty years – is still a living issue of profound significance in Ireland, and in the relations between Ireland and Britain, is in itself sufficient proof that it is not a good, nor likely to prove a permanent, arrangement'[27]); but at others he showed himself able to break free from orthodox anti-partitionism, and even to offer some nuanced subtlety in his approach to the painful subject of northern discrimination against the Catholic minority. His famously innovative meetings with Northern Ireland Prime Minister Terence O'Neill in 1965 – first in Belfast, then in Dublin – were echoed also by his less famous achievements of better Anglo-Irish relations.[28] Lemass was not in power long enough to make all of the changes that he wanted to effect. But he did inaugurate a new period of nationalist struggle for the people of independent Ireland: he recognized the urgency of their actual economic needs, and he was prepared to amend nationalist orthodoxy as necessary. In this, as in his and Whitaker's scepticism about traditionally aggressive anti-partitionism, he was deeply patriotic. For the various aspects of nationalist thinking could make rival demands upon you; and nationalism, for those holding power, often involved the choice between competing inherited assumptions. Lemass had grown up politically with the idea that Sinn Féinish protectionism and all-island unity alike were deeply embedded in Irish nationalism; yet he now had sovereign authority – and therefore daily responsibility – for the people within one part of the putative national territory, and had no effective power over events in the other. Like some other of his ex-revolutionary Fianna Fáil colleagues, therefore, he decided to modify both parts of this inheritance, in the actual interests of those over whom he held power.

2

Is it politic to claim a sovereignty [over Northern Ireland]
that one is powerless to assert? . . . the frontal attack on the
northern position, in which governments on this side of the
border engaged themselves for almost fifty years, has failed
dismally. The time, I feel, has come when another approach
should be considered. And here I think full account must be
taken of the hard fact that the unionist party in north-
eastern Ireland does represent the traditions and deeply-held
convictions of a large majority of the people in that area.

Fianna Fáil politician, and ex-IRA man, Sean MacEntee (1969)[29]

There has been an understandable tendency for historians to focus
more attention on the two periods of Northern Ireland's 'Troubles' –
in the early 1920s, and then from the late 1960s onwards – than on
the era which fell in between. Another instinct for some has been to
assume that Ulster's violent episodes were somehow the norm, and
that the late-twentieth-century eruption of violence was inevitable. For
these reasons, the period from the mid-1940s to the mid-1960s has
often been treated less seriously than it deserves: as an era in which
nothing much happened, while everyone waited for the unstoppable
conflict to emerge again.

But is this a justifiable view? At the University in Belfast I have
often set my politics students a question about Northern Ireland along
the lines of 'Was the Collapse of Stormont Inevitable?' The majority
of students answer 'yes', and then outline very plausible explanations
as to why this was so: the disaffection of the Catholic minority, the
structural imbalance of power in the north, the troubled Anglo-Irish
historical relationship, and so on. In our seminar discussions of this
subject, I have then sometimes asked a similar question relating to
contemporary events – in the late 1990s, for example, asking students
whether they considered the success or failure of the Good Friday
Agreement to be inevitable. Understandably, the answer to this question has tended to be far more hesitant ('How can we be sure?'); and

when I've suggested that in thirty years' time a group of university students might be sitting around confidently declaring how inevitable the Agreement's success or failure was, there has often been a wry smile. For inevitability seems far more clear looking back than looking forward, and this should cause us some pause for thought. In the 1950s, northern nationalists certainly did not think that the coming carnage was inevitable, or even – for the most part – imaginable.[30] And even in the late 1960s it was possible to think that consensual rather than aggressive politics might determine the north's next generation.

Not that there weren't profound problems with Northern Ireland as far as its nationalist inhabitants were concerned. In the theology of nationalism, the very existence of this state transgressed against the proper rules of united territory and people (dividing both in ways which nationalists considered to be mutilations), and the state sinned again by elevating in place of Irish nationalist ideas, unionist versions of culture, descent-myth, history, ethics and exclusivism. Here indeed was the politics of sovereignty and state – but within a UK framework rather than the one which nationalist Ireland assumed to be legitimate. And, day to day, the supposed illegitimacy of Northern Ireland for northern nationalists was compounded by a range of symbolic, political and economic experiences of marginalization.[31] Only part of this marginality was caused by discrimination – choices made and cultures sustained within northern nationalist community also contributed to the process – but it seems clear that discrimination did play a part.[32] Yet discrimination itself must be explained, of course, rather than merely condemned. Unionist insecurity was in itself understandable, and this led the state to tolerate some abuses, in a spirit of self-protection. In the long run, this mid-century toleration helped to cause late-century crisis, but in an Ireland in which informal discrimination had become the norm among both political communities, it should not surprise. Unionists could recall that the Revolutionary IRA had indeed used people from their own community who worked, for example, in the civil service, in order to acquire information which had then been used with deadly, murderous effect. Rather casually, Irish nationalist memory tends simultaneously to celebrate the achievements of, for example, Michael Collins's spies in ensuring the killing of British targets, and also to denounce with outraged anger the reluctance of some within the Northern Ireland authorities subsequently to employ nationalists.

Nationalist experience within Northern Ireland was, of course, in some respects unfair, and we should not understate the corrosive effect of the discrimination and disadvantage experienced by the north's minority within a state which had been designed to possess a durable unionist majority. Clearly, the notion of nationalist suffering under the north's 1921–72 regime (and beyond) did not arise without a material basis to it. But the key point for our purposes is to see the strength which this gave to nationalism, as an ideology which stressed the central emancipation of having an equal share in the sovereignty which allowed for the running of your community. Unionists could say that the minority shared freedoms of expression, cultural and political, and – within limits – this was true. Yet it also missed the point: for the attraction of nationalism is that the various aspects of people's lives (culture, people, economic success and so forth) all seem to be enhanced and protected and advanced if people live in a polity whose government reflects their own background and culture, and within a state whose sovereignty they endorse. So it wasn't a question *either* of people feeling that their employment opportunity, or electoral equality,[33] was infringed *or* that they wanted to be part of a state within which they would be a sovereign-powerful majority rather than a powerless majority: it was both, because the first reinforced the importance of the second. So while Catholic experience under the Stormont regime should not be exaggerated – comparisons with South African apartheid or Nazi Germany have always been offensive and absurd – that experience did still reflect one of the key features of nationalism: that daily experience of economic or social matters reinforced a nationalist attachment which was seen as offering a powerful, communal means of redress.

And until the day when nationalism delivered the sovereign state run by your own majority – in other words, a united and independent Ireland – nationalism offered also the means of distinctive expression and ennoblement. Thus language and culture were to be celebrated, and as parts of the same whole. One prominent speaker (Joseph Skeffington) at the Tyrone County Convention of the GAA in 1955 lamented that 'For all the good we are doing for the language we might as well be a Chinese Athletic Association.' Not enough money was being collected for the language, he said, in places where there were active GAA clubs, and there should be closer cooperation between the GAA and the Gaelic League. For his own part, the GAA County Secretary (P. K. O'Neill) reinforced the idea that 'It is our duty to support and encourage every aspect of our national culture and to cooperate in every way possible with our local Gaelic League branch.'[34] The Gaelic Athletic Association indeed offered a kind of sublimated republic: it was an all-Ireland organization, basically Catholic and, of course, proudly and distinctively Gaelic. A counterlife, linking locality to nation and both to recreation.

Catholic religion in mid-century Northern Ireland also offered rewards which were tied in with the imagination of the Irish nation. The northern nationalist press was full of Church matters, and the idea that Catholicism was central to Irish nationalism was one shared by many: 'For Catholics their religion *was* their political identity, and the Church provided all the necessary institutional infrastructure.'[35] Without effective political representation in the Belfast parliament – a body with a permanent unionist majority – northern nationalists understandably looked more keenly to their clergy for a political and communal lead; and nationalist politicians long relied on clerical support as a basis for their own success. Nationalist groups such as the Ancient Order of Hibernians (AOH) again echoed this confessionalization of politics. At an AOH function in Cookstown, County Tyrone, in August 1955 a new banner was ceremoniously unfurled (with accompanying parade, marching, bandsmen and so on): on one side the banner carried a portrait of Blessed Oliver Plunkett (1625–81, Archbishop of Armagh and Catholic martyr), and on the other the portraits of five deceased AOH National Presidents.[36] Nationalist politics and the Catholic faith were two sides of the one public banner. (Although banners and marching tend to be more commonly associated in the public mind with Orangeism and unionism in Northern Ireland, there is a long and strong tradition of such cultural expressions on the part of nationalists there also.[37]) One local AOH pilgrimage (the annual one to the Shrine of Our Lady, Moneyglass), saw members of the Order from Antrim, Derry and Tyrone process with banners, march with bands and celebrate an emphatically Catholic nationalist ritual. When they reached the Shrine they were welcomed by the Very Rev. J. Macmullan, who observed that the faith faced great dangers in

Ireland as elsewhere. Ireland, he declared, had had 'her own dark night of persecution but the union of faith and fatherland, through the mercies of God, and the Rosary of Mary, saved the faith. . . . It is our earnest prayer,' he continued, 'that the union of faith and fatherland which that afternoon's procession reflected in no small way, would never be broken.'[38] And faith and fatherland could be reflected in that most famous of all of Ulster's Irish nationalist groups in struggle, the IRA: Lurgan barman Leonard Magill, sentenced in January 1957 to eighteen months' imprisonment for IRA membership and activities, declared in court that he 'hoped and prayed that God would give his comrades strength to carry on the work until the last vestiges of British imperialism had been banished from Ireland'.[39] (When picked up by the RUC near Dungannon in December 1956, Magill had on him – among other things – two sets of Rosary beads.)

The IRA were not the only nationalist group struggling to undo partition. The Anti-Partition League (APL), founded in November 1945, sought by propaganda, publicity and on-the-ground political organization to further the cause of reuniting national territory, and of achieving republican sovereignty for Ireland. It failed (having begun its life with some naive ideas about the north, and also about the extent of support likely to be forthcoming from Dublin and London[40]), and it broke up in 1953, its traditional, conservative nationalism having yielded little fruit. It might be thought that the harvest from IRA violence at this point might have seemed similarly meagre in prospect, as clear-sighted observers could see that unionist opposition to Irish unity represented too serious an obstacle to be overcome except by trust and consent. (Even John F. Kennedy, hardly the closest observer of Ulster politics, crisply noted in 1945 that it would be by 'cooperating and the building of mutual trust' that the ending of partition might be achieved.[41])

And yet aggressive nationalism was to engage in another round of struggle in the 1950s, tied integrally as it was to republican political ambition. For the 1955 General Election the Sinn Féin candidate for Fermanagh–South Tyrone (Dublin civil servant Phil Clarke) was then serving a ten-year sentence in Belfast's Crumlin Road Prison for his part in a republican raid on Omagh Barracks. The 26 May election saw eight of the twelve Sinn Féin abstentionist candidates in jail at the time of the poll. In the event Clarke (and another prisoner, Tom Mitchell, in Mid-Ulster) were elected, and while this might be judged only to provide the barest foundation for a restarting of a violent campaign, that is precisely what was to follow from the republican movement. The Sinn Féin election manifesto for the 1955 election had stated that 'Sinn Féin candidates seek the votes of the electorate and the support of the Irish people as the representatives of the Republican movement now on the onward march towards achievement of the national ideal – the enthronement of the sovereign Irish Republic.'[42]

The mid-century IRA itself didn't seem, perhaps, on much of an onward march anywhere. The 1940s Irish Republican Army was described by one Belfast Catholic writer as 'a minor confraternity of dedicated men who wore slouch hats and trench coats, and conducted manoeuvres on the back-roads of the Antrim hills above Belfast, like distant Irish deputies of Legs Diamond, transported by their one motor-car, which had two rusted pistols and a ceremonial sword concealed beneath its gaping floor-boards'.[43] Moreover, many in the northern nationalist community during the 1950s began to exhibit 'an acquiescence in the constitutional status quo. Very slowly but clearly Catholic aspirations began to focus on Northern rather than a united Ireland.'[44] Yet 1956–62 was to see 'Operation Harvest', an IRA border campaign with a traditional aim: 'an independent, united, democratic Irish republic. For this we shall fight until the invader is driven from our soil and victory is ours.'[45] The struggle here was to involve flying columns from the south, attacking Northern Ireland in guerrilla-warfare style. The border campaign involved over 500 incidents, some of them resulting in fatalities. But it made little impact on the Northern Ireland state, and resonated little with the northern nationalist population. Recognizing this, the IRA called the campaign off in 1962. An army order of 5 February directed all IRA units to dump arms, while an IRA statement later in the month publicly announced the end of the feeble, bloody campaign: the latter statement acknowledged the central reason for calling off the war to have been 'the attitude of the general public whose minds have been deliberately distracted from the supreme issue facing the Irish people – the unity and freedom of Ireland'.[46]

As noted, the IRA's campaign had its grim, serious aspect. But the archives now available for this period illustrate the comparatively mild nature of the nationalist-versus-unionist conflict in Northern Ireland

during these years. The papers of Newry's Joseph Connellan (Nationalist MP for South Down from 1949 to 1967) serve as one telling
example. Connellan engaged in extensive lobbying for the release or
good treatment of those from the Newry area who were interned or
jailed during the IRA's border campaign. He dealt with the Ministry of
Home Affairs at Stormont and did so with some considerable success,
getting people released or achieving better conditions of treatment for
them. Here, then, was a Nationalist MP doing very effective work in a
cooperative manner, under a comparatively moderate regime. Contrary
to the image sometimes given of an unapproachably ruthless policy of
Northern Ireland internment, for example, Connellan did actually get
people released or better treated, and the exchanges between himself
and the Stormont Ministry were cordial.[47]

The IRA's own violence, of course, had been intended to effect
the end of Northern Ireland. How did unionists in fact respond?
There was predictable enough anger and anxiety. Captain L. P. S.
Orr (Unionist MP for South Down from 1950 to 1974, and leader of
the Unionist MPs at Westminster for many years), told the County
Armagh Unionist Association Annual Meeting at Portadown in January
1957 that there was a need for tighter security at military establishments, and greater knowledge of 'who is employed where' in regard to
pivotal jobs at post office and telephone exchanges. Furthermore, Orr
identified what he saw as a root problem behind IRA activity: 'the
main cause of the trouble was the attitude of the Eire government who
were continually giving sanctuary to raiders. The Eire government had
condoned the behaviour by allowing the IRA to grow for a long time
and drill on the border.'[48] To Irish nationalists, discrimination in
Northern Ireland helped to justify republican violence and southern
equivocation about the legitimacy of the northern state; to unionists,
such IRA violence and Dublin ambivalence were in fact the conditions
which necessitated concern that loyal people should occupy key jobs.

Nor did IRA violence make unionists, in fact, more likely to
concede what nationalists required of them. Local responses to the
beginning of the 1950s IRA border campaign perhaps even suggested
the opposite. A well-attended meeting of Strabane Orangemen unanimously praised the Northern Ireland government's strong stand against
this latest assault 'by murderers and thugs from across the border',
enthusing in particular over 'the defence of the Province provided by

the RUC and the Ulster Special Constabulary'. Resolve was not shaken: 'We reiterate the strongest determination of the people of Ulster to remain part of the United Kingdom, and pledge ourselves to fight in every possible manner to maintain our cherished heritage.'[49]

Had nationalists misread unionism entirely? Late-nineteenth- and early-twentieth-century unionism might have been 'not quite a nationalism',[50] the two communities in Northern Ireland (as ever) not being neat mirror images of each other. But unionist concerns about culture, economy, power and symbolism echoed much that was powerful within nationalisms and, more importantly, demonstrated that unionists did not fit into the kind of Irish nation which had been defined by Irish nationalists themselves. The border which partitioned Ireland had been created in the 1920s, but, flawed though this was as a remedy, it did represent a response to pre-existing divisions. Ulster distinctiveness had been evident through much of the pre-twentieth-century period, and while partition clearly reinforced and deepened and institutionalized division between nationalist and unionist in Ireland, no serious observer could argue that it had created it.

For their part, Irish nationalists did think the northern state to be both illegitimate and doomed – they forthrightly said as much – and this was what unionists saw at local as well as national level from mid-century northern nationalists. At a St Patrick's Day demonstration at Drumquin in County Tyrone in 1955 (impressively attended by over 10,000 AOH members), a prominent figure from within the Order referred in his address to partition as 'the unnatural division of their country for the benefit of a foreign power against the manifest desire of the nation', and argued 'that the complete inability of the Northern government to maintain control of this area by other means than naked force was established beyond doubt by the events of the years since partition was imposed'.[51] At a nationalist demonstration at Carrickmore in the same county in April 1955, ex-IRA leader Sean MacBride addressed the 1,000-strong crowd with the claim that 'everyone today, including the most firm opponents of Irish freedom and Irish unity, recognized the inevitability of the re-union of the country. No responsible spokesman in either Dublin or Belfast could even attempt to justify the continuance of partition on the basis of any recognized democratic principle.'[52]

The enemy was clear here, as were the principles of territorial and

popular unity, democratic and sovereign independence, ethical superiority, religio-cultural enthusiasm and organized struggle. And as
Northern Ireland's intercommunal cold war entered the early 1960s,
northern nationalists still only grudgingly accepted the legitimacy and
authority of the Stormont parliament. An alternative northern nationalist culture effectively existed: Church, schools, newspapers, sports,
business firms, and culture. But did the problem for northern nationalists become easier with the arrival in 1963 of a seemingly more
conciliatory Unionist Prime Minister, Terence O'Neill, in Belfast,
together with a sympathetic London premier in Labour's Harold
Wilson from 1964 onwards? In some senses, yes, although the seeds of
the soon-to-flower conflict were already in the ground, and shoots
were beginning visibly to sprout.

In 1964 republicans in Belfast displayed an Irish tricolour in their
Divis Street Westminster election headquarters, a gesture which could
be undone if the police so chose, under the provisions of the north's
Flags and Emblems Act. The flag was hardly conspicuous, and the
RUC – probably wisely – had decided not to intervene. By late
September, however, a zealous unionist politician called Ian Paisley
had learned of the flag, and threatened that he and his supporters
would go to west Belfast to remove it themselves were the police not
to do something about the tricolour. And so the police did remove the
flag, riots ensued, the flag was restored, more rioting developed, and
the north had begun to erupt. Looking back, it's easy to see that the
violent clashes of this episode were avoidable. And this kind of insight
was, of course, obvious enough at the time also. For the dangers of
creating a worse situation, and of generating subversion by unneces-
sarily meddling with trivial affairs, were easy enough to identify. As the
archives again show, South Down's Nationalist MP Joseph Connellan
had observed in a letter to the Ministry of Home Affairs in 1957
(during the IRA's border campaign) that 'the overwhelming majority'
of the people of Newry and its surrounding area were strongly opposed
to politically violent methods; but, he tellingly continued,

> interference with trifling events could tend to create very bad
> feeling. It would be better to ignore the carrying of the tricolour in
> areas which are predominantly nationalist and where no offence
> could thereby be given to those opposed to its display. There are

many ways in which the interests of the public peace could be well served and I believe that this is one of them.[53]

If northern nationalists were hardly helped by the bullish intervention of unionists such as Ian Paisley, nor were they necessarily always aided by their fellow-nationalists to the south. Eddie McAteer, the Nationalist Party leader who in February 1965 led his party into Stormont as Northern Ireland's official opposition, recalled Taoiseach Sean Lemass offering him far from enthusiastic support:

> Lemass said it appeared to him that Catholics in the North were just as intractable as the Protestants. It was hardly the reaction I expected from a Taoiseach with his republican background to the representative of the oppressed Irish minority in the six counties ... I came away with the conviction that as far as Sean Lemass was concerned, the Northern Irish were very much on their own.[54]

3

> There is no doubt that I owe the dawn of political feeling to my father. One way in which he was more involved in family life than most Irish fathers was in telling us bedtime stories. ... The stories he told us then were not about fairies and pixies but the whole parade of Irish history from its beginnings with the Firbolgs and the Tuatha de Danain, the supposedly magical people of Irish mythology. He told us bedtime stories from recorded history as well – the battles and invasions, the English oppression and the risings, the English–Irish trade agreement which crippled the country's economy. Naturally, he didn't attempt to be objective about all this: this was Ireland's story, told by an Irishman, with an Irishman's feelings.
>
> Bernadette Devlin[55]

Looking back from the war-weary Ulster of the early twenty-first century, the striking thing about 1960s Northern Ireland is how much optimism and hope there actually was. One of my own university tutors had much earlier, in 1968, published a book in which it had seemed plausible to suggest that ancient Irish hostilities had significantly thawed: 'it would appear', he suggested, 'that the once all-powerful bigotry of Ireland is at last on the wane'; 'the impetus behind amelioration is very formidable'.[56] In fact, 1968 was to be the year in which the Northern Ireland troubles were to erupt, and even four decades later the fire of nationalist anger has far from burned out in Irish politics.

It is conventional to see the 1960s civil rights movement in Northern Ireland as part of the contemporary zeitgeist: the preoccupation with establishing fair treatment. This preoccupation is often held to have echoed that of, for example, blacks in the United States, in ways which in Northern Ireland eclipsed the traditional nationalist emphasis of Catholics. There is something in this, but perhaps not as much as people would like to believe. The discrimination experienced by the Northern Irish minority was, in fact, far more mild than that known to US blacks; articulate Sinn Féiners might lately like to style themselves as the Irish versions of Langston Hughes,[57] but the severity of American black suffering greatly exceeded that known by northern Catholics.[58] Moreover, there was a further huge difference between the two cases: the US civil rights movement did not involve an historic battle over the legitimacy or existence of the United States itself; the Northern Irish version clearly did involve precisely such a war over state legitimacy. Key figures among those who initiated the northern civil rights agitation were undoubtedly keen on using it as a route towards the undoing of Northern Ireland,[59] while prominent civil rights leaders could be emphatically and explicitly anti-unionist in their politics.[60] Moreover, the interweaving of cultural division and nationalist assumption ran deep: civil rights activism could take on a decidedly Catholic flavour (as even its own leaders acknowledged[61]), while anti-partitionism was conspicuous enough (the influential grandfather of the civil rights idea, the historian Desmond Greaves, was himself emphatic about the need to end partition: 'Of course the only basis for a liberal democracy is a united Ireland'[62]).

It is true that there were important civil rights injustices to be redressed, and that the 1960s campaign focused primarily on rights within the United Kingdom; it might be the case that immediate and full satisfaction of these demands would have been enough to accom-

modate nationalists within the northern state. But there is no doubt
that the lines of Northern Ireland's civil rights battle very quickly
became those of nationalist-versus-unionist and, in this sense, the
1960s civil rights episode did involve a phase in the ever-evolving
politics of nationalist Ireland. The more emollient Northern Irish
Prime Minister, Terence O'Neill, wanted to modernize the Ulster
economy, and to win back unionist votes from the Northern Ireland
Labour Party. He did also make some gestures towards the Catholic
minority, but suffered a fate familiar to many benign politicians in an
era of hasty change: he raised Catholic hopes without being able to
satisfy them, and he prompted unnecessary fears from the Protestant
majority. This recipe, so often repeated in Northern Ireland's febrile
history, led to disaffection all round, and it helped to ignite the fires of
nationalist grievance. The new Prime Minister had hoped that economic modernization would be the means by which Catholics were
won over to the Northern Ireland state; by the time of his resignation
in 1969, this hope had effectively been killed off.

A variety of initiatives (including the left-republican vision of
radicals like Roy Johnston, as well as the equally sincere crusading
of enthusiasts such as the 'reasonable, respectable, righteous, solid,
non-violent and determined'[63] schoolteacher John Hume), coalesced
to produce a civil rights agitation, and in 1967 there was formed the
Northern Ireland Civil Rights Association (NICRA), a movement
which pursued a range of reforms: the establishment of one-man-one-
vote in local elections; mechanisms for preventing discrimination by
public authorities, and for dealing with complaints; fairer organization
of electoral boundaries; fair allocation of public housing; the disbandment of the unionist Ulster Special Constabulary (or B Specials); and
the repeal of the extensive Special Powers Act.

Many nationalists held that the Nationalist Party's failure to achieve
reform during several decades in Northern Ireland provided the
condition and the need for new and different initiatives; and this is
what the civil rights movement involved. What were the issues most
pressing upon people as they lived their daily lives? Employment
and housing, yes, but also matters of power, equality and dignity for
the community. When Nationalist MP Austin Currie in June 1968
occupied a house in the small County Tyrone village of Caledon, in
protest against alleged discrimination in housing ('a non-violent

protest against the system of house allocation'[64]), the gesture attracted attention because individual experience was taken to involve the disadvantage which one experienced as part of the community. If electoral boundaries were unfair, then this reflected a limitation upon communal access to power, to the allocation of resources, and ultimately to community respect. The civil rights movement might have been a campaign which sought to avoid explicit reference to the traditional nationalist rejection of the Northern Ireland state, but it related to this struggle in several key ways. It was precisely the disadvantage experienced by nationalists in a non-nationalist state which caused them so to reject Northern Ireland. Unsurprisingly, the movement was effectively one without unionists; but it was also one which had a nationalist spine to it: for some of the key players in this campaign, indeed, it was axiomatic that the unionist state simply could not reform itself, and that its welcome collapse would be precipitated by civil rights agitation. In this sense, once again, we see the relevance of nationalism to the interwoven politics of community, struggle and power. Here was communal struggle for redress of grievance, for the empowering of a disadvantaged nationalist people, and against the abusive deployment of power.

The debate on the causes, extent and undoing of discrimination in Northern Ireland is extensive, and it ranges across a wide spectrum of analytical interpretation. It seems clear that anti-Catholic discrimination, though not as extensive as some have suggested, did exist ('In so far as there is a consensus in the literature [on discrimination in Northern Ireland], then, it is that the picture is not black, nor white, but grey'[65]); and it seems unsurprising that, in the context of the turbulent 1960s, opposition to it would arise. Much (perhaps too much?[66]) has been said about the importance in all this of a new Catholic middle class, one emancipated by post-war British educational reform (1947 had brought free and potentially universal secondary education, while the 1960s had seen the expansion of free university education). But it was to be the working class in the north with which the British state was to have its primary difficulties, and this was made most clear in the history of one of nationalist Ireland's most durable and brutal organizations, the Provisional IRA.

The IRA emerged at the same time as the Northern Ireland troubles, and both were the product of many interlocking factors at the end of the 1960s, matters within and beyond the region which interacted in malign fashion. It is futile to single out one factor, one group or one individual on which or whom to focus undue attention; for it is possible and more valuable to produce a fairly comprehensive list of those things that between them produced the conflict.

The problem partly lay in the failure of two competing nationalisms (and their respective states) to deal with Irish minorities. The UK state and its accompanying British nationalism had found it difficult to accommodate Catholic Ireland, and this had remained a problem in the six north-eastern counties after partition. But nationalist Ireland, and its post-1922 state, had never appealed to unionists. Culture, economy, symbols, religion and politics all combined to produce, therefore, the worst combination in the north: a disaffected minority and an under-confident majority. The unionist majority faced irredentist neighbours to the south, potentially fickle regimes in London, and a growing and hostile nationalist minority inside its own borders: it decided to prize loyalty above all, and in the confessional politics of Northern Ireland this meant a certain protection of Protestant space and privilege. Yet, explicable and even understandable as this was, it did reinforce among northern nationalists the sense that Northern Ireland was both illegitimate and unfair. When civil rights agitation – for some, just that; for other participants, a means of continuing the war against unionism by other means – prompted hostile, violent loyalist reaction in the 1960s, communal friction ensued and the centrifugal instincts of the rival peoples of Ulster were triggered. The Belfast government did produce reform. In 1968 it announced that an Ombudsman was to be appointed to investigate grievances relating to central-governmental administration; that local authorities were to publish a scheme for housing allocation; that the business vote in local government elections was to be abolished; that comprehensive local government reform was to follow; and that the Special Powers Act was to be reviewed. The following year, still further reforms were announced in the fields of housing, community relations, local government and local-election suffrage.

But by 1969 relations between nationalists and unionists were too tautly strained for easy relaxation, and certain actors reinforced this tension. Some republicans saw the chance to vindicate their traditional argument about the irreformable nature of the sectarian state, and to initiate appropriate hostilities against that state; some loyalists acted brutally in trying to extirpate republicanism (only, in practice, to stimulate its growth); some civil rights agitators unwisely acted in provocative manner at tense moments. For its own part, London – which had for years ignored Northern Ireland by hiding behind the wall of Belfast government – took too long to assume direct control, and allowed a sluggish unionist regime to preside over disastrous choices in the crucial 1968–72 period: so a one-sided curfew in Catholic Belfast in 1970, the introduction of equally one-sided and clumsy internment in 1971, and the disaster of the Bloody Sunday killings in 1972 all backfired, and helped destroy the chance of a rapprochement between the British state and the Catholic working class.

> From 1970 I had sold *Republican News* from underneath my coat outside Mass but it was only after the British Army curfew of the Falls Road in July 1970 that I decided to go one step further and hold guns for the IRA ... Any moral resistance I had to violence was being rapidly undermined by the actions of the British Army and the RUC during and after the introduction of internment.[67]

Why join the IRA? Partly because of 'the reaction of the security forces within the nationalist areas'[68] in those early days of chaos. As security force action involved increasing friction with the Catholic community, the latter turned in some numbers to a nationalist group which claimed to understand what was going on – and to know how to solve the problem.

For the republican tradition had been kept alive by a minority of zealots, and at times they had been given new energy, as with the opportunity provided by the 1966 fiftieth anniversary of the Easter Rising. This helped to alert some young people to the glories of republican politics, though many in nationalist Ireland must surely have taken a lighter, less engaged view (as gloriously hinted at in one of Roddy Doyle's novels, when schoolchildren laugh at their teacher's solemn 1966 celebration of the Rising, the youthful Paddy Clarke claiming that his grandfather is the executed 1916 rebel Thomas Clarke – and that the latter is alive and well in Clontarf).[69] There was nothing light, however, about the crisis which had fallen on working-class areas of Belfast and Derry by mid-1969, when intercommunal violence threatened both communities, and when many Catholic northerners were, for their part, left very vulnerable to loyalist attack. Republicans had maintained that the northern state was irretrievably sectarian, that non-violent attempts at reform were futile, and that the IRA was needed both to defend Catholic communities and to end the existence of this corrupt and artificial polity. And here one could see, by 1969, loyalist anger and violence having been generated by civil rights reformism, and one could seem to justify the need for a defensive and liberating IRA form of struggle.

Thus it was that, bolstered by some support from Dublin and from Irish-American nationalists, the Provisional IRA was born in December 1969. Initially seeking to defend their local communities, the Provisionals also espoused the use of violence in offensive manner, to undo a Northern Ireland state which they considered to be beyond reform or repair. The civil rights movement had produced intercommunal turbulence and out of this heightened sectarian tension emerged the new IRA, which became a serious paramilitary force within a very short time: they were able to kill 235 people in 1972 alone, and 690 during the 1969–75 period as a whole.

The IRA were both a symptom and, in the actions and attitudes of their founding clique, a partial cause of the outbreak of the Troubles. And they reflected our deeper explanation of the power of nationalism. Here was the politics of urgent self-protection as a community: the impulsion behind the split in the IRA which produced the Provisionals was the intercommunal violence of the north, and in particular the loyalist attacks on some working-class Catholic areas in 1969. As it turned out, the new IRA were unable in practice to defend their community from attack: but one deep cause behind their creation was the understandable sense of a need for protection, for communal and individual defence (after the clashes of August 1969 republicans were, in the words of the Provos' first Chief of Staff, 'determined that they would not be caught defenceless again'[70]). And the Provos also represented a politics firmly based in daily ties to actual people as well as (more than?) to an imagined national community, whether in the comradeship to be found in this newly forged republican army ('Now I felt I was one of the boys'[71]), or in the family relations which sometimes played a part in IRA careers ('I was born into a very staunch republican family';[72] 'My father had been a life-long republican';[73] with the IRA 'there's an element of the extended family even involved'[74]).

It was very much a politics of attachment to particular place and space (such as west Belfast[75]), and of particular culture: whether ethno-linguistic ('Learn Irish, speak Irish, be Irish'[76]), or at times religious ('We were reared in the nationalist, Catholic tradition, with the greater emphasis being on Catholic'[77]). The IRA was an organization with a sharp, if starkly teleological, sense of national history (it frequently, for example, celebrated former republican heroes and martyrs such as Kevin Barry and Liam Mellows[78]); and it was a movement which exuded a preoccupation with communal self-respect, prestige, dignity and pride: 'If we do not respect ourselves, we need not expect our British overlords to respect us';[79] there was 'a fierce pride' in one's own area as 'everybody felt a part of something' in the IRA's struggle.[80] That struggle was held to possess ethical dimensions too; for villainy – in this case, for example, sectarianism – was the preserve of the other, morally dubious side: 'Who started sectarianism? The English murderers who invaded Ireland.'[81] And the community's self-definition was in practice exclusivist (as well as unique, special and vulnerable for those who were inside its boundaries): if being truly Irish involved speaking Irish, then what of those who did not want to do so?

But the Provisional IRA's violent nationalism was also about a community in struggle; indeed, it was one largely defined by a particular kind of struggle. Constitutional politics were held to have failed, reformism to have been proved futile. Northern Ireland could not be reformed – as was held to have been shown by loyalist resistance to civil rights demands – and so it had instead to be destroyed and replaced by a non-partitioned, independent Ireland. How was this to be achieved? Through necessary force: 'The IRA strategy is very clear. At some point in the future, due to the pressure of the continuing and sustained armed struggle, the will of the British government to remain in this country will be broken. That is the objective of the armed struggle.'[82]

The Provos were never just about violence; various kinds of political argument, propaganda and campaigning were involved even in their early years. But the necessity and practice of violent nationalist struggle were central and distinctive features of their mission. Violence was considered essential to the production of necessary change – from the unacceptable 'is' to the sought-after 'ought'. More viscerally, it simul-taneously met needs for revenge, for hitting back: security force violence and harassment of the Catholic community produced an intensified, rage-filled response, whether against the British Army, the RUC or loyalists: there was a strong 'desire to fight back';[83] when faced with loyalist attacks on Catholics, 'There was no way to defend against these things. So the only way to appear to be defending, to appear to be active, was to take out other people.'[84] There was already a measure of support available at the start of the Provisionals' existence. At one of their founders' earliest meetings (on 17 January 1970) a 'detailed analysis' was made of how the republican army stood after the recent split in the movement, and people from various areas in Ireland gave their respective accounts: 'The situation in the six counties was not very clear but their is definate [sic] support in Derry, Belfast, north and south Armagh and south Down and Fermanagh.'[85] After the friction between the British Army and the Catholic working class during 1970–72, this support had been deeply intensified.

As a self-conscious community of nationalists, the IRA brutally exercised power in its campaign; and its struggle was itself very much one for the attainment of power. How were you to produce a society in which your individual and communal grievances would be redressed, and your lack of dignity and of fair treatment amended? If life in Northern Ireland for Irish nationalists was unacceptable, in terms of daily disadvantage and communal lack of power, then how was this to be reversed? Republican nationalism provided an answer, in the classic model of the congruence of nation and political unit, of your own nation coinciding with your own state.[86] To the IRA, it seemed that the best solution to their various problems lay in the creation of a united and independent Ireland in which their national community would be a dominant majority, rather than a disadvan-taged and effectively powerless minority. So, as elsewhere in the history of nationalism,[87] individual self-image and self-respect suffered if one's national community – in this case, northern, Irish nationalism within the UK – lacked appropriate status and power.

So you pursued national self-determination, the achievement of fully independent, sovereign statehood for Ireland, in the hope that this newly legitimate polity would be one in which you as an individual, enjoying an equal, democratic share of national power, could take your

part in a free community. In this new order, power would be held by
your own community, and would from then onwards protect rather
than undermine your own interests. So Provisional IRA nationalism
was not about *either* the response to northern nationalist daily disadvantage *or* pursuing the historic reunification of Ireland: it was about
both, because each made pressing sense of the other. And this was why
members of the republican movement repeatedly, year after year,
stressed the centrality of unity and self-determination: 'There is an
urgent need to build an all-Ireland movement which would be open to
everyone committed to the principle and objective of Irish national
self-determination.'[88] And so what happened to people in your family,
or in your street, was interpreted and potentially redeemed or remedied
through its incorporation into wider nationalist argument and organization. How would you deal with employment or housing, how would
you protect yourself against sectarian attack, how would you help build
a non-sectarian Ireland in which your own culture was treated with
due respect? A confident, defiant nationalism held the answers, or so it
seemed.

Thus the social and the political, as so often, became interwoven (a
not unfamiliar occurrence in revolutionary situations: 'Class and economic grievances do usually play an important role in revolutions, but
the roots of revolutionary movements are found in the political context
in which class relationships and economic institutions (among other
factors) are embedded'[89]). And the conflict within which this developed
in the north was one of a kind familiar to those studying nationalism
more broadly. It echoed, for example, the triangular pattern identified
by sociologist Rogers Brubaker, a three-way relationship between
'distinct and mutually antagonistic nationalisms'. There had been the
'nationalizing' nationalism of the newly established state (Northern
Ireland): this had made claims for a core group (in this case, unionists),
who legitimately owned the state and whose vulnerability justified the
use of state power to promote core-group interests. There was also the
'external national "homeland"' (in this case, the Republic of Ireland),
characterized by a trans-border nationalism which felt obliged 'to
monitor the condition, promote the welfare, support the activities and
institutions, assert the rights, and protect the interests of "their"
ethnonational kin' in another state (in this case, nationalists in
Northern Ireland). In particular, such trans-border nationalism

becomes operative when those kin are threatened by the actions or power of a nationalizing nationalism. The third actor in Brubaker's triangular relationship was the 'national minority' (in this case, northern nationalists), possessing its own distinct nationalism and asserting its own national, communal rights: 'Although national minority and homeland nationalisms both define themselves in opposition to the "nationalizing" nationalisms of the state in which the minorities live, they are not necessarily harmoniously aligned.' Brubaker's book[90] does not apply this model to Northern Ireland, but the latter clearly does fit the pattern which he outlines, and the notion of these three antagonistic nationalisms usefully illuminates the nature of the relationships within which the IRA found itself.

The IRA's campaign has frequently been narrated elsewhere,[91] and it involved a mixture of commitment, suffering, courage and futile brutality. The Provos' armed struggle certainly involved horrific episodes; even mainstream republicans have acknowledged that the IRA during the sectarian mid-1970s carried out some appalling acts,[92] and IRA actions from Belfast to Enniskillen to Warrington to Brighton between them caused too many fatalities and mutilations for anyone to be able to ignore their horror. (And the violence was not only in the north of Ireland, but extended frequently enough to England also, where the Provisionals' twenty-five-year campaign from 1973 onwards involved nearly 500 recorded incidents, causing 115 deaths as well as injury to 2,134 other people.[93]) Those scholars who have articulately stressed the broader, positive qualities of nationalism and its associated identities (the ethical and political benefits of nationality) must also face the unquestionable ugliness and viciousness of these phenomena in areas where they have been sharply contested. For example, the Ulster conflict between Irish and British nationalisms should, perhaps, form a crucial part of any assessment of nationalism and nationality in the Irish and British islands (a challenge which is sometimes simply avoided[94]).

Certainly, the important justifications for the IRA's political violence need to be set against the experience of those who were on the receiving end of their vicious and violent use of power. In an area such as south Armagh, where Protestant unionists very much felt besieged, and vulnerable to the Provos, this was perhaps particularly marked: 'You can live in this area as a Protestant as long as you see nothin', hear nothin', or tell nothin'. You live under the rule of the Provisional IRA. They'll let you live here as long as you do what they say'; 'There was a [Provisional IRA] campaign of ethnic cleansing where they tried to move the Protestant community further back from the border.'[95] And such perceptions were reinforced by the very marked actual decline in the Armagh border Protestant population between the early 1970s and the 1990s.

Nor were the IRA's serious and articulate arguments in defence of their violence necessarily persuasive on close examination. They presented themselves as a communal defence force, and yet much-vaunted episodes such as the republican defence in 1970 of St Matthew's Church in Belfast's Catholic Short Strand (a skirmish still celebrated in republican memory thirty-five years later[96]) were in fact very atypical. The IRA could not protect Catholic civilians during the Troubles (at least 1,227 being killed in the period after the Provos' foundation, many of them indeed being killed by the IRA itself[97]) any more than they could erase sectarian division in Ireland (a phenomenon from which they derived much momentum, and which they in turn helped to exacerbate). Many other Provo claims were highly dubious: Northern Ireland demonstrably was not, *pace* republicans, anything like Nazi Germany or apartheid South Africa. And while the Provos claimed a moral high ground, few beyond their own ranks and enthusiasts shared such a view of the ethics of Ulster during the vicious, late-twentieth-century war.

Moreover, it could be argued that the IRA's central political argument was itself suspect in some respects. They held that the key problem in Ireland lay in a British colonial desire to hold on to part of the island: the focus of attention was therefore on British attitudes, rather than on what might better be seen as the real obstacle to Irish unity, namely the existence of a large and concentrated group of Ulster unionists who simply wanted nothing to do with it. However much violent pressure was deployed against Britain, there would still remain the problem of unionists who could not realistically be coerced – and didn't seem about to be persuaded – into joining a united, nationalist Ireland.

It's not that the Provos started the northern conflict – they didn't even exist as an organization when the first killings occurred in 1966 – nor that the seriousness or importance of their nationalism should be disputed. But the legacy of the Provisional IRA's 1969–94 campaign against the British state was one of making the northern problem simultaneously more urgently prominent and more difficult to resolve. The intercommunal trust required to produce satisfactory compromise had been rendered even more elusive after years of killing, and the IRA had killed more than any other agent in the conflict.

Republicans have sometimes portrayed the IRA's violent nationalism as having been inevitable as well as justified ('I think that it was inevitable that the nationalist people took up arms. There was no viable democratic alternative'[98]). But the choices made – on all sides – were choices to which there were alternatives. Unionists could have acted with riskier magnanimity during the 1920–72 era; militant civil rights leaders could have avoided provocative, destabilizing gestures such as their 1969 Burntollet march; the London government could have intervened directly in Northern Ireland more speedily and effectively than it did; security deployments and actions of 1970–72 could have been handled far better than they were. And there was nothing inevitable about the IRA's violence: not all working-class Catholics responded to Bloody Sunday in 1972 by joining the Provisionals and killing people; some people saw far earlier than the Provos that violence in Northern Ireland would bring not nationalist victory but futile, bloodstained stalemate. And there's no inevitability about daily grievances being expressed through nationalism or, as in this case, through violent nationalism on the part of IRA supporters. We need to explain why, when the crisis came in the late 1960s, it was through nationalism that responses were channelled. And here the inheritance of community (people, culture, sense of history, boundaries of exclusion) within the northern state was one which cemented national ties: it was a British state which discriminated against you as part of a nationalist Irish community. And when the struggle became clarified in local battle lines (police from beyond your community clashing with neighbours from within it), and when it was nationalists who offered both explanation and seemingly powerful defence and remedy, it was nationalism which became the vehicle for your urgent struggle.

As with earlier generations of IRA violence, conflict, once begun, could help to sustain itself through antiphonal, attritional prompting. A classic instance of this was the 1976–81 republican prison protest, as much of a stimulus to IRA support as the bungled security policy had been in Belfast and Derry during 1970–72. Keen to delegitimize their IRA opponents, the mid-1970s London government defined them as criminal, removing from republican prisoners the effective political status with which they had been treated in the jails. This prompted republican prison protests, which escalated from a refusal to wear prison clothing to the extreme tactic of hunger-striking in 1980 and 1981. The latter of these strikes – in which ten republicans died on their fast – was famously to arouse nationalist rage, and it generated much energy for the Provisional movement to use in the coming years.

This remains a highly charged period even when viewed decades later, and the commitment evident from sources such as the diary of Bobby Sands (the first prisoner to die, in May 1981 on his sixty-sixth day without food) can prompt both sadness and a sense of futility. The latter can seem more sharp when viewed through other lenses: it has, for example, been claimed by one pivotal republican ex-prisoner that, after only four deaths, the IRA authorities outside the jail rejected a compromise deal which had been agreed by the republican prisoners themselves,[99] a claim which has been disputed by some but which might tend to suggest an avoidability to much of the tragedy of those days.

At the time of the protracted hunger strikes themselves there was a coming together of normally divided sections of the northern nationalist family. Many of the 30,492 people who voted for IRA man Sands in the April 1981 election which saw him win a House of Commons seat for Fermanagh–South Tyrone were people who did not support his or his comrades' violence. But they did, in the Manichean tussle of 1981, side with the prisoners in their demand to be treated as political rather than as criminal actors. The hunger-strikes could also reflect and intensify some divisions within the Irish nationalist community, however. This was true regarding the relationship between republicans and the Catholic Church (the former thinking that elements within the latter tried to undermine the strike). And it was also true regarding relations between republicans and the Dublin nationalist regime. In May 1981 one republican prisoner in the H-Blocks of Northern Ireland's Maze Prison (writing on the day of the funeral for Francis Hughes, the second hunger-striker to die), articulated republican rage towards established Dublin nationalism in a letter to the then Taoiseach (Prime Minister) there, Fianna Fáil's Charles Haughey:

As I write Frank Hughes, one of the finest Irish patriots this country has ever produced, is being buried. He was the second Irish political prisoner to have died in these Hell Blocks in the space of a week. The first was Bobby Sands, MP, fluent Irish speaker, writer and poet. Neither of them need have died had you and your government taken a real stand against the arrogant and callous government of [UK Prime Minister] Margret [sic] Thatcher.

The letter – from Sean Coleman in H6 – was intended to force Haughey to do something positive for republicans: it demanded that he sever diplomatic and trade links with Britain, and that he call for all governments to support the prisoners' demands. Coleman's prison epistle ended plaintively, 'How many more of my friends will you let die through your inaction?'[100]

It is sometimes assumed that there was something inherently old-Irish about the hunger-strikes (presented by some as 'an ancient weapon in Ireland'[101]), and again that there was something inevitable – or even foreseen and intended – about the development from hunger-strike election success in 1981 to the 1990s peace process and to the IRA's eventual cessation of its military campaign against Britain. But we should probably beware of such assumptions. It's clear enough that the hunger-strike of 1981 was very much a means of struggle determined by contemporary exigency as the prisoner community saw it (and that it was part of their pragmatic attempt to use prison resistance as another part of their nationalist struggle, a collective political effort to challenge existing power relations[102]). It is equally clear that, at the time that the strike ended, the lesson drawn by the prisoners themselves was not that peaceful politics would work, but rather that it was 'energy-wasting, futile and unproductive'.[103] For, while Bobby Sands's election in April 1981 and his martyr-apotheosis in the following month did strengthen the hand of those republicans who had wanted to build up the movement's politics (after Sands, who could denounce elections and politics as necessarily bad?), the evidence from the 1980s suggests firmly that republicans envisaged politics complementing rather than replacing violence. It's tempting to look in the past for those signs of what we now know to have emerged as the present, and to isolate these as the matters of historic importance; but this does no justice to the complexity and contingency of the past itself. Other futures were possible, and republican leaders were no more aware than other people of how the new century was likely to emerge.

There can be no doubt, however, that the 1981 strike and its associated mobilization – communal, intense, widespread, sharply felt – represented something of a watershed in militant republican Irish nationalism. At the Provos' initial foundation, Sinn Féin had been constituted as a political mask for the IRA; during the 1970s the two partners in the republican movement – the party and the army – were interwoven in terms of personnel, organization, goals and ideology; but Sinn Féin was very much the subordinate member of the relationship, often enough just a public mouthpiece and a legal convenience.[104] The 1981 experience, with Sands's electoral success, helped to overcome some republicans' instinctive suspicion of the political, and to usher in a period in which the balance of power in the republican marriage would be able to change. Sinn Féin's role became expanded, a process reinforced by the movement's abandonment of abstentionism in relation to the Dublin Dáil, and the evolution in the 1990s of the Northern Ireland peace process.

The right to self-determination still, in republican eyes, legitimated the use of force: 'We demand the basic right of every nation to national self-determination. The denial of that right by armed might will always legitimize and give rise to armed struggle in pursuit of that right.'[105] But post-1981 Provisional republican nationalism moved, jaggedly and slowly, towards a more argumentative-electoral form of struggle. In this it involved a political community coming to terms with its own capacity for effective mobilization by other means – the Sinn Féin vote was to rise most conspicuously once the IRA had stopped killing soldiers and police officers – but also coming to terms with some political realities which its earlier zealotry had tended to eclipse from view. The Provos had argued that the central Irish problem lay with London, implying that there would be little difficulty in overcoming unionist opposition in the north once Britain announced its impending departure from Northern Ireland, and that there would be little problem in joining Ireland's north-eastern six to her southern twenty-six counties. But each of these assumptions was almost certainly flawed. In reality, London's commitment to Northern Ireland owed far more to a recognition that there was no other serious option while the unionist population there remained attached to UK membership; in this sense, Secretary of State for Northern Ireland Peter Brooke's famous statement in 1990 that 'the British government has no selfish strategic or economic interest in Northern Ireland'[106] was merely a reiteration of what any calmly observant analyst had been able to see for many years. (What could be the possible selfish interest in maintaining hold over a territory which drained resources, offered international embarrassment, and occasioned bombing and other attacks on your country?)

And the problem of unionism became more and more obvious to thoughtful republicans too. 'When you're engaged in a struggle, you fight with basics in mind: it's a united Ireland or nothing; the unionists are basically tools of British imperialism; they don't know what they're doing; they'll come into a united Ireland like sheep once you break the will of the British. That was a very simplistic view of unionism.'[107] 'In a way we made them [unionists] a non-people. We just said: you can't move the unionists until you move the Brits. So we didn't even see them as part of the problem, never mind as being part of the solution.'[108]

> The vision of an Ireland that is at peace with itself and with our nearest neighbours in Britain is a shared aspiration for most of the people of Ireland. There are many different expressions of that ideal and on the constitutional, political, social and economic future of the island of Ireland. Decisions on these matters, in our view, can ultimately only be arrived at through the most thorough and inclusive dialogue, political discourse and negotiation by the people of Ireland. Clearly that includes unionists. We have a responsibility to build an inclusive society which addresses the political allegiances of unionists and guarantees their rights and entitlements so that they have a sense of security and a stake in the new Ireland.[109]

Republicans certainly hadn't come to reconceptualize their conflict as an Ulster civil war against unionists, rather than a war against Britain; but they had more clearly than before seen the importance of the unionists and of their views for any serious forward movement politically in the north.

The historical inheritance of religious, economic, cultural and political difference left unionists with a rich store of reasons for resisting absorption into a nationalist Ireland; and, in truth, unionist resistance had probably been hardened rather than softened by the aggressive nationalism of the IRA. Objection to a united Ireland probably had less to do with the specifics of what such a state might look like (specifics to which most unionists had given little extended thought), and more to do with not losing to local nationalist enemies, neighbours, rivals, or coming under their (or their community's) nationalist power and control. In this sense, IRA violence merely made the likelihood of unionist acquiescence even more remote.

And what of Dublin anyway? Leading Fine Gael politician Garret FitzGerald recalled how, as an Irish government minister in January 1975, he had told US politician Henry Kissinger in Washington 'of our worries' about British policy regarding Northern Ireland. These were worries which would have annoyed northern republicans: 'in the event,' FitzGerald said, 'of a shift in British policy towards withdrawal from Northern Ireland in advance of an agreed political solution we would then seek US assistance in persuading Britain not to embark on a course of action that could be so fraught with dangers not just to Northern Ireland but to the whole of Ireland'. Kissinger 'agreed that he would be open to an approach from us in the event of such a grave development'.[110] Should the British agree to grant what the IRA demanded, then Dublin – powerfully backed by Washington – would oppose it.

The republican recognition of some of these realities – regarding London, Ulster unionism and Dublin – implied that an alternative method of communal struggle was required, since the armed version was not solving the problem. And here lay one of the tangled roots of the Northern Ireland peace process. For republicans were no less rational than anyone else in the conflict, in their desire for political momentum in their struggle. The Provisionals had early on believed that their violence – and, after 1981, their violence tinged with electoralism – would bring victory. But, year after year, it became clear that even the nationalist people in the north emphatically preferred their politicians to espouse non-violent methods. People only came to vote for Sinn Féin in dominant numbers once the IRA's war against the British state had effectively ended, as is clear from long-term voting patterns. In pre-ceasefire Northern Ireland, the constitutional-nationalist Social Democratic and Labour Party (SDLP) clearly and repeatedly defeated republicans at the polls:

General Election 1983	SDLP 17.9%	SF 13.4%
General Election 1987	SDLP 21.1%	SF 11.4%
General Election 1992	SDLP 23.5%	SF 10.0%
District Council Elections 1985	SDLP 17.8%	SF 11.8%
District Council Elections 1989	SDLP 21.0%	SF 11.2%[111]

Observers of Irish nationalism and of the Northern Ireland troubles sometimes assume them to exemplify the politics of extremism and violence; in some ways, as the above figures demonstrate, it is towards the triumph of constitutional moderation that modern Ulster politics actually points.

4

> The combination of social and national demands, on the whole, proved very much more effective as a mobilizer of independence than the pure appeal of nationalism.
>
> Eric Hobsbawm[112]

For some Provisionals, the appeal of revolutionary struggle partly involved the supposed prospect of social reorganization along left-wing lines. As far as hard-left politics went, these hopes effectively died by the end of the 1980s and the early 1990s, with the collapse of formal Marxism and the disintegration of the Soviet Union. (Even so committed a leftist as the great historian Eric Hobsbawm himself has frankly and tersely acknowledged that 'Communism is now dead.'[113])

But some within the republican family had adopted a leftist path very different from that of the Provos. When the 1969 split in the republican movement produced the Provisional IRA, those remaining in the old movement continued their politics and their violence as the Official IRA (OIRA). This group declared a ceasefire in 1972, although some aggressive actions continued in subsequent years. The 1960s IRA

Chief of Staff Cathal Goulding (who became a leading figure in Official republicanism after the split with the Provos) had himself been clear for years that violent struggle was probably not the best means of achieving the kind of nationalist progress that Ireland required. In the pre-Troubles years he had attempted to shift the IRA towards a more leftist, mass-popular brand of politics, and long after the split with the Provos he remained eloquent in his denunciations of what he saw as the latter's sectarian, bankrupt militarism. In June 1975, in an oration at the Bodenstown grave of Theobald Wolfe Tone, Goulding celebrated the United Irishman's philosophy, and also offered a sharp attack on his Provisional rivals:

> By their campaign of military action against non-military targets, the Provisionals ... alienated the Protestant workers of the six counties, diverted attention from the struggle for democratic reform, produced the stimulus the loyalists needed to recover Orange unity, excused the replacement of the B Specials with an equally vicious, equally corrupt force, the UDR, lent weight to arguments for rearming the RUC and did more than anything else to destroy the sympathy of the British working class. And the campaign gave the enemies of the Irish people – the ruling classes of Britain and Ireland – the opportunity to impose on all who resisted their will a kind of repression that was even more vicious than the repression we had fought to destroy. The Provisionals' campaign once more diverted attention, North and South, from the struggle for democratic rights and social advance. The ruling class could hardly have been better served if they had planned the campaign themselves.[114]

Certainly, it was difficult to see how the killing of working-class Protestants or the bombing of the state that they loved would help to produce intercommunal class unity. But there were those besides the Provisionals who combined aggression with socialist hope. In December 1974 a break-away group from the OIRA formed a new vehicle for nationalist struggle, with the emergence of the Irish Republican Socialist Party (IRSP). In this new group's view, 'British imperialist interference in Ireland constitutes the most immediate obstacle confronting the Irish people in their struggle for democracy, national liberation and socialism.' The IRSP therefore demanded 'that Britain must immediately renounce all claims to sovereignty over any part of Ireland and its coastal waters, and should immediately specify an early date for the total withdrawal of her military and political presence from Ireland'.[115]

The IRSP Constitution declared the party's objectives to be 'to end imperialist rule in Ireland and establish a thirty-two-county democratic socialist republic, with the working class in control of the means of production, distribution and exchange'. As to method, the party realized 'that socialism can only be built by a conscious working class'; accordingly, they would 'seek an active working alliance of all radical forces within the context of a broad front to ensure the ultimate success of the Irish working class in their struggle for national libera- tion and socialism'.[116] Indeed, the IRSP form of republican nationalism was crisp in its working-class definition of community, of anti-British grievance, and of the changes in power relations necessary if Irish national problems were to be solved:

> The continuation of direct rule from Westminister [sic] is a continuation of the attacks on the lives of the working class by way of mass unemployment, rising prices, harassment and repres- sion. . . . In our view, an immediate end to the British military, political and economic presence is a prerequisite for a solution to the northern conflict.[117]

Echoing this, on 13 December 1974, a statement from the newly- formed Derry IRSP put things crisply: 'there is a need for a real socialist alternative.'[118]

This party was to sustain such a class-communal politics, even into the period during which obituaries were being written for Marxism. Marking the twentieth anniversary of British troops' deployment in Northern Ireland, the IRSP newspaper declared on its front page in August 1989: 'BRITS OUT! SELF-DETERMINATION': traditional enough nationalist sentiments in themselves. But the paper's editorial explained lucidly that the IRSP had a very distinctive reading of what self-determination should entail. The previous twenty years had seen the nationalist community in the north 'subjected to every weapon in the British arsenal'. But the story had not just been one of repression, 'but of a heroic working class fighting back, taking blow for blow and often giving six in return'. The people had shown their resilience. But, asked the IRSP, 'is this enough, how nearer are the Brits to withdrawing than say ten years ago? The reality is that whilst an active section of the people continue to resist, the vast majority of the working class, whilst wanting a British withdrawal, do not feel they have a role to play in the struggle.'

So military force on its own would not get the British out; nor, indeed, was it sufficient merely to say 'Brits out' and leave it at that. What was required was a communally self-conscious, class-based reading of the Irish national struggle. Only this would prove effective.

> The working class are not only suffering under British repression, but under capitalism as a whole. . . . So we are not only fighting to get the Brits out but our goal has to be the overthrow of the present corrupt system and to replace it with socialism. That is the only basis on which the working class as a whole will mobilize and play an active part in the national liberation struggle . . . The IRSP is the only revolutionary socialist party in Ireland who is trying to build a genuine communist party, that recognizes that the fight for national liberation and socialism are part of the same struggle. It is only by building such a party that can give direction and leadership to the working class that the struggle for national liberation and socialism can be won.[119]

A couple of months later, the IRSP paper tersely summarized the party's philosophy in the front-page declaration: 'FOR NATIONAL LIBERATION AND A SOCIALIST REVOLUTION'.[120]

So here we are back to 1916 Marxist rebel James Connolly, to the supposedly inseparable politics of working class and nation, to the utopian appeal of a supposed remedy for social and national ills at one stroke. And, as with Connolly himself, there was a violent edge to this leftist struggle: whatever the limitations of violence in the view of the IRSP, their affiliated military wing – the Irish National Liberation Army (INLA) – carried out a very bloody campaign,[121] not least against their former comrades in the OIRA.

The fissiparous and violent world of left republicanism exemplified one of the key truths of Irish nationalist history: that it has very often involved struggle against other nationalists as much as against Britain. For rival versions of nationalist struggle again and again demonstrate that – even on this comparatively small Irish canvas – it is nationalisms rather than nationalism that we are attempting to paint. This was clear also from the case of less aggressive nationalist politics in the north during the Troubles. For while the INLA and rival IRAs were killing people, other Irish nationalists – far more, in fact – spent the 1970s and 1980s supporting more peaceful and conciliatory forms of struggle in Northern Ireland. Pre-eminent here was the SDLP, formed in 1970 with a view to offering a strong and constitutionally-oriented northern nationalist movement. The SDLP were committed by their Constitution 'To promote the cause of Irish unity based on the consent of the majority of people in Northern Ireland'.[122] The Stormont MPs who formed the new party – Gerry Fitt, John Hume, Paddy Devlin, Austin Currie, Ivan Cooper and Paddy O'Hanlon – sought to infuse life into the constitutional-nationalist tradition at this early-Troubles moment of unfolding crisis. Their politics involved a dialogue between the social and the national (with the latter normally prevailing[123]), and their programme was far too green for any section of unionism to accept: by the end of 1972, for example, the party was strenuously arguing for joint London–Dublin sovereignty over Northern Ireland.

Yet the SDLP analysis did offer a far less coercive approach to solving the problems of the north than was on offer from belligerent republicanism. The party consistently and courageously opposed violence (numerous party figures themselves being threatened and attacked by the IRA for their trouble); and they long championed some of the ideas which would, eventually, lie at the heart of the 1998 Good Friday Agreement: a recognition of the rights of both unionist and nationalist traditions, the need for the local sharing of power, the necessity of compromise rather than victory, and the eschewing of violence.[124] According to the SDLP, the two political communities in the north – nationalist and unionist – needed to work together in ways that would remove hostility and in its place build trust: according to the SDLP argument, IRA violence destroyed such possibilities for trust and for relationships to grow. And while the Provos considered that it was London which blocked the way to a united Ireland, the SDLP recognized that the main obstacle to the ending of partition lay not in Britain, but with the British in Ulster: the northern unionists.

If the SDLP early on identified the eventual destination of nationalist thinking on the north, they also suggested before others did the route by which to reach it. While republicans were pursuing victory and bloodily rejecting reconciliation, the SDLP were arguing for a very different means of struggle. Their 1979 Annual Conference heard calls for the party to pursue reconciliation and peace by 'publicly inviting unionist and loyalist politicians to debate with us either publicly or privately the future of Northern Ireland either at meetings called by them or the SDLP or jointly', and by establishing contact with 'the leadership of all political and paramilitary organizations who belong to the Irish tradition with a view to establishing a common ground upon which that tradition could move forward towards reconciliation and peace with those of the British tradition'.[125] Here were pre-echoes of a much later peace-process politics. Two years earlier, in 1977, party Chairman Denis Haughey had presciently called for 'a realistic effort' by both communities in Northern Ireland 'to grasp the fears and misgivings of "the other side" in a spirit of generosity and tolerance. For our part', he continued, 'we understand the genuine fears and misgivings of the "Ulster-Scots" community.'[126] (And these fears – justified or not – lay at the heart of the problem for Irish nationalists as they understandably sought redress of grievance from unionists. Traditionally presented in militant nationalist rhetoric as bullying and dominant, Northern Irish unionists were in fact feeling increasingly vulnerable and politically insecure: a sense of insecurity rather than a sense of superiority more effectively explained their politics.[127] And, in part, this was to do with the realities of local community demographics: the Catholic majority in County Tyrone, for example, had been 55 per cent in 1926; by 1991 this had risen to 63 per cent; in County Fermanagh, the Catholic majority in 1926 had been 56 per cent; by 1991 this too had risen, to 59 per cent.)

Much that end-of-century Irish republicans were to endorse, therefore, had long (and much earlier) been advocated by the SDLP. This was true of the argument that the absence of violence would increase the chances of nationalist progress: 'The Provisional IRA can achieve nothing by carrying on their campaign of violence but they can achieve almost anything they desire by knocking it off',[128] as the SDLP pithily put it in the mid-1970s. And it was true also of the fundamental principles which were to lie at the very heart of the eventual 1998 settlement: the recognition of two national traditions, and the shared access to decision-making and power. As early as 1974 the SDLP had set out what it considered to be key 'realities and principles'. Northern

Ireland was not, they held, 'an economic, social, cultural or geographic unit', but rather a place where divided loyalties prevented necessary consensus: 'The minimal consensus which enables other communities to erect a framework within which to contain their political conflicts and regulate their social and economic life is here absent.' In setting out what was to be done to remedy this situation, the SDLP prefigured the central elements of the late-1990s settlement:

> If the people of Northern Ireland are to govern themselves peace-fully, democratically and liberally, their institutions of government must reflect these realities. They must take account of the divisions within Northern Ireland, the conflicting national identities and the special relationships that Northern Ireland will always have with Great Britain and the Republic of Ireland. . . . SDLP policy has consistently recognized these realities. It is based on two principles: that all sections of the Northern people should have access, by right, to the decision-making process at all levels, and that the two national identities must be recognized in Northern Ireland's rela-tions with Great Britain and the Republic of Ireland.[129]

It was to take a long time for more aggressive northern nationalists to accept these as the key truths in the situation: the politics of struggle could blind people to wider realities, and had a self-sustaining dyna-mism to it in republican areas.

At local level, one can explain this: wars tend to generate their own myopic limitations on all sides. But it now seems fairly clear that the sort of compromise and blurring of certainty implied in the political initiatives of the 1970s and 1980s – endorsed by the SDLP, rejected by republicans – pointed the way forward for Irish nationalism more helpfully than did the politics of bombs and bullets. The SDLP supported the 1973 Sunningdale deal between unionists, nationalists, the British and Irish governments and the cross-community Northern Irish Alliance Party – an agreement according to which a power-sharing executive for Northern Ireland would be complemented by the establishment of a cross-border Council of Ireland (the latter compris-ing representatives from both Irish states, and possessing an ambigu-ously defined remit). For their part, the SDLP were delighted with this Sunningdale deal, seeing in the Council of Ireland the potential for forward-movement in a nationalist direction (something which contributed, of course, towards unionist and loyalist suspicion and anger). And Sunningdale reaffirmed that the achievement of nationalist goals should be reached by peaceful means and through consent rather than coercion.

So too the 1983–4 New Ireland Forum – a gathering of the four main Irish nationalist parties (the SDLP, Fianna Fáil, Fine Gael, Labour) with a view to their developing a shared approach to a settlement in the north – was an initiative based on constitutional, peaceful struggle towards nationalist goals. The Forum's 1984 Report set out options for a united Ireland, for joint authority between Dublin and London, and for a federal answer to the Northern Ireland question; all three were unacceptable to unionists, of course, and famously also to UK Prime Minister Margaret Thatcher ('The unified Ireland was one solution – that is out. A second solution was a confederation of the two states – that is out. A third solution was joint authority – that is out'[130]).

Yet, despite such resounding denunciation, Thatcher herself was to sign late in 1985 the Anglo-Irish Agreement which, once again, reflected the politics of constitutional nationalist advance as favoured by the SDLP and their leader after 1979, John Hume. The 1985 Agreement between London and Dublin reaffirmed the guarantee of Northern Ireland's place within the United Kingdom (as long as a majority there wished to retain it), and made noises about security cooperation between the United Kingdom and the Republic of Ireland to deal with paramilitary violence; it also set out a preference for devolution as the way forward in the north, and expressed intentions regarding rights and identities; but the main innovation was to give the Dublin government a formal, institutional, consultative role in Northern Irish affairs, with the establishment of a joint-ministerial conference of Irish and British ministers, to be serviced by a permanent secretariat. This was a major shift in British policy, one which horrified unionist opinion and which seemed to suggest that SDLP-style politics could yield powerful results for nationalists in Ireland. For Dublin was now institutionally involved in monitoring the redress of nationalist grievance in the north. This might have reflected a recognition of something reasonably obvious, namely, that there had to be some input from Dublin if any lasting resolution in the north was to be achieved; as one British Conservative politician with long experience

in Ulster was to put it, regarding the mid-1980s, 'the British government had long since realized that defeating the IRA was impossible
without the wholehearted commitment of the South and unless and
until the Republic could be drawn into taking some responsibility for
what was happening in the North.'[131] But the announcement of
Dublin's new role, together with the manner of the 1985 Agreement's
production, alarmed unionists sharply (unlike the unionist parties, the
SDLP had been kept informed by Dublin of what was brewing).

The 1985 Anglo-Irish Agreement was to change the terms of
Northern Ireland politics, and it seemed emphatically to reinforce
SDLP thinking. Hume and his comrades were able to produce results,
it seemed to suggest, and their arguments had thus perhaps been
validated. For the SDLP had read 1970s loyalism (with its bruising
destruction of the 1973 Sunningdale deal, for example) as having
demonstrated the impossibility of an internal, power-sharing strategy.
The game had therefore to be widened out. As one of their politicians
had put it in 1978,

> Loyalist intransigence has made it pointless for the SDLP to
> continue debating about and working for the acceptability of
> power-sharing. That intransigence leaves us with little option but
> to henceforth work in an all-Ireland context with the two sovereign
> governments. This involves firstly getting an acceptance by both
> sovereign governments of the fact that each are [sic] prepared to
> work towards the same objective, namely the ending of British
> involvement and the setting up of a new and an agreed Irish nation.
> This involves a much greater change than either the Irish govern-
> ment or probably the people of the South appreciate.[132]

Not all the matters set out here were fulfilled, but the broad point
about expanding the scale of the answer to the north's questions was
reflected in the newly defined politics of 1985.

Yet there were ambiguities here as well. Republicans were to read
the lessons of 1985 both as showing their own marginalization and
also as reflecting what they saw as the rewards of their own aggressive
pressure. And within the SDLP's own argument itself, there long
remained a tension characteristic of Irish constitutional nationalism,
between stressing northern reform as the crucial thing, and simultaneously holding that a united Ireland remained a key nationalist

aspiration. And the party was emphatically not one to accept the status quo. They were clear that direct rule from Westminster – which had been introduced in 1972 – remained a deeply inadequate answer to the Ulster question. SDLP Chairman Denis Haughey made this lucidly clear at the opening of the party's 1977 Annual Conference:

> politics have come to a standstill. Direct rule has removed from the hands of local politicians, the power to solve the most important problem facing the people of Northern Ireland – the divisions in our society. Power has been transferred into the hands of people who have neither the will nor the knowledge to solve it. It is clear to most people that direct rule is inadequate to our needs, that it does not offer any hope of an acceptable settlement, and that it does not offer any hope of a cessation of violence. In this much, at least, there is general agreement on both sides of the political divide. We need a strong central government here in Northern Ireland to deal with the problem of our society.[133]

This last sentence rightly implied that the politics of nationalism would only continue to appeal if it did address what people daily and urgently faced in their lives. SDLP appeal – as with that of all success-ful and lasting nationalist movements – included broad constitutional and national issues, but also much else of daily relevance to voters. For the 1987 UK General Election, the party's South Down candidate Eddie McGrady stressed his local credentials ('I was born in South Down. I live here'), but also set out a range of would-be vote-catching claims: 'The Anglo-Irish Agreement: forward together. Job Creation: top priority – jobs for South Down ... Health Services: I'll fight for a new hospital ... Pollution: stop dumping nuclear waste in our sea.' (McGrady ended his message to potential voters with the catchphrase: 'PS I win – you win' – which he narrowly did, unseating the UUP's Enoch Powell in the process.)[134] The party tried to offer a range of policies attractive in many directions (they had long considered issues relating directly to women, a policy discussion document concerning anti-female violence featuring at their 1986 Annual Conference, for example).[135]

And the SDLP looked also to internationalize the northern question, another very important feature of Irish nationalist support and lever-age. Prominent party figure Seamus Mallon set things out crisply in

November 1974, when speaking at an SDLP meeting in Armagh: 'Look
to Brussels – not Bodenstown [Theobald Wolfe Tone's burial place] or
the Boyne'. The EEC was providing the context for the transcendence
of old hatreds, and this provided the best model for Northern Irish
rivals: 'At a time when traditional enemies like England and Germany
are working together for their mutual good, we in the North are
allowing ourselves to be riveted to an irrelevant past. At present,'
Mallon continued, 'when we need the vision and moral courage to
meet the challenges of a Europeanized Ireland, we have reverted to the
type of siege mentality which keeps us lurking in the shadows of
Bodenstown and the Boyne and blinds us to the realities of Brussels.'[136]

Crucial in building the international strength of SDLP nationalism
was Derry-born ex-civil rights politician John Hume.[137] By the time
that Hume became SDLP leader in 1979, he was already well
acquainted and well integrated with key US-Irish figures such as
Edward Kennedy, and these links were to prove important in the
States: 'His influence was unparalleled because his was the one consistent voice that spoke out against violence and offered an alternative
strategy.'[138] Hume saw his role as one of dissuading Irish-Americans
from helping to sustain IRA-style nationalism; he argued powerfully
that, instead, they should further the cause of a more moderate and
peaceful nationalist politics. On 17 March 1981 the Friends of Ireland
was founded as a kind of antidote to the more aggressive style of US-
Irish politics associated with IRA sympathizers. And US government
support for the 1985 Anglo-Irish Agreement reflected something of
Hume's impact: for here was the politics of inclusion and compromise,
rather than that of rejectionist bombing, and this more peaceful style
of nationalist advance had the blessing of Washington. Long before 9/
11, and even before the United States so emphatically won the Cold
War, it was clear to all who would see it that serious American
endorsement was only available to those Irish nationalists who
eschewed terror campaigns.

As a Member of the European Parliament (MEP) from 1979
onwards, Hume was also well placed to internationalize the problems
of Northern Ireland in Europe (and also to promote there his own
brand of nationalist medicine for dealing with them). While his
proclamations on such matters could at times sound rather platitudi-
nous – his desire, for example, to see 'an Ireland that is whole in a

Europe that is whole, in a world that is whole'[139] – it's vital to grasp how important a role Hume played in these years in furthering a northern nationalism based on consent rather than coercion. For there were far more martial tunes being played. Irish Northern Aid (Noraid) was founded in 1970 following meetings between Provisional IRA representatives and Irish-American activists in New York (including Michael Flannery); the group was for years to fund-raise and engage in publicity, both in support of the militant republican struggle in the north of Ireland.[140] Closer to home, the English-based Troops Out Movement had emerged in the early 1970s and for decades attempted to mobilize opinion around the interwoven notions of 'Troops out now' and 'self-determination for the Irish people as a whole'. Based on rather simplistic premises, their argument was clearly articulated for many years (deep, indeed, into the latter-day peace-process period:

> The Troops Out Movement is made up of people who believe that the cause of all conflict in the north of Ireland is the continuing British presence there, both military and political. We believe that the British troops are in Ireland not as a peacekeeping force, but in order to maintain British rule. Britain's presence in Ireland is the most serious obstacle to a lasting peace with justice.[141])

SDLP nationalism did not focus purely on the northern Troubles or their political resolution. Its appeal was broader and more capacious than that. In campaigning for the June 1994 European elections, the party highlighted its priorities for the European parliament with a stress on the issue of employment: 'with twenty million people in the European Union out of work and an unemployment rate of 13.3 per cent overall in Northern Ireland, job creation is the number one priority for the SDLP'. Other themes highlighted were poverty, regional development, agriculture and fisheries.[142] Economic grievance remained central here to Irish nationalist politics. And this approach had long roots. An SDLP election leaflet for the 1979 UK General Election listed the difficulties which Northern Ireland was suffering after some years of direct rule, with the *economic* problems ('the highest unemployment level in the history of the state; the lowest average wage in the UK; the highest prices in the UK; the greatest dependence on social security payments in the UK; the rapid decline of employment in manufacturing; the lowest growth rate of any region in Europe') preceding the more obviously *political* items in the list ('the resurgence of paramilitary violence; brutality in the interrogation centres; chaos in the prisons ... the complete absence of any political initiative').[143]

Could it, indeed, be argued that by the 1990s the politics of the SDLP had effectively moved beyond nationalism? In December 1993 Hume stated that it had been the SDLP's consistent position 'that the British Irish quarrel of old, the quarrel of sovereignty, has changed fundamentally in the evolution of the new, interdependent and post-nationalist Europe of which we are members'.[144] And yet nationalism – dealing with constitutional issues as well as quotidian matters – remained central to the SDLP's politics. And part of John Hume's mission was to persuade fellow-nationalists of all kinds that the consensual, constitutional road was the one most likely to lead the community forward. His central, insistent role in the politics of the Northern Ireland peace process was founded, in part, on just this desire to draw away from the violent path those republicans who had so bloodily gone down it. In May 1994, for example, Hume lucidly clarified his own view of the true goal of his lengthy dealings with Sinn Féin: 'I would underline that throughout my dialogue with Gerry Adams the bottom line has been a total cessation of violence, followed by dialogue involving both governments and all parties whose objective was agreement among our divided people, an agreement that must earn the allegiance and agreement of all our traditions.'[145] Fittingly, Mo Mowlam (British Labour Party Secretary of State after 1997) was to observe that 'The important start to the peace process, talking with Sinn Féin, was achieved by John [Hume]. He took a lot of criticism for it, but it was his work and his vision which made the later progress possible. I think his contribution to the peace process will never be forgotten. It would be true to say he gave his life to finding peace.'[146]

By the time of Hume's retirement as SDLP leader in 2001, some of that job had been done. And crucial here had been his personal relationship – yet again, the politics of actual rather than imagined community relationships – with the only other contemporary northern nationalist leader of comparable influence and fame, Gerry Adams. Hume and Adams met numerous times during the late 1980s and early 1990s, and their developing relationship played a major part in the evolution of a new kind of nationalist-political architecture in Ireland.

Their dialogue focused significantly on the issue of the Irish people's right to national self-determination, as was clear from their 1993 joint statements: 'the Irish people as a whole have a right to national self-determination ... The exercise of self-determination is a matter for agreement between the people of Ireland.'[147]

Both Hume and Adams had faced difficulties in their respective brands of nationalist struggle. The problem for the SDLP was the dilemma about how far to accept the reality of the problematic Northern Ireland state (thereby hoping to achieve things in practice), and how far to reject it (thereby losing purchase on the mechanisms of actual political power). The first path risked a loss of legitimacy with one's own community at times when the state seemed harsh or unresponsive or biased; the second could lead to a futility of protest, and might seem to validate the rejectionism espoused by more aggressive nationalist rivals. But by the late 1980s those rivals had their own problems, and this was partly why Sinn Féin leader Adams was now more receptive to the kind of sermon being preached by his SDLP counterpart. Armed struggle was not bringing anticipated victory; indeed, it seemed to be stumbling badly: twenty-six IRA Volunteers died violently during 1987–8, and the IRA unintentionally killed twenty-seven civilians during the same two-year period; each of these grim statistics pointed towards the stagnation and futility of the violent campaign, and reinforced the fact that violence brought with it huge problems. These were underlined by Hume's argument that, *pace* the Provisionals, the main obstacle to Irish unity was not, in fact, opinion in London, but rather the existence of a large number of Irish people (Ulster's unionist community) who refused to enter the kind of political arrangements favoured by nationalist Ireland. If the problem was not London's desire to stay in the north, then what was the point of trying to bomb London into leaving? If the real problem lay more with unionist opinion, was there any evidence that years of killing had weakened unionist opposition to a united Ireland? (In 1968, 20 per cent of Northern Irish Protestants had described themselves as Irish, a figure which had dropped to only 3 per cent by 1986, where it remained until the end of the century.[148])

It was not that the SDLP couldn't recognize the political roots of violence: however appalling and misjudged, paramilitary actions had their origins in political problems. 'Violence has erupted periodically in Northern Ireland since the foundation of the state,' the Party's Executive Committee observed in 1978, 'because of injustices in the political, social and economic systems. All attempts to remedy those injustices were met with repression by the Stormont government through the Special Powers Act. Since the abolition of the Stormont government there has been change. A start has been made on some of the social and economic problems of our society. However,' they continued, 'stable political institutions have not been established, and currently the government is doing nothing to create them. Violence continues, therefore, because of the unsatisfactory political situation.'[149]

And yet the battle within nationalism was ultimately clear enough in terms of rival preferences for the appropriate mode of struggle. In his successful campaign to hold on to his West Belfast Westminster seat in 1974, the then SDLP leader Gerry Fitt had stressed that a vote for him would be seen as favouring 'the ballot box instead of the bomb and the bullet', and 'partnership instead of conflict'.[150] His party repeatedly condemned the horrific violence of the IRA. After the 27 August 1979 Provo operations which were to claim twenty-two lives – including that of Lord Mountbatten in County Sligo, and eighteen paratroops in County Down, Northern Ireland, whose deaths were welcomed with 'euphoria' and 'elation' by IRA prisoners[151] – the SDLP were impressively lucid in their own stance:

> We wish to reiterate again our utter revulsion at the acts of murder and carnage carried out by the Provisional IRA. We are confident that our sense of revulsion, outrage and shame is shared by the mass of the Irish people. Who would want to live in an Ireland created by people who are capable of such acts?[152]

5

> Republicanism as an ideology based itself on the rights of self-determination, which had been denied to the Irish people by centuries of British rule.
>
> Gerry Adams[153]

Easily the most important figure in the history of the Provisional movement, Gerry Adams here, in the above quotation, sets out his view of Irish republicanism with a classic version of the central nationalist argument about power as validated by self-determination (one of the most central of all nationalist articles of faith throughout the world, and crucial to its lasting appeal[154]). Indeed, Adams's rhetoric as a whole has been very much that of the familiar nationalist, his arguments couched in the democratic and the self-determining: 'the task of democratic opinion in Ireland and Britain and further afield – and this includes the USA – is to get a change of British policy from upholding partition and the Union to a policy of ending partition and the Union in consultation with the people of this island'.[155] In this very traditional view, the day-to-day problems faced by northern nationalists are seen as being best solved by ending the artificial partition of what should properly be a united territory and people:

> Ireland is historically, culturally and geographically one single unit. The partition of Ireland, established by the British 'Government of Ireland Act' and subsequent British Acts, divides Ireland into two artificial statelets, the boundaries of which were determined by a sectarian head-count and can be maintained only by continuing sectarianism.[156]

Adams has consistently been clear about the communal nature of his support and about the localized focus of his nationalist constituency and formation: 'The reality is that I have always felt very much a part of a community in struggle. . . . I am rewarded with the support and protection of our community in struggle.'[157] With deep family roots in republicanism, Adams has commented of his background in west

Belfast that 'The Falls, with its own pubs, its own shops, the library and the schools, generated a specific sense of community.'[158] In regard to his 1960s republicanism in his own part of Belfast, he acknowledged that 'To a large extent, my political world was Ballymurphy',[159] as late as 1999 still claiming that 'Ballymurphy was a state of mind. It still is.'[160]

Over his long years of struggle, that world and that state of mind have expanded greatly, to the extent that Adams the Ballymurphy nationalist has been transformed into a politician frequently seen in Downing Street, the White House, or among establishment politicians in Dublin. As his politics have shifted somewhat away from the aggressive towards the constitutional, so London and Dublin have come to view him differently; where once civil servants were keen to stress that Adams was no Nelson Mandela, more recently some of them have begun to hope that in fact he might prove just that. Adams himself has taken great inspiration from Mandela's very different kind of struggle. But it's important to be clear about what has not been involved: Adams did not spend most of the Troubles advocating the kind of politics now preached in the early twenty-first century by Sinn Féin; he did not single-handedly choreograph a lengthy peace process, or predict its contours long ago; and he did not betray pure republicanism so much as adapt his politics at each changing set of circumstances in order to maximize his own, and his followers', interests. In the 1970s it was the SDLP, rather than Gerry Adams, who recognized the potential for nationalist forward-movement were the IRA's armed campaign to be brought to a close. Adams himself had argued for the necessity of IRA violence, and had stressed in the 1970s the inevitability of IRA victory ('That the British face military defeat is inevitable and obvious'[161]). Adams anticipated British withdrawal and a united and republican Ireland, brought about primarily by IRA violence; he later came to the view that much more ambiguous achievements were the best that could be attained (stating in 2003 that 'There can be no escape from the reality that the conditions in which we will all have to live are those contained in the Good Friday Agreement'[162]), and that an end to the IRA's war against Britain had been a necessary condition for even this.

As early as 1973 Adams clearly foresaw the likelihood of a long IRA war (alarming some republican prisoners in Long Kesh with the rhetorical question, 'Does anybody think this war's going to be over in twenty years?'[163]) He was prepared for a long conflict even then. Irish republicans are repeatedly vocal about the suffering which they have undergone and about the superior morality of their, rather than their opponents', cause. But there has to be some doubt about the broad morality of this kind of stubbornly long-sustained campaign in circumstances in which victory was clearly unlikely. Others within the nationalist family could, even at the start of the Troubles, see the probable futility of pursuing nationalist struggle through killing. It should not be through violent coercion, wrote southern politician Garret FitzGerald in 1972, but 'with the freely given consent of a majority in Northern Ireland' that Irish unity should be pursued.[164] Even earlier, before the Provisional movement had even been born, Irish civil servant T. K. Whitaker had in 1968 observed that the Republic had rightly given up force as a means of undoing partition because '(1) the use of force to overcome northern unionists would accentuate rather than remove basic differences and (2) it would not be militarily possible in any event'. Political violence in pursuit of Irish unity would only prove counterproductive: 'Force will get us nowhere,' Whitaker advised, 'it will only strengthen the fears, antagonisms and divisions that keep north and south apart.'[165]

So the flaws in Provisional-style thinking were open to view even before the Provisionals themselves as an organization existed. Yet, flawed though it was in key regards, the approach of those who worked for so many years in the republican movement did represent a powerful and – for many – a very compelling one. Its appeal lay in the manner of its seeming to satisfy so many demands at once. It offered a large-scale promise of defence of person, property and interests, as well as the ultimate reward of sharing in sovereignty as part of a national majority. In the arguments of somebody like Gerry Adams, the main elements of nationalism as a global philosophy were on view: attachment to territory (both in the integrity of the island nation, and in the local Belfast community in struggle) and to people (again, imagined, but also very neighbourly and real), culture and history;[166] a sense of the nation's superior ethics when compared with villainous opponents (Adams compared loyalism to fascism, Northern Ireland to a fascist state or to South African apartheid,[167] and the republican prisoners during the blanket protest to 'characters from Solzhenitsyn's Gulag'[168]);

the idea that republicans were morally righteous, while their enemies were tyrants and oppressors. And his movement offered organized, large-scale struggle for power, in the form of a self-determining, sovereign state.

Each of these elements held an appeal for some, and while Provisional thinking was ultimately flawed, our understanding of nationalism in this book has focused often on the very local (my family, my friends, my neighbours, my community); and the repeated curse of escalating, tit-for-tat violence of the kind known in Northern Ireland during the Troubles is that it can induce myopia about things which lie beyond one's immediate vision. Yes, republican arguments were dubious; but their appeal, on the ground, can easily enough be explained, against a background of disaffection from a cold state, loyalist attack, soldierly roughness, and so on. There was, it is true, a solipsism to northern republican thinking in the 1970s, as though self were the only really existing thing, and as though the issues that mattered to one's own republican people could be conflated with the concerns and interests of the Irish people as a whole – north and south, nationalist and unionist. They could not. But this might not have been so clear from within the context of attritional friction with enemy forces. Adams's own reading of the early days of the Troubles would back this up:

> By their approach the British Army had generated in the residents of Ballymurphy a willingness and an eagerness to meet head on the violence of the soldiers who now strutted their streets with riot shields, batons, helmets and guns. No one could look on and passively accept having their doors kicked in, their houses wrecked, their family members beaten up.[169]

Clumsiness and brutality by the Army in the early years of the conflict helped to sustain that which it was supposed to crush: as one ex-IRA man was later to put it, 'the British Army, the British government, were our best recruiting agents'.[170]

The republican self-image of a nationalist community in struggle is one which must be interrogated sharply. How many people in the Irish nation actually agreed with the Provos' methods? What would have happened to those in your own areas who might publicly have dared to disagree? And yet it is clear that the lasting momentum for

Provisional republicanism did come from the motor of shared, communal anger and aspiration; from the sense of a need for practical resistance; and from a drive towards the maintenance of communal dignity amid grievance and suffering. As one Sinn Féin activist (Lily Fitzsimons, whose mother had been burned out of her Belfast home in 1969, and four of whose own five children had been arrested by the security forces) was later to interpret things, 'like many of our people, who live in nationalist areas in the six counties, my entire family have had first hand experience of loyalist sectarianism and blatant discrimination'. In Fitzsimons's view, political resistance was to be accompanied by the maintenance of communal self-respect: 'In spite of all the murders and repression that our communities have suffered at the hands of the British Army, RUC and loyalist killer gangs; in spite of the imprisonment and brutal treatment of our husbands, sons and daughters, we have always attempted to keep our pride and dignity intact.'[171]

Such aspects of Troubles republicanism – the positive, communal, humanly sympathetic – should be included in any serious historical assessment of this kind of nationalism, and should accompany in our minds the more brutal and offensive actions practised. It was a very vicious war, with acts such as the IRA's October 1993 Shankill bomb (which killed nine Protestants in Belfast) being condemned even by Adams himself ('The IRA operation on the Shankill was wrong; there can be no doubt'[172]). But the movement which could produce such horror clearly also made sense to many ordinary people in a more positive and communal sense. One H-Block republican (Alex Comerford, writing in November 1976 to supporters beyond the jail 'on behalf of POWs, H-Block Hell Hole, Long Kesh'), made the standard contemporary case for political treatment ('If we submit to abide by the criminal rules we will be granted "privileges" such as visits, parcels etc. But we are POWs, not criminals; we are soldiers and demand to be treated as such'), and then more tellingly set out a vision of the importance, appeal and nature of nationalist, communal solidarity: 'So we are depending on you, the people, our people, to stand by us – by supporting us in our struggle, by protesting, by going out on to the streets. Get as many people behind you as possible. March, rally, and petition, agitate. But please, please, in the name of humanity, stand firmly behind us. Remember you are the people.'[173]

14. Patrick Henry Pearse (1879–1916), writer, educator and nationalist politician. Pearse led the ill-fated Easter Rising in April 1916, becoming the first president of the Provisional Irish Republic. After surrendering to the British in the same month, he was arrested, court-martialled and shot.

15. A commemorative postcard honouring the seven signatories of the Proclamation of the Irish Republic, engraved by P. P. O'Malley c.1916. Pearse is in the centre, surrounded by Thomas J. Clarke, Sean MacDiarmada, Thomas MacDonagh, Eamonn Ceannt, James Connolly and Joseph Plunkett.

16. *Left*. Sir Roger Casement (1864–1916) in the dock at Bow Street court, London, in 1916. His attempts to support the Easter Rising cost him his life. Arrested shortly after landing in Ireland, he was stripped of his knighthood, tried for treason and hanged in Pentonville Prison in August 1916.

17. *Below*. In 1965 Casement's body was repatriated and, on 2 March, after a state funeral, was buried with full military honours in the Republican Plot in Glasnevin Cemetery in Dublin. The President of Ireland, Eamon de Valera, who in his mid-eighties was the last surviving leader of the Easter Rising, defied the advice of his doctors to attend the ceremony, along with an estimated 30,000 Irish citizens.

18. *Above.* The arrest of Eamon de Valera (1882–1975) in 1916. After the Easter Rising, de Valera was court-martialled, convicted, and sentenced to death, but the sentence was immediately commuted to penal servitude for life. He was, however, released under an amnesty in June 1917, and shortly thereafter was elected to the House of Commons.

19. *Right.* Constance Markievicz (1868–1927). Countess Markievicz was a passionate Nationalist, joining Sinn Féin in 1908. She took part in the Easter Rising, was arrested and imprisoned. Like de Valera she was released in 1917 under an amnesty and was subsequently elected to both the House of Commons and the first Dail Eirann. She later became the first Irish female cabinet minister.

20. *Above, left*. Ethna Carbery – the pseudonym of Anna Johnson (1866–1902) – was a nationalist writer, and the favourite poet of hunger striker, Bobby Sands. Together with Alice Milligan, Carbery founded the nationalist *Shan Van Vocht* in 1896.

21. *Above, right*. Mary MacSwiney (1872–1942), sister of republican martyr Terence MacSwiney and founder member of the Cumann na mBan, pictured at St Ita's, the school she founded after being dismissed from her teaching post following her arrest during the Easter Rising. She was vociferously opposed to the Anglo-Irish Treaty, calling it 'the grossest act of betrayal that Ireland ever endured'.

22. *Left*. Eithne Coyle O'Donnell (1897–1987), like Mary MacSwiney an anti-treaty republican. Born in County Donegal, she founded the first unit of the Cumann na mBan in that county in 1918 and was national president throughout the 1930s.

23. *Above.* Harry Boland (1887–1922), Michael Collins (1890–1922) and Eamon de Valera in February 1922.

24. *Right.* Sean Lemass (1899–1971). Lemass joined the Irish Volunteers in 1915 and was an active participant in the Easter Rising and the Civil War of 1922–3. He was elected to the Dail in 1924 and, when de Valera became President of Ireland in 1959, Lemass was appointed Taoiseach, a position he held until 1966.

25. *Above.* John Hume, then vice-chairman of the Derry Citizens' Action Committee, Gerry Fitt, MP for Belfast West, and Ivan Cooper, chairman of the Derry Citizens' Action Committee, outside the House of Commons, January 1969. They were in London to hand in a petition demanding an inquiry into alleged police terrorism in the Bogside of Derry earlier that month.

26. *Opposite, top.* John Hume, Austin Currie, Paddy O'Hanlon, all Stormont opposition MPs, and Bernadette Devlin, Independent MP for Mid-Ulster, on a sit-in hunger strike outside 10 Downing Street in London in October 1971. They were demanding a public enquiry into the treatment of the detainees in Northern Ireland.

27. *Opposite, bottom.* John Hume, SDLP leader, with Seamus Mallon, Deputy First Minister of the new Northern Ireland government, in November 1999.

28. Sinn Féin Chief Negotiator,
Martin McGuinness,
July 2005.

29. Gerry Adams,
Sinn Féin President,
in May 2005, backed
by a Belfast mural
of hunger-striker
Bobby Sands.

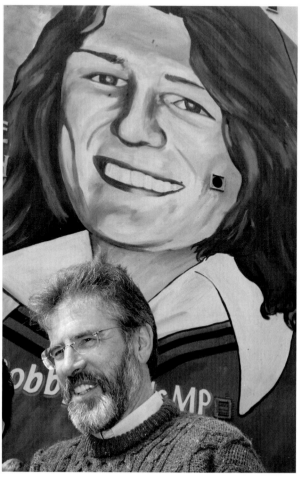

The story of the Northern Ireland peace process is a familiar one, and has frequently been well told.[174] Sinn Féin's Gerry Adams had apparently been in indirect dialogue with British politicians during 1986–7, and had known for many years people such as the Catholic priest Father Alec Reid, who had been involved in the 1970s in negotiating an end to Belfast intra-republican feuds, and who now pressed republicans towards a shift away from their violent struggle. More weighty still, in practice, was the engagement of constitutional-nationalist leader John Hume, whose 1990s arguments stressed both the justification for, and the genuine promise of, a return to more peaceful nationalist politics. The SDLP leader had been involved in Reid's own initial attempts to refashion nationalism and nationalist relationships: 'In 1986 ... Fr Alex Reid of Clonard monastery approached the Fianna Fáil leader and subsequent Taoiseach Charles Haughey, together with John Hume, to encourage dialogue with Sinn Féin up to the highest level, centred on the concept of self-determination.'[175] And, in Hume's view, there now existed no justification for the IRA's violence, none whatever:

> The stated reasons by the IRA for armed struggle were that the British were in Ireland defending their own interests by force – economic and strategic interests – and that they were preventing the Irish people from exercising the right to self-determination. I have argued that while these reasons were historically correct, they are no longer true in today's new Europe.[176]

And he saw peace as something which would emerge from community will: 'there now exists', Hume had proclaimed in November 1993, 'the best opportunity for peace in many years ... there is a burning desire for peace in both sections of our community and I hope that both governments will bring it to fruition as soon as possible'.[177] At the start of 1995 he repeated the same conviction: 'As we enter 1995, in a totally peaceful atmosphere, there can be no doubt of the enormous commitment of all sections of our community to the peace process.'[178]

Liaison between republicans and the British was ongoing, and in public the framework was established by the London and Dublin governments for an inclusive process of politics in the north. The December 1993 Joint Declaration of Prime Minister John Major and Taoiseach Albert Reynolds (the Downing Street Declaration) committed both governments to working for a new northern politics founded on consent and also on relationships within Northern Ireland, across Ireland as a whole, and between Ireland and Britain. When a Provisional IRA cessation of military operations emerged at the end of August 1994, the peace process received an injection of energy. This remained a fragile situation (the IRA Army Council's decision in favour of the ceasefire had not, for example, been unanimous). But even after a break in the IRA cessation – with a brief return to violence during 1996–7 – there seemed real momentum towards change, and a renewed IRA ceasefire of July 1997 allowed for inclusive talks which, in April 1998, produced the Belfast (or Good Friday) Agreement. This promised equality, respect and partnership as the basis for the three-stranded (Northern Irish, Irish, Irish-British) relationships involved, and it set out the framework for the new politics of Northern Ireland: recognition of the legitimacy of majority opinion in the north regarding the constitutional position of Northern Ireland; the establishment of a Northern Irish Assembly and a power-sharing Executive; the creation of north–south and east–west Councils, to reflect Irish, and Irish–British, realities and interests; and commitment to human rights, equality, prisoner release, the decommissioning of paramilitary weapons, and the pursuit of policing reform.

For all of its flaws, the peace process did involve a lower level of Troubles-related deaths. In 1999 there were 7 Troubles-generated fatalities; a decade earlier in 1989, the figure had been 81; a decade before that in 1979, it had been 125, with the IRA alone killing 91 people. For our purposes, however, the key questions concern the changes which all of this involved within Irish nationalism, and the reasons behind those shifts. For the great change which made possible the Northern Ireland peace process was the new direction in which Provisional republican nationalism turned in the 1990s, easily the most significant change in Irish politics in the last decades of the twentieth century. The republican movement had based its politics on the necessity of violence, on the futility of more conventional methods, on the impossibility of accepting a reformed Northern Ireland, and on the refusal to recognize the implications of unionist majority opposition to republican advance. All these aspects of their thinking were now to change, as the nature of republican struggle was judged in need of dramatic overhaul.

The new Sinn Féin not only became far more conspicuous and powerful within the Sinn Féin–IRA marriage, but it also altered its ideas of what the goals of the marriage were to be. Ideas which had long been part of constitutional-nationalist (and, indeed, British-governmental) thinking – such as devolved power-sharing in Belfast, recognition of the consent principle for northern unionists, a moderate Irish dimension in terms of institutional relationships between north and south – were all now adopted by militant republicanism. Socialism was still mentioned, but far less prominently than before. Sinn Féin Youth – the official youth wing of the party – held its first National Congress in Dublin in 1998, and proclaimed goals which reflected socialism's less than pre-eminent position within the reformed ideology: 'Sinn Féin Youth are committed to Irish independence, the ending of partition and a complete British withdrawal from our country. We believe that an independent Irish republic is a fundamental right of the Irish people.... Sinn Féin Youth is committed to a socialist Irish republic'; 'We are clear in our goals ... We want Irish independence, we want peace, we want democracy and we want socialism. We will not rest until we have achieved all this.'[179] Even more emphatically, a Sinn Féin economic policy document from the previous year had declared that 'In essence, Sinn Féin's vision is a socialist society that grants economic justice to all its people', while simultaneously stating the party's economic objectives for Ireland in terms that had nothing necessarily socialist about them at all: 'to provide sustainable and dignified livelihoods for all its citizens; to develop economic resources, human and material, to their fullest; and to create an economic base which reflects the social and cultural values of all the Irish people and which fulfils their material needs and aspirations'.[180] The party now tended to focus more prominent attention than before on the politics of communal equality (regarding health, housing, transport) rather than on the violent overthrow of the state itself. This was still, of course, communally-rooted nationalist struggle. Certainly, 1990s northern republicans saw the notion of community as central to their nationalism: in 1997, for example, Sinn Féin declared 'the role of community' to be 'the core starting point of any economic policy'.[181]

The republican movement presented the 1998 Agreement as a transitional one, a stepping stone on the road to traditional sovereign unity and independence for Ireland: 'We are Irish republicans,' Gerry

Adams declared in 1998. 'We want an end to partition . . . The reality is that the Good Friday Agreement is not a peace settlement. It does not claim to be. However, it is a basis for advancement. It is transitional.'[182] Yet the logic of the Agreement most pressingly involved the advancing of nationalist communal interests within the north itself, since there was no immediate prospect of a majority of Northern Irish people opting out of the UK (a point reinforced by the fact that only 50 per cent of SDLP members themselves declare that a united Ireland is the best solution for the north[183]).

And the central ideas of nationalism, such as rights of self-determination, could surely themselves be furthered in novel ways, in a fashion which reflected the northern reality of coexisting, rival nationalities. This was, perhaps, one of the most significant ways in which the peace process amended the nature of Irish nationalist thinking, and the idea of self-determination is indeed the crucial example. Traditionally, republicans had understood the concept as legitimating an independent, all-island state, completely free from British control and mandated by a single-majority preference across Ireland. Now, in the nationalism of the peace process, this was to become reformulated. National self-determination remained central to republican rhetoric, but after the 1993 Downing Street Declaration, and the 1998 Belfast Agreement itself, the concept was doubly changed in content. First, it had now been reformulated to involve simultaneous expressions of majority opinion in the two parts of Ireland: if a united Ireland was to emerge, there now had to be expressions of self-determination in this direction both from a majority in the Republic and, separately, from a majority in the north. Paragraph Four of the Downing Street Declaration spelled it out in the very precise politics of the comma (a style which now emerged as those drafting documents sought to balance out the competing demands of nationalism and unionism). Sovereignty was still central, and Irish rights of self-determination accepted, but the latter had now been reimagined:

> The Prime Minister, on behalf of the British government, reaffirms that they will uphold the democratic wish of the greater number of the people of Northern Ireland on the issue of whether they prefer to support the Union or a sovereign united Ireland. . . . The British government agree that it is for the people of the island of Ireland

alone, by agreement between the two parts respectively, to exercise their right of self-determination on the basis of consent, freely and concurrently given, North and South, to bring about a united Ireland, if that is their wish.[184]

Sinn Féin leader Gerry Adams considered this 1993 Downing Street Declaration to be innovative, in that it involved the British government addressing the issue of Irish national self-determination. In Adams's view this pointed in a hopeful direction: 'A nation cannot have half a right or a quarter right to self-determination. There can be no justification for trying to instruct the people whose right to self-determination you have just conceded, how they are to use it.' So, having addressed the self-determination issue, the British 'should now move to permit the Irish people to take up that challenge and they should seek to persuade the unionists that their future lies in that context'.[185]

But the 1993 shift had, in fact, diluted the traditional republican understanding of self-determination as a single, all-island mechanism for establishing a unitary state. This shift was again evident in the republican acceptance of the 1998 Good Friday Agreement. Adherents to this latter deal recognized

> that it is for the people of the island of Ireland alone, by agreement between the two parts respectively and without external impediment, to exercise their right to self-determination on the basis of consent, freely and concurrently given, North and South, to bring about a united Ireland, if that is their wish, accepting that this right must be achieved and exercised with and subject to the agreement and consent of a majority of the people of Northern Ireland.[186]

And the 1998 Agreement also involved a second reformulation of self-determination – more welcome to nationalist eyes, perhaps – in that it established mechanisms by which the communities in the north could self-determine the nature of that state, while it existed. Self-determination now related, not just to the establishment of a new state, but also to there being communal control over what did or did not happen within the existing one. So, under the Belfast Agreement, the workings of the proposed Northern Ireland Assembly were to be conducted, in regard to key decisions at least, on the basis of substantial support from each community; if enough representatives from one or other community didn't like something, then they would have the formal power in this newly imagined Northern Ireland to veto it. In effect, the 1998 deal institutionalized a duality of identity in many areas of life: Irish as well as British. Indeed, might Northern Ireland even follow here the examples of other parts of the United Kingdom, where dual (Scottish-British, Welsh-British, English-British) national identity had remained widespread even into the very modern period in Scotland, Wales and England?[187]

Those who have studied self-determination and nationalism are far from agreed that a right to self-determination in itself necessarily involves, for all peoples, an automatic right to territorial sovereignty;[188] so some form of rethinking of this aspect of traditional Irish nationalism possibly made sense. In any case, Irish republicans' acceptance of this subtler version of self-determination merely involved a more pragmatic kind of politics on their part. There had been no immediate prospect of old-style self-determination producing a united Ireland anyway; now, there was at least internal self-determination of the kind of state in which one had to live. Nationalists in the north seem unlikely simply to jettison the ideal of a future united Ireland: the allure of such victory and of such unambiguous power is too strong. But within a refashioned Northern Ireland, in which nationalists co-wield power and within which communal identity and interests are secured, the possibilities for a satisfactory partitioned nationalist outcome perhaps seem greater.

Pragmatism did indeed lie at the heart of the momentous shift in late-twentieth-century Irish republican nationalism.[189] Republicans had stated that their armed struggle would not end until the British declared a will to leave Northern Ireland; now a different policy had been adopted, and greater flexibility demonstrated. As early as 1992 leading Sinn Féiner Martin McGuinness conceded openly that, in the republican movement's eyes, there need be no strict adherence to the idea that British withdrawal from Northern Ireland should occur within the lifetime of a parliament: 'in a situation where you would get a British government becoming amenable to a policy of withdrawal, and in favour of the reunification of Ireland, then the period of time which it would take for them to disengage would have to be negotiated between the Irish people and that government'.[190] And ensuing years would see republicans shifting far further than that, suggesting perhaps that all along there had been more potential for fluidity and pragmatism in republican thinking than some observers had acknowledged.

But why had the Provos changed their mind so significantly? Why had they decided to end their campaign of violence against the British state, and on terms so far short of their traditional demands?[191] In part, the change in approach was born of a recognition that violence was not bringing its anticipated success. By the late 1980s it was clear to the more sharp-sighted in the movement that armed struggle was bringing, not victory, but merely stalemate. All sides – republican, loyalist, state forces – could fight on. But none could militarily win. So if the struggle was to move forward, something new was required. And there was evidence to suggest that much could be gained by republicans were their violence to be soft-pedalled. More people from the nationalist community, south as well as north of the border, would be prepared to vote for a Sinn Féin free from the opprobrium caused by frequent IRA murder and maiming.[192] The post-ceasefire years were to vindicate this assumption, as was hinted at, for example, by the party/seat share in the Northern Ireland Assembly at the time of its October 2002 Dissolution:

Ulster Unionist Party	26 seats
SDLP	24 seats
Democratic Unionist Party	22 seats
Sinn Féin	18 seats
Alliance Party	6 seats
Northern Ireland Unionist Party	3 seats
United Unionist Assembly Party	3 seats
Progressive Unionist Party	2 seats
Women's Coalition	2 seats
United Kingdom Unionist Party	1 seat
Independent Unionist	1 seat

Indeed, in June 2001 the SDLP had been overtaken by Sinn Féin in the Westminster General Election, winning only three seats to the republicans' four; and this trend was reinforced at the UK General Election on Thursday, 5 May 2005, which resulted in the following distribution of seats: DUP 9; Sinn Féin 5; SDLP 3; UUP 1. In votes, too, this 2005 Westminster election showed republican strength at the polls: Sinn Féin – 174,530 votes (24.3 per cent of the vote, and a rise of 2.6 per cent); the SDLP – 125,626 votes (17.5 per cent of the vote, and a fall of 3.5 per cent).[193]

With the end of their ghettoization, post-IRA republicans could – conceivably – enjoy not merely the rewards of prisoner release or northern police reform but, ultimately, the prospect of being in coalition government both in Belfast and Dublin. Not a united Ireland, but nearer to this than the movement had been getting through the use of violence. And within the refashioned north, republican adoption of a new form of struggle would wrong-foot unionists (who would find it difficult to deal with the suspect situation of peace-process republicanism), and would allow for Sinn Féin to become the muscular defenders of daily nationalist interests: in the communal battle between two sullen political communities, nationalists could push to maximize peace-process advantage (in terms of economic, social, political and symbolic concessions).

Given that republican vision had now taken in some key realities (that unionism rather than London was the key obstacle to a united Ireland, that the economic subvention provided to the north by the United Kingdom was currently essential), there was much to recommend this new departure. Rather than republicans being outnumbered and outmanoeuvred by the combined forces of London, Dublin, Washington and constitutional northern nationalism, Sinn Féin might now be able to reverse the pattern: with these other players so keen to draw republicans away from the gun, the leverage existed for republicans themselves to be closer to the centre of mainstream politics, with Ulster's unionists being the ones who were marginalized and excluded.

None of these republican changes of mind occurred in isolation, of course. International contexts had shifted in various ways: the European Union had provided a different setting within which the United Kingdom and the Republic of Ireland could harmoniously work together and build the axis which stabilized the peace process; the involvement of the Bill Clinton regime in Washington provided a player in the 1990s negotiations who was more powerful than the British state, and a player instinctively nearer to nationalist than unionist politics; the death of Marxism suggested that the most radical of revolutionary roads had been closed down, and therefore clarified the logic of compromise;[194] the South African example suggested that oppositional groups might obtain more from peace processes than their governmental antagonists had anticipated; and so on. But the real dynamic for change lay closer to home, and the other players whose activities mattered most to republicans were those nearby. These included the British state, which had come to adopt a policy of engagement with a republican movement judged ready to move towards a different style of politics. Here, once again, Ireland presents a pattern familiar to students of conflict between state and anti-state forces internationally. For there was logic, on both sides, in attempting to build a politics within which republicans played a part, and here we are back to the practical politics of power. If a protest group can be recognized as legitimate then there is, perhaps, more chance of curtailing the escalation of aggressive protest mobilization against the state: 'Rejection by the established authorities and the denial of any legitimate part in the exercise of power, on the other hand, tends to encourage a protest organization to persist in its opposition and, perhaps, to raise its demands.'[195] Indeed, comparative reflection suggests that 'Even if aggrieved groups direct their claims at the state, they are unlikely to seek its overthrow (or radical reorganization) if they manage to attain some significant share – or believe they *can* attain such a share – of state power or influence.'[196] In a position of bloody and futile stalemate, it made sense for republicans and governments alike to work towards the incorporation of the rebels into the system; where in 1981 a leading republican had famously suggested the viability of using a combination of violence and electoralism ('with a ballot paper in this hand, and an Armalite [rifle] in this hand'[197]), now the logic lay far more with elections. In 1982 one former IRA hunger-striker was clear that Sinn Féin was needed in order to supplement violence ('the armed struggle in fact needed a sound political machine geared to use itself as another weapon to help rid us of foreign imperialism north and south of our falsely divided country'[198]); now, the sound political machine was to be the main vehicle.

And, as so often in our story, personal relationships played a key part here as the process developed, whether in Gerry Adams's good relationship with Fianna Fáil leaders Albert Reynolds and Bertie Ahern, and indeed with British politician Mo Mowlam; or in Martin Mc-Guinness's amiable dealings with Reynolds also; or in the Dublin–London relationships which provided the framework for so much change (evident, for example, in the often good relations between Taoiseach and UK Prime Minister[199]).

So when republicans faced a choice between continued violent struggle and a more promising change in strategy, they chose the latter. It was not that violence was entirely or urgently eschewed: for years, the leverage derived from promising the final abandonment of the gun was played to full effect. But the change in republican terminology did reflect a material alteration in Provo nationalism. Where in the past words such as 'peace' had been used – understandably enough – against the IRA, and had been monopolized by republicans' opponents, now the republican movement itself deployed such eirenic terms again and again, presenting themselves (not without irony or justification) as the key initiators of the peace process in Ireland. Thus Gerry Adams, whose earlier career had been in a very aggressive and bloody republicanism,[200] now produced a shelf of books with peaceful titles (*Towards a Lasting Peace, A Pathway to Peace, The Quest for Peace, Making Peace in Ireland*). Rhetorically, republicans had become peace-makers. The IRA repeatedly affirmed its commitment to the peace process ('Oglaigh na hEireann [the IRA] supports the peace process. We want it to work. We affirm that our cessation is intact'; 'The IRA leadership is committed to making the peace process work'[201]); and the 1998 Belfast Agreement had been founded on a verbal adherence to non-violence ('We reaffirm our total and absolute commitment to exclusively democratic and peaceful means of resolving differences on political issues, and our opposition to any use or threat of force by others for any political purpose, whether in regard to this agreement or otherwise'[202]).

Republicans' verbal commitment to the ending of physical-force methods was complemented by some public gestures of symbolic prominence. Sinn Féin's Alex Maskey, as Lord Mayor of Belfast, took part along with senior members of the British Army in an April 2003 service, in Belfast's St Anne's Cathedral, to commemorate the First World War dead. Maskey's own grandfather had been in the British Army in the 1914–18 war, and in July 2002 he and other party colleagues had already laid a wreath at the City Hall Cenotaph in Belfast to commemorate the dead of that conflict. This was a new gesture by republicans, for whom celebration of the British Army's suffering clearly jarred. And Maskey's claim to be keen to 'build a relationship between republicans and the unionist community', and to have made 'efforts to promote reconciliation',[203] should not be too casually dismissed. From an Irish republican point of view, the gestures made during Maskey's year as Belfast Mayor were significant: 'I do think people have taken note of my theme of office, which was Belfast, a city of equals.'[204]

In all of this, the appeal of power in a personal sense (political office, with its associated influence and blandishments) played its part. But there had also to be more to it than that, in order to bring so many nationalist voters along in the same direction. Unlike a unionist community which greeted the peace process suspiciously and which grew to dislike and distrust it more year by year, nationalist Ireland – and certainly the nationalist north – has enthused over the 1998 Good Friday arrangement. The referendum on the Good Friday Agreement in Northern Ireland in 1998 itself saw 71.1 per cent of people vote yes – but this included only a bare majority of unionists, and rested on huge nationalist support (98.6 per cent of SDLP party members, for example, voted for the Agreement in this referendum[205]). Even after enthusiasm began to dim in subsequent years, nationalist support remained comparatively high: one opinion poll published in October 2002 suggested that unionist support for the Belfast Agreement had fallen to 33 per cent, but that nationalist support stood at 82 per cent.[206]

For many nationalists saw momentum taking them in their pre-ferred direction. If the police were reformed, if equality legislation were reinforced, if symbolism in the north became dually Irish-British rather than British alone, then all these things showed that history was moving in the right direction. The Good Friday Agreement was not an end to the nationalist struggle, but rather a redefinition of it: and within the new game, nationalists seemed to be gaining.

It was not that everything had changed in northern nationalism, of course. For years after 1998 the republican movement not only retained the capacity for renewed violence, but also carried out intimidation, organization and violent actions in practice. This caused concern among some constitutional-nationalist rivals about the bullying meth-ods used by republicans to acquire and maintain power. SDLP MP for South Down Eddie McGrady was very lucid on this point, being highly critical of the 'green fascists' of the republican movement: 'Sinn Féin politically is the IRA on the ground when it suits them. Every community knows that. They know who they are. So this takeover of community worries me sick.'[207] As the party whose arguments had won the day in 1998, the SDLP could legitimately feel aggrieved that it was Sinn Féin who were gaining ground in post-Agreement politics in the north. The SDLP did fare rather better in the 2005 UK General Election than some had feared, winning three seats; and they had done this on the back of arguments for the Good Friday Agreement, for a full ending to republican violence, and for unionists moving faster towards accommodation with their nationalist neighbours. As post-Hume party leader Mark Durkan put it, 'We stand for the whole of the [Belfast] Agreement ... the SDLP has worked to make a success of every part of the Agreement'; 'The only way to force the peace from paramilitaries and force the pace from unionists is by voting for a stronger SDLP.'[208]

As ever, the appeal of constitutional nationalism related partly, therefore, to its non-violent expression of communal politics (not now quite as decisive an advantage over Sinn Féin, given that many in the electorate no longer saw republicans through bloodstained lenses: anyone aged eighteen when voting in the 2005 General Election had been only a young child at the time of the 1994 IRA ceasefire). And – again, as ever – SDLP politics involved more than anti-partitionism. In the November 2003 Northern Ireland Assembly elections the party still described itself as '100 per cent for a United Ireland', but this commitment to constitutional change was only made as the last item of a list of pledges: the prior issues on this list (policing, economic growth, jobs, poverty, schools, hospitals, roads, rates, and water charges[209]) were all of them ones which could be as effectively dealt with within as without a Northern Ireland context. The quotidian politics of reform had, perhaps, triumphed within nationalism at last, and this was reinforced at the 2005 UK General Election too: 'My priorities for South Belfast,' declared the (in the event, successful) SDLP candidate Dr Alasdair McDonnell,

are:
Water – No to extra water charges
Crime – No to crime
Health – No to waiting lists

Planning – Stop over-development; Protect open green spaces
Education – Committed to improving education provision for all
Housing – Assistance for first-time home buyers.[210]

The battle within nationalism remained a crucial one, if one which was often obscured by the conflict between unionist and nationalist politics. And there continued to be key differences between the two northern nationalist parties. Despite their great shift in emphasis at the end of the twentieth century, much within republicans' politics still remained familiar, and these continuities helped the movement to retain heartland support. Republicans still stressed that the most significant responsibility for producing and facilitating progress in the north lay with the British government; they still retained a rhetorical commitment, at least, to the achievement of a united and independent Ireland; they still complained about British or unionist wrongs in the past (state-loyalist collusion, for example); and they retained a veneration for the struggle waged in their previous phase. Indeed, as new violence diminished, so the matter of appropriate memory of past battles became of symbolic importance, particularly as an issue of local remembrance. This was reflected in the 1990s aims set out by the Tyrone National Graves Association: 'to erect and maintain fitting graves and memorials in honour of all patriot dead in Tyrone; to organize fitting commemorations in honour of the patriot dead in Tyrone; to compile and keep records of such graves and memorials'. To this end, during 1996, the Tyrone NGA held twenty-three commemorations and twelve wreath-laying ceremonies (speakers at commemorations including prominent Sinn Féiners Jim Gibney and Francie Molloy[211]). So, while the new Sinn Féin redefined itself as it flourished (being, by 2001, the largest single party in Belfast City Hall in terms of the number of its Councillors), there remained continuities with an aggressive past.

Certainly, the IRA retained well into the peace-process period sufficient weapons and ammunition and explosive material for them to be militarily able to restart their war if they judged it advantageous to do so. As late as 2002 the Provisionals were still active (in terms, for example, of intelligence-gathering), and this helped to strengthen unionist fears about republican intentions: the IRA might not be fighting its war against the British state, but neither was it utterly dormant. As the intelligence war continued, so too did the north's culture of mistrust. It was true that there seemed no imminent threat to the mainstream republican ceasefire policy: dissident republicans had been unable to construct a seriously threatening assault on the Provo leadership's hold on republican minds and sympathies, and during the peace process the Provisional IRA had demonstrated a brutal willingness and capacity to silence republican opinion which differed from its own orthodoxy:[212] where the British had long condemned the IRA for its violent silencing of opinion and its ruthlessly authoritarian style of command-politics, it could perhaps now implicitly welcome aspects of this, as one means of preventing the peace process from fragmenting on the republican side. This had its ugly aspect, as the state effectively closed its eyes to some of the intracommunal intimidation and violence practised by republicans in their own areas. And yet broad reflection on the nature of the state should, at least, cause us to feel no surprise at such an approach. If 'order maintenance'[213] is indeed the primary function of state government, then one might not be surprised to find that the authorities have tolerated in Northern Ireland the intimidation of local communities as a price for preventing large-scale disorder in the form of bombings and killings in a major campaign.

None of this diminishes the horror of what victims of modern republican violence have experienced. As so often, a nationalism framed as a struggle for freedom has also constricted key liberties. The IRA was still very much alive in 2005: the Northern Ireland Independent Monitoring Commission noted in May of that year that the IRA was still recruiting and training members, gathering intelligence, and involving itself very heavily in criminality.[214] This all had sharp echoes of recent experience, with republican involvement in a major (£26.5 million) Belfast bank robbery in December 2004, and in the killing outside a central Belfast bar in January 2005 of a thirty-three-year-old Belfast father of two, Robert McCartney. He and a friend had become involved in an argument one night in Magennis's Bar, and the two men were stabbed and brutally beaten – McCartney fatally so – in an horrific attack involving many people, some of whom were members of the Provisional movement. Popular revulsion at the murder focused clear light on what had by now become the central political problem in the politics of the north, that of having a major political party (Sinn Féin) whose share of electoral support clearly meant that it had to be involved in any Northern Ireland government, but whose links to a brutal paramilitary army meant that it could not at present become part of such a regime.

To many, the argument and the path seemed clear. 'Nothing less than complete and open surrender of weapons and disbandment of the IRA will now be sufficient' to relaunch the peace process, declared the *Financial Times*.[215] Taoiseach Bertie Ahern voiced his view that Sinn Féin now faced 'total exclusion' in the United States unless the IRA disbanded and ended criminality.[216] A March 2005 opinion poll recorded that 60 per cent of northern nationalists (77 per cent of SDLP voters and 44 per cent of Sinn Féin voters) thought that the IRA should disband immediately, while 70 per cent of nationalist voters (82 per cent SDLP, 59 per cent Sinn Féin) thought that they should decommission all their weapons.[217] The decommissioning issue had plagued the peace process for years: despite Gerry Adams's claim that the issue of IRA weapons-decommissioning had not been mentioned before the first IRA ceasefire,[218] his own words showed that the issue of 'how the IRA can hand over its weapons' had been raised prior to August 1994.[219]

Now, over a decade later and in the midst of pressure on republicans in the wake of the multi-million-pound Belfast bank robbery and the Robert McCartney killing, Adams on 6 April 2005 made a speech in Belfast, in which he stated that in his view there was now a better road for republicans to take than that of paramilitary violence:

> In the past I have defended the right of the IRA to engage in armed struggle. I did so because there was no alternative for those who would not bend the knee, or turn a blind eye to oppression, or for those who wanted a national republic. Now there is an alternative.... The way forward is by building political support for republican and democratic objectives across Ireland and by winning support for these goals internationally. I want to use this occasion therefore to appeal to the leadership of Oglaigh na hEireann [the IRA] to fully embrace and accept this alternative. Can you take courageous initiatives which will achieve your aims by purely political and democratic activity?[220]

There was no doubt that the bank robbery and the Magennis's Bar killing – together with the less than candid responses to each from republican leaders – had reinforced a sense of scepticism about republican political honesty. Longstanding sceptics such as the leading Irish poet Paul Durcan found the IRA and Sinn Féin's equivocations during the spring of 2005 unbelievable:

> Every day Sinn Féin and the IRA have come out with a new batch of lies ... Obviously they've murdered a lot of people over the years, but they're in the business of murdering language. Almost every day there's a new set of lies ... Words have become devalued. If there was a Nobel Prize for propaganda, Sinn Féin would have long ago won that prize.[221]

Even a long-term interlocutor with republicans such as Denis Bradley was driven to comment, 'There was a time when if the Provos said something, 98% of the time you believed them. I think that they have gone down in the credibility stakes. I think that the McCartney situation was badly handled from that perspective.'[222]

So republican words were not widely trusted. Yet significant-sounding words were forthcoming. On 28 July 2005 the IRA delivered a much-anticipated statement which, by republican-historical stand-ards, was clear and highly significant. The IRA leadership had 'formally ordered an end to the armed campaign', to take effect that afternoon. 'All volunteers have been instructed,' the statement continued, 'to assist the development of purely political and democratic programmes through exclusively peaceful means. Volunteers must not engage in any other activities whatsoever.'[223] IRA units had been ordered to dump arms, and decommissioning was promised to follow. Had militant Irish nationalism's long twentieth century finally come to an end?

Irish Taoiseach Bertie Ahern promptly hailed the significance of the IRA announcement (it had inaugurated 'a new era' for Ireland), and called for decommissioning to follow ('I'd like to see it happening sooner rather than later'[224]). Broadly, Irish nationalists agreed on the grand scale of the IRA's gesture: 'there can be little doubt this statement is a watershed in terms of the history of violent republicanism', declared the *Irish News*: it was an 'enormously positive step' towards peace.[225] Beyond the Irish nationalist family, however, responses were more cautious. 'NO MORE DECEIT, WE WANT ACTION', loudly proclaimed the unionist *News Letter*: the IRA's July 2005 statement 'contained too many gaps and omissions for law-abiding people in Northern Ireland to take comfort. They did not say the war was over nor apologize to their victims, while the IRA structure is to remain in place.'[226] The *Belfast Telegraph* commented that

> After so many false dawns, there is bound to be a degree of doubt about yesterday's statement by the IRA announcing an end to the 'armed struggle'. But taken at face value, it means that one of the longest and bloodiest terrorist campaigns in Europe is finally over, and that must be a reason for relief. . . . The IRA's actions still have to match its words, but there is no doubt that internationally, this statement will be regarded as a major step forward.[227]

Democratic Unionist Party (DUP) leader Ian Paisley was predictably more forthright: 'The IRA statement is neither historic nor credible,' he said. 'Remember, the words of the IRA count for nothing. . . . We have had these words all before. The proof of this IRA pudding will be in the eating. They can wrap this statement up any way they want, but it is action, not words, that will count.'[228]

But even when action came, it still appeared too ambiguous to some. On Monday, 26 September 2005 the Independent International Commission on Decommissioning (IICD) Chairman, John de Chastelain, announced that the IRA had – in his view, as well as that of his IICD colleagues Tauno Nieminen and Andrew Sens, and two clergy witnesses (Methodist Harold Good and Catholic Alec Reid) – met their obligation to decommission their entire weaponry (an arsenal which had included handguns, rifles, machine guns, rocket-launchers, flame-throwers, bomb detonators and Semtex). Responses were predictably varied: 'momentous stuff', asserted the nationalist *Daily Ireland*;[229] 'It's Just a Cover-Up', proclaimed the front-page headline of the unionist *News Letter*. DUP leader Ian Paisley was far from happy in public: 'There were no photographs, no detailed inventory and no detail of the destruction of these arms. To describe today's act as being transparent would be the falsehood of the century.'[230] The credibility of this grand act of decommissioning was certainly not helped when, at an October 2005 public meeting in Belfast, Father Reid likened Ulster's unionists to the Nazis (hardly a comparison likely to strengthen his credentials with a unionist audience, or one justified by historical reality). And even into 2006 there was evidence that at least some IRA weapons had been retained by the organization, and that low-level IRA activity continued.[231]

Yet this decommissioning moment surely was a significant symbol of the great change which had occurred in republican Irish nationalism. Had it been suggested fifteen years earlier (when the IRA were killing fifty people in a year) that by 2005 the Provisionals would not only have ended their war against the British state, but would also have decommissioned most of their weapons in the verifying presence of British-appointed officials, it would have seemed a revolutionary prospect indeed. The republican struggle had, quite simply, changed, the demands of the community and the realities of contemporary opportunities for power necessitating as much.

Some issues did remain the same. The establishment of a Northern Irish police force acceptable to both political communities remained a challenge now, just as it had been at the start of the Troubles, and just as it had been recognized by nationalists for so long. John Hume, as deputy leader of the SDLP in 1975, had argued that 'The problem of providing effective policing in all parts of Northern Ireland remains central to any lasting solution to our problems.'[232] And he had surely been right, the police being arguably the most significant practical and symbolic example of the relation of the state to its people. Yet could those people – in the north, peoples – be reconciled over such matters? It seemed clear from the 2001 Northern Ireland Census that neither community was going to enjoy a sufficient majority to enable it to win the intercommunal battle (44 per cent of the people having a Catholic community background, 53 per cent Protestant, and 3 per cent other). These peoples were as divided as ever into sectarian confessional-political camps: it remained a chilling fact for Sinn Féin's ostensibly non-sectarian strategists that as late as 2004 Ian Paisley's DUP had more Catholic support than Sinn Féin had Protestant.[233] But the nature of the nationalist struggle had crucially altered, with militant republicans having been brought much closer to the mainstream of northern politics.

6

Few Catholics and nationalists born in what is now the
Republic of Ireland have ever cared all that much about what
is now Northern Ireland.

Conor Cruise O'Brien[234]

How far has the existence of Northern Ireland for the best part of a
century led to the emergence of two different nationalisms in Ireland,
north and south respectively? Do northern nationalists now have more
in common with northern unionists (in terms of experience, context,
preoccupations, culture) than they do with Irish nationalists in the
Republic of Ireland? Has nationalism in Ireland been partitioned?

One way of beginning to answer these questions is to consider
evolving attitudes to the north within southern nationalism in recent
decades. Late-twentieth-century southern nationalism retained an irredentist flavour,[235] and even from the start of the post-1960s Troubles,
there have been elements within southern life supportive of militant
northern nationalism. Yet mainstream nationalists in the Republic
have long eschewed violence as the appropriate northern way forward.
Jack Lynch (as Fianna Fáil Taoiseach in early 1973) had made it quite
clear to UK Prime Minister Edward Heath that Dublin simply could
not afford to assume responsibility for Northern Ireland[236] (one of the
key realities blocking the path to a united Ireland being the question
of its economic practicality). But the picture emerging from close
inspection of southern attitudes towards the north is complicated and
rather fluid.

Levels of support in the Republic for British withdrawal of troops
and rule from Northern Ireland dropped significantly as the conflict
there progressed: in 1978, 78 per cent of southerners stated a desire for
British withdrawal; by 1988, only 53 per cent said they wanted even
British troops to be withdrawn. Yet the southern Irish aspiration
towards Irish unity apparently remained, levels of declared support for
ultimate unification being as high as 82 per cent in 1991.[237] Indeed,
rhetorical keenness for an end to Irish partition has been relatively

persistent: opinion polls in the Republic showed, in 1968, that 85 per cent of a sample of people in the south expressed a preference for Irish unity; in 1983 the equivalent figure was 76 per cent (although that same year saw only a quarter of people in the Republic saying that they actually expected unification to happen within twenty-five years).[238] So there were varying but clearly high levels of support for the idea that, ultimately, Irish unity should emerge (in 1989, 73 per cent in the Republic said that they favoured a united Ireland).[239]

How much of a priority was this? In the 1987 Republic of Ireland General Election campaign, when asked, 'In this general election campaign what are the main issues which the parties should be concerned about?' (2 February 1987), only 3 per cent mentioned Northern Ireland (compared, for example, with 84 per cent mentioning unemployment). Even among Fianna Fáil voters, only 2 per cent mentioned Northern Ireland as such a main issue.[240] Only once in the entire 1969–92 period was Northern Ireland considered the most important issue in a southern election by more than 1 per cent of voters (the exception was 1973, and even then only 12 per cent so cited it).[241] So while the north was never off the southern political agenda, it only very rarely managed to dominate it in terms of people's electoral priorities. Just as partition was not discussed much in the Treaty debates of the early 1920s, so partition was largely ignored in practice by governments and people in the south in terms of urgent political priorities.

When people in the Republic were asked, in the early 1990s, whether they would be prepared to pay higher taxes in the event of a settlement in Northern Ireland bringing about a closer relationship between north and south, a striking 75 per cent of respondents said no (19 per cent yes, 6 per cent don't know).[242] And it's easy enough to see why nationalists in the south would consider the north to represent a destabilizing influence on their settled community: the irruption of violence, of anti-state unionists, and indeed of aggressive northern nationalists, would all threaten the stable democratic evolution of a state which could also hardly bear the necessary economic burden of unity. Southern politicians of nationalist hue – Charles J. Haughey, Fianna Fáil leader from 1979 to 1992, among them – could play a green card when not in power, only to do little about it should the responsibility of government return. For even Haughey's party – the most obviously nationalistic of the main southern parties – has in practice again and again showed itself to be more concerned with the stability and well-being of the Republic of Ireland than with the potentially damaging prospect of trying in practice to unite the divided island.

Until Sean Lemass met Terence O'Neill in 1965, there had been little direct contact between Ireland's two high-political elites. None of this should really surprise us. Newly independent states tend to guard their sovereignty and security and culture carefully, and the independent Irish state was no exception. If there was a choice to be made between sovereignty and unity, then there was little hesitation in choosing the former; and such attitudes were pervasive and enduring. (It is, perhaps, telling that it was not until its fourth edition that the leading modern textbook on politics in the Republic came to include a chapter on the question of Northern Ireland.[243])

As in Britain, so also in nationalist southern Ireland there remains much ignorance and indifference regarding the north; and in the south there is comparatively little enthusiasm in practice for doing all that much about the uniting of the divided island. Opinion in the Republic tends to support the idea of unification as an aspiration but it is very much a low-level priority, and there seems no obvious practical route to attaining it anyway. So it took many years for Dublin to grant the idea of Northern Ireland's legitimacy, and it was simpler to combine several responses at once: to engage in selective rhetorical intervention, to ignore the question of unity in practice, and to demand that Britain deal with the undoubted and serious problems which existed for nationalists north of the border. By the time of the 1998 Belfast Agreement, southern opinion was almost unanimous in backing a deal which seemed to resolve the violent conflict, to give nationalists a better deal in the north, and to promise no immediate change at all in the border. Yet despite this – and in spite of suggestions by articulate unionists that 'an unrealistic adherence to Irish unity' be sidelined by northern nationalists[244] – the goal of a united Ireland still remains part of nationalist political rhetoric and imagination.

And southern political parties were reluctant to jettison the whole tradition of aggressive republicanism, symbolically at least. In October 2001 Fianna Fáil instigated Dublin state funerals for ten IRA men who had been executed during the 1919–21 War for Independence. The bodies having been exhumed from Mountjoy Jail, tricolour-draped coffins and a formal military cortège reflected the post-northern Troubles desire of the main southern party to celebrate and claim some of Irish nationalism's fighting history. Key Fianna Fáil adviser Martin Mansergh was himself clear that southern, constitutional nationalists had to lay claim to what might otherwise be seen as a legacy of history to paramilitary republicans: 'I think it's very import-ant that the state should not make a present of the various elements that went to make it up; it shouldn't make a present of all that to radical or militant republicanism. . . . I think the state is the heir to the War of Independence.'[245]

There were pre-echoes of this in earlier Fianna Fáil politics, a shrewd player such as Charles Haughey – 'always a colourful and controversial figure'[246] – at times utilizing a republican posture to advantageous effect. One scholar has suggested that two key themes defined Haughey's career: 'the need to generate income by reducing the tax burden on business and the need to develop a distinctive position on the national question in order to differentiate himself from his rivals'.[247] In the post-Haughey era, Fianna Fáil now faced the prospect of persistent pressure from another republican party campaigning in the south, and this reinforced their need to claim republican heritage for themselves. For the peace-process version of Sinn Féin was slowly growing stronger in the south. The Republic's general election in 2002 saw Sinn Féin raise its number of Dáil seats from one to five, while with high-profile events to mark the 2005 centenary of the original Sinn Féin's foundation, the Gerry Adams-led party itself laid claim to nationalism's past.[248] And the modern-day Sinn Féin was well funded: the party's candidate had, for example, the highest level of spending for any individual candidate in the March 2005 by-elections.[249]

Like Sinn Féin, but on a far grander scale south of the border, Fianna Fáil itself had managed to change its central politics while retaining much support among nationalists. The party had gained power in the 1930s promising economic self-sufficiency through the discouragement of foreign investment, the creation of tariff barriers and the promotion of native industry; yet by the 1960s the same party (with, in some cases, the same leaders) was opening up the economy to Britain and to the rest of Europe, and offering incentives to foreign capital. The project of making Irish the first national language in practice had clearly died long before the end of the twentieth century, while the decline in the political power of the Catholic Church,[250] and the effective end of any but the vaguest irredentism concerning the north, also bore witness to the huge changes in Fianna Fáil's politics and context. As one leading political scientist crisply put it regarding this most powerful of Irish nationalist parties, 'The hallmarks of its earlier nationalist platform had been discarded entirely, yet the party remained as powerful as before and still claimed a monopoly of the nationalist credentials.'[251]

For the pragmatism at the heart of nationalist struggle demanded that changes be made, and that relevance to daily reality should be maintained. An imagined all-island territory was comforting, but if the longevity and success of a twenty-six-county state clashed with it, then territorial claims could be amended. If it was clear, as it was by the 1960s, that the idea of reviving the Irish language through schools had not worked, and that the use of Irish beyond schools was not spreading as widely as had been hoped, then again there was little point in pursuing something which – in this form, at least – the community did not consider to be an urgent priority. If Sinn Féinish, Griffithite economics were leading to practical problems of state survival, then they could be discarded. It has recently been argued that the central reason behind Ireland being so economically poor for so long after independence was a coalition of small farmers, Catholic Church and Irish-language lobbyists, for all of whom modernization represented a threatening force.[252] Significantly, none of these three groups now holds anything like the power they once wielded – in a then poorer Ireland – over the nationalist means of struggle.

As nationalism has changed, it has brought people with it, since it has again addressed their pressing concerns. At the Republic's General Election of 17 May 2002, Fianna Fáil won 770,748 votes out of a total 1,857,902 which were cast (a share of 41.5 per cent of the vote). In so doing, the party captured 39.1 per cent of the middle-class vote, 44.2 per cent of the working-class vote, and 48.2 per cent support among farmers. Here was cross-class neo-nationalism, rural as well as urban (Fianna Fáil under its leader Bertie Ahern won 38.4 per cent of urban votes in this election, and 47.8 per cent of rural votes.) And what had been the issues cited as important in determining people's vote? Northern Ireland enjoyed only 3 per cent here as an issue of importance, whereas the health service, for example, won 70 per cent citation.[253] Again, opinion poll evidence early in 2002 suggested that Fianna Fáil enjoyed the support of 47 per cent of the electorate: this backing was equally strong among social classes ABC1 (47 per cent) as among C2DE voters (47 per cent), and it comprised impressive levels of urban (41 per cent) as well as rural (55 per cent) support.[254]

The community had effectively contracted, for southern Irish nationalists, from thirty-two to twenty-six counties. And it was the management of the latter which demanded attention. Content analysis of party manifestoes for the 1997 General Election showed the economy to be highly significant (for Fianna Fáil, 26.7 per cent) and welfare and quality of life prominent also (Fianna Fáil, 26.7 per cent).[255] In the 1992 General Election, jobs and unemployment were persistently and easily the most important of issues in determining people's voting intention.[256]

So a party whose nationalism had evolved dramatically since its early, de Valera-led days, could still command huge support (with eighty-one seats in a Dáil of 166 members in 2003, for example), and did so by shaping its nationalism to suit changing community priorities. This approach enjoyed much success for the Republic as a whole. Having long suffered appallingly high levels of unemployment, by May 2000 1.67 million people were employed in a state whose population was around 3.75 million; the unemployment rate in August 2000 was a very low 4.4 per cent.

And modern Irish nationalism in the south had shifted from an anglocentric-anglophobic political obsession born of lengthy tensions with the British neighbour, to a much more Europeanized focus. It is true that the great enthusiasm long shared by so many in southern Ireland for the European Union and its precursors (born, in part, of the economic gains which Europe repeatedly brought) has now begun to alter. Opinion poll evidence from 2001 suggested a marked ambivalence towards Europe among the Republic's population. Asked whether Ireland should 'unite fully' with, or 'do all it can to protect its independence' from, the European Union, a poll of 14–15 May produced figures of 46 per cent for the former position and 41 per cent for the latter. A similar poll held later in the same month produced respective figures of 40 per cent and 43 per cent. Supporters of the traditionally Irish nationalist Fianna Fáil party were themselves markedly split in these polls, the figures from the two surveys being (14–15 May) 51/38 per cent and (29–30 May) 41/43 per cent.[257] Other twenty-first-century evidence pointed in the same direction.[258] But there is no doubt that European Union membership had profoundly affected Irish political life,[259] not least in helping to mould Irish nationalist self-image in a less British-determined shape. The confidence born of long independence, and the cultural and economic successes of the late twentieth century,[260] had produced a southern nationalism which only partly overlapped with its troubled, northern counterpart.

PART FOUR

CONCLUSION

SEVEN
EXPLAINING IRISH NATIONALISM

1

> Nation, nationality, nationalism – all have proved notoriously difficult to define, let alone to analyse.
>
> Benedict Anderson[1]

In the Introduction to this book, I set out a briefly expressed theory of nationalism, a theory which tried to explain why nationalism has so dominated modern world history. In the Conclusion, I think we need to look more closely at this argument, and at how it explains the Irish nationalist story which we have just narrated.

So what, at root, *is* nationalism? The term has arguably been both under- and over-analysed. In everyday speech and in media reportage, it's a word much more frequently used than it is defined; indeed, for most of us and for most of the time this vital concept is employed in very loose, ill-fitting and ill-considered fashion. We use it to refer to a great range of different phenomena around the world and across historical periods, casually including under this one term people and movements and ideologies and episodes of marked variety; and we tend to do so without considering the precise meaning of the word, or indeed its relevance or explanatory usefulness regarding the things we so describe.

But the term so ill-defined in popular usage is one to which vast amounts of academic attention have been devoted. If anything, scholars have so over-analysed this concept that it is difficult simultaneously to grasp all the features and qualities which are attributed to it, and to reach a single understanding of what nationalism is and what it does.[2]

So what, precisely, do we mean when we use the term nationalism? When did nationalism arise as a force in human history, and why, and where did it do so? Why has it been so powerful and pervasive a feature of the lives of so many people and communities across the world? In what ways has it changed over time, and what has remained consistent within it despite these transformations? Why has nationalism so eclipsed other organizing, mobilizing ideologies (such as socialism or feminism), why has it so transcended other units of identity (the region, the sub-culture, the generation), and why has it managed to rival and – for many – to outlive even its most powerful rival, religion?

The term 'nationalism' is far more recent than 'nation': although there are claims that it appeared much earlier,[3] the word 'nationalism' seems to have emerged properly in the 1770s, with its more fully political sense only gaining expression in the 1840s.[4] Dictionary definitions of the word offer some introductory help as to its range of meanings: '*1a* patriotic feeling, principles, etc. *b* an extreme form of this; chauvinism. *2* a policy of national independence';[5] 'Devotion to one's nation; a policy of national independence'.[6] But these provide only a sketchy outline of the word's richly detailed connotations, and they do nothing to explain why nationalism arose, what purposes it serves, how it has changed over time through history, or why it has been so varied across different geographical settings. Nor do they address the fact that nationalism can be seen as an ideology and also as an interwoven set of practices, campaigns or actions.[7]

The true explanation for nationalism lies with the concepts of community, struggle and power; and **community**[8] must be our starting-point.

> To belong to a given community, to be connected with its members by indissoluble and impalpable ties of common language, historical memory, habit, tradition and feeling, is a basic human need no less natural than that for food or drink or security or procreation. One nation can understand and sympathize with the institutions of another only because it knows how much its own mean to itself.[9]

Although people understandably sometimes resist the idea of a restrictive human nature, it is now clear from scientific research that we humans are sociable by nature, that our brain is a 'social organ'.[10]

In understanding why we engage in social action as we do, it's vital to recognize that the human instinct towards sociality and group aggregation has well-established biological dimensions: 'The biological reason why species acquire the adaptations necessary for sociality is that aggregating and living in groups foster their fitness (that is to say, chances of surviving, reproducing, and propagating their genes) better than living alone.'[11] This is not to say that all our activity can be mechanically explained in terms of our doing something in order to maximize the chances of genetic survival. It does mean, however, that the mind which makes choices (in favour of group identity or nationalism, for example) is a mind which has been moulded through a process of evolutionary adaptation, and that unless we acknowledge this we are only offering a partial explanation of what happens when a nationalist movement arises.

If we want to explain the interrelated phenomena of nationalist ideology and activity (rather than merely to describe their history in interesting ways), then we need to note what physically happens when the mind makes choices, and to reflect on how that process might inform our understanding of the choices that are made, the constraints upon those choices and the impulses which drive and determine them.[12] Historians have tended to be much better at those materialist explanations which relate to economic structures or social contexts than they have been at addressing the more immediate material question of what happens when we actually have a thought, make a choice, and so on. But we need to consider both these materialist dimensions, rather than neglecting what scientific research can offer to our understanding of social activity.[13] It is not that everything can be simply explained, for example, in terms of biological adaptation. A sociobiologist might argue that genetic impulsion pushes humans towards nepotistic, group behaviour of the kind that we find in nationalism, in order to further the replication and survival of one's own genes and characteristics; in essence, such a case would involve the assumption that nations are a natural extension of those kinship groups selected by genetic evolution, and that nationalism is a mechanism biologically evolved in order to promote individual self-interest.[14] But that is not the argument offered here. For one thing, evolutionary natural selection seems to proceed at the level of the gene or, at most, that of the individual; as such, there is no direct biological link explaining why one should be genetically driven to act as a nationalist (certainly not as a nationalist who sacrifices himself or herself for the sake of the nation: the ruthlessly selfish gene would, in fact, militate against such a course of action).[15]

In fact, it's better not to seek too neat a biological explanation for a phenomenon as protean and vast as nationalism. It's clear that the mind has a great measure of autonomy from genetic impulsion (hence the enormous range of human responses to a phenomenon such as nationalism). And even evolutionary psychologists (with their emphasis on genetic programming, and their depictions of the mind as a computational system of organs produced by natural selection) openly concede the explanatory importance of contextually-generated ideas, aspirations, beliefs and influences of precisely the kind with which historians normally deal. The genetically-programmed mind processes these pieces of information in physical ways, but such information – our varied and distinctive beliefs and so on – is still crucially part of our explanation of political and other changes.[16] So what is suggested here is not that biology in itself will explain all the varied complexities of actual human behaviour;[17] but rather that scientific understanding of the mind and of the brain does allow us to talk about human nature, and that this has implications for our explanation of historical change and therefore of nationalism. Indeed, we can't properly understand the power of nationalism without it. To the normal historical subjects of individual circumstance, influence, inheritance, decision-making, ambition and so forth, must be added a recognition of the broader, scientifically-established human instincts which delimit those circumstances, influences and so on, and which undermine the notion of the infinite plasticity of human behaviour.

So we *can* ask – and indeed need to ask – what it is that humans want.[18] Survival, security, protection and safety are clearly dominant instincts, as scientists who study genes forcefully point out. 'We are all survival machines'; the individual is 'a survival machine built by a short-lived confederation of long-lived genes'.[19] So neo-Darwinian evolutionary theory does contribute towards our explanation of nationalist dominance in the modern world, in helping to explain the physical context within which complex ideas such as 'nationalism' thrive and outdo their rivals. Part of the appeal of nationalism lies with human group instinct; behind this lies a desire for security; behind this lies our understanding of the genes.

Survival instinct is inbuilt and so too is a need for belonging: more particularly, the need to belong to a stable and coherent community. Such belonging is necessary not only for self-protection and for the practical achievement of necessarily cooperative goals (producing food and other goods, creating mechanisms for economic exchange); it is needed also for the building of that self-definition and identity necessary for life to become meaningfully productive and purposeful.[20] The need for belonging, bonding and attachment within groups is now very widely attested to in the psychological literature (into which historians all too rarely delve). And belonging to distinctive communities matches a deep affiliative instinct towards group life, towards effective social groups – and especially towards, not social association in general, but particular association with a perceivedly special and distinctive group.[21] Community – of the kind associated with nationalism – appears to suit human nature, collectivity meeting the needs of what are instinctively group creatures.

If we are to understand the appeal and power and nature of nationalism – to address the explanatory 'why?' of nationalism as well as the more descriptive 'what?' – then we need to consider the psychological processes which underlie it, and to grasp the emotional as well as the material rewards which it offers. Our physical needs (food, protection, the exchange of goods) cannot be met by acting singly, and our sense of meaning through identity again demands our belonging to a group – and ideally our belonging to one which we perceive to be special. So social interaction, integration, identification and relationship are all necessary;[22] familiarity, solidarity, likeness and mutual sympathy provide comforting reinforcement and make contextual sense of individual lives in ways that transcend the limitations of isolation. The essence of all this is the consensual loyalty which people give to a community, a community with which one can communicate in ways which in turn provide the foundations for meaningful lives, as we organize and interpret our knowledge of the surrounding world.

So when people seek to define nationalism by saying that it is characterized by commitment to a set of shared features (territory, descent, culture, history, and so on), they are – in a sense – doubly missing the point. First, nationalists tend not, in fact, to share actual descent, or homogeneous culture, or truly continuous history. Second, and more importantly, none of these features of perceivedly shared life is in itself essential to nationalism. There are nationalist groups which have long lacked possession of a territory (Jewish nationalists, for example), and also nationalists whose relation to their territory is far from intimate (diaspora nationalisms such as the Irish, and again the Jewish, suggest themselves). There are nations (such as the American) in which even the notion of shared and discrete descent is evidently absurd. There are many nationalist groups whose culture (religious attachment, linguistic medium) is profoundly divided within the nation, but whose national attachment remains powerful (America provides a strong and convenient example). Nor is it the case that each nation has required its own separate language (English, Irish, American, Australian and some other nationalists too have all been able to make their respective cases in English). And many nationalist groups have histories which, in fact, reflect extremely divergent rather than common relationships to their nation's history.

But the point about these perceivedly shared dimensions of national and nationalist communities is neither their objective reality (which is frequently dubious) nor their value as an essentialist checklist (since none of the listed features is in fact essential to nationalism). The importance for nationalism of these supposedly shared aspects of life is that *some* such effective media of communication are necessary as ways of creating and sustaining and giving meaning and coherence to the communities which we all (in some form) require if we are practically and emotionally and psychologically to survive.[23] These languages of communication allow us to belong, and to commit ourselves, to a mutually recognized and comprehensible group, a community with common meanings.

How does this work in fine-grained practice? The commonly cited features of nationalism are, of course, so commonly cited precisely because they do relate to the practicalities of what nationalists so often think and do. And, despite the romantic and invented nature of so much nationalist history, much of this has a deeply practical and physical quality. Individuals grouping themselves together will, of necessity, have to relate to and make sense of their physical surroundings, and thus *territory* understandably becomes crucial to national communities, most of which lastingly inhabit an identifiable homeland. Emotional attachment to familiar place or home; utilization of the land that one occupies and shares with one's neighbours; celebration of distinctive topographical features – all of this can quite predictably lead to more nationalistic interpretations of the relationship between community and specific, special territory. If this is our land, where we as a community interdepend on one another, then our claim to possession of that territory becomes vitally important. Hence the important role of map-making in the development of nationalisms.[24] Hence also the significance of first-occupancy (whether historically valid or demonstrable or not): as nationalists stress their prior historical rights to their particular territory, the cry of 'We were here first' becomes central to nationalists' territorial claim and to their perceived rights – a fact well known to those familiar with Ireland.

Territory therefore has both a practical meaning and a symbolic, historic quality: the nationalist community occupies and works this land, but it also fiercely defends particular association with and ownership of it. For some nationalists, this can lead to a supposed linkage between the specific territory occupied and the distinctive soul, identity and personality of the national community: soil and people become organically bonded in the imaginative world of the romantic nationalist. So specific, distinctive, unique geographical place is often foundational to nationalist community, in practical and imaginative fashion alike. The quotidian necessities (where you physically are, what surrounds you, how you survive, how you shape your economic life, and so on), lead to the development of more elaborate interpretations of hills, fields, mountains, sea, rivers, and, indeed, of towns, architecture and other constructed features of the national territory as you see and inhabit it. (And even the most untouched aspects of our landscape tend, of course, to be apprehended, moulded and interpreted through human eyes and culture.[25])

So the physicality of immediate surroundings is the foundation for an emotional attachment and identification, and this can increase with historical layers of communal association and activity over time. If *our* community is the one which has cultivated this land, built this economy or created these buildings, then our communal possessiveness towards this territory becomes ever more intense with time, and our sense of the value of this particular place is sharpened. If our land defines our community and our sense of self, then the unity of our territory – so important a theme in many nationalisms – becomes vital. While nationalist communities are often theorized in rather abstract terms, therefore, it is initially their very physical dimensions which help to explain them. The centrality of particular place, and the spatial-historical details of nationalist experience, must be acknowledged.[26]

So in Ireland we've seen nationalist attachment to particular territory: to the land from which survival is to be guaranteed (in the late-nineteenth-century Land War, for example); to the locality which is lyrically or sentimentally celebrated (as in Charles Kickham's local loyalties, Ernie O'Malley's Arcadian Revolutionary memoirs, or the association of later republicans such as Gerry Adams or Danny Morrison with their local, troubled Belfast streets); and to the territory of the whole island, imagined and claimed for the nation (as in the 1937 Constitution). And we've seen the marking out of territory in terms of physical nationalist symbols, as with those Donegal rebel memorials to Theobald Wolfe Tone and Thomas D'Arcy McGee with which we opened the book.

But if our necessary response to physical surroundings often leads to a unique attachment to place, then equally pressing is some way of engaging with other *people*. Again, this has been a key part of the Irish story, during which there has been a deep association among the nation's people, a bond born of necessary belonging. Much of the coherence and durability of nationalism in Ireland has been built out of human intimacies. Again and again in these pages we have encountered the politics of family, literal or metaphorical, within nationalist Irish community: Mary Anne and her brother Henry Joy McCracken; Martha McTier and her brother William Drennan; the intimacy of Thomas Russell with Tone, Emmet and McCracken; the great friendship between Thomas Moore and Robert Emmet; Redmondite MP Stephen Gwynn being a grandson of William Smith O'Brien. W. B. Yeats was a friend of John O'Leary, but also faced into a new generation through knowing people such as Peadar O'Donnell and Ernie O'Malley; Alice Stopford Green was a friend of both Roger Casement and Erskine Childers; Alice Milligan's brother Ernest was a member of James Connolly's small band in the ISRP; Daniel Corkery had extremely moving friendships with those doomed republicans,

Tomas MacCurtain and Terry MacSwiney. Later, too, the same pattern emerged: 1960s radical republican Roy Johnston revered his Home Ruler father, Joseph; Bernadette Devlin imbibed something of her nationalism from her own father; Gerry Adams enjoyed a republican lineage on both his father's and his mother's side of the family tree. In the moving comradeship of the hunger-striking IRA volunteers in jail in the 1980s we see the creation of new kinds of family, and there has frequently been much poignant experience in such episodes, even among the most aggressive. IRA men Sean Russell and Frank Ryan had taken different paths in their 1930s careers – one towards militarism, the other towards the politics of the left – but even in their unappealing, shared relationship with England's enemy Nazi Germany, there was to be some personal sadness, with Russell's death in 1940 as he and Ryan travelled by submarine towards an Ireland which neither of them would ever see again. Ryan encapsulated something of this when he later recalled of Russell that 'He and I were always good personal friends – and never more so than during his last days. He died in my arms.'[27] From the intense comradeship of prison struggle among anti-Treaty republicans in their futile 1920s war against the Free State, to the more fruitful trust and respect developed in peace-process Northern Ireland between figures as different as John Hume, Gerry Adams and Alec Reid, it has been the politics of actual community which has most decisively defined and driven the Irish version of the world's most powerful force.

This has all involved the actual community which you protect (as in Belfast or Derry in 1969) and also the comradeship which has tied people meaningfully together, and the actual people whom you love. But it has also involved the broader group so brilliantly depicted in Benedict Anderson's *Imagined Communities*, 'an imagined political community'[28] which has been evident in the inclusive claims to all of Ireland's people – and to their unity – made by the United Irishmen in the 1790s, the Young Irelanders in the 1840s, the 1916 Proclamation, or de Valera's Fianna Fáil; an Irish nationalist such as Alice Stopford Green placed great stress on the supposedly ancient and continuous unity of the Irish people; the SDLP in Northern Ireland repeatedly emphasized the importance of healing divisions within the Irish people as a whole. And this broad community of the imagination was interwoven with the physically knowable group: the initial building-block towards the nation lay precisely with those whom one knew, those with whom one worked, and with whom one developed actual ties of friendship, attachment and identification.

One means of such identification, of marking out those with whom we are exclusively involved, is assumedly shared *descent*, and again we can see this operating within Irish nationalism: the idea of ethnic roots has been persistent, not least in attachment to the practices and symbols of an assumedly authentic Gaelicism. Although the etymology of 'nation' relates to birth, genealogically discrete groups – all neatly descended through hermetically-sealed lineages – are precisely what modern nationalist groups are not. And while race and nation have frequently been used as interchangeable terms by nationalists (including many Irish ones), we are in fact all much more hybrid than that would suggest and nationalisms have little, in practice, to do with sealed racial categories.[29] (In some cases, indeed, modern nationalists are demonstrably *not* descended from their putative ancestors.[30])

Equally, however, it is untrue that birth connection is irrelevant either to the original emergence of national communities or to the inheritance (even in a modern nationalist context) of a particular identity: to that extent, the organic notion of automatically belonging to a unique nation through birth has some merit for many people. Where and to whom you are born *do* affect and help to determine your sense of national identification and belonging, however hybrid your community's historical descent-line in fact turns out to have been. Even if the myth of common descent distorts historical reality, in many national cases it retains credibility because it expresses part of the historical truth of relatedness: many people within a given nation *will* have blood-ties with others of their nation in greater measure than they will have with people from other nations. In this sense, the distorting and powerful myth of blood-based belonging is sustained because it possesses sufficient reality to remain both useful and (just about) plausible.

Moreover, as with attachment to territory or to those around you, the idea of shared descent, of blood-belonging, offers a powerful way of making communication both easier and more meaningful. The notion of biological purity of descent may be ahistorical (as well as pernicious, in terms of the use to which such ideas have at times been put); but the myth of shared descent does intensify the attachment to those around you. It is not an idea to which nationalists will rigorously adhere (if one forces the issue, even most zealots will acknowledge a measure of hybridity to be their national reality); but neither is descent irrelevant to national communities, and this allows for a casually assumed myth of actual ties of blood, ties which seem to root and ennoble our sense of attachment within our special group. We are, if we sustain this national myth, a kind of extended family, and our identity as such seems all the more powerful and purposeful and lasting.

As so often, what carries social power here is less the scientific or historical reality than that which people allow themselves to believe – simplified or profoundly distorted though this may be. As an historian (or a biologist) one might want to demolish such wrong-headed notions; but as supportive members of a national group one probably needs to leave them in place. A similar series of points can be made about those languages of communication included under the term *culture*. Indeed, in explaining what nationalism is and why it has proved so dominant in human history, the facilitative languages of shared and public culture are absolutely central. Nationalists may not all speak the same actual language (Irish nationalists themselves have been English-speaking, Irish-speaking, or both; the Swiss speak numerous languages), and they do not necessarily even share any particular cultural form homogeneously (nations can have various religious allegiances, or various attachments to music, or diet); but it could not be the case that a nationalism flourished which did not possess some powerful cultural languages for communication between the members of its nation. Some kind of communicative media are required, some means which allow people to share sufficiently to be able to communicate reciprocally and associatively.

The habitual preferences, assumptions, customs, values, beliefs, behaviours and understandings which – when shared – we call culture, offer just such means of social communication, integration and shared identity, and are crucial to understanding why nationalist communities arise and persist as they do. The range of possible shared beliefs, shibboleths, activities and patterns of behaviour is clearly very broad (the actual language we speak,[31] the religion to which we adhere, the sports which we play, the music to which we listen, the oral or folk traditions which we sustain, the food we tend to eat, the drinks we like to drink, and so on); but they all represent ways of dealing with information and with one another, and if they resonate meaningfully with common experience then they allow for the sameness, unity and cooperation necessary for essential social communication. And the Irish nationalist story is full of them. Religion has been to the fore: 'Catholicism provided Irish nationalism with a distinctive character within the United Kingdom.'[32] From the medieval proto-nation could be drawn later communal-religious identity and tradition, a vital resource for Irish nationalism. And from the Reformation onwards, Catholic faith and Irish distinctiveness were interwoven, and religion rather than ethnic unity was the binding element in the seventeenth-century Irish proto-nation. Later on, nationalist battles themselves were often focused on Catholic grievance (Emancipation in the 1820s, for example, during a period when Daniel O'Connell shrewdly recognized that Catholic grievance, organization and identity were vital to successful mobilization; but self-consciously Catholic nationalism was prominent too even in the movement led by the Protestant Parnell); and although nationalists did not necessarily obey their Church (there were tensions in the 1860s as in the 1920s and the 1980s), they did – whether Fenian or IRA or constitutional-nationalist – tend to exhibit a Catholic identity and to associate this with Irishness. At times, as in much of the nineteenth century, priests were central to nationalist struggle; and great nationalist leaders (whether themselves Protestant, like Parnell, or Catholic, like de Valera) shrewdly kept the Church on their side. From the vibrant AOH, to 1920s IRA prisoners, to the newly formed Irish Free State of the early twentieth century, to interwar Northern Irish nationalists, to the republican hunger-strikers of 1981, Catholic religion has been a meaningful and profound part of the Irish national story. In overwhelming composition, in terms of many of the goals pursued, in terms of the vision of what made the nation special, and in terms of identifying what you were not (Protestant, atheistic) – in all these ways, and despite rhetorical non-sectarianism, Irish nationalism has been deeply Catholic. Even at the one moment at which a large number of non-Catholics were involved – the 1790s – we have seen that religious conviction and thinking were vital to an understanding of nationalist politics. And at many points (from the 1790s to the 1990s, and beyond), what we find is a nationalist rhetoric and vision of non-sectarian inclusiveness, complemented by a frequent enough sectarianism on the ground. Both need to be acknowledged and explained as part of the story.

Culture has played its part in other ways too, in the appeal and rewards of a poetic expression (from Robert Emmet to Thomas Moore to Young Ireland to Patrick Pearse to Bobby Sands), or in the value placed on education (whether of the formal CBS variety, or the auto-didacticism of IRA prisoners in jail in the Northern Ireland Troubles[33]), or in the understandable attachment to symbols as the markers of what is special about the nation (as in the debates around the 1921 Treaty). And in all this we find the powerful attraction of nationalist means of shared communication, and a preference for ways of achieving this which involve the ennoblement of self and community. So Gaelic Ireland has been prized and praised – as in the Gaelic League or the GAA – and debates on national identity (common elsewhere too, of course[34]) have in Ireland focused so frequently on what is distinctively non-British and unique and dignified. Thus, to the Young Irelanders as to the IRA, Irish culture has been special, worth defending and preserving and celebrating; Gaelic Ireland has been zealously protected by D. P. Moran as also by the 1930s Blueshirts and by disaffected northern nationalists in the 1950s.

If culture allows for sufficient sameness and understanding to enable us to form community and to sustain it relatively stably, then its appeal and value also go far beyond this. The mechanisms of culture to which we voluntarily subscribe not only allow us to relate to and communicate with others, but our communal and cultural identity – our collective pride in our culture – also ennobles us in our own estimation. Our national culture and group and identity are held to be unique and special, and as nationalists we are deeply proud of them and prioritize them and resent their being patronized. The layered value, therefore, of nationalist culture is that it both enables us to find ways of dealing with those with whom we have to cooperate and interact, *and* simultaneously offers us enhanced meaning as we do so. Our self-conception, our self-definition, are rendered more coherent and more extensive and more positive by our identification with our special culture. If I am a nationalist, then my community is an extension of myself; the distinctiveness and exceptionalism of its personality are deeply mine also; its purpose and prestige lend greater value to my own achievements and allow for functional engagement with those around me and for a more celebratory self-image at the same time. The affirmation of one's own culture is the affirmation – among other things – of oneself.[35]

Thus the rationally instrumental and the emotionally appealing coalesce together. And just as it is convenient to forget that my community is not a discrete racial group neatly descended through history, so also – if I am a nationalist – I can comfortingly assume that my community's culture somehow *is* more special, important, complete and desirable than others' alternatives. Thus when we celebrate our national language, sports, dress, ritual, religious beliefs, diet, art, music, symbols, and so on, when we decide to continue to share what we inherit of all these cultural expressions, we are sustaining norms which have both practical and psychological value. How else are we to deal with one another as we must, except in communities sharing culture as a means of communication? And how better to think of ourselves in augmented ways than to celebrate the distinctiveness and dignity of our special, our unique and authentic cultural identity?

Given this, the supposedly bizarre emotional attachment so commonly felt by people towards the symbols of their nation seems much less perplexing. Such intense sentiment emerges because people are thereby attached to a magnified, dignified version of themselves and their interests. If I am a nationalist, then my culture is special, distinctive and – despite the ubiquity of nations – unique; it bestows prestige upon my individual life; it enjoys my loyalty, and I will strive that it should receive both protection and also due recognition of its special value. All this relates nationalist community to the deepest human instincts, since the perceived specialness of each nation and each nationalism reflects the universal human desire for status, dignity, self-respect, pride and prestige.[36] The supposed superiority and even sanctity of one's nation, the defence of its interests against threats to its condition, the obsession with the fortunes and purity and unity of its culture – all this makes sense in the light of nationalism's strong psychological dimensions. Why does one become a nationalist? In part, because communal-national culture has so much to offer in response to the deepest human instincts.

A particularly significant aspect of this pervasive nationalist culture is a sense of the community's special *history*; 'Every nation has its own understanding of its distinctive past that is conveyed through stories, myths and history.'[37] The nation is held not just to be a community existing in the present, but one whose distinctive meaning and identity have evolved through a continuous, shared, unique past. The stories people tell or assume about that past may, as the nineteenth-century French historian Ernest Renan (1823–92) famously pointed out,[38] involve considerable amounts of amnesia, distortion or anachronism; but the myths or memories of such a common history represent another means of communicating with and about one another. In further answer to the question of who we are, the historically recognizable group can celebrate glorious past achievements or it can draw strength from past endurance of soon-to-be-redeemed suffering; it can meaningfully relate past to future, as the decline and decay of the past are replaced by heady national redemption; it can identify as a group through the ties of past experience and destiny, and by means of traditions which supposedly embody common experiences or historically ordained character; it can enjoy the augmented self-image which comes from a deployment of shared past community; and it can focus emotionally upon heroes and emblems and values located in its special history.

Thus nationalists so frequently focus upon education (as the means of inculcating certain readings of a distinctive national past), and on archaeology and antiquities and their supposed preciousness for the national community. Nationalist sermons frequently draw on the glories and lessons of the past; and nationalist movements very often build on revivals of interest in the nation's actual or supposed historical experiences together. So nationalists tend to celebrate an historical community, and nationalist conceptions of time frequently involve a teleological dimension. To the nationalist, the assumed future can be as vital as the imagined past: history as read through nationalist lenses often possesses a direction or purpose, a destiny or mission, and at times an inevitable progression towards a determined end-point. Again, this tendency is rooted in the nature of the human mind, which has an orientation towards the creation of narrative interpretations of important events around us, and towards the moral or sense which those events embody for us:

We know that human minds are narrative or literary minds. That is, minds strive to represent events in their environment, however trivial, in terms of causal *stories*, sequences where each event is the result of some other event and paves the way for what is to follow. People everywhere make up stories, avidly listen to them, are good judges of whether they make sense. But the narrative drive goes deeper. It is embedded in our mental representation of whatever happens around us.[39]

In the Irish case, there have certainly been, generation after generation, a wide range of narratives told and retold.[40] And our stories about supposed national pasts – if they are to be widely accessible to the community and easily transmitted across time – need to be relatively simple (hence the much-lamented historical distortion and anachronism associated with so much nationalist history).

We have seen all this clearly woven into our tale of nationalist Ireland. A vital strain within the appeal of nationalist culture has been nationalists' attachment to and reading of history, hinted at by our opening Donegal memorials. This can involve imaginative raids back into the pre-nationalist period, as modern imaginations seize on the sufferings of those from one's own proto-nation: if the Catholic Irish suffered under Cromwell's English hands or through the Penal Laws, and if even twelfth-century invasion still offered grounds for communal grievance, then history was a valuable resource indeed; again, republicans during 1919–21 sometimes drew on an historical notion of pre-Norman Ireland having been paradigmatically united and free. So nationalism might need to be partly amnesiac; but it needs also not to be entirely so. The glory of a national past, the struggle for redress of historical grievance, the education of people into an attachment to the national past – all these have played a part. Young Irelanders such as Thomas Davis exuded a zeal for such things (Young Ireland frequently celebrating inspiring heroes from the past), and IRA figures throughout the twentieth century were avid history-readers. Historical heroes – Tone, Emmet, Mitchel, Collins, Sands – became icons of struggle (1916 heroes Sean MacDiarmada and Patrick Pearse shared something of an obsession with Robert Emmet, and then themselves entered the national-historical memory as heroes in turn); cults developed around great leaders such as O'Connell, Parnell or de Valera. Episodes of past suffering were lastingly powerful in the present – whether associated with Cromwellian slaughter, Penal Law discrimination or 1840s Famine – and cultural-historical arguments were central to the work of nationalist historians such as Alice Stopford Green.

Irish nationalist readings of history often involved a teleology, the notion that there was a purpose, direction or even design to the nation's story. The idea of history as progress was there in the United Irish conviction about reason triumphing over authoritarian superstition, in the confident expectations typical of the Fenians, and again in the republican politics of the early twentieth century. The idea that history was on the side of nationalism was there, explicitly, among northern nationalists during the late-twentieth-century peace process too ('The tide of history is with Irish nationalists'[41]). At times, there was a declinist quality to nationalist argument: a golden age had been lost or betrayed, the present was flawed, but villains could be defeated and necessary remedies applied: this kind of thinking was evident in the Gaelic cultural nationalism of D. P. Moran, but also in the redemptive politics of the 1916 Patrick Pearse. And the early twentieth century witnessed a profound belief among nationalists in Ireland that an historically embedded national culture could be – indeed, must be – awakened in the present.

Some developments in Irish nationalism have often been seen as inevitable, such as the decline of John Redmond's Irish Parliamentary Party,[42] or the eruption of violent republican campaigns against British rule in Ireland, or the eventual emergence in the future of an independent and united Ireland. For their part, however, professional scholars tend to be much more sceptical about teleology, about the certainty of historically determined end-points in the future, and about inevitability more generally; and the Irish experience might justify their caution.[43] As we've seen here in this book, the crucial Reformation episode – or, more particularly, its Irish failure – does not seem to have been inevitable; again, what we now know about the 1919–21 War for Independence suggests the importance, not of inevitability, but rather of the contingency associated with varied local or even individual republican action; yet again, there were other available choices in the north of Ireland during 1968–72, from which a very different nationalism might well have emerged. Much of what Irish nationalists have anticipated about inevitable futures has in fact failed to materialize, from the achievement of Home Rule at the start of the twentieth century to the IRA-driven expulsion of Britain from the north at its end. Did those who started the 1960s civil rights movement in the north anticipate that they would help to produce the Troubles? Did culture produce the kind of shared Irish nationality envisaged by Thomas Davis? Did the Ireland of Pearse's mystical imagination come true? In practice, the historical development of Irish nationalism has been contingent and jagged and varied rather than inevitable and smooth and uniform; any teleology identified has been very much that of nationalist faith, rather than that born from coldly factual observation. Novelist Philip Roth's 'unfolding of the unforeseen' is surely the right key to play in here: 'the relentless unforeseen was what we schoolchildren studied as "History", harmless history, where everything unexpected in its own time is chronicled on the page as inevitable. The terror of the unforeseen is what the science of history hides, turning a disaster into an epic.'[44]

There is likely always to be a certain distance between the forensic precision sought after by historians, and the needs of us all as part of a wider public understandably keen on what popular memory can supply in terms of making sense of communal lives. We've noted that the human mind is formed to think narratively and causally and through the telling of moral stories, and it would be surprising if historians' justifiable dismantling of popular myths (the exceptional awfulness of the Cromwellian episode, the ruthlessness of the Penal Laws, the Nazi-like quality of Ulster unionist rule, and so on) were to be entirely welcome.

Nor is there anything uniquely Irish in all this. Irish nationalists are no more trapped or governed by the past than are those in other countries, and there is nothing exceptional in their understandably using the past in order to legitimize certain strategies in the present. This happens all over the world (evident, for example, in late-twentieth-century Iran and Iraq,[45] and also in the way in which national pasts have been used in France, the United States, Britain, Germany, Israel/Palestine and elsewhere). So the debates over Irish historians' scepticism regarding nationalist myth[46] should recognize the familiarity of such processes elsewhere. The idea that professional historians' scepticism might undermine popular notions of the past, and that scholarship might thereby remove the historical foundations of contemporary coherence and conviction, was a notion hardly new or unique to late-twentieth-century Ireland: historian Jack Plumb had said as much in the 1960s, long before the Irish revisionist debate had gained momentum.[47]

Of course, historians will – and should – correct errors: whether Gerry Adams's misdating of the battle of the Boyne or (more surprisingly) of James Connolly's execution;[48] or wider nationalist assumptions about the United Irishmen being secularist, the 1916 rebels socialist, or the Famine a product of British genocidal intention. But a more interesting divergence between historians and some nationalists regarding approaches to the past probably does concern this question of teleology or destiny; although few will want to express the case quite as brutally as the great philosopher Karl Popper ('the belief in historical destiny is sheer superstition'[49]), there is surely something in what he claimed.

Nationalist community can also often involve *ethical* attitudes.[50] For one's territory, people, descent, culture and history to be special, the values which they embody cannot be considered merely typical. The community which makes meaning of my life must be a special one, involving superior moral claims and values and therefore deserving my utter loyalty. Nationalist morality involves not just the sense that one's nation has a distinctive purpose or unique (perhaps even divinely chosen) mission in the world, but also that one owes a supervening loyalty, duty, obligation to that national purpose and community.[51] For nationalists, the nation has a special moral claim upon a person. Yes, there may be other layers of identity (sexual, intimate, regional, social, professional, and so forth), but – from a nationalist view – all these are ultimately subsumed under and superseded by one's devotion to the nation. In fighting and dying for one's nation one might be fighting with friends, among one's social class, and perceivedly to defend one's family's freedom: but it is the nation which is the dominant community demanding one's warlike sacrifice, and it is the nation which possesses an overarching or supreme moral authority and righteousness.

How has this worked in Ireland? Irish nationalists' sense of community has often enough been made more alluring by its repeated self-image of ethical superiority, by an effective moralization of politics. Natives have been held to be good, and settlers bad (and so, yet again, the lessons drawn from the pre-modern era of the proto-nation retain some force, as the politics of early-modern Plantation continue to resonate even centuries later); the United Irishmen thought the forces of Democracy morally superior to those of Aristocracy; the Young Irelanders held Irish culture to be, in key respects, superior to its rivals', and exuded a sense of high morality and ethical responsibility; late-nineteenth-century nationalist peasants held their moral claims to land and to land-related rights to be morally superior to landlord claims; republicanism has been seen by its adherents, and by some of its chroniclers, as involving 'a form of political morality';[52] England was held, again and again by generations of Irish nationalist, to be villainous; figures such as Charles Kickham thought those taking different political paths to be less morally motivated than himself; Constance Markievicz displayed a haughty self-righteousness; Gaelic culture has been held as morally superior to English culture, and Catholicism to non-Catholicism (as in Ernie O'Malley's typically candid point about pitying those not belonging to the true faith); late-twentieth- and early-twenty-first-century republicans have invoked a pious rhetoric of victimhood with which to assail their opponents (over state-loyalist collusion, Bloody Sunday killings, and so forth). The supposedly paramount moral claim which the nation has on the loyalty of the individual has been matched by a sense of superior morality associated with that nation's own cause. Victimhood at the hands of enemy villains has been crucial here (even if this has at times involved some distorted argument: contrary to some republican propaganda about the north of Ireland under unionist rule, there has been nothing in Northern Ireland which has come close to matching the horrific experiences of those who suffered under the apartheid or Nazi regimes).

Beyond all this, to the nationalist there is a proper division of humanity itself into nations, and in the nationalist's view international morality demands recognition of this specially important fact. Embedded in the nation's own vision of itself and its purpose are ethical ambitions and commitments: religion often features here (not least, of course, in Ireland), as do claims that one's national system of values or culture is morally superior to that of rivals. And there is also a frequently recurring motif of the demand for justice, for equality, for the rightful recognition of the nation's cause, or for restitution for supposed historical wrongs suffered in the past.[53]

You can, therefore, have a national community which speaks

different languages, or attends different religious services, or listens to various different kinds of music. But a national community does require some such shared social languages of communication: languages which facilitate necessary interaction, which provide the basis for reciprocal trust and obligation,[54] and which appeal because they do not merely possess this functional value, but also ennoble members of the community in the process.

Vital to these self-definitions is the (often uglier) *exclusivism* of national community. If one defines – for practical and psychological and emotional purpose – what one is, then one is also defining what one is not.[55] Put more practically, if there are those who will be included in my special community (because they share my culture, history and so on), then for this to have any meaning, there must be those whom the group excludes, those who are not the same. The bonded in-group must have an out-group, and here lies much of the understandable anxiety felt by many observers (this author included) when considering the phenomenon of nationalism. Can I praise what I am through celebration of my national territory, culture, history and superior value system, without implicitly or explicitly condemning you – if you are not a member of my community – as being inferior in these regards? At many points in nationalist histories, this problem has had brutal and pernicious outcomes (Nazi Germany providing the most obvious illustration of the dangerous potential of xenophobic nationalist politics[56]); as a consequence, some observers have held nationalism to have been the main cause of violence and conflict in the modern world, and it's certainly easy enough to present a case to this effect.[57] In particular, some liberals have frequently seen nationalism as a chauvinistic, illiberal force, one to be fought against rather than embraced.[58]

It would be wrong to take appalling examples of nationalism – such as the Nazi case – as necessarily paradigmatic: there are myriad shades of national community, some more civic and relaxed and inclusive than others, some exhibiting more liberal forms of nationalism and others more illiberal varieties.[59] But frequently one finds that civic and ethnic definitions of the nation compete, coexist and mingle with one another within the same nationalism, and that distinctions between the two tend not to be absolute in practice. Certainly, it is difficult to ignore the dual reality, first, that the communal definition of what and who we are involves defining what and who we are not; and, second, that such boundary-marking relates to our human instinct to set out what we are (and that this is good) and what we are not (and that this is bad). Perhaps grimly, it seems a pervasive feature of human thinking to assume that people can be classified according to what might be termed innate attributes or properties;[60] and in terms of national or racial exclusiveness this can have appallingly destructive effects.

There's no doubt that many nationalisms have drawn strength from stark emphasis on what the community is not, on what it opposes, and on a Manichean image of good opposing evil. This can operate at different levels of anger and conflict: Scottish nationalists' emphatic non- and anti-Englishness, though sharp, have tended not to have been expressed in the same form as, for example, Basque commitment to non- or anti-Spanishness. But nationalism has appealed, and does appeal, to aggressive, hostile instincts as well as to our more attractive ones, and sophisticated arguments have been offered in defence of the notion that focused resentment, hatred, envy and anger against another, perhaps prior, nationalist nation have been crucial in the spread of nationalisms around the world.[61]

Nationalists often focus on achieving or maintaining the unity of their national community: the prevention of cultural dilution, and the menace of national apathy, appear again and again in nationalist rhetoric (not least in Ireland). The maintenance of cultural and other frontiers is vital to this process, and solidarity among fellow-nationals is most easily and most often pursued through exclusivism and the use of the pejorative regarding those who are outside the community. All this is sharpened and intensified during war, conflict, and campaigns for national liberation. But it is evident also in descriptions of our culture, our music, our diet, our sport and sporting achievements. These are presented not as just another set of national habits, but as special and superior. And, again, this persistently appeals because it can bestow added dignity, grandeur and worth to us all as individuals.

In a sense, such views have been an outgrowth from the supposed moralization of politics involved in nationalist self-image: if Gaelicism and Catholicism are morally superior, as early-twentieth-century Irish nationalists so often thought they were, then what do we make of those who are neither Gaelic nor Catholic? All too often, indeed, the fact that Irish nationalists have seen themselves as inhabiting a higher moral ground than their adversaries has at times fed into the exclusivist strain within nationalist Ireland. Anglophobia has, of course, been a key part of the philosophy, from Wolfe Tone through John Mitchel and Roger Casement to the Provisional IRA. England (at times, the target becomes Britain) has been seen as the cause of Irish grievance and suffering and division;[62] and Britain has been seen as treacherous and hypocritical (Michael Davitt: 'Nothing has been more consistent in the policy of British statesmen in their rule of Ireland than their inconsistency. There has not been a Prime Minister from Pitt to Arthur James Balfour who did not apply principles of government to the rule of the Irish people at complete variance with his own convictions, spoken or written, on some contingency or occasion.'[63])

But if anglicization has been a problem and the English or British the clear villains, then another key out-group for nationalist Ireland has been the non-nationalist community on the island itself. There are obvious rewards in all this, in terms of the sustenance of clarifying and comforting self-images, but there has also been on all sides much ugliness and chauvinism. Just as unionists in the north have at times dismissed the legitimacy of nationalist argument and grievance, so too the legitimacy of unionism has been largely dismissed by most nationalist observers throughout our story. It has been (wrongly) assumed that unionists are effectively descended from early-modern Planters and that their British version of Irishness is therefore necessarily unauthentic. In both directions, nationalist towards unionist and back, violence has often enough accompanied such exclusivist lines of division, in the conflicts of 1919–23, for example, or the post-1968 Northern Ireland Troubles. As far as nationalist Ireland has been concerned, the difference and commitment of unionist Ulster have long created an insoluble problem. For many northern nationalists, the answer has been simply to see bigotry as something which is the preserve of the Protestants,[64] and to assume some future dissolution of unionist politics. Yet it's difficult to read the now vast literature on unionist Ulster[65] and still to deny the depth, sincerity, and long-rootedness of this political tradition, in just the same kinds of area in which nationalism itself has found its legitimacy (territory, people, myth of descent, attachment to culture and history, and so on).

2

> Indeed, nationalist visions of internally uniform and sharply
> bounded cultural and political identities often have to be
> produced or maintained by struggle.
>
>   Craig Calhoun[66]

In assessing community, we can identify not only what this involves
(territory, people, descent, culture, history, ethics, exclusivism), but
also why all this makes such appealing sense to so many people.[67]
Nations are necessarily self-defining and self-aware groups (you simply
cannot have a group of people who do not think of themselves as a
nation and yet qualify as one); and the nature of that collective choice
or will, that self-conscious group identification, must be explained in
part by the ways in which it maps on to pervasive, practical, emotional
and psychological needs alike. It powerfully mixes the rational and the
visceral, and in all this the national community is a key foundation to
our understanding nationalism. Paradoxically, perhaps, the needs of a
universal human nature seem very effectively to be met by attachment
to unique and partial national communities.

But nationalism must involve more than membership of such a
meaningful community. It crucially also involves **struggle**. The term
'nationalist' should not be restricted purely to describing organizations,
but nationalism does involve movement and activity and collective
mobilization; in its most powerful, mass moments it has been a
phenomenon with goals, characterized by a programmatic striving; it
means more to its adherents than identification with a community,
but calls also for action, for change, or for the creation of momentum.
It is, in short, political.[68]

What is it for which nationalists strive? Why do they pursue such
objectives? And how do they struggle towards the achievement of their
goals?

Nationalism can involve a wide range of communal agendas for
struggle, not least because nationalisms are not static, but changing
and dynamic according to period and place. The establishment of

sovereign independence for the national community is the most obvious goal to be attained or, once attained, to be defended and sustained. If, as Ernest Gellner once put it, 'Nationalism is primarily a political principle, which holds that the political and the national unit should be congruent',[69] then nationalists' struggles will most conspicuously be directed towards the achievement of such a reality, and this has indeed been close to the heart of much political nationalism. It might involve the struggle for minority secession from a larger political unit (Basque secession from the Spanish or French states), for independence from a world imperial power (as in anti-colonial struggles against various international empires), for the integration or reintegration of territory and people currently separated yet – in nationalist thinking – rightfully one (pan-German nationalism of the early twentieth century), or for the assimilation or absorption of territories and peoples[70] that one considers it appropriate and right to control (as in the case of expanding empires). All of this involves the struggle, often passionate, for freedom: freedom from wrongly dominant political rulers, freedom for united expression of historic national destiny, freedom for the flourishing of cultural identity.

But these struggles for autonomy and freedom contain within them kaleidoscopic possibilities, such is nationalism's protean quality. At times the struggle is for survival, whether literal (in war or other brutal conflict with enemies, or with fellow-nationalist rivals), or cultural (in terms of preserving the essential ingredients and life of the nation, or seeking the formal recognition or protection of a national culture and its associated rights). The struggle of nationalists can be for very practical, material, economic advantage; with political power in the hands of our own community, so the argument frequently runs, our own prosperity and economic opportunity will improve in terms of jobs, income, wealth, land, and so on. Or it can involve more abstract, but no less important, struggle towards the recognition of group rights, of equal treatment for one's community, and of the freedom for particular cultural expression.

Nationalist struggle frequently appeals and succeeds in mobilizing communal forces precisely because it offers a direct and powerful means of furthering the interests of the group whose advantage will benefit individual self-interest and communal self-perception alike. Cultural marginalization is to be overcome, freedom of group expression must be defended through ongoing campaigns, dilution and apathy must be guarded against, the proper national ways must be codified and institutionalized and strengthened, and the nation must be built or fortified.

In all this, rectification is surely the key feature of nationalist struggle. What *is* must become what it *ought* to be (often involving the supposed restoration of a previously existing order); nationalist restlessness with current imperfection must be assuaged through a grievance-driven struggle for redress. This can involve the re-establishment of past independence or former cultural glory and greatness, the rebirth and renewal of true national culture. And it often enough involves a quasi-religious sense of time: nationalist struggle can be seen as producing an historical redemption out of which will spring a wonderful future period, seen in chiliastic, millenarian terms.

And this nationalist struggle for transformation is a potentially ongoing one. One might achieve independence for the national community; but that independence may in future need to be guarded against enemies both within and without, while the cultural priorities and practices of the community will need to be rendered fitting, and sufficient uniformity of authentic cultural practice and allegiance will need to be maintained. So all of this will require ongoing struggle and organization and programmatic nationalism. The establishing of political or cultural boundaries is one aspect of nationalist struggle, but their ongoing defence and delineation can prove much more lasting.

Many of these kinds of struggle can be seen in the Irish nationalist tale: reform and the redress of specific grievance (in the 1790s, from the 1820s through to the 1840s, in the land struggle of the late nineteenth century, or the anti-discrimination campaign within modern Northern Ireland); sovereignty and separatism (in 1798, in 1803 with Robert Emmet's struggle against English dominion, in the Fenian campaigns for liberation from Britain during the nineteenth century, in the various IRAs of the twentieth century and their pursuit of a united Irish republic); measures of political autonomy short of full separation from Britain (Repeal of the Union, Home Rule, pro-Treaty politics in the 1920s); the unity of the people (the United Irishmen, Sinn Féin during 1917–21, Fianna Fáil in the 1920s and 1930s); the survival of national culture (through Moranite cultural campaigns, or the work of the GAA); properly legitimate arrangements for economic organization (regarding nineteenth-century land ownership, for example), or representative government with power and sovereignty resting in the people; defence in times of crisis (whether economic in the 1950s, or intercommunal in the north in 1969). And, through all this, liberty: freedom from English domination or from social or economic or cultural injustice.

Why, at root, do nationalists struggle for the attainment of these goals? Why has such struggle appealed and occurred? At times, it has been driven in Ireland by economic or other very practical, day-to-day exigency (as in the agricultural crisis of the 1870s, the desire for land redistribution which drove support for the UIL, the response to wartime economics during 1917–18, or the land annuities struggle of the 1920s Free State; or in the daily, cyclical traumas of the spiralling northern conflict of the 1960s and 1970s), with the politics of competition over land having been long prominent (even as early as the Wexford of the 1790s, for example). Competition over control of resources has been complemented at times by the desire for greater prestige to accompany economic advantage (as in the politics of communal competition over jobs and the like in early-twentieth-century Ireland, or the attractions of O'Connellite or Parnellite or Griffithite dignity); and here the individual's desires and needs have found meaning and possible fulfilment through association with the national community. On occasion, it has been a matter of intellectual influence which has contributed to nationalist appeal, as with the impact of the alluring ideas of Locke, Rousseau or Paine in the eighteenth century, or of Romanticism in the mid-nineteenth, or of poetic-sacrificial patriotism in the period of the First World War. On others, family has been a crucial vehicle for the inculcation of nationalist struggle (very variously, as the careers of Parnell, Davitt, Peadar O'Donnell, Bernadette Devlin and Gerry Adams each distinctively testify). Personal influences could also involve teachers; and at times the allure of struggle lay in the immediacy of highly personalized revenge (evident in the 1790s, in 1919–23, and in the north after the 1960s), or in the broader cultures of communal rage and revanchism seen among embittered American post-Famine emigrant-zealots, or those involved in the violence of 1919–21 or 1968–98. And the yearning to prevent the decline or death of distinctive culture could energize nationalist action (as in the case of late-nineteenth-century cultural nationalist protectionism).

The struggle could be attractive not just for what it promised as an end-result, but for its value in itself: nationalist struggle can be explained partly by its perceivedly intrinsic, inherent worth. It need not merely be that struggle will move your community from unaccept-able Point A to desirable Point B; the process of struggle, and what it reflects and creates in the form of national character and attitude, might in itself be of profound attraction and value in nationalists' view. It might offer an escape from quotidian boredom; as something producing defiance rather than deference and servility; as a means of inculcating or demonstrating the truly noble values inherent in Irish nationhood; or as something (in the Fenian case, for example, or the world of the GAA) which offered conviviality and a truly social life. If economics was of great importance in explaining the emergence of nationalist struggle (land hunger in the west at the end of the nineteenth century, or the anticipated economic benefits of Home Rule at the start of the twentieth), then it also of course explained the shape which it took. You wished, especially in the wake of the Famine, to consolidate your hold on the land; you fought to own it, and having so acquired your farm, you would definitely not hand it over to a Connollyite or O'Donnellite socialist state.

And central to the appeal of nationalist struggle lay the question of freedom, as it could be achieved through the establishment of egalitar-ian sovereignty over the community and its decisions. Once that central principle had been established, then all sorts of possible routes could be seen as legitimate, and these would often enough involve a very British style of Irish independence in practice, as we have seen. No matter. As a free Irish nationalist, you shared equally now in the decisions which produced law and culture, and nationalism offered the way to achieve this.

Broadening this out to nationalism as a whole, one could of course say that nationalists struggle for their goals for precisely the reasons that they themselves cite as self-justifications for their various struggles. The world, nationalists argue, should properly and justly be divided into distinct, authentic nations, each free to live as they choose; my national culture is rich and unique and it should be given appropriate recognition and free expression; the restrictions on my liberty imposed by a dominant imperial power are insufferable and immoral; my nation has an historic destiny and international mission which must be fulfilled; all people should belong to a nation, for it is only a world of free and sovereign national units which will provide stability and order for the world; and so on. But these self-justifications, important though they are to any proper understanding of nationalism, are only part of the answer; behind them lie some ulterior assumptions, preferences, instincts and understandable needs to be fulfilled. ('Nationalism is not what it seems, and above all it is not what it seems to itself.'[71]) In part, we are back again to psychological and practical impulses of the deepest kind: self-preservation, the advancement of economic interests ('virtually all political questions today revolve around economic ones'[72]), the desire for prestige or dignity or mean-ing-bestowing activity, the search for reinforcement through seeing one's own ways widely accepted and legitimized – all of these and other urges find valuable expression through nationalist struggle and make it comprehensible.

Nationalist struggle can be stimulated by direct and urgent threats: the aggression of a neighbouring group; the perceived danger of cultural erosion and dilution; the threat of great social or cultural change. It can be stimulated (as so often in Ireland) by a sharp sense of prior wrongs committed against one's own kind, wrongs considered insufferable and thus demanding urgent redress; this can in part be driven itself by impulses towards revenge, by the satisfaction of rage, reprisal and anger against a transgressing opponent. The struggles of nationalists often make such attractive sense because of the logic involved in dealing with enemies: 'History would not be a meaningful drama if there were no deep conflict at the heart of it.'[73] Nationalist struggle can involve the pursuit or defence of honour or dignity: a redemption for past humiliation.

In practice, perhaps the most common generator of nationalist struggle is a sharpened sense of relative group grievance. Calculation (we will have more jobs, land, money, power) here interweaves with more visceral impulses (jealousy, resentment, revanchism, anger, in-furiation at one's perceived social dislocation) in the midst of what is probably itself a mixture of actual and exaggerated deprivation. Typic-ally, a communal elite enjoying some socially-upward momentum might reach a perceived ceiling of opportunity, a ceiling which forms part of the intercommunal architecture of power relations between two national groups. Repeatedly, such blocked mobility has inflamed latent national sentiment, and has been the occasion for programmatic struggle to redress injustice, discrimination and inequality, and – ultimately – to achieve power for the community suffering unequal opportunity. (The classic example of this in Ireland lies in the sectarian, communal conflicts of the early twentieth century.)

Such a pattern helps to explain both the timing of the genesis of nationalist struggles and also the profile for communal leadership and activism. For, while nationalist movements tend to stress their own egalitarianism, and to emphasize their cross-class dimension, clearly they also operate according to internal hierarchies of power and elite-dominance. There have been nationalisms which explicitly stress the particular cause of one class (the working class, for instance), and many which have implicitly reflected the interests of one section of the supposedly unified nation; in these cases, economic impulsion towards nationalist struggle has been particularly important, and class tensions within the nation have been of profound importance.

The collective struggle is often presented by nationalist zealots as natural, and as merely reflective of timeless national realities. In historical practice, however, it often tends to be at least partly contingent upon social stimuli which, in origin, have nothing to do with the national character or cause at all. Shifts in the pattern of educational qualification can produce rising but unfulfilled levels of professional expectation; changes in demography or economy, and therefore in social or class structure, can produce a sense of communal eclipse and group demotion which require redress. These shifts are not created by nationalism but, extraneous though they are, they produce the context within which discontented social elites can effectively lead nationalist movements. Status resentment, anger and dissatisfaction (all focused on a non-national opponent who currently thwarts the progress of the national community) have repeatedly generated nationalist attempts to address communal grievance, whether in the form of achieving cultural freedoms, the establishment of an independent or autonomous national state, or some other much-desired remedy.

Crucial to explaining why nationalist struggle occurs is the frequently misrepresented phenomenon of relative deprivation. A concept used in academic analysis for many decades, relative deprivation involves the idea that people agitate to remedy alleged injustices because of their perceived disadvantage relative to relevant comparators. One can – in global terms – be extraordinarily well-off in terms of prosperity, opportunity, goods, and so on; but if the group which one considers to be one's real comparator (a neighbour, a persistently visible rival) seems to enjoy privileges which are denied to oneself, then relative deprivation might be held to explain agitation towards necessary change. The concept has perhaps been overused by social scientists (to explain virtually every kind of social transformation in history!), and it has certainly been deployed rather loosely and casually on occasions. But, as part of our explanation for the emergence and persistence of nationalist struggles, relative deprivation is an important concept as long as it is used sensitively. The sense of unfair and avoidable relative disadvantage characterizing one national group as opposed to a comparator and rival, the stigma and resulting anger thus generated, and the intergroup conflict that can ensue, have all frequently played important roles in the generation of nationalist struggle and momentum.

Relative deprivation is not the sole cause for organized nationalist pursuit of goals, but rather one link in a chain of concatenation; and it is not so much the individual's perception of deprivation that is relevant, but rather the individual's sense of such deprivation experienced as a representative group member. Again, it must be seen that the relations between actual and perceived disadvantage, and between the alleged causes (discrimination, abuse of power by opponents) and the actual range of causes, are likely to be varied and complex (as in the politics of Northern Ireland, where Catholic disadvantage arose not purely from Protestant discrimination). And it has to be realized not only that relative deprivation can help lead people to engage in collective action, but also that engagement in such action can then reinforce and even strengthen discontented activists' sense of relative deprivation – it is a complex, and far from simply linear, process.

But, if sufficient note is taken of these points, then the widespread and varied communal experience of relative deprivation is important for our understanding of nationalist struggle: the most recent research on the subject clearly reinforces the view that rising or accentuated relative deprivation is indeed part of what makes people engage in social, collective action of precisely the kind practised by nationalists in struggle.[74]

The complex causation behind collective nationalist struggle involves, therefore, individual engagement with the organized pursuit of communal goals. This engagement develops because of the individual's self-identification as an integral part of the nationalist community, and also because a mixture of rational and visceral impulses makes nationalist struggle seem appealing or necessary or just. The calculated and the instinctive interweave powerfully here: various kinds of psychological gratification of need (often not consciously identified as such by nationalists themselves), complement more self-conscious choices in favour of pursuing material or practical benefits through nationalist struggle.

But in what ways do nationalists, in practice, struggle for the achievement of such collective goals? At its most brutal, nationalist struggle can take very violent shape: wars between nations, wars of liberation, wars of annexation or expansion. The infliction and suffering of great loss have all too frequently formed part of the story. Less horrifically, nationalist struggle can be calmly political in form (a political party engaging in an election), culturally-oriented (campaigns for the extension of national language use, for the establishment of norms of cultural practice), and frequently reflected even in daily routines and rituals. Though nationalism's most powerful, visible and history-defining moments tend to lie in extreme action (wars to achieve national independence, for example), it is also true that struggles for national self-assertion often enough relate to the quotidian rather than the exceptional. Shrewd nationalists recognize that national consciousness, cultural practice and the like must be embedded in daily routines and habits and assumptions; and so campaigns can revolve around not merely the exalted, intensified, violent or passionate, but also around the reinforcing and reproducing of nationalist consciousness through day-to-day language and practice: the people and events commemorated in the names of streets, buildings, stations, airports, sports stadia; the frequency and location of the flying of the national flag; the attention paid to specifically national dimensions in media news reporting; and so forth.[75]

In these comparatively banal reiterations and in moments of grand national struggle alike, the mass mobilization of the community around the organized pursuit of national goals exists centrally within nationalist experience. Whether routine or exceptional, nationalist struggle tends to involve demand rather than request, for things which are perceived as rights rather than as privileges; and it is this demand for rights which defines the attitude of so much nationalist struggle in practice.

It is here that the important distinction lies between nationalism and ethnicity. The latter term – as elusive as any in the lexicon[76] – relates to the near-ubiquitous attachment people have to an ethnic group. Derived from the Greek word 'ethnos' (meaning 'nation' in its original sense of a people of common, shared descent), ethnicity refers to many of the same human linkages as are included under the term 'national'. An ethnic group shares perceivedly common descent, or a myth of collective, shared ancestry; assumptions about, or memories of, a common history; shared cultural forms or preferences, in terms of (perhaps) language, religion, music, sport, ritual; a link with a homeland.[77] The ethnos is, effectively, the nation.

But nationalism involves something more than ethnicity. It is true that ethnicity is defined and sharpened through social interaction and transaction.[78] But, still, one can be part of an ethnic group without necessarily engaging in struggles towards the achievement of programmatic goals, without the political self-consciousness and ambition and struggle which are vital features of nationalism; indeed, many ethnic groups do not explicitly identify themselves as nations or strive after national self-government or power. The term 'ethnicity' is comparatively recent (a mid-twentieth-century neologism in the English language and, for some, a more polite and modern way of saying 'race'), and it has understandably become central to much social-scientific analysis. But while nationalism does involve the ethnic, it should not casually be conflated with it since the ethnic group is not necessarily nationalist also. Discussions which blur the concepts of 'nationalism' and 'ethnicity' are unhelpful: ethnicity does not necessarily involve organized struggle; nationalism, by contrast, does.[79]

How has this practicality of struggle been manifested in Ireland? Such struggle could be violent (1798, 1803, 1867, 1916, 1919–21, 1969 onwards) or constitutional-reformist (the early days of the United Irishmen, O'Connell, Parnell, Redmond, the SDLP); or both. It could be domestically produced or – as in the case of the Fenians – stimulated and supported by emigrant rage and commitment; it could gain support from foreign allies, whether eighteenth-century France, twentieth-century World War Germany (twice), or Colonel Gaddafi's Libya (a significant friend of the Provisional IRA). It could involve land agitation, or literary struggle (Tone, Kickham, O'Leary, O'Malley, O'Donnell, Morrison, Adams), or heroic sacrifice; violence against the British, or the unionists, or – often enough – against fellow-nationalists (as in 1916–23, or after 1969). It could involve the cultivation of martyrs (Tone, Emmet, the Fenians, Pearse, Sands) or of cults around the personalities of political leaders (O'Connell, Parnell, de Valera, Collins); it could necessitate political propaganda (the United Irishmen and the Fenians), cultural-nationalist publicity and mobilization, agrarian protest, and journalism (spectacularly in *The Nation* or in the brilliant yet narrow arguments of D. P. Moran); and it could again and again involve prison struggle (as with the Fenians or the twentieth-century IRA). Nationalism could be transmitted through family, school, ritual, organization (parliamentary as well as extra-parliamentary), poetry, ballads, and friends. And this process of transmission did not stop once independent statehood was achieved: the kind of daily reinforcement of nationalist assumption and context identified by scholars such as Michael Billig[80] has helped give coherence and sense to – for example – the physical world of modern Dublin: Parnell Avenue, Parnell Place, Parnell Road, Parnell Square, Parnell Street, Pearse Square, Pearse Street, Pearse Station, Connolly Station, Connolly Avenue, and so on throughout the city. And in all this, again and again from the United Irishmen through the Fenians to the Northern Irish civil rights enthusiasts or the IRA or the SDLP, the role of committed activists has changed history – though frequently enough not in the ways which were intended or preferred.

3

A nationalist movement seeks to bind together people in a particular territory in an endeavour to gain and use state power.

John Breuilly[81]

And nationalist struggle clearly and crucially relates to questions of **power**. This is so in two main senses. First, power (of various specific kinds) is what nationalist struggle seeks to achieve; second, power is definingly wielded in the nationalist attempt to achieve it.

It might be claimed, indeed, that nationalism is essentially a politics of power: of coordinated action which transforms the world, produces different reality, makes great change happen; of deliberately acting in order to bring about effects on those with whom one is linked in social relation. This can have political, violent, cultural, intellectual and other forms, and it lies right at the centre of nationalism.

Nationalism has rightly been recognized by many scholarly observers as an organizing and legitimizing principle behind power, and nationalists tend to assume that the nation is indeed the appropriate source of political power and authority. If we are to regulate our communal life together, then authority and order are required, and these in turn demand that we set up units and agents of government which are widely accepted as legitimate. Nationalism has an answer to this problem: it is the nation which is the proper political unit; and it is a national government, composed of fellow-nationals, which enjoys true legitimacy. Nationalism crucially relates, therefore, to the establishment, the legitimation and the consolidation of power. And the three crucially interlocking ideas here are the state, sovereignty, and self-determination. We need to consider each in turn.

All too frequently there remains some confusion regarding the distinction between nation and state. The terms are often used as though they were interchangeable (which they are not) and very frequent reference is made to nation-states; yet, historically, the latter represent rather a recent idea (as, indeed, does the state itself).[82]

Moreover, in the literal sense of a state whose border and population exactly match the nation, nation-states almost certainly never exist. None the less, the state is a vital aspect of modern nationalist politics, since the most common political goal of nationalist movements at the high points of their struggle has been the establishment or re-establishment or defence of their national state. The nation can exist without its own state. But independence, autonomy, the freedom to establish cultural and other norms in accordance with nationalist preference, the opportunity for maintaining order and regulating national, communal life – all this seems much more easily attainable with control over one's own state structures than it would be without such control.

So nationalists tend to want to institutionalize their own national identities and associations within state structures. Those structures themselves might be more diverse than is often assumed (relating variously to governmental, legislative, judicial, administrative, military, and other features of group life);[83] but each of these features clearly relates to issues of power over a particular, demarcated community. Now almost universal in its reach across the planet, the state is a term referring to organizational structures of power within a given territory, to a political and public and legal entity: it can – and almost always does – differ from the nation, in that the people within the state's boundaries are likely never to be homogeneously national (and, indeed, the members of a state's perceived nation will always include people who are non-resident within that state).

But, though they are different phenomena, the relation between nation and state has been close and complex. If nationalists are to enjoy independence and self-government within a political unit coterminous with the nation, then state power is almost irresistibly alluring; especially so, given that nationalists so frequently pursue the amending of perceivedly unjust imbalances in access to power – how better to make such amendments than by gaining control over your own state? Even at its most basic, the attraction of legitimating physical control over the community is enticing (as in Weber's classic definition of the state as an organization successfully claiming a monopoly of legitimate force within a given territory).

Some eminent scholars, indeed, have argued that it is in the context of the modern state that one truly finds the best explanation for nationalism: that nationalism makes its most important sense in conditions moulded by the modern state, and that it should be read as political behaviour explained by the context established by the modern state system.[84] Certainly, possession of state power (and the opportunity thus to control and allocate resources and opportunities in the community) has been and remains a central aim of nationalist movements. And, once state power has been attained, nationalist struggle can continue to be played out – albeit at a lower pitch of intensity – within the day-to-day state context. Is the independence of the state's nation under threat from a rival power, in war or the threat of war? Do aspects of the nation's life require amendment so that national culture (language, morals, religion, sport) be properly respected in daily practice? In each of these cases, nationalist struggle within the state can remain prominent, and even in cases which involve something other than a traditional independent state (some kind of multi-national or federal arrangement), the same kinds of question concerning autonomy, resources and nationalist struggle re-emerge.

So the state should not casually be equated with the nation, and indeed the confusion of the two phenomena (and of loyalty to one with loyalty to the other) has been one of the great failings of some scholarly as well as popular thinking about nationalism.[85] But while this state–nation relationship involves subtle distinctions between an organizational unit and a popular community, it is also one involving deep linkages too. Nationalist movements have tended to be most conspicuous in those painful situations (the Irish-British famous among them) in which state and nation fail to overlap as neatly as the nationalist imagination would like. The mismatch between 'your' state and 'my' nation has generated throughout the modern world much tension, conflict and nationalist struggle: nationalists have again and again wanted their own state, as the most effective mechanism for protecting or developing their national culture and life.

And states want nations also. The state is an organizational, bureaucratic creature, promulgating and enforcing and basing itself upon formal laws. But how do you legitimize and give authenticity to the boundaries and identity and structures of such a state? More importantly, how do you produce the necessary identification between inhabitants and their state, and how do you get people to feel loyalty or devotion to its causes? One answer is that, historically, states have frequently emerged out of nationalist struggle and have therefore been interwoven in their inhabitants' and rulers' minds alike with that more emotionally alluring concept of the nation. So, after all, the confusion in popular usage between 'nation' and 'state' – though infuriating to analytical purists – does reflect key realities: that members of states do tend to see those states through the refracting lens of the nation; and that, in practice, the separation of nationalism from the state is often far from easy.[86]

Certainly, it seems that states function far more effectively if they possess some reservoir of national sentiment from which to sustain cohesive allegiance to themselves, some means of establishing legitimacy and emotional attachment among their people. Those aspects of national community which we have already discussed (territory, people, descent, culture, history, ethics and exclusivism) all offer rich soil in which to grow just such a sense of attachment to the state which nationalists have produced. If we do consider the importance of Weber's legitimate-force notion of the state, then we can recognize how crucial communal legitimacy is for those wanting to run states – and hence much of the importance of the nation. For if you're going to allow that only the state can legitimately use force – and if you are going to trust that it will do so in your defence and interests – then you need a good reason for believing that you are integrally a part of that state. National identification offers one such reason.

And so state-building and nation-building alike represent forms of nationalist struggle towards stronger and more legitimate forms of power, their interwoven processes strengthening state and nation simultaneously. As the symbols of authority – the daily emblems and rituals of shared life – are shaped and embedded, so the nation and the state both take form and become more sturdy: so state media are given a national identity, while the symbolic dimensions of the headship of state, national anthems, governmental induction and military organization all come to possess a national quality while yet relating to state forms and occasions; the laws of the state reinforce national self-image; and so on.

Yet the state's most prized asset of all is its sovereignty, and again this provides a very important part of our understanding of the nature and appeal of nationalism. Arguably the central of all nationalist notions is the idea that political sovereignty is a right held by the nation, and that the nation should possess sovereignty over itself as a free, independent, autonomous, self-governing and united unit.[87] Here again, therefore, power is absolutely central to nationalism (power being the defining feature of states).[88] To a nationalist, human communities must be not only separate and distinct, and defined according to their own peculiar culture; they should also be sovereign and independent, holding communal power over themselves.

There are subtler aspects to this nationalist argument as it has evolved over time, and they relate especially to the issue of legitimacy and to the question of freedom. If power is lastingly to work, then it must be considered legitimate by the community within which it operates.[89] The nationalist solution to this problem involves the vesting of political and cultural power in the hands of people who are drawn from (and representative of) the community over which such power is wielded. If those who rule over me are like me, and if they share my national culture, habits and assumptions, then they are more likely to frame a world which is in accordance with my interests, and within which I will be able to flourish. So if the national and the political boundaries are as neatly matched as is realistically possible, then one problem of power is appealingly resolved by sovereignty residing in a community which will be ruled by its own kind.

Yet there is another level also to this nationalist argument, and it relates to the nature of consent, democracy and freedom as they are embodied in nationalist conceptions of power. Perhaps the most telling way of considering this is through looking at the innovative and influential ideas of two men: John Locke and Jean-Jacques Rousseau.

An Oxford-educated English philosopher and political theorist, John Locke challenged then-existing arguments in favour of absolute monarchy and the divine right of the monarch. In his own political theory (famously articulated in his *Two Treatises of Government* (1690)), he asserted that political power existed for the public good, and that legitimate political authority rested on the consent of the governed. If the basis of proper government was indeed consent, then the power held by rulers was held as a trust for the people who so consented; and power could legitimately be removed by the people if that trust was not respected by the rulers who held it.

In such a view, society represented a form of contract with proto-democratic dimensions. Each individual, together with every other individual, agreed to give up to the community the right of enforcing the law of reason, for the purpose of preserving life, liberty, peace and property. A legislative power would thus be established, with popular consent, and for the good of the people. So the people effectively delegated power to a legislative authority which could be altered or removed, were it to act contrary to the popular interest and thereby to betray the trust vested in it. Lockeian emphasis upon the communal consent of the governed, upon power being properly legitimated only by the consent of the people, allowed for supreme power to rest with the community, and it emphasized a communal liberty to deal with wrongful rulers.

The relevance of this to nationalist conceptions of power is profound. For what is to be the unit of such free expression of popular will? What is to be the community over which such rightfully established legislative authority will prevail? How will such arrangements be struggled for and set up and then guarded? In each case, the historical answer has led to the nation and to nationalist struggle on the nation's behalf. Moreover, this emphasis on consensual power – effectively self-government – not only holds within it the embryo of later, fuller theories of national self-determination; this Lockeian argument also interweaves communal consent, power, equality and freedom in a manner which has been central to modern nationalism: 'freedom of men under government is to have a standing rule to live by, common to every one of that society, and made by the legislative power erected in it'. The power to make laws is one vested in rulers by freely expressed communal will, and – just as we are equal in the state of nature – so too in society as it is envisaged by Locke, the laws produced are ones that are experienced equally and applied impartially. There will, in Locke's words, be 'a settled legislative and a fair and impartial execution of the laws made by it'.[90] Law, in this view, could ultimately be seen to emancipate rather than restrict people, and Locke's precise mechanism for this involved the community – the nation – bestowing authority on a legislative power whose laws were applied equally to all in the community. Thus freedom.

This idea that sovereign power rests with the people's freely expressed will (and that the interweaving of sovereignty, equality and freedom lies at the heart of nationalism and helps to explain its appeal) is one which becomes even more crisp if we examine the thinking of the great Geneva-born political philosopher, Jean-Jacques Rousseau.

The latter's ideas vitally developed concepts which were to define much nationalist thinking, and it was in the period shortly after his death that nationalism truly emerged. Popular sovereignty was prominent here, and it was the late-eighteenth-century French Revolution which most influentially marked the new world order. 'Each people is independent and sovereign,' the 1795 French Declaration of Rights proclaimed; 'This sovereignty is inalienable.'[91] Indeed, it was only in the post-French Revolutionary period that the nation became politically central as the dominant unit of political allegiance, and as the main vehicle for popular political expression. For the Revolution challenged the previously pervasive assumption that rulers could rule without requiring the supportive endorsement or will of the people over whom they ruled; and so sovereignty effectively now shifted from monarch to national people. In 1700 most of Europe lay under the rule of people whose power was hereditary, and who felt that they owed their authority to God and not to the people over whom they ruled; by 1800 rulers were aware of the idea (and the threat) of power resting in popular sovereignty, and of sovereignty lying with the nation of equal and free citizens rather than in the person of the monarch or ruler. A new world had been born. State-centred, and based on the idea of popularly-determined national sovereignty, the post-Revolutionary world embodied a transformation in political imagination. Monarchical rights and hierarchies were replaced with a nation possessing sovereign power and participative, representative rights; the people could now replace the ruler as the focus for sovereign power.

Rousseau himself is often too closely associated with French Revolutionaries who, in truth, adopted some of his ideas rather than necessarily implementing them appropriately. But this new, post-French Revolutionary world of national sovereignty was one whose central idea, as far as nationalism is concerned, can indeed be seen to derive from Rousseau's innovative arguments, especially in his extraordinary *Social Contract* (1762). Equality and liberty ran deeply through Rousseau's thinking, and it was his interlocking together of sovereignty, equality and freedom which lay at the heart of his contribution to modern nationalism. For the Rousseauan vision involved a community which offered a distinctive kind of freedom, and which therefore held a special appeal. There was a profound liberty, he argued, to be found in obeying laws which one had, as an equal part of the sovereign people, oneself effectively prescribed – 'obedience to a law one prescribes to oneself is freedom'.[92] Laws may on occasion restrict my liberty (forbidding certain actions, insisting on the performance of others); but since the sovereign power which devises and implements all these laws enjoys a sovereignty in which I share equally with everybody else in the community, I am therefore emancipated by the very process of law being created and sustained effectively by my own will and authority. As equal citizens, we share popular sovereign power in equal measure, and we are emancipated as a result.

For the nation and for nationalists, this argument has had the most profound importance: for, although Rousseau wrote explicitly for Geneva and the city-state, it was the nation which was the community within which this Rousseauan logic was historically to be played out. It is significant that Rousseau himself assumed a national framework to be appropriate and necessary, for purposes of unity and stability, and that he therefore strongly favoured nation-building as providing a communal foundation for political sovereignty. The nation was the community within which sovereign power resided, legitimated in equal measure by all the members of that nation. Thus individual attachment to national sovereignty can be seen to make individual sense: according to Rousseau's argument, it is through an equal share in national sovereign power that we can all be freed.

This point leads us to our third crucial aspect of nationalist power, for in nationalism the state and sovereignty tend also to be joined by the concept of self-determination. If Rousseau's ideas legitimated the determination of political organization or government by the people, then, by extension, this suggested that a wider process – involving all peoples – might also be justified. Behind nationalist enthusiasm for one's own national freedom lies the assumption of an international order which is modelled according to the universal principle of all nations self-determining their political future; for nationalists tend to assume that the world is properly divided into nations, each possessing its own distinctiveness and rights. Indeed, nationalism has been a doctrine of self-determination ('the power of a population to decide its own government and political relations'[93]), as much as it has been almost anything else. Nationalists have defended the right of national majorities within a territory collectively to decide their own political lives and, in doing so, to enjoy freedom from outside control or power or domination. Hence the importance to nationalists of the collective will (or, at least, of something which comes as close as possible to this, or which can be plausibly presented as such) and of collective self-rule.

This notion of the national group possessing the right to decide and to manage its collective actions and rules and behaviour has defined much modern world politics. Its combination of the ideas of autonomy, consent and freedom has rendered it appealing to many; and US President Woodrow Wilson's influential 1918 declaration in favour of this concept of self-determination famously inaugurated an era in which the principle was seen by many as the proper foundation for the international order. For nationalists, there has long been a tendency to pursue the expression of self-determination through the medium of the sovereign state; but the legitimizing power of this principle need not express itself only through that form of power, or through states which neatly match national borders. In practice, some nationalists (many Irish people among them) have not demanded independent statehood, being satisfied instead with autonomy within wider states. More flexible patterns of expression have often enough offered perfectly feasible ways of matching popular will to political realities, and as a result federal or multi-national arrangements have at times emerged to prominence. For all its difficulties with competing nationalisms, the United Kingdom offers one possible example, many in Wales, Scotland and Ireland having been nationalist yet satisfied with less than full separation from England. And if, for example, a Scottish parliament possessing powers far short of full independence for a purely national state might satisfy the rights of Scottish people to political self-determination within the multi-national United Kingdom, then a similar case could be made in relation to Catalan or Basque nationalisms also in their relationship with Spain, since in each case many adherents have stated an acceptance of limited autonomy rather than absolute separatist independence as the national goal.

So, while self-determination still lies at the heart of the argument, it might be that the actual expression of national, communal will could produce structures far short of traditional nationalist expectations, and that this might involve, for example, the right of communal veto over certain political or cultural developments, on behalf of a national group within a multi-national state (something which began to emerge at the end of the twentieth century in the case of Northern Ireland, for example).

Certainly, history tells us that, for all its undoubted allure, self-determination as traditionally understood (a sovereign, independent state for each nation) has in fact failed to solve the problem that it was set. The places in which self-determination was most urgently tried as the key to unlocking a national problem, have often tended to be the very places in which it has been least easily used. Where the concept seems most required – to solve a problem of disputed legitimacy, power, sovereignty and nationalism – is exactly where there tends to be least agreement about which 'self' should do the 'determining'. (Where there exists no such dispute, there probably doesn't exist a problem requiring solution.) So in Ireland, Israel/Palestine, Spain, the former Yugoslavia and many other conflict areas around the world, the identification of an agreed communal self has proved elusive and reflective of the very conflict requiring resolution. Indeed, it may well be (as some have powerfully argued) that the attempt to apply the principle of national self-determination in fact produces, not order, but rather disorder in international affairs.[94]

As far as nationalists themselves tend to be concerned, however, self-determination (whether in the traditional nation-state form, or through more sophisticated veto-style arrangements) remains a central political right; nationalists still tend to assume that the world is naturally divided into nations, each of which possesses inalienable self-determining rights. Part of the point, and much of the appeal, here is the question of authenticity. If those ruling over you are to enjoy your support, then they must be seen authentically to represent your identity and your interests; if the government under which you live is one chosen by the communal will of those like yourself, then it will not only be assumed to reflect your own communal (and therefore individual) self-image in comforting ways, but also powerfully to pursue your own advantage. The power for which nationalist communities struggle is a special and hypnotic kind of power: it is legitimate because it is authentically representative of the community itself, pursuant of its interests and determined by the free expression of its will. So nationalist movements typically tend not merely to demand that their culture be tolerated, but rather that there be created a government in their own self-image which will have the power to sustain communal culture.

This is where nationalism and democracy so significantly intersect.[95] Despite the frequent and understandable hostility of some liberal observers towards nationalism and towards its uglier, anti-democratic features, an argument could also be made that nationalism has been the foundation stone upon which much effective, democratic experience has historically been built.[96] In this sense, liberal democrats have themselves frequently relied (perhaps unwittingly) on nationalism.[97] For if democratic politics are to flourish, then one requires some agreed, sustainable, meaningful unit or set of units within which they will do so. A single world community – with decisions made across global elections – clearly cannot prove workable; the hope that we might all – under globalization, or socialism, or Marxism, or a universally shared religion – become world-citizens in a single democratic unit has not happened and shows no sign of coming to pass. Similarly, however, democratic decisions about allocating power and resources cannot sensibly be made in tiny political units (democracy by the street, for example). No: some reasonably sized and clearly specified political community is required, one which possesses meaningful identity and power, is able to engage in collective communication, and sees itself as a continuous entity. Nationalists and their nations, for all their undoubted flaws, have often provided that entity (or have, at least, provided the basis upon which states have built such lasting communities). Indeed, the nation – or something like it – has often been invisibly presumed in discussions of democracy, justice and equality, by commentators who have celebrated these phenomena while sneering at nationalism itself.

The case is not, of course, a simple one. Nationalists have frequently displayed a cavalier or even hostile attitude towards the democratic expression of particular will within their respective nations (and we've seen this in the Irish story, as with the attitudes of republicans during 1916–23 or 1968–98, for example). Nationalist regimes have all too often been authoritarian in practice; and there has frequently emerged a clash between the imagined popular will of the nationalist zealot's mind (in accordance with which aggressive action is often taken), and the (usually more mild and mixed) will of the actually existing people of that zealot's nation. Much of what liberal-democratic observers understandably find distasteful about nationalist experience arises from this tension: as when nationalist movements bully supposed or actual fellow-nationals into activity or conformity which the latter clearly resent and oppose.

There is also a second problem, alluded to above, that while nations might be necessary to the effective functioning of democracy, establishing the appropriate boundaries of such nations can prove and has proved an often bloody and difficult process, generative of further conflict and cruelty. But the point is not that nationalism is purely democratic; rather that, for all the practical difficulties in establishing national boundaries, and for all the anti-democratic action of nationalists in historical practice, nations and nationalists have proved the basis for much modern democratic decision-making and governance. Paradoxically, nationalism may be seen historically to have proved both essential to democracy and – all too often, in political practice – deeply anti-democratic.

Among Irish nationalists, much of the appeal of nationalist community and struggle has certainly involved their combined capacity to offer power, both as the mechanism for achieving things and as the goal which must be delivered. Repeatedly, this has involved acquiring control over, or at the very least redefining the power structures within, the state. Why pursue land-related goals through nationalism? In part, because nationalism – in the Parnellite case, for instance – offered a means of effecting redress through the state's mechanism of power: parliament. How best would you protect your own people (in settings of intercommunal conflict like the north) or culture (in early-twentieth-century Ireland) or economic opportunity? Through creating a state in which you – or people like you – were in charge of police and army and cultural organization and law and economy. So nationalism has again and again involved the reinvention, or the gaining of access to, or the acquiring of state power: the United Irishmen, Daniel O'Connell, the Fenians, the IPP, Sinn Féin, the IRA, young Fianna Fáil, the INLA and IRSP all exemplify this trend. The message has been often repeated: struggle for a legitimate state, and then defend it.

Sovereignty was vital here. The birth of nationalism in Ireland coincided with the eighteenth-century emergence of the idea at the very heart of nationalism itself: that equality, sovereignty and freedom were interlinked in the democratic nation, in which power now rested with the sovereign people. This detonating argument resounded as the French Revolution helped bring nationalism to Ireland, a process aided by the fact that the radicalism of that other great contemporary Revolution – in America – again involved the flowering of such radical notions. Personal connections were crucial here: many in Ulster, for example, had relatives in America. And it was through personal linkages that this central nationalist egalitarianism took such deep root: Drennan and Russell were directly influenced by Rousseau's ideas; Tone and Emmet had read Locke; Tom Paine and his works had appealed to many Irish radicals; and so on, Locke, Rousseau and Paine being the routes by means of which nationalism arrived in late-eighteenth-century Ireland in egalitarian, emancipatory form. Once embedded in Irish nationalist thinking, this central notion – the welding together of sovereignty, equality and liberty – then became seemingly ineradicable, evident in epochal moments such as the 1919 Declaration of Independence. In pre-nationalist Ireland sovereignty had been a less prominent matter (the mid-seventeenth-century Confederate Catholics had not, for example, claimed it); but in the struggles of nationalist Ireland, it became the emblem of freedom. So the sovereignty of Ireland repeatedly takes prominent place in our narrative (with equality and freedom again and again to be seen); the material dimensions of sovereignty were evident in the writings of James Fintan Lalor, and the symbols of sovereignty emerged again and again conspicuously among nationalists' own concerns (as in the debate over the Treaty of 1921).

And the bedrock for this representative sovereign arrangement has been self-determination. For popular sovereignty to work, agreed boundaries for self-determining people are required, and the banner of self-determination has been flown repeatedly in Ireland. The case for Home Rule rested upon it. Irish nationalists in the early twentieth century argued that theirs was an ancient nation which had been subjected unwillingly to foreign domination, and which had an historic right to self-determination and freedom. IRA man Dan Breen was confident in the logic of self-determination and, again, pro- and anti-Treatyite both claimed it in the 1920s – as did so many nationalist movements pursuing independence, or those defending it once it had been won, or those eventually claiming a modified form of communal veto within the refashioned Northern Ireland of the Belfast Agreement of 1998. And, while we have seen just how anti-democratic some vanguardist nationalists have been in Ireland at times, there surely remains an intersection between self-determination, sovereignty and democracy. If democracy is to work, it requires a political unit to which people give respect and lasting allegiance, and the nation has – in Ireland as elsewhere – answered this call. It has not been a neat process, for the island and the nation are not coterminous. From O'Connell onwards, Ireland has had a democratic mass nationalism; but from O'Connell onwards, it has effectively coincided only with Catholic Ireland. Thus nationalists – whether John Hume or Gerry Adams, Michael Collins or Eamon de Valera – have proclaimed self-determination as the basis for democracy and nation alike, only to see a partial fulfilment achieved. The very logic which underpinned Irish independence for most of the country – popular will – proved an insuperable barrier to nationalist progress in the unionist north-east.

The achievements here should be respected, just as the flaws must be acknowledged, in the nationalist record. Liberal democracy is clearly flawed in some ways,[98] but of the various possible contexts for creating nations and nationalism (imperial, absolutist, state-totalitarian, fascist, communist, Islamist), it is hard to see that we have yet come up with a better one. Nationalism in Ireland has not been consistently democratic; but it has been the basis upon which an impressive democratic tradition – from O'Connell through Parnell and Redmond to de Valera and Lemass and beyond – has been built.

Taking power in Ireland has, then, been an appealing nationalist goal. And nationalism has appealed also because it has offered the scale of operation on which basis major change could be effected. This was true of the O'Connellite mass mobilization for Catholic Emancipation, the Parnellite campaigns for land revolution and progress towards Home Rule, the Revolutionism of Sinn Féin during and after the First World War, and the organized, rival nationalist movements of Northern Ireland after the 1960s. Power as nationalist goal, and power as means of getting what you want to get effectively, have both been central to the appeal of nationalism. For the broader explanation of nationalism relates, not merely to the power which nationalists seek to attain, but also to the power which they use in order to pursue, achieve or maintain it. Frequently, nationalism involves the enforcing or attempted reversal of power imbalances (imposing a national empire, liberating a colony from imperial control), by means of the use of power as leverage. Much of the practical definition of nationalism – what it does, day to day; how it affects people's lives; why it appeals so much to people – involves questions of the deployment of power as attempted leverage. The nationalist community engaged in struggle is one which must have some means of pursuing or producing the change which nationalist thinking considers to be essential, and this involves social power.[99] This can take the form of a wide range of mechanisms (violent, propagandist, electoral-parliamentary, intimidatory, economic, administrative; but also verbal, ideological and through other methods of forceful persuasion or presentation); and it implies a certain scale of activity. Not only does the active or target community need to be of significant size, but the mechanisms of mobilization require also to be more than merely parochial.

And nationalism is defined by questions of power even once initial goals (an independent state, a cultural renaissance) have been realized: the national state itself will hold political and physical power (and many nationalists are attracted by the possibility of wielding this); the cultural rebirth will need to be enforced or maintained; dissidents within the community will have to be prevented from diluting the true national customs; and so on. Ideological as well as physical power will frequently play its part in this latter process of nationalist activity: for nationalists will ideally establish for themselves such legitimacy for the national and the national authority that no mechanical application of force or threat is required in order for nationalist power to be exerted.

4

In all belligerent countries [in the First World War], the vast majority of socialists and trade unionists supported their respective national governments.

David Howell[100]

Community, struggle and power. These three themes, intricately interwoven, represent the key to defining and understanding nationalism and to explaining its immense historical importance and appeal. Human nature and instincts, psychological and material needs, at deep levels point us towards meaningful and special community. We want security, safety, belonging, purpose, self-worth and cooperation; we require effective and affective means of communication with those around us; and in the national community (variously through territory, people, assumed descent, culture, history, ethics and exclusivism) we frequently find all of this. Yet nationalism involves not just community but community in organized struggle: for independence or for expansion, for cultural rebirth or purity – for a wide variety of goals and through a range of methods, as a national group. And that struggle is ultimately focused on power, in terms of the goal to be pursued (very often the self-determined, sovereign and independent state) and also of the means of pursuing it (the leverage by which change is to be wrought).

But why is it *nationalism* which so widely and lastingly answers these needs? Can we not find distinctive community at the smaller-scale level of family, or village, or cultural enthusiasm (such as musical sub-group, or sporting identification)? Can we not obtain and exert power through our job, or struggle for the redress of wrongs on a less grand scale than the national? The answer lies in appreciating the interlinked nature of community, struggle and power, and the extra-ordinary force and varied capacity of this combination. The family can and does offer profound belonging and meaning: but it cannot possibly provide a sufficiently large scale of social interaction and communication (to meet the needs of exchange and safety); it cannot provide the means for struggle of a significant kind (for effective protection, or for the allocation of large-scale resources), since its scale (like that of the village, or even the city) is far too limited; and it cannot provide access to serious power. One can wield power through the medium of one's prominent role in a business, but not anything like the kind of power which nations (larger, stronger, better-resourced) can deploy. Again, dignity can be achieved through many non-national routes, but nationalism offers a more durable, large-scale association which bolsters individual dignity in extremely powerful fashion, not least because of its very long-term history and ancient gravity. Part of the appeal of nationalism is that its particular combination of community, struggle and power makes it more durably coherent than any larger-scale alternative (the world community), and yet so much more effective and powerful than smaller rivals (the musical sub-culture, the allegiance to a football team, and so on).

And its capacity simultaneously to meet such an extraordinary variety of needs, and to offer such a wide range of possibilities, also undermines its rivals in a more absorptive manner. For nationalism can be the means through which one meets all those other needs too. The family to be protected, the economic and other interests of the local town, the success of the business in which one is employed – none of these units (family, town, business) can do what nationalism can do; but nationalism presents itself successfully as being able indeed to meet the demands of these other units of attachment in its furtherance of the nation's well-being, and therefore to subsume these other allegiances within itself. This, I think, is the key to understanding why nationalism has so outshone competitors in the modern world: that through its interweaving of particular kinds of community, struggle and power it has persuaded people that it can meet the needs of – for example – region, sex or class in ways that regionalism, feminism or socialism have been unable to do; in tying together so many aspects of human life, nationalism has been able to seem to meet the needs of those whom such rival 'isms' seem necessarily to exclude (with regionalism, those from other regions; with feminism, men; with socialism, the non-working class). The nation suggests that it can accommodate all classes, while socialism cannot plausibly claim to treat equally all within the nation; religion can offer the most profound of beliefs and understandings and attachments, but it cannot – as itself – offer the kind of structures of meaningful power that the nation can provide (since neither a small-church local government, nor a world-government of one religion, is feasible).

For the issue is not so much why people group themselves according to identity or allegiance, but rather why national identity and allegiance have so predominated over all rival forms of group identification. Despite all its undoubted flaws, nationalism has appeared to provide a richer, more powerful, more comprehensive and more varied set of possibilities than its rivals have managed to do. It has promised, seemingly, everything. The persistent contagiousness of nationalism lies in its success in persuading so many people for so much of the time that it can deal with everything at once, and that it can meet many differing needs and agendas under the same grand banner: the economic and the material as well as the psychological and the spiritual; the cultural as well as the political; the individual and local and the most banal of necessities, but also the demands of the grandest teleological thinking; the rational as well as the visceral or emotional; millenarian hope as well as daily practicality. The nationalist is not seeking *either* to obtain more land for himself *or* greater respect for her local culture *or* institutional representation as a guarantee of future well-being *or* protection from and revenge upon enemies – but all these things at once. And it is that mixture of apparent efficacy and multi-dimensional appeal which makes nationalism the world's dominant force.

It should be stressed that I write this, not as a nationalist, but rather as someone offering an explanation for nationalism's immense and durable strength. And there seems to me to be one further point that needs to be highlighted at this stage: for one melody which links together many of the themes which have emerged so far in this argument about nationalism is freedom. Nationalism has frequently constricted as well as liberated. But for nationalists themselves, one of the key, attractive features of so much nationalist thought, ambition and action is that it involves the pursuit or maintenance of freedom. The freedom to express oneself through one's own, unrestricted culture; freedom from the external restraint of alien power; the freedom embodied in the Rousseauan chain of sovereignty, equality and liberty; the freedom found in economic advantage delivered by nationalist victory; the formal freedom embodied in independent state power and open representation – in seeking all these and many other forms of liberty, the nationalist world is one to which freedom is perceivedly central, and which further attracts many people as a result.

In Ireland we have seen all this clearly as it has historically evolved in detail. Community (territory, people, descent, culture, history, ethics, exclusivism); struggle; and power. And all three elements have been so alluring as part of the nationalist process because all three have been so intimately, inextricably interwoven together within it, between them allowing for satisfaction of the very many motivations and desires of those who have constituted nationalist Ireland through history.

5

> Nationalism is a doctrine invented in Europe at the begin-
> ning of the nineteenth century.
>
> Elie Kedourie[101]

Perhaps the central debate in recent decades concerning the nature of
nationalism has revolved around the question of its modernity.[102] Is
nationalism a modern phenomenon, created in the world of the French
Revolution and only relevant in the period inaugurated by the late
eighteenth century? Or does it in fact enjoy a much older vintage, with
roots into the early-modern or medieval periods? Is it a phenomenon
created comparatively recently, and reflecting voluntary choices, allegiances and instrumental inventions? Or is it something more organic
and perennial – even primordial – in nature?

In concluding our attempt to understand the true nature of nationalism, it might be helpful briefly to examine this debate, to try to
resolve it by means of the arguments offered above concerning community, struggle and power, and to see how things have worked in
practice in Ireland.

The extraordinarily large literature of theories of nationalism defies
easy classification, but one three-fold way of making sense of it is to
talk respectively of 'perennialists', 'modernists' and 'ethno-symbolists'.
Perennialists are those who would stress the longevity and seamless
continuity of the nation deep into history, some even adopting what
might be termed a primordial approach (namely, one which considers
nations to have existed effectively from the beginning of human
community). In this light, nations seem natural and innate, perhaps
even timeless, and they tend to be seen effectively as one of the givens
of human experience; allegiance to the nation transcends the material,
the instrumental and the rational, and has something of a spiritual and
timeless dimension to it. More moderately, some scholars who might
be labelled perennialist hold that the nation existed in ancient or
medieval history, rather than being a modern creation. They might
point to the existence, for example, of biblical nations and even

nationalisms.[103] They might stress the importance of recognizing medieval or early-modern nations or nationalisms, identifying communal, national identity as pre-modern rather than modern,[104] and arguing that – in terms of defined territory, ecclesiastical unification, language and literature, economic forces and bureaucracy – there existed in the medieval period a recognizable nation. Thus understood, modern nations are just the recent versions of something very, very old. Certainly, some scholars have stressed the deep medieval roots of peoples' self-images as given political communities, possessing solidarity, shared collective culture, and myths of common origin.[105]

These perennialist or primordial[106] readings of nationalism clearly reinforce and overlap with the assumptions held by very many nationalists themselves about what they assume to be their organic and ancient nations. For one committed to the cause of the nation, it is far more comforting to believe that the nation possesses a given, even timeless quality, rather than to see it as something artificially conjured to suit late-eighteenth-century needs. Nationalist language is full of images of sleeping nations needing to be awakened, and these notions of long-pre-existing entities are in turn supported by perennialist arguments.

But such views have generated fierce debate,[107] and they have certainly not been dominant within the scholarly understanding of nationalism in the last generation. Rather, most writers on nationalism have presented it as an emphatically recent, modern phenomenon, rather lacking in ancient depth. Just as some historians have been sceptical about the application of the word 'nationalism' to pre-eighteenth-century periods,[108] so too most theorists of nationalism have tended to see it as a creature of the period which began around the late eighteenth century,[109] while some would locate its birth even later.[110] Nations are seen by such modernists to be modern creations, produced by modern conditions to suit distinctively modern needs.

For the important point about this modernist school of nationalism is not just its argument about the timing of nationalism's emergence, but also the causal explanation offered to explain that timing. Arguably the most influential modernist scholar of all was the brilliant sociologist, anthropologist and philosopher Ernest Gellner, who scathingly dismissed nationalist self-images in a series of important books and essays. It was not, Gellner argued, that nations produced nationalists but entirely the other way around. Nations were not timeless, ancient entities, but artificial and deceptive modern creations which served a specifically modern purpose. 'The central mistake committed both by the friends and the enemies of nationalism is the supposition that it is somehow *natural*. . . . The truth is, on the contrary, that there is nothing natural or universal about possessing a "nationality".'[111]

The argument ran as follows. In pre-modern times, association was local: family, kin and tribe were satisfactory units if one lived in small, agrarian, contained, self-sufficient, stable communities and therefore had no need of wider interaction or affiliation. (In sixteenth-century Europe, for example, the vast majority of people lived in very small communities indeed, only a tiny fraction of the population inhabiting towns of 20,000 or more people.) With the onset of modern technological change, however, and with the consequent industrialization of society, these older bonds no longer sufficed. If modern society were to be effective, then people needed to be mobile rather than to live in static communities: they were now required to migrate in large numbers into industrial towns and cities, and so they needed to be able to communicate across much wider sections of humanity, to share a culture with the people with whom they would now be living and working and economically exchanging in much larger numbers. For those societies which had modernized in this way, there had to be a larger frame of meaningful association than the purely local, and this – the need for a new nexus linking together larger numbers of people, and for a more extensive shared culture – explained the origins of nationalism. This is what made nations and nationalism necessary and what explained their emergence and power.

It was and remains an ingenious argument. How would newly industrial society work? By a shift from an old world, in which high culture, literacy and education were the preserve of an elite minority, to a new world – modernity – in which such things were pervasive, standardized and widely shared. In the new world of nations there existed – and there had to exist – 'a literate codified culture' permitting 'context-free communication'.[112] Members of the new and much wider community would be educated in and would all now share what had previously been an elite high culture: they would acquire the standardized skills necessary to enable them to move around and communicate within necessarily mobile industrial society; centrally-controlled education would produce this new uniformity and this pervasively shared idiom. Local bonds having been eroded by industrialization and by accompanying social change, what would bind this newly integrating, larger body of people together if not the shared assumptions, languages and culture which are nationalism? In Gellner's view, therefore, nationalism emerged as a function of industrialization, a response to the structural needs of industrial society;[113] pre-industrial society had produced a pre-nationalist community, industrial society a nationalist one, and nationalism was effectively a result of the shift 'from an earlier condition of mankind, when high culture was a speciality and a privilege, to a new condition when high culture becomes universalized and pervades entire societies'.[114]

But if nationalism was indeed merely a functional response to new social conditions, then it clearly isn't what its enthusiasts have claimed, believed and assumed it to be. For a scholar such as Ernest Gellner, nations were not timeless and self-evident and given, but were instead contingent upon specific historical circumstances and exigencies, and they were therefore open to cold social explanation: 'modernists like myself believe that the world was created round about the end of the eighteenth century, and nothing before that makes the slightest difference to the issues we face'.[115] 'The cultures [nationalism] claims to defend and revive are often its own inventions, or are modified out of all recognition ... nationalism is *not* the awakening of an old, latent, dormant force, though that is how it does indeed present itself. It is in reality the consequence of a new form of social organization, based on deeply internalized, education-dependent high cultures, each protected by its own state.'[116]

There is no single, monolithic modernist school of interpretation, but rather a family of approaches which share similarities. Some present nations as the product of industrialization, others of capitalism itself. But Gellner's own very powerful arguments epitomize some of the main aspects of this kind of approach: the nation is created by nationalists in a modern world inaugurated by the late eighteenth century; it can be explained by forces other than those which its enthusiasts invoke; modernization explains not just the timing but the meaning of its arrival.

Another highly influential member of this modernist family is Benedict Anderson, who – with his Irish father and a childhood partly spent in Waterford ('Waterford was home'[117]) – might be considered Ireland's only theorist of nationalism of genuine world influence and standing. Anderson's stress on the importance of print capitalism for the emergence and development of nationalism has been overshadowed by his famous, much-quoted depiction of the nation as an imagined community. Both are telling points. The historical convergence of capitalism and print technology had dire implications for utterly local, multiply diverse languages since a larger unit could now be imagined and communicated with, in ways which had previously been impossible. And the concept of an imagined community clearly does represent one key feature of modern nations: for mass nationalism to be successful, it was obviously necessary for there to be more than an actual intimacy with fellow members of one's community. The modern nation is a mass phenomenon, requiring large-scale assent and mobilization; it thus involves not just association with those immediately around you, but identification with a much broader, imagined, largely anonymous group of people with whom you form the nation.[118]

According to this argument, mass literacy and new print technology combined to facilitate this imagined community, to produce a large-scale public opinion central to nationalist movements. And so the legitimizing potential of nationalism could be realized in our democratic age: popular sovereignty could only make sense if the people could imagine themselves to be part of a large community, and newspapers, periodicals and books all contributed here to the emergence of nationalism, allowing for the spread of ideas and identity over a far wider range than was possible before.

But are either of these positions – the perennialist/primordialist, or the modernist – ultimately persuasive? If nations and nationalisms are as ageless as perennialists sometimes suggest, then how are we to account for the profundity of the difference between nations in different historical eras? As modernists rightly point out, it's only in the modern period that nation-states with mass-based nationalisms historically emerged (1789 for France, 1860 for Italy, 1870 for Germany); and the term 'nationalism' itself is a relatively recent one[119] (as is the formalized ideology to which this term is applied). To read nations and nationalisms further back into history risks anachronism and distortion, and such readings can dubiously assume an innate, ahistorical quality to the nation. It was only in the eighteenth century,

Ernest Gellner would have reminded us, that nationalism was born; and it was only in the nineteenth that it spread and came to dominate political life. If nations are such perennial entities, then why is it that, as a philosophical justification for political legitimacy, involving free and collective popular rule expressed in state form, it is only in the post-eighteenth-century world that we have encountered nationalism? Moreover, there are clear cases of emphatically modern rather than ancient national constructions: the Afrikaners and their language did not exist, for example, until the late nineteenth century and yet they came to embody a very forceful nationalism.

On the other hand, there are several possible problems also with modernist arguments. If one defines nationalism in terms of what we have known since the French Revolution, then yes, it is indeed a modern phenomenon; but can we simply assume that only this, rather than earlier historical phenomena, is worthy of the word 'nationalism'? Does one have to share modern nationalist notions in order to qualify for that description, or might more flexible definitions be allowed? Again, while print and literacy rendered possible a wider diffusion of ideas and identity, they did not necessitate that it was *national* ideas and identities which therefore flourished. In itself, mass literacy would have been just as necessary for and just as facilitative of a global rather than a national identity. Anderson's print capitalism might have been necessary for the emergence and development of nationalism, but it might have yielded other, non-national outcomes just as effectively.

Yet again, is the modernist industrialization argument a sound one? In terms of timing, there is certainly a problem. In some cases (the Estonian, for example) it is clear that modern nationalism created a nation anew. But it is also true that there were some nations existing prior to the industrialization which Gellner and others held to have been their cause;[120] moreover, there are nationalisms which, though modern in period, flourish amid economic settings which are still pre-industrial. And in terms of causality there might be difficulties too: even if one substituted a more flexible variable than industrialization itself (the expansion of economic markets and mobility, for example), there still seems a suspiciously monocausal quality to this explanation of such a vast and varied phenomenon. Can nationalism really be accounted for by this unwitting mass response to the modernization of economic relationships? Is there not far more – and a far more conscious process – involved? Yes, nationalism may serve a function, but it is probable that its success lies in its having the capacity to serve far more than just one, and that nationalists themselves do indeed recognize precisely what some of these functions are.

So there are difficulties with each of these approaches; 'we should not allow ourselves to be seduced by either the modernist or the perennialist paradigms of nationality'.[121] And so some observers have sought to harmonize the insights of the perennialist and the modernist schools of thought (and to address some of the inadequacies of each approach) by suggesting that the key to understanding nationalism is what Anthony Smith has termed ethno-symbolism.[122] This approach stresses that modern nationalisms – though distinctive – can possess ancient depths; that they draw – in ways which feed but which also constrain them – on important pre-existing, pre-modern attachments and inheritances; that there is a great debt on modern nationalists' part towards their pre-modern ethnic culture and inheritance. For Smith, modern nations are successful only if they build on foundations which are deeply and distinctively pre-modern: there are continuities, roots and pre-echoes in the history of the nations and nationalisms we witness today. In particular, there is an ethnic core, and ethnicity is vital to appreciating the nature and evolution of nationalism. What exists in the modern period is not created from nothing, nor free from the bonds which are inherited from older ethnic pasts.

So ethno-symbolists stress that one can trace elements of national structures and attitudes and symbols in, for example, the medieval period. Modern nations, they contend, draw on earlier ethnically inherited symbols, attachments, traditions, memories, myths and practices: 'we can best grasp the character, role and persistence of the nation in history if we relate it to the symbolic components and ethnic models of earlier collective cultural identities'.[123] In this view, nationalism 'derives its force from its historical embeddedness',[124] resonating so powerfully with people today precisely because of the richness of a particular, historically located set of cultural inheritances. It is the layers of history and tradition and values and inherited symbolism which help to explain nationalism's power and its resonance.

So where modernists stress historical novelty and discontinuity, ethno-symbolists emphasize long-term continuities in national development, seeing nationalism as involving the reconstitution of something inherited rather than the creation of something entirely anew. These ethnic foundations, of course, allow not only for strong links between modern nationalisms and ancient ethnic communities, but also for at least the possibility of pre-modern nations.

So ethno-symbolist arguments might be seen as a compromise between perennialism and modernism. They recognize the important differences between ancient and modern nations, but they acknowledge – more than modernists tend to do – that we require long-term history and an analysis which looks back deep into the past if we are to understand nationalism; and they hold that it's not enough to study the nation-creating ideas of modern nationalist elites on their own. The inherited ties and sentiments and assumptions of mass, popular, pre-modern ethnicity are duly weighted as we try to understand how older attachments have helped to shape, strengthen and define what later nationalists have celebrated. As so often, Anthony Smith has expressed the argument with sharp lucidity:

> Although the nation, as a named community of history and culture, possessing a common territory, economy, mass education system and common legal rights, is a relatively modern phenomenon, its origins can be traced back to pre-modern ethnic communities. Such named *ethnies* with their myths of common descent, common memories, culture and solidarity, and associations with a homeland, are found in both the ancient and the medieval periods in many areas of the world.[125]

This approach helps to explain the importance of the symbolic dimension to nationalist thinking, and it also allows room for nationalists' own sense of the profound linkages between past and present. It accords with the way in which, for instance, the modern Russian and French nations have drawn respectively on the reservoirs of medieval Russia and France in terms of symbols and traditions and identities. For ethno-symbolists, the nation is best understood as an ethno-cultural community of old vintage.

There is clearly much weight in this argument about modern nations having ethnic origins, and an older ethnic core on which to build. It's not uncommon for examples of supposedly ancient or traditional folk cultures to be created or invented in the modern period;[126] but on many other occasions, contemporary nationalists often do have a powerful resource in the older ethnic traditions and roots on which they draw, and which survive (albeit modified) into the modern period. But this kind of approach involves not just the claim that old ethnic communities (*ethnies*) offer resources, but also that they are in some way limiting of what later happens. Put another way, if pre-modern history is – as people like Gellner seem to suggest – unimportant for the development of nationalism, then why did the specific nations that did come into existence actually do so? For Smith, the answer lies partly in the powerful historical resources open to some rather than to all potential nations. And if these older ties, sentiments and symbols are indeed important, then this might help to explain not only why modern nations have taken the particular shape that they have, but also why they have possessed such strong emotional hold over people who associate with such durable, transgenerational traditions. A considerable body of scholarly research has now been done examining those pre-modern cultures, ideas and beliefs which have given modern nationalism its persistence, intensity and wide prevalence.[127]

Powerful though it is, however, the ethno-symbolist case is not entirely persuasive. The term itself is arguably unhelpful, and not just for its inelegance. For it and its associated arguments seem to elevate the symbolic to an exaggerated position of importance. Sentiments, symbols and so on are indeed rightly stressed as crucial (and it might be said that modernist theories about industrialization tend to underestimate their role). But the long-rootedness of nations in the past surely relates not just – or even primarily – to the symbolic or the imagined. It relates also to very material questions: the inheritance (or not) of land; the attachment to particular territory in practical, possessive ways for very economic and physical, rather than symbolic, reasons.

And if 'ethno-symbolism' exaggerates the symbolic, then it might also be said to place unhelpful emphasis on the ethnic too. If an *ethnie* is a population with an identifying name, a myth of shared ancestry, common traditions, memories and culture, a link with a homeland, and some solidarity – and this is how such ethnic communities are defined by Smith himself[128] – then what is the analytical value in calling this an *ethnie* rather than simply calling it a nation?[129] (Smith himself acknowledges that his 'definitions of the nation and of the *ethnie* are closely aligned'.[130]) Why not call these ethnic myths, memories, symbols and so forth national myths, memories and symbols? And this suggests that there might be a certain circularity in the ethno-symbolist argument that nationalism derives much of its strength from its ethnic roots and ethnic past: we still need to explain the emergence and power of these very ethnic roots and pasts themselves, and this is highlighted if we honestly call them national rather than ethnic. To say that nationalism draws strength from the roots of its old nation might indeed be accurate: but calling it a 'nation' rather than an *ethnie* clarifies for us how important it is to explain this older phenomenon rather than assuming its existence and using it to help account for later nationalism.

Yet despite such objections to the arguments of ethno-symbolists – and they are partly objections to the term 'ethno-symbolism' itself – their attempt to combine rather than to polarize the varying schools of nationalist interpretation is surely the right approach to adopt. For the apparent dilemma about whether nations are modern or ancient probably misses the point, namely, that post-eighteenth-century nationalism is indeed a modern phenomenon, but that in very many cases it is a force built upon, constrained by and deriving power from earlier expressions of its associated nation. While perennialists tend to underestimate the degree to which something genuinely new was created in the eighteenth century, and modernists sometimes offer too historically shallow a reading of nationalism, a rounded approach will acknowledge that nationalism is neither ancient nor utterly, discretely modern: long historical roots and distinctively modern conditions have both been vital parts of the story.

So, as with the argument about whether nations are abstractions or a reality, so also this debate over whether they are old or new can be resolved by recognizing that, in fact, they are both. It does seem to me important to recognize the depth of the eighteenth-century fault-line: the Rousseauan notion of intersecting equality, popular sovereignty and freedom within the context of a nation represented something genuinely new, and this is central to nationalism as such. So we might want to clarify that nationalism emerges in the eighteenth century, and to distinguish therefore between the nation promoted by such nationalism, and the preceding proto-nation (first, primitive, ancestral) on which it built. But both nation and proto-nation are important aspects of the evolving story.

In Ireland as elsewhere, nationalists have at times misread the proto-national past on which they have built. But these pre-existing materials with which they work are not limitlessly malleable and they are not entirely false. It's been fashionable in recent decades to emphasize the 'inventedness' of nations and their associated traditions.[131] It has rightly (almost axiomatically) been stated by many observers that modern nationalists create the beliefs, traditions, symbols and arguments that constitute their nationalist ideology. But such a process (if it is to be successful) is far from unconstricted. Not all inventions work, not all inventions become popular and durable, and such truths apply in the realm of nationalist as well as scientific invention.[132] Just like other inventors, so too those who wish to create a nation or nationalism do so with limited rather than unlimited resources and materials; with ingredients which tend to act upon one another in some ways rather than in others; with an eye on those to whom the invention must appeal and seem useful if it is to succeed; and so on. Inventors of nations, like inventors of machines, are limited by their inheritance and by the context of their invention; the fact that something has been invented does not mean that it could have been successfully invented in just any shape or form chosen by its inventor.

So nationalism is clearly in crucial ways modern, and as such effectively arose in the eighteenth century. But certain aspects of nationalists' nations have deep and important roots in proto-national history. This is true of aspects of community (regarding territory, for example, or language and other key parts of culture), and also of pre-nationalist experiences of struggling for power in a proto-national setting. Prior to the eighteenth century, there might not have been a modern conception of popular sovereignty, but the notion of sovereign power over a nationally imagined territory was not unknown – and nor was it entirely irrelevant to later nationalist ideas and self-images. The Bible clearly possesses within it the idea of the nation, in ways that relate to modern Jewish nationalist politics, for example; but the idea of the masses as the egalitarian embodiment of sovereignty was clearly absent from the Old and the New Testament alike. Even some of those who disagree on when to date the appearance of nation or nationality seem able to agree that nationalism itself emerged as a post-French Revolutionary phenomenon;[133] and it seems clear that the emergence of late-eighteenth-century nationalism was a major fault-line in human history, as is acknowledged even by those who emphasize the long historical roots of the modern nation.[134]

The modernists are surely justified in claiming that national*ism*, as a doctrine and an ideological movement, is a modern phenomenon dating from the late eighteenth century and that many nations are also of fairly recent vintage. Equally, perennialists are right to point to the premodern continuities of at least *some* nations and to the recurrence, in different historical epochs, of a kind of collective cultural identity that may resemble the modern nation – resemble, but not be identical with the modern nation ... these modern nations are not created *ex nihilo*; they have premodern antecedents that require investigation in order to establish the basis on which they were formed.[135]

And what of Ireland? To what extent had there emerged – during the medieval period, for example – an Irish nation? In regard to the late-medieval period, this question of national frameworks has become a sharply contested one, with battle lines at times firmly drawn. Some have suggested that it is anachronistic to study late-medieval Ireland as a discrete, integral unit in itself, since it was only later that an Irish nation emerged to fit this model. Rather than projecting an Irish nation backwards from modern times, such arguments suggest that we would do better to look through lenses more historically appropriate to the period; we should acknowledge, for example, the existence of a Gaelic world which included part of Ireland but which also extended beyond it, and in thus understanding Gaelic Ireland as part of a wider Gaelic world, we are effectively undermining the idea that a discrete Ireland is the best framework within which to work.[136] In contrast, some have argued that Ireland did indeed exist as a meaningful entity in the late-medieval era (constitutionally, for example, as a lordship under the English Crown), and that to ignore or to dismiss this is to miss an important aspect of medieval Irish experience, namely, an Irish national consciousness.[137]

To those familiar with studying the more recent past, the sources available for medieval Ireland seem disconcertingly limited and patchy;

conclusions drawn from them concerning nations and nationalism might, as a consequence, appear elusive as it is very difficult to acquire the data upon which to base a thoroughly grounded judgment of what most people actually thought at the time. But it is possible, I think, to paint a portrait which interprets this period in light of our central, national question.

One part of that portrait seems to obscure any sense of a nation, nationality and certainly a nationalism.[138] From earliest times the inhabitants of Ireland were racially mixed rather than joined by ties of blood; and what did tie them together often undermined a discrete island framework. Catholic Christianity linked Irish identity into a wider, transnational network of authority and belief and community; and even the emergence of a Gaelic culture resistant to post-conquest Englishness involved an identification with a Gaelic world which covered only part of Ireland, and parts of the neighbouring island as well. There was certainly no modern-style popular self-determination nor, clearly, any Rousseauan concept of linking freedom, sovereignty and equality (far from it), or any arguments about mass nationalism being the foundation of political legitimacy. There was no rejection of royal rule; there was no self-conscious, popular mobilization of the kind familiar to nationalists in struggle; nor was there any equivalent of the modern state in terms of its depersonalized structures of permanent national authority (though there were, at least by the twelfth century, some royal ministers to carry out daily tasks of governing business). So, set against definitions of what we might now take to be a nation – 'a named community of history and culture, possessing a unified territory, economy, mass education system and common legal rights'[139] – it is clear that medieval Ireland fails to match up. Again, for the thirteenth and fourteenth centuries, even those who do identify a clear Irish nation and national identity tend not to posit the existence of a nationalism,[140] and this is surely right.

Units of allegiance remained largely local, with loyalty and power being highly personalized. In part this reflected the limited extent of population concentration and mobility: it was only really in the ninth century that towns and villages emerged in Ireland, and only after the twelfth-century invasion that more weighty urban centres such as Kilkenny began to flourish. So we can understand the doubts expressed by many scholars about whether the nation, and certainly nationalism, can generally be found in antiquity and in the early medieval era, especially since the role of modernization and of mass education has been stressed as key to the development of both phenomena.[141]

Even as late as the ninth century in Ireland, sovereignty remained rather fragmented. At the start of the tenth century, overlordships coexisted with smaller units which retained their own distinctive notions of identity. And even the strong and ambitious Brian Bóruma had not effectively established by the time of his death in 1014 a meaningful kingship of all Ireland. (As we've seen, the occasion for the Anglo-Norman invasion in the twelfth century itself was rivalry between competing Irish kings in a fragmented world of personalized power.)

So we should beware of too neat an insular reading of medieval Ireland, as though an embryonic Irish nation and nationality are necessarily the best context within which to understand the island in this period. The fact that we know Ireland later to have produced a strong nationalist movement focusing on independence and separateness should not lead us to assume anything of the sort for an earlier era in which no such nationalist sense dominated (or could have dominated) contemporary perceptions.

And yet, for all these limitations to any medieval Irish nation, there is another part of the picture to be painted, and it is plausible to suggest that there was something of a proto-nation in medieval Ireland. It's true that nationalism was a word never used in this period, and that much that was celebrated by later nationalists (the existence of the ancient Irish Celts, for example) now appears highly dubious. But while it might be acknowledged that nationalism did not exist in medieval Ireland, it remains true that there were, at least, embryonic elements of an Irish nationality and of an Irish nation present (certainly by the thirteenth century).[142] There seem to have been faintly drawn contours of what later was to emerge: in terms, for instance, of a tenth- to twelfth-century self-consciousness as *natio* or wider national community of ultimately shared descent;[143] or in terms of the perception by others – such as the incoming Anglo-Normans – that the inhabitants of the island were ethnically or racially other (and we have seen that one key part of nation formation has often related to the boundary between self and others).[144] Moreover, if it is dangerous to read too much back into earlier periods on the basis of what we now know to have ensued, then it is equally unsatisfactory to assume that earlier events have no relevance or importance for our understanding of the later evolution of political and cultural life.

So it is worth noting that the early Irish long enjoyed a standard language throughout the island, and that this gave them a certain cohesion – and awareness of cohesion – as a cultural unit. It is worth remembering that (while the attainment of political power throughout the island remained elusive until, perhaps, just before the Anglo-Norman incursion undermined it) the very pursuit of such all-Ireland power in itself displays an early sense of something like national identity and ambition. And, within the limitations of medieval possibility, the extent of the power wielded across much of Ireland by Turlough O Brien by the late eleventh century, or Turlough O Connor during the twelfth, should not be casually dismissed. As with later nationalism itself, there was a connection between power and struggle, with the growth of medieval kingship co-developing with the emergence of warfare, standing armies and the hiring of mercenaries. As so often elsewhere, the notion (in thirteenth- or fourteenth-century Ireland, for instance) that one was fighting against the foreigner could help to sharpen self-image as a unified or unifying nation.

Certainly, the *idea* of Ireland as a distinct political entity is evident from at least the twelfth century,[145] and this included a sense that the place might require defence against outsiders. Even the fact that some of those who arrived as conquerors in the twelfth century saw the event in terms of gaining sovereignty over the whole island, might paradoxically point us towards a sense of Irish unity and distinctiveness.

And we should not demand that medieval politics and culture interweave as they have done in more recent centuries. In modern polities, state and culture have very often been interwoven parts of the nation's world; but it would be anachronistic to demand of the Middle Ages that there exist a modern-style state or bureaucracy, and I think it's possible in the absence of such a state still to identify meaningful aspects of medieval proto-national culture and identity. By the late seventh century it was being claimed that the authority of the archbishop of Armagh extended over the whole of Ireland: in practice this may not have been the case, but in terms of a proto-national imagination it still possesses some significance. By the later medieval period of the thirteenth century, there was definitely at least some sense of national identity, and even earlier one can detect traces of it. Religious peregrination – *peregrinatio*, wandering, exile or pilgrimage – offers an example: for the *peregrinus* was thought to engage in more meaningful peregrination (making oneself a foreigner by leaving home) if they left Ireland,[146] rather than if they merely moved between Irish kingdoms. During the twelfth century a distinct, self-consciously Irish Church had developed. By the time we reach the thirteenth and fourteenth centuries, there is evidence from bardic poetry of at least a proto-national sense of shared history, tradition and geographical space.[147]

Such incipient notions of nation and national identity do not, of course, involve the kind of interweaving of community, struggle and power which later produced nationalism. But they do carry strong pre-echoes of each of these themes, and might be taken to indicate the existence in medieval Ireland of a proto-nation. Just as there were, in pre-modern settings elsewhere, traces of the proto-national,[148] so also there was in medieval Ireland a sense of Irish community, and of struggles for power extending across the island. There were aspects of culture (language, for example, or a distinctive Irish Christianity) which reflected a belonging and cooperation which were to be central to nationalism as it later developed and grew. These senses did increasingly relate to the territory of the island as such, in terms of royal and ecclesiastical power. And while elements of Gaelic Irish identity, for example, extended beyond the island – and while there were people in late-medieval Ireland outside that Gaelic identity – this need not entirely undermine the suggestion that elements upon which later Irish nationalism built can be discerned in the medieval period. (Even in the modern period Irish nationalist community stretches beyond the territory itself, and of course there exist many in modern Ireland who are not nationalist.)

In itself, there is nothing inherently misguided about identifying proto-national sense and identity in the medieval period. Some eminent scholars consider that Englishness, for example, is an ancient phenomenon, stretching back deep into the Middle Ages,[149] while the most famous of medieval English scholars, Bede, himself wrote in the eighth century in terms of a national history for England. Again, there was clearly a meaningful idea of nationhood in Scotland by at least the fourteenth century. Despite the limitations on medieval travel and movement, it was clearly possible for people to imagine themselves part of meaningful communities which extended far beyond those which they actually knew (Christianity provides the obvious illustration). Indeed, since the Bible was so long central to medieval Christianity, its record of ancient biblical nations might further strengthen our sense that medieval people could have imagined themselves part of something like a nation. And this might certainly have been true in Ireland itself, where scriptural scholarship was so central.

Of course, it's important not to exaggerate the links between the proto-nation of early Ireland and its modern counterpart, the nation; certainly, we should not assume that the existence of certain traits in early Ireland necessitated the later development of modern Ireland as it eventually evolved: matters were more contingent than that. Understanding the past primarily in its own terms and in terms appropriate to the period under scrutiny, we should recognize that much of what later emerged as Irish nationalism would have been not only unpredictable but unimaginable to medieval people. But it does seem to me just as important that we recognize the continuities which do clearly help to explain the nature of later Irish developments. Modern Irish nationalism was not the only possible outcome – there was nothing inevitable about it – but it did grow out of the roots of pre-modern Ireland and we should not shy away from that fact and its implications. This was true of an emergent Gaelic communal identity, of struggles for all-island political authority, and perhaps most tellingly in terms of the importance of Catholic Christianity for the later development of Irish nationalism. As we move from the medieval to the early-modern period, we see the vital and defining significance of the last of these elements – Irish Catholicism – when we consider the extent to which nation and nationalism had emerged in Ireland by the early-modern period.

The scholar of nationalism Liah Greenfeld has suggested that 'The original modern idea of the nation emerged in sixteenth-century England, which was the first nation in the world ... It is possible to locate the emergence of national sentiment in England in the first third of the sixteenth century.'[150] Statements such as this demonstrate the possibility of locating the national (in Greenfeld's own argument, indeed, the nationalist) as early as the sixteenth century. How valid is this for Ireland? Were nation, national identity or even nationalism evident in early-modern Irish life?

There was clearly no nationalism if the term is taken to mean our intersection of community, struggle and power, with its associated notions of mass mobilization, egalitarian-sovereign liberty, or large-scale, modern-style state self-determination. The early sixteenth century, for example, was a period during which most people in Ireland primarily understood the world very much in local terms. Again, the monarchical conception of sovereignty clashed with the popular understanding at the heart of nationalism. And early-modern government was not representative in any recognizably nationalist sense; even foreign policy in contemporary Europe could be seen as much in dynastic as in national terms.[151]

And yet, while we might not be persuaded by those theorists of nationalism[152] who argue a primordialist case, there was before 1700 a growing sense of an Irish identity and of Ireland as a political entity. This was traceable in clear terms at least to the end of the sixteenth century, and its implications were even more evident in the seventeenth: Confederate Catholic Patrick Darcy (1598–1668) could argue in 1643 that no English statute could be enforced in Ireland unless it had been enacted by an Irish parliament, an assertion containing strong indications of political self-image and identity.[153] And a reasonably detailed sense of a physically discrete island-Ireland was evident repeatedly in more than one seventeenth-century map.[154] Moreover, the existence of a form of public opinion dates back at least to the era of the Reformation in Europe, so the idea of something resembling a shared national imagination and identity is not intrinsically implausible. There were also clear traces of the kind of conflict which was later to become so central to nationalist politics. Colonial arguments offer an important illustration: nationalism in Ireland was to involve an ambiguously anti-colonial stance in the modern period, and something of this was evident even in this proto-national, pre-eighteenth-century era. That Anglo-Irish relations in the early-modern period had a colonial dimension has been accepted by different shades of scholarly and political opinion;[155] and yet even in this period Ireland's status was tellingly ambiguous ('constitutionally a kingdom with its own legislature, but economically a colonial dependency'[156]). As in so much

else, the proto-national foundations for nation and nationalism had
been laid.

By the time we reach the eighteenth century, the shape of nationalism was emerging more clearly within its proto-national shell. During
this century, indeed, we near and then we reach actual nationalism in
Ireland. Swift is ambiguous. He argued the case for Irish economic
interests against England, for greater Irish legislative independence, for
the defence of Irish rights, and out of a sense of an affronted dignity
in Ireland. Yet he did not imagine the Catholic majority in Ireland to
be truly part of his nation, owed primary loyalty to the Church of
Ireland rather than to Ireland itself, did not hold the people as a whole
to be sovereign, and saw himself as an Englishman. (As the feline D.
P. Moran later noted, describing Swift as 'This Englishman, whom,
with characteristic latter-day Irish cringe we claim for ourselves': 'that
great Irishman [Swift], as we love to call him, who had not a drop of
Irish blood in his veins, no Irish characteristics, and an utter contempt
for the entire pack of us'.[157]) With Sheridan we see an enthusiasm for
a measure of Irish independence, and the influence of Lockeian ideas;
in Edmund Burke we hear the case made regarding Catholic grievance,
but find no link established between this and the search for Irish
independence – quite the contrary. The Patriots exhibited what we
might term a proto-nationalism, but this too was Protestant rather
than inclusive, and in the case of someone like Henry Grattan it did
not involve a desire to weaken the Anglo-Irish connection.

So it was with the late-eighteenth-century United Irishmen that we
truly see the birth of nationalist Ireland. In contrast to what preceded
them, we have here mass politicization, the cause of popular sovereignty, the case for representative government, the struggle for power
on behalf of a self-consciously national community, the politics of
independence and democracy, and the powerful cocktail of Lockeian,
Rousseauan and Paineite argument decisively reaching Ireland. In part,
these developments were so timed because of social and technological
changes: print dissemination, literacy, the development of more commercial and even industrial culture with consequent effect on population mobility and concentration. And now a new world had been
imagined. In the pre-modern era power was still very localized, whereas
the era of nationalist Ireland would see this alter; sovereignty for
nationalists could now be held to rest in the people rather than in the

monarch, and egalitarianism began to write itself into Irish nationalist politics.

Some of this echoes and reinforces (and some of it demands modification of) the arguments of key theorists of nationalism. For the United Irishmen, the importance of communication, printing and dissemination was certainly striking (an echo of the arguments of Anderson and Deutsch[158]), the movement's *Northern Star* newspaper being highly influential in spreading the new nationalist word, and reaching an impressive peak circulation of around 4,000. In other respects, perhaps, the arguments of broader theorists of nationalism require slight modification to fit the Irish case. Those like Ernest Gellner[159] who stressed that the onset of industrialization brought about nationalism would find ambiguous evidence in Ireland. As in other places (Mexico, Japan, Serbia, Finland, Greece, the Balkans), so too in Ireland the emergence of modern-style nationalism predated large-scale industrialization. In 1800 only 7 per cent of Irish people lived in cities of 10,000 or more,[160] and well into the nineteenth century it was agriculture rather than industry which dominated the Irish economy. So late-eighteenth-century Irish nationalism certainly predated full industrialization.[161]

And yet we should not dismiss the importance, in the Irish nationalist birth, of industrialization, urbanization and the expansion of markets and economic integration. Eighteenth-century Ireland did possess significant cities and towns (Dublin, Cork, Limerick, Belfast, Derry and Galway among them). Admittedly, these tended to be small: Lisburn, with around 4,000 inhabitants, was in the early eighteenth century the eighth largest town on the island. But the eighteenth century had indeed witnessed a crucial economic change in the emergence of a much more substantial commercial society: a community within which people engaged in the market and were bound together in wider market relations. Moreover, the nationalism which had emerged by 1800 in Ireland clearly rested upon a self-conscious public community which could feel and express patriotic sentiment on a reasonably large scale, and the increased aggregation and association of people for economic reasons played its vital part here. This shouldn't be seen as too sudden or abrupt a process, perhaps. It was not that pre-industrial society in Ireland had been entirely localized or non-mobile, for there had been social movement even in the medieval period (towards

Dublin from far afield, towards the towns which had emerged in the twelfth and thirteenth centuries, and so on). But the expansion of communication, the growth of markets and of more concentrated centres of population in the eighteenth century did between them signify a major shift in terms of creating possibilities for wider association. And the broader economic context of the British and Irish islands was important here too.

For Britain undoubtedly had industrialized significantly towards the end of the eighteenth century, and marked progress had been made there also in terms of mobility by means of road and river travel. As noted, the United Irishmen drew heavily upon ideas and influences from Britain,[162] and it could be argued that there was a process of diffusion to Ireland, from the more industrialized neighbour-island, of ideas which had grown partly from such industrialization and which then formed the basis of nationalism in Ireland. To that extent, the modernization thesis of nationalism could perhaps be redeemed in the Irish case.

It might seem ironic that economic changes in Britain would prove partly responsible for the development of anti-British Irish nationalism, but it is well known that eighteenth-century Irish radicals drew upon British political ideas, and in other ways too it has long been the proximity and complex intimacy of the two islands which has explained their respective political and ideological developments. And, just as ideas from industrialized Britain spread to Ireland, so too during the eighteenth century there was a sharpening sense among some Irish figures that clear definition of Ireland and her interests had become more urgently pressing as Britain was forged,[163] and as Britain grew more and more powerful. If Britain gained in economic power, then definition of Irish community and of Irish interests and of Irish struggles for autonomy became necessarily more important. The struggles born of such recognition were the struggles which gave birth to modern Irish nationalism, a phenomenon born in direct and indirect response to British change (just as so many nationalisms have arisen in direct and rivalrous response to competitor nations[164]).

Other echoes (and modifications) of the theoretical literature can also be heard in this eighteenth-century birth period of nationalist Ireland. The imagined community of cross-denominational unity – rhetorically enduring and powerful as it has been – involved precisely the kind of imaginary world depicted by Benedict Anderson.[165] (Wolfe Tone conjured an image of Catholic participation in the nation, without any real acquaintance with Irish Catholics.) Yet this new nationalism grew, it should be stressed, also from the soil of real community and far from anonymous interlocutors: the actual and the imagined were both required. The United Irishmen did have a sense of a wider Ireland; but it was also vital that they were personally bonded together, and this often drove, influenced and inspired them. Thomas Russell was a close friend of Tone, of Robert Emmet, of Henry Joy McCracken, and he was a key, vital influence over all three; William Drennan's father had known Francis Hutcheson, a human link by means of which new ideas could reach their Irish destination; and so on.

In the end, then, Irish nationalism has been a modern phenomenon. But it has possessed historically embedded, constricting and defining roots, which go back into the pre-modern period of an Irish proto-nation. As noted, there has now emerged a broad consensus among most scholars studying nationalism that the phenomenon represents something which is comparatively recent in human history.[166] But this need not rule out the importance of what we have called here the proto-nation, a pre-modern phenomenon which has influenced and helped to shape later Irish nationalism. The Irish ancientness celebrated by modern nationalists such as Thomas D'Arcy McGee or Patrick Pearse might have been seen through sentimental and anachronistic lenses, but that does not mean that there was nothing there to be seen in the first place. There was indeed a pre-modern, proto-national consciousness, and as we have seen this was evident even in medieval Ireland: in a self-conscious Gaelic Ireland existing beyond the Anglo-Norman lordship; in the pre-Anglo-Norman traditions which remained vibrant in some parts of the island even after Henry II's famous arrival here; in a medieval Gaelic culture and identity; in there being a standard language across the island; in the establishment of medieval Irish Catholic Christianity (strongly rooted by the eighth century as an expressly Irish Church); in the clear signs of a self-consciousness, by the tenth- to twelfth-century period, as a wider Irish community of shared descent; in the notion of all-island rule, attempts to make this a reality, and the measure of success actually achieved by some in such struggles for power.

Some aspects of supposedly ancient Irish culture – the Irish Celticism celebrated by nationalists like Michael Davitt, for example – might be deeply suspect. But others, therefore, were foundations on which later nationalists could build the edifice of nationalism in terms of territory, people, descent, culture and so on. In the early-modern era this was again clear: the survival of Catholicism, and its increasing identification with distinctive, non-English Irishness, was highly important, as was the growing early-modern sense of an Irish identity. On all of this, later nationalists were able to build, and to do so in a manner which would have been far less sturdy and appealing had this pre-modern experience not been precisely as it was.

So, while there was nothing inevitable about Catholic or Gaelic Irish nationalism emerging, nor was the prehistory of nationalism – in terms of Gaelic identity and Catholic survival – merely incidental. Those later nationalists who tried to build nationalist identity around different kinds of self-image (Marxists, for example, for whom class supposedly transcended Gaelic ethnicity, and materialism was to replace God as the framework for understanding history) found themselves unable to invent a nation in which any but a handful believed.[167] The contrast with a nationalism rooted in Gaelic, Catholic Ireland could hardly be greater. When Daniel O'Connell gained strength from his personal Gaelic identity, or from his emphatically Catholic politics, he was building a nationalism which was defined and sustained by pre-modern realities, as well as one which was informed by an urgent contemporary context. Similar patterns can be seen in Parnellite politics, in IRA nationalism, in the collective self-image of northern nationalists in the twentieth century, and so on through much of our story.

And there still surely rests far too much appeal in such politics for nationalism to become superseded very quickly. There are those who have thoughtfully examined the possibilities for a post-nationalist era,[168] but it seems to me that the politics of nationalism in Ireland offers too much to too many people for such post-nationalism to become anything but an eccentric, minority taste at present. And there are wider international echoes to this too. Some have suggested that the most important unit of historical momentum and conflict has now become, not the nation, but the civilization. In Samuel Huntington's words, 'patterns of cohesion, disintegration and conflict' in the post-

Cold War period are being shaped by culture and identity at the civilizational rather than the national level; a 'clash of civilizations' – involving seven or eight rivals – has arrived and now determines history. But even Huntington acknowledges that 'States are and will remain the dominant entities in world affairs',[169] and the nations and nationalisms which feed into those states are almost certainly still the decisive units of allegiance for many the world over. Even in the world of Islam (which one scholar has described as involving 'not a nation subdivided into religious groups but a religion subdivided into nations'[170]), the role of nation and nationalism – as evident in the twenty-first-century Iraq war and its aftermath – has been striking and powerful. Globalization occurred at the same period as did the resurgence of ethnic nationalisms throughout much of the world in the 1990s, and of ethno-national conflict as the determinant of much political reality; so any idea that globalization itself has spelled the end of nationalism must surely seem suspect. Yet again, the growth of a meaningful European Union has not implied the end of nationalist identity within that region. In all these cases, recent decades have seen, not the withering, but the flowering of nationalism across much of the globe.[171] In Ireland, as elsewhere, nationalism – enjoying the combined force of a particular kind of community, struggle and power – seems unlikely to evaporate in the foreseeable future.

Notes and References

Introduction

1. A. L. Milligan, *Life of Theobald Wolfe Tone* (Belfast: Boyd, 1898), p. 97.
2. E. O'Malley, *On Another Man's Wound* (Dublin: Anvil Press, 1979; 1st edn, 1936), p. 93.
3. P. O'Donnell, *Islanders* (Cork: Mercier Press, 1963; 1st edn, 1927), p. 11.
4. In the words of one of the most distinguished students of the phenomenon (Anthony Smith), the story of nationalism is 'the central thread binding, and dividing, the peoples of the modern world' (A. D. Smith, *Nationalism and Modernism: A Critical Survey of Recent Theories of Nations and Nationalism* (London: Routledge, 1998), p. 1). Cf. 'Nationalism was the most powerful and recurring political idea of the nineteenth and twentieth centuries and it starts off the twenty-first century in a lead position' (R. Taras, *Liberal and Illiberal Nationalisms* (Basingstoke: Palgrave Macmillan, 2002), p. xii); see also the excellent J. Hutchinson, *Modern Nationalism* (London: Fontana, 1994), p. 1.
5. Cf. 'the key language of our age is ethnic nationalism' (M. Ignatieff, *Blood and Belonging: Journeys into the New Nationalism* (London: Vintage, 1994; 1st edn, 1993), p. 2).
6. Numerous of these books first appeared many years ago, and cannot therefore reflect either recent scholarship or the full range of archive sources which have been made available since their publication. This is true of D. G. Boyce, *Nationalism in Ireland* (London: Routledge, 1995; 1st edn, 1982); S. Cronin, *Irish Nationalism: A History of Its Roots and Ideology* (Dublin: Academy Press, 1980); R. Kee, *The Green Flag: A History of Irish Nationalism* (Harmondsworth: Penguin, 2000; 1st edn, 1972); T. Garvin, *The Evolution of Irish Nationalist Politics* (Dublin: Gill and Macmillan, 2005; 1st edn, 1981). R. V. Comerford's *Ireland* (London: Arnold, 2003) is a more recent book, but is a brilliantly thematic, oblique argument, rather than a book comprehensively reflecting the literature on Irish nationalism as a whole.

7. Among the very best are R. F. Foster, *Modern Ireland 1600–1972* (Harmondsworth: Penguin, 1988); K. T. Hoppen, *Ireland Since 1800: Conflict and Conformity* (Harlow: Longman, 1999; 1st edn, 1989); C. Townshend, *Ireland: The Twentieth Century* (London: Arnold, 1999); F. S. L. Lyons, *Ireland Since the Famine* (London: Fontana, 1973; 1st edn, 1971); J. J. Lee, *Ireland 1912–1985: Politics and Society* (Cambridge: Cambridge University Press, 1989); A. Jackson, *Ireland 1798–1998: Politics and War* (Oxford: Blackwell, 1999); D. Ferriter, *The Transformation of Ireland 1900–2000* (London: Profile, 2005; 1st edn, 2004).

8. As one thoughtful observer has put it, in relation to what he sees as the parochial limitations of Irish history-writing, 'Irish historians give prominence to nationalism, but make little attempt to flesh out the concept in any rigorous social scientific manner' (M. Suzman, *Ethnic Nationalism and State Power: The Rise of Irish Nationalism, Afrikaner Nationalism and Zionism* (Basingstoke: Palgrave, 1999), p. 2). And this has reflected a broader international pattern, within which historians have 'continued to chronicle the story of nationalist movements, but did not enquire too closely into the nature of nationalism itself' (G. Schöpflin, *Nations, Identity, Power* (London: Hurst, 2000), p. 2).

9. George Boyce's superb *Nationalism in Ireland* starts with a brief discussion of definitions, but avoids any systematic integration of theoretical considerations into the broad narrative of the book, arguing that the historian 'can take comfort in the reflection that nationalism is something that he recognizes when he sees it' (p. 17). Vincent Comerford, in his own fine study, explicitly eschews systematic engagement with theory: 'the intention is to explore the particularity and complexity of the subject . . . rather than to test, much less to elaborate, any theory. . . . There is no intention here to emulate social scientists by elaborating or reworking definitions of key concepts such as nation, nationalism and nationality' (*Ireland*, pp. 2–3). Tom Garvin's excellent book, *The Evolution of Irish Nationalist Politics*, likewise avoids systematic discussion of the theoretical literature on nationalism; so too do Garvin's *Nationalist Revolutionaries in Ireland, 1858–1928* (Oxford: Oxford University Press, 1987), Cronin's *Irish Nationalism*, and Kee's *Green Flag*.

10. The most that tends to be offered in conceptual terms is a brief salute to a few theorists (most commonly, Ernest Gellner, Benedict Anderson, Eric Hobsbawm or Anthony Smith), rather than any more sustained, systematic or integrated engagement with the vast literature on nationalism or with what it might mean for our understanding and explanation of nationalist Ireland.

11. There have been occasional attempts to deploy nationalist theory in an Irish context, but these have tended not to involve sufficiently detailed empirical-

historical research; see, for example, J. Mac Laughlin, *Reimagining the Nation-State: The Contested Terrains of Nation-Building* (London: Pluto, 2001).

12. It has sometimes been assumed that Ireland is simply exceptional to wider patterns, and that there is little point in, or need for, comparison with other cases. But while it is quite correct to recognize that Ireland – like any other country – is unique, it is also necessary to ask whether there are wider social and historical patterns at work here which can only be established by reflection on the broader phenomenon of nationalism beyond Ireland's shores. Indeed, it is only by reflecting on other cases that we can assess the extent to which, and the reasons why, Ireland has been unique.

13. E. J. Hobsbawm, *The Age of Revolution 1789–1848* (London: Weidenfeld and Nicolson, 1995; 1st edn, 1962), p. ix.

14. G. B. Shaw, 'Preface' to *Plays Unpleasant* (Harmondsworth: Penguin, 1946; 1st edn. 1898), p. v.

15. *Radicals and the Republic: Socialist Republicanism in the Irish Free State 1925–1937* (Oxford: Oxford University Press, 1994); *Ernie O'Malley: IRA Intellectual* (Oxford: Oxford University Press, 1999; 1st edn, 1998); *Armed Struggle: The History of the IRA* (London: Pan, 2004; 1st edn, 2003).

16. *The Shorter Oxford English Dictionary* (vol. II) (Oxford: Oxford University Press, 1980; 1st edn, 1933), p. 1386.

17. E. J. Hobsbawm, *Nations and Nationalism Since 1780: Programme, Myth, Reality* (Cambridge: Cambridge University Press, 1990), p. 8.

18. Certain other terms might helpfully be defined at this stage, in relation to their specifically Irish use. **Republicanism** in a modern Irish context should be understood to indicate either specific attachment to a republican form of government and/or an aggressive pursuit of such an arrangement in Ireland. **Separatism** will be used to refer to the tradition favouring or pursuing the establishment of a fully separate Ireland, entirely politically independent from Britain. **Unionism** denotes the political tradition espousing Ireland's – and subsequently Northern Ireland's – continued membership of the United Kingdom. **Loyalism** will be used to refer to a more aggressively defined and expressed version of unionism.

One – 'A Wild and Inhospitable People'? Pre-1700 Ireland

1. T. D. McGee, *A Popular History of Ireland: From the Earliest Period to the Emancipation of the Catholics* (Glasgow: Cameron, Ferguson and Co., n.d.) (vol. I), pp. 11–12.

2. M. Elliott, *The Catholics of Ulster: A History* (Harmondsworth: Allen Lane, 2000), p. 4.

3. M. Davitt, *The Fall of Feudalism in Ireland or the Story of the Land League*

Revolution (London: Harper and Brothers, 1904), Dedication, and pp. xii–xiii, xv, xvii, and so on.

4. See, for example, the influential historian Edmund Curtis, *A History of Ireland* (London: Methuen, 1950; 1st edn, 1936), pp. viii, 1, 19, 21. Cf. also, for one more example among very many, P. A. Sheehan, *The Intellectuals: An Experiment in Irish Club-Life* (London: Longmans, Green and Co., 1911), p. 55.

5. M. Richter, *Medieval Ireland: The Enduring Tradition* (Dublin: Gill and Macmillan, 1988), pp. 1–3; F. J. Byrne, 'Early Irish Society (1st–9th Century)', in T. W. Moody and F. X. Martin (eds), *The Course of Irish History* (Cork: Mercier Press, 1994; 1st edn, 1967), p. 43; P. B. Ellis, *The Ancient World of the Celts* (London: Constable, 1998), pp. 25, 222.

6. S. James, *The Atlantic Celts: Ancient People or Modern Invention?* (London: British Museum Press, 1999), p. 12.

7. B. Cunliffe, *The Celts* (Oxford: Oxford University Press, 2003); James, *Atlantic Celts*; A. T. Q. Stewart, *The Shape of Irish History* (Belfast: Blackstaff Press, 2001), pp. 41–4.

8. Tacitus, *Tacitus on Britain and Germany* (West Drayton: Penguin, 1948), p. 74.

9. Curtis, *A History of Ireland*, p. v.

10. Bede, *A History of the English Church and People* (Harmondsworth: Penguin, 1955), p. 39.

11. S. Duffy, *Ireland in the Middle Ages* (Basingstoke: Macmillan, 1997), pp. 15–16.

12. R. Fletcher, *The Conversion of Europe: From Paganism to Christianity AD 371–1386* (London: HarperCollins, 1997), p. 80.

13. C. Etchingham, *Church Organization in Ireland AD 650–1000* (Maynooth: Laigin Publications, 1999).

14. T. M. Charles-Edwards, *Early Christian Ireland* (Cambridge: Cambridge University Press, 2000), p. 185.

15. Fletcher, *The Conversion of Europe*, p. 81.

16. C. Townshend, *Easter 1916: The Irish Rebellion* (London: Penguin, 2005), p. 125.

17. R. V. Comerford, *Ireland* (London: Arnold, 2003), p. 21.

18. Gerald of Wales, *The History and Topography of Ireland* (Harmondsworth: Penguin, 1982), p. 89.

19. J. O'Leary, *Recollections of Fenians and Fenianism* (London: Downey and Company, 1896) (vol. I), p. 78.

20. George Harrison, interviewed by the author, New York, 30 October 2000.

21. H. E. Butler (ed.), *The Autobiography of Gerald of Wales* (Woodbridge: Boydell Press, 2005; 1st edn, 1937), p. 35.

22. H. Morgan, 'Giraldus Cambrensis and the Tudor Conquest of Ireland', in

H. Morgan (ed.), *Political Ideology in Ireland, 1541–1641* (Dublin: Four Courts Press, 1999).

23. Gerald of Wales, *History and Topography*, pp. 99–102, 106.

24. Quoted in R. F. Foster (ed.), *The Oxford Illustrated History of Ireland* (Oxford: Oxford University Press, 1989), p. 101.

25. S. G. Ellis, 'Nationalist Historiography and the English and Gaelic Worlds in the Late Middle Ages', *Irish Historical Studies* 25, 97 (1986), p. 12.

26. D. MacCulloch, *Reformation: Europe's House Divided 1490–1700* (London: Allen Lane, 2003), p. 394.

27. C. Lennon, *Sixteenth-Century Ireland: The Incomplete Conquest* (Dublin: Gill and Macmillan, 1994).

28. C. Marsh, *Popular Religion in Sixteenth-Century England* (Basingstoke: Macmillan, 1998), p. 33.

29. Cecily Stonor, quoted in C. Haigh, 'The Continuity of Catholicism in the English Reformation', in C. Haigh (ed.), *The English Reformation Revised* (Cambridge: Cambridge University Press, 1987), p. 176.

30. D. MacCulloch, 'Putting the English Reformation on the Map', *Transactions of the Royal Historical Society* (sixth series) 15 (2005), p. 75.

31. Quoted in C. S. L. Davies, *Peace, Print and Protestantism 1450–1558* (St Albans: Paladin, 1977), p. 44.

32. M. D. Palmer, *Henry VIII* (London: Longman, 1971), p. 119.

33. S. G. Ellis, 'Economic Problems of the Church: Why the Reformation Failed in Ireland', *Journal of Ecclesiastical History* 41, 2 (1990), p. 242.

34. H. A. Jefferies, 'The Early Tudor Reformations in the Irish Pale', *Journal of Ecclesiastical History* 52, 1 (2001).

35. Germany provides one obvious example (S. Ozment, *Protestants: The Birth of a Revolution* (London: Fontana, 1993; 1st edn, 1992)), Britain another (L. Colley, *Britons: Forging the Nation 1707–1837* (London: Pimlico, 1994; 1st edn. 1992)).

36. P. Mitchell, 'Futures', in P. Mitchell and R. Wilford (eds), *Politics in Northern Ireland* (Boulder: Westview Press, 1999), p. 266.

37. B. Bradshaw, 'Sword, Word and Strategy in the Reformation in Ireland', *Historical Journal* 21, 3 (1978).

38. D. G. Boyce, *Nationalism in Ireland* (London: Routledge, 1995; 1st edn, 1982), p. 46.

39. Ellis, 'Economic Problems of the Church'.

40. On the history of the Black Abbey, see H. Fenning, *The Black Abbey: The Kilkenny Dominicans 1225–1996* (Kilkenny: Kilkenny People Printing, n.d.).

41. M. Tanner, *Ireland's Holy Wars: The Struggle for a Nation's Soul, 1500–2000* (New Haven: Yale University Press, 2001), pp. 83–4.

42. Barnaby Rich, quoted in J. Lydon, *The Making of Ireland: From Ancient Times to the Present* (London: Routledge, 1998), p. 141.

43. See the thoughtful treatment offered by Alan Ford in *The Protestant Reformation in Ireland, 1590–1641* (Dublin: Four Courts Press, 1997; 1st edn, 1985).

44. A. S. Green, *Irish Nationality* (London: Williams and Norgate, n.d.), p. 164.

45. An attempt meticulously recounted in N. Canny, *Making Ireland British 1580–1650* (Oxford: Oxford University Press, 2003; 1st edn, 2001).

46. B. Mac Cuarta, 'Introduction', in B. Mac Cuarta (ed.), *Ulster 1641: Aspects of the Rising* (Belfast: Institute of Irish Studies, 1993), p. 1.

47. M. Ó Siochrú, *Confederate Ireland 1642–1649: A Constitutional and Political Analysis* (Dublin: Four Courts Press, 1999), p. 11.

48. A point ably demonstrated by Toby Barnard in his *Cromwellian Ireland: English Government and Reform in Ireland 1649–1660* (Oxford: Oxford University Press, 2000; 1st edn, 1975).

49. On well-publicized Catholic violence in the early-modern period, see E. Cameron, *Waldenses: Rejections of Holy Church in Medieval Europe* (Oxford: Blackwell, 2000), pp. 261–2, 274, 287–8, 294.

50. C. Calhoun, *Nationalism* (Buckingham: Open University Press, 1997), pp. 51–2.

51. T. Bartlett, '"This Famous Island Set in a Virginian Sea": Ireland in the British Empire, 1690–1801', in P. J. Marshall (ed.), *The Eighteenth Century* (The Oxford History of the British Empire, vol. II) (Oxford: Oxford University Press, 1998), pp. 253–4.

Two – 'Rational Ideas of Liberty and Equality': The Eighteenth Century

1. Quoted in C. C. O'Brien, *The Great Melody: A Thematic Biography and Commented Anthology of Edmund Burke* (London: Minerva, 1993; 1st edn, 1992), p. 459.

2. John Wesley (19 July 1756), in E. Jay (ed.), *The Journal of John Wesley: A Selection* (Oxford: Oxford University Press, 1987), p. 135.

3. Among a vast literature, see: I. Higgins, *Swift's Politics: A Study in Disaffection* (Cambridge: Cambridge University Press, 1994); F. P. Lock, *The Politics of Gulliver's Travels* (Oxford: Oxford University Press, 1980); F. P. Lock, *Swift's Tory Politics* (London: Duckworth, 1983).

4. J. Coakley (ed.), *The Social Origins of Nationalist Movements: The Contemporary West European Experience* (London: Sage, 1992).

5. J. Swift, *The Drapier's Letters to the People of Ireland* (London: Oxford University Press, 1935 edn), p. 10.

6. Molyneux's Dublin-published 1698 tract, *The Case of Ireland's Being Bound by Acts of Parliament in England*, had itself drawn upon earlier debates in order to argue against the English parliament's claim to control Irish affairs.

Arguing that Ireland was a separate and distinct kingdom and that, as such, it should not be subject to the English parliament, Molyneux held that those of English blood shouldn't lose their English freedoms simply as a result of being across the sea in Ireland. Irishmen, Molyneux asserted, had the right to submit only to those laws and taxes to which they had given their consent.

7. Swift, *Drapier's Letters*, p. 40.

8. Y. Tamir, *Liberal Nationalism* (Princeton: Princeton University Press, 1993), p. 73.

9. Jonathan Swift, quoted in Higgins, *Swift's Politics*, p. 151.

10. Especially in Robert Mahony's excellent *Jonathan Swift: The Irish Identity* (New Haven: Yale University Press, 1995).

11. See Fintan O'Toole's compelling study, *A Traitor's Kiss: The Life of Richard Brinsley Sheridan* (London: Granta, 1997).

12. T. Moore, *Memoirs of the Life of the Right Honourable Richard Brinsley Sheridan* (London: Longman, Rees, Orme, Brown and Green, 1826) (vol. II), pp. 349–50.

13. Edmund Burke, *Reflections on the Revolution in France* (Oxford: Oxford University Press, 1993; 1st edn, 1790), pp. 25, 31, 49, 61.

14. Edmund Burke (29 September 1773), quoted in O'Brien, *The Great Melody*, p. 70.

15. This is a powerful theme ibid., but it is clearly noted, if more briefly, in much earlier works such as C. B. Macpherson, *Burke* (Oxford: Oxford University Press, 1980), or T. H. D. Mahoney, *Edmund Burke and Ireland* (Cambridge, Mass.: Harvard University Press, 1960).

16. For a strong argument that Richard Burke had been a recent Catholic convert to Anglicanism at the time of Edmund's birth, see O'Brien, *Great Melody*.

17. Edmund Burke, quoted ibid., p. 41.

18. Burke to Langrishe (3 January 1792), quoted ibid., p. 480.

19. J. Mitchel, *Jail Journal; Or, Five Years in British Prisons* (London: R. and T. Washbourne, n.d.), p. 10.

20. A. S. Green, *Irish Nationality* (London: Williams and Norgate, n.d.), pp. 170, 205.

21. R. F. Foster, *W. B. Yeats: A Life. II: The Arch-Poet 1915–1939* (Oxford: Oxford University Press, 2003), pp. 297, 409, 424.

22. L. G. Redmond-Howard, *Home Rule* (London: T. C. and E. C. Jack, n.d. [1912?]), pp. 13–14, 31, 45–6.

23. J. C. Beckett, 'Burke, Ireland and the Empire', in O. MacDonagh, W. F. Mandle and P. Travers (eds), *Irish Culture and Nationalism, 1750–1950* (Dublin: Gill and Macmillan, 1983), p. 1.

24. D. Trimble, *To Raise Up a New Northern Ireland: Articles and Speeches*

1998–2000 (Belfast: Belfast Press, 2001), pp. 55–60; R. McCartney, *Reflections on Liberty, Democracy and the Union* (Dublin: Maunsel, 2001), p. 5. Edward Carson had also been a youthful admirer of Burke.

25. T. Paulin, *The Day-Star of Liberty: William Hazlitt's Radical Style* (London: Faber and Faber, 1998).

26. Quoted in N. L. York, *Neither Kingdom Nor Nation: The Irish Quest for Constitutional Rights, 1698–1800* (Washington, DC: Catholic University of America Press, 1994), p. 39.

27. K. Whelan, *The Tree of Liberty: Radicalism, Catholicism and the Construction of Irish Identity 1760–1830* (Cork: Cork University Press, 1996), p. 56.

28. The case for the ancien régime is powerfully made in S. J. Connolly, *Religion, Law, and Power: The Making of Protestant Ireland 1660–1760* (Oxford: Oxford University Press, 1995; 1st edn, 1992).

29. For an impressive corrective to this misunderstanding, see T. Barnard, *A New Anatomy of Ireland: The Irish Protestants, 1649–1770* (New Haven: Yale University Press, 2003).

30. See the thoughtful essays of D. W. Hayton, gathered together as *Ruling Ireland, 1685–1742: Politics, Politicians and Parties* (Woodbridge: Boydell Press, 2004).

31. P. McNally, *Parties, Patriots and Undertakers: Parliamentary Politics in Early Hanoverian Ireland* (Dublin: Four Courts Press, 1997), p. 23.

32. J. Kelly, *Henry Grattan* (Dundalk: Dundalgan Press, 1993), p. 3.

33. W. J. O'Neill Daunt (4 July 1870), quoted in D. Thornley, *Isaac Butt and Home Rule* (London: MacGibbon and Kee, 1964), p. 104.

34. 'It is now universally accepted among academic historians that many of these laws (those relating to religious worship, for example) were rarely, unevenly or only half-heartedly enforced' (McNally, *Parties, Patriots and Undertakers*, p. 26).

35. It should be noted that contemporary legislation in Ireland discriminated also against Dissenters.

36. Theobald Wolfe Tone, *Memoirs*, in T. Bartlett (ed.), *Life of Theobald Wolfe Tone: Memoirs, Journals and Political Writings, Compiled and Arranged by William T. W. Tone, 1826* (Dublin: Lilliput Press, 1998), pp. 85–6.

37. *Declaration and Resolutions of the Society of United Irishmen of Belfast*, in Bartlett (ed.), *Life of Theobald Wolfe Tone*, pp. 298–9.

38. *Northern Star* 28 January–1 February 1796.

39. T. Graham, 'Dublin in 1798: The Key to the Planned Insurrection', in D. Keogh and N. Furlong (eds), *The Mighty Wave: The 1798 Rebellion in Wexford* (Blackrock: Four Courts Press, 1996), p. 65.

40. D. Dickson, 'Smoke Without Fire? Munster and the 1798 Rebellion', in T. Bartlett, D. Dickson, D. Keogh and K. Whelan (eds), *1798: A Bicentenary Perspective* (Dublin: Four Courts Press, 2003).

41. T. Bartlett (ed.), *Revolutionary Dublin, 1795–1801: The Letters of Francis Higgins to Dublin Castle* (Dublin: Four Courts Press, 2004).

42. Whelan, *Tree of Liberty*, p. 95.

43. K. Whelan, 'Reinterpreting the 1798 Rebellion in County Wexford', in Keogh and Furlong (eds), *The Mighty Wave*, p. 34.

44. A story powerfully told in T. Dunne, *Rebellions: Memoir, Memory and 1798* (Dublin: Lilliput Press, 2004).

45. 'The Address of the Roman Catholics of Ireland, Presented to His Excellency the Lord Lieutenant, on Wednesday May 30 1798', Stewart Papers, PRONI D/3167/2/143.

46. B. Clifford, *Edmund Burke and the United Irishmen: Their Relevance in Ireland Today* (Aubane: Aubane Historical Society, 1994), p. 3.

47. Whelan, *Tree of Liberty*, p. ix.

48. I. McBride, *Scripture Politics: Ulster Presbyterians and Irish Radicalism in the Late Eighteenth Century* (Oxford: Oxford University Press, 1998), p. 230.

49. N. J. Curtin, *The United Irishmen: Popular Politics in Ulster and Dublin 1791–1798* (Oxford: Oxford University Press, 1994), p. 289.

50. On Russell, see James Quinn's excellent biography: *Soul on Fire: A Life of Thomas Russell* (Dublin: Irish Academic Press, 2002).

51. McBride, *Scripture Politics*, p. 13.

52. T. Paine, *Rights of Man* (London: Watts and Co., 1937; 1st edn, 1791–2), p. 117.

53. Theobald Wolfe Tone, *Memoirs*, in Bartlett (ed.), *Life of Theobald Wolfe Tone*, p. 39.

54. McTier to Drennan (28 October 1791), quoted in D. Dickson, 'Paine and Ireland', in D. Dickson, D. Keogh and K. Whelan (eds), *The United Irishmen: Republicanism, Radicalism and Rebellion* (Dublin: Lilliput, 1993), p. 140.

55. Theobald Wolfe Tone, *Journals* (March 1797), in Bartlett (ed.), *Life of Theobald Wolfe Tone*, p. 734.

56. Paine, *Rights of Man*, pp. xv, xvii, 2, 114.

57. P. Kelly, 'Perceptions of Locke in Eighteenth-Century Ireland', *Proceedings of the Royal Irish Academy* 89, C, 2 (1989).

58. I. McBride, 'The School of Virtue: Francis Hutcheson, Irish Presbyterians and the Scottish Enlightenment', in D. G. Boyce, R. Eccleshall and V. Geoghegan (eds), *Political Thought in Ireland Since the Seventeenth Century* (London: Routledge, 1993), p. 91; A. T. Q. Stewart, *A Deeper Silence: The Hidden Origins of the United Irish Movement* (London: Faber and Faber, 1993), p. 101.

59. J. Connolly, *Labour in Irish History*, in *Collected Works* (vol. I) (Dublin: New Books, 1987), p. 88.

60. P. O'Donnell, *There Will Be Another Day* (Dublin: Dolmen, 1963), p. 11.

61. E. Hobsbawm, *On History* (London: Weidenfeld and Nicolson, 1997), p. 7.

62. Theobald Wolfe Tone, quoted in J. Smyth, *The Men of No Property: Irish Radicals and Popular Politics in the Late Eighteenth Century* (Dublin: Gill and Macmillan, 1992), p. ix.

63. 75 per cent of Dublin United Irishmen during 1791–4 were from the professional, business or shop-keeping classes (T. Garvin, *The Evolution of Irish Nationalist Politics* (Dublin: Gill and Macmillan, 2005; 1st edn, 1981), p. 26).

64. Mary Anne McCracken (16 March 1797), quoted in M. McNeill, *The Life and Times of Mary Ann McCracken 1770–1866* (Dublin: Allen Figgis, 1960), p. 126.

65. Mary Anne McCracken, quoted in J. Gray, 'Mary Anne McCracken: Belfast Revolutionary and Pioneer of Feminism', in D. Keogh and N. Furlong (eds), *The Women of 1798* (Dublin: Four Courts Press, 1998), p. 53.

66. W. E. H. Lecky, *A History of Ireland in the Eighteenth Century* (vol. V) (London: Longmans, Green and Co., 1913; 1st edn, 1892), p. 79.

67. I. McBride (ed.), *History and Memory in Modern Ireland* (Cambridge: Cambridge University Press, 2001), p. 32.

68. Connolly Association, *Radicals and Revolutionaries: Essays on 1798* (London: Connolly Association, n.d.), p. 5.

69. F. MacDermot, *Theobald Wolfe Tone and His Times* (Tralee: Anvil Books, 1969; 1st edn, 1939), p. v.

70. J. N. Molony, *A Soul Came Into Ireland: Thomas Davis 1814–1845* (Dublin: Geography Publications, 1995), pp. 234–6; R. English, *Ernie O'Malley: IRA Intellectual* (Oxford: Oxford University Press, 1999; 1st edn, 1998), pp. 8, 111–12; R. D. Edwards, *Patrick Pearse: The Triumph of Failure* (Dublin: Poolbeg Press, 1990; 1st edn, 1977), p. 174; D. Fitzpatrick, *Harry Boland's Irish Revolution* (Cork: Cork University Press, 2003), p. 102; *AP* 20 June 1925.

71. S. O'Faoláin, *The Irish* (West Drayton: Penguin, 1947), p. 99.

72. See, for example, C. D. Greaves, *Theobald Wolfe Tone and the Irish Nation* (Dublin: Fulcrum Press, 1991; 1st edn, 1961).

73. S. MacEntee, *Episode at Easter* (Dublin: Gill and Son, 1966), pp. 11–12.

74. H. Butler, *Wolfe Tone and the Common Name of Irishman* (Mullingar: Lilliput, 1985), p. 9.

75. M. Elliott, *Wolfe Tone: Prophet of Irish Independence* (New Haven: Yale University Press, 1989), p. 1.

76. E. O'Malley, *On Another Man's Wound* (Dublin: Anvil Press, 1979; 1st edn, 1936), pp. 58–9.

77. T. W. Tone, *The Autobiography of Theobald Wolfe Tone 1763–1798* (London: T. Fisher Unwin, 1893) (vol. I), pp. 7, 10.

78. Ibid., p. 21.

79. Theobald Wolfe Tone, quoted in T. Bartlett, *Theobald Wolfe Tone* (Dundalk: Dundalgan Press, 1997), p. 9.

80. Theobald Wolfe Tone, *Memoirs*, p. 11.

81. Theobald Wolfe Tone, quoted in Bartlett, *Theobold Wolfe Tone*, p. 23.

82. Theobald Wolfe Tone (11 July 1793), in Bartlett (ed.), *Life of Theobald Wolfe Tone*, p. 399.

83. For differing views on this, see Elliott, *Wolfe Tone*, and Bartlett, *Theobald Wolfe Tone*.

84. Tone, *Journals*, in Bartlett (ed.), *Life of Theobald Wolfe Tone*, p. 649.

85. A. L. Milligan, *Life of Theobald Wolfe Tone* (Belfast: Boyd, 1898), p. 5; Elliott, *Wolfe Tone*, p. 1.

86. Theobald Wolfe Tone, *Memoirs*, in Bartlett (ed.), *Life of Theobald Wolfe Tone*, p. 46.

87. W. Bruce and H. Joy, *Belfast Politics: Thoughts on the British Constitution* (Dublin: UCD Press, 2005; 1st edn, 1794).

88. Theobald Wolfe Tone, *Memoirs*, in Bartlett (ed.), *Life of Theobald Wolfe Tone*, p. 43.

89. T. D. McGee, *A Popular History of Ireland: From the Earliest Period to the Emancipation of the Catholics* (Glasgow: Cameron, Ferguson and Co., n.d.) (vol. II), p. 276.

90. U. Ozkirimli, *Theories of Nationalism: A Critical Introduction* (Basingstoke: Macmillan, 2000), p. 40.

91. Theobald Wolfe Tone, *An Argument on Behalf of the Catholics of Ireland*, in Bartlett (ed.), *Life of Theobald Wolfe Tone*, p. 289.

92. M. Guibernau, *Nationalisms: The Nation-State and Nationalism in the Twentieth Century* (Cambridge: Polity Press, 1996), p. 45.

93. S. J. Connolly, 'Eighteenth-Century Ireland: Colony or *ancien régime*?', in D. G. Boyce and A. O'Day (eds), *The Making of Modern Irish History: Revisionism and the Revisionist Controversy* (London: Routledge, 1996).

94. Certainly for the early eighteenth century (Hayton, *Ruling Ireland*, p. 278).

95. See, for example, E. Kedourie, *Nationalism* (Oxford: Blackwell, 1993; 1st edn, 1960), p. 1; E. J. Hobsbawm, *Nations and Nationalism Since 1780: Programme, Myth, Reality* (Cambridge: Cambridge University Press, 1990), p. 14; J. G. Kellas, *The Politics of Nationalism and Ethnicity* (Basingstoke: Macmillan, 1998; 1st edn, 1991), p. 89.

96. A. D. Smith, 'The Problem of National Identity: Ancient, Medieval and Modern?', *Ethnic and Racial Studies* 17, 3 (1994), p. 375.

Three – Catholic Reform and Cultural Nationalism, 1800–1850

1. M. Edgeworth, *Castle Rackrent* (1800), in *Castle Rackrent/The Absentee* (Ware: Wordsworth, 1994 edn), p. 56.

2. D. Keogh and K. Whelan (eds), *Acts of Union: The Causes, Contexts and Consequences of the Act of Union* (Dublin: Four Courts Press, 2001).

3. J. Leerssen, *Mere Irish and Fíor-Ghael: Studies in the Idea of Irish Nationality, its Development and Literary Expression Prior to the Nineteenth Century* (Cork: Cork University Press, 1996; 1st edn, 1986), p. 376.

4. R. O'Donnell, *Remember Emmet: Images of the Life and Legacy of Robert Emmet* (Bray: Wordwell, 2003), p. 100.

5. 'Proclamation of the Provisional Government', quoted in P. M. Geoghegan, *Robert Emmet: A Life* (Dublin: Gill and Macmillan, 2004; 1st edn, 2002), pp. 288–96.

6. Quoted in M. Elliott, *Robert Emmet: The Making of a Legend* (London: Profile, 2003), pp. 82, 85.

7. Ibid., p. 151.

8. For a sample of the range, see L. Robinson, *Patriots: A Play in Three Acts* (Dublin: Maunsel and Company, 1912), p. 4; P. A. Sheehan, *The Graves at Kilmorna: A Story of '67* (London: Longmans, Green and Company, 1926; 1st edn, 1914), pp. 23, 110; D. Morrison, *Then the Walls Came Down: A Prison Journal* (Cork: Mercier Press, 1999), pp. 104–5; 'Emmet and Tone Commemoration Documents', McGarrity Papers, NLI MS 17, 641.

9. *Shan Van Vocht*, 6 March 1896.

10. *Saoirse*, October 2003.

11. Robert Emmet, quoted in Geoghegan, *Robert Emmet*, p. 250.

12. See the images reproduced in Elliott, *Robert Emmet*.

13. The Whiteboys were an episodic, agrarian protest movement which emerged in the 1760s in County Tipperary, but which spread further afield in response to regional and immediate grievances. The latter included the enclosure of common land, tithes and evictions, and Whiteboyism mainly tended towards the conservative, and towards the averting of unwelcome change.

14. D. Lloyd, *Ireland After History* (Cork: Cork University Press, 1999), p. 3.

15. For recent, conflicting views, see G. K. Peatling, 'The Whiteness of Ireland Under and After the Union', *Journal of British Studies* 44, 1 (2005); L. P. Curtis, 'The Return of Revisionism', *Journal of British Studies* 44, 1 (2005).

16. T. Dunne, *Rebellions: Memoir, Memory and 1798* (Dublin: Lilliput Press, 2004), pp. 76–7, 91, 95; T. Garvin, *The Evolution of Irish Nationalist Politics* (Dublin: Gill and Macmillan, 2005; 1st edn, 1981), pp. vii, 4.

17. T. McDonough (ed.), *Was Ireland a Colony? Economics, Politics and Culture in Nineteenth-Century Ireland* (Dublin: Irish Academic Press, 2005).

18. E. W. Said, *Culture and Imperialism* (London: Vintage, 1994; 1st edn, 1993), pp. xi, 8.

19. T. Bartlett, '"This Famous Island Set in a Virginian Sea": Ireland in the British Empire, 1690–1801', in P. J. Marshall (ed.), *The Eighteenth Century*

(The Oxford History of the British Empire, vol. II) (Oxford: Oxford University Press, 1998), p. 273.

20. See Stephen Howe's judicious discussion in *Ireland and Empire: Colonial Legacies in Irish History and Culture* (Oxford: Oxford University Press, 2000).

21. Thomas Moore, quoted in Geoghegan, *Robert Emmet*, p. 70.

22. Listen, for example, to the excellent 1990s recording by Invocation, directed by Timothy Roberts: *Thomas Moore's Irish Melodies* (Hyperion CDA66774).

23. S. J. Connolly (ed.), *The Oxford Companion to Irish History* (Oxford: Oxford University Press, 1998).

24. From Moore's *Irish Melodies*, in B. Clifford (ed.), *The Life and Poems of Thomas Moore (Ireland's National Poet)* (London: Athol Books, 1984), p. 102.

25. R. V. Comerford, *Ireland* (London: Arnold, 2003), p. 187.

26. T. Moore, *Letters and Journals of Lord Byron: With Notices of His Life* (Paris: Baudry, 1833).

27. D. G. Boyce, *Nineteenth-Century Ireland: The Search for Stability* (Dublin: Gill and Macmillan, 1990), p. 23.

28. M. Davitt, *The Fall of Feudalism in Ireland or the Story of the Land League Revolution* (London: Harper and Brothers, 1904), p. 35.

29. W. E. H. Lecky, *Democracy and Liberty* (vol. I) (New York: Longmans, Green and Co., 1896), p. 18.

30. D. G. Boyce, *Nationalism in Ireland* (London: Routledge, 1995; 1st edn, 1982), p. 137.

31. V. Crossman, *Politics, Law and Order in Nineteenth-Century Ireland* (Dublin: Gill and Macmillan, 1996).

32. M. R. O'Connell, *Daniel O'Connell: The Man and His Politics* (Blackrock: Irish Academic Press, 1990), pp. 11–12.

33. Daniel O'Connell, quoted ibid., p. 65.

34. Quoted ibid., p. 83.

35. R. Kee, *The Green Flag: A History of Irish Nationalism* (Harmondsworth: Penguin, 2000; 1st edn, 1972), p. 203.

36. Garvin, *The Evolution of Irish Nationalist Politics*, p. 57.

37. Jeremy Bentham (1748–1832): English philosopher and exponent of utilitarianism, the view that one should pursue courses of action calculated to produce the greatest happiness or pleasure for the greatest number.

38. S. O'Faoláin, *King of the Beggars: A Life of Daniel O'Connell* (Dublin: Poolbeg Press, 1986; 1st edn, 1938), pp. 37, 329.

39. Daniel O'Connell, quoted in R. Davis, *The Young Ireland Movement* (Dublin: Gill and Macmillan, 1987), p. 38.

40. S. T. Kingon, 'Ulster Opposition to Catholic Emancipation, 1828–9', *Irish Historical Studies* 34, 134 (2004).

41. M. Elliott, *The Catholics of Ulster: A History* (Harmondsworth: Allen Lane, 2000), pp. 269–70.

42. Daniel O'Connell, quoted in O. MacDonagh, *O'Connell: The Life of Daniel O'Connell 1775–1847* (London: Weidenfeld and Nicolson, 1991), p. 231.

43. Daniel O'Connell, quoted ibid., p. 11.

44. Garvin, *The Evolution of Irish Nationalist Politics*, p. 16.

45. Boyce, *Nationalism in Ireland*, p. 171.

46. Reproduced in R. F. Foster and F. Cullen (eds), *'Conquering England': Ireland in Victorian London* (London: National Portrait Gallery, 2005), p. 41.

47. *IT*, 7 August 1875.

48. D. G. Boyce, *Ireland 1828–1923: From Ascendancy to Democracy* (Oxford: Blackwell, 1992), p. 22.

49. T. Davis, 'Our National Language', in *Literary and Historical Essays* (Dublin: James Duffy, 1854), p. 175.

50. 'Mazzini's romantic nationalism had little appeal for O'Connell' (S. Cronin, *Irish Nationalism: A History of its Roots and Ideology* (Dublin: Academy Press, 1980), p. 66).

51. Garvin, *The Evolution of Irish Nationalist Politics*, p. 62.

52. K. W. Deutsch, *Nationalism and Social Communication: An Inquiry into the Foundations of Nationality* (Cambridge, Mass.: MIT Press, 1966; 1st edn, 1953).

53. C. G. Duffy, *My Life in Two Hemispheres* (Shannon: Irish University Press, 1969; 1st edn, 1898) (vol. I), pp. 80–81.

54. M. Doheny, *The Felon's Track: A Narrative of '48* (Glasgow: Cameron and Ferguson, 1875), pp. 21–2.

55. *Irish Felon*, 1 July 1848.

56. Davis, *The Young Ireland Movement*, p. 206.

57. See, for example, the discussion in U. Ozkirimli, *Theories of Nationalism: A Critical Introduction* (Basingstoke: Macmillan, 2000).

58. Davis's father's family had Welsh and English roots, and his mother was descended from Cromwellian settlers in Ireland.

59. T. Davis, 'Ancient Ireland', in *Literary and Historical Essays*, pp. 41–2.

60. C. Calhoun, *Nationalism* (Buckingham: Open University Press, 1997), p. 51.

61. Quoted in Elliott, *Robert Emmet*, p. 141.

62. J. Chuto, R. P. Holzapfel, P. Mac Mahon and E. Shannon-Mangan (eds), *The Collected Works of James Clarence Mangan: Poems: 1838–1844* (Blackrock: Irish Academic Press, 1996), p. 362.

63. J. Chuto, R. P. Holzapfel and E. Shannon-Mangan (eds), *The Collected Works of James Clarence Mangan: Poems: 1845–1847* (Dublin: Irish Academic Press, 1997), p. 234.

64. See E. Kedourie, *Nationalism* (Oxford: Blackwell, 1993; 1st edn, 1960), pp. 57–61, for discussion of the argument of German philosopher Johann

Gottlieb Fichte (1762–1814) that distinctive language lay at the heart of distinctive nationhood.

65. T. Davis, 'Our National Language', in *Literary and Historical Essays*, pp. 173–4.

66. T. Davis, 'Irish Music and Poetry', in *Thomas Davis: Selections from his Prose and Poetry* (London: T. Fisher Unwin, n.d.), p. 205.

67. William Vincent Wallace, *Maritana* (Marco Polo: 8.223406–7; 1996 recording).

68. Comerford too makes a plea that figures such as Wallace be seen as truly Irish: *Ireland*, p. 267.

69. Davis, 'Irish Music and Poetry', pp. 205–6.

70. T. Davis, 'Hints for Irish Historical Paintings', in *Thomas Davis: Selections from his Prose and Poetry*, p. 169.

71. See Benedict Anderson's sharp-eyed identification of such paradoxes: 'The formal universality of nationality as a socio-cultural concept – in the modern world everyone can, should, will "have" a nationality, as he or she "has" a gender – vs. the irremediable particularity of its concrete manifestations, such that, by definition, "Greek" nationality is *sui generis*' (B. Anderson, *Imagined Communities: Reflections on the Origin and Spread of Nationalism* (London: Verso, 1983), p. 14).

72. N. Doumanis, *Italy* (London: Arnold, 2001), p. 9.

73. William Smith O'Brien to Charlotte O'Brien (10 March 1819), in R. Davis and M. Davis (eds), *The Rebel in His Family: Selected Papers of William Smith O'Brien* (Cork: Cork University Press, 1998), p. 21.

74. T. Davis, 'The History of Ireland', in *Literary and Historical Essays*, pp. 28, 31.

75. J. N. Molony, *A Soul Came Into Ireland: Thomas Davis 1814–1845: A Biography* (Dublin: Geography Publications, 1995).

76. L. Fogarty (ed.), *James Fintan Lalor: Patriot and Political Essayist (1807–1849)* (Dublin: Talbot Press, 1918), pp. 2–3.

77. Ibid., p. 43.

78. Ibid., p. 44.

79. Ibid., pp. 74–6.

80. A. Griffith (1918), 'Preface', ibid., p. xi.

81. James Fintan Lalor, quoted in D. N. Buckley, *James Fintan Lalor: Radical* (Cork: Cork University Pres, 1990), p. 36.

82. *United Irishman*, 12 February 1848.

83. Davitt, *Fall of Feudalism*, p. 73.

84. R. Davis, *William Smith O'Brien: Ireland – 1848 – Tasmania* (Dublin: Geography Publications, 1989), p. 1.

85. T. Davis, 'Our Parliament – A Street Ballad', in M. MacDermott (ed.), *The New Spirit of the Nation* (London: T. Fisher Unwin, 1894), p. 173.

86. S. McConville, *Irish Political Prisoners, 1848–1922: Theatres of War* (London: Routledge, 2003), pp. 55–6.

87. T. F. Meagher, 'Prison Thoughts', in A. Griffith (ed.), *Meagher of the Sword: Speeches of Thomas Francis Meagher in Ireland 1846–1848* (Dublin: M. H. Gill and Son, 1916), p. 330.

88. The description of Mitchel given by the *Irish Felon* on 24 June 1848.

89. John Mitchel (1852), quoted in McConville, *Irish Political Prisoners*, p. 93.

90. 6 August 1855, Pinkerton Papers, PRONI D/1078/M/5A.

91. J. Mitchel, *Jail Journal; Or, Five Years in British Prisons* (London: R. and T. Washbourne, n.d.), pp. 9, 14.

92. Markievicz to Gore-Booth, 5 July 1919, Lissadell Papers, PRONI D/4131/K/7/5.

93. *IT*, 11 November 1861.

94. R. Wagner, *Judaism in Music and Other Essays* (Lincoln: University of Nebraska Press, 1995 edn); P. L. Rose, *Wagner: Race and Revolution* (London: Faber and Faber, 1992); B. Magee, *Wagner and Philosophy* (Harmondsworth: Penguin, 2000).

95. On Crispi's career, see C. Duggan, *Francesco Crispi 1818–1901: From Nation to Nationalism* (Oxford: Oxford University Press, 2002).

96. T. Carlyle, *Chartism* (1839), in *Selected Writings* (Harmondsworth: Penguin, 1971), p. 170.

97. Carlyle, *Signs of the Times* (1829), ibid., pp. 72–4.

98. Ibid., p. 83.

99. H. D. Thoreau, *Walden* (Oxford: Oxford University Press, 1999; 1st edn, 1854).

100. Carlyle, *The French Revolution* (1837), in *Selected Writings*, p. 143.

101. 10 April 1859, Pinkerton Papers, PRONI D/1078/M/7A.

102. A. Griffith, 'Preface', in Griffith (ed.), *Meagher of the Sword*, p. v.

103. A. Hastings, *The Construction of Nationhood: Ethnicity, Religion and Nationalism* (Cambridge: Cambridge University Press, 1997), p. 4.

104. Cronin, *Irish Nationalism*, p. 69.

105. Davis, *The Young Ireland Movement*, p. 264.

106. A. Jackson, *Home Rule: An Irish History, 1800–2000* (London: Weidenfeld and Nicolson, 2003), pp. 18–19.

107. C. Woodham-Smith, *The Great Hunger: Ireland 1845–9* (London: Hamish Hamilton, 1962), p. 20. For balanced evaluation of the historiography of the Famine, see M. Daly, 'Revisionism and Irish History: The Great Famine', in D. G. Boyce and A. O'Day (eds), *The Making of Modern Irish History: Revisionism and the Revisionist Controversy* (London: Routledge, 1996).

108. Woodham-Smith, *The Great Hunger*, p. 75.

109. Ibid., p. 76.

110. P. McGregor, '"Insufficient for the Support of a Family": Wages on the

Public Works During the Great Irish Famine', *Economic and Social Review* 35, 2 (2004).

111. Alexis Soyer, quoted in R. Brandon, *The People's Chef: Alexis Soyer, A Life in Seven Courses* (Chichester: Wiley, 2005; 1st edn, 2004), pp. 173–4.

112. *FJ*, 5 April 1847.

113. C. Kinealy, *A Death-Dealing Famine: The Great Hunger in Ireland* (London: Pluto, 1997); C. Kinealy, *The Great Irish Famine: Impact, Ideology and Rebellion* (Basingstoke: Palgrave, 2002).

114. 'It is unquestionable that during the Famine the Russell administration failed the people of Ireland in what it publicly accepted as being the first duty of government – preventing mass Famine mortality' (P. Gray, *Famine, Land and Politics: British Government and Irish Society 1843–1850* (Dublin: Irish Academic Press, 1999), p. 331).

115. S. Gwynn, *Ireland* (London: Ernest Benn, 1924), p. 37.

116. Duffy, *My Life in Two Hemispheres* (vol. I), p. 199.

117. *FJ*, 9 June 1874.

118. K. Marx, *Capital: A Critique of Political Economy* (London: Lawrence and Wishart, 1954 edn) (vol. I), p. 652.

119. See the thoughtful assessment offered in C. Ó Gráda, *Ireland: A New Economic History 1780–1939* (Oxford: Oxford University Press, 1994), pp. 236–54.

120. P. Hart, *Mick: The Real Michael Collins* (London: Macmillan, 2005), p. 7.

121. J. Mitchel, *The Last Conquest of Ireland (Perhaps)* (Dublin: UCD Press, 2005; 1st edn, 1861), p. 151.

Four – Fenians and Parliamentary Nationalism, 1850–1900

1. Engels to Marx (27 September 1869), in K. Marx and F. Engels, *Ireland and the Irish Question* (Moscow: Progress Publishers, 1971), p. 387.

2. 14 December 1869, in Marx and Engels, *Ireland and the Irish Question*, p. 251.

3. Ibid., pp. 253–4.

4. Marx to Lafargue and Lafargue (5 March 1870), ibid., p. 404.

5. Ibid., p. 304.

6. Engels, 'Letters from London', ibid., p. 43.

7. Engels, 'Preface to the English Edition of 1888', in K. Marx and F. Engels, *Manifesto of the Communist Party* (Moscow: Progress Publishers, 1977; 1st edn, 1848), p. 20.

8. On the relations between nationalism and Marxism, see E. Nimni, *Marxism and Nationalism: Theoretical Origins of a Political Crisis* (London: Pluto Press, 1991).

9. E. Gellner, *Thought and Change* (Chicago: University of Chicago Press, 1965; 1st edn, 1964), p. 147.

10. Marx and Engels, *Manifesto of the Communist Party*, p. 56.

11. Ibid., p. 35.

12. Engels to Marx (23 May 1856), in Marx and Engels, *Ireland and the Irish Question*, p. 93.

13. See, for example, their comments on the Fenians' Clerkenwell explosion of 1867: ibid., p. 159.

14. F. Engels, *The Condition of the Working Class in England* (London: Granada, 1969; 1st edn, 1845), pp. 153, 285, 299.

15. E. Gellner, *Nations and Nationalism* (Oxford: Basil Blackwell, 1983).

16. As David Cannadine has crisply suggested, the dichotomous approach to class relations – so deeply ingrained in Marx's arguments – was grossly simplifying and distorting when compared to the much more complicated historical reality: *Class in Britain* (New Haven: Yale University Press, 1998).

17. J. S. Mill, *England and Ireland* (London: Longmans, Green, Reader and Dyer, 1868), p. 2.

18. J. McCarthy, *Reminiscences* (London: Chatto and Windus, 1899) (vol. I), p. 104.

19. J. S. Mill, *On Liberty* (Harmondsworth: Penguin, 1974; 1st edn, 1859), pp. 61–3.

20. Ibid., pp. 59, 68, 72.

21. 16 December 1867, in Marx and Engels, *Ireland and the Irish Question*, p. 136.

22. *Irish People*, 20 January 1866.

23. O. McGee, *The IRB: The Irish Republican Brotherhood, From the Land League to Sinn Féin* (Dublin: Four Courts Press, 2005), p. 15.

24. *Irish People*, 20 January 1866.

25. *Irish People*, 10 February 1866.

26. *FJ*, 8 March 1867.

27. *IT*, 14 December 1867.

28. *IT*, 16 December 1867.

29. *Irish People*, 3 February 1866.

30. W. B. Yeats, *Autobiographies: Memories and Reflections* (London: Bracken Books, 1995; 1st edn, 1955), p. 209.

31. J. O'Leary, *Recollections of Fenians and Fenianism* (London: Downey and Company, 1896) (vol. I), p. 3.

32. J. B. Yeats, 'John O'Leary', National Gallery of Ireland.

33. O'Leary, *Recollections of Fenians and Fenianism* (vol. I), pp. 78–9.

34. Ibid., p. 30.

35. Ibid., p. 47.

36. C. McGlinchey, *The Last of the Name* (Belfast: Blackstaff, 1986), p. 47.

37. J. S. Casey, *The Galtee Boy* (Dublin: UCD Press, 2005), pp. 42, 61, 98.

38. Yeats, *Autobiographies*, p. 35.

39. *Irish People*, 27 January 1866.

40. J. H. Whyte, *The Independent Irish Party 1850–9* (London: Oxford University Press, 1958), p. vi.

41. *FJ*, 23 February 1864.

42. McGee, *The IRB*, p. 329.

43. C. Townshend, *Ireland: The Twentieth Century* (London: Arnold, 1999), pp. 26–7.

44. J. Mullin, *The Story of a Toiler's Life* (Dublin: UCD Press, 2000; 1st edn, 1921), p. 68.

45. See, for example, L. Greenfeld, *Nationalism: Five Roads to Modernity* (Cambridge, Mass.: Harvard University Press, 1992), pp. 224–7.

46. J. Coakley (ed.), *The Social Origins of Nationalist Movements: The Contemporary West European Experience* (London: Sage, 1992).

47. As brilliantly demonstrated in R. V. Comerford, *The Fenians in Context: Irish Politics and Society, 1848–82* (Dublin: Wolfhound Press, 1985).

48. R. V. Comerford, 'Comprehending the Fenians', *Saothar* 17 (1992), p. 52.

49. O'Leary, *Recollections of Fenians and Fenianism* (vol. II), p. 15.

50. J. H. Whyte, *Church and State in Modern Ireland 1923–1979* (Dublin: Gill and Macmillan, 1980; 1st edn, 1971).

51. *IT*, 25 November 1867.

52. *FJ*, 18 March 1874.

53. D. Thornley, *Isaac Butt and Home Rule* (London: MacGibbon and Kee, 1964), p. 9.

54. *FJ*, 4 March 1874.

55. Charles Stewart Parnell (1877), quoted in F. S. L. Lyons, *Charles Stewart Parnell* (London: Fontana, 1978; 1st edn, 1977), p. 69.

56. T. Parnell, 'To Dr Swift', in *The Poetical Works of Thomas Parnell* (London: George Bell and Sons, 1894), p. 132.

57. See Roy Foster's pioneering study of this theme, *Charles Stewart Parnell: The Man and His Family* (Hassocks: Harvester, 1979; 1st edn, 1976).

58. A. Jackson, *Ireland 1798–1998: Politics and War* (Oxford: Blackwell, 1999), p. 142.

59. *DJ*, 4 January 1882, 6 January 1882.

60. *DJ*, 16 January 1882.

61. *DJ*, 23 January 1882.

62. *GE*, 31 January 1880, 6 March 1880.

63. Mill, *England and Ireland*, p. 13.

64. L. Fogarty (ed.), *James Fintan Lalor: Patriot and Political Essayist (1807–1849)* (Dublin: Talbot Press, 1918), p. 29.

65. P. Bull, *Land, Politics and Nationalism: A Study of the Irish Land Question* (Dublin: Gill and Macmillan, 1996).

66. J. Caird, *The Irish Land Question* (London: Longmans, Green, Reader and Dyer, 1869), pp. 5–6.

67. J. Sanderson, *The Irish Land Question* (London: Edward Stanford, 1870), pp. 3, 53.

68. M. Keane, *The Irish Land Question: Suggestions for Legislation* (Dublin: Hodges, Smith and Co., 1868), pp. 3, 6.

69. R. M. Heron, *The Irish Difficulty, and Its Solution, by a System of Local Superintendence* (London: Hatchard and Co., 1868), pp. 3, 8.

70. Duke of Argyll, *Irish Nationalism: An Appeal to History* (London: John Murray, 1893), pp. 265–6.

71. Charles Stewart Parnell, quoted in Foster, *Charles Stewart Parnell*, p. 316.

72. Charles Stewart Parnell, quoted in L. Kennedy, 'The Economic Thought of the Nation's Lost Leader: Charles Stewart Parnell', in D. G. Boyce and A. O'Day (eds), *Parnell in Perspective* (London: Routledge, 1991), p. 173.

73. The Ulster custom or tenant right was, in varying forms, common across much of mid-nineteenth-century Ireland. It centrally involved the payment by an incoming tenant, to an outgoing one, often without the landlord's knowledge. Effectively, it involved a sale of a perceived interest in the land, symbolizing a sense of at least partial tenant ownership.

74. Michael Davitt, quoted in C. King, *Michael Davitt* (Dundalk: Dundalgan Press, 1999), p. 11.

75. *FJ*, 22 October 1879.

76. Fixity of tenure meant that the tenant could not be evicted for inefficiency, Catholicism, or a lack of obedience or deference towards the landlord; free sale involved the right of the tenant to sell their interest in a farm, not necessarily relating to actual improvements which the tenant had made, but in time coming to be presented and understood as involving precisely this.

77. M. Davitt, *The Fall of Feudalism in Ireland or the Story of the Land League Revolution* (London: Harper and Brothers, 1904), p. xii.

78. Ibid., pp. xi–xii.

79. *FJ*, 1 January 1885.

80. Most thoroughly expounded in a series of important books by Paul Bew: *Land and the National Question in Ireland, 1858–82* (Dublin: Gill and Macmillan, 1978); *C. S. Parnell* (Dublin: Gill and Macmillan, 1980); *Conflict and Conciliation in Ireland, 1890–1910: Parnellites and Radical Agrarians* (Oxford: Oxford University Press, 1987).

81. Charles Stewart Parnell, quoted in A. O'Day, *Charles Stewart Parnell* (Dundalk: Dundalgan Press, 1998), p. 37.

82. W. Dillon, *Life of John Mitchel* (vol. I) (London: Kegan Paul, Trench and Co., 1888), p. 184.

83. Quoted in J. M. Côté, *Fanny and Anna Parnell: Ireland's Patriot Sisters* (Basingstoke: Macmillan, 1991), p. 260.

84. Charles Stewart Parnell, quoted in T. Claydon, 'The Political Thought of Charles Stewart Parnell', in Boyce and O'Day (eds), *Parnell in Perspective*, p. 166.

85. *FJ*, 14 March 1874.

86. William Ewart Gladstone, quoted in J. Morley, *The Life of William Ewart Gladstone* (London: Macmillan, 1903) (vol III), p. 51.

87. See the lucid treatment of these and other themes in E. F. Biagini, *Gladstone* (Basingstoke: Macmillan, 2000).

88. P. Murray, *From the Shadow of Dracula: A Life of Bram Stoker* (London: Jonathan Cape, 2004), p. 139.

89. B. Stoker, *The Snake's Pass* (Dingle: Brandon, 1990; 1st edn, 1890), p. 37.

90. Justin McCarthy, quoted in G. Morton, *Home Rule and the Irish Question* (Harlow: Longman, 1980), p. 97.

91. P. Maume, 'Parnell and the IRB Oath', *Irish Historical Studies* 29, 115 (1995).

92. Parnell had been arrested in October 1881 for attacking the Land Act of that year.

93. Charles Stewart Parnell, quoted in Morton, *Home Rule*, pp. 88–9; cf. Job 38:11.

94. M. Davitt, *Leaves from a Prison Diary; Or, Lectures to a 'Solitary' Audience* (London: Chapman and Hall, 1885), p. 329.

95. R. Kee, *The Green Flag: A History of Irish Nationalism* (Harmondsworth: Penguin, 2000; 1st edn, 1972), p. 383.

96. *FJ*, 6 January 1885.

97. *FJ*, 14 March 1874.

98. *IN*, 1 January 1895.

99. J. Mitchel, *Jail Journal; Or, Five Years in British Prisons* (London: R. and T. Washbourne, n.d.), p. 25.

100. *FJ*, 28 October 1879.

101. A pattern of influence which was long to prevail beyond the nineteenth century in Irish nationalist politics: see John Whyte's powerful study, *Church and State in Modern Ireland*.

102. J. MacVeagh, *A Sketch of the Donegal Land War* (London: Home Rule Union, n.d.), pp. 6–7.

103. *FJ*, 16 March 1885.

104. *FJ*, 18 March 1885.

105. *FJ*, 18 March 1874. On the broader history of St Patrick's Day, see M. Cronin and D. Adair, *The Wearing of the Green: A History of St Patrick's Day* (London: Routledge, 2002).

106. *DJ*, 9 January 1882.

107. R. F. Foster, *The Story of Ireland* (Oxford: Oxford University Press, 1995), p. 11.

108. J. Mac Laughlin, 'The Politics of Nation-Building in Post-Famine Donegal', in W. Nolan, L. Ronayne and M. Dunlevy (eds), *Donegal: History and Society* (Dublin: Geography Publications, 1995).

109. E. Larkin, *The Roman Catholic Church and the Emergence of the Modern Irish Political System 1874–1878* (Blackrock: Four Courts, 1996), pp. xvii–xviii.

110. B. Bradshaw, in B. Bradshaw and D. Keogh (eds), *Christianity in Ireland: Revisiting the Story* (Blackrock: Columba Press, 2002), p. 76.

111. Across much of Ireland the division between landlord and tenant was also one between Anglican and Catholic.

112. R. Dawkins, *The Selfish Gene* (London: Granada, 1978; 1st edn, 1976).

113. *DJ*, 13 January 1882.

114. *FJ*, 6 January 1885.

115. Aristotle, *Politics* (Oxford: Oxford University Press, 1995 edn), p. 47.

116. S. Clark, *Social Origins of the Irish Land War* (Princeton: Princeton University Press, 1979).

117. The phenomenon of 'established industrialism' which so defined mid- to late-nineteenth-century English life (K. T. Hoppen, *The Mid-Victorian Generation 1846–1886* (Oxford: Oxford University Press, 1998), p. 3), had no mirror image in Ireland, save for part of the ever-divergent north-east.

118. Davitt, *Leaves from a Prison Diary*, pp. 292–3.

119. Lyons, *Charles Stewart Parnell*, p. 616.

120. McCarthy, *Reminiscences* (vol. II), p. 105.

121. On this episode, see F. Callanan, *The Parnell Split, 1890–91* (Cork: Cork University Press, 1992).

122. Poster advertising anti-Parnellite demonstration at Lislea, Camlough, County Armagh, 8 March 1891, Pinkerton Papers, PRONI D/1078/P/52.

123. See, for example, *Armagh Guardian*, 31 January 1890.

124. D. G. Boyce, *Nationalism in Ireland* (London: Routledge, 1995; 1st edn, 1982), p. 388.

125. J. J. Bergin, *History of the Ancient Order of Hibernians* (Dublin: AOH, n.d. [1910?]), p. 85.

126. *Donegal Vindicator*, 27 January 1899.

127. J. Leerssen, *Remembrance and Imagination: Patterns in the Historical and Literary Representation of Ireland in the Nineteenth Century* (Cork: Cork University Press, 1996), p. 24.

128. *Shan Van Vocht*, 7 February 1896.

129. T. Garvin, *The Evolution of Irish Nationalist Politics* (Dublin: Gill and Macmillan, 2005; 1st edn, 1981), p. 76.

130. S. Ó Riain, *Maurice Davin (1842–1927): First President of the GAA* (Dublin: Geography Publications, n.d.), pp. 113–14.

131. And again, therefore, echoing the arguments of people such as Liah Greenfeld (in her *Nationalism: Five Roads to Modernity* (Cambridge: Har-

vard University Press, 1992)) concerning the emulatory, responsive politics of nationalist movements in regard to their enemies.

132. D. P. McCracken, *The Irish Pro-Boers, 1877–1902* (Johannesburg: Perskor, 1989).

133. J. H. Murphy, *Abject Loyalty: Nationalism and Monarchy in Ireland During the Reign of Queen Victoria* (Cork: Cork University Press, 2001).

134. See Senia Păseta's fascinating article, 'Nationalist Responses to Two Royal Visits to Ireland, 1900 and 1903', *Irish Historical Studies* 31, 124 (1999).

135. P. Gray, 'Introduction' to P. Gray (ed.), *Victoria's Ireland? Irishness and Britishness, 1837–1901* (Dublin: Four Courts Press, 2004), p. 10.

Five – World Wars and Revolutions, 1900–1945

1. G. B. Shaw, Preface (1906) to *John Bull's Other Island*, in *Prefaces* (London: Odhams Press, 1938), p. 457.

2. Ibid.

3. As in Eric Hobsbawm's marvellous *Age of Extremes: The Short Twentieth Century 1914–1991* (London: Abacus, 1995; 1st edn, 1994).

4. A. S. Green, *Irish Nationality* (London: Williams and Norgate, n.d.), pp. 21, 29.

5. See, for example, S. James, *The Atlantic Celts: Ancient People or Modern Invention?* (London: British Museum Press, 1999).

6. Green, *Irish Nationality*, p. 222; for a more thorough and complex depiction, see D. G. Boyce, *Nationalism in Ireland* (London: Routledge, 1995; 1st edn, 1982).

7. 'Childers took cocaine' (O'Malley Papers, ADUCD P17b/100).

8. On Yeats, above all see Roy Foster's magnificent two-volume biography: *W. B. Yeats: A Life. I: The Apprentice Mage 1865–1914* (Oxford: Oxford University Press, 1997); *W. B. Yeats: A Life. II: The Arch-Poet 1915–1939* (Oxford: Oxford University Press, 2003).

9. W. B. Yeats, *Autobiographies: Memories and Reflections* (London: Bracken Books, 1995; 1st edn, 1955), p. 570.

10. W. B. Yeats (13 November 1898), quoted in Foster, *The Apprentice Mage*, p. 162.

11. D. P. Moran, quoted in Boyce, *Nationalism in Ireland*, p. 242.

12. D. P. Moran, *The Philosophy of Irish Ireland* (Dublin: James Duffy, n.d.), p. 1; cf. E. Kedourie, *Nationalism* (Oxford: Blackwell, 1993; 1st edn, 1960), p. 56.

13. M. Hroch, *Social Preconditions of National Revival in Europe: A Comparative Analysis of the Social Composition of Patriotic Groups among the Smaller European Nations* (Cambridge: Cambridge University Press, 1985).

14. See, for example, the discussions contained in R. English and M. Kenny, (eds), *Rethinking British Decline* (Basingstoke: Macmillan, 2000).

15. F. S. L. Lyons, *Culture and Anarchy in Ireland 1890–1939* (Oxford: Oxford University Press, 1982; 1st edn, 1979), p. 27.

16. A. Clery, *The Idea of a Nation* (Dublin: UCD Press, 2002; 1st edn, 1907), p. 5.

17. See Kedourie, *Nationalism*, pp. 52–9.

18. P. A. Sheehan, *The Intellectuals: An Experiment in Irish Club-Life* (London: Longmans, Green and Co., 1911), p. v.

19. On the essential probity of the Irish Party, see P. Bew, *Ideology and the Irish Question: Ulster Unionism and Irish Nationalism 1912–1916* (Oxford: Oxford University Press, 1994), p. 20.

20. P. A. Sheehan, *The Graves at Kilmorna: A Story of '67* (London: Longmans, Green and Company, 1926; 1st edn, 1914), p. 5.

21. J. Devlin, 'Introduction' (1910) to J. J. Bergin, *History of the Ancient Order of Hibernians* (Dublin: AOH, n.d. [1910?]), p. v.

22. *Irish Freedom*, April 1911.

23. *Donegal Vindicator*, 13 January 1899.

24. *Donegal Vindicator*, 7 July 1899.

25. See, for example, Harry Johnson's suggestion that nationalism attaches 'utility or value to having certain jobs held or certain property owned by members of the national group rather than by non-members of the national group', and that it is thought 'that the utility accrues to members of the national group whether or not they themselves hold the jobs or the property in question' (quoted in A. D. Smith and J. Hutchinson (eds), *Nationalism* (Oxford: Oxford University Press, 1994), p. 236).

26. For fine treatment of this subject, see S. Pašeta, *Before the Revolution: Nationalism, Social Change and Ireland's Catholic Élite, 1879–1922* (Cork: Cork University Press, 1999), pp. 5–27.

27. *Donegal Vindicator*, 5 January 1900.

28. Yeats, *Autobiographies*, p. 559.

29. R. Kee, *The Green Flag: A History of Irish Nationalism* (Harmondsworth: Penguin, 2000; 1st edn, 1972), pp. 411–12.

30. Bew, *Ideology and the Irish Question*; P. Bew, *John Redmond* (Dundalk: Dundalgan Press, 1996); J. P. Finnan, *John Redmond and Irish Unity, 1912–1918* (Syracuse: Syracuse University Press, 2004); P. Maume, *The Long Gestation: Irish Nationalist Life 1891–1918* (Dublin: Gill and Macmillan, 1999); M. Wheatley, *Nationalism and the Irish Party: Provincial Ireland 1910–1916* (Oxford: Oxford University Press, 2005).

31. J. E. Redmond, 'Home Rule: Its Real Meaning' (July 1883), in *Historical and Political Addresses 1883–1897* (Dublin: Sealy, Bryers and Walker, 1898), pp. 179, 181.

32. E. O'Duffy, *The Wasted Island* (Dublin: Martin Lester, n.d.), p. 137.

33. Kee, *The Green Flag*, p. 752.
34. A. D. Smith, *The Nation in History: Historiographical Debates about Ethnicity and Nationalism* (Hanover: University Press of New England, 2000), pp. 63–4.
35. L. G. Redmond-Howard, *Home Rule* (London: T. C. and E. C. Jack, n.d. [1912?]), pp. 12, 30.
36. J. MacVeagh, *Home Rule in a Nutshell* (London: Daily Chronicle, 1912), pp. 1, 3.
37. UIL Lurgan Branch: To the Nationalists of Lurgan (1911), UIL Papers (Lurgan Branch), PRONI T/2530/5.
38. Albert Lewis, quoted in A. N. Wilson, *C. S. Lewis: A Biography* (London: Flamingo, 1991; 1st edn, 1990), p. 5.
39. J. Johnston, *Civil War in Ulster: Its Objects and Probable Results* (Dublin: UCD Press, 1999; 1st edn, 1913), p. 5.
40. *IN*, 25 September 1911.
41. G. Lewis, *Carson: The Man Who Divided Ireland* (London: Hambledon, 2005), pp. 88, 107; A. Jackson, *Sir Edward Carson* (Dundalk: Dundalgan Press, 1993); A. T. Q. Stewart, *Edward Carson* (Dublin: Gill and Macmillan, 1981); H. M. Hyde, *Carson* (London: Constable, 1987; 1st edn, 1953).
42. Modern scholarship has tended to reinforce the view that a simple one-nation reading of Ireland is simplistic and misleading: M. Gallagher, 'How Many Nations are there in Ireland?', *Ethnic and Racial Studies* 18, 4 (1995).
43. J. Lynch, *A Tale of Three Cities: Comparative Studies in Working-Class Life* (Basingstoke: Macmillan, 1998).
44. Clery, *The Idea of a Nation*, pp. 62–4.
45. On Clery, see the perceptive article by Patrick Maume: 'Nationalism and Partition: The Political Thought of Arthur Clery', *Irish Historical Studies* 31, 122 (1998).
46. D. Ó Cróinín, *Early Medieval Ireland 400–1200* (London: Longman, 1995), p. 44.
47. *Irish Freedom*, November 1910.
48. C. Townshend, *Easter 1916: The Irish Rebellion* (London: Penguin, 2005), p. 19.
49. J. O'Neill, *At Swim, Two Boys* (London: Scribner, 2001), p. 141. Another recent novelist has movingly depicted the imagined sacrifice of one Irish soldier in the First World War British Army (S. Barry, *A Long Long Way* (London: Faber and Faber, 2005)), although the hero of this novel comes not from a Redmondite but from a Catholic unionist background.
50. Of course, concern over Irish Home Rule was not necessarily the only motivation behind Home Rulers' involvement in the War; see S. Páseta, 'Thomas Kettle: "An Irish Soldier in the Army of Europe"', in A. Gregory and S. Páseta (eds), *Ireland and the Great War: 'A War to Unite Us All'* (Manchester: Manchester University Press, 2002).

51. M. Kelly, '"Parnell's Old Brigade": The Redmondite-Fenian Nexus in the 1890s', *Irish Historical Studies* 33, 130 (2002).

52. Redmond, 'Irish Protestants and Home Rule' (November 1886), in *Historical and Political Addresses*, p. 118.

53. A. D. Smith, *National Identity* (Harmondsworth: Penguin, 1991), p. 14.

54. R. O'Loughran, *Redmond's Vindication* (Dublin: Talbot Press, 1919), Foreword (9 May 1918), p. xiii.

55. See the fine treatment of this in F. Campbell, *Land and Revolution: Nationalist Politics in the West of Ireland 1891–1921* (Oxford: Oxford University Press, 2005).

56. J. B. Keane, *The Field* (Cork: Mercier, 1966), p. 16.

57. S. Schama, *Landscape and Memory* (London: Fontana, 1996; 1st edn, 1995).

58. Charles Dolan, quoted in C. Ó Duibhir, *Sinn Féin: The First Election 1908* (Manorhamilton: Drumlin Publications, 1993), p. 59.

59. R. English, *Radicals and the Republic: Socialist Republicanism in the Irish Free State 1925–1937* (Oxford: Oxford University Press, 1994).

60. F. McCourt, *Angela's Ashes: A Memoir* (New York: Scribner, 1996), p. 181.

61. D. Corkery, *The Hidden Ireland: A Study of Gaelic Munster in the Eighteenth Century* (Dublin: Gill and Macmillan, 1967; 1st edn, 1924), pp. 5, 11.

62. Tomas MacCurtain (1884–1920) was a Cork Volunteer leader shot dead in 1920 by Crown forces; Terence MacSwiney (1879–1920) was another IRA man, who died in 1920 in a British prison after a lengthy hunger-strike.

63. D. Corkery, Foreword to M. Chavasse, *Terence MacSwiney* (Dublin: Clonmore and Reynolds, 1961), p. 14.

64. See Patrick Maume's fine study, *'Life That is Exile': Daniel Corkery and the Search for Irish Ireland* (Belfast: Institute of Irish Studies, 1993).

65. R. Tagore, *Nationalism* (London: Papermac, 1991; 1st edn, 1917).

66. Maume, *Long Gestation*, p. 52.

67. 4 May 1916, Lissadell Papers, PRONI D/4131/K/4. Though a less defiant court-martial Markievicz emerges from the account offered by one contemporary observer, who recalled her protesting, 'I am only a woman and you cannot shoot a woman. You must not shoot a woman' (L. Ó Broin, *W. E. Wylie and the Irish Revolution 1916–1921* (Dublin: Gill and Macmillan, 1989), p. 27).

68. Most fully now in Charles Townshend's superb *Easter 1916*.

69. S. MacEntee, *Easter Fires: Personal Records of 1916 by Sean MacEntee and Dr James Ryan* (Waterford: St Carthage Press, 1943), p. 20.

70. 'Easter Week, 1916: British Government Reports', Files of the Department of the Taoiseach, NAD S14060.

71. O'Loughran, *Redmond's Vindication*, p. 34.

72. Maire Comerford, quoted in U. MacEoin (ed.), *Survivors* (Dublin: Argenta, 1987; 1st edn, 1980), p. 41.

73. W. B. Yeats, 'Easter 1916', in *Yeats's Poems* (Dublin: Gill and Macmillan, 1989), pp. 288–9.

74. P. Pearse, 'Little Lad of the Tricks', quoted in E. Sisson, *Pearse's Patriots: St Enda's and the Cult of Boyhood* (Cork: Cork University Press, 2004), pp. 142–3.

75. J. Dudgeon, *Roger Casement: The Black Diaries with a Study of his Background, Sexuality, and Irish Political Life* (Belfast: Belfast Press, 2002), p. 222.

76. ISRP 1896 Programme, quoted in D. Lynch, *Radical Politics in Modern Ireland: The Irish Socialist Republican Party 1896–1904* (Dublin: Irish Academic Press, 2005), p. 166.

77. J. W. Boyle, *The Irish Labor Movement in the Nineteenth Century* (Washington, DC: Catholic University of America Press, 1988), p. 201.

78. J. Connolly, *Labour in Irish History*, in *Collected Works* (vol. I) (Dublin: New Books, 1987), p. 25.

79. J. Connolly, 'The Irish Flag' (8 April 1916), in *Collected Works* (vol. II) (Dublin: New Books, 1988), p. 175.

80. J. Connolly, 'North-East Ulster' (2 August 1913), in *Collected Works* (vol. I), pp. 383–4.

81. V. I. Lenin, *On Religion* (Moscow: Progress Publishers, 1969), pp. 8, 21.

82. P. Maume, 'Lily Connolly's Conversion', *History Ireland* 2, 3 (1994).

83. J. Connolly, *Labour, Nationality and Religion*, in *Collected Works* (vol II).

84. P. Yeates, *Lockout: Dublin 1913* (New York: Palgrave, 2001).

85. For extended discussion of Connolly's thinking and of the debate around his participation in 1916, see English, *Radicals and the Republic.*

86. See the discussion, for example, in E. Nimni, *Marxism and Nationalism: Theoretical Origins of a Political Crisis* (London: Pluto, 1991); or in W. Connor, *The National Question in Marxist-Leninist Theory and Strategy* (Princeton: Princeton University Press, 1984).

87. V. Geoghegan, 'The Emergence and Submergence of Irish Socialism, 1821–51', in D. G. Boyce, R. Eccleshall and V. Geoghegan (eds), *Political Thought in Ireland Since the Seventeenth Century* (London: Routledge, 1993).

88. On Casement, for example, see B. Inglis, *Roger Casement* (Belfast: Blackstaff, 1993; 1st edn, 1973); Dudgeon, *Roger Casement*; R. Sawyer, *Casement, the Flawed Hero* (London: Routledge and Kegan Paul, 1984); W. J. McCormack, *Roger Casement in Death, or, Haunting the Free State* (Dublin: UCD Press, 2002). On Connolly, see A. Morgan, *James Connolly: A Political Biography* (Manchester: Manchester University Press, 1988); R. D. Edwards, *James Connolly* (Dublin: Gill and Macmillan, 1981); C. D. Greaves, *The Life and Times of James Connolly* (London: Lawrence and Wishart, 1972; 1st edn, 1961); Howell, *A Lost Left*; J. L. Hyland, *James Connolly* (Dundalk: Dundalgan Press, 1997); J. Newsinger, 'Connolly and his Biographers', *Irish Political Studies* 5 (1990); P. Bew, P. Gibbon, P. and H. Patterson, *The State in*

Northern Ireland, 1921–72: Political Forces and Social Classes (Manchester: Manchester University Press, 1979); Lynch, *Radical Politics in Modern Ireland*; D. Nevin, *James Connolly: 'A Full Life'* (Dublin: Gill and Macmillan, 2005).

89. P. Bew, 'The Real Importance of Sir Roger Casement', *History Ireland* 2, 2 (1994), p. 42.

90. Ethel Mannin, quoted in Foster, *The Arch-Poet*, p. 683.

91. W. B. Yeats, quoted ibid., p. 572.

92. W. B. Yeats, 'Roger Casement', in *Yeats's Poems*, p. 423.

93. Roger Casement (1916), quoted in H. M. Hyde, *Roger Casement* (Harmondsworth: Penguin, 1964; 1st edn, 1960), pp. 156–7.

94. 'In the tragic divisions which befell Ireland during the ten years after Pearse's death, it was he whose name appeared most often . . . in republican propaganda' (R. D. Edwards, *Patrick Pearse: The Triumph of Failure* (Dublin: Poolbeg Press, 1990; 1st edn, 1977), p. 338).

95. On St Enda's, see Sisson, *Pearse's Patriots*.

96. L. Greenfeld, *Nationalism: Five Roads to Modernity* (Cambridge, Mass.: Harvard Univesity Press, 1992).

97. P. H. Pearse, 'The Sovereign People' (1916), in *Political Writings and Speeches* (Dublin: Phoenix, n.d.), p. 337.

98. P. H. Pearse, 'Why We Want Recruits' (1915), in *Political Writings and Speeches*, p. 121.

99. See English and Kenny (eds), *Rethinking British Decline*.

100. P. H. Pearse, 'Ghosts' (1915), in *Political Writings and Speeches*, p. 223.

101. J. Connolly, 'Trust your Leaders!' (4 December 1915), in *Collected Works* (vol. II), p. 117.

102. S. Robson, *The First World War* (Harlow: Longman, 1998), p. 33.

103. On whom, see the valuable biography by Gerard MacAtasney, *Seán MacDiarmada: The Mind of the Revolution* (Manorhamilton: Drumlin Publications, 2004).

104. Michael Collins (26 July 1915), quoted in MacAtasney, *Seán MacDiarmada*, p. 92.

105. F. X. Martin, 'The Evolution of a Myth: The Easter Rising, Dublin 1916', in E. Kamenka (ed.), *Nationalism: The Nature and Evolution of an Idea* (New York: St Martin's Press, 1976), p. 59; cf. W. I. Thompson, *The Imagination of an Insurrection: Dublin, Easter 1916. A Study of an Ideological Movement* (West Stockbridge: Lindisfarne Press, 1982; 1st edn, 1967).

106. See, for example, Kedourie, *Nationalism*; or Hroch, *Social Preconditions*.

107. T. MacDonagh, *The Poetical Works of Thomas MacDonagh* (Dublin: Talbot Press, 1916), p. 91.

108. E. Young, *Flowering Dusk: Things Remembered Accurately and Inaccurately* (London: Dennis Dobson, 1947; 1st edn, 1945), p. 131.

109. 'Proclamation of the Republic', in R. F. Foster, *Modern Ireland 1600–1972* (Harmondsworth: Penguin, 1988), pp. 597–8.

110. M. Canovan, *Nationhood and Political Theory* (Cheltenham: Edward Elgar, 1996).

111. F. Shaw, 'The Canon of Irish History: A Challenge', *Studies* 61 (1972), p. 119.

112. For discussion of this theme, see English, *Radicals and the Republic.*

113. Boyce, *Nationalism in Ireland*, p. 310.

114. Dudgeon, *Roger Casement*, p. 9.

115. Quoted in *IT*, 4 February 2006.

116. 'Public Attitude and Opinion in Ireland as to the Recent Outbreak' (15 May 1916), Bonar Law Papers, HLRO BL 63/C/3.

117. J. J. Lee, 'In Search of Patrick Pearse', in M. Ní Dhonnchadha and T. Dorgan (eds), *Revising the Rising* (Derry: Field Day, 1991), p. 137.

118. Roger Casement (1916), quoted in Hyde, *Roger Casement*, p. 118.

119. Roger Casement (1912), quoted in R. MacColl, *Roger Casement* (London: Four Square, 1960; 1st edn, 1956), p. 96.

120. C. Townshend, *Political Violence in Ireland: Government and Resistance Since 1848* (Oxford: Oxford University Press, 1984; 1st edn, 1983), p. 281.

121. L. Robinson, *Patriots: A Play in Three Acts* (Dublin: Maunsel and Company, 1912), p. 24.

122. O'Malley to Childers (26 November/1 December 1923), in R. English and C. O'Malley (eds), *Prisoners: The Civil War Letters of Ernie O'Malley* (Dublin: Poolbeg Press, 1991), pp. 72–3.

123. Among them, M. Caulfield, *The Easter Rebellion* (London: Frederick Muller, 1964); M. Foy and B. Barton, *The Easter Rising* (Stroud: Sutton, 1999); Townshend, *Easter 1916.*

124. Including L. O'Flaherty, *Insurrection* (Dublin: Wolfhound Press, 1993; 1st edn, 1950); and B. Tóibín, *The Rising* (Dublin: New Island Books, 2001).

125. Bax had met Pearse, who liked him, and wrote in the 1916 martyr's memory, both musically (*In Memoriam Pádraig Pearse*) and – as Dermot O'Byrne – in poetic response to the Easter Rising (see *IT*, 23 August 2003).

126. M. Tierney, *Eoin MacNeill: Scholar and Man of Action 1867–1945* (Oxford: Oxford University Press, 1980), p. 19.

127. Markievicz to Gore-Booth (16 May 1916), Lissadell Papers, PRONI D/4131/K/7/1.

128. Markievicz to Gore-Booth (c. July 1911), Lissadell Papers, PRONI D/4131/K3.

129. *FJ*, 1 October 1917.

130. D. Fitzpatrick, *Politics and Irish Life 1913–1921: Provincial Experience of War and Revolution* (Cork: Cork University Press, 1998; 1st edn, 1977), p. 99.

131. Barry, *A Long Long Way*, p. 281.

132. Eithne Coyle, quoted in MacEoin (ed.), *Survivors*, pp. 151–2.

133. Peadar O'Donnell, quoted ibid., p. 22.

134. S. Gwynn, *Ireland* (London: Ernest Benn, 1924), p. 193.

135. Such slips even occur in some highly intelligent books: C. Bell, *Peace Agreements and Human Rights* (Oxford: Oxford University Press, 2000), p. 137; P. Magee, *Gangsters or Guerrillas? Representations of Irish Republicans in "Troubles Fiction"* (Belfast: Beyond the Pale, 2001), p. 11.

136. D. Breen, *My Fight for Irish Freedom* (Dublin: Anvil Press, 1989; 1st edn, 1924), p. 30.

137. Ó Duibhir, *Sinn Féin*, p. 15.

138. J. Augusteijn, *From Public Defiance to Guerrilla Warfare: The Experience of Ordinary Volunteers in the Irish War of Independence 1916–1921* (Blackrock: Irish Academic Press, 1996), p. 16.

139. D. Macardle, *Without Fanfares: Some Reflections on the Republic of Eire* (Dublin: M. H. Gill and Son, 1946), pp. 3–4.

140. M. Moore, *The Ethics of Nationalism* (Oxford: Oxford University Press, 2001), p. 1.

141. See, for example, the views exchanged over what actually happened at the IRA's Kilmichael ambush of November 1920 in County Cork: P. Hart, *The IRA and Its Enemies: Violence and Community in Cork, 1916–1923* (Oxford: Oxford University Press, 1998), ch. 2; *Kilmichael: The False Surrender* (Aubane: Aubane Historical Society, 1999); M. Ryan, *Tom Barry: IRA Freedom Fighter* (Cork: Mercier Press, 2003), pp. 49–67; *Irish Political Review* 20, 7 (2005); *History Ireland* 13, 4 (2005).

142. On which, see A. Mitchell, *Revolutionary Government in Ireland: Dáil Éireann, 1919–22* (Dublin: Gill and Macmillan, 1995).

143. Quoted in D. Macardle, *The Irish Republic: A Documented Chronicle of the Anglo-Irish Conflict and the Partitioning of Ireland, with a Detailed Account of the Period 1916–1923* (London: Corgi, 1968; 1st edn, 1937), pp. 252–4.

144. R. English, *Ernie O'Malley: IRA Intellectual* (Oxford: Oxford University Press, 1999; 1st edn, 1998), p. 79.

145. Brilliantly chronicled for Cork in Peter Hart's *The IRA and Its Enemies* (quotation at p. 17). On the 1919–21 conflict more broadly, see M. Hopkinson, *The Irish War of Independence* (Dublin: Gill and Macmillan, 2002).

146. J. Augusteijn, *From Public Defiance to Guerrilla Warfare: The Experience of Ordinary Volunteers in the Irish War of Independence 1916–1921* (Blackrock: Irish Academic Press, 1996), pp. 269–70, 278; C. Townshend, *The British Campaign in Ireland, 1919–1921: The Development of Political and Military Policies* (Oxford: Oxford University Press, 1975), p. 206.

147. P. Hart (ed.), *British Intelligence in Ireland, 1920–21: The Final Reports* (Cork: Cork University Press, 2002).

148. Townshend, *British Campaign*, pp. 192–3; Augusteijn, *From Public Defiance*, p. 352; Hart, *The IRA and Its Enemies*, pp. 107–8, 261.

149. Seán MacEoin, quoted in M. Coleman, *County Longford and the Irish Revolution 1910–1923* (Dublin: Irish Academic Press, 2003), p. 134.

150. B. O'Connor, *With Michael Collins in the Fight for Irish Independence* (London: Peter Davies, 1929), p. 173.

151. Harry Boland, quoted in D. Fitzpatrick, *Harry Boland's Irish Revolution* (Cork: Cork University Press, 2003), p. 83.

152. Liam Mellows, quoted in C. D. Greaves, *Liam Mellows and the Irish Revolution* (London: Lawrence and Wishart, 1971), p. 152.

153. Maire Comerford, quoted in U. MacEoin (ed.), *Survivors* (Dublin: Argenta, 1987; 1st edn, 1980), p. 41.

154. Eamon de Valera, quoted in T. R. Dwyer, *De Valera's Darkest Hour: In Search of National Independence 1919–1932* (Cork: Mercier Press, 1982), p. 11.

155. *IT*, 26 October 1917.

156. E. O'Malley, *On Another Man's Wound* (Dublin: Anvil Press, 1979; 1st edn, 1936), p. 332.

157. F. Gallagher, *The Indivisible Island: The History of the Partition of Ireland* (Westport: Greenwood Press, 1974; 1st edn, 1957), p. 16.

158. J. Scharzmantel, *The State in Contemporary Society: An Introduction* (Hemel Hempstead: Harvester Wheatsheaf, 1994), p. 184.

159. Liam Lynch, quoted in M. Ryan, *Liam Lynch: The Real Chief* (Cork: Mercier Press, 1986), p. 9.

160. F. McGarry, *Eoin O'Duffy: A Self-Made Hero* (Oxford: Oxford University Press, 2005), p. 25; English, *Ernie O'Malley*, pp. 73–4.

161. Devlin to Moloney (1920), Devlin Papers, PRONI T/2257/7.

162. Augusteijn, *From Public Defiance*, p. 270.

163. Macardle, *The Irish Republic*, p. 277.

164. Summary of Police Reports (1 August 1920), NAL CO 904/142.

165. Augusteijn, *From Public Defiance*, pp. 293–4; Hart, *The IRA and Its Enemies*, pp. 150, 273–92, 303–4, 313.

166. As far as the Volunteers/IRA were concerned, Ulster was tellingly quiet. In some parts (including Tyrone, Derry and Armagh) the 1919–21 expansion of Sinn Féin was not matched by an equivalent growth in the Volunteers; and out of over 500 IRA casualties during 1920–21, only twenty-five were from the six counties which were to form Northern Ireland (E. Staunton, *The Nationalists of Northern Ireland 1918–1973* (Blackrock: Columba Press, 2001), pp. 30–33, 286).

167. M. Hopkinson, 'Biography of the Revolutionary Period: Michael Collins and Kevin Barry', *Irish Historical Studies* 28, 111 (1993), p. 313; P. Hart, *Mick: The Real Michael Collins* (London: Macmillan, 2005), pp. 193, 242–3.

168. S. Joy, *The IRA in Kerry 1916–1921* (Cork: Collins Press, 2005), p. 126.

169. P. Hart, *The IRA at War 1916–1923* (Oxford: Oxford University Press, 2003), p. 123.

170. M. Dragojevic, 'Competing Institutions in National Identity Construction: The Croatian Case', *Nationalism and Ethnic Politics* 11, 1 (2005).

171. P. S. O'Hegarty, *A Short Memoir of Terence MacSwiney* (Dublin: Talbot Press, 1922), p. 3.

172. M. Chavasse, *Terence MacSwiney* (Dublin: Clonmore and Reynolds, 1961), p. 170.

173. F. Gallagher, *Days of Fear* (London: John Murray, 1928), pp. 13, 35–6, 57, 60–61, 75, 110.

174. P. Béaslaí, *Michael Collins and the Making of a New Ireland* (vol. I) (Dublin: Phoenix, 1926), p. 78.

175. M. G. Valiulis, *Portrait of a Revolutionary: General Richard Mulcahy and the Founding of the Irish Free State* (Blackrock: Irish Academic Press, 1992), p. 2.

176. McGarry, *Eoin O'Duffy*, pp. 4, 31, 39, 56.

177. M. Brennan, *The War in Clare 1911–1921: Personal Memoirs of the Irish War of Independence* (Dublin: Four Courts Press, 1980), p. 81.

178. Ernie O'Malley, quoted in R. English and C. O'Malley (eds), *Prisoners: The Civil War Letters of Ernie O'Malley* (Dublin: Poolbeg Press, 1991), p. 110.

179. Constance Markievicz (4 December 1918) in *Prison Letters of Countess Markievicz* (London: Virago, 1987; 1st edn, 1934), p. 188.

180. Gallagher, *Days of Fear*, pp. 25, 29, 67; English and O'Malley (eds), *Prisoners*, p. 48.

181. MacSwiney to Brugha (23 January 1935), Brugha Papers, ADUCD P15/8.

182. B. M. Coldrey, *Faith and Fatherland: The Christian Brothers and the Development of Irish Nationalism 1838–1921* (Dublin: Gill and Macmillan, 1988), pp. 4–5, 98, 109, 113, 139, 248, 253, 257–9, 272; Hart, *The IRA at War*, pp. 56–7.

183. M. Billig, *Banal Nationalism* (London: Sage, 1995).

184. Tom Barry, quoted in Ryan, *Tom Barry: IRA Freedom Fighter*, p. 295.

185. O'Malley, *On Another Man's Wound*, p. 24.

186. Hart, *The IRA and Its Enemies*; McGarry, *Eoin O'Duffy*.

187. E. Gellner, *Nations and Nationalism* (Oxford: Basil Blackwell, 1983).

188. On the social profile of the Revolutionary generation, see Hart, *The IRA at War*; T. Garvin, *Nationalist Revolutionaries in Ireland, 1858–1928* (Oxford: Oxford University Press, 1987); Augusteijn, *From Public Defiance*.

189. Although this need not offer much comfort to the Marxists: there clearly were important tensions between nationalism's various classes in some places, including the rural west, during the 1919–21 period (F. Campbell, *Land and Revolution: Nationalist Politics in the West of Ireland 1891–1921* (Oxford: Oxford University Press, 2005)). But these did not stem from the

kind of anti-capitalist instincts or desires of somebody like the Marxist republican Peadar O'Donnell. Indeed, small farmers and labourers (and Sinn Féin, where they were supportive) helped to consolidate private ownership in these years: precisely the kind of conservative barrier which blocked the Marxist path in Ireland. See R. English, *Radicals and the Republic: Socialist Republicanism in the Irish Free State 1925–1937* (Oxford: Oxford University Press, 1994); and cf. Sean Cronin's judgment that 'Socially-radical republicanism had no influence during the "War of Independence" (1919–21)' (S. Cronin, *Irish Nationalism: A History of its Roots and Ideology* (Dublin: Academy Press, 1980), p. 218).

190. Garvin, *Nationalist Revolutionaries*, p. 90.
191. F. Fukuyama, *Trust: The Social Virtues and the Creation of Prosperity* (Harmondsworth: Penguin, 1995), p. 358.
192. See, for example, Gallagher to Briscoe (29 November 1928), Gallagher Papers, NLI MS 18,353.
193. P. R. Brass, *Ethnicity and Nationalism: Theory and Comparison* (London: Sage, 1991), p. 33.
194. Valiulis, *Portrait of a Revolutionary*; Hart, *Mick*; English, *Ernie O'Malley*.
195. O'Malley, *On Another Man's Wound*, p. 85.
196. Chief Secretary of Ireland to War Cabinet (24 February 1918), Files of the Department of the Taoiseach, NAD S14049.
197. F. O'Connor, *An Only Child* (Belfast: Blackstaff, 1993; 1st edn, 1961), p. 202.
198. O'Malley, *On Another Man's Wound*, p. 126.
199. B. Anderson, *Imagined Communities: Reflections on the Origin and Spread of Nationalism* (London: Verso, 1983).
200. Handwritten notes of Sean MacBride (14 April 1923), Cormac O'Malley Papers.
201. R. E. Childers, *The Riddle of the Sands* (Ware: Wordsworth, 1993; 1st edn, 1903), pp. 95, 179.
202. K. Clarke, *Revolutionary Woman: Kathleen Clarke 1878–1972 – An Autobiography* (Dublin: O'Brien Press, 1991).
203. C. S. Andrews, *Man of No Property: An Autobiography (Volume Two)* (Cork: Mercier Press, 1982), p. 11.
204. Eithne Coyle, quoted in M. Ward, *Unmanageable Revolutionaries: Women and Irish Nationalism* (London: Pluto Press, 1983), p. 100.
205. IRA Report, 3rd Southern Division (2 October 1922), Twomey Papers, ADUCD P69/94 (41). Often enough, Cumann na mBan spent time celebrating the martial heroics of the boys: see their 1929 document, *The Story of Liam Mellows* (Coyle O'Donnell Papers, ADUCD P61/6 (2)).
206. Francis Stuart, interviewed by the author, Dublin, 24 February 1987.
207. G. Gilmore, *Labour and the Republican Movement* (Dublin: Repsol, n.d.; 1st edn, 1966), p. 12.
208. *Workers' Republic*, 26 August 1922.

209. 'Constance G. Markievicz: letter from Russian Consul, Glasgow, 1919', Files of the Department of the Taoiseach, NAD S14058.

210. M. Hroch, *Social Preconditions of National Revival in Europe: A Comparative Analysis of the Social Composition of Patriotic Groups among the Smaller European Nations* (Cambridge: Cambridge University Press, 1985).

211. T. Barry, *Guerilla Days in Ireland* (Dublin: Anvil, 1989; 1st edn, 1949), p. 2.

212. Tom Barry, quoted in Ryan, *Tom Barry: IRA Freedom Fighter*, p. 15.

213. Hart, *Mick*, pp. xxi, 33, 70.

214. O'Malley to Humphreys (12 April 1923), Humphreys Papers, ADUCD P106/754.

215. *Irish People*, 27 January 1866.

216. D. G. Boyce, *Nationalism in Ireland* (London: Routledge, 1995; 1st edn, 1982), pp. 388–9.

217. L. Greenfeld, *Nationalism: Five Roads to Modernity* (Cambridge, Mass.: Harvard University Press, 1992).

218. C. S. Andrews, *Dublin Made Me: An Autobiography* (Cork: Mercier Press, 1979), p. 7.

219. S. O'Fáolain, *The Irish* (West Drayton: Penguin, 1947), p. 106.

220. S. O'Fáolain, *Constance Markievicz* (London: Sphere, 1967; 1st edn, 1934), p. 74.

221. See, in particular, O'Malley, *On Another Man's Wound*.

222. Gallagher, *Days of Fear*, p. 122.

223. A. de Blacam, *Towards the Republic: A Study of New Ireland's Social and Political Aims* (Dublin: Kiersey, 1918), p. 13.

224. Gerald Boland, quoted in Fitzpatrick, *Harry Boland's Irish Revolution*, p. 32.

225. Fitzpatrick, *Harry Boland's Irish Revolution*; Hart, *Mick*; Valiulis, *Portrait of a Revolutionary*; English, *Ernie O'Malley.*; McGarry, *Eoin O'Duffy*.

226. W. B. Yeats, quoted in R. F. Foster, *W. B. Yeats: A Life. II: The Arch-Poet 1915–1939* (Oxford: Oxford University Press, 2003), p. 165.

227. Childers, *Riddle of the Sands*, p. 15.

228. Brass, *Ethnicity and Nationalism*.

229. O. Wilde, *Lady Windermere's Fan*, in *Complete Works of Oscar Wilde* (vol. II) (London: Heron Books, 1966), p. 107.

230. Michael Collins, quoted in Hart, *Mick*, p. 334.

231. M. Collins, *The Path to Freedom* (Cork: Mercier Press, 1968; 1st edn, 1922), pp. 11, 13.

232. *Private Sessions of Second Dáil* (17 December 1921) (Dublin: Dáil Éireann), p. 245.

233. Aiken to all Ranks (12 November 1923), O'Malley Papers, ADUCD P17a/43.

234. M. Gallagher (ed.), *Irish Elections 1922–44: Results and Analysis* (Limerick: PSAI Press, 1993), pp. 2, 4, 6, 8.

235. *IT*, 28 June 1922.

236. B. Kissane, *The Politics of the Irish Civil War* (Oxford: Oxford University Press, 2005), p. 237.

237. Constitution of the Irish Free State, in S. Gwynn, *Ireland* (London: Ernest Benn, 1924), p. 225.

238. Hart, *The IRA at War*, p. 21; English, *Radicals and the Republic*, pp. 52–65.

239. On the Civil War, see especially M. Hopkinson, *Green Against Green: The Irish Civil War* (Dublin: Gill and Macmillan, 1988), and Kissane, *The Politics of the Irish Civil War*.

240. O'Connor, *An Only Child*, p. 211.

241. D. Macardle, *Tragedies of Kerry 1922–1923* (Dublin: Irish Freedom Press, 1988; 1st edn, 1924); A. Dolan, *Commemorating the Irish Civil War: History and Memory, 1923–2000* (Cambridge: Cambridge University Press, 2003).

242. C. Calhoun, 'Neither Individualism Nor "Groupism"', *Ethnicities* 3, 4 (2003).

243. P. O'Donnell, *The Gates Flew Open* (London: Jonathan Cape, 1932), p. 44.

244. C. Ó Gráda, *Ireland: A New Economic History 1780–1939* (Oxford: Oxford University Press, 1994), pp. 307–8, 314–15.

245. Gwynn, *Ireland*, p. 12.

246. J. Baker, *The McMahon Family Murders* (Belfast: Glenravel Local History Project, n.d.), pp. 5, 42.

247. O. MacDonagh, *States of Mind: Two Centuries of Anglo-Irish Conflict, 1780–1980* (London: Pimlico, 1992; 1st edn, 1983), p. 22; L. Kennedy, 'Repartition', in B. O'Leary and J. McGarry (eds), *The Future of Northern Ireland* (Oxford: Oxford University Press, 1990).

248. See C. O'Halloran, *Partition and the Limits of Irish Nationalism: An Ideology under Stress* (Dublin: Gill and Macmillan, 1987).

249. Harry Boland, quoted in Fitzpatrick, *Harry Boland's Irish Revolution*, p. 130.

250. 'Address to the Electors of the Six Counties, Issued by the Nationalist Candidates', *IN*, 7 May 1921.

251. T. Garvin, *The Evolution of Irish Nationalist Politics* (Dublin: Gill and Macmillan, 2005; 1st edn, 1981), p. 9.

252. Although the sharp-eyed Joe Devlin recognized that, once a northern parliament had been set up, there would be established a certain momentum working lastingly against Irish unity (E. Phoenix, *Northern Nationalism: Nationalist Politics, Partition and the Catholic Minority in Northern Ireland 1890–1940* (Belfast: Ulster Historical Foundation, 1994), pp. 76–7).

253. As the most thorough chronicler of Belfast's early-1920s violence has noted, 'the boycott was singularly unsuccessful and even counter-productive' (A. F. Parkinson, *Belfast's Unholy War: The Troubles of the 1920s* (Dublin: Four Courts Press, 2004), p. 81).

254. C. C. O'Brien, *Ancestral Voices: Religion and Nationalism in Ireland* (Dublin: Poolbeg Press, 1994), p. 152.

255. D. Trimble, *The Easter Rebellion of 1916* (Lurgan: Ulster Society, 1992), p. 35.

256. A. Conan Doyle, *His Last Bow: Some Reminiscences of Sherlock Holmes* (London: Pan, 1955; 1st edn, 1917), p. 175.

257. Hart, *The IRA at War*.

258. 'James Connolly', from 'Sing a Song of Irish Freedom' (Recording: CSDBL 515).

259. 'Kevin Barry', ibid.

260. 'Michael Collins', from P. Woods, 'A Tribute to Michael Collins' (Recording: TRAMC 012).

261. Hart, *The IRA at War*, pp. 30–1.

262. Moore Papers, NLI MS 10,560 (5 January 1931).

263. *AP*, 17 December 1927.

264. As has now become more widely noted in our post-Marxist world, culture determines economics as often as the latter determines the former (Fukuyama, *Trust*, p. 15).

265. M. E. Daly, *Industrial Development and Irish National Identity, 1922–1939* (Dublin: Gill and Macmillan, 1992), p. 102.

266. A process central to nationalism throughout the world: Billig, *Banal Nationalism*.

267. R. V. Comerford, *Ireland* (London: Arnold, 2003), p. 145.

268. N. Whyte, *Science, Colonialism and Ireland* (Cork: Cork University Press, 1999), pp. 180–1. It is now well recognized that there is a geography of science – specific, local conditions of politics and society determining the ways in which scientific innovation and knowledge flourish in various settings (D. N. Livingstone, *Putting Science in Its Place: Geographies of Scientific Knowledge* (Chicago: University of Chicago Press, 2003)) – and independent Ireland's record here is far from impressive.

269. See Comerford's fine treatment of this in *Ireland*, pp. 113–15.

270. T. Brown, *Ireland: A Social and Cultural History 1922–1985* (London: Fontana, 1985; 1st edn, 1981), p. 45.

271. G. FitzGerald, *Reflections on the Irish State* (Dublin: Irish Academic Press, 2003), p. 144.

272. D. Kennedy, *The Widening Gulf: Northern Attitudes to the Independent Irish State, 1919–49* (Belfast: Blackstaff Press, 1988).

273. Comerford, *Ireland*, p. 115.

274. *AP*, 6–7 January 1934.

275. Sean O'Faoláin (1948), quoted in M. Harmon, *Sean O'Faoláin* (London: Constable, 1994), p. 181. Cf. English, *Ernie O'Malley*.

276. S. Beckett, *Murphy* (London: Picador, 1973; 1st edn, 1938), p. 75.

277. Quoted in M. Doorley, *Irish-American Diaspora Nationalism: The Friends of Irish Freedom, 1916–1935* (Dublin: Four Courts Press, 2005), p. 38.

278. P. J. Waller, *Town, City and Nation: England 1850–1914* (Oxford: Oxford University Press, 1991; 1st edn, 1983), pp. 27, 150.

279. For stunning visual record of this process, see Foster and Cullen (eds), *'Conquering England'*.

280. M. Cronin and D. Adair, *The Wearing of the Green: A History of St Patrick's Day* (London: Routledge, 2002), pp. 66–7.

281. O. Wilde, 'The Soul of Man Under Socialism', in *Complete Works of Oscar Wilde* (vol. III), p. 379.

282. 'Civil society is that set of diverse non-governmental institutions which is strong enough to counterbalance the state and, while not preventing the state from fulfilling its role of keeper of the peace and arbitrator between major interests, can nevertheless prevent it from dominating and atomizing the rest of society' (E. Gellner, *Conditions of Liberty: Civil Society and Its Rivals* (London: Hamish Hamilton, 1994), p. 5).

283. See the very valuable treatment of this theme in B. Kissane, *Explaining Irish Democracy* (Dublin: UCD Press, 2002).

284. L. Kennedy, 'Modern Ireland: Post-Colonial Society or Post-Colonial Pretensions?', *Irish Review* 13 (1992–3); Kissane, *Explaining Irish Democracy*, pp. 38–9.

285. J. M. Regan, *The Irish Counter-Revolution 1921–1936* (Dublin: Gill and Macmillan, 1999), p. 100.

286. T. Garvin, *1922: The Birth of Irish Democracy* (Dublin: Gill and Macmillan, 1996).

287. R. Dunphy, *The Making of Fianna Fáil Power in Ireland 1923–1948* (Oxford: Oxford University Press, 1995).

288. De Valera to McGarrity (13 March 1926), McGarrity Papers, NLI MS 17,441.

289. S. O'Faoláin, *De Valera* (Harmondsworth: Penguin, 1939), p. 40.

290. Clarke, *Revolutionary Woman*, pp. 218–19; Files of the Department of the Taoiseach, NAD S9880; see also M. Luddy, 'A "Sinister and Retrogressive" Proposal: Irish Women's Opposition to the 1937 Draft Constitution', *Transactions of the Royal Historical Society* (sixth series) 15 (2005).

291. *Bunreacht na hÉireann (Constitution of Ireland)*, pp. 136–8.

292. Interview with Sean MacBride, *Irish America* 2, 4 (1986), p. 34.

293. *Bunreacht na hÉireann (Constitution of Ireland)*, p. 4.

294. L. O'Flaherty, *Famine* (London: Four Square, 1959; 1st edn, 1937), pp. 216, 274, 278.

295. Sheila Humphreys, interviewed by the author, Dublin, 26 February 1987.

296. *AP*, 6–7 January 1934.

297. Government and Cabinet Minutes, Files of the Department of the Taoiseach, NAD G3/3.

298. Sinn Féin to all Republican Citizens (January 1929), Files of the Department of the Taoiseach, NAD S5880.

299. *Constitution of Oglaigh na hEireann (IRA) as Amended by General Army Convention 14–15 November 1925*, Blythe Papers, ADUCD P24/165 (10).

300. *AP*, 20 June 1925.

301. Oglaigh na h-Eireann (IRA) to the People of Ireland (October 1938), Files of the Department of the Taoiseach, NAD S11564A.

302. *AP*, 10 August 1929.

303. Gannon Statement, NAD 999/951.

304. Charlotte Despard, quoted in M. Mulvihill, *Charlotte Despard: A Biography* (London: Pandora, 1989), p. 157.

305. See, for example, G. Gilmore, *The Relevance of James Connolly in Ireland Today* (Dublin: Fodhla Printing Company, n.d. [1970?]).

306. Sheila Humphreys, interviewed by the author, Dublin, 26 February 1987.

307. Nora Connolly O'Brien, quoted in MacEoin (ed.), *Survivors*, p. 213.

308. Minutes of IRA General Army Convention (17 March 1934), MacEntee Papers, ADUCD P67/525.

309. G. Gilmore, *The Irish Republican Congress* (New York: United Irish Republican Committees of US, 1935), p. 3.

310. For this broader point, see J. Mac Laughlin, *Reimagining the Nation-State: The Contested Terrains of Nation-Building* (London: Pluto, 2001). On O'Donnell's Donegal-rooted radicalism, see English, *Radicals and the Republic*, pp. 72–86.

311. H. Tracy, *Mind You, I've Said Nothing! Forays in the Irish Republic* (Harmondsworth: Penguin, 1961; 1st edn, 1953), p. 52.

312. See, for example, Constitution (Special Powers) Tribunal: Attorney General v. Sheila Humphreys (15 January 1932), Files of the Department of the Taoiseach, NAD S2846.

313. For one such amusing description, see Oliver St. John Gogarty's quirky volume, *As I Was Going Down Sackville Street: A Phantasy in Fact* (Harmondsworth: Penguin, 1954; 1st edn, 1937), pp. 40–5.

314. Patsy O'Hagan, quoted in MacEoin (ed.), *Survivors*, p. 170.

315. B. Levitas, *The Theatre of Nation: Irish Drama and Cultural Nationalism 1890–1916* (Oxford: Oxford University Press, 2002), p. 228.

316. *Catholic Mind*, January 1934, February 1934.

317. *Republican Congress*, 5 May 1934.

318. 'Liberal-democracy now seems to command universal admiration as the model of the desirable political system' (J. Schwarzmantel, *The State in Contemporary Society: An Introduction* (Hemel Hempstead: Harvester Wheatsheaf, 1994), p. 5).

319. M. Cronin, *The Blueshirts and Irish Politics* (Dublin: Four Courts Press, 1997); McGarry, *Eoin O'Duffy*; F. McGarry, *Irish Politics and the Spanish Civil War* (Cork: Cork University Press, 1999); R. A. Stradling, *The Irish*

and the Spanish Civil War 1936–1939 (Manchester: Manchester University Press, 1999); Regan, *The Irish Counter-Revolution 1921–1936.*

320. McGarry, *Eoin O'Duffy*, pp. 234–5.
321. J. J. Lee, *Ireland 1912–1985: Politics and Society* (Cambridge: Cambridge University Press, 1989), p. 181; cf. M. Manning, *The Blueshirts* (Dublin: Gill and Macmillan, 1970).
322. Cronin, *The Blueshirts and Irish Politics*, pp. 53, 62.
323. F. McGarry, *Frank Ryan* (Dundalk: Dundalgan Press, 2002), p. 70.
324. O'Faoláin, *De Valera*, p. 176.
325. *War News*, 22 March 1940.
326. G. Walker, *A History of the Ulster Unionist Party: Protest, Pragmatism and Pessimism* (Manchester: Manchester University Press, 2004), pp. 100–2.
327. H. Patterson, 'Nationalism', in A. Aughey and D. Morrow (eds), *Northern Ireland Politics* (Harlow: Longman, 1996), p. 39.
328. A. Jackson, *Ireland 1798–1998: Politics and War* (Oxford: Blackwell, 1999), p. 337.
329. Parkinson, *Belfast's Unholy War*, p. 239.
330. *Irish Press*, 25 January 1933.
331. 'Arrest of Mrs. Sheehy-Skeffington in Northern Ireland', Files of the Department of the Taoiseach, NAD S2280.
332. Minutes of IRA General Army Convention (17 March 1934), MacEntee Papers, ADUCD P67/525.
333. O'Neill Papers, PRONI D/2720/1/4, D/2720/1/6, D/2720/1/7–10.
334. Joseph Devlin Memorial Leaflet: 'Souvenir of Our Friend and Leader', Devlin Papers, PRONI T/2257/15.

Six – Cold Wars and Revolutionaries, 1945–2005

1. D. Macardle, *Without Fanfares: Some Reflections on the Republic of Eire* (Dublin: M. H. Gill and Son, 1946), p. 14.
2. Dylan Thomas (1946), quoted in P. Ferris, *Dylan Thomas* (London: Hodder and Stoughton, 1977), p. 208.
3. J. V. Kelleher, 'Irish Literature Today', *The Bell* 10, 4 (1945), pp. 344–5.
4. H. Hamilton, *The Speckled People* (London: Fourth Estate, 2003), quotations at pp. 12, 190.
5. See the elegant treatment of this broad theme in S. Schama, *Landscape and Memory* (London: Fontana, 1996; 1st edn, 1995).
6. R. Monk, *Ludwig Wittgenstein: The Duty of Genius* (London: Jonathan Cape, 1990), pp. 516, 520–21, 524–5; R. Wall, *Wittgenstein in Ireland* (London: Reaktion, 2000), pp. 89–91.
7. Quoted in R. English, *Ernie O'Malley: IRA Intellectual* (Oxford: Oxford University Press, 1999; 1st edn, 1998), pp. 131, 187.

8. Ibid.

9. M. Walsh, *The Quiet Man and Other Stories* (Belfast: Appletree Press, 1992), pp. 148–9.

10. M. Walsh, *The Key Above the Door* (Harmondsworth: Penguin, 1958; 1st edn, 1923), pp. 172–3.

11. R. Sinnott, *Irish Voters Decide: Voting Behaviour in Elections and Referendums Since 1918* (Manchester: Manchester University Press, 1995), p. 7.

12. D. Fitzpatrick, *The Two Irelands 1912–1939* (Oxford: Oxford University Press, 1998), p. vii.

13. Ludwig Wittgenstein, quoted in Wall, *Wittgenstein in Ireland*, p. 117.

14. S. O'Faoláin, *De Valera* (Harmondsworth: Penguin, 1939), pp. 155–6.

15. D. Macardle, *The Irish Republic: A Documented Chronicle of the Anglo-Irish Conflict and the Partitioning of Ireland, with a Detailed Account of the Period 1916–1923* (London: Corgi, 1968; 1st edn, 1937); D. Macardle, *The Unforeseen* (London: Corgi, 1966; 1st edn, 1945), pp. 159, 162.

16. J. M. Skelly, *Irish Diplomacy at the United Nations 1945–1965: National Interests and the International Order* (Dublin: Irish Academic Press, 1997), p. 15.

17. D. H. Akenson, *The Irish Diaspora: A Primer* (Belfast: Institute of Irish Studies, 1993), p. 257.

18. D. O'Reilly (ed.), *Accepting the Challenge: The Memoirs of Michael Flannery* (Dublin: Irish Freedom Press, 2001), p. 131. Though, broadly, Irish America had little interest in this campaign (A. J. Wilson, *Irish America and the Ulster Conflict 1968–1995* (Belfast: Blackstaff Press, 1995), p. 16).

19. M. Doorley, *Irish-American Diaspora Nationalism: The Friends of Irish Freedom, 1916–1935* (Dublin: Four Courts Press, 2005), p. 159.

20. *Dungannon Observer*, 22 January 1955.

21. On which, see E. Mac Dermott, *Clann na Poblachta* (Cork: Cork University Press, 1998).

22. N. Browne, *Church and State in Modern Ireland* (Belfast: Queen's University, 1991), p. 3.

23. Quoted in H. Patterson, *Ireland Since 1939* (Oxford: Oxford University Press, 2002), p. 95.

24. *Dáil Debates* 67: 1890. The 1936 Census recorded that out of a total Free State population of 2,968,420 there were 2,773,920 Catholics (93.4 per cent) (Eire/Ireland, *Census of Population 1936* (vol. III), p. 3).

25. J. Bowman, '"The Wolf in Sheep's Clothing": Richard Hayes's Proposal for a New National Library of Ireland, 1959–60', in R. J. Hill and M. Marsh (eds), *Modern Irish Democracy* (Blackrock: Irish Academic Press, 1993).

26. O'Faoláin, *De Valera*, p. 117.

27. Sean Lemass (15 October 1959), quoted in M. O'Sullivan, *Sean Lemass: A Biography* (Dublin: Blackwater Press, 1994), p. 196.

28. R. Savage, *Sean Lemass* (Dundalk: Dundalgan Press, 1999), p. 61.

29. MacEntee to Lynch (6 November 1969), Lynch Papers, NAD 2001/8/5.
30. As is movingly suggested in the photographic and written accounts contained in Belfast Exposed Photography, *Portraits from a 50s Archive* (Belfast: Belfast Exposed Photography, 2005).
31. A. McIntyre, 'Modern Irish Republicanism: The Product of British State Strategies', *Irish Political Studies* 10 (1995).
32. D. J. Smith and G. Chambers, *Inequality in Northern Ireland* (Oxford: Oxford University Press, 1991); P. J. Roche and B. Barton (eds), *The Northern Ireland Question: Myth and Reality* (Aldershot: Avebury, 1991); B. O'Leary and J. McGarry, *Explaining Northern Ireland: Broken Images* (Oxford: Blackwell, 1995).
33. There was universal suffrage at parliamentary elections in Northern Ireland; for local government elections, however, there were property and residence qualifications for voting, and multiple votes for some business people. A higher percentage of people was as a consequence disadvantaged within the Catholic, than within the Protestant, community.
34. *Dungannon Observer*, 5 February 1955.
35. M. Elliott, *The Catholics of Ulster: A History* (Harmondsworth: Allen Lane, 2000), p. 450.
36. *Dungannon Observer*, 13 August 1955.
37. N. Jarman, *Displaying Faith: Orange, Green and Trade Union Banners in Northern Ireland* (Belfast: Institute of Irish Studies, 1999), pp. 33–6.
38. *Dungannon Observer*, 3 September 1955.
39. *Lurgan Mail*, 1 February 1957.
40. E. Staunton, *The Nationalists of Northern Ireland 1918–1973* (Blackrock: Columba Press, 2001), p. 175.
41. John F. Kennedy, quoted in N. Hamilton, *JFK: Reckless Youth* (London: BCA, 1993; 1st edn, 1992), p. 715.
42. 'Sinn Féin Election Manifesto, Westminster Elections, 1955' in *Dungannon Observer*, 21 May 1955.
43. C. Carson, *The Star Factory* (London: Granta, 1997), p. 117.
44. S. Wichert, *Northern Ireland Since 1945* (Harlow: Longman, 1991), p. 75.
45. IRA Proclamation of December 1956, quoted in J. B. Bell, *The Secret Army: The IRA 1916–1979* (Dublin: Poolbeg, 1989; 1st edn, 1970), p. 291.
46. *IN*, 27 February 1962.
47. See, for example: Walker to Connellan, 4 October 1956; Parkes to Connellan, 11 January 1957; Walker to Connellan, 26 April 1957; Connellan to Walker, 27 April 1957, Connellan Papers, PRONI D/2355/1/2.
48. *Lurgan Mail*, 18 January 1957.
49. *Strabane Weekly News*, 5 January 1957.
50. A. Jackson, *The Ulster Party: Irish Unionists in the House of Commons, 1884–1911* (Oxford: Oxford University Press, 1989), p. 17.
51. *Dungannon Observer*, 19 March 1955.

52. *Dungannon Observer*, 16 April 1955.
53. Connellan to Walker, 27 April 1957, Connellan Papers, PRONI D/2355/1/2.
54. Eddie McAteer, quoted in B. Lynn, 'Revising Northern Nationalism, 1960–1965: The Nationalist Party's Response', *New Hibernia Review* 4, 3 (2000), pp. 91–2.
55. B. Devlin, *The Price of My Soul* (London: Pan, 1969), p. 38.
56. M. Hurst, *Parnell and Irish Nationalism* (London: Routledge and Kegan Paul, 1968), p. 2.
57. M. Ó Muilleoir, *Belfast's Dome of Delight: City Hall Politics 1981–2000* (Belfast: Beyond the Pale, 1999), p. iv.
58. H. Sitkoff, *The Struggle for Black Equality, 1954–1992* (New York: Hill and Wang, 1993; 1st edn, 1981).
59. On this, see R. English, *Armed Struggle: The History of the IRA* (London: Pan, 2004; 1st edn, 2003), pp. 85–92.
60. E. McCann, *War and an Irish Town* (London: Pluto Press, 1993; 1st edn, 1974), pp. 79–80, 91, 102.
61. Devlin, *The Price of My Soul*, p. 91.
62. C. D. Greaves, *Reminiscences of the Connolly Association* (London: Connolly Association, 1978), p. 34.
63. McCann, *War and an Irish Town*, p. 103.
64. A. Currie, *All Hell Will Break Loose* (Dublin: O'Brien Press, 2004), p. 97.
65. J. H. Whyte, *Interpreting Northern Ireland* (Oxford: Oxford University Press, 1990), p. 168.
66. See, for example, the scepticism shown regarding the new middle-class thesis by Michael Morgan in 'Post-War Social Change and the Catholic Community in Northern Ireland', *Studies* 77, 308 (1988).
67. D. Morrison, *All the Dead Voices* (Cork: Mercier Press, 2002), pp. 121, 123.
68. Ex-IRA man, interviewed by the author, Belfast, 31 October 2001.
69. R. Doyle, *Paddy Clarke Ha Ha Ha* (London: BCA, 1993), pp. 20–23.
70. Seán MacStiofáin, *Memoirs of a Revolutionary* (Edinburgh: Gordon Cremonesi, 1975), p. 123.
71. E. Collins, *Killing Rage* (London: Granta, 1997), p. 96.
72. Marian Price, interviewed by the author, Belfast, 28 February 2002.
73. R. O'Rawe, *Blanketmen: An Untold Story of the H-Block Hunger Strike* (Dublin: New Island, 2005), p. 4.
74. Tommy McKearney, interviewed by the author, Belfast, 20 September 2000.
75. D. Morrison, *Then the Walls Came Down: A Prison Journal* (Cork: Mercier, 1999), p. 66.
76. *RN*, May 1971.
77. Martin McGuinness, quoted in L. Clarke and K. Johnston, *Martin McGuinness: From Guns to Government* (Edinburgh: Mainstream, 2001), p. 15.
78. *AP/RN*, 3 November 1979, 8 December 1979.
79. *RN*, September/October 1970.

80. Patrick Magee, interviewed by the author, Belfast, 5 March 2002.

81. *RN*, 19 May 1973.

82. IRA spokesperson, quoted in *AP/RN* 17 August 1989.

83. Pat McGeown, quoted in L. Clarke, *Broadening the Battlefield: The H-Blocks and the Rise of Sinn Féin* (Dublin: Gill and Macmillan, 1987), p. 16.

84. Anthony McIntyre, interviewed by the author, Belfast, 23 August 2000.

85. Minutes of Provisional Committee Meeting (17 January 1970), LHLPC, Provisional Minutes 1970 Folder.

86. E. Gellner, *Nations and Nationalism* (Oxford: Basil Blackwell, 1983), p. 1.

87. Y. Tamir, *Liberal Nationalism* (Princeton: Princeton University Press, 1993), p. 73.

88. G. Adams, *A Pathway to Peace* (Cork: Mercier Press, 1988), p. 77.

89. J. Goodwin, *No Other Way Out: States and Revolutionary Movements, 1945–1991* (Cambridge: Cambridge University Press, 2001), p. 23.

90. R. Brubaker, *Nationalism Reframed: Nationhood and the National Question in the New Europe* (Cambridge: Cambridge University Press, 1996), pp. 4–6.

91. For fuller analysis of the Provisional IRA, see English, *Armed Struggle*; H. Patterson, *The Politics of Illusion: A Political History of the IRA* (London: Serif, 1997; 1st edn, 1989); E. Moloney, *A Secret History of the IRA* (London: Penguin, 2002); K. Toolis, *Rebel Hearts: Journeys within the IRA's Soul* (London: Picador, 1995); P. Bishop and E. Mallie, *The Provisional IRA* (London: Corgi, 1988; 1st edn, 1987); M. O'Doherty, *The Trouble with Guns: Republican Strategy and the Provisional IRA* (Belfast: Blackstaff Press, 1998); M. L. R. Smith, *Fighting For Ireland? The Military Strategy of the Irish Republican Movement* (London: Routledge, 1995). For a terrorologist or counter-terrorist perspective, see J. C. Woewoda, *The IRA: Death by Deception* (Vancouver: Lausanne Institute, 1994).

92. See G. Murray and J. Tonge, *Sinn Féin and the SDLP: From Alienation to Participation* (Dublin: O'Brien Press, 2005), p. 79.

93. G. McGladdery, *The Provisional IRA in England: 'Terrorizing the Heartland' with the Bombing Campaign: 1973–1997* (Dublin: Irish Academic Press, 2006).

94. It might, for example, seem rather avoidant for a scholar as rigorous and intelligent as David Miller to stress the beneficent aspects of nationality, and then to refuse engagement with that part of the United Kingdom in which it has displayed its most cruel nature: 'The Northern Irish raise special problems when British national identity is being discussed, and since I could not hope to do justice to these problems I shall simply set them to one side' (D. Miller, *On Nationality* (Oxford: Oxford University Press, 1995), p. 173). There are glancing references to Northern Ireland in a later, equally valuable work (D. Miller, *Citizenship and National Identity* (Cambridge: Polity Press, 2000)), but again there is no attempt here to consider in any detail the problems raised by the Ulster conflict for Miller's philosophical defence of nationality.

95. South Armagh Protestants, quoted in H. Donnan, 'Material Identities: Fixing Ethnicity in the Irish Borderlands', *Identities* 12 (2005), pp. 86–7.

96. On which, see *Daily Ireland*, 25 June 2005.

97. D. McKittrick, S. Kelters, B. Feeney and C. Thornton, *Lost Lives: The Stories of the Men, Women and Children Who Died as a Result of the Northern Ireland Troubles* (Edinburgh: Mainstream, 2001; 1st edn, 1999), p. 1494. Cf. M. Fay, M. Morrissey and M. Smyth, *Northern Ireland's Troubles: The Human Costs* (London: Pluto Press, 1999), p. 169.

98. Alex Maskey, quoted in B. McCaffrey, *Alex Maskey: Man and Mayor* (Belfast: Brehon Press, 2003), p. 217.

99. O'Rawe, *Blanketmen*.

100. Coleman to Haughey (15 May 1981), IRSP Comms Folder, LHLPC.

101. D. Beresford, *Ten Men Dead: The Story of the 1981 Irish Hunger Strike* (London: Grafton, 1987), p. 14.

102. K. McEvoy, *Paramilitary Imprisonment in Northern Ireland: Resistance, Management and Release* (Oxford: Oxford University Press, 2001).

103. Statement from Republican POWs in H-Block (29 September 1981), LHLPC.

104. On the intimacy of Sinn Féin–IRA overlap, see B. Feeney, *Sinn Féin: A Hundred Turbulent Years* (Dublin: O'Brien Press, 2002), and K. Rafter, *Sinn Féin 1905–2005: In the Shadow of Gunmen* (Dublin: Gill and Macmillan, 2005).

105. IRA GHQ spokesperson, quoted in *AP/RN*, 28 June 1990.

106. Statement made on 9 November 1990; see *IN*, 10 November 1990.

107. Danny Morrison, interviewed by the author, Belfast, 26 May 2000.

108. Tom Hartley, interviewed by the author, Belfast, 24 October 2001.

109. Gerry Adams Press Release, 'Rights for All Charter', January 2004.

110. G. FitzGerald, *All in a Life: An Autobiography* (Dublin: Gill and Macmillan, 1992; 1st edn, 1991), pp. 258–9.

111. W. D. Flackes and S. Elliott, *Northern Ireland: A Political Directory 1968–1993* (Belfast: Blackstaff Press, 1994; 1st edn. 1980), pp. 393, 397, 401, 404, 408.

112. E. J. Hobsbawm, *Nations and Nationalism Since 1780: Programme, Myth, Reality* (Cambridge: Cambridge University Press, 1990), p. 125.

113. E. J. Hobsbawm, *Interesting Times: A Twentieth-Century Life* (London: Penguin, 2002), p. 127.

114. Official Sinn Féin Press Release (21 June 1975): Text of Oration to be Delivered by Cathal Goulding at the Wolfe Tone Commemoration, Bodenstown, LHLPC.

115. IRSP Press Statement (13 December 1974), LHLPC.

116. Constitution of the IRSP, copy in LHLPC.

117. IRSP Press Statement (2 March 1976), LHLPC.

118. *IN*, 14 December 1974.

119. *Starry Plough* 6 (August 1989).

120. *Starry Plough* 7 (October 1989).

121. See J. Holland and H. McDonald, *INLA: Deadly Divisions* (Dublin: Torc, 1994).

122. SDLP Constitution, quoted in I. McAllister, *The Northern Ireland Social Democratic and Labour Party: Political Opposition in A Divided Society* (London: Macmillan, 1977), p. 168.

123. Although socialism itself was at times rhetorically prominent with the SDLP. An election leaflet on behalf of Gerry Fitt – then the SDLP's leader – in 1974 had prominently quoted James Connolly's 1916 declaration that 'The cause of labour is the cause of Ireland, the cause of Ireland is the cause of labour' (SDLP Election Leaflet, Gerry Fitt, Westminster General Election, West Belfast Constituency (10 October 1974), LHLPC, SDLP Box 3).

124. For lucid exposition of this point, see Murray and Tonge, *Sinn Féin and the SDLP*.

125. Emergency Motion Submitted by all Branches in Mid-Ulster Constituency (for SDLP Annual Conference, 2–4 November 1979), LHLPC, SDLP Box 1.

126. Statement by SDLP Chairman Denis Haughey at opening of Party's Seventh Annual Conference, Friday (4 November 1977), in the Slieve Donard Hotel, Newcastle, LHLPC, SDLP Box 1.

127. A point clearly expounded in S. Bruce, *The Edge of the Union: The Ulster Loyalist Political Vision* (Oxford: Oxford University Press, 1994).

128. SDLP Press Release (26 September 1974), LHLPC, SDLP Box 2.

129. Joint Statement by the SDLP Executive Committee and Assembly Party (3 September 1974), LHLPC, SDLP Box 2.

130. *BT*, 20 November 1984.

131. R. Needham, *Battling for Peace* (Belfast: Blackstaff, 1998), p. 37. Richard Needham: born 1942; Conservative MP from 1979; 1983–4, Parliamentary Private Secretary to Northern Ireland Secretary of State James Prior; 1985–92 Minister at the Northern Ireland Office.

132. Text of Speech by Paddy Duffy (SDLP Constituency Representative for Mid-Ulster) to a Meeting of Party Members in Cookstown (5 April 1978), LHLPC, SDLP Box 2.

133. Statement by SDLP Chairman Denis Haughey at opening of Party's Seventh Annual Conference, Friday (4 November 1977), in the Slieve Donard Hotel, Newcastle, LHLPC, SDLP Box 1.

134. SDLP Election Leaflet, 1987 UK General Election, South Down Constituency: 'Vote McGrady', LHLPC, SDLP Box 2.

135. Hanna to Delegates and Visitors to the Sixteenth Annual SDLP Conference (13 November 1986), LHLPC, SDLP Box 1.

136. SDLP Press Release (27 November 1974), LHLPC, SDLP Box 2.

137. On whom, see G. Drower, *John Hume: Peacemaker* (London: Victor Gollancz, 1995).

138. P. Arthur, *Special Relationships: Britain, Ireland and the Northern Ireland Problem* (Belfast: Blackstaff Press, 2000), p. 139. See also J. Dumbrell, 'The United States and the Northern Irish Conflict 1969–94: From Indifference to Intervention', *Irish Studies in International Affairs* 6 (1995).

139. John Hume, quoted in M. Cunningham, 'The Political Language of John Hume', *Irish Political Studies* 12 (1997), p. 17.

140. B. Hanley, 'The Politics of Noraid', *Irish Political Studies* 19, 1 (2004).

141. *Troops Out of Ireland* 21, 1 (1999), p. 2.

142. Statement from SDLP Headquarters: SDLP Launches Manifesto for European Elections (16 May 1994), LHLPC, SDLP Box 3.

143. SDLP Election Leaflet, Alasdair McDonnell, Westminster General Election, South Belfast Constituency (3 May 1979), LHLPC, SDLP Box 3.

144. Statement by John Hume (15 December 1993), LHLPC, SDLP Box 3.

145. Statement from SDLP Party Leader, John Hume (26 May 1994), LHLPC, SDLP Box 3.

146. M. Mowlam, *Momentum: The Struggle for Peace, Politics and the People* (London: Hodder and Stoughton, 2002), pp. 148–9.

147. Hume/Adams Joint Statement, quoted in *IT*, 26 April 1993.

148. J. Coakley, 'Religion, National Identity and Political Change in Modern Ireland', *Irish Political Studies* 17, 1 (2002), p. 15.

149. Statement by SDLP Executive Committee on the Emergency Provisions Act (1 Sep. 1978), LHLPC, SDLP Box 3.

150. SDLP Election Leaflet, Gerry Fitt, Westminster General Election, West Belfast Constituency (10 October 1974), LHLPC, SDLP Box 3.

151. O'Rawe, *Blanketmen*, pp. 52, 58.

152. Statement from SDLP (10 September 1979), LHLPC, SDLP Box 1.

153. G. Adams, *Before the Dawn: An Autobiography* (London: Heinemann, 1996), p. 73.

154. E. Kedourie, *Nationalism* (Oxford: Blackwell, 1993; 1st edn, 1960), p. 56.

155. G. Adams, *An Irish Journal* (Dingle: Brandon, 2001), p. 22.

156. G. Adams, *The Politics of Irish Freedom* (Dingle: Brandon, 1986), pp. 88–9.

157. G. Adams, *Hope and History: Making Peace in Ireland* (Dingle: Brandon, 2003), pp. 160–61.

158. Adams, *Before the Dawn*, p. 28; cf. G. Adams, *Falls Memories* (Dingle: Brandon, 1983; 1st edn, 1982).

159. Adams, *Before the Dawn*, p. 122.

160. 22 November 1999, in Adams, *An Irish Journal*, p. 195.

161. Gerry Adams (17 June 1979), quoted in *AP/RN*, 23 June 1979.

162. Adams, *Hope and History*, p. 388.

163. Recollection of Patrick Magee, interviewed by the author, Belfast, 5 March 2002.

164. G. FitzGerald, *Towards a New Ireland* (Dublin: Torc Books, 1973; 1st edn, 1972), p. viii.

165. T. K. Whitaker, *A Note on North-South Policy* (11 November 1968), Lynch Papers, NAD 2001/8/1.

166. See, for example, G. Adams, *Who Fears to Speak...? The Story of Belfast and the 1916 Rising* (Belfast: Beyond the Pale, 2001; 1st edn, 1991). Adams as a child read works such as Charles Kickham's *Knocknagow*, although too much should not perhaps be made of such things: like his fellow republican leader Danny Morrison, he seems also to have had a youthful enthusiasm for Enid Blyton.

167. Adams, *Hope and History*, p. 83.

168. Adams, *Before the Dawn*, p. 273.

169. Ibid., p. 136.

170. Tommy Gorman, interviewed by the author, Belfast, 2 May 2001.

171. L. Fitzsimons, *Does Anybody Care? A Personal Journal 1976–81* (Belfast: Glandore, n.d.), pp. 4, 12.

172. Adams, *Hope and History*, p. 138.

173. Alex Comerford to Relatives Action Committee (18 November 1976), quoted in Fitzsimons, *Does Anybody Care?*, pp. 16–17.

174. M. Elliott (ed.), *The Long Road to Peace in Northern Ireland* (Liverpool: Liverpool University Press, 2002); R. Wilford (ed.), *Aspects of the Belfast Agreement* (Oxford: Oxford University Press, 2001); M. Cox, A. Guelke, and F. Stephen (eds), *A Farewell to Arms? Beyond the Good Friday Agreement* (Manchester: Manchester University Press, 2006; 1st edn, 2000); T. Hennessey, *The Northern Ireland Peace Process: Ending the Troubles?* (Dublin: Gill and Macmillan, 2000); D. de Bréadún, *The Far Side of Revenge: Making Peace in Northern Ireland* (Cork: Collins Press, 2001).

175. M. Mansergh, 'Mountain-Climbing Irish-Style: The Hidden Challenges of the Peace Process', in Elliott (ed.), *The Long Road to Peace in Northern Ireland*, p. 110.

176. Statement by John Hume, SDLP Leader (4 January 1994), LHLPC, SDLP Box 3.

177. Statement from John Hume (16 November 1993), LHLPC, SDLP Box 3.

178. Statement from SDLP Leader, John Hume: New Year Message for Start of 1995, LHLPC, SDLP Box 3.

179. Sinn Féin Youth, First National Congress, Dublin (17 October 1998), *Congress Book*, pp. 1, 7.

180. Sinn Féin, *Putting People First: The Role of the Community in Economic Development* (1997), p. 25.

181. Ibid., p. 24.

182. *AP/RN*, 6 August 1998.

183. Murray and Tonge, *Sinn Féin and the SDLP*, p. 204.

184. *Joint Declaration on Peace (Downing Street Declaration)* (15 December 1993), in Cox, Guelke and Stephen (eds), *A Farewell to Arms?*, p. 486.

185. Adams, *Hope and History*, p. 165.

186. *The Belfast Agreement: Agreement Reached in the Multi-Party Negotiations* (10 April 1998), p. 3.

187. J. G. Kellas, *The Politics of Nationalism and Ethnicity* (Basingstoke: Macmillan, 1998; 1st edn, 1991), pp. 21–2.

188. C. Gans, 'Historical Rights: The Evaluation of Nationalist Claims to Sovereignty', *Political Theory* 29, 1 (2001).

189. A point well brought out in Rafter, *Sinn Féin 1905–2005*.

190. Interview with Martin McGuinness, *Troops Out* 15, 4 (1992), p. 16.

191. For sustained explanation of the shift in Provisional thinking, see English, *Armed Struggle*, and Moloney, *A Secret History of the IRA*.

192. See Rafter, *Sinn Féin 1905–2005*, pp. 3, 151, 218.

193. *BT*, 7 May 2005.

194. It is true that there were (and remain) inconsistencies in what might be termed republican foreign policy, between a support base in the USA and a set of alliances with radical groups throughout much of the world (M. Frampton, '"Squaring the Circle": The Foreign Policy of Sinn Féin, 1983–1989', *Irish Political Studies* 19, 2 (2004)). But these inconsistencies should not, perhaps, be overstated: first, it would be wrong to exaggerate the degree to which radical Marxism or Third-Worldist revolutionism really drove or defined the Provos, even in the 1980s; second, after the collapse of communism, the dilemma effectively ended, as US support was clearly of far more weight than radical alliances; third, some of those in the US support base themselves held views in conflict with US mainstream politics anyway; and, fourth, foreign policy alliances are rarely consistent (for discussion of these themes, see English, *Armed Struggle*).

195. J. Scott, *Power* (Cambridge: Polity Press, 2001), p. 126.

196. Goodwin, *No Other Way Out*, p. 46.

197. Danny Morrison (31 October 1981), quoted in *AP/RN*, 5 November 1981.

198. Raymond McCartney (to editor, *AP/RN*, 23 November 1982, LHLPC).

199. See, for example, Bertie Ahern's enthusiasm about the 'great privilege' of working with Tony Blair in relation to Northern Ireland (Preface to British Council Ireland, *Britain and Ireland: Lives Entwined* (Dublin: British Council Ireland, 2005)).

200. See English, *Armed Struggle*, pp. 109–11.

201. IRA Statements, 13 April 2003, 6 May 2003, quoted in B. Rowan, *The Armed Peace: Life and Death after the Ceasefires* (Edinburgh: Mainstream, 2003), pp. 245, 248.

202. *Belfast Agreement*, p. 1.

203. Alex Maskey, quoted in McCaffrey, *Alex Maskey*, pp. 200, 209.

204. *AP/RN*, 5 June 2003.

205. J. Tonge and J. Evans, 'Party Members and the Good Friday Agreement in Northern Ireland', *Irish Political Studies* 17, 2 (2002), p. 61.

206. R. Wilford, R. MacGinty, L. Dowds and G. Robinson, 'Northern Ireland's Devolved Institutions: A Triumph of Hope over Experience?', *Regional and Federal Studies* 13, 1 (2003), p. 53.

207. Eddie McGrady, quoted in *Fortnight* 434 (2005), p. 11.

208. Mark Durkan, SDLP Manifesto Launch Speech ('A Better Way to a Better Ireland'), 2005.

209. SDLP Election Leaflet, South Belfast, Assembly Election, November 2003.

210. SDLP Election Communication, Belfast South, 2005.

211. Tyrone National Graves Association, *Annual Report 1996.*

212. See Anthony McIntyre's chilling essay ('Provisional Republicanism: Internal Politics, Inequities and Modes of Repression'), in F. McGarry (ed.), *Republicanism in Modern Ireland* (Dublin: UCD Press, 2003).

213. C. Townshend, *Making the Peace: Public Order and Public Security in Modern Britain* (Oxford: Oxford University Press, 1993), p. 4.

214. *Guardian*, 25 May 2005.

215. *Financial Times*, 11 March 2005.

216. *IT*, 18 March 2005.

217. *BT*, 10 March 2005.

218. Adams, *Hope and History*, p. 213.

219. Gerry Adams, quoted in *IN*, 8 January 1994.

220. *IN*, 7 April 2005.

221. Paul Durcan, quoted in *Fortnight* 435 (2005), p. 22.

222. Denis Bradley, quoted in *Fortnight* 436 (2005), p. 15.

223. IRA Statement (28 July 2005), copy in author's possession.

224. Bertie Ahern, quoted in *IT*, 29 July 2005.

225. *IN*, 29 July 2005.

226. *News Letter*, 29 July 2005.

227. *BT*, 29 July 2005.

228. Ian Paisley, in *News Letter*, 29 July 2005.

229. *Daily Ireland*, 27 September 2005.

230. *News Letter*, 27 September 2005.

231. *BT*, 1 February 2006.

232. SDLP Press Release, 29 January 1975, LHLPC, SDLP Box 2.

233. *Northern Ireland Life and Times Survey 2004* (Question: Which Northern Ireland political party would you support? DUP 1 per cent Catholic support; Sinn Féin 0 per cent Protestant support).

234. C. C. O'Brien, *Memoir: My Life and Themes* (Dublin: Poolbeg, 1998), p. 7.

235. 'Irredentism was at the heart of Irish policy after 1945. Successive Irish governments could not accept any arrangement which acknowledged the existence of partition' (B. Girvin, *From Union to Union: Nationalism, Democracy and Religion in Ireland – Act of Union to EU* (Dublin: Gill and Macmillan, 2002), p. 175).

236. *Irish Independent*, 2 January 2004.

237. B. C. Hayes and I. McAllister, 'British and Irish Public Opinion Towards the Northern Ireland Problem', *Irish Political Studies* 11 (1996), pp. 76–8.

238. T. Garvin, 'The North and the Rest', in C. Townshend (ed.), *Consensus in Ireland: Approaches and Recessions* (Oxford: Oxford University Press, 1988), pp. 106–7.

239. 'Irish Political Data 1989', *Irish Political Studies* 5 (1990), p. 151.

240. 'Data Section', *Irish Political Studies* 3 (1988), p. 138.

241. R. Sinnott, *Irish Voters Decide: Voting Behaviour in Elections and Referendums Since 1918* (Manchester: Manchester University Press, 1995), p. 178.

242. 'Irish Political Data 1993', *Irish Political Studies* 9 (1994), pp. 209–10.

243. The first three editions of this excellent volume appeared in 1992, 1993 and 1999 respectively; the fourth edition is J. Coakley and M. Gallagher (eds), *Politics in the Republic of Ireland* (London: Routledge, 2005; 1st edn, 1992).

244. Cadogan Group, *Beyond Belfast: Where Now in Northern Ireland?* (Belfast: Cadogan Group, 2005), p. 11.

245. Martin Mansergh, quoted in J. O'Brien, *The Modern Prince: Charles J. Haughey and the Quest for Power* (Dublin: Merlin, 2002), p. 172.

246. J. Joyce and P. Murtagh, *The Boss: Charles J. Haughey in Government* (Dublin: Poolbeg Press, 1983), p. 20.

247. O'Brien, *The Modern Prince*, p. 4.

248. *IT*, 7 November 2005.

249. *IT*, 16 July 2005.

250. On which, see the excellent treatment in D. Ferriter, *The Transformation of Ireland 1900–2000* (London: Profile Books, 2005; 1st edn, 2004).

251. P. Mair, *The Changing Irish Party System* (London: Pinter, 1987), p. 182.

252. T. Garvin, *Preventing the Future: Why Was Ireland So Poor for So Long?* (Dublin: Gill and Macmillan, 2004).

253. M. Gallagher, M. Marsh and P. Mitchell (eds), *How Ireland Voted 2002* (Basingstoke: Palgrave Macmillan, 2003), pp. 126, 131, 248–9.

254. Opinion Poll 25–26 February 2002, in F. Kennedy and C. Farrington (eds), *Irish Political Studies Data Yearbook 2003* (Abingdon: Taylor and Francis, 2003), p. 45. A similar picture of substantial cross-class support for Fianna Fáil is repeatedly evident from other sources also; see, for example, Sinnott, *Irish Voters Decide*, p. 182.

255. M. Marsh and P. Mitchell (eds), *How Ireland Voted 1997* (Boulder: Westview Press, 1999), pp. 95–6.

256. M. Gallagher and M. Laver (eds), *How Ireland Voted 1992* (Dublin: Folens, 1993), p. 99.

257. K. Gilland and F. Kennedy (eds), *Irish Political Studies Data Yearbook 2002* (London: Frank Cass, 2003), p. 62.

258. 'Ireland should do all it can to unite fully with the EU' (endorsed by 45 per cent), 'Ireland should do all it can to protect its independence from the EU'

(40 per cent) (F. Kennedy and C. Farrington (eds), *Irish Political Studies Data Yearbook 2004* (Abingdon: Taylor and Francis, 2005), p. 70).

259. Coakley and Gallagher (eds), *Politics in the Republic of Ireland*; Y. Galligan, *Women and Politics in Contemporary Ireland: From the Margins to the Mainstream* (London: Pinter, 1998).

260. For thoughtful analysis of which, see N. J. Smith, *Showcasing Globalization? The Political Economy of the Irish Republic* (Manchester: Manchester University Press, 2005).

Seven – Explaining Irish Nationalism

1. B. Anderson, *Imagined Communities: Reflections on the Origin and Spread of Nationalism* (London: Verso, 1983), p. 12.

2. For an excellent introduction to the vast extent of such analysis, see A. D. Smith and J. Hutchinson (eds), *Nationalism* (Oxford: Oxford University Press, 1994).

3. Kecmanovic suggests that the term first appeared in 1409 (D. Kecmanovic, *The Mass Psychology of Ethnonationalism* (New York: Plenum Press, 1996), p. 198), although it could hardly have carried fully modern resonances at this stage.

4. *Shorter Oxford English Dictionary* (vol. II), p. 1386; J. C. D. Clark, *Our Shadowed Present: Modernism, Postmodernism and History* (London: Atlantic Books, 2003), p. 269.

5. *The Concise Oxford Dictionary* (Oxford: Oxford University Press, 1991; 1st edn, 1911), p. 789.

6. *Shorter Oxford English Dictionary* (vol. II), p. 1386.

7. The definition of 'ideologies' adumbrated by Michael Freeden seems valuably capacious yet concise: 'sets of political ideas, beliefs and attitudes that involve the adoption of practices which explain, support, justify or contest socio-political arrangements, and which provide plans of action for public political institutions' ('Is Nationalism a Distinct Ideology?', *Political Studies* 46, 4 (1998), p. 749).

8. For valuable theoretical reflections on the idea of community, see E. Frazer, *The Problems of Communitarian Politics: Unity and Conflict* (Oxford: Oxford University Press, 1999); W. Kymlicka, *Liberalism, Community and Culture* (Oxford: Oxford University Press, 1991; 1st edn, 1989); S. Kautz, *Liberalism and Community* (Ithaca: Cornell University Press, 1995); A. Etzioni (ed.), *New Communitarian Thinking: Persons, Virtues, Institutions, and Communities* (Charlottesville: University Press of Virginia, 1995); Z. Bauman, *Community: Seeking Safety in an Insecure World* (Cambridge: Polity Press, 2001).

9. Isaiah Berlin, quoted in D. Miller, 'Crooked Timber or Bent Twig? Isaiah Berlin's Nationalism', *Political Studies* 53, 1 (2005), pp. 100–101.

10. S. Gerhardt, *Why Love Matters: How Affection Shapes a Baby's Brain* (Hove: Brunner-Routledge, 2004), p. 15.

11. D. Krebs and M. Janicki, 'Biological Foundations of Moral Norms', in M. Schaller and C. S. Crandall (eds), *The Psychological Foundations of Culture* (Mahwah: Lawrence Erlbaum, 2004), p. 127.

12. Such an approach is necessitated, in part, by the advances made in scholarly psychological research, on which see H. Whitehouse, *Modes of Religiosity: A Cognitive Theory of Religious Transmission* (Walnut Creek: Altamira Press, 2004), pp. 16–17, 26.

13. Thankfully, it's now becoming more common for the division between scientific and other kinds of research to be challenged (see Gerhardt, *Why Love Matters*).

14. For forceful statements of such a case (essentially, the application of Darwinian evolutionary theory to human social behaviour, and the assertion that nationalism emerges from processes of genetic selection), see P. L. van den Berghe, *The Ethnic Phenomenon* (New York: Elsevier, 1981); for example, 'Ethnicity and "race", I will argue, are extensions of kinship, and, therefore, the feelings of ethnocentrism and racism associated with group membership are extensions of nepotism between kinsmen' (p. xi). Again: 'My central thesis is that both ethnicity and "race" (in the social sense) are, in fact, extensions of the idiom of kinship, and that, therefore, ethnic and race sentiments are to be understood as an extended and attenuated form of kin selection' (P. L. van den Berghe, 'Race and Ethnicity: A Sociobiological Perspective', *Ethnic and Racial Studies* 1, 4 (1978), p. 403).

15. It is the good of the gene or, perhaps, the individual (rather than that of the species or the group), which determines evolutionary development: 'A population is not a discrete enough entity to be a unit of natural selection, not stable and unitary enough to be "selected" in preference to another population' (R. Dawkins, *The Selfish Gene* (London: Granada, 1978; 1st edn, 1976), pp. 2, 8–12, 35, 48; quotation at p. 36). We might be genetically driven to act selflessly in order to protect the survival of our actual kin (who share genetic relatedness), but nations are not genetically linked together in this tight way, and I don't agree that genetically-driven nepotism would extend beyond actual kin.

16. S. Pinker, *How the Mind Works* (Harmondsworth: Penguin, 1998; 1st edn, 1997).

17. As Steven Pinker himself puts it, 'To say that the mind is an evolutionary adaptation is not to say that all behaviour is adaptive in Darwin's sense ... there is no need to strain for adaptive explanations for everything we do' (*How the Mind Works*, pp. 41–2).

18. As Alan Finlayson has rightly noted, many theorists of nationalism implicitly and unreflectively assume certain things about pervasive human nature as the basis for their arguments (A. Finlayson, 'Psychology, Psychoanalysis and

Theories of Nationalism', *Nations and Nationalism* 4, 2 (1998)). My own argument is that it is far better to be explicit and reflective on matters of such importance.

19. Dawkins, *Selfish Gene*, p. x; quotations at pp. 22 and 46.

20. We know that the brain has considerable autonomy from the genes, and can therefore determine far more than mere survival (ibid., pp. 64–7).

21. Kecmanovic, *Mass Psychology*, pp. 27–8.

22. As has long been explicitly recognized by some students of nationalism; see, for example, Royal Institute of International Affairs, *Nationalism* (London: Oxford University Press, 1939), p. xiii.

23. 'Processes of communication are the basis of the coherence of societies, cultures, and even of the personalities of individuals; and it may be worth while to see whether concepts of communication may not help us to understand the nature of peoples and of nations' (K. W. Deutsch, *Nationalism and Social Communication: An Inquiry into the Foundations of Nationality* (Cambridge: MIT Press, 1966; 1st edn, 1953), p. 87).

24. C. Calhoun, *Nationalism* (Buckingham: Open University Press, 1997), pp. 12–18.

25. S. Schama, *Landscape and Memory* (London: Fontana, 1996; 1st edn, 1995).

26. A point sharply made by the political geographer Jim Mac Laughlin in his *Reimagining the Nation-State: The Contested Terrains of Nation-Building* (London: Pluto, 2001).

27. Ryan to Kerney (14 January 1942), Files of the Department of Foreign Affairs (Secretary's Office), NAD A20/4.

28. Anderson, *Imagined Communities*, p. 15.

29. 'Races as objectively existing biological entities do not exist. The traditional concept of "race" cannot be reconciled with current understanding of the genetic nature of human diversity' (G. Richards, *'Race', Racism and Psychology: Towards a Reflexive History* (London: Routledge, 1997), p. x).

30. Modern Greeks being a case in point (J. Hutchinson, *Modern Nationalism* (London: Fontana, 1994), p. 4).

31. Language has, for some, occupied an extremely important place within the nationalist cultural argument: Herder's emphasis on the distinctiveness of language groups, and Fichte's argument that linguistic groups each represent a distinct nation, have been very influential examples.

32. B. Girvin, *From Union to Union: Nationalism, Democracy and Religion in Ireland – Act of Union to EU* (Dublin: Gill and Macmillan, 2002), p. 19.

33. On the latter, see English, *Armed Struggle*, pp. 228–37.

34. See, for one example from very many, S. Chen and T. Wright (eds), *The English Question* (London: Fabian Society, 2000).

35. 'The self-image of individuals is highly affected by the status of their national community' (Y. Tamir, *Liberal Nationalism* (Princeton: Princeton University Press, 1993), p. 73).

36. 'The concept of the nation presupposed a sense of respect toward the individual, an emphasis on the dignity of the human being' (L. Greenfeld, *Nationalism: Five Roads to Modernity* (Cambridge: Harvard University Press, 1992), p. 31).

37. S. Grosby, *Nationalism* (Oxford: Oxford University Press, 2005), p. 8.

38. 'Forgetting, I would even go so far as to say historical error, is a crucial factor in the creation of a nation' (Ernest Renan, quoted in Calhoun, *Nationalism*, p. 52).

39. P. Boyer, *Religion Explained: The Human Instincts that Fashion Gods, Spirits and Ancestors* (London: William Heinemann, 2001), p. 233.

40. R. F. Foster, *The Story of Ireland* (Oxford: Oxford University Press, 1995), p. 4.

41. *AP/RN*, 27 October 1994.

42. M. Wheatley, *Nationalism and the Irish Party: Provincial Ireland 1910–1916* (Oxford: Oxford University Press, 2005), p. 3.

43. A. Aughey, *The Politics of Northern Ireland: Beyond the Belfast Agreement* (London: Routledge, 2005), p. 10.

44. P. Roth, *The Plot Against America* (London: Jonathan Cape, 2004), pp. 113–14.

45. B. Lewis, *The Crisis of Islam: Holy War and Unholy Terror* (New York: Modern Library, 2003), p. xxiii.

46. See the useful essays contained in D. G. Boyce and A. O'Day (eds), *The Making of Modern Irish History: Revisionism and the Revisionist Controversy* (London: Routledge, 1996).

47. J. H. Plumb, *The Death of the Past* (Basingstoke: Palgrave Macmillan, 2004; 1st edn, 1969).

48. G. Adams, *Hope and History: Making Peace in Ireland* (Dingle: Brandon, 2003), pp. 220, 374.

49. K. Popper, *The Poverty of Historicism* (London: Routledge, 1991; 1st edn, 1957), p. v.

50. Cf. David Miller: 'nations are ethical communities. They are contour lines in the ethical landscape. The duties we owe to our fellow-nationals are different from, and more extensive than, the duties we owe to human beings as such' (*Citizenship and National Identity* (Cambridge: Polity Press, 2000), p. 27); see also Calhoun, *Nationalism*, p. 6.

51. As one scholar has phrased it, nationalism 'confers moral value on national membership, and on the past and future existence of the nation' (M. Moore, *The Ethics of Nationalism* (Oxford: Oxford University Press, 2001), p. 5).

52. O. McGee, *The IRB: The Irish Republican Brotherhood, From the Land League to Sinn Féin* (Dublin: Four Courts Press, 2005), p. 11.

53. This has become an increasingly marked feature of nationalist argument; see Elazar Barkan's fascinating treatment in *The Guilt of Nations: Restitution*

and Negotiating Historical Injustices (Baltimore: Johns Hopkins University Press, 2001; 1st edn, 2000).

54. F. Fukuyama, *Trust: The Social Virtues and the Creation of Prosperity* (Harmondsworth: Penguin, 1995.)

55. U. Ozkirimli, *Theories of Nationalism: A Critical Introduction* (Basingstoke: Macmillan, 2000), p. 111.

56. M. Burleigh, *The Third Reich: A New History* (London: Macmillan, 2000); R. J. Evans, *Telling Lies about Hitler: The Holocaust, History and the David Irving Trial* (London: Verso, 2002).

57. See the observations of Partha Chatterjee in *Nationalist Thought and the Colonial World: A Derivative Discourse?* (London: Zed Books, 1986), pp. 2–3.

58. Though some liberals have produced more positive readings of nationalism, an impressive example being Yael Tamir's *Liberal Nationalism*.

59. R. Taras, *Liberal and Illiberal Nationalisms* (Basingstoke: Palgrave Macmillan, 2002).

60. Whitehouse, *Modes of Religiosity*, p. 78.

61. Greenfeld, *Nationalism*.

62. See J. H. Whyte, *Interpreting Northern Ireland* (Oxford: Oxford University Press, 1990), ch. 6.

63. M. Davitt, *The Fall of Feudalism in Ireland or the Story of the Land League Revolution* (London: Harper and Brothers, 1904), p. 229.

64. F. O Connor, *In Search of a State: Catholics in Northern Ireland* (Belfast: Blackstaff Press, 1993), pp. 171–2.

65. For telling examples, from very many: G. Walker, *A History of the Ulster Unionist Party: Protest, Pragmatism and Pessimism* (Manchester: Manchester University Press, 2004); S. Bruce, *God Save Ulster! The Religion and Politics of Paisleyism* (Oxford: Oxford University Press, 1989; 1st edn, 1986); S. Bruce, *The Edge of the Union: The Ulster Loyalist Political Vision* (Oxford: Oxford University Press, 1994); D. Godson, *Himself Alone: David Trimble and the Ordeal of Unionism* (London: Harper Perennial, 2005; 1st edn, 2004); A. Jackson, *Colonel Edward Saunderson: Land and Loyalty in Victorian Ireland* (Oxford: Oxford University Press, 1995); H. McDonald, *Trimble* (London: Bloomsbury, 2000); F. Millar, *David Trimble: The Price of Peace* (Dublin: Liffey Press, 2004); S. Nelson, *Ulster's Uncertain Defenders: Loyalists and the Northern Ireland Conflict* (Belfast: Appletree Press, 1984); R. English and G. Walker (eds), *Unionism in Modern Ireland: New Perspectives on Politics and Culture* (Basingstoke: Macmillan, 1996).

66. Calhoun, *Nationalism*, p. 19.

67. Some might suggest that nationalism appeals to people simply because they inherit it from their parents or their parents' generation, that it is not something people choose but something that they unquestioningly accept. Yet this seems to me doubly to avoid the issue: first, at some stage an initial

choice in favour of this kind of identity had to be made by one generation and we must explain why; second, for people to sustain a nationalism with which they were presented at birth, they presumably have to continue to find it of value or it would be jettisoned (as is so much that we inherit from previous generations).

68. 'Nationalism is a political movement by definition' (P. R. Brass, *Ethnicity and Nationalism: Theory and Comparison* (London: Sage, 1991), p. 48).

69. E. Gellner, *Nations and Nationalism* (Oxford: Basil Blackwell, 1983), p. 1.

70. O. Zimmer, *Nationalism in Europe, 1890–1940* (Basingstoke: Palgrave Macmillan, 2003), p. 65.

71. Gellner, *Nations and Nationalism*, p. 56.

72. Fukuyama, *Trust*, p. xiii.

73. E. Gellner, *Conditions of Liberty: Civil Society and Its Rivals* (London: Hamish Hamilton, 1994), p. 138.

74. I. Walker and H. J. Smith (eds), *Relative Deprivation: Specification, Development and Integration* (Cambridge: Cambridge University Press, 2002).

75. As sustainedly argued in M. Billig, *Banal Nationalism* (London: Sage, 1995).

76. For a flavour of the range of understandings of the term, see M. Banks, *Ethnicity: Anthropological Constructions* (London: Routledge, 1996), pp. 4–5.

77. For a valuable collection of writings on this subject, see A. D. Smith and J. Hutchinson (eds), *Ethnicity* (Oxford: Oxford University Press, 1996).

78. R. Jenkins, 'Rethinking Ethnicity: Identity, Categorization and Power', *Ethnic and Racial Studies* 17, 2 (1994), p. 198.

79. On the dangers of confusing political community with ethnicity, when considering national identity, see B. Parekh, 'Discourses on National Identity', *Political Studies* 42, 3 (1994).

80. In his excellent *Banal Nationalism*.

81. J. Breuilly, *Nationalism and the State* (Manchester: Manchester University Press, 1993; 1st edn, 1982), p. 381.

82. 'It is clear that, for most of its history, humankind functioned without even a very primitive form of state' (C. Pierson, *The Modern State* (London: Routledge, 1996), p. 2).

83. For extended discussion of the state, see R. English and C. Townshend (eds), *The State: Historical and Political Dimensions* (London: Routledge, 1999).

84. An argument powerfully developed in Breuilly, *Nationalism and the State*. Cf. 'Nationalism is inconceivable without the state and vice versa' (J. Breuilly, 'The State and Nationalism', in M. Guibernau and J. Hutchinson (eds), *Understanding Nationalism* (Cambridge: Polity Press, 2001), p. 32).

85. As forcibly pointed out by Walker Connor: *Ethnonationalism: The Quest for Understanding* (Princeton: Princeton University Press, 1994), pp. 91–2.

86. 'The modern state therefore bases itself on the idea of a national group, a nation ruling itself, and the state is the institution or set of institutions

appropriate to the task of national security and national defence' (J. Schwarzmantel, *The State in Contemporary Society: An Introduction* (Hemel Hempstead: Harvester Wheatsheaf, 1994), p. 13).

87. Though it should be noted that nationalists do not always stress the need for an absolutely independent and sovereign state. Welsh and Scottish (and very many Irish) nationalists have been happy to see their nationalist rights of self-determination expressed far short of this goal. On sovereignty, and in particular its relations to the state, see J. Hoffman, *Sovereignty* (Minneapolis: University of Minnesota Press, 1998).

88. 'The modern state emerged as a specialized apparatus of power' (Schwarzmantel, *The State in Contemporary Society*, p. 8).

89. 'All regimes capable of effective action must be based on some principle of legitimacy' (F. Fukuyama, *The End of History and the Last Man* (New York: Free Press, 1992), p. 15).

90. J. Locke, *Two Treatises of Government* (London: Dent, 1924; 1st edn, 1690), pp. 127, 228.

91. Quoted in E. J. Hobsbawm, *Nations and Nationalism Since 1780: Programme, Myth, Reality* (Cambridge: Cambridge University Press, 1990), p. 19.

92. J. Rousseau, *The Social Contract* (Harmondsworth: Penguin, 1968; 1st edn, 1762), quotation at p. 65.

93. *Chambers C20th Dictionary* (Edinburgh: Chambers, 1983), p. 1176.

94. E. Kedourie, *Nationalism* (Oxford: Blackwell, 1993; 1st edn, 1960), p. xvi.

95. Indeed some observers identify the interwoven politics of democracy, collective responsibility and nation-state nationalism as the essence of what is to be valued about the western, as opposed to other, forms of politics; see R. Scruton, *The West and the Rest: Globalization and the Terrorist Threat* (London: Continuum, 2002).

96. M. Canovan, *Nationhood and Political Theory* (Cheltenham: Edward Elgar, 1996).

97. This is frequently true even where liberals assume that the state, rather than the nation, is their preferred unit; 'Liberals often rely at least tacitly on the idea of "nation" to give an account of why particular people belong together as the "people" of a particular state' (C. Calhoun, ' "Belonging" in the Cosmopolitan Imaginary', *Ethnicities* 3, 4 (2003), p. 533).

98. A. Guelke, 'Democracy and Ethnic Conflict', in A. Guelke (ed.), *Democracy and Ethnic Conflict: Advancing Peace in Deeply Divided Societies* (Basingstoke: Palgrave Macmillan, 2004).

99. 'Social power . . . involves the socially significant affecting of one agent by another in the face of possible resistance' (J. Scott, *Power* (Cambridge: Polity Press, 2001), p. 3). It commonly involves not merely the discrete action of one group or representative individual, but also the structures which allow for that action to occur: if a soldier or paramilitary, for example, deploys threatened or actual violence in order to exert power over another person

or persons, then a military or paramilitary infrastructure lies behind this act and facilitates it.

100. D. Howell, *A Lost Left: Three Studies in Socialism and Nationalism* (Manchester: Manchester University Press, 1986), p. 128.

101. Kedourie, *Nationalism*, p. 1.

102. One leading scholar of nationalism rightly pointed out some years ago that it was becoming 'the most contested issue in the recent literature ... whether the nation is a peculiarly modern social formation or is embedded in history' (Hutchinson, *Modern Nationalism*, p. xi).

103. B. M. Metzger and M. D. Coogan (eds), *The Oxford Companion to the Bible* (Oxford: Oxford University Press, 1993), p. 343.

104. For the argument that the nation predates modernity in England, for example, see J. Campbell, *The Anglo-Saxon State* (London: Hambledon, 2000), pp. xxi, xxiii, 10, 31–2, 47; Clark, *Our Shadowed Present*, p. 30; A. Hastings, *The Construction of Nationhood: Ethnicity, Religion and Nationalism* (Cambridge: Cambridge University Press, 1997), pp. 9, 15, 17–18, 36, 42–3. See also Greenfeld, *Nationalism*, pp. 42, 47, for the argument that nationalism itself, as well as national feeling, existed in early-sixteenth-century England. Other striking examples also exist: G. Williams, 'Wales: The Cultural Bases of Nineteenth and Twentieth Century Nationalism', in R. Mitchison (ed.), *The Roots of Nationalism: Studies in Northern Europe* (Edinburgh: John Donald, 1980), p. 119.

105. S. Reynolds, 'Medieval *Origines Gentium* and the Community of the Realm', *History* 68 (1983).

106. These two terms differ in aspects of their precise meaning and have rightly therefore been separated out from each other by some authors. But they surely overlap significantly: the 'primordial' exists from the beginning and so, in the case of a still-surviving phenomenon such as the nation or nationalism, 'primordialism' must imply 'perennialism' (an enduring, long-lasting or even indefinite quality). If 'perennialism' is interpreted as referring to indefinite existence, then the two terms do greatly overlap; if perennialism were, however, taken merely to refer to something which was very long-lasting, then it might be distinguished from primordialism, since the perennialist could hold that the nation or nationalism were phenomena which originated, for instance, in the medieval or early-modern periods at a specific moment of creation, rather than being primordial.

107. J. D. Eller and R. M. Coughlan, 'The Poverty of Primordialism: The Demystification of Ethnic Attachments', *Ethnic and Racial Studies* 16, 2 (1993); S. Grosby, 'The Verdict of History: The Inexpungeable Tie of Primordiality', *Ethnic and Racial Studies* 17, 1 (1994).

108. 'I doubt whether one can use the word "nationalism" to any great purpose in the fifteenth to seventeenth centuries' (D. MacCulloch, *Reformation: Europe's House Divided 1490–1700* (London: Allen Lane, 2003), p. 43).

109. 'For most writers on nationalism, nationalism is a modern political ideology which can be found only from the late eighteenth century' (J. G. Kellas, *The Politics of Nationalism and Ethnicity* (Basingstoke: Macmillan, 1998; 1st edn, 1991), p. 89); M. Guibernau, *Nationalisms: The Nation-State and Nationalism in the Twentieth Century* (Cambridge: Polity Press, 1996), p. 45; Hobsbawm, *Nations and Nationalism*, p. 14; M. Hechter, *Containing Nationalism* (Oxford: Oxford University Press, 2000), p. 24; Kedourie, *Nationalism*, p. 1.

110. K. Kumar, *The Making of English National Identity* (Cambridge: Cambridge University Press, 2003).

111. E. Gellner, *Thought and Change* (Chicago: University of Chicago Press, 1965; 1st edn, 1964), pp. 150–51.

112. E. Gellner, 'Do Nations Have Navels?', *Nations and Nationalism* 2 (1996), p. 368.

113. 'The roots of nationalism in the distinctive structural requirements of industrial society are very deep indeed' (Gellner, *Nations and Nationalism*, p. 35).

114. E. Gellner, 'Nations, States and Religions', in English and Townshend (eds), *The State*, p. 235.

115. Gellner, 'Do Nations Have Navels?', p. 366.

116. Gellner, *Nations and Nationalism*, pp. 48, 56.

117. B. Anderson, 'Selective Kinship', *Dublin Review* (2003), p. 9. I'm very grateful to Roy Foster for drawing my attention to this fascinating essay.

118. Anderson, *Imagined Communities*.

119. Though this, in itself, does not seem to me to decide the issue of the concept's modernity. There are many words of comparatively recent coinage which refer to phenomena that we assume to have predated the actual term which describes them, and nationalism could, in theory, be such a word.

120. A. D. Smith, *Nationalism in the Twentieth Century* (Oxford: Martin Robertson, 1979), p. 47; R. Poole, *Nation and Identity* (London: Routledge, 1999), pp. 20–22; A. D. Smith, *Nations and Nationalism in a Global Era* (Cambridge: Polity Press, 1995), p. 35; A. D. Smith, *Myths and Memories of the Nation* (Oxford: Oxford University Press, 1999), p. 47; A. D. Smith, *Nationalism and Modernism: A Critical Survey of Recent Theories of Nations and Nationalism* (London: Routledge, 1998), p. 36; Hutchinson, *Modern Nationalism*, p. 21.

121. A. D. Smith, 'The Problem of National Identity: Ancient, Medieval and Modern?', *Ethnic and Racial Studies* 17, 3 (1994), p. 387.

122. A. D. Smith, *Nationalism* (Cambridge: Polity, 2001); A. D. Smith, 'The Poverty of Anti-Nationalist Modernism', *Nations and Nationalism* 9, 3 (2003). Elsewhere, Smith has used the term 'historical ethno-symbolism' to refer to his argument (Smith, *Myths and Memories of the Nation*, p. 10); John Hutchinson adopts a similar approach but has used the term 'ethni-

cists'. This kind of argument has been tested and found by some scholars to be valid in relation to numerous case studies: see, for example, H. Gerber, 'The Limits of Constructedness: Memory and Nationalism in the Arab Middle East', *Nations and Nationalism* 10, 3 (2004).

123. A. D. Smith, *The Nation in History: Historiographical Debates about Ethnicity and Nationalism* (Hanover: University Press of New England, 2000), pp. 62–6, 70 and quotation at p. 77.

124. Smith, *Nations and Nationalism in a Global Era*, p. viii.

125. A. D. Smith, 'The Origins of Nations', *Ethnic and Racial Studies* 12, 3 (1989), p. 340.

126. See, for example, M. Stokes, *The Arabesk Debate: Music and Musicians in Modern Turkey* (Oxford: Oxford University Press, 1992), p. 56.

127. Most notably, perhaps, John A. Armstrong in his impressive *Nations Before Nationalism* (Chapel Hill: University of North Carolina Press, 1982).

128. Smith, *Myths and Memories of the Nation*, p. 13.

129. 'By the twelfth century several populations in western Europe had already been recognized by themselves and by others as possessing a distinctive existence of enduring character, and it seems reasonable to refer to these as "nations"' (R. V. Comerford, *Ireland* (London: Arnold, 2003), pp. 3–4).

130. Smith, *Nationalism and Modernism*, p. 196.

131. A trend stimulated, in part, by a brilliant and influential book: E. J. Hobsbawm and T. Ranger (eds), *The Invention of Tradition* (Cambridge: Cambridge University Press, 1983).

132. As anyone who has studied the unsuccessful invention of an Irish socialist republican nationalism will be able to tell you. See, for example, R. English, *Radicals and the Republic: Socialist Republicanism in the Irish Free State 1925–1937* (Oxford: Oxford University Press, 1994), or H. Patterson, *The Politics of Illusion: A Political History of the IRA* (London: Serif, 1997; 1st edn, 1989).

133. Clark, *Our Shadowed Present*, p. 61; Kumar, *The Making of English National Identity*, p. 23.

134. Smith, 'The Problem of National Identity', p. 391.

135. Smith, *The Nation in History*, pp. 63, 65.

136. S. G. Ellis, 'Nationalist Historiography and the English and Gaelic Worlds in the Late Middle Ages', *Irish Historical Studies* 25, 97 (1986); S. G. Ellis, 'Representations of the Past in Ireland: Whose Past and Whose Present?', *Irish Historical Studies* 27, 108 (1991).

137. B. Bradshaw, 'Nationalism and Historical Scholarship in Modern Ireland', *Irish Historical Studies* 26, 104 (1989).

138. 'Medievalists are generally aware of the dangers of anachronism when investigating questions of nationality in their period' (R. Bartlett, *Gerald of Wales 1146–1223* (Oxford: Oxford University Press, 1982), p. 10).

139. Smith, 'The Origins of Nations', p. 342.

140. T. Finan, *A Nation in Medieval Ireland? Perspectives on Gaelic National Identity in the Middle Ages* (Oxford: Archaeopress, 2004).

141. Gellner, *Nations and Nationalism*.

142. Finan, *A Nation in Medieval Ireland?*, p. 114.

143. D. Ó Corráin, 'Nationality and Kingship in Pre-Norman Ireland', in T. W. Moody (ed.), *Nationality and the Pursuit of National Independence* (Belfast: Appletree Press, 1978), pp. 4–6. The term *natio* could be used to refer to powerful family groups or political factions, but also to indicate wider ethnic groups more akin to the modern sense of 'nation'.

144. Ozkirimli, *Theories of Nationalism*, p. 111.

145. Some date the notions of national identity and its necessary rival, 'otherness', as early as the seventh century (Ó Corráin, 'Nationality and Kingship', p. 35).

146. A practice well noted in the available sources: S. Keynes and M. Lapidge (eds), *Alfred the Great: Asser's Life of King Alfred and other Contemporary Sources* (Harmondsworth: Penguin, 1983), pp. 113–14, 282–3.

147. Finan, *A Nation in Medieval Ireland?*, p. 28.

148. The Greeks and the Jews provide examples (Grosby, *Nationalism*, pp. 2, 71).

149. Clark, *Our Shadowed Present*, pp. 75–7.

150. Greenfeld, *Nationalism*, pp. 14, 42.

151. R. Briggs, *Early Modern France 1560–1715* (Oxford: Oxford University Press, 1998; 1st edn, 1977), pp. 142–3.

152. Such as Grosby in 'The Verdict of History'.

153. R. F. Foster, *Modern Ireland 1600–1972* (Harmondsworth: Penguin, 1988), p. 84.

154. Willem and Johan Blaeu's 'Theatrum Orbis Terrarum' (1635), for example, or William Petty's 'Hiberniae Regnum' (c. 1685); more proof of the possible connection between map-making and the potential for nationalist imagination (cf. Calhoun, *Nationalism*, pp. 12–18).

155. Foster, *Modern Ireland*, p. 3; D. Miller, (ed.), *Rethinking Northern Ireland: Culture, Ideology and Colonialism* (Harlow: Longman, 1998), pp. 3–4.

156. D. Armitage, *The Ideological Origins of the British Empire* (Cambridge: Cambridge University Press, 2000), pp. 148–9.

157. D. P. Moran, *The Philosophy of Irish Ireland* (Dublin: James Duffy, n.d.), pp. 34–5.

158. Anderson, *Imagined Communities*; Deutsch, *Nationalism and Social Communication*.

159. Gellner, *Nations and Nationalism*.

160. T. C. W. Blanning (ed.), *The Eighteenth Century: Europe 1688–1815* (Oxford: Oxford University Press, 2000), p. 101.

161. C. Ó Gráda, *Ireland: A New Economic History 1780–1939* (Oxford: Oxford University Press, 1994); T. Garvin, *The Evolution of Irish Nationalist Politics* (Dublin: Gill and Macmillan, 2005; 1st edn, 1981), p. 49.

162. J. Smyth, *The Men of No Property: Irish Radicals and Popular Politics in the Late Eighteenth Century* (Dublin: Gill and Macmillan, 1992), p. 80; M. H. Thuente, *The Harp Re-Strung: The United Irishmen and the Rise of Irish Literary Nationalism* (Syracuse: Syracuse University Press, 1994), p. 21.

163. L. Colley, *Britons: Forging the Nation 1707–1837* (London: Pimlico, 1994; 1st edn, 1992).

164. Greenfeld, *Nationalism*.

165. Anderson, *Imagined Communities*.

166. 'That nationalism is a genuinely modern phenomenon that made its first appearance in Europe shortly before or after 1800 has almost assumed the status of a scholarly consensus' (Zimmer, *Nationalism in Europe*, p. 5).

167. English, *Radicals and the Republic*.

168. R. Kearney, *Postnationalist Ireland: Politics, Literature, Philosophy* (London: Routledge, 1997).

169. S. P. Huntington, *The Clash of Civilizations and the Remaking of World Order* (London: Touchstone, 1998; 1st edn, 1997), pp. 20, 28, 34.

170. Lewis, *The Crisis of Islam*, p. xx.

171. R. Brubaker, *Nationalism Reframed: Nationhood and the National Question in the New Europe* (Cambridge: Cambridge University Press, 1996), p. 2.

Bibliography

MANUSCRIPTS AND ARCHIVES

Linen Hall Library, Political Collection, Belfast – H-Block/Hunger Strike Papers, IRSP/INLA Papers, Northern Ireland Civil Rights Association Papers, Peace Process Papers, SDLP Papers, Sinn Féin Papers

Public Record Office of Northern Ireland, Belfast – Cabinet Files, Joseph Connellan Papers, Joseph Devlin Papers, Matthew Keating Papers, Lissadell Papers, Patrick O'Neill Papers, John Pinkerton Papers, Stewart of Killymoon Papers, United Irish League Papers (Lurgan Branch)

Archives Department, University College, Dublin – Ernest Blythe Papers, Caithlin Brugha Papers, Daniel Bryan Papers, Eithne Coyle O'Donnell Papers, Desmond FitzGerald Papers, Mabel FitzGerald Papers, Sheila Humphreys Papers, Sean MacEntee Papers, Mary MacSwiney Papers, Terence MacSwiney Papers, Richard Mulcahy Papers, Ernie O'Malley Papers, Moss Twomey Papers

National Archives, Dublin – Defence Forces Files, Files of the Department of the Taoiseach, Files of the Department of Foreign Affairs, Jack Lynch Papers

National Library of Ireland, Dublin – Joe Clarke Papers, Michael Collins Papers, Frank Gallagher Papers, Joseph McGarrity Papers, Maurice Moore Papers, Austin Stack Papers

National Archives, London – Colonial Office Files

House of Lords Record Office, London – Andrew Bonar Law Papers

Private Possession – Cormac O'Malley Papers

NEWSPAPERS AND MAGAZINES

An Phoblacht, An Phoblacht/Republican News, An t-Oglach, Armagh Guardian, Belfast Telegraph, Bell, Blueshirt, Catholic Mind, Daily Ireland, Daily Telegraph, Derry Journal, Donegal Vindicator, Dungannon Observer, Financial Times, Fortnight, Freeman's Journal, Galway Express, Guardian, Irish America, Irish Democrat (Belfast), Irish Democrat (London), Irish Echo, Irish Felon, Irish Freedom, Irish Independent, Irish News, Irish People, Irish Press, Irish Times, Irish Voice, Irish Workers' Voice, Freeman's Journal, Leader, Lurgan Mail, Magill, News Letter, Northern Star, Observer, Republican Congress, Republican File, Republican News, Saoirse, Shan Van Vocht, Sinn Fein, Sligo–Leitrim Liberator, Starry Plough, Strabane Weekly News, Sunday Business Post, Sunday Independent, Times, Troops Out, Village, Voice of Labour, United Irishman (mid-nineteenth century), United Irishman (late twentieth century), War News, Wolfe Tone Weekly, Workers' Republic, Workers' Voice

BOOKS, ARTICLES AND OTHER PUBLISHED MATERIAL

Adams, G., *Falls Memories* (Dingle: Brandon, 1983; 1st edn, 1982).
—— *The Politics of Irish Freedom* (Dingle: Brandon, 1986).
—— *Free Ireland: Towards a Lasting Peace* (Dingle: Brandon, 1995; 1st edn, 1986).
—— *A Pathway to Peace* (Cork: Mercier Press, 1988).
—— *Cage Eleven* (Dingle: Brandon, 1990).
—— *Before the Dawn: An Autobiography* (London: Heinemann, 1996).
—— *An Irish Voice: The Quest for Peace* (Dingle: Mount Eagle, 1997).
—— *An Irish Journal* (Dingle: Brandon, 2001).
—— *Hope and History: Making Peace in Ireland* (Dingle: Brandon, 2003).
—— *Who Fears to Speak . . .? The Story of Belfast and the 1916 Rising* (Belfast: Beyond the Pale, 2001; 1st edn, 1991).
—— *The New Ireland: A Vision for the Future* (Dingle: Brandon, 2005).
Adams, M., *Censorship: The Irish Experience* (Dublin: Scepter Books, 1968).
Akenson, D. H., *The Irish Diaspora: A Primer* (Belfast: Institute of Irish Studies, 1993).
Anderson, B., *Imagined Communities: Reflections on the Origin and Spread of Nationalism* (London: Verso, 1983).
—— 'Selective Kinship', *Dublin Review* (2003).
—— *Joe Cahill: A Life in the IRA* (Dublin: O'Brien Press, 2003; 1st edn, 2002).
Andrews, C. S., *Dublin Made Me: An Autobiography* (Cork: Mercier Press, 1979).
—— *Man of No Property: An Autobiography (Volume Two)* (Cork: Mercier Press, 1982).

Archard, D., 'Myths, Lies and Historical Truth: A Defence of Nationalism', *Political Studies* 43, 3 (1995).

Aretxaga, B., *Shattering Silence: Women, Nationalism and Political Subjectivity in Northern Ireland* (Princeton: Princeton University Press, 1997).

——, Dworkin, D., Gabilondo, J., and Zulaika, J. (eds), *Empire and Terror: Nationalism/Postnationalism in the New Millennium* (Reno: Center for Basque Studies, 2004).

Argyll, Duke of, *Irish Nationalism: An Appeal to History* (London: John Murray, 1893).

Aristotle, *Politics* (Oxford: Oxford University Press, 1995 edn).

Armitage, D., *The Ideological Origins of the British Empire* (Cambridge: Cambridge University Press, 2000).

Armstrong, J. A., *Nations Before Nationalism* (Chapel Hill: University of North Carolina Press, 1982).

Arnold, B., *Haughey: His Life and Unlucky Deeds* (London: HarperCollins, 1993).

Arnold, M., *The Works of Matthew Arnold* (Ware: Wordsworth Editions, 1995).

Arthur, P., *Special Relationships: Britain, Ireland and the Northern Ireland Problem* (Belfast: Blackstaff Press, 2000).

Ashcroft, B. and Ahluwalia, P., *Edward Said* (London: Routledge, 2001; 1st edn, 1999).

Aughey, A., *Nationalism, Devolution and the Challenge to the United Kingdom State* (London: Pluto Press, 2001).

—— *The Politics of Northern Ireland: Beyond the Belfast Agreement* (London: Routledge, 2005).

—— and Morrow, D. (eds), *Northern Ireland Politics* (Harlow: Longman, 1996).

Augusteijn, J., *From Public Defiance to Guerrilla Warfare: The Experience of Ordinary Volunteers in the Irish War of Independence 1916–1921* (Blackrock: Irish Academic Press, 1996).

—— (ed.), *Ireland in the 1930s: New Perspectives* (Dublin: Four Courts Press, 1999).

—— (ed.), *The Irish Revolution, 1913–1923* (Basingstoke: Palgrave, 2002).

Bairner, A. (ed.), *Sport and the Irish: Histories, Identities, Issues* (Dublin: UCD Press, 2005).

Baker, J., *The McMahon Family Murders* (Belfast: Glenravel Local History Project, n.d.).

Balliett, C. A., 'The Lives – and Lies – of Maud Gonne', *Eire–Ireland* 14, 3 (1979).

Ballymacarrett Research Group, *Lagan Enclave: A History of Conflict in the Short Strand 1886–1997* (Belfast: BRG, 1997).

Banks, M., *Ethnicity: Anthropological Constructions* (London: Routledge, 1996).

Bardon, J., *A History of Ulster* (Belfast: Blackstaff Press, 1992).

Barkan, E., *The Guilt of Nations: Restitution and Negotiating Historical Injustices* (Baltimore: Johns Hopkins University Press, 2001; 1st edn, 2000).

Barnard, T., *Cromwellian Ireland: English Government and Reform in Ireland 1649–1660* (Oxford: Oxford University Press, 2000; 1st edn, 1975).

—— *A New Anatomy of Ireland: The Irish Protestants, 1649–1770* (New Haven: Yale University Press, 2003).

Barrington, B. (ed.), *The Wartime Broadcasts of Francis Stuart 1942–1944* (Dublin: Lilliput, 2000).

Barry, S., *A Long Long Way* (London: Faber and Faber, 2005).

Barry, T., *Guerilla Days in Ireland* (Dublin: Anvil, 1989; 1st edn, 1949).

Bartlett, R., *Gerald of Wales 1146–1223* (Oxford: Oxford University Press, 1982).

Bartlett, T., *Theobald Wolfe Tone* (Dundalk: Dundalgan Press, 1997).

—— (ed.), *Life of Theobald Wolfe Tone: Memoirs, Journals and Political Writings, Compiled and Arranged by William T. W. Tone, 1826* (Dublin: Lilliput Press, 1998).

—— (ed.), *Revolutionary Dublin, 1795–1801: The Letters of Francis Higgins to Dublin Castle* (Dublin: Four Courts Press, 2004).

—— and Jeffery, K. (eds), *A Military History of Ireland* (Cambridge: Cambridge University Press, 1996).

——, Dickson, D., Keogh, D., and Whelan, K. (eds), *1798: A Bicentenary Perspective* (Dublin: Four Courts Press, 2003).

Bauman, Z., *Community: Seeking Safety in an Insecure World* (Cambridge: Polity Press, 2001).

Béaslaí, P., *Michael Collins and the Making of a New Ireland* (Dublin: Phoenix, 1926).

Beckett, S., *Murphy* (London: Picador, 1973; 1st edn, 1938).

—— *Dream of Fair to Middling Women* (Monkstown: Black Cat Press, 1992).

—— *The Expelled and Other Novellas* (Harmondsworth: Penguin, 1980).

Bede, *Ecclesiastical History: Book III, Text* (Oxford: Oxford University Press, 1896).

—— *A History of the English Church and People* (Harmondsworth: Penguin, 1955).

Belfast Exposed Photography, *Portraits from a 50s Archive* (Belfast: Belfast Exposed Photography, 2005).

Bell, C., *Peace Agreements and Human Rights* (Oxford: Oxford University Press, 2000).

Bell, J. B., *The Secret Army: The IRA 1916–1979* (Dublin: Poolbeg, 1989; 1st edn, 1970).

Benjamin, W., *The Arcades Project* (Cambridge, Mass.: Harvard University Press, 1999).

Benner, E., *Really Existing Nationalisms: A Post-Communist View from Marx and Engels* (Oxford: Oxford University Press, 1995).

Beresford, D., *Ten Men Dead: The Story of the 1981 Irish Hunger Strike* (London: Grafton, 1987).

Bergin, J. J., *History of the Ancient Order of Hibernians* (Dublin: AOH, n.d. [1910?]).

Bernstein, G. L., 'Liberals, the Irish Famine and the Role of the State', *Irish Historical Studies* 29, 116 (1995).

Bew, P., *Land and the National Question in Ireland, 1858–82* (Dublin: Gill and Macmillan, 1978).

—— *C. S. Parnell* (Dublin: Gill and Macmillan, 1980).

—— *Conflict and Conciliation in Ireland, 1890–1910: Parnellites and Radical Agrarians* (Oxford: Oxford University Press, 1987).

—— *Ideology and the Irish Question: Ulster Unionism and Irish Nationalism 1912–1916* (Oxford: Oxford University Press, 1994).

—— 'The Real Importance of Sir Roger Casement', *History Ireland* 2, 2 (1994).

—— *John Redmond* (Dundalk: Dundalgan Press, 1996).

—— 'The Role of the Historical Adviser and the Bloody Sunday Tribunal', *Historical Research* 78, 199 (2005).

——, Gibbon, P., and Patterson, H., *The State in Northern Ireland, 1921–72: Political Forces and Social Classes* (Manchester: Manchester University Press, 1979).

—— and Gillespie, G., *Northern Ireland: A Chronology of the Troubles 1968–1999* (Dublin: Gill and Macmillan, 1999).

——, Hazelkorn, E., and Patterson, H., *The Dynamics of Irish Politics* (London: Lawrence and Wishart, 1989).

Biagini, E. F., *Gladstone* (Basingstoke: Macmillan, 2000).

—— (ed.), *Citizenship and Community: Liberals, Radicals and Collective Identities in the British Isles, 1865–1931* (Cambridge: Cambridge University Press, 1996).

Billig, M., *Banal Nationalism* (London: Sage, 1995).

Bishop, P., and Mallie, E., *The Provisional IRA* (London: Corgi, 1988; 1st edn, 1987).

Blake, J. W., *Northern Ireland in the Second World War* (Belfast: Blackstaff Press, 2000; 1st edn, 1956).

Blanning, T. C. W. (ed.), *The Eighteenth Century: Europe 1688–1815* (Oxford: Oxford University Press, 2000).

—— (ed.), *The Nineteenth Century: Europe 1789–1914* (Oxford: Oxford University Press, 2000).

—— and Wende, P. (eds), *Reform in Great Britain and Germany 1750–1850* (Oxford: Oxford University Press, 1999).

Bloomfield, K., *Stormont in Crisis: A Memoir* (Belfast: Blackstaff Press, 1994).

Bosworth, C. E. (ed.), *A Century of British Orientalists 1902–2001* (Oxford: Oxford University Press, 2001).

Bottigheimer, K., 'Revisionism and the Irish Reformation', *Journal of Ecclesiastical History* 51, 3 (2000).

Bourke, R., *Peace in Ireland: The War of Ideas* (London: Pimlico, 2003).

Boyce, D. G., *Nationalism in Ireland* (London: Routledge, 1995; 1st edn, 1982).

—— *Nineteenth-Century Ireland: The Search for Stability* (Dublin: Gill and Macmillan, 1990).

—— *Ireland 1828–1923: From Ascendancy to Democracy* (Oxford: Blackwell, 1992).

—— and O'Day, A. (eds), *Parnell in Perspective* (London: Routledge, 1991).

——, Eccleshall, R., and Geoghegan, V. (eds), *Political Thought in Ireland Since the Seventeenth Century* (London: Routledge, 1993).

—— and O'Day, A. (eds), *The Making of Modern Irish History: Revisionism and the Revisionist Controversy* (London: Routledge, 1996).

—— and Swift, R. (eds), *Problems and Perspectives in Irish History Since 1800: Essays in Honour of Patrick Buckland* (Dublin: Four Courts Press, 2004).

Boyd, A., *Jack White: First Commander, Irish Citizen Army* (Belfast: Donaldson Archives, 2001).

—— *Marx, Engels and the Irish* (Belfast: Donaldson Archives, 2004).

Boyer, P., *Religion Explained: The Human Instincts that Fashion Gods, Spirits and Ancestors* (London: William Heinemann, 2001).

Boylan, H., *Wolfe Tone* (Dublin: Gill and Macmillan, 1981).

—— (ed.), *A Dictionary of Irish Biography* (Dublin: Gill and Macmillan, 1998).

Boyle, J. W., *The Irish Labor Movement in the Nineteenth Century* (Washington, DC: Catholic University of America Press, 1988).

Bradshaw, B., 'Sword, Word and Strategy in the Reformation in Ireland', *Historical Journal* 21, 3 (1978).

—— 'Nationalism and Historical Scholarship in Modern Ireland', *Irish Historical Studies* 26, 104 (1989).

—— 'Revisionism and the Irish Reformation: A Rejoinder', *Journal of Ecclesiastical History* 51, 3 (2000).

—— and Keogh, D. (eds), *Christianity in Ireland: Revisiting the Story* (Blackrock: Columba Press, 2002).

Brandon, R., *The People's Chef: Alexis Soyer, A Life in Seven Courses* (Chichester: John Wiley, 2005; 1st edn, 2004).

Brass, P. R., *Ethnicity and Nationalism: Theory and Comparison* (London: Sage, 1991).

Breen, D., *My Fight for Irish Freedom* (Dublin: Anvil Press, 1989; 1st edn, 1924).

Brennan, M., *The War in Clare 1911–1921: Personal Memoirs of the Irish War of Independence* (Dublin: Four Courts Press, 1980).

Brennan-Whitmore, W. J., *With the Irish in Frongoch* (Dublin: Talbot Press, 1917).

Breuilly, J., *Nationalism and the State* (Manchester: Manchester University Press, 1993; 1st edn, 1982).

Briggs, R., *Early Modern France 1560–1715* (Oxford: Oxford University Press, 1998; 1st edn, 1977).

British Council Ireland, *Britain and Ireland: Lives Entwined* (Dublin: British Council Ireland, 2005).

Brown, D., *Contemporary Nationalism: Civic, Ethnocultural and Multicultural Politics* (London: Routledge, 2000).

Brown, M. E., Coté, O. R., Lynn-Jones, S. M., and Miller, S. E. (eds), *Nationalism and Ethnic Conflict* (Cambridge, Mass.: MIT Press, 1997).

Brown, T., *Ireland: A Social and Cultural History 1922–1985* (London: Fontana, 1985; 1st edn, 1981).

Browne, N., *Against the Tide* (Dublin: Gill and Macmillan, 1986).

—— *Church and State in Modern Ireland* (Belfast: Queen's University, 1991).

Brubaker, R., *Nationalism Reframed: Nationhood and the National Question in the New Europe* (Cambridge: Cambridge University Press, 1996).

—— 'Neither Individualism Nor "Groupism"', *Ethnicities* 3, 4 (2003).

Bruce, S., *God Save Ulster! The Religion and Politics of Paisleyism* (Oxford: Oxford University Press, 1989; 1st edn, 1986).

—— *The Edge of the Union: The Ulster Loyalist Political Vision* (Oxford: Oxford University Press, 1994).

Bruce, W. and Joy, H., *Belfast Politics: Thoughts on the British Constitution* (Dublin: UCD Press, 2005; 1st edn, 1794).

Buckley, D. N., *James Fintan Lalor: Radical* (Cork: Cork University Press, 1990).

Bull, P., *Land, Politics and Nationalism: A Study of the Irish Land Question* (Dublin: Gill and Macmillan, 1996).

Burke, E., *Reflections on the Revolution in France* (Oxford: Oxford University Press, 1993; 1st edn, 1790).

Burleigh, M., *The Third Reich: A New History* (London: Macmillan, 2000).

Burnett, M. T. and Wray, R. (eds), *Shakespeare and Ireland: History, Politics, Culture* (Basingstoke: Macmillan, 1997).

Butler, H., *Wolfe Tone and the Common Name of Irishman* (Mullingar: Lilliput Press, 1985).

Butler, H. E. (ed.), *The Autobiography of Gerald of Wales* (Woodbridge: Boydell Press, 2005; 1st edn, 1937).

Byron, R., *Irish America* (Oxford: Oxford University Press, 1999).

Cadogan Group, *Beyond Belfast: Where Now in Northern Ireland?* (Belfast: Cadogan Group, 2005).

Caird, J., *The Irish Land Question* (London: Longmans, Green, Reader and Dyer, 1869).

Calhoun, C., *Nationalism* (Buckingham: Open University Press, 1997).

—— '"Belonging" in the Cosmopolitan Imaginary', *Ethnicities* 3, 4 (2003).

—— 'The Variability of Belonging', *Ethnicities* 3, 4 (2003).

Callanan, F., *The Parnell Split, 1890–91* (Cork: Cork University Press, 1992).

Cameron, E., *The European Reformation* (Oxford: Oxford University Press, 1991).

—— *Waldenses: Rejections of Holy Church in Medieval Europe* (Oxford: Blackwell, 2000).

Campbell, B., McKeown, L., and O'Hagan, F. (eds), *Nor Meekly Serve My Time: The H-Block Struggle 1976–1981* (Belfast: Beyond the Pale, 1994).

Campbell, C., *Emergency Law in Ireland 1918–1925* (Oxford: Oxford University Press, 1994).

—— and Connolly, I., 'A Model for the "War Against Terrorism"? Military Intervention in Northern Ireland and the 1970 Falls Curfew', *Journal of Law and Society* 30, 3 (2003).

—— and Ní Aoláin, F., 'The Paradox of Transition in Conflicted Democracies', *Human Rights Quarterly* 27, 1 (2005).

Campbell, F., *Land and Revolution: Nationalist Politics in the West of Ireland 1891–1921* (Oxford: Oxford University Press, 2005).

Campbell, J., *The Anglo-Saxon State* (London: Hambledon, 2000).

Canefe, N., 'Turkish Nationalism and Ethno-Symbolic Analysis: The Rules of Exception', *Nations and Nationalism* 8, 2 (2002).

Cannadine, D., *Class in Britain* (New Haven: Yale University Press, 1998).

Canny, N., 'Why the Reformation Failed in Ireland: *Une Question Mal Posée*', *Journal of Ecclesiastical History* 30, 4 (1979).

—— *Making Ireland British 1580–1650* (Oxford: Oxford University Press, 2003; 1st edn, 2001).

Canovan, M., *Nationhood and Political Theory* (Cheltenham: Edward Elgar, 1996).

Carens, J. H., *Culture, Citizenship, and Community: A Contextual Exploration of Justice as Evenhandedness* (Oxford: Oxford University Press, 2000).

Carey, T. and de Burca, M., 'Bloody Sunday 1920: New Evidence', *History Ireland* 11, 2 (2003).

Carlyle, T., *Selected Writings* (Harmondsworth: Penguin, 1971).

Carr, E. H., *The Twenty Years' Crisis* (Basingstoke: Palgrave, 2001; 1st edn, 1939).

—— *Nationalism and After* (London: Macmillan, 1945).

—— *What Is History?* (Basingstoke: Palgrave, 2001; 1st edn, 1961).

Casey, J. S., *The Galtee Boy* (Dublin: UCD Press, 2005).

Caulfield, M., *The Easter Rebellion* (London: Frederick Muller, 1964).

Champion, J. A. I., 'John Toland, the Druids, and the Politics of Celtic Scholarship', *Irish Historical Studies* 32, 127 (2001).

Charles-Edwards, T. M., *Early Christian Ireland* (Cambridge: Cambridge University Press, 2000).

Chatterjee, P., *Nationalist Thought and the Colonial World: A Derivative Discourse?* (London: Zed Books, 1986).

Chavasse, M., *Terence MacSwiney* (Dublin: Clonmore and Reynolds, 1961).

Chen, S. and Wright, T. (eds), *The English Question* (London: Fabian Society, 2000).

Childers, R. E., 'Law and Order in Ireland', *Studies* 8 (1919).

—— *The Riddle of the Sands* (Ware: Wordsworth, 1993; 1st edn, 1903).

Chrimes, S. B., *Henry VII* (London: Eyre Methuen, 1977; 1st edn, 1972).

Chuto, J., Holzapfel, R. P., Mac Mahon, P., Ó Snodaigh, P., Shannon-Mangan,

E, and Van de Kamp, P. (eds), *The Collected Works of James Clarence Mangan: Poems: 1818–1837* (Blackrock: Irish Academic Press, 1996).

——, Holzapfel, R. P., Mac Mahon, P., Shannon-Mangan, E. (eds), *The Collected Works of James Clarence Mangan: Poems: 1838–1844* (Blackrock: Irish Academic Press, 1996).

——, Holzapfel, R. P., Shannon-Mangan, E. (eds), *The Collected Works of James Clarence Mangan: Poems: 1845–1847* (Dublin: Irish Academic Press, 1997).

——, Van de Kamp, P., Martin, A., and Shannon-Mangan, E. (eds), *The Collected Works of James Clarence Mangan: Prose: 1832–1839* (Dublin: Irish Academic Press, 2002).

Clark, J. C. D., *English Society 1688–1832: Ideology, Social Structure and Political Practice During the Ancien Regime* (Cambridge: Cambridge University Press, 1985).

—— *Revolution and Rebellion: State and Society in England in the Seventeenth and Eighteenth Centuries* (Cambridge: Cambridge University Press, 1986).

—— *The Language of Liberty 1660–1832: Political Discourse and Social Dynamics in the Anglo-American World* (Cambridge: Cambridge University Press, 1994).

—— *Our Shadowed Present: Modernism, Postmodernism and History* (London: Atlantic Books, 2003).

—— (ed.), (Edmund Burke,) *Reflections on the Revolution in France: A Critical Edition* (Stanford: Stanford University Press, 2001).

Clark, S., *Social Origins of the Irish Land War* (Princeton: Princeton University Press, 1979).

Clarke, K., *Revolutionary Woman: Kathleen Clarke 1878–1972 – An Autobiography* (Dublin: O'Brien Press, 1991).

Clarke, L., *Broadening the Battlefield: The H-Blocks and the Rise of Sinn Féin* (Dublin: Gill and Macmillan, 1987).

—— and Johnston, K., *Martin McGuinness: From Guns to Government* (Edinburgh: Mainstream, 2001).

Clasen, C-P., *Anabaptism: A Social History, 1525–1618 – Switzerland, Austria, Moravia, South and Central Germany* (Ithaca: Cornell University Press, 1972).

Clery, A., *The Idea of a Nation* (Dublin: UCD Press, 2002; 1st edn, 1907).

Clifford, B., *Canon Sheehan: A Turbulent Priest* (Aubane: Aubane Historical Society, 1990).

—— *Edmund Burke and the United Irishmen: Their Relevance in Ireland Today* (Aubane: Aubane Historical Society, 1994).

—— *Daniel O'Connell and Republican Ireland* (Aubane: Aubane Historical Society, 1995).

—— (ed.), *The Life and Poems of Thomas Moore (Ireland's National Poet)* (London: Athol Books, 1984).

Coakley, J., 'Religion, National Identity and Political Change in Modern Ireland', *Irish Political Studies* 17, 1 (2002).

—— (ed.), *The Social Origins of Nationalist Movements: The Contemporary West European Experience* (London: Sage, 1992).

—— (ed.), *Changing Shades of Orange and Green: Redefining the Union and the Nation in Contemporary Ireland* (Dublin, UCD Press, 2002).

—— (ed.), *The Territorial Management of Ethnic Conflict* (London: Frank Cass, 2003).

—— and Gallagher, M. (eds), *Politics in the Republic of Ireland* (London: Routledge, 2005; 1st edn, 1992).

Coldrey, B. M., *Faith and Fatherland: The Christian Brothers and the Development of Irish Nationalism 1838–1921* (Dublin: Gill and Macmillan, 1988).

Coleman, M., *County Longford and the Irish Revolution 1910–1923* (Dublin: Irish Academic Press, 2003).

Colley, L., *Britons: Forging the Nation 1707–1837* (London: Pimlico, 1994; 1st edn, 1992).

—— *Captives: Britain, Empire and the World 1600–1850* (London: Pimlico, 2003; 1st edn, 2002).

Collins, E., *Killing Rage* (London: Granta, 1997).

Comerford, M., *The First Dáil: January 21st 1919* (Dublin: Joe Clarke, 1969).

Comerford, R. V., *Charles J. Kickham: A Study in Irish Nationalism and Literature* (Portmarnock: Wolfhound Press, 1979).

—— *The Fenians in Context: Irish Politics and Society, 1848–82* (Dublin: Wolfhound Press, 1985).

—— 'Comprehending the Fenians', *Saothar* 17 (1992).

—— *Ireland* (London: Arnold, 2003).

Conan Doyle, A., *His Last Bow: Some Reminiscences of Sherlock Holmes* (London: Pan, 1955; 1st edn, 1917).

Connolly Association, *Radicals and Revolutionaries: Essays on 1798* (London: Connolly Association, n.d.).

Connolly, J., *Collected Works* (vol. I) (Dublin: New Books, 1987).

—— *Collected Works* (vol. II) (Dublin: New Books, 1988).

Connolly, N., *The Unbroken Tradition* (New York: Boni and Liveright, 1918).

—— [as Connolly O'Brien, N.] *Portrait of a Rebel Father* (London: Rich and Cowan, 1935).

Connolly, S. J., *Religion, Law, and Power: The Making of Protestant Ireland 1660–1760* (Oxford: Oxford University Press, 1995; 1st edn, 1992).

—— 'Reconsidering the Irish Act of Union', *Transactions of the Royal Historical Society* (sixth series) 10 (2000).

—— (ed.), *The Oxford Companion to Irish History* (Oxford: Oxford University Press, 1998).

Connor, W., *The National Question in Marxist-Leninist Theory and Strategy* (Princeton: Princeton University Press, 1984).

—— *Ethnonationalism: The Quest for Understanding* (Princeton: Princeton University Press, 1994).

Conversi, D. (ed.), *Ethnonationalism in the Contemporary World: Walker Connor and the Study of Nationalism* (London: Routledge, 2002).

Coogan, O., *Politics and War in Meath 1913–23* (Dublin: Folens, 1983).

Corkery, D., *The Hidden Ireland: A Study of Gaelic Munster in the Eighteenth Century* (Dublin: Gill and Macmillan, 1967; 1st edn, 1924).

Côté, J. M., *Fanny and Anna Parnell: Ireland's Patriot Sisters* (Basingstoke: Macmillan, 1991).

Coulter, C., *The Hidden Tradition: Feminism, Women and Nationalism in Ireland* (Cork: Cork University Press, 1993).

Cox., M. (ed.), *E. H. Carr: A Critical Appraisal* (Basingstoke: Palgrave, 2000).

——, Guelke, A., and Stephen, F. (eds), *A Farewell to Arms? Beyond the Good Friday Agreement* (Manchester: Manchester University Press, 2006; 1st edn, 2000).

Cregan, D. F., 'The Confederate Catholics of Ireland: The Personnel of the Confederation, 1642–9', *Irish Historical Studies* 29, 116 (1995).

Creighton, A., 'The Remonstrance of December 1661 and Catholic Politics in Restoration Ireland', *Irish Historical Studies* 34, 133 (2004).

Crimmins, J. E., 'Jeremy Bentham and Daniel O'Connell: Their Correspondence and Radical Alliance, 1828–1831', *Historical Journal* 40, 2 (1997).

Cronin, M., *The Blueshirts and Irish Politics* (Dublin: Four Courts Press, 1997).

—— and Adair, D, *The Wearing of the Green: A History of St Patrick's Day* (London: Routledge, 2002).

Cronin, S., *Marx and the Irish Question* (Dublin: Repsol, 1977).

—— *Frank Ryan: The Search for the Republic* (Dublin: Repsol, 1980).

—— *Irish Nationalism: A History of Its Roots and Ideology* (Dublin: Academy Press, 1980).

Crooke, E., *Politics, Archaeology and the Creation of a National Museum of Ireland: An Expression of National Life* (Dublin: Irish Academic Press, 2000).

Crossman, V., *Politics, Law and Order in Nineteenth-Century Ireland* (Dublin: Gill and Macmillan, 1996).

Cunliffe, B., *The Celts* (Oxford: Oxford University Press, 2003).

Cunningham, M., 'The Political Language of John Hume', *Irish Political Studies* 12 (1997).

Curran, J., *Pagan City and Christian Capital: Rome in the Fourth Century* (Oxford: Oxford University Press, 2002; 1st edn, 2000).

Currie, A., *All Hell Will Break Loose* (Dublin: O'Brien Press, 2004).

Curtin, N. J., *The United Irishmen: Popular Politics in Ulster and Dublin 1791–1798* (Oxford: Oxford University Press, 1994).

Curtis, E., *A History of Ireland* (London: Methuen, 1950; 1st edn, 1936).

Curtis, L. P., 'The Return of Revisionism', *Journal of British Studies* 44, 1 (2005).

Daly, M. E., *Social and Economic History of Ireland Since 1800* (Dublin: Educational Company of Ireland, 1981).

——— *Industrial Development and Irish National Identity, 1922–1939* (Dublin: Gill and Macmillan, 1992).

Darwin, C., *The Origin of Species* (New York: New American Library, 1958; 1st edn, 1859).

Davies, C. S. L., *Peace, Print and Protestantism 1450–1558* (St Albans: Paladin, 1977).

Davis, R., *Arthur Griffith and Non-violent Sinn Féin* (Dublin: Anvil, 1974).

——— *The Young Ireland Movement* (Dublin: Gill and Macmillan, 1987).

——— *William Smith O'Brien: Ireland – 1848 – Tasmania* (Dublin: Geography Publications, 1989).

——— and Davis, M. (eds), *The Rebel in His Family: Selected Papers of William Smith O'Brien* (Cork: Cork University Press, 1998).

Davis, T., *Literary and Historical Essays* (Dublin: James Duffy, 1854).

——— *Thomas Davis: Selections from his Prose and Poetry* (London: T. Fisher Unwin, n.d.),

Davitt, M., *Leaves from a Prison Diary; Or, Lectures to a 'Solitary' Audience* (London: Chapman and Hall, 1885).

——— *The Fall of Feudalism in Ireland or the Story of the Land League Revolution* (London: Harper and Brothers, 1904).

Dawkins, R., *The Selfish Gene* (London: Granada, 1978; 1st edn, 1976).

——— *The Blind Watchmaker* (London: Penguin, 1988; 1st edn, 1986).

Deane, S., *Strange Country: Modernity and Nationhood in Irish Writing Since 1790* (Oxford: Oxford University Press, 1998; 1st edn, 1997).

——— *Reading in the Dark* (London: Jonathan Cape, 1996).

Deasy, L., *Brother Against Brother* (Cork: Mercier Press, 1982).

de Blacam, A., *Towards the Republic: A Study of New Ireland's Social and Political Aims* (Dublin: Kiersey, 1918).

de Bréadún, D., *The Far Side of Revenge: Making Peace in Northern Ireland* (Cork: Collins Press, 2001).

de-Shalit, A., 'National Self-determination: Political, not Cultural', *Political Studies* 44, 5 (1996).

Deutsch, K. W., *Nationalism and Social Communication: An Inquiry into the Foundations of Nationality* (Cambridge, Mass.: MIT Press, 1966; 1st edn, 1953).

Devlin, B., *The Price of My Soul* (London: Pan, 1969).

Dickson, D., Keogh, D., and Whelan, K. (eds), *The United Irishmen: Republicanism, Radicalism and Rebellion* (Dublin: Lilliput Press, 1993).

Dillon, W., *Life of John Mitchel* (two volumes) (London: Kegan Paul, Trench and Co., 1888).

Doheny, M., *The Felon's Track: A Narrative of '48* (Glasgow: Cameron and Ferguson, 1875).

Dolan, A., *Commemorating the Irish Civil War: History and Memory, 1923–2000* (Cambridge: Cambridge University Press, 2003).

Donnan, H., 'Material Identities: Fixing Ethnicity in the Irish Borderlands', *Identities* 12 (2005).

Donnelly, J. S., *The Land and the People of Nineteenth-Century Cork: The Rural Economy and the Land Question* (London: Routledge and Kegan Paul, 1975).

Donnelly, J., *Charlie Donnelly: The Life and Poems* (Dublin: Dedalus Press, 1987).

Doob, L. W., *Patriotism and Nationalism: Their Psychological Foundations* (New Haven: Yale University Press, 1964).

Doorley, M., *Irish-American Diaspora Nationalism: The Friends of Irish Freedom, 1916–1935* (Dublin: Four Courts Press, 2005).

Doumanis, N., *Italy* (London: Arnold, 2001).

Doyle, D. N., 'Irish Elites in North America and Liberal Democracy, 1820–1920', *Radharc* 3 (2002).

Doyle, E. J., *Justin McCarthy* (Dundalk: Dundalgan Press, 1996).

Doyle, R., *Paddy Clarke Ha Ha Ha* (London: BCA, 1993).

Dragojevic, M., 'Competing Institutions in National Identity Construction: The Croatian Case', *Nationalism and Ethnic Politics* 11, 1 (2005).

Drower, G., *John Hume: Peacemaker* (London: Victor Gollancz, 1995).

Dudgeon, J., *Roger Casement: The Black Diaries with a Study of his Background, Sexuality, and Irish Political Life* (Belfast: Belfast Press, 2002).

Duffy, C. G., *My Life in Two Hemispheres* (Shannon: Irish University Press, 1969; 1st edn, 1898).

Duffy, S., 'King John's Expedition to Ireland, 1210: The Evidence Reconsidered', *Irish Historical Studies* 30, 117 (1996).

—— *Ireland in the Middle Ages* (Basingstoke: Macmillan, 1997).

Duggan, C., *Francesco Crispi: From Nation to Nationalism* (Oxford; Oxford University Press, 2002).

Dumbrell, J., 'The United States and the Northern Irish Conflict 1969–94: From Indifference to Intervention', *Irish Studies in International Affairs* 6 (1995).

Dunn, J., 'Crisis of the Nation State?', *Political Studies* 42, Special Issue (1994).

Dunne, T., *Rebellions: Memoir, Memory and 1798* (Dublin: Lilliput Press, 2004).

Dunphy, R., *The Making of Fianna Fáil Power in Ireland 1923–1948* (Oxford: Oxford University Press, 1995).

Dwyer, T. R., *De Valera's Darkest Hour: In Search of National Independence 1919–1932* (Cork: Mercier Press, 1982).

—— *De Valera's Finest Hour: In Search of National Independence 1932–1959* (Cork: Mercier Press, 1982).

—— *Tans, Terror and Troubles: Kerry's Real Fighting Story 1913–23* (Cork: Mercier Press, 2001).

Eagleton, T., *Nationalism: Irony and Commitment* (Derry: Field Day, 1988).

—— *Ideology: An Introduction* (London: Verso, 1991).

—— *Heathcliff and the Great Hunger: Studies in Irish Culture* (London: Verso, 1995).

Edgeworth, M., *Castle Rackrent/The Absentee* (Ware: Wordsworth, 1994 edn).

Edwards, O. D., *Eamon de Valera* (Cardiff: University of Wales Press, 1987).

Edwards, R. D., *Patrick Pearse: The Triumph of Failure* (Dublin: Poolbeg Press, 1990; 1st edn, 1977),

—— *James Connolly* (Dublin: Gill and Macmillan, 1981).

Eller, J. D. and Coughlan, R. M., 'The Poverty of Primordialism: The Demystification of Ethnic Attachments', *Ethnic and Racial Studies* 16, 2 (1993).

Elliott, M., *Wolfe Tone: Prophet of Irish Independence* (New Haven: Yale University Press, 1989).

—— *The Catholics of Ulster: A History* (Harmondsworth: Allen Lane, 2000).

—— *Robert Emmet: The Making of a Legend* (London: Profile, 2003).

—— (ed.), *The Long Road to Peace in Northern Ireland* (Liverpool: Liverpool University Press, 2002).

Elliott, S. and Flackes, W. D., *Northern Ireland: A Political Directory 1968–1993* (Belfast: Blackstaff Press, 1994; 1st edn, 1980).

Ellis, P. B., *The Ancient World of the Celts* (London: Constable, 1998).

Ellis, S. G., 'Nationalist Historiography and the English and Gaelic Worlds in the Late Middle Ages', *Irish Historical Studies* 25, 97 (1986).

—— 'Economic Problems of the Church: Why the Reformation Failed in Ireland', *Journal of Ecclesiastical History* 41, 2 (1990).

—— 'Representations of the Past in Ireland: Whose Past and Whose Present?', *Irish Historical Studies* 27, 108 (1991).

—— *Ireland in the Age of the Tudors 1447–1603: English Expansion and the End of Gaelic Rule* (London: Longman, 1998; 1st edn, 1985).

Ellmann, R., *Oscar Wilde* (Harmondsworth: Penguin, 1988; 1st edn, 1987).

Engels, F., *The Condition of the Working Class in England* (London: Granada, 1969; 1st edn, 1845).

English, R., *Radicals and the Republic: Socialist Republicanism in the Irish Free State 1925–1937* (Oxford: Oxford University Press, 1994).

—— *Ernie O'Malley: IRA Intellectual* (Oxford: Oxford University Press, 1999; 1st edn, 1998).

—— *Armed Struggle: The History of the IRA* (London: Pan, 2004; 1st edn, 2003).

—— and O'Malley, C. (eds), *Prisoners: The Civil War Letters of Ernie O'Malley* (Dublin: Poolbeg Press, 1991).

—— and Walker, G., (eds), *Unionism in Modern Ireland: New Perspectives on Politics and Culture* (Basingstoke: Macmillan, 1996).

—— and Skelly, J. M. (eds), *Ideas Matter: Essays in Honour of Conor Cruise O'Brien* (Dublin: Poolbeg, 1998).

—— and Townshend, C. (eds), *The State: Historical and Political Dimensions* (London: Routledge, 1999).

—— and Kenny, M. (eds), *Rethinking British Decline* (Basingstoke: Macmillan, 2000).

Etchingham, C., *Church Organization in Ireland AD 650 to 1000* (Maynooth: Laigin Publications, 1999).

Etzioni, A. (ed.), *New Communitarian Thinking: Persons, Virtues, Institutions, and Communities* (Charlottesville: University Press of Virginia, 1995).

Evans, R. J., *In Defence of History* (London: Granta, 1997).

—— *Telling Lies about Hitler: The Holocaust, History and the David Irving Trial* (London: Verso, 2002).

Fallon, C., 'The Civil War Hungerstrikes: Women and Men', *Eire–Ireland* 22, 3 (1987).

Fanning, R., *Independent Ireland* (Dublin: Helicon, 1983).

Farrell, M., *Northern Ireland: The Orange State* (London: Pluto Press, 1980; 1st edn, 1976).

Farry, M., *The Aftermath of Revolution: Sligo 1921–23* (Dublin: UCD Press, 2000).

Fauske, C. J., *Jonathan Swift and the Church of Ireland 1710–1724* (Dublin: Irish Academic Press, 2002).

Fay, M., Morrissey, M., and Smyth, M., *Northern Ireland's Troubles: The Human Costs* (London: Pluto Press, 1999).

Feeney, B., *Sinn Féin: A Hundred Turbulent Years* (Dublin: O'Brien Press, 2002).

Feldman, A., 'Music of the Border: The Northern Fiddler Project, Media Provenance and the Nationalization of Irish Music', *Radharc* 3 (2002).

Fenning, H., *The Black Abbey: The Kilkenny Dominicans 1225–1996* (Kilkenny: Kilkenny People Printing, n.d.).

Ferris, P., *Dylan Thomas* (London: Hodder and Stoughton, 1977).

Ferriter, D., 'On the State Funerals', *Dublin Review* (2001–2).

—— *The Transformation of Ireland 1900–2000* (London: Profile Books, 2005; 1st edn, 2004).

Finan, T., *A Nation in Medieval Ireland? Perspectives on Gaelic National Identity in the Middle Ages* (Oxford: Archaeopress, 2004).

Finlayson, A., 'Psychology, Psychoanalysis and Theories of Nationalism', *Nations and Nationalism* 4, 2 (1998).

Finnan, J. P., *John Redmond and Irish Unity, 1912–1918* (Syracuse: Syracuse University Press, 2004).

FitzGerald, G., *Towards a New Ireland* (Dublin: Torc Books, 1973; 1st edn, 1972).

—— *All in a Life: An Autobiography* (Dublin: Gill and Macmillan, 1992; 1st edn, 1991).

—— *Reflections on the Irish State* (Dublin: Irish Academic Press, 2003).

Fitzpatrick, D., *Politics and Irish Life 1913–1921: Provincial Experience of War and Revolution* (Cork: Cork University Press, 1998; 1st edn, 1977).

—— 'The Logic of Collective Sacrifice: Ireland and the British Army, 1914–1918', *Historical Journal* 38, 4 (1995).

—— *The Two Irelands 1912–1939* (Oxford: Oxford University Press, 1998).

—— *Harry Boland's Irish Revolution* (Cork: Cork University Press, 2003).

Fitzsimons, L., *Does Anybody Care? A Personal Journal 1976–81* (Belfast: Glandore, n.d.).

Fleischmann, R., *Catholic Nationalism in the Irish Revival: A Study of Canon Sheehan, 1852–1913* (Basingstoke: Macmillan, 1997).

Fletcher, R., *The Conversion of Europe: From Paganism to Christianity 371–1386 AD* (London: HarperCollins, 1997).

Fogarty, L. (ed.), *James Fintan Lalor: Patriot and Political Essayist (1807–1849)* (Dublin: Talbot Press, 1918).

Ford, A., *The Protestant Reformation in Ireland, 1590–1641* (Dublin: Four Courts Press, 1997; 1st edn, 1985).

Foster, R. F., *Charles Stewart Parnell: The Man and His Family* (Hassocks: Harvester, 1979; 1st edn, 1976).

—— *Modern Ireland 1600–1972* (Harmondsworth: Penguin, 1988).

—— *The Story of Ireland* (Oxford: Oxford University Press, 1995).

—— *W. B. Yeats: A Life. I: The Apprentice Mage 1865–1914* (Oxford: Oxford University Press, 1997).

—— *The Irish Story: Telling Tales and Making It Up in Ireland* (Harmondsworth: Penguin, 2001).

—— *W. B. Yeats: A Life. II: The Arch-Poet 1915–1939* (Oxford: Oxford University Press, 2003).

—— (ed.), *The Oxford Illustrated History of Ireland* (Oxford: Oxford University Press, 1989).

—— and Cullen, F. (eds), *'Conquering England': Ireland in Victorian London* (London: National Portrait Gallery, 2005).

Foy, M., and Barton, B., *The Easter Rising* (Stroud: Sutton, 1999).

Frame, R., *Colonial Ireland, 1169–1369* (Dublin: Helicon, 1981).

Frampton, M., ' "Squaring the Circle": The Foreign Policy of Sinn Féin, 1983–1989', *Irish Political Studies* 19, 2 (2004)).

Frazer, E., *The Problems of Communitarian Politics: Unity and Conflict* (Oxford: Oxford University Press, 1999).

Freeden, M., 'Is Nationalism a Distinct Ideology?', *Political Studies* 46, 4 (1998).

Freud, S., *Totem and Taboo* (Harmondsworth: Penguin, 1938; 1st edn, 1919).

—— *Jokes and their Relation to the Unconscious* (Harmondsworth: Penguin, 1976).

—— *On Psychopathology* (Harmondsworth: Penguin, 1979).

—— *The Origins of Religion* (Harmondsworth: Penguin, 1985).

—— *Civilization, Society and Religion* (Harmondsworth: Penguin, 1985).

Fukuyama, F., *The End of History and the Last Man* (New York: Free Press, 1992).

—— *Trust: The Social Virtues and the Creation of Prosperity* (Harmondsworth: Penguin, 1995).

Gallagher, F., *Days of Fear* (London: John Murray, 1928).

—— *The Indivisible Island: The History of the Partition of Ireland* (Westport: Greenwood Press, 1974; 1st edn, 1957).

—— *The Anglo-Irish Treaty* (London: Hutchinson, 1965).

Gallagher, M., 'How Many Nations are there in Ireland?', *Ethnic and Racial Studies* 18, 4 (1995).

—— (ed.), *Irish Elections 1922–44: Results and Analysis* (Limerick: PSAI Press, 1993).

—— and Laver, M. (eds), *How Ireland Voted 1992* (Dublin: Folens, 1993).

——, Marsh, M., and Mitchell, P. (eds), *How Ireland Voted 2002* (Basingstoke: Palgrave Macmillan, 2003).

Gallagher, T. (ed.), *Nationalism in the Nineties* (Edinburgh: Polygon, 1991).

Galligan, Y., *Women and Politics in Contemporary Ireland: From the Margins to the Mainstream* (London: Pinter, 1998).

Gans, C., 'Historical Rights: The Evaluation of Nationalist Claims to Sovereignty', *Political Theory* 29, 1 (2001).

Gargett, G., and Sheridan, G. (eds), *Ireland and the French Enlightenment, 1700–1800* (Basingstoke: Macmillan, 1999).

Garnham, N., 'Accounting for the Early Success of the Gaelic Athletic Association', *Irish Historical Studies* 34, 133 (2004).

Garvin, T., *The Evolution of Irish Nationalist Politics* (Dublin: Gill and Macmillan, 2005; 1st edn, 1981).

—— *Nationalist Revolutionaries in Ireland, 1858–1928* (Oxford: Oxford University Press, 1987).

—— 'The Politics of Language and Literature in Pre-Independence Ireland', *Irish Political Studies* 2 (1987).

—— *1922: The Birth of Irish Democracy* (Dublin: Gill and Macmillan, 1996).

—— *Preventing the Future: Why Was Ireland So Poor for So Long?* (Dublin: Gill and Macmillan, 2004).

Gellner, E., *Thought and Change* (Chicago: University of Chicago Press, 1965; 1st edn, 1964).

—— *Nations and Nationalism* (Oxford: Basil Blackwell, 1983).

—— *Conditions of Liberty: Civil Society and Its Rivals* (London: Hamish Hamilton, 1994).

—— *Encounters with Nationalism* (Oxford: Blackwell, 1994).

—— 'Do Nations Have Navels?', *Nations and Nationalism* 2 (1996).

Geoghegan, P. M., *The Irish Act of Union: A Study in High Politics 1798–1801* (Dublin: Gill and Macmillan, 2001; 1st edn, 1999).

—— 'The Catholics and the Union', *Transactions of the Royal Historical Society* (sixth series) 10 (2000).

—— *Robert Emmet: A Life* (Dublin: Gill and Macmillan, 2004; 1st edn, 2002).

Gerald of Wales, *The History and Topography of Ireland* (Harmondsworth: Penguin, 1982).

Gerber, H., 'The Limits of Constructedness: Memory and Nationalism in the Arab Middle East', *Nations and Nationalism* 10, 3 (2004).

Gerhardt, S., *Why Love Matters: How Affection Shapes a Baby's Brain* (Hove: Brunner-Routledge, 2004).

Gibbons, L., *Edmund Burke and Ireland: Aesthetics, Politics, and the Colonial Sublime* (Cambridge: Cambridge University Press, 2003).

Gilmore, G., *The Irish Republican Congress* (New York: United Irish Republican Committees of US, 1935).

—— *Labour and the Republican Movement* (Dublin: Repsol, n.d.; 1st edn, 1966).

—— *The Relevance of James Connolly in Ireland Today* (Dublin: Fodhla Printing Company, n.d. [1970?]).

Girvin, B., *From Union to Union: Nationalism, Democracy and Religion in Ireland – Act of Union to EU* (Dublin: Gill and Macmillan, 2002).

Godson, D., *Himself Alone: David Trimble and the Ordeal of Unionism* (London: Harper Perennial, 2005; 1st edn, 2004).

Gogarty, O. St J., *As I Was Going Down Sackville Street: A Phantasy in Fact* (Harmondsworth: Penguin, 1954; 1st edn, 1937).

Goodwin, J., *No Other Way Out: States and Revolutionary Movements, 1945–1991* (Cambridge: Cambridge University Press, 2001).

Gorringe, T. J., *Karl Barth: Against Hegemony* (Oxford: Oxford University Press, 1999).

Grand Orange Lodge of Ireland, *The Formation of the Orange Order 1795–1798: The Edited Papers of Colonel William Blacker and Colonel Robert H. Wallace* (Belfast: GOLI Publications, 1994).

Gray, J., *Mill on Liberty: A Defence* (London: Routledge, 1996; 1st edn, 1983).

Gray, P., *Famine, Land and Politics: British Government and Irish Society 1843–1850* (Dublin: Irish Academic Press, 1999).

—— 'Famine and Land in Ireland and India, 1845–1880: James Caird and the Political Economy of Hunger', *Historical Journal* 49, 1 (2006).

—— (ed.), *Victoria's Ireland? Irishness and Britishness, 1837–1901* (Dublin: Four Courts Press, 2004).

Greaves, C. D., *The Life and Times of James Connolly* (London: Lawrence and Wishart, 1972; 1st edn, 1961).

—— *Theobald Wolfe Tone and the Irish Nation* (Dublin: Fulcrum Press, 1991; 1st edn, 1961).

—— *Liam Mellows and the Irish Revolution* (London: Lawrence and Wishart, 1971).

—— *Reminiscences of the Connolly Association* (London: Connolly Association, 1978).

—— *Sean O'Casey: Politics and Art* (London: Lawrence and Wishart, 1979).

Green, A. S., *Ourselves Alone in Ulster* (Dublin: Maunsel and Company, 1918).

—— *Irish Nationality* (London: Williams and Norgate, n.d.).

Greenfeld, L., *Nationalism: Five Roads to Modernity* (Cambridge, Mass.: Harvard University Press, 1992).

Gregory, A. and Pašeta, S. (eds), *Ireland and the Great War: 'A War to Unite Us All'* (Manchester: Manchester University Press, 2002).

Griffith, A. (ed.), *Meagher of the Sword: Speeches of Thomas Francis Meagher in Ireland 1846–1848* (Dublin: M. H. Gill and Son, 1916).

Grosby, S., 'The Verdict of History: The Inexpungeable Tie of Primordiality', *Ethnic and Racial Studies* 17, 1 (1994).

—— *Nationalism* (Oxford: Oxford University Press, 2005).

Guelke, A. (ed.), *Democracy and Ethnic Conflict: Advancing Peace in Deeply Divided Societies* (Basingstoke: Palgrave Macmillan, 2004).

Guibernau, M., *Nationalisms: The Nation-State and Nationalism in the Twentieth Century* (Cambridge: Polity Press, 1996).

—— and Hutchinson, J. (eds), *Understanding Nationalism* (Cambridge: Polity Press, 2001).

Gwynn, S., *Ireland* (London: Ernest Benn, 1924).

Hackett, F., *Ireland: A Study in Nationalism* (New York: Huebsch, 1920).

Haigh, C., *English Reformations: Religion, Politics, and Society under the Tudors* (Oxford: Oxford University Press, 1993).

—— (ed.), *The English Reformation Revised* (Cambridge: Cambridge University Press, 1987).

Hall, D., *Women and the Church in Medieval Ireland, c. 1140–1540* (Dublin: Four Courts Press, 2003).

Hall, J. A. (ed.), *The State of the Nation: Ernest Gellner and the Theory of Nationalism* (Cambridge: Cambridge University Press, 1998).

Hamilton, N., *JFK: Reckless Youth* (London: BCA, 1993; 1st edn, 1992).

Hanley, B., *The IRA, 1926–1936* (Dublin: Four Courts Press, 2002).

—— 'The Politics of Noraid', *Irish Political Studies* 19, 1 (2004).

—— '"Oh Here's to Adolph Hitler"? The IRA and the Nazis', *History Ireland* 13, 3 (2005).

Hardiman, A., 'The (Show?) Trial of Robert Emmet', *History Ireland* 13, 4 (2005).

Harmon, M., *Seán O'Faoláin* (London: Constable, 1994).

Hart, P., *The IRA and Its Enemies: Violence and Community in Cork, 1916–1923* (Oxford: Oxford University Press, 1998).

—— *The IRA at War 1916–1923* (Oxford: Oxford University Press, 2003).

—— *Mick: The Real Michael Collins* (London: Macmillan, 2005).

—— (ed.), *British Intelligence in Ireland, 1920–21: The Final Reports* (Cork: Cork University Press, 2002).

Hastings, A., *The Construction of Nationhood: Ethnicity, Religion and Nationalism* (Cambridge: Cambridge University Press, 1997).

Hayes, B. C., and McAllister, I., 'British and Irish Public Opinion Towards the Northern Ireland Problem', *Irish Political Studies* 11 (1996).

Hayes, C. J. H., *The Historical Evolution of Modern Nationalism* (New York: Richard R. Smith, 1931).

Hayton, D. W., *Ruling Ireland, 1685–1742: Politics, Politicians and Parties* (Woodbridge: Boydell Press, 2004).

Hazelkorn, E., 'Reconsidering Marx and Engels on Ireland', *Saothar* 9 (1983).

Heal, F., *Reformation in Britain and Ireland* (Oxford: Oxford University Press, 2003).

Healy, D., *A Goat's Song* (London: Harvill Press, 1997; 1st edn, 1994).

Heaney, S., *Station Island* (London: Faber and Faber, 1984).

—— *Seeing Things* (London: Faber and Faber, 1991).

—— *The Redress of Poetry: Oxford Lectures* (London: Faber and Faber, 1995).

—— *The Spirit Level* (London: Faber and Faber, 1996).

—— *Electric Light* (London: Faber and Faber, 2001).

Hechter, M., *Containing Nationalism* (Oxford: Oxford University Press, 2000).

Hennessey, T., *A History of Northern Ireland 1920–1996* (Dublin: Gill and Macmillan, 1997).

—— *The Northern Ireland Peace Process: Ending the Troubles?* (Dublin: Gill and Macmillan, 2000).

Hepburn, A. C., 'The Ancient Order of Hibernians in Irish Politics, 1905–14', *Cithara* 10 (1971).

Herman, N., 'Henry Grattan, the Regency Crisis and the Emergence of a Whig Party in Ireland, 1788–9', *Irish Historical Studies* 32, 128 (2001).

Heron, R. M., *The Irish Difficulty, and Its Solution, by a System of Local Superintendence* (London: Hatchard and Co., 1868).

Hewitt, J., *Loose Ends* (Belfast: Blackstaff, 1983).

Higgins, I., *Swift's Politics: A Study in Disaffection* (Cambridge: Cambridge University Press, 1994).

Hill, J. R. (ed.), *A New History of Ireland, Volume VII: Ireland, 1921–84* (Oxford: Oxford University Press, 2003).

Hill, R. J. and Marsh, M. (eds), *Modern Irish Democracy* (Blackrock: Irish Academic Press, 1993).

Hobsbawm, E. J., *The Age of Revolution 1789–1848* (London: Weidenfeld and Nicolson, 1995; 1st edn, 1962).

—— *Nations and Nationalism Since 1780: Programme, Myth, Reality* (Cambridge: Cambridge University Press, 1990).

—— *Age of Extremes: The Short Twentieth Century 1914–1991* (London: Abacus, 1995; 1st edn, 1994).

—— *On History* (London: Weidenfeld and Nicolson, 1997).

—— *Interesting Times: A Twentieth-Century Life* (London: Penguin, 2002).

—— and Ranger, T. (eds), *The Invention of Tradition* (Cambridge: Cambridge University Press, 1983).

Hoffman, J., 'James Connolly and the Theory of Historical Materialism', *Saothar* 2 (1976).

—— *Sovereignty* (Minneapolis: University of Minnesota Press, 1998).

Holland, J., *The American Connection: US Guns, Money and Influence in Northern Ireland* (Boulder: Roberts Rinehart, 1999; 1st edn, 1987).

—— and McDonald, H., *INLA: Deadly Divisions* (Dublin: Torc, 1994).

Holland, V., *Son of Oscar Wilde* (Harmondsworth: Penguin, 1957; 1st edn, 1954).

Holmes, J., *John Bowlby and Attachment Theory* (London: Routledge, 1993).

Hooper, G., and Litvack, L. (eds), *Ireland in the Nineteenth Century: Regional Identity* (Dublin: Four Courts Press, 2000).

Hopkinson, M., *Green Against Green: The Irish Civil War* (Dublin: Gill and Macmillan, 1988).

—— 'Biography of the Revolutionary Period: Michael Collins and Kevin Barry', *Irish Historical Studies* 28, 111 (1993).

—— *The Irish War of Independence* (Dublin: Gill and Macmillan, 2002).

Hoppen, K. T., *Ireland Since 1800: Conflict and Conformity* (Harlow: Longman, 1999; 1st edn, 1989).

—— *The Mid-Victorian Generation 1846–1886* (Oxford: Oxford University Press, 1998).

Horowitz, D. L., *Ethnic Groups in Conflict* (Berkeley: University of California Press, 2000; 1st edn, 1985).

Howe, S., *Ireland and Empire: Colonial Legacies in Irish History and Culture* (Oxford: Oxford University Press, 2000).

Howell, D., *A Lost Left: Three Studies in Socialism and Nationalism* (Manchester: Manchester University Press, 1986).

Hroch, M., *Social Preconditions of National Revival in Europe: A Comparative Analysis of the Social Composition of Patriotic Groups among the Smaller European Nations* (Cambridge: Cambridge University Press, 1985).

Huntington, S. P., *The Clash of Civilizations and the Remaking of World Order* (London: Touchstone: 1998; 1st edn, 1997).

Hurley, M. (ed.), *Reconciliation in Religion and Society* (Belfast: Institute of Irish Studies, 1994).

Hurst, M., *Parnell and Irish Nationalism* (London: Routledge and Kegan Paul, 1968).

Hutchinson, J., *The Dynamics of Cultural Nationalism: The Gaelic Revival and the Creation of the Irish Nation State* (London: Allen and Unwin, 1987).

—— *Modern Nationalism* (London: Fontana, 1994).

—— 'Ethnicity and Modern Nations', *Ethnic and Racial Studies* 23, 4 (2000).

Hyde, H. M., *Carson* (London: Constable, 1987; 1st edn, 1953).

Hyland, J. L., *James Connolly* (Dundalk: Dundalgan Press, 1997).

Ignatieff, M., *Blood and Belonging: Journeys into the New Nationalism* (London: Vintage, 1994; 1st edn, 1993).

Inglis, B., *Roger Casement* (Belfast: Blackstaff, 1993; 1st edn, 1973).

Ingram, M. and Harkin, G., *Stakeknife: Britain's Secret Agents in Ireland* (Dublin: O'Brien Press, 2004).

Jackson, A., *The Ulster Party: Irish Unionists in the House of Commons, 1884–1911* (Oxford: Oxford University Press, 1989).

—— *Sir Edward Carson* (Dundalk: Dundalgan Press, 1993).

—— *Colonel Edward Saunderson: Land and Loyalty in Victorian Ireland* (Oxford: Oxford University Press, 1995).

—— *Ireland 1798–1998: Politics and War* (Oxford: Blackwell, 1999).

—— *Home Rule: An Irish History, 1800–2000* (London: Weidenfeld and Nicolson, 2003).

James, S., *The Atlantic Celts: Ancient People or Modern Invention?* (London: British Museum Press, 1999).

Jarman, N., *Displaying Faith: Orange, Green and Trade Union Banners in Northern Ireland* (Belfast: Institute of Irish Studies, 1999).

Jay, E. (ed.), *The Journal of John Wesley: A Selection* (Oxford: Oxford University Press, 1987).

Jefferies, H. A., 'The Early Tudor Reformations in the Irish Pale', *Journal of Ecclesiastical History* 52, 1 (2001).

Jeffery, K., *Ireland and the Great War* (Cambridge: Cambridge University Press, 2000).

—— (ed.), *'An Irish Empire'? Aspects of Ireland and the British Empire* (Manchester: Manchester University Press, 1996).

Jenkins, R., 'Rethinking Ethnicity: Identity, Categorization and Power', *Ethnic and Racial Studies* 17, 2 (1994).

Johnson, B. (ed.), *Freedom and Interpretation: The Oxford Amnesty Lectures 1992* (New York: Basic Books, 1993)

Johnston, E., 'Early Irish History: The State of the Art', *Irish Historical Studies* 33, 131 (2003).

Johnston, E. M., *Ireland in the Eighteenth Century* (Dublin: Gill and Macmillan, 1974).

Johnston, J., *Civil War in Ulster: Its Objects and Probable Results* (Dublin: UCD Press, 1999; 1st edn, 1913).

Jones, S., *The Language of the Genes: Biology, History and the Evolutionary Future* (London: Flamingo, 1994; 1st edn, 1993).

Joy, S., *The IRA in Kerry 1916–1921* (Cork: Collins Press, 2005).

Joyce, J. *A Portrait of the Artist as a Young Man* (Harmondsworth: Penguin, 1960; 1st edn, 1916).

—— *Ulysses* (Harmondsworth: Penguin, 1968; 1st edn, 1922).

Joyce, J. and Murtagh, P., *The Boss: Charles J. Haughey in Government* (Dublin: Poolbeg Press, 1983).

Jupp, P., *British Politics on the Eve of Reform: The Duke of Wellington's Administration, 1828–30* (Basingstoke: Macmillan, 1998).

—— 'Britain and the Union, 1797–1801', *Transactions of the Royal Historical Society* (sixth series) 10 (2000).

Kabdebo, T., *Ireland and Hungary: A Study in Parallels* (Dublin: Four Courts Press, 2001).

Kamenka, E. (ed.), *Nationalism: The Nature and Evolution of an Idea* (New York: St Martin's Press, 1976).

Kautz, S., *Liberalism and Community* (Ithaca: Cornell University Press, 1995).

Keable, K., *The Missing Piece in the Peace Process* (London: Connolly Publications, 2004; 1st edn, 2003).

Keane, J. B., *The Field* (Cork: Mercier, 1966).

Keane, M., *The Irish Land Question: Suggestions for Legislation* (Dublin: Hodges, Smith and Co., 1868).

Kearney, R., *Postnationalist Ireland: Politics, Literature, Philosophy* (London: Routledge, 1997).

Keating, M., *Nations Against the State: The New Politics of Nationalism in Quebec, Catalonia and Scotland* (Basingstoke: Palgrave, 2001; 1st edn, 1996).

Kecmanovic, D., *The Mass Psychology of Ethnonationalism* (New York: Plenum Press, 1996).

Kedourie, E., *Nationalism* (Oxford: Blackwell, 1993; 1st edn, 1960).

Kee, R., *The Green Flag: A History of Irish Nationalism* (Harmondsworth: Penguin, 2000; 1st edn, 1972).

Kellas, J. G., *The Politics of Nationalism and Ethnicity* (Basingstoke: Macmillan, 1998; 1st edn, 1991).

Kelleher, J. V., 'Irish Literature Today', *The Bell* 10, 4 (1945).

—— 'Early Irish History and Pseudo-History', *Studia Hibernica* 3 (1963).

Kelly, A. C., *Jonathan Swift and Popular Culture: Myth, Media, and the Man* (Basingstoke: Palgrave, 2002).

Kelly, J., *Henry Grattan* (Dundalk: Dundalgan Press, 1993).

Kelly, P., 'Perceptions of Locke in Eighteenth-Century Ireland', *Proceedings of the Royal Irish Academy* 89, C, 2 (1989).

Kennedy, D., *The Widening Gulf: Northern Attitudes to the Independent Irish State, 1919–49* (Belfast: Blackstaff Press, 1988).

Kennedy, L., *The Modern Industrialization of Ireland 1940–1988* (Dublin: Economic and Social History Society of Ireland, 1989).

—— 'Modern Ireland: Post-Colonial Society or Post-Colonial Pretensions?', *Irish Review* 13 (1992–3).

Kenny, M., *The Politics of Identity: Liberal Political Theory and the Dilemmas of Difference* (Cambridge: Polity Press, 2004).

Keogh, D. [Dáire] and Furlong, N. (eds), *The Mighty Wave: The 1798 Rebellion in Wexford* (Blackrock: Four Courts Press, 1996).

—— and Furlong, N. (eds), *The Women of 1798* (Dublin: Four Courts Press, 1998).

—— and Whelan, K. (eds), *Acts of Union: The Causes, Contexts and Consequences of the Act of Union* (Dublin: Four Courts Press, 2001).

Keogh, D. [Dermot], *Twentieth-Century Ireland: Nation and State* (Dublin: Gill and Macmillan, 1994).

Keynes, S. and Lapidge, M. (eds), *Alfred the Great: Asser's* Life of King Alfred *and Other Contemporary Sources* (Harmondsworth: Penguin, 1983).

Kiberd, D., *Irish Classics* (London: Granta, 2000).

Kickham, C., *Knocknagow or, The Homes of Tipperary* (Otley: Woodstock Books, 2002).

Kinealy, C., *A Death-Dealing Famine: The Great Hunger in Ireland* (London: Pluto, 1997).

—— *The Great Irish Famine: Impact, Ideology and Rebellion* (Basingstoke: Palgrave, 2002).

King, C., *Michael Davitt* (Dundalk: Dundalgan Press, 1999).

Kingon, S. T., 'Ulster Opposition to Catholic Emancipation, 1828–9', *Irish Historical Studies* 34, 134 (2004).

Kirwin, B., *Thomas D'Arcy McGee: Visionary of the Welfare State in Canada* (Calgary: University of Calgary, 1981).

Kissane, B., *Explaining Irish Democracy* (Dublin: UCD Press, 2002).

—— *The Politics of the Irish Civil War* (Oxford: Oxford University Press, 2005).

Kleinrichert, D., *Republican Internment and the Prison Ship Argenta 1922* (Dublin: Irish Academic Press, 2001).

Knowlson, J., *Damned to Fame: The Life of Samuel Beckett* (London: Bloomsbury, 1996).

Kotsonouris, M., *Retreat from Revolution: The Dáil Courts, 1920–24* (Blackrock: Irish Academic Press, 1994).

Kumar, K., *The Making of English National Identity* (Cambridge: Cambridge University Press, 2003).

Kuzio, T., 'Nationalism in Ukraine: Towards a New Theoretical and Comparative Perspective', *Journal of Political Ideologies* 7, 2 (2002).

Kymlicka, W., *Liberalism, Community and Culture* (Oxford: Oxford University Press, 1991; 1st edn, 1989).

Laffan, M., *The Resurrection of Ireland: The Sinn Féin Party, 1916–1923* (Cambridge: Cambridge University Press, 1999).

Larkin, E., *The Roman Catholic Church and the Emergence of the Modern Irish Political System 1874–1878* (Blackrock: Four Courts Press, 1996).

Lecky, W. E. H., *Democracy and Liberty* (New York: Longmans, Green and Co., 1896).

—— *A History of Ireland in the Eighteenth Century* (London: Longmans, Green and Co., 1913 edn).

Lee, J. J., *The Modernization of Irish Society 1848–1918* (Dublin: Gill and Macmillan, 1973).

—— *Ireland 1912–1985: Politics and Society* (Cambridge: Cambridge University Press, 1989).

Leerssen, J., *Mere Irish and Fíor-Ghael: Studies in the Idea of Irish Nationality, its Development and Literary Expression Prior to the Nineteenth Century* (Cork: Cork University Press, 1996; 1st edn, 1986).

—— *Remembrance and Imagination: Patterns in the Historical and Literary Representation of Ireland in the Nineteenth Century* (Cork: Cork University Press, 1996).

—— *The Cultivation of Culture: Towards a Definition of Romantic Nationalism in Europe* (Amsterdam: University of Amsterdam, 2005).

Lenin, V. I., *On Religion* (Moscow: Progress Publishers, 1969).

Lennon, C., *Sixteenth-Century Ireland: The Incomplete Conquest* (Dublin: Gill and Macmillan, 1994).

Lever, C., *Charles O'Malley: The Irish Dragoon* (Belfast: Olley and Co., n.d.).

Levitas, B., *The Theatre of Nation: Irish Drama and Cultural Nationalism 1890–1916* (Oxford: Oxford University Press, 2002).

Lewis, B., *The Crisis of Islam: Holy War and Unholy Terror* (New York: Modern Library, 2003).

Lewis, G., *Carson: The Man Who Divided Ireland* (London: Hambledon, 2005).

Lewis, S., *Counties Londonderry and Donegal: A Topographical Dictionary of the Parishes, Villages and Towns of these Counties in the 1830s* (Belfast: Friar's Bush Press, 2004).

Livingstone, D. N., *Putting Science in its Place: Geographies of Scientific Knowledge* (Chicago: University of Chicago Press, 2003).

Lloyd, D., *Ireland After History* (Cork: Cork University Press, 1999).

Lobell, S. E. and Mauceri, P. (eds), *Ethnic Conflict and International Politics: Explaining Diffusion and Escalation* (Basingstoke: Palgrave Macmillan, 2004).

Lock, F. P., *The Politics of Gulliver's Travels* (Oxford: Oxford University Press, 1980).

—— *Swift's Tory Politics* (London: Duckworth, 1983).

—— *Edmund Burke, Volume I: 1730–1784* (Oxford: Oxford University Press, 1998).

Locke, J., *Two Treatises of Government* (London: Dent, 1924; 1st edn, 1690).

Longley, E. (ed.), *Culture in Ireland: Division or Diversity?* (Belfast: Institute of Irish Studies, 1991).

Luddy, M., 'A "Sinister and Retrogressive" Proposal: Irish Women's Opposition to the 1937 Draft Constitution', *Transactions of the Royal Historical Society* (sixth series) 15 (2005).

—— and Murphy, C. (eds), *Women Surviving: Studies in Irish Women's History in the Nineteenth and Twentieth Centuries* (Swords: Poolbeg Press, 1989).

Lydon, J., *The Making of Ireland: From Ancient Times to the Present* (London: Routledge, 1998).

—— (ed.), *The English in Medieval Ireland* (Dublin: Royal Irish Academy, 1984).

Lyman, W. W., 'Ella Young: A Memoir', *Eire–Ireland* 8, 3 (1973).

Lynch, D., *Radical Politics in Modern Ireland: The Irish Socialist Republican Party 1896–1904* (Dublin: Irish Academic Press, 2005).

Lynch, J., *A Tale of Three Cities: Comparative Studies in Working-Class Life* (Basingstoke: Macmillan, 1998).

Lynn, B., *Holding the Ground: The Nationalist Party in Northern Ireland, 1945–72* (Aldershot: Ashgate, 1997).

—— 'Revising Northern Nationalism, 1960–1965: The Nationalist Party's Response', *New Hibernia Review* 4, 3 (2000).

Lyons, F. S. L., *Ireland Since the Famine* (London: Fontana, 1973; 1st edn, 1971).

—— *Charles Stewart Parnell* (London: Fontana, 1978; 1st edn, 1977).

—— *Culture and Anarchy in Ireland 1890–1939* (Oxford: Oxford University Press, 1982; 1st edn, 1979).

McAllister, I., *The Northern Ireland Social Democratic and Labour Party: Political Opposition in a Divided Society* (London: Macmillan, 1977).

Macardle, D., *Tragedies of Kerry 1922–1923* (Dublin: Irish Freedom Press, 1988; 1st edn, 1924).

—— *Earth-Bound: Nine Stories of Ireland* (Worcester: Harrigan Press, 1924).

—— *The Irish Republic: A Documented Chronicle of the Anglo-Irish Conflict and the Partitioning of Ireland, with a Detailed Account of the Period 1916–1923* (London: Corgi, 1968; 1st edn, 1937).

—— *The Unforeseen* (London: Corgi, 1966; 1st edn, 1945).

—— *Without Fanfares: Some Reflections on the Republic of Eire* (Dublin: M. H. Gill and Son, 1946).

MacAtasney, G., *Seán MacDiarmada: The Mind of the Revolution* (Manorhamilton: Drumlin Publications, 2004).

Macaulay, A., *The Holy See, British Policy and the Plan of Campaign in Ireland, 1885–93* (Dublin: Four Courts Press, 2002).

McBride, I., ' "When Ulster Joined Ireland": Anti-Popery, Presbyterian Radicalism and Irish Republicanism in the 1790s', *Past and Present* 157, (1997).

—— *Scripture Politics: Ulster Presbyterians and Irish Radicalism in the Late Eighteenth Century* (Oxford: Oxford University Press, 1998).

—— 'Reclaiming the Rebellion: 1798 in 1998', *Irish Historical Studies* 31, 123 (1999).

—— (ed.), *History and Memory in Modern Ireland* (Cambridge: Cambridge University Press, 2001).

MacBride, S. (ed.), *Ireland's Right to Sovereignty, Independence and Unity Is Inalienable and Indefeasible* (Dublin: Hyland, n.d.).

McCaffrey, B., *Alex Maskey: Man and Mayor* (Belfast: Brehon Press, 2003).

McCall, S., *Irish Mitchel: A Biography* (London: Thomas Nelson, 1938).

McCann, E., *War and an Irish Town* (London: Pluto Press, 1993; 1st edn, 1974).

McCarthy, J., *Reminiscences* (London: Chatto and Windus, 1899).

McCartney, D., *W. E. H. Lecky: Historian and Politician 1838–1903* (Dublin: Lilliput Press, 1994).

McCartney, R., *Reflections on Liberty, Democracy and the Union* (Dublin: Maunsel, 2001).

McCone, K. and Simms, K. (eds), *Progress in Medieval Irish Studies* (Maynooth: Cardinal Press, 1996).

McConnel, J., '"Fenians at Westminster": The Edwardian Irish Parliamentary Party and the Legacy of the New Departure', *Irish Historical Studies* 34, 133 (2004).

—— '"Jobbing with Tory and Liberal": Irish Nationalists and the Politics of Patronage 1880–1914', *Past and Present* 188 (2005).

McCormack, W. J., *Roger Casement in Death, or, Haunting the Free State* (Dublin: UCD Press, 2002).

MacCormick, N., 'Justice as Impartiality: Assenting with Anti-Contractualist Reservations', *Political Studies* 44, 2 (1996).

McCourt, F., *Angela's Ashes: A Memoir* (New York: Scribner, 1996).

McCourt, M., *A Monk Swimming: A Memoir* (New York: Hyperion, 1998).

McCracken, D. P., *The Irish Pro-Boers, 1877–1902* (Johannesburg: Perskor, 1989).

Mac Cuarta, B., 'The Plantation of Leitrim, 1620–41', *Irish Historical Studies* 32, 127 (2001).

—— (ed.), *Ulster 1641: Aspects of the Rising* (Belfast: Institute of Irish Studies, 1993).

MacCulloch, D., *The Later Reformation in England 1547–1603* (Basingstoke: Macmillan, 1990).

—— *Reformation: Europe's House Divided 1490–1700* (London: Allen Lane, 2003).

—— 'Putting the English Reformation on the Map', *Transactions of the Royal Historical Society* (sixth series) 15 (2005).

MacDermot, F., *Theobald Wolfe Tone and His Times* (Tralee: Anvil Books, 1969; 1st edn, 1939).

Mac Dermott, E., *Clann na Poblachta* (Cork: Cork University Press, 1998).

McDermott, F. C., *Taking the Long Perspective: Democracy and 'Terrorism' in Ireland: The Writings of W. E. H. Lecky and After* (Sandycove: Glendale, 1991).

MacDonagh, O., *States of Mind: Two Centuries of Anglo-Irish Conflict, 1780–1980* (London: Pimlico, 1992; 1st edn, 1983).

—— *O'Connell: The Life of Daniel O'Connell 1775–1847* (London: Weidenfeld and Nicolson, 1991).

——, Mandle, W. F., and Travers, P. (eds), *Irish Culture and Nationalism, 1750–1950* (Dublin: Gill and Macmillan, 1983).

MacDonagh, T., *The Poetical Works of Thomas MacDonagh* (Dublin: Talbot Press, 1916).

McDonald, H., *Trimble* (London: Bloomsbury, 2000).

——— and Cusack, J., *UDA: Inside the Heart of Loyalist Terror* (London: Penguin, 2004).

MacDonncha, M. (ed.), *Sinn Féin: A Century of Struggle* (Dublin: Sinn Féin, 2005).

McDonough, T. (ed.), *Was Ireland a Colony? Economics, Politics and Culture in Nineteenth-Century Ireland* (Dublin: Irish Academic Press, 2005).

MacEntee, S., *Easter Fires: Personal Records of 1916 by Sean MacEntee and Dr James Ryan* (Waterford: St Carthage Press, 1943).

——— *Episode at Easter* (Dublin: Gill and Son, 1966).

MacEoin, U. (ed.), *Survivors* (Dublin: Argenta, 1987; 1st edn, 1980).

McEvoy, K., *Paramilitary Imprisonment in Northern Ireland: Resistance, Management and Release* (Oxford: Oxford University Press, 2001).

McGarry, F., *Irish Politics and the Spanish Civil War* (Cork: Cork University Press, 1999).

——— *Frank Ryan* (Dundalk: Dundalgan Press, 2002).

——— *Eoin O'Duffy: A Self-Made Hero* (Oxford: Oxford University Press, 2005).

——— (ed.), *Republicanism in Modern Ireland* (Dublin: UCD Press, 2003).

McGarry, J. (ed.), *Northern Ireland and the Divided World: Post-Agreement Northern Ireland in Comparative Perspective* (Oxford: Oxford University Press, 2001).

McGee, O., *The IRB: The Irish Republican Brotherhood, From the Land League to Sinn Féin* (Dublin: Four Courts Press, 2005).

McGee, T. D., *A Popular History of Ireland: From the Earliest Period to the Emancipation of the Catholics* (Glasgow: Cameron, Ferguson and Co., n.d.).

McGladdery, G., *The Provisional IRA in England: 'Terrorizing the Heartland' with the Bombing Campaign: 1973–1997* (Dublin: Irish Academic Press, 2006).

McGlinchey, C., *The Last of the Name* (Belfast: Blackstaff, 1986).

McGregor, P., '"Insufficient for the Support of a Family": Wages on the Public Works During the Great Irish Famine', *Economic and Social Review* 35, 2 (2004).

Macintyre, A., *The Liberator: Daniel O'Connell and the Irish Party 1830–1847* (London: Hamish Hamilton, 1965).

McIntyre, A., 'Modern Irish Republicanism: The Product of British State Strategies', *Irish Political Studies* 10 (1995).

McKee, E., 'Church–State Relations and the Development of Irish Health Policy: The Mother-and-Child Scheme, 1944–53', *Irish Historical Studies* 25, 8 (1986).

McKenzie, F. A., *The Irish Rebellion: What Happened – And Why* (London: C. Arthur Pearson, 1916).

McKittrick, D., Kelters, S., Feeney, B., and Thornton, C., *Lost Lives: The Stories of the Men, Women and Children Who Died as a Result of the Northern Ireland Troubles* (Edinburgh: Mainstream Publishing, 2001; 1st edn, 1999).

Mac Laughlin, J., *Reimagining the Nation-State: The Contested Terrains of Nation-Building* (London: Pluto, 2001).

McLellan, D., *The Thought of Karl Marx* (London: Macmillan, 1980; 1st edn, 1971).

—— *Karl Marx: His Life and Thought* (London: Granada, 1976; 1st edn, 1973).

—— *Marx* (Glasgow: Fontana, 1975).

—— *Engels* (Glasgow: Fontana, 1977).

McLoughlin, T., *Contesting Ireland: Irish Voices against England in the Eighteenth Century* (Dublin: Four Courts Press, 1999).

McMahon, D., *Republicans and Imperialists: Anglo-Irish Relations in the 1930s* (New Haven: Yale University Press, 1984).

MacMillan, G. M., *State, Society and Authority in Ireland: The Foundations of the Modern State* (Dublin: Gill and Macmillan, 1993).

McNally, P., *Parties, Patriots and Undertakers: Parliamentary Politics in Early Hanoverian Ireland* (Dublin: Four Courts Press, 1997).

—— 'Wood's Halfpence, Carteret, and the Government of Ireland, 1723–6', *Irish Historical Studies* 30, 119 (1997).

McNeill, M., *The Life and Times of Mary Ann McCracken 1770–1866* (Dublin: Allen Figgis, 1960).

Macpherson, C. B., *Burke* (Oxford: Oxford University Press 1980).

MacStiofáin, S., *Memoirs of a Revolutionary* (Edinburgh: Gordon Cremonesi, 1975).

MacVeagh, J., *A Sketch of the Donegal Land War* (London: Home Rule Union, n.d.).

—— *Home Rule in a Nutshell* (London: Daily Chronicle, 1912).

Magee, B., *Wagner and Philosophy* (Harmondsworth: Penguin, 2000).

Magee, P., *Gangsters or Guerrillas? Representations of Irish Republicans in "Troubles Fiction"* (Belfast: Beyond the Pale, 2001).

Maghtochair [Michael Harkin], *Inishowen: Its History, Traditions and Antiquities* (Carndonagh: Michael Harkin, 1935; 1st edn, 1867).

Mahoney, T. H. D., *Edmund Burke and Ireland* (Cambridge, Mass.: Harvard University Press, 1960).

Mahony, R., *Jonathan Swift: The Irish Identity* (New Haven: Yale University Press, 1995).

Maillot, A., *IRA: Les Républicains Irlandais* (Caen: Presses Universitaires de Caen, 1996).

Mair, P., *The Changing Irish Party System* (London: Pinter, 1987).

Mandle, W. F., *The Gaelic Athletic Association and Irish Nationalist Politics 1884–1924* (London: Christopher Helm, 1987).

Manning, M., *The Blueshirts* (Dublin: Gill and Macmillan, 1970).

Markievicz, C., *Prison Letters of Countess Markievicz* (London: Virago, 1987; 1st edn, 1934).

Marsh, C., *Popular Religion in Sixteenth-Century England* (Basingstoke: Macmillan, 1998).

Marsh, M. and Mitchell, P. (eds), *How Ireland Voted 1997* (Boulder: Westview Press, 1999).

Marshall, P. J. (ed.), *The Eighteenth Century* (The Oxford History of the British Empire, vol. II) (Oxford: Oxford University Press, 1998).

Marwick, A., *The New Nature of History: Knowledge, Evidence, Language* (Basingstoke: Palgrave, 2001).

Marx, K., *Capital: A Critique of Political Economy* (London: Lawrence and Wishart, 1954 edn).

—— and Engels, F., *Manifesto of the Communist Party* (Moscow: Progress Publishers, 1977; 1st edn, 1848).

—— and Engels, F., *Ireland and the Irish Question* (Moscow: Progress Publishers, 1971).

—— and Engels, F., *The German Ideology* (London: Lawrence and Wishart, 1974).

Mason, R., *Paying the Price* (London: Robert Hale, 1999).

Maume, P., *'Life That Is Exile': Daniel Corkery and the Search for Irish Ireland* (Belfast: Institute of Irish Studies, 1993).

—— 'Lily Connolly's Conversion', *History Ireland* 2, 3 (1994).

—— *D. P. Moran* (Dundalk: Dundalgan Press, 1995).

—— 'Parnell and the IRB Oath', *Irish Historical Studies* 29, 115 (1995).

—— 'In the Fenians' Wake: Ireland's Nineteenth-Century Crises and their Representation in the Sentimental Rhetoric of William O'Brien MP and Canon Sheehan', *Bullán* 4, 1 (1998).

—— 'Nationalism and Partition: The Political Thought of Arthur Clery', *Irish Historical Studies* 31, 122 (1998).

—— *The Long Gestation: Irish Nationalist Life 1891–1918* (Dublin: Gill and Macmillan, 1999).

—— and O'Leary, C., *Controversial Issues in Anglo-Irish Relations 1910–1921* (Dublin: Four Courts Press, 2004).

Meenan, J. (ed.), *Centenary History of the Literary and Historical Society of University College Dublin 1855–1955* (Tralee: The Kerryman, n.d.).

Meisels, T., ' "A Land without a People": An Evaluation of Nations' Efficiency-based Territorial Claims', *Political Studies* 50, 5 (2002).

Merquior, J. G., *Foucault* (London: Fontana, 1991; 1st edn, 1985).

Metzger, B. M. and Coogan, M. D. (eds), *The Oxford Companion to the Bible* (Oxford: Oxford University Press, 1993).

Mill, J. S., *On Liberty* (Harmondsworth: Penguin, 1974; 1st edn, 1859).

—— *England and Ireland* (London: Longmans, Green, Reader and Dyer, 1868).

Millar, F., *David Trimble: The Price of Peace* (Dublin: Liffey Press, 2004).

Miller, D. [David Leslie], *On Nationality* (Oxford: Oxford University Press, 1995).

—— *Citizenship and National Identity* (Cambridge: Polity Press, 2000).

—— 'Crooked Timber or Bent Twig? Isaiah Berlin's Nationalism', *Political Studies* 53, 1 (2005).

Miller, D. (ed.), *Rethinking Northern Ireland: Culture, Ideology and Colonialism* (Harlow: Longman, 1998).

Milligan, A. L., *Life of Theobald Wolfe Tone* (Belfast: Boyd, 1898).

Mitchel, J., *Jail Journal; Or, Five Years in British Prisons* (London: R. and T. Washbourne, n.d.).

—— *The Last Conquest of Ireland (Perhaps)* (Dublin: UCD Press, 2005; 1st edn, 1861).

Mitchell, A., *Revolutionary Government in Ireland: Dáil Éireann, 1919–22* (Dublin: Gill and Macmillan, 1995).

Mitchell, P. and Wilford, R. (eds), *Politics in Northern Ireland* (Boulder: Westview Press, 1999).

Mitchison, R. (ed.), *The Roots of Nationalism: Studies in Northern Europe* (Edinburgh: John Donald, 1980).

Mokyr, J., *Why Ireland Starved: A Quantitative and Analytical History of the Irish Economy, 1800–1850* (London: Allen and Unwin, 1983).

Moloney, E., *A Secret History of the IRA* (London: Penguin, 2002).

Molony, J. N., *A Soul Came into Ireland: Thomas Davis 1814–1845: A Biography* (Dublin: Geography Publications, 1995).

Monk, R., *Ludwig Wittgenstein: The Duty of Genius* (London: Jonathan Cape, 1990).

Moody, T. W. (ed.), *The Fenian Movement* (Cork: Mercier, 1978; 1st edn, 1968).

—— (ed.), *Nationality and the Pursuit of National Independence* (Belfast: Appletree Press, 1978).

—— and Martin, F. X. (eds), *The Course of Irish History* (Cork: Mercier Press, 1994; 1st edn, 1967).

Moore, M., *The Ethics of Nationalism* (Oxford: Oxford University Press, 2001).

—— 'Normative Justifications for Liberal Nationalism: Justice, Democracy and National Identity', *Nations and Nationalism* 7, 1 (2001).

Moore, T., *Memoirs of the Life of the Right Honourable Richard Brinsley Sheridan* (London: Longman, Rees, Orme, Brown and Green, 1826).

Moran, D. P., *The Philosophy of Irish Ireland* (Dublin: James Duffy, n.d.).

Morgan, A., *James Connolly: A Political Biography* (Manchester: Manchester University Press, 1988).

Morgan, H., ' "Never Any Realm Worse Governed": Queen Elizabeth and Ireland', *Transactions of the Royal Historical Society* (sixth series) 14 (2004).

—— (ed.), *Political Ideology in Ireland, 1541–1641* (Dublin: Four Courts Press, 1999).

Morgan, M., 'Post-War Social Change and the Catholic Community in Northern Ireland', *Studies* 77, 308 (1988).

Morley, J., *The Life of William Ewart Gladstone* (London: Macmillan, 1903).

Morris, E., *Our Own Devices: National Symbols and Political Conflict in Twentieth-Century Ireland* (Dublin: Irish Academic Press, 2005).

Morrison, D., *Then the Walls Came Down: A Prison Journal* (Cork: Mercier Press, 1999).

—— *All the Dead Voices* (Cork: Mercier Press, 2002).

Morton, G., *Home Rule and the Irish Question* (Harlow: Longman, 1980).

Morton, H. V., *In Search of Ireland* (London: Methuen, 1942; 1st edn, 1930).

Mowlam, M., *Momentum: The Struggle for Peace, Politics and the People* (London: Hodder and Stoughton, 2002).

Muldoon, P., *New Selected Poems 1968–1994* (London: Faber and Faber, 1996).

Mullin, J., *The Story of a Toiler's Life* (Dublin: UCD Press, 2000; 1st edn, 1921).

Mulvihill, M., *Charlotte Despard: A Biography* (London: Pandora, 1989).

Murphy, B. P., *Patrick Pearse and the Lost Republican Ideal* (Dublin: James Duffy, 1991).

—— (ed.), *Michael Collins: Some Original Documents in His Own Hand* (Aubane: Aubane Historical Society, 2004).

Murphy, J. A., *Ireland in the Twentieth Century* (Dublin: Gill and Macmillan, 1975).

Murphy, J. H., *Abject Loyalty: Nationalism and Monarchy in Ireland During the Reign of Queen Victoria* (Cork: Cork University Press, 2001).

Murray, G. and Tonge, J., *Sinn Féin and the SDLP: From Alienation to Participation* (Dublin: O'Brien Press, 2005).

Murray, P., *From the Shadow of Dracula: A Life of Bram Stoker* (London: Jonathan Cape, 2004).

Musée de Pont-Aven, *Peintres Irlandais en Bretagne* (Pont-Aven: Musée de Pont-Aven, 1999).

Needham, R., *Battling for Peace* (Belfast: Blackstaff, 1998).

Nelson, I. F., '"The First Chapter of 1798?": Restoring a Military Perspective to the Irish Militia Riots of 1793', *Irish Historical Studies* 33, 132 (2003).

Nelson, S., *Ulster's Uncertain Defenders: Loyalists and the Northern Ireland Conflict* (Belfast: Appletree Press, 1984).

Nevin, D., *James Connolly: 'A Full Life'* (Dublin: Gill and Macmillan, 2005).

Newsinger, J., 'Revolution and Catholicism in Ireland, 1848–1923', *European Studies Review* 9, 4 (1979).

—— 'Connolly and his Biographers', *Irish Political Studies* 5 (1990).

—— 'Fenianism Revisited: Pastime or Revolutionary Movement?', *Saothar* 17 (1992).

Ní Chatháin, P. and Richter, M. (eds), *Ireland and Europe in the Early Middle Ages: Texts and Transmission* (Dublin: Four Courts Press, 2002).

Ní Dhonnchadha, M. and Dorgan, T. (eds), *Revising the Rising* (Derry: Field Day, 1991).

Nimni, E., *Marxism and Nationalism: Theoretical Origins of a Political Crisis* (London: Pluto, 1991).

Nolan, E., *James Joyce and Irish Nationalism* (London: Routledge, 1995).

Nolan, W., Ronayne, L., and Dunlevy, M. (eds), *Donegal: History and Society* (Dublin: Geography Publications, 1995).

Nye, J. S., *Understanding International Conflicts: An Introduction to Theory and History* (New York: Pearson, 2005).

O'Brien, C. C., *States of Ireland* (St Albans: Panther, 1974; 1st edn, 1972).

—— *God Land: Reflections on Religion and Nationalism* (Cambridge, Mass.: Harvard University Press, 1988).

—— *Passion and Cunning and Other Essays* (London: Weidenfeld and Nicolson, 1988).

—— *The Great Melody: A Thematic Biography and Commented Anthology of Edmund Burke* (London: Minerva, 1993; 1st edn, 1992).

—— *Ancestral Voices: Religion and Nationalism in Ireland* (Dublin: Poolbeg Press, 1994).

—— *Memoir: My Life and Themes* (Dublin: Poolbeg, 1998).

O'Brien, F., *The Poor Mouth* (London: Paladin, 1988; 1st edn, 1941).

O'Brien, J., *The Modern Prince: Charles J. Haughey and the Quest for Power* (Dublin: Merlin Publishing, 2002).

O'Brien, P., 'Shelley and Catherine Nugent: Spirits of the Age', *History Ireland* 13, 3 (2005).

Ó Broin, L., *Charles Gavan Duffy: Patriot and Statesman – The Story of Charles Gavan Duffy (1816–1903)* (Dublin: James Duffy, 1967).

—— *W. E. Wylie and the Irish Revolution 1916–1921* (Dublin: Gill and Macmillan, 1989).

O'Callaghan, M., *British High Politics and a Nationalist Ireland: Criminality, Land and the Law under Forster and Balfour* (Cork: Cork University Press, 1994).

Ó Cathaoir, B., *John Mitchel* (Dublin: Clódhanna Teoranta, 1978).

O'Connell, M. R., *Daniel O'Connell: The Man and His Politics* (Blackrock: Irish Academic Press, 1990).

O'Conner, R., *Jenny Mitchel – Young Irelander: A Biography* (Tucson: O'Conner Trust, 1985).

O'Connor, B., *With Michael Collins in the Fight for Irish Independence* (London: Peter Davies, 1929).

O'Connor, F., *In Search of a State: Catholics in Northern Ireland* (Belfast: Blackstaff Press, 1993).

O'Connor, F., *The Big Fellow: A Life of Michael Collins* (London: Thomas Nelson, 1937).

—— *An Only Child* (Belfast: Blackstaff, 1993; 1st edn, 1961).

Ó Cróinín, D., *Early Medieval Ireland 400–1200* (London: Longman, 1995).

O'Day, A., *Charles Stewart Parnell* (Dundalk: Dundalgan Press, 1998).

O'Dea, J., *History of the Ancient Order of Hibernians and Ladies' Auxiliary* (three volumes) (Notre Dame: University of Notre Dame Press, n.d.; 1st edn, 1923).

O'Doherty, M., *The Trouble with Guns: Republican Strategy and the Provisional IRA* (Belfast: Blackstaff Press, 1998).

O'Donnell, P., *Storm: A Story of the Irish War* (Dublin: Talbot Press, n.d. [1926?])

—— *Islanders* (Cork: Mercier Press, 1963; 1st edn, 1927).

—— *Adrigoole* (London: Jonathan Cape, 1929).

—— *The Knife* (Dublin: Irish Humanities Centre, 1980; 1st edn, 1930).

—— *The Gates Flew Open* (London: Jonathan Cape, 1932).

—— *There Will Be Another Day* (Dublin: Dolmen, 1963).

—— *Not Yet Emmet* (Dublin: New Books, n.d.).

O'Donnell, R., *Remember Emmet: Images of the Life and Legacy of Robert Emmet* (Bray: Wordwell, 2003).

O'Duffy, E., *The Wasted Island* (Dublin: Martin Lester, n.d.).

Ó Duibhir, C., *Sinn Féin: The First Election 1908* (Manorhamilton: Drumlin, 1993).

O'Faoláin, S., *Constance Markievicz* (London: Sphere, 1967; 1st edn, 1934).

—— *King of the Beggars: A Life of Daniel O'Connell* (Dublin: Poolbeg Press, 1986; 1st edn, 1938).

—— *De Valera* (Harmondsworth: Penguin, 1939).

—— *The Irish* (West Drayton: Penguin, 1947).

O'Flaherty, L., *Thy Neighbour's Wife* (Dublin: Wolfhound, 1992; 1st edn, 1923).

—— *The Assassin* (Dublin: Wolfhound, 1988; 1st edn, 1928).

—— *Famine* (London: Four Square, 1959; 1st edn, 1937).

—— *Insurrection* (Dublin: Wolfhound Press, 1993; 1st edn, 1950).

Ó Gráda, C., *Ireland: A New Economic History 1780–1939* (Oxford: Oxford University Press, 1994).

O'Halloran, C., *Partition and the Limits of Irish Nationalism: An Ideology under Stress* (Dublin: Gill and Macmillan, 1987).

O'Hegarty, P. S., *A Short Memoir of Terence MacSwiney* (Dublin: Talbot Press, 1922).

O'Leary, B. and McGarry, J., *Explaining Northern Ireland: Broken Images* (Oxford: Blackwell, 1995).

—— and McGarry J. (eds), *The Future of Northern Ireland* (Oxford: Oxford University Press, 1990).

O'Leary, J., *Recollections of Fenians and Fenianism* (London: Downey and Company, 1896).

O'Loughlin, M., *Frank Ryan: Journey to the Centre* (Dublin: Raven Arts Press, 1987).

O'Loughran, R., *Redmond's Vindication* (Dublin: Talbot Press, 1919).

O Mahony, S., *Frongoch: University of Revolution* (Killiney: FDR Teoranta, 1987).

O'Malley, E., *On Another Man's Wound* (Dublin: Anvil Press, 1979; 1st edn, 1936).

—— *The Singing Flame* (Dublin: Anvil Press, 1978).

O'Malley, P., *Biting at the Grave: The Irish Hunger Strikes and the Politics of Despair* (Belfast: Blackstaff Press, 1990).

Ó Muilleoir, M., *Belfast's Dome of Delight: City Hall Politics 1981–2000* (Belfast: Beyond the Pale, 1999).

O'Neill, J., *At Swim, Two Boys* (London: Scribner, 2001).

O'Rawe, R., *Blanketmen: An Untold Story of the H-Block Hunger Strike* (Dublin: New Island, 2005).

O'Reilly, D. (ed.), *Accepting the Challenge: The Memoirs of Michael Flannery* (Dublin: Irish Freedom Press, 2001).

Ó Riain, S., *Maurice Davin (1842–1927): First President of the GAA* (Dublin: Geography Publications, n.d.).

Ó Siochrú, M., *Confederate Ireland 1642–1649: A Constitutional and Political Analysis* (Dublin: Four Courts Press, 1999).

O'Sullivan, M., *Sean Lemass: A Biography* (Dublin: Blackwater Press, 1994).

O'Toole, F., *A Mass for Jesse James: A Journey Through 1980s Ireland* (Dublin: Raven Arts Press, 1990).

—— *A Traitor's Kiss: The Life of Richard Brinsley Sheridan* (London: Granta, 1997).

Otway-Ruthven, A. J., *A History of Medieval Ireland* (New York: Barnes and Noble Books, 1993; 1st edn, 1968).

Ozkirimli, U., *Theories of Nationalism: A Critical Introduction* (Basingstoke: Macmillan, 2000).

—— 'The Nation as an Artichoke? A Critique of Ethnosymbolist Interpretations of Nationalism', *Nations and Nationalism* 9, 3 (2003).

Ozment, S., *Protestants: The Birth of a Revolution* (London: Fontana, 1993; 1st edn, 1992).

Paine, T., *Rights of Man* (London: Watts and Co., 1937; 1st edn, 1791–2).

Palmer, M. D., *Henry VIII* (London: Longman, 1971).

Parekh, B., 'Discourses on National Identity', *Political Studies* 42, 3 (1994).

Parkinson, A. F., *Belfast's Unholy War: The Troubles of the 1920s* (Dublin: Four Courts Press, 2004).

Parnell, T., *The Poetical Works of Thomas Parnell* (London: George Bell and Sons, 1894).

Pašeta, S., *Before the Revolution: Nationalism, Social Change and Ireland's Catholic Élite, 1879–1922* (Cork: Cork University Press, 1999).

—— 'Nationalist Responses to Two Royal Visits to Ireland, 1900 and 1903', *Irish Historical Studies* 31, 124 (1999).

—— *Modern Ireland* (Oxford: Oxford University Press, 2003).

Patten, A., 'The Autonomy Argument for Liberal Nationalism', *Nations and Nationalism* 5, 1 (1999).

Patten, E. (ed.), *Returning to Ourselves: Second Volume of Papers from the John Hewitt International Summer School* (Belfast: Lagan Press, 1995).

Patterson, H., 'James Larkin and the Belfast Dockers' and Carters' Strike of 1907', *Saothar* 4 (1978).

—— 'Reassessing Marxism on Ulster', *Saothar* 5 (1979).

—— *The Politics of Illusion: A Political History of the IRA* (London: Serif, 1997; 1st edn, 1989).

—— 'Sean Lemass and the Ulster Question, 1959–65', *Journal of Contemporary History* 34, 1 (1999).

—— *Ireland Since 1939* (Oxford: Oxford University Press, 2002).

Paulin, T., *The Day-Star of Liberty: William Hazlitt's Radical Style* (London: Faber and Faber, 1998).

Pearse, P. H., *Political Writings and Speeches* (Dublin: Phoenix, n.d.).

Peatling, G. K., 'The Whiteness of Ireland Under and After the Union', *Journal of British Studies* 44, 1 (2005).

Phillips, J. R. S., 'Edward II and Ireland (in Fact and in Fiction)', *Irish Historical Studies* 33, 129 (2002).

Phoenix, E., *Northern Nationalism: Nationalist Politics, Partition and the Catholic Minority in Northern Ireland 1890–1940* (Belfast: Ulster Historical Foundation, 1994).

Pierson, C., *The Modern State* (London: Routledge, 1996).

Pinker, S., *The Language Instinct: The New Science of Language and Mind* (Harmondsworth: Penguin, 1994).

—— *How the Mind Works* (Harmondsworth: Penguin, 1998; 1st edn, 1997).

Plumb, J. H., *The Death of the Past* (Basingstoke: Palgrave Macmillan, 2004; 1st edn, 1969).

Pollak, A. (ed.), *A Citizens' Inquiry: The Opsahl Report on Northern Ireland* (Dublin: Lilliput Press, 1993).

Pollock, J., *John Wesley* (Oxford: Lion Publishing, 1989).

Poole, R., *Nation and Identity* (London: Routledge, 1999).

Popper, K., *The Open Society and Its Enemies: The Spell of Plato* (London: Routledge, 1966; 1st edn, 1945).

—— *The Open Society and Its Enemies: Hegel and Marx* (London: Routledge, 1966; 1st edn, 1945).

—— *The Poverty of Historicism* (London: Routledge, 1991; 1st edn, 1957).

Probert, B., 'Marxism and the Irish Question', *Saothar* 6 (1980).

Purdie, B., 'The Irish Anti-Partition League, South Armagh and the Abstentionist Tactic 1945–58', *Irish Political Studies* 1 (1986).

—— *Politics in the Streets: The Origins of the Civil Rights Movement in Northern Ireland* (Belfast: Blackstaff Press, 1990).

Quinn, J., *Soul on Fire: A Life of Thomas Russell* (Dublin: Irish Academic Press, 2002).

Quinn, R. J., *A Rebel Voice: A History of Belfast Republicanism 1925–1972* (Belfast: Belfast Cultural and Local History Group, 1999).

Rafter, K., *Sinn Féin 1905–2005: In the Shadow of Gunmen* (Dublin: Gill and Macmillan, 2005).

Redmond, J. E., *Historical and Political Addresses 1883–1897* (Dublin: Sealy, Bryers and Walker, 1898).

Redmond-Howard, L. G., *Home Rule* (London: T. C. and E. C. Jack, n.d. [1912?])

Regan, J. M., *The Irish Counter-Revolution 1921–1936* (Dublin: Gill and Macmillan, 1999).

Reynolds, S., 'Medieval *Origines Gentium* and the Community of the Realm', *History* 68 (1983).

Richards, G., *'Race', Racism and Psychology: Towards a Reflexive History* (London: Routledge, 1997).

Richey, A. G., *A Short History of the Irish People, Down to the Date of the Plantation of Ulster* (Dublin: Hodges, Figgis and Co., 1887).

Richter, M., *Medieval Ireland: The Enduring Tradition* (Dublin: Gill and Macmillan, 1988).

Ring, J., *Erskine Childers* (London: John Murray, 1996).

Robbins, K., *The First World War* (Oxford: Oxford University Press, 1984).

Robinson, L., *Patriots: A Play in Three Acts* (Dublin: Maunsel and Company, 1912).

Robson, S., *The First World War* (Harlow: Longman, 1998).

Roche, P. J. and Barton, B. (eds), *The Northern Ireland Question: Myth and Reality* (Aldershot: Avebury, 1991).

Rose, P. L., *Wagner: Race and Revolution* (London: Faber and Faber, 1992).

Roth, P., *The Plot Against America* (London: Jonathan Cape, 2004).

Rousseau, J., *The Social Contract* (Harmondsworth: Penguin, 1968; 1st edn, 1762).

Rowan, B., *Behind the Lines: The Story of the IRA and Loyalist Ceasefires* (Belfast: Blackstaff Press, 1995).

—— *The Armed Peace: Life and Death after the Ceasefires* (Edinburgh: Mainstream, 2003).

Royal Institute of International Affairs, *Nationalism* (London: Oxford University Press, 1939).

Ryan, M., *The Tom Barry Story* (Cork: Mercier Press, 1982).

—— *Liam Lynch: The Real Chief* (Cork: Mercier Press, 1986).

—— *Tom Barry: IRA Freedom Fighter* (Cork: Mercier Press, 2003).

Saddlemyer, A., *Becoming George: The Life of Mrs W. B. Yeats* (Oxford: Oxford University Press, 2002).

Said, E. W., *Culture and Imperialism* (London: Vintage, 1994; 1st edn, 1993).

—— *Representations of the Intellectual* (London: Vintage, 1994).

—— *Orientalism: Western Conceptions of the Orient* (Harmondsworth: Penguin, 1995; 1st edn, 1978).

Sanderson, J., *The Irish Land Question* (London: Edward Stanford, 1870).

Sands, B., *The Diary of Bobby Sands* (Dublin: Sinn Féin, 1981).

Sarbaugh, T. J., 'Eamon de Valera and the *Irish Press* in California, 1928–1931', *Eire–Ireland* 20, 4 (1985).

Sathyamurthy, T. V., *Nationalism in the Contemporary World: Political and Sociological Perspectives* (London: Frances Pinter, 1983).

Savage, R., *Sean Lemass* (Dundalk: Dundalgan Press, 1999).

Sawyer, R., *Casement, the Flawed Hero* (London: Routledge and Kegan Paul, 1984).

Schaller, M. and Crandall, C. S. (eds), *The Psychological Foundations of Culture* (Mahwah: Lawrence Erlbaum, 2004).

Schama, S., *Landscape and Memory* (London: Fontana, 1996; 1st edn, 1995).

Schöpflin, G., *Nations, Identity, Power* (London: Hurst, 2000).

Schwarzmantel, J., *The State in Contemporary Society: An Introduction* (Hemel Hempstead: Harvester Wheatsheaf, 1994).

Scott, J., *Power* (Cambridge: Polity Press, 2001).

Scruton, R., *The West and the Rest: Globalization and the Terrorist Threat* (London: Continuum, 2002).

Shannon-Mangan, E., *James Clarence Mangan: A Biography* (Blackrock: Irish Academic Press, 1996).

Sharrock, D. and Devenport, M., *Man of War, Man of Peace: The Unauthorized Biography of Gerry Adams* (London: Pan, 1998; 1st edn, 1997).

Shaw, F., 'The Canon of Irish History: A Challenge', *Studies* 61 (1972).

Shaw, G. B., *Plays Unpleasant* (Harmondsworth: Penguin, 1946; 1st edn, 1898).

—— *Plays Pleasant* (Harmondsworth: Penguin, 1946; 1st edn, 1898).

—— *Prefaces* (London: Odhams Press, 1938).

Sheehan, P. A., *The Intellectuals: An Experiment in Irish Club-Life* (London: Longmans, Green and Co., 1911).

—— *The Graves at Kilmorna: A Story of '67* (London: Longmans, Green and Company, 1926; 1st edn, 1914).

Sheeran, P. F., *The Novels of Liam O'Flaherty: A Study in Romantic Realism* (Dublin: Wolfhound, 1976).

Shelley, P. B., *The Works of P. B. Shelley* (Ware: Wordsworth Editions, 1994).

Sheridan, R. B., *The Rivals/The School for Scandal* (London: Blackie and Son, n.d.).

Shirlow, P. and McGovern, M., 'Language, Discourse and Dialogue: Sinn Féin and the Irish Peace Process', *Political Geography* 17, 2 (1998).

Sigurdsson, D. L., '"A Parallel Much Closer": The 1918 Act of Union Between Iceland and Denmark and Ireland's Relations with Britain', *Irish Historical Studies* 34, 133 (2004).

Sinnott, R., *Irish Voters Decide: Voting Behaviour in Elections and Referendums Since 1918* (Manchester: Manchester University Press, 1995).

Sisson, E., *Pearse's Patriots: St Enda's and the Cult of Boyhood* (Cork: Cork University Press, 2004).

Skelly, J. M., *Irish Diplomacy at the United Nations 1945–1965: National Interests and the International Order* (Dublin: Irish Academic Press, 1997).

Sloan, J., *Oscar Wilde* (Oxford: Oxford University Press, 2003).

Small, S., *Political Thought in Ireland 1776–1798: Republicanism, Patriotism, and Radicalism* (Oxford: Oxford University Press, 2002).

Smith, A. D., *Theories of Nationalism* (London: Duckworth, 1971).

—— *Nationalism in the Twentieth Century* (Oxford: Martin Robertson, 1979).

—— *The Ethnic Revival* (Cambridge: Cambridge University Press, 1981).

—— 'The Origins of Nations', *Ethnic and Racial Studies* 12, 3 (1989).

—— *National Identity* (Harmondsworth: Penguin, 1991).

—— 'The Problem of National Identity: Ancient, Medieval and Modern?', *Ethnic and Racial Studies* 17, 3 (1994).

—— *Nations and Nationalism in a Global Era* (Cambridge: Polity Press, 1995).

—— *Nationalism and Modernism: A Critical Survey of Recent Theories of Nations and Nationalism* (London: Routledge, 1998).

—— *Myths and Memories of the Nation* (Oxford: Oxford University Press, 1999).

—— *The Nation in History: Historiographical Debates about Ethnicity and Nationalism* (Hanover: University Press of New England, 2000).

—— *Nationalism* (Cambridge: Polity Press, 2001).

—— 'The Poverty of Anti-Nationalist Modernism', *Nations and Nationalism* 9, 3 (2003).

—— and Hutchinson, J. (eds), *Nationalism* (Oxford: Oxford University Press, 1994).

—— and Hutchinson, J. (eds), *Ethnicity* (Oxford: Oxford University Press, 1996).

Smith, D. J. and Chambers, G., *Inequality in Northern Ireland* (Oxford: Oxford University Press, 1991).

Smith, M. L. R., *Fighting for Ireland? The Military Strategy of the Irish Republican Movement* (London: Routledge, 1995).

Smith, N. J., *Showcasing Globalization? The Political Economy of the Irish Republic* (Manchester: Manchester University Press, 2005).

Smyth, J., *The Men of No Property: Irish Radicals and Popular Politics in the Late Eighteenth Century* (Dublin: Gill and Macmillan, 1992).

—— 'Robert Emmet's Copy of John Locke's *Two Treatises of Government*', *History Ireland* 11, 3 (2003).

Snyder, L. L., *The Meaning of Nationalism* (New York: Greenwood Press, 1968).

Southern, R. W., *Western Society and the Church in the Middle Ages* (Harmondsworth: Penguin, 1970).

Spence, J., 'Isaac Butt, Nationality and Irish Toryism, 1833–1852', *Bullán* 2, 1 (1995).

Staunton, E., *The Nationalists of Northern Ireland 1918–1973* (Blackrock: Columba Press, 2001).

Stewart, A. T. Q., *Edward Carson* (Dublin: Gill and Macmillan, 1981).
—— *A Deeper Silence: The Hidden Origins of the United Irish Movement* (London: Faber and Faber, 1993).
—— *The Shape of Irish History* (Belfast: Blackstaff Press, 2001).
Stoker, B., *The Snake's Pass* (Dingle: Brandon, 1990; 1st edn, 1890).
—— *Dracula* (Harmondsworth: Penguin, 1979; 1st edn, 1897).
Stokes, M., *The Arabesk Debate: Music and Musicians in Modern Turkey* (Oxford: Oxford University Press, 1992).
—— and Bohlman, P. V. (eds), *Celtic Modern: Music at the Global Fringe* (Lanham: Scarecrow Press, 2003).
Stradling, R. A., *The Irish and the Spanish Civil War 1936–1939* (Manchester: Manchester University Press, 1999).
Strauss, E., *Irish Nationalism and British Democracy* (London: Methuen, 1951).
Sullivan, T. D., *Prison Poems; Or, Lays of Tullamore* (Dublin: *The Nation*, 1888).
Suzman, M., *Ethnic Nationalism and State Power: The Rise of Irish Nationalism, Afrikaner Nationalism and Zionism* (Basingstoke: Palgrave, 1999).
Swift, J., *Gulliver's Travels/The Tale of a Tub/Battle of the Books* (London: Oxford University Press, 1919 edn).
—— *The Drapier's Letters to the People of Ireland* (London: Oxford University Press, 1935 edn).
—— *A Tale of A Tub* (London: Oxford University Press, 1958 edn)
Tacitus, *Tacitus on Britain and Germany* (West Drayton: Penguin, 1948).
Tagore, R., *Nationalism* (London: Papermac, 1991; 1st edn, 1917).
Takagami, S., 'The Fenian Rising in Dublin, March 1867', *Irish Historical Studies* 29, 115 (1995).
Tamir, Y., *Liberal Nationalism* (Princeton: Princeton University Press, 1993).
Tanner, M., *Ireland's Holy Wars: The Struggle for a Nation's Soul, 1500–2000* (New Haven: Yale University Press, 2001).
Taras, R., *Liberal and Illiberal Nationalisms* (Basingstoke: Palgrave Macmillan, 2002).
TeBrake, J. K., 'Irish Peasant Women in Revolt: The Land League Years', *Irish Historical Studies* 28, 109 (1992).
Thompson, W. I., *The Imagination of an Insurrection: Dublin, Easter 1916. A Study of an Ideological Movement* (West Stockbridge: Lindisfarne Press, 1982; 1st edn, 1967).
Thoreau, H. D., *Walden* (Oxford: Oxford University Press, 1999; 1st edn, 1854).
Thornley, D., *Isaac Butt and Home Rule* (London: MacGibbon and Kee, 1964).
Thuente, M. H., *The Harp Re-Strung: The United Irishmen and the Rise of Irish Literary Nationalism* (Syracuse: Syracuse University Press, 1994).
Thurschwell, P., *Sigmund Freud* (London: Routledge, 2000).
Tierney, M., *Eoin MacNeill: Scholar and Man of Action 1867–1945* (Oxford: Oxford University Press, 1980).

Tóibín, B., *The Rising* (Dublin: New Island Books, 2001).

Tóibín, C., *Lady Gregory's Toothbrush* (London: Picador, 2003; 1st edn, 2002).

Tone, T. W., *The Autobiography of Theobald Wolfe Tone 1763–1798* (London: T. Fisher Unwin, 1893) (two vols).

Tonge, J., *The New Northern Irish Politics?* (Basingstoke: Palgrave Macmillan, 2005).

—— and Evans, J., 'Party Members and the Good Friday Agreement in Northern Ireland', *Irish Political Studies* 17, 2 (2002).

Tönnies, F., *Community and Society: Gemeinschaft and Gesellschaft* (New York: Dover Publications, 2002; 1st edn, 1887).

Toolis, K., *Rebel Hearts: Journeys within the IRA's Soul* (London: Picador, 1995).

Townshend, C., *The British Campaign in Ireland, 1919–1921: The Development of Political and Military Policies* (Oxford: Oxford University Press, 1975).

—— *Political Violence in Ireland: Government and Resistance Since 1848* (Oxford: Oxford University Press, 1984; 1st edn, 1983).

—— *Making the Peace: Public Order and Public Security in Modern Britain* (Oxford: Oxford University Press, 1993).

—— *Ireland: The Twentieth Century* (London: Arnold, 1999).

—— *Easter 1916: The Irish Rebellion* (London: Penguin, 2005).

—— (ed.), *Consensus in Ireland: Approaches and Recessions* (Oxford: Oxford University Press, 1988).

Tracy, H., *Mind You, I've Said Nothing! Forays in the Irish Republic* (Harmondsworth: Penguin, 1961; 1st edn, 1953).

Trimble, D., *The Easter Rebellion of 1916* (Lurgan: Ulster Society, 1992).

—— *To Raise Up a New Northern Ireland: Articles and Speeches 1998–2000* (Belfast: Belfast Press, 2001).

Valiulis, M. G., *Portrait of a Revolutionary: General Richard Mulcahy and the Founding of the Irish Free State* (Blackrock: Irish Academic Press, 1992).

van den Berghe, P. L., 'Race and Ethnicity: A Sociobiological Perspective', *Ethnic and Racial Studies* 1, 4 (1978).

—— *The Ethnic Phenomenon* (New York: Elsevier, 1981).

Vincent, A., 'Liberal Nationalism: An Irresponsible Compound?', *Political Studies* 45, 2 (1997).

Wagner, R., *Judaism in Music and Other Essays* (Lincoln: University of Nebraska Press, 1995 edn).

Walker, G., 'The Northern Ireland Labour Party in the 1920s', *Saothar* 10 (1984).

—— 'Propaganda and Conservative Nationalism During the Irish Civil War, 1922–1923', *Eire–Ireland* 22, 4 (1987).

—— *A History of the Ulster Unionist Party: Protest, Pragmatism and Pessimism* (Manchester: Manchester University Press, 2004).

Walker, I. and Smith, H. J. (eds), *Relative Deprivation: Specification, Development and Integration* (Cambridge: Cambridge University Press, 2002).

Wall, R., *Wittgenstein in Ireland* (London: Reaktion, 2000).

Waller, P. J., *Town, City and Nation: England 1850–1914* (Oxford: Oxford University Press, 1991; 1st edn, 1983)

Walsh, M., *The Key Above the Door* (Harmondsworth: Penguin, 1958; 1st edn, 1923).

—— *The Quiet Man and Other Stories* (Belfast: Appletree Press, 1992).

Ward, B., *Nationalism and Ideology* (New York: Norton, 1966).

Ward, M., *Unmanageable Revolutionaries: Women and Irish Nationalism* (London: Pluto Press, 1983).

—— *Hanna Sheehy Skeffington: A Life* (Cork: Attic Press, 1997).

Warrender, H., *The Political Philosophy of Hobbes: His Theory of Obligation* (London: Oxford University Press, 1957).

Warwick-Haller, S., *William O'Brien and the Irish Land War* (Blackrock: Irish Academic Press, 1990).

Watson, C., *Modern Basque History: Eighteenth Century to the Present* (Reno: Centre for Basque Studies, 2003).

Welch, R. (ed.), *The Oxford Companion to Irish Literature* (Oxford: Oxford University Press, 1996).

Wellings, B., 'Empire-Nation: National and Imperial Discourses in England', *Nations and Nationalism* 8, 1 (2002).

Wheatley, M., *Nationalism and the Irish Party: Provincial Ireland 1910–1916* (Oxford: Oxford University Press, 2005).

Whelan, K., *The Tree of Liberty: Radicalism, Catholicism and the Construction of Irish Identity 1760–1830* (Cork: Cork University Press, 1996).

Whitehouse, H., *Inside the Cult: Religious Innovation and Transmission in Papua New Guinea* (Oxford: Oxford University Press, 1995).

—— *Arguments and Icons: Divergent Modes of Religiosity* (Oxford: Oxford University Press, 2000).

—— *Modes of Religiosity: A Cognitive Theory of Religious Transmission* (Walnut Creek: Altamira Press, 2004).

Whyte, J. H., *The Independent Irish Party 1850–9* (London: Oxford University Press, 1958).

—— *Church and State in Modern Ireland 1923–1979* (Dublin: Gill and Macmillan, 1980; 1st edn, 1971).

—— *Interpreting Northern Ireland* (Oxford: Oxford University Press, 1990).

Whyte, N., *Science, Colonialism and Ireland* (Cork: Cork University Press, 1999).

Wichert, S., *Northern Ireland Since 1945* (Harlow: Longman, 1991).

—— (ed.), *From the United Irishmen to Twentieth-Century Unionism* (Dublin: Four Courts Press, 2004).

Wilde, O., *Complete Works of Oscar Wilde* (London: Heron Books, 1966).

Wilford, R. (ed.), *Aspects of the Belfast Agreement* (Oxford: Oxford University Press, 2001).

——, MacGinty, R., Dowds, L., and Robinson, G., 'Northern Ireland's Devolved

Institutions: A Triumph of Hope over Experience?', *Regional and Federal Studies* 13, 1 (2003).

Williams, P., *The Later Tudors: England 1547–1603* (Oxford: Oxford University Press, 1998; 1st edn, 1995).

Williams, W., *Pilgrimage and Narrative in the French Renaissance: 'The Undiscovered Country'* (Oxford: Oxford University Press, 1998).

Wilson, A. J., *Irish America and the Ulster Conflict 1968–1995* (Belfast: Blackstaff Press, 1995).

Wilson, A. N., *C. S. Lewis: A Biography* (London: Flamingo, 1991; 1st edn, 1990).

Woewoda, J. C., *The IRA: Death by Deception* (Vancouver: Lausanne Institute, 1994).

Wokler, R., *Rousseau* (Oxford: Oxford University Press, 1995).

Woodham-Smith, C., *The Great Hunger: Ireland 1845–9* (London: Hamish Hamilton, 1962).

Wright, F., *Northern Ireland: A Comparative Analysis* (Dublin: Gill and Macmillan, 1992; 1st edn, 1987).

Yeates, P., *Lockout: Dublin 1913* (New York: Palgrave, 2001).

Yeats, W. B., *Autobiographies: Memories and Reflections* (London: Bracken Books, 1995; 1st edn, 1955).

—— *Selected Poetry* (London: Pan, 1974; 1st edn, 1962).

—— *Yeats's Poems* (Dublin: Gill and Macmillan, 1989).

York, N. L., *Neither Kingdom Nor Nation: The Irish Quest for Constitutional Rights, 1698–1800* (Washington, DC: Catholic University of America Press, 1994).

Young, E., *Flowering Dusk: Things Remembered Accurately and Inaccurately* (London: Dennis Dobson, 1947; 1st edn, 1945).

Younger, C., *Ireland's Civil War* (Glasgow: Fontana, 1979; 1st edn, 1968).

—— *Arthur Griffith* (Dublin: Gill and Macmillan, 1981).

Zalewski, M., 'Gender Ghosts in McGarry and O'Leary and Representations of the Conflict in Northern Ireland', *Political Studies* 53, 1 (2005).

Zimmer, O., *Nationalism in Europe, 1890–1940* (Basingstoke: Palgrave Macmillan, 2003).

Zubaida, S., 'Nations: Old and New – Comments on Anthony D. Smith's "The Myth of the 'Modern Nation' and the Myths of Nations"', *Ethnic and Racial Studies* 12, 3 (1989).

Zulaika, J., *Basque Violence: Metaphor and Sacrament* (Reno: University of Nevada Press, 1988).

Index